CONTEMPORARY READINGS IN AMERICAN GOVERNMENT

D.C. Heath and Company
Lexington, Massachusetts, Toronto

CONTEMPORARY READINGS IN AMERICAN GOVERNMENT

Edited by

Byron W. Daynes
DePauw University

Raymond Tatalovich
Loyola University of Chicago

320.973
C761

International Standard Book Number: 0-669-01163-0

Library of Congress Catalog Card Number: 791214

PREFACE

★★

This collection of essays has the dual purpose of presenting a series of contemporary political issues while at the same time encouraging students to reflect on and analyze the political and social impact of these issues on the political system. To accomplish this purpose, the anthology is made up of an outstanding selection of contemporary articles, essays, and Supreme Court cases accompanied by pedagogical aids that direct the students' attention to the major concerns of politics.

Recognized scholars, journalists, jurists, and political officeholders have all been contributors to the volume. The anthology includes essays written from a number of perspectives. Each selection is thoughtfully written, insightful, and stimulating and should be understandable to all readers regardless of background. Thought-provoking descriptions and searching questions accompany each essay, pointing to the primary themes of the article and encouraging the reader to weigh the viewpoints presented and to draw his or her own conclusions about the problems posed.

The anthology is organized by topics rather than by themes. All the topics selected are found in virtually every standard American government textbook. Each topic is treated in a separate chapter, and each chapter is written as a complete, self-contained unit. This will allow the anthology not only to complement a primary textbook but also to become a valuable addition to basic American government courses regardless of the particular approach used in the course.

Anyone who has ever engaged in a project of this magnitude immediately realizes that the task could not be accomplished without the valuable assistance of others. We would like to thank our publisher, D. C. Heath and Company, and its editorial staff for valuable guidance and support in the preparation of the manuscript. We are grateful to the following people for their many helpful suggestions that guided us in the preparation of this volume: James Brooks, New Mexico State University; Marvin J. Folkerstma, Grove City College; and Ted Neima, Los Angeles Pierce College. We are also grateful for the sound advice offered by Larry Elowitz, Georgia College; Mark S. Frankel, Wayne State University; J. P. Heim, University of Wisconsin—La Crosse; William P. Kinney, Foothill College; Peter R. Manoogian, Pennsylvania State University; Ronald M. Mason, Southern Illinois University; Robert C. McIntire, Millikin University; William P. McLauchlan, Purdue University; and J. Douglas Nelson, Anderson College. In addition, we extend our thanks to Elizabeth Bottorff, who offered an invaluable student perspective in criticizing the readings selected. Finally, we would most sincerely like to thank our wives—Kathryn Daynes and Anne Tatalovich—for their criticisms of the manuscript, for their editing abilities, and most important, for their patience with us as we completed the project.

Byron W. Daynes
Raymond Tatalovich

65075

v

CONTENTS

★★★

CHAPTER ONE

***

The American Political Community

Every now and again a nation is fortunate to experience a constitutional crisis that forces its leadership to reassess the basic fundamental values of the political system. Such a reassessment happened in the United States during the impeachment hearings of Richard Nixon and again in the bicentennial year. During the impeachment hearings the House Judiciary Committee spent as much or more time discussing democracy and such fundamental concepts as executive privilege, separation of powers, and universal suffrage, as it did discussing presidential deception, concealment, and perjury. The bicentennial year of 1976 gave to many thoughtful scientists and analysts another opportunity to consider America's future in terms of its past.

One such analyst was Robert M. Hutchins, who in his article "Is Democracy Possible?" raises some very pointed questions about American democracy. Is democracy possible? If so, is it also possible to utterly destroy it? Hutchins feels certain that democracy *is* possible but is dubious about its present condition. Democracy, according to him, is a system of government in which "people rule and are ruled in turn for the good life of the whole." It cannot survive, he argues, without a firm grasp of

the "common good." Hutchins questions whether we have such an understanding.

In fact, he contends that we have a government ruled by special interests rather than for the common good. The difficulty posed by Hutchins calls to mind the research of another political scientist who indicated that interest groups' domination of government can eventually destroy the system. Their domination is debilitating to democracy because expectations about democratic institutions are confused, government is demoralized, and formal procedures are weakened. As Diane Ravitch in "Color-Blind or Color-Conscious?" suggests, this focus on group interests may also take our attention from the more important social issues such as race relations. She indicates that public policy has encouraged group consciousness by formalizing and distinguishing the group. As a result, Ravitch contends, the "color-blind" racial policies and politics of the 1950s and 1960s have given way to "color-conscious" politics of the 1970s, weakening the original intent of *Brown v. Board of Education.* Robert Hutchins' solution to this situation of group domination of governmental procedures extends well beyond the Framers' vision for American democracy. He suggests that the only way democracy will survive is by applying the goals and principles in our Constitution's Preamble to *all* the inhabitants on earth.

Today we are operating in a political system somewhat changed since the days of the Framers. Federalism—the relationship between federal and state government—is an ever-changing part of that system. Although it is still the system of divided powers conceived of by James Madison, federalism may take on a different hue and meaning with each presidential administration. It may even be known by different names. Before Franklin Roosevelt, for example, federalism was known as "dual federalism," conveying the idea of separate and competing centers of power. To Franklin Roosevelt it was "cooperative federalism," in which the various levels of government were thought of as related parts of a single governmental system of shared functions. Lyndon Johnson's Great Society program encouraged intimate contact between federal and state governments in a relationship he called "creative federalism," wherein the federal government expanded its role to handle such concerns as public school education and poverty which had previously been state and local matters. Under Nixon's "new federalism," more power was again returned to the state through revenue sharing, allowing more financial independence on the part of the state vis-à-vis the federal government.

Martin Diamond in his article *"The Federalist* on Federalism" indicates that although *The Federalist* appears to convey an image of federalism different from the popular image, Madison, Hamilton, and Jay reveal a national and a federal component to federalism that best explains why our institutions were structured as they were and why they now behave as they do. Diamond suggests that *The Federalist* still offers us the best commentary on our system of government, because it is not time-bound to the period in which it was written. As he suggests, it focuses on the so-called "perennial" political issues and especially on those indigenous to American politics.

As there have been changes in the relationship between the federal government and state governments, so there have also been fundamental changes in other aspects of the political system. But, as James Q. Wilson in his article "American Politics, Then & Now" emphasizes, no structural change has been as extensive as the change in attitude on the part of citizens and policy-makers toward the political system. There has been a change in attitude over time, he suggests, from support for institution-building in the period 1890–1920 to the potential dismantling of institutions in the last decade. Accompanying this change in attitude, Wilson argues, there has been a major alteration in political power that seems to have been encouraged by this new ethos.

The repercussions of such power redistribution are of major interest to Kirkpatrick Sale in his article on "The Cowboy Challenge: The Rise of the Southern Rim." Since the 1780s, he argues, we have had five of these shifts of power that have altered the course of political history. They have included the consolidation of federal power during the eighteenth century, the introduction of Jacksonian democracy, the expansion of industrialization, the introduction of New Deal politics and, now, the expansion of Southern Rim politics. He sees in Southern Rim politics a refocusing of political power from the Northeastern region of the country, a region that has long dominated our politics and culture, to the major cities and regional centers of the Southern Rim—an area reaching from Southern California, continuing through the Southwest and Texas, and terminating in the Deep South and Florida. The political consequences of this shift are yet to be fully appreciated. We have seen Presidents Nixon and Carter elected from this Southern Rim, and the 1980 census should also reveal a greater proportional increase in population from this area that will guarantee additional congressional representation.

With all of these alleged changes to our democratic system occurring since the founding of the nation, one might ask whether the Constitution is still adequate to the needs of the system. A constitutional convention has never been called to consider this question, but, as Bertram M. Gross in "The Con-Con Con: Unbalancing the Constitution" explains, we are closer now than ever before to convening such a convention. In 1973 some forty-five states called for a convention, though on separate items of concern. Although the Constitution states in Article V that two-thirds of the state legislatures may petition Congress to call a convention, it is unclear whether those thirty-four states calling the convention must first agree on a single issue of concern before the convention can convene. An answer to this question may soon be forthcoming

★★

since, as Gross reminds us, twenty-nine states have already requested a convention to consider a balanced-budget amendment.

Support for this "budget-balancing" convention has come primarily from the state and local levels. Apprehension has come essentially from the national policy-makers. Their concerns about calling a new constitutional convention call to mind the first Constitutional Convention. The Founders, with the exception of a few, fully intended to go to Philadelphia to *revise* the Articles of Confederation. Instead, at the urging of those few, they designed a totally new governmental system *replacing* the Articles of Confederation with the Constitution. There are no guarantees that the "new framers," who would be considering alterations to the present Constitution, would not do the very same thing. We would do well to recall the concerns of Robert Hutchins, who asked whether democracy is really possible. If the present Constitution were replaced, would democracy be any stronger than it is today? Would protections for individual liberty, equality, and justice be incorporated into a "new" constitution? These are the vital questions that any new framers would necessarily have to address.

★★

★★

1

Is Democracy Possible?   Robert M. Hutchins

Throughout this article Hutchins places emphasis on the necessity of the citizen learning to live in a democracy, learning to seek the common good, and learning to form that "more perfect union." How does Hutchins define "democracy" in this essay? Does government by pressure group fit his definition of democracy? Why is it necessary to spend time learning to live in this system? Should all systems of government demand the same of their citizens, or is there something peculiar about democracy that this seems to be a prerequisite? How best can we learn to live in this system? Can we learn in the schools, from television, or from the city as the early Greeks did?

Hutchins suggests that in Lincoln's day government was dedicated to the proposition that "all men are created equal." Is government today still committed to this proposition? Are the concepts of freedom and justice well served in the United States today? Without a firm commitment to these principles, can we honestly say we have a "political community"?

Threatening the vitality of the political community, Hutchins indicates, is the exclusion of the poor and minorities from the political system. Since it is they who bring diversity to the system and help the rich and the majority learn about "community," it is crucial to devise ways to include them. How might we begin to bring them back into the political system? Can this be done without undermining the present power structure? If it cannot, what repercussions to the system would you anticipate?

Hutchins argues that it is crucial for the United States to learn to understand and operate the political community within the nation in order to assume the awesome task of organizing the world political community. Is it really possible to expand our notion of democracy and political community beyond our borders? Are our political concepts translatable to the world community?

★ ★ ★

ROBERT M. HUTCHINS

IS DEMOCRACY POSSIBLE?

Sixteen years ago I wrote an essay on this topic that was published in the *Saturday Review*. The very nice lady who acted for the *Review* objected strongly to the title. She said it was so shocking that nobody would take the paper seriously. She may have been right. At any rate nobody *did* take the article seriously.

If nobody takes this article seriously, it will not be because of the title. If we look almost anywhere in the world, we find people asking whether democracy is possible and usually giving a negative answer. The dictatorships in Latin America, Africa, and Asia leave the Western world with an almost complete monopoly of self-government. Only Europe and North America make serious claims to democracy as we understand it. The peoples' democracies that burden the Eastern world need not detain us, for they are clearly not within the range of our subject. The difficulties besetting the governments of Europe and North America are serious enough to raise the question whether democracy is possible even when these countries actually have governments democratic in form. Britain, for example, is a democracy, but it is a fair question whether it can escape a temporary interruption of its democratic course. And for ourselves, we have only to remember the narrow escape of Watergate.

Democracy is a system of government by which people rule and are ruled in turn for the good life of the whole. It is a system of self-government. It is government by the consent of the governed, who have consented, among other things, to majority rule. Nothing excludes a system of representation, though a system of full-time politicians and indifferent citizens can hardly be a democracy except in name. The aim of any democracy must be the common good, which is that good which no member of the community would enjoy if he did not belong to the community.

The exact opposite of democracy is government by pressure groups. This is a government under which special interests, by deals and propaganda, endeavor to exploit the community for their own benefit. For example, everybody ought to have a chance to live in a decent environment. Everybody ought to have a chance to live in a decent home. Those who destroy the environment in order to provide homes and those who would preserve the environment by refusing to provide homes are equally guilty of perverting democracy; for they must see that the common good requires both.

A community is of course composed of diverse people with diverse interests. These people become a

From *The Center Magazine*, January/February 1976. Reprinted with permission from *The Center Magazine*, a publication of the Center for the Study of Democratic Institutions, Santa Barbara, California.

Instead of being a citizen the American individual is a consumer, an object of propaganda, and a statistical unit. In view of the condition of our education, our mass media, and our political parties, the outlook for democracy, the free society, and the political community seems dim.

All the studies the Center has been carrying on have come out at the same place. We are entering a new world, and we are not very well prepared for it.

ح

In 1934 Mr. Chief Justice Hughes said, delivering the opinion of the Court, "The vast body of law which has been developed was unknown to the fathers, but it is believed to have preserved the essential content and spirit of the Constitution. . . . This is a growth from the seeds the fathers planted."

In this view, the founding fathers meant us to learn. They meant us to learn how to form a more perfect union, to establish justice, to insure domestic tranquillity, to provide for the common defense, to promote the general welfare, and to secure the blessings of liberty to ourselves and our posterity. They founded a political community; a community learning together to discover and achieve the common good, the elements of which they set forth, but did not elucidate, in the Preamble. The reliance on us to continue learning is evident in every line of the Constitution and in the brevity of the whole.

The Constitution is to be interpreted, therefore, as a charter of learning. We are to learn how to develop the seeds the fathers planted under the conditions of our own time. This political botany means that nothing we have learned and no process of learning could be unconstitutional. What would be unconstitutional would be limitations or inhibitions on learning.

Learning is a rational process. Law is an ordinance of reason, directed to the common good. If the Constitution is to teach us, and we are to learn under its instruction, the dialogue that goes on about its meaning must be about what is reasonable and unreasonable, right and wrong, just and unjust. The question is not what interests are at stake, not what are the mores of the community, not who has the power or who is the dominant group, not what the courts will do or what the legislature has done, but what is reasonable, right, and just.

What are the prospects of learning?

Not too long ago the Resource Guide for English and the Social Studies for the tenth grade in Pasadena announced: "In the tenth grade, study is concen-

The founding fathers formed a political community, a community learning together to discover and achieve the common good. "The reliance on us to continue learning is evident in every line of the Constitution and in the brevity of the whole."

community through their dedication to the common good. They have to be dedicated to the common good, or there will be no community, and they will lose that good which would accrue to them if they did not belong to it.

Tocqueville remarked that the individual is a defaulted citizen, that democracy fosters individualism, and that individualism first saps the virtues of public life and ends in pure selfishness. Tocqueville said that democracy, by way of individualism, throws every man "back forever upon himself alone and threatens in the end to confine him entirely within the solitude of his own heart." The citizens of the United States, Tocqueville thought, would escape this fate because our Constitution required us to learn together to seek the common good. We would be forced, he said, by the necessity of cooperating in the management of our free institutions, and by our desire to exercise our political rights, into the habit of attending to the interests of the public. This was, indeed, the hope of the founding fathers.

Tocqueville's expectations have not been fulfilled. The people of the United States are in fact defaulted citizens, with an indifference and even a hostility to government, politics, and law that would have astounded Tocqueville — and the founding fathers.

trated on the growth of democracy, and especially on the form of government which developed. Such a study should be brief and to the point, in order to allow time for the unit on Driver Education."

We have triumphantly invented, perfected, and distributed to the humblest cottage throughout the land one of the greatest technical marvels in history, television, and used it for what? To bring Coney Island into every home. It is as though movable type had been devoted exclusively since Gutenberg's time to the publication of comic books.

William Berkeley, governor of Virginia in the seventeenth century, said, "Thank God there are no free schools or printing, for learning has brought disobedience into the world, and printing has divulged it. God keep us from both." We are combining Berkeley's ideal of no communications at all with the

> *"We must say that the political community required by democracy has disappeared...."*

democratic ideal of communications for everybody by having mass communications without content. In the same way it sometimes seems as though we were trying to combine the ideal of no schools at all with the democratic ideal of schools for everybody by having schools without education.

Lincoln once referred to us as the "Almighty's almost chosen people." Whether he meant that the Almighty had given us careful consideration and decided to pass us by, or whether Lincoln was simply being modest, I do not know. He probably meant that the Almighty had provided us with all the materials necessary for us to display a great experiment on a world stage. He was not forcing us to play such a role. But He was giving us a chance to be the last best hope of earth.

If we look at ourselves in this light, as trustees for democracy, the means for which have been lavishly supplied to us, we have not been doing very well by ourselves or others. Domestic and foreign policy appear to be conducted without regard to the democratic history or intentions of our country. Now that the Cold War may be over, foreign policy seems to be carried on in the light of the needs of the munitions makers, the Pentagon, the C.I.A., and the multinational corporations. These corporations must, among other things, be allowed to make enough money to bribe foreign governments, political parties, and purchasing agents. Domestic policy is conducted according to one infallible rule: the costs and burdens of whatever is done must be borne by those least able to bear them. What is the price of gasoline to me? To a blue-collar worker who must commute two hours a day — usually because he can't find a home nearer to his job — the coming price of gasoline may have all the charm of a heart attack.

Against the poor, and especially the black and Chicano poor, the forces of what we call the community are massed. Since the poor are a majority of the people, we must say that the political community required by democracy has disappeared and that what we have is what the Athenians called a timocracy, a government by money. We must say also that the political community must be restored. If it isn't, we shall experience a period of disruptive violence the like of which we have not seen since the Civil War.

The procession of corporate executives who have pleaded guilty to violating the laws of this country and who have admitted spending millions on paying off foreigners, suggests, like Watergate, that wealth and college degrees have no connection with morality or with the common good. The power of wealth includes the power to get a college degree. But a college degree provides no assurance that its recipient will have any faint glimmer of the dedication to the common good that democracy demands.

❧

We are without leadership because that dedication is missing — political power is simply power, the object of which can be either good or evil.

Contrast this to Werner Jaeger's description of the consequences for democracy of the conviction of the greatest Greeks that they were the servants of the community. Jaeger says, "In that atmosphere of spiritual liberty, bound by deep knowledge (as if by a divine law) to the service of the community, the Greek creative genius conceived and attained that lofty educational ideal which sets it far above the more superficial artistic and intellectual brilliance of our individualistic civilization." The Athenians did not have much of an educational system. They did not need one. They learned from the City, not merely what it was, but what it ought to be, a political community dedicated to the common good.

So to Abraham Lincoln this was a government not merely of, by, and for the people. It was a government dedicated to a proposition. The proposition was that all men are created equal. This proposition, which we neither understand nor apply, is likely to be the battleground of the future as it was in Lincoln's day. At that time the most conspicuous manifestation of inequality was slavery. Democracy demanded that all men be free; justice made the same demand. Today freedom and justice demand that equality be applied to opportunities for each citizen to achieve his fullest possible development. This means equal educational opportunity. It also means access to the legal system, to the health system, to housing. The political community cannot be restored or maintained unless minorities and the poor are given that equality to which this community was originally dedicated.

The exclusion of minorities and the poor from the political, economic, and social system means that the diversity out of which the community is formed is so restricted that the rich and the majority cannot learn through the community. We should ponder the words of a justice of the New Jersey Supreme Court, who said the other day, "A homogeneous community . . . is culturally dead, aside from being downright boring."

Hence the basic theoretical question with which the Center is now dealing is equality in relation to freedom and justice. Take any subject on which we have worked in the last six months: the revision of the federal criminal code; the possibilities of accommodation as against those of litigation; planning; electoral reform; the press, its freedom and its responsibility; the penal system (now called corrections); the community and the schools; the British experience with the privatization of profits and the socialization of losses; growth and the right to housing; and world organization. The central issue has been equality in relation to freedom and justice. These appear to be the central elements of the common good.

Democracy today has all the problems Tocqueville saw in it, but it has them on a world scale. The atrocities of which the C.I.A. has been guilty may not show that democracy is impossible worldwide. But they do show that merely having a democratic form of government is no guarantee that atrocities will not be committed.

We know that freedom, justice, and equality — the common good — must be preserved worldwide because all our problems are world problems. But we have not even begun to think about them as such. Sixteen years ago I was able to say that reality was concealed from us by our current remarkable prosperity, which resulted in part from our new way of getting rich, which was to buy things from one another that we did not want because of advertising we did not believe at prices we could not pay on terms we could not meet. We know better now.

Perhaps we shall learn also that our preoccupation with Russia is also somewhat exaggerated. Russia has played a curious double role in our lives as the

> *"There is no apparent limit to the greed of those who want to exploit the oceans...."*

devil in our world and as the standard by which we measure our own progress. If we weren't getting ahead of Russia, or falling behind her, how would we tell where we were? History will smile sardonically at the spectacle of this great country getting interested, slightly and temporarily, in education only because of Sputnik, and then being able to act as a nation only by assimilating education to the Cold War and calling an education bill a defense act.

The pursuit of the common good on a world scale presents special difficulties. When nations see something to gain, the pursuit seems bound to fail. The Center for the Study of Democratic Institutions plunged into the oceans eight years ago. What I have principally learned from the resulting studies is that there is no apparent limit to the greed of those who want to exploit the oceans, which used to be called the common heritage of mankind.

Of course we have to keep trying, and we have to see the world situation as it is, and not as this morning's headlines present it. The French historian and philosopher, Etienne Gilson, describes what is actually going on as follows: "The throes of the contemporary world are those of a birth. And what is being born with such great pain is a universal human society. . . . What characterizes the events we witness . . . is their global character. . . . The unity of the planet is already accomplished. For reasons economic, industrial, and technical, reasons all linked to the practical applications of science, such a solidarity is established among the peoples of the earth that their vicissitudes are integrated into a universal history of which they are particular moments . . . These peoples are in fact parts of a Humanity . . . , something of which they must now become conscious in order to will it instead of being subject to it, in order to think it, with a view to organizing it."

World order is not, then, something that we can ignore or pay attention to as we choose. It is here, and it will be good or bad depending on whether or not we will it instead of being subject to it, and whether or not we think it, persistently, patiently, in spite of the newspaper headlines, with a view to organizing it.

As we have learned to our sorrow from the Vietnamese and the Organization of Petroleum Exporting Countries, things do not always go our way merely because, as Mr. Nixon liked to say, we are the most powerful nation on earth. Power is more complicated than it used to be. We are going to have to learn how to live under unprecedented conditions.

When it comes to learning through the political community, the object is to learn how to be a responsible citizen, enjoying liberty under law. The freedom of the individual must be protected, but in addition the citizen must grow in responsibility if our country is to become conscious of itself as a part of Humanity and to think Humanity in order to organize it. Individual freedom and liberty under law are not incompatible, and they are both indispensable.

Law is a great teacher. It does not represent that minimum of morality necessary to hold the community together. It stands rather for such moral truth as the community has discovered that can and should be supported by the authority of the community. The conception of law as coercion, or the command of the sovereign, or the expression of power, or what the courts will do leads to the conclusion that it is proper to do anything that nobody can compel you to abstain from doing — or that you can get away with.

Some such misconceptions must have been in the minds of our governmental agencies that have planned crimes against our citizens and against other nations and their leaders. These offenses suggest either that our officials are hypocritical when they talk about the rule of law or that when they use the words "rule of law" they don't know what they are talking about.

ℰ

The principles of world law are the principles of thinking Humanity in order to organize it. I think they will be found to be the principles embodied in the Preamble to the Constitution of the United States.

We must revive, reconstruct, and learn to operate the political community in the United States because the task we confront on our two-hundredth anniversary is nothing less than the organization of the world political community. We have thought that we have had hold of some truths that would mean something in the universal history of mankind. The founding fathers rightly believed that the truths in which America was conceived would stir the aspirations of all men everywhere. And so they did until it began to look as though we were losing our grip on our original ideas and ideals.

If today we are called on to exemplify these truths, we have to keep our hold on them. We have to keep learning them. We have to learn all they can imply for today and tomorrow. Only if we can do this is democracy possible. Meanwhile, the proposition to which the Declaration of Independence and Lincoln dedicated us now extends to the whole world. Once more, on a new scale, Americans have the duty of forming a more perfect union, which will involve establishing justice, promoting the general welfare, and securing the blessings of liberty to ourselves and all the people of the earth.

Mr. Hutchins is President of the Center.

★★

2   Color-Blind or Color-Conscious?   Diane Ravitch

Diane Ravitch argues that while Brown v. Board of Education *provided a strong precedent to prohibit racial discrimination, its effect was greatly strengthened by the passage of the Civil Rights Act of 1964 ten years later. What was the Supreme Court's ruling in the* Brown *case? What were the provisions of the 1964 Civil Rights Act? How were they supportive of one another? Was Court action effective from 1954 to 1964 without the enactment of the Civil Rights Act? Could the civil rights movement have survived on the basis of* Brown *alone?*

Ravitch maintains that part of the appeal the civil rights movement had in the 1950s and 1960s was the clear-cut issue of discrimination against blacks that was readily understood by the public. But, as she asserts, civil rights issues of the 1970s have become much more complex. They now include busing, affirmative action, racial balancing, and quotas, none of which are as precise. What has resulted from this change? How do the complexities of these issues affect their possible resolutions?

The Supreme Court, Ravitch argues, has generally tried to use the research of social scientists in making decisions involving social questions. The decision concerning whether policy should be color-blind or color-conscious, however, was an exception. No attempt was made by the Court to use social science research before the Court drew its conclusion. If no appeal is made to the social sciences, then what area or field could contribute helpful data to answer such social questions? Is it better for the Court to decide these issues without reference to any scientific data?

The author points to the difficulties posed by a Supreme Court decision like Brown *that was written so it could be interpreted in several ways. Right now, she suggests, both the supporters of integration as well as those who do not recognize race as a factor in assigning students to schools look to* Brown *as a source of legitimacy. Would integration have proceeded more rapidly had the Court's language in* Brown *been more precise?*

★ ★ ★

Twenty-five years after the *Brown* decision, its real meaning is still elusive.

Color-Blind or Color-Conscious?

by Diane Ravitch

In 1954 the Supreme Court declared that state-imposed school segregation was unconstitutional, and invalidated state laws that assigned children to school on the basis of their race. Today that decision, *Brown* v. *Board of Education*, is cited as authority for a network of judicial decisions, laws and administrative regulations that specifically require institutions to classify people on the basis of their group identity and to deal with them accordingly.

By denying states the power to differentiate among its citizens by race, the *Brown* decision provided a strong precedent to bar racial discrimination in every realm of civic and public acitivity. Its effect was strengthened and extended by the Civil Rights Act of 1964, which prohibited discrimination based on race, color, religion, sex or national origin. The Civil Rights Act embodied the fundamental principle that everyone should be considered as an individual without regard to social origin. This idea attracted the support of a broad alliance composed of blacks, liberals, organized labor, Catholics, Jews and others who perceived that the black cause was the common cause of everyone who wanted to eliminate group bias from American life. The particular genius of the civil rights movement was its successful forging of a coalition led by blacks but far more numerous than the black population alone; at the height of its power, in 1964-65, the coalition was potent enough to win passage of the Civil Rights Act, federal aid to education, the Voting Rights Act and the anti-poverty program.

The recent shift in focus from anti-discrimination to group preference has splintered the civil rights coalition of the 1960s and has changed the nature of civil rights issues. The issues of the late 1970s are far more complex than were those of the 1950s and 1960s, when the public could readily understand the denial of the civil and political rights of black people. Issues such

as racial balancing, busing, affirmative action and quotas are not nearly so clear-cut. People of good will of all races and both sexes can be found on different sides of these questions.

But this disagreement arises between one-time allies in the struggle for universalism and equal rights not just because the issues today are complicated, but also because there is an essential dilemma: the group-based concepts of the present are in conflict with the historic efforts of the civil rights movement to remove group classifications from public policy. And at the heart of this dilemma is the *Brown* decision.

The *Brown* case was one of several school segregation suits brought before the Supreme Court in the early 1950s by the NAACP Legal Defense Fund. The cases were intended to challenge the "separate but equal" doctrine of statutory racial segregation that was upheld in the *Plessy* v. *Ferguson* decision in 1896. The Supreme Court then held that a state law requiring the separation of the races in railway coaches was no violation of the Constitution as long as the races had equal facilities. The decision of the majority gave legal reinforcement to social customs and "black codes" based on the presumption of black inferiority.

Only Justice John Marshall Harlan dissented from the *Plessy* decision, and his dissent was for many decades a foundation-stone of the civil rights movement. Harlan denied that the states had the power to regulate their citizens solely on the basis of race: "Our Constitution is color-blind, and neither knows nor tolerates classes among citizens. . . . The law regards man as man, and takes no account of his surroundings or of his color when his civil rights as guaranteed by the supreme law of the land are involved."

The city of Topeka, Kansas, where the *Brown* case originated in 1951, maintained racially segregated schools for the first six grades. The Topeka School District contained 18 elementary schools for white students and four elementary schools for black students. White children attended their neighborhood school, but many black children were required to

---

Diane Ravitch is associate professor of history and education at Columbia Teachers College.

From *The New Republic*, May 5, 1979. Reprinted by permission of *The New Republic*, © 1979 The New Republic, Inc.

travel long distances by school bus to attend a designated "colored" school.

The arguments against racial segregation were of two kinds: those derived from constitutional objections, and those derived from social science. The constitutional arguments explicitly rejected the power of the state to recognize racial differences. The social science arguments were ambivalent, asserting both that color was irrelevant and that interracial experiences were valuable.

In building their case, the NAACP lawyers stressed the fact that blacks were denied the right to send their children to the nearest school. Segregation imposed on black children the handicap of spending extra time traveling to and from school, which was detrimental to the children's development. Oliver Brown, the named plaintiff, testified about the inconvenience and lack of safety which resulted from busing his daughter, Linda Carol Brown, to a "colored school" 21 blocks away, instead of the neighborhood school only seven blocks from his home.

Among the social scientists who testified, there were contradictory themes. Some held that blacks were deprived by lack of contact with whites. But others emphasized that segregation was wrong because it accorded different treatment to children on the basis of their ancestry. Thus the social scientists' testimony left unresolved a major dilemma: should policy be color-blind or color-conscious? Were black parents suing for the right to gain admission to their neighborhood school or for the right to an integrated education? Was the constitutional wrong to blacks the denial of liberty or the denial of integration?

The constitutional argument contained no such ambivalence. Robert Carter, chief counsel for Topeka's black plaintiffs, rested the case against school segregation on two grounds: first, that "the state has no authority and no power to make any distinction or any classification among its citizenry based upon race and color alone"; and second, that "the rights under the Fourteenth Amendment are individual rights," and not group rights.

When the unfavorable decision in Kansas was appealed to the Supreme Court in 1952, the chief argument in the appellants' brief was the unconstitutionality of racial classification by the state: "The Fourteenth Amendment precludes a state from imposing distinctions or classifications based upon race and color alone." The NAACP conceded that the state may "confer benefits or impose disabilities upon selected groups of citizens," but the selection of such groups must be related to real differences. Race, the NAACP said, is not a real difference.

Black organizations have maintained in the 1970s that the 14th Amendment bans legislation that discriminates against blacks but does not ban legislation intended to confer benefits on blacks. But this was not the position of the NAACP in its *Brown* brief. On the contrary, the appellants' brief is a cogent, tightly reasoned documentation of the view that the 14th Amendment was written specifically to ensure that all state action would henceforth be color-blind. There was no suggestion in the brief that racial distinctions might, in some circumstances, be tolerable.

The NAACP said, "The evidence makes clear that it was the intent of the proponents of the Fourteenth Amendment, and the substantial understanding of its opponents, that it would, of its own force, prohibit all state action predicated upon race or color. . . . [A]s a matter of law, race is not an allowable basis of differentiation in governmental action."

In the oral arguments before the Supreme Court, Thurgood Marshall for the NAACP described the kind of remedy that he sought, and he was clear that race should play no part in school assignment. Marshall said the Court should forbid explicit segregation and segregation by gerrymandering of school district lines, but, "If the lines are drawn on a natural basis, without regard to race or color, then I think that nobody would have any complaint." Thurgood Marshall made the most conclusive and unambiguous statements about the constitutional issues before the Court. Marshall said that under the Constitution, "the state is deprived of any power to make any racial classification in any governmental field."

When the Brown decision was announced on May 17, 1954, it appeared that the grounds for it were more sociological than constitutional. In retrospect this seems surprising in light of the solidity of the constitutional argument and the controvertible nature of sociological evidence. The Court did not, in its *Brown* decision, declare the Constitution to be color-blind, which explains some of the present-day confusion about the meaning of the decision. The decision can be read, as it was then, as removing from the states the power to use race as a factor in assigning children to public schools. It can also be read, as it is now, as a mandate to bring about racial integration in the public schools by taking race into account in making assignments.

But it was the former interpretation that the NAACP lawyers used at the time. In 1955, Robert Carter asked for a decree from the Surpeme Court that would order the Topeka school board "to cease and desist at once from basing school attendance and admission on the basis of race or color." James M. Nabrit Jr. argued in the same vein for a Supreme Court decree for the District of Columbia public schools: ". . . . Do not deny any child the right to go to the school of his choice on the grounds of race or color within the normal limits of your districting system. . . . Do not assign them on the basis of race or color, and we have no complaint."

Today the *Brown* decision is considered the progenitor of a host of color-conscious and group-specific policies. The decision that was supposed to remove from the states the power to assign children to school on the basis of race has become the authority for assigning children to school solely on the basis of race, even where official segregation never existed. One western school district, which contains 19 variants of the HEW-designated minority groups, has voluntarily undertaken to maintain a racial-ethnic balance of these groups in its schools for both students and teachers.

For at least the first 10 years after the *Brown* decision, belief in color-blind policy was the animating force behind the civil rights movement. In the hearings on the Civil Rights Act in 1963, Roy Wilkins denounced employment quotas as "evil" and predicted that they would be used to restrict the opportunities of black workers. In the same hearings, Attorney General Robert Kennedy, in a heated sparring match with Senator Sam Ervin, forced the senator to agree with him that the *Brown* decision established the right of the individual to attend his neighborhood school. The Civil Rights Act ultimately included an unequivocal definition of desegregation:

'Desegregation' means the assignment of students to public schools and within such schools without regard to their race, color, religion, or national origin, but 'desegregation' shall not mean the assignment to public schools in order to overcome racial imbalance.

Not long after Congress passed into law the color-blind principle embodied in the Civil Rights Act of 1964, several trends converged to undermine it.

First, white southern intransigence had effectively preserved segregation despite the *Brown* decision. The dismantling of state-segregated school systems was occurring at a snail's pace; by 1964, only two percent of the black students in the deep South attended schools with white students. Southern politicans boasted of their success in frustrating the implementation of the *Brown* mandate, and southern legislatures devised ingenious schemes to protect the dual school systems. In some cities, white students were allowed to transfer away from their neighborhood schools to avoid desegregation. Some districts were gerrymandered to conform to the racial division of neighborhoods. In some districts, blacks who applied to attend white schools were required to pass special tests to prove their fitness.

Second, the Civil Rights Act of 1964 authorized federal officials to cut off federal funds from districts that failed to desegregate their schools. This meant little in 1964, when federal funds for elementary and secondary schools were minor, but it became a powerful weapon to compel desegregation after 1965, when federal aid to education was passed by the Congress. The United States Office of Education moved swiftly to establish guidelines by which it might determine whether a district was obeying the Civil Rights Act. For a year, the guidelines required free-choice plans. By 1966, unhappy with the slow pace of the first year, education officials promulgated new guidelines which set out in detail the numerical range of proportions of each race that had to be in integrated schools in each district in order to assure the flow of federal funds. The Fifth Circuit Court of Appeals rejected challenges to the HEW guidelines, holding that freedom of choice was permissible only so long as it brought about integration. By 1968, the Supreme Court invalidated a free-choice plan that did not produce substantial integration. And by 1971, the high court directed the schools of Charlotte-Mecklenburg, North Carolina, to do whatever was necessary—including busing children away from their neighborhood schools, gerrymandering of districts and creation of noncontiguous attendance zones—in order to bring about "truly non-discriminatory assignments."

Third, just as the federal bureaucracy and the federal judiciary began to abandon the color-blind principle, the black power movement emerged. Black power spokesmen ridiculed the leaders of the civil rights movement as Uncle Toms and accommodationists. It was not their rejection of integration that gave them mass appeal, however, but rather their open advocacy of black self-interest. While civil rights leaders championed policies of non-discrimination, the black advocacy movement demanded black principals, black teachers, specific jobs, here and now, period. Even after the more flamboyant black activists passed from the national scene, many of their ideas and goals were absorbed into the programs of the traditional organizations of the civil rights movement.

Fourth, the color-blind principle lost much of its luster for the civil rights organizations as soon as it was established in law. Once it was a fact, it ceased to be a goal. Organizations either generate new goals or become defunct. One cannot keep a mass movement excited about goals that have already been attained. Nor can a revolution of rising expectations be satisfied by non-discrimination policies alone.

Fifth, some of those who had led the fight against segregation came to believe that color blindness is an abstract principle with no power to alter the status quo and no possibility of making up for the effects of past discrimination, either in institutional or in personal terms. One of the champions of color-blind policy, Robert Carter, now a federal district judge, believes that group preferences will in time cause the nation's institutions, professions and work force to reflect the racial, ethnic, religious and gender composition of the population. In his view, the color-conscious policy brings about by compulsion what the color-blind policy should have brought about if implemented in good faith.

Thus it was that the idea of a color-blind society fell out of fashion almost as soon as it was enacted into law and well before it became part of custom. This is a turn of events with consequence for American society. We do not have a broad-based civil rights movement in the United States today precisely because the only common purpose that could bind dozens of minorities together is the goal of preventing discrimination against *all* minorities. The fight to ban discrimination, which gathered to its banners a powerful coalition of diverse groups, has been replaced for now by group-ism, or every interest group for itself. The idea of universalism is in retreat, an idea whose time came and went with amazing speed.

Black civil rights leaders fear that color blindness today means a willful refusal to recognize exclusionary practices that operate under the guise of racial neutrality. Opponents of group-conscious policies fear that to replace old-fashioned racism with well-intentioned racialism is divisive and wrong. Somewhere between total color blindness and extreme color-consciousness, there must be a reconciliation of democratic values. Strict neutrality in admissions and hiring, with no effort to remedy the effects of past discrimination, will leave many blacks right where they are, at the bottom. The alternative to racial quotas is the kind of program that prepares blacks to succeed without racial preferences, such as special tutoring for college admission or for union apprenticeship tests. A remarkable example is the Recruitment and Training Program (RTP), a New York-based national organization which since 1965 has recruited and trained more than 30,000 blacks for well-paid apprenticeships in construction trade unions. As a result of RTP's efforts, minority membership in the affected unions has grown from three percent to 19 percent. Similarly, educational programs that upgrade academic skills have enabled black students not only to gain admission to colleges and graduate schools, but to complete their studies successfully. One noteworthy example is the ABC (A Better Chance) program, now in its 16th year. ABC identifies promising minority youngsters from economically disadvantaged backgrounds and helps them to get high quality college preparation, either in their own communities or in boarding schools. About 6000 students have received financial aid from ABC for their secondary schooling, and more than 90 percent have entered college. Most ABC students are accepted in the most selective colleges, where their preparation enables them to compete as equals.

Such creative interweaving of color-conscious and racially neutral approaches recognizes the need to overcome the effects of past discrimination by supplying the skills and motivation to achieve without regard to race or social origins. In the long run, the ability of minorities to sustain the occupational and educational gains of the past 15 years depends not only on those who enter higher education but on those who can hold their own academically, and not only on those who win union jobs but on those who can do the job well.

Whether it is possible to treat people as individuals rather than as group members is as uncertain today as it was in 1954. And whether it is possible to achieve an integrated society without distributing jobs and school places on the basis of group identity is equally uncertain. What does seem likely, though, is that the trend toward formalizing group distinctions in public policy has contributed to a sharpening of group consciousness and group conflict. As a people, we are still far from that sense of common humanity to which the civil rights movement appealed. We may yet find that just such a spirit is required to advance a generous and broad sense of the needs and purposes of American society as a whole.

★★

3

The Federalist on Federalism   Martin Diamond

There is no way to overstate the importance of federalism to our political system. Not only are each of the 81,209 separate governments and governmental units in the United States affected, but interest groups, professional groups, and political parties are also organized on a "federal" basis with units at the national, state, and local levels. In truth, the entire political process is federalized. As Martin Diamond indicates, federalism was probably the Framers' most important contribution to democratic government.

The first and primary commentary on federalism is the collection of essays known as the The Federalist, *written by the very persons who were most intimately involved with its design. The thrust of these essays, Diamond argues, is that federal government has both a national and a federal identity. Since the Framers were attempting to overcome the weaknesses of the Articles of Confederation and trying to infuse more of a national identity into the new government, their focus on the national component is not surprising. How did the Framers distinguish "national" from "federal"? What effect did the Framers' concern with the "national component" of government have on the composition of federal institutions? Does each institution reveal both federal and national elements?*

In his discussion Diamond refers to John C. Calhoun's theory of "concurrent majority," a notion that would disallow government from initiating legislation that was in opposition to any identified major interests. Does Calhoun's theory help differentiate the meaning of the terms "confederalism" and "federalism"? Is the theory of "concurrent majority" applicable to the contemporary political system? Does this theory help explain how policy sometimes fails to pass in Congress because of the strong opposition of some interest groups?

Finally, Diamond urges us to take care that we do not unnecessarily disturb the federal-national components of federalism since, if we do, we risk affecting important interconnecting links of the political system. If this is the case, what do you feel we should do about the Electoral College? What would happen to the political system should we choose to elect a president by direct election? Would other elements of the system be affected?

★ ★ ★

Commentaries on *The Federalist*

The Federalist on Federalism: "Neither a National Nor a Federal Constitution, But a Composition of Both"

Martin Diamond†

Something surprising confronts the contemporary reader who turns to *The Federalist* to see what it has to say about federalism. Expecting to find the original source of his view of American federalism, he finds instead a very different understanding from ours of the nature of federalism and of the federal character of American government. We think that the invention of federal government was the most important contribution made by the American founders to the art of government and we thus regard the system they devised as the very paradigm of what we call "federal government." Indeed, as we shall see, most contemporary definitions of federalism are little more than generalized descriptions of the way we Americans divide governing power between the states and the central government. It is surprising, therefore, to discover that *The Federalist* does not likewise characterize the American constitutional system as a "federal government." Instead, it tells us that the "proposed Constitution . . . is in strictness neither a national nor a federal constitution; but a composition of both."[1]

This formulation is typical of the way the entire founding generation saw the matter. For example, the proceedings of the Federal Convention—especially in the famous compromise regarding the House and Senate—show that the delegates likewise understood the terms federal and national in a way that required characterizing the Con-

† Leavey Professor of the Foundations of American Freedom, Georgetown University. The Editors regret the passing of Professor Diamond not long after this essay was completed. All students of the Constitution are greatly indebted to him for what he taught us about the thought and aspirations that inspired our existing form of government.

1. THE FEDERALIST No. 39, at 257 (J. Cooke ed. 1961) [hereinafter cited to this edition without reference to editor]. Professor Cooke's edition is the definitive modern edition of *The Federalist*.

stitution as a compound or composition of both elements. But what Madison and the founding generation carefully distinguished as partly federal and partly national, we have for a long time blended or blurred under the single term federal. Alexis de Tocqueville saw this happening: "Clearly here we have not a federal government but an incomplete national government. Hence a form of government has been found which is neither precisely national nor federal; but things have halted there, and the new word to express this new thing does not yet exist."[2] Although it may well have been politically salutary that things "halted" at the old word federal, much may thereby have been lost in precision. And that is the concern of this review of what *The Federalist* teaches about federalism, namely, to suggest that it would be analytically useful to restore *The Federalist*'s "strict" distinction between the federal and the national elements in our compound political system, and therewith to restore also *The Federalist*'s understanding of federalism in general.

The Federalist was operating with a typology, so to speak, composed of two fundamental modes of political organization, the federal and the national. The founders thought that they had combined these two fundamental modes or "elements" into a "compound" system. We disagree and think, instead, that they invented a third fundamental mode or element, which we call federal government. In so thinking, we are operating with a typology composed of three elemental forms: confederation, federal government, and national or unitary government. The difference between our thinking and that of the founders evidently turns on the distinction that we make, and they did not, between confederalism and federalism. That familiar distinction will be found in almost all contemporary writing on federalism. But *The Federalist* and the whole founding generation saw no more difference between confederalism and federalism than we see, say, between the words inflammable and flammable; nothing more was involved than the accidental presence or absence of a nonsignifying prefix. For the founders, then, there were only two basic modes to choose from: confederal/federal as opposed to national/unitary; confederal/federal being that mode which preserves the primacy and autonomy of the states, and the national/unitary being that mode which gives unimpeded primacy to the government of the whole society. Given their bipartite typology or framework, the founders had to view the Constitution as being a "composition" of the two elemental modes and, given our tripartite one, we have to see the Constitution as elementally federal. The question is who is right, we or they? Which is the more useful mode of analysis?

It is instructive, and perhaps disconcerting, to learn that our modern distinction between confederalism and federalism derives from John Calhoun. His *Discourse on the Constitution and Government of the United States* begins with a severe and systematic attack on *The Federalist*'s view of federalism. In particular, Calhoun argues that its view of American government as compoundly federal and national is

---

2.   A. DE TOCQUEVILLE, DEMOCRACY IN AMERICA 143 (J. Mayer & M. Lerner eds. 1966).

a "deep and radical error."[3] Now Calhoun had some very practical reasons for rejecting the "compound" view. He could not admit that there was anything national at all about the central government because that would open the door to an effective national jurisdiction over South Carolina's slave interests. Yet, because the central government under the Constitution was so palpably stronger than under the Articles of Confederation, Calhoun could not characterize it as confederal/federal, which was the only category left to him according to the bipartite typology then still universally accepted. Moreover, Calhoun did not really want to return to the old Articles; he was not averse to having a government as powerful as that under the Constitution, provided it could be rendered safe for southern interests. Calhoun solved all of his problems by inventing a new category of "federal government" which he contradistinguished from both a confederacy and a national government.

Not surprisingly, Calhoun saw "federal government" as differing rather more from the national form, which posed the threat to southern interests, than from the confederal form. Indeed, Calhoun's new "federal government" turns out to be nothing but a confederacy in all respects save one; unlike a confederacy, which has at its center "a mere congress of delegates,"[4] it has a real central government to carry its powers into execution. This becomes clear if we examine his famous and shrewdly labeled theory of the "concurrent majority." The concurrent *majority* is in fact a system of *unanimous* concurrence; according to Calhoun's scheme, the central government can act only when its measures have the unanimous concurrence of majorities in every sovereign sub-unit of the system. This requirement of unanimity (an exaggeratedly confederal requirement) guaranteed that nothing could be done without the voluntary concurrence of South Carolina. Whatever South Carolina concurred in, however, would then be executed, not with confederal weakness, but directly upon individuals throughout the country with the full force of a national government. Is it not clear, then, that far from being contradistinguished from confederation and national government, Calhoun's "federal government" is in fact nothing but a compound of these two fundamental forms? He combined an exaggeratedly confederal/federal means of arriving at central decisions with a wholly national means of execution, and then arbitrarily assigned to his peculiar compound the new label of federal government.

This appears to have been an important source of our contemporary understanding of federalism. While we have largely rejected his theory of the concurrent majority, we have nonetheless taken over Calhoun's tripartite framework and the elemental status it assigns to federal government. Many scholars have, of course, been perfectly aware that the founding generation conceived their handiwork differently than Calhoun did and we do. But the difference has not been taken seriously.

---

3. J. Calhoun, A Disquisition on Government and a Discourse on the Constitution and Government of the United States 156 (R. Cralle ed. 1851).
   4. *Id.* at 163.

Either there has been a patronizing assumption that our understanding has scientifically superseded theirs, or the difference has been shrugged off as a mere matter of their having their terminology and we ours.[5] But this is surely too serious a matter to be so quickly dismissed; if *The Federalist* is analytically right in its compound view, then we have lost ground in our understanding of federalism. After all, is it not as obscurantist in political things, as it would be in, say, physics or chemistry, to confuse as a new element what in fact is only a compound? In both cases, it would be rendered difficult if not impossible to see how the essential parts of the compound worked and, thereby, to know how to achieve, preserve, or improve it.

To resolve our dispute with *The Federalist*, as to whether our political system is compoundly federal and national or integrally federal, we need a satisfactory definition of federalism. Unfortunately, the current conventional definition will not do. Consider the following from the standard contemporary work on federalism by Professor K. C. Wheare. Like Calhoun, Wheare disagrees with *The Federalist*'s compound theory and also sees federal government as a distinctive form differing from both the confederal and the national forms. He defines this distinctive federal principle as "the method of dividing powers so that the general and regional governments are each, within a sphere, co-ordinate and independent."[6] Nearly all contemporary definitions concur in the single point of this one, namely, the reduction of federalism solely to the idea of the division of the governing power.[7] Indeed, the "division of power" definition of federalism is so familiar that it is hard to force ourselves to examine it closely. But its shortcomings will become evident if we ask precisely what is federal about such a division of power. Clearly there is nothing federal at all about the "general" government; it is just a national government like every other one, save that its jurisdiction is not complete. The only thing federal, then, is the retention by the "regional governments" of some portion of the governing power. But this is manifestly nothing more than to define arbitrarily as uniquely federal what is merely the combination of an incomplete national government with the retention in the member units of a confederal/federal autonomy in some respects. In short, the modern theory turns out to be an arbitrarily unacknowledged and hence obscuring version of *The Federalist*'s compound theory. *The Federalist* openly alerts us to the national and federal elements in the compound, enabling us to see when it is becoming more simply na-

5. A recent example of the latter is Gunther, *Toward "A More Perfect Union": Framing and Implementing the Distinctive Nation-Building Elements of the Constitution*, 2 STAN. LAW., Fall 1976, at 5. In this otherwise very thoughtful essay, Professor Gunther takes note of *The Federalist*'s compound theory, but then treats it only as belonging to "the terminology of that day." *Id.*

6. K. WHEARE, FEDERAL GOVERNMENT 11 (3d ed. 1953).

7. An example in a recent American textbook can be found in M. CUMMINGS & D. WISE, DEMOCRACY UNDER PRESSURE (3d ed. 1977): "[T]he United States has a *federal* system of government, in which power is constitutionally shared by a *national* government and fifty state governments." *Id.* at 63 (emphasis added). *See also* W. BENNETT, AMERICAN THEORIES OF FEDERALISM 10 (1964) (The "essence of federalism" is evidenced by any "political system in which there is a constitutional distribution of powers between provincial governments and a common central authority."); W. RIKER, FEDERALISM 5 (1964) ("The essential institutions of federalism are, of course, a government of the federation and a set of governments of the member units . . . .")

tional or more simply federal, and thereby enabling us to take appropriate action. By lumping together under the term federal government what *The Federalist* keeps separately visible, the modern definition makes it harder for us to see and evaluate such changes in the compound system.

But more importantly, the modern definition is a badly truncated version of *The Federalist*'s compound theory. It blinds us to a whole range of federal phenomena that *The Federalist*'s understanding of federalism properly comprehends. A moment's reflection reminds us what is left out. Consider the Senate; every school child knows (or at least used to be taught) that the Senate is a peculiarly federal part of American government. *The Federalist*, as we shall see, can readily explain what is federal about the Senate. And so can we all, unless we take seriously the modern definition of federalism, which makes the federalness of the Senate quite inexplicable. After all, the Senate has nothing to do with the reserved powers of the states, which is the sole federal desideratum according to the modern definition. The Senate is a part of the general government of the whole society. But it is a *federal* part of that government. And that is what the truncated modern definition cannot reach—the federal elements in the structure and procedures of the central government itself. By limiting federalism to the reserved jurisdiction of the states, the modern definition obliges us, insofar as we take it seriously, to conceive the central government as purely national. It thus contradicts what our commonsense tells us about the federal character of the Senate and, as we shall see, it tends to blind us to other federal elements in the design of our central government.

The Federalist's compound theory offers a clearer and fuller account of federalism, albeit not in the handy form of a definition. We must glean that definition from the various ways *The Federalist* replies to the main charge made by the opponents of the proposed Constitution, namely, that it had departed from the federal form in favor of the "consolidated" national form. In *Federalist* 39, where the charge is most systematically dealt with, Madison examines five ways to "ascertain the real character of the government" relative to the federal-national question.[8] By examining them closely, we will be able to piece together *The Federalist*'s understanding of federalism.

First, the mode by which the Constitution is to be ratified, Madison argues, is federal and not national, because only the voluntary assent of each state, taken as a distinct and independent body politic, joins it to the Union. Second, Madison examines the sources of the legislative and executive branches of the central government. The House of Representatives is national because it derives from the whole people treated as a single body politic; the people will be represented in it, Madison says, exactly as they would be in any unitary state. Contrarily, the Senate is a federal element in the central government because it derives from, and represents equally, the states treated as "political and coequal societies." The Presidency has a "very com-

---

8. The quotations in the analysis that follows are taken from THE FEDERALIST No. 39, at 250-57. The concept of federalism is discussed throughout *The Federalist;* other papers that are especially relevant are numbers 15-17, 23, 27, 45, and 46.

pound source" because the electoral votes allotted to the states "are in a compound ratio, which considers them partly as distinct and coequal societies, partly as unequal members of the same society." The presidential aspect of the central government thus "appears to be of a mixed character presenting at least as many *federal* as *national* features."[9] Third, the government's mode of operation, in exercising its enumerated powers, is national because it reaches directly to individual citizens like any other national government (like any *government*, one might say). Fourth, as to the extent of its powers, Madison cautiously says that the government "cannot be deemed a national one," because it has a limited, enumerated jurisdiction. Madison means that the new system is national as to the extent of powers entrusted, but is federal insofar as a substantial portion of the governing powers autonomously remains with the states as distinct political societies. (Notice that Madison is here treating as but one aspect of federalism what the modern definition treats as the whole of it. In his first three considerations, Madison had been inquiring into what was federal in the formation, structure, and operation of the central government, that is, into crucial aspects of federalism which the modern definition excludes from its purview.)

Fifth, and finally, Madison judges the amending process to be neither wholly federal nor wholly national. His argument on this brings to the fore the logic and language of his theory of federalism.

> [Were the amending process] wholly national, the supreme and ultimate authority would reside in the *majority* of the people of the Union; and this authority would be competent at all times, like that of a majority of every national society, to alter or abolish its established Government. Were it wholly federal on the other hand, the concurrence of each State in the Union would be essential to every alteration that would be binding on all. . . . In requiring more than a majority, and particularly in computing the proportion by *States*, not by *citizens*, it departs from the *national*, and advances toward the *federal* character: In rendering the concurrence of less than the whole number of States sufficient, it loses again the *federal*, and partakes of the *national* character.[10]

This is the way the federal principle was understood in 1787 and, for that matter, in all earlier political writings. We are now in a position to summarize it. Having the nature of a "league or contract,"[11] federalism is a relation of independent, equal bodies politic that join together for limited purposes and carry those out, as the Latin root (*foedus, fides*) of the word reminds us, only by the obligation of good faith, rather than by governmental, which is to say coercive, authority. Insofar as any governmental structure, process, power, or practice conforms to the primacy of the separate bodies politic, to their equal status within the federal association, to the limited nature of that

---

9. THE FEDERALIST No. 39, at 255 (emphasis in original).

10. *Id*. at 257 (emphasis in original).

11. Samuel Johnson's dictionary defined "confederacy" as: "A league; a contract by which several persons or bodies of men engage to support each other; union; engagement; federal compact." The definition of "federal" said: "Relating to a league or contract." The entry for "federate" said: "Leagued; joined in confederacy." 1 S. JOHNSON, A DICTIONARY OF THE ENGLISH LANGUAGE (Philadelphia 1818) (1st Amer. ed. from 11th London ed.).

association, and to its operational dependence upon faithful compliance rather than political coercion, the structure, process, power, or practice is federal; insofar as it departs toward the principle of a complete, coercive government of a single body politic, it is national. Indeed, one may even contrast federalism, not only with national government, but with government as such. This is in fact what Alexander Hamilton argues in *Federalist* 15. The Constitution differs from the Articles of Confederation, he argues, because it incorporates "those ingredients which may be considered as forming the characteristic difference between a league and a government."[12]

Because they thus understood federalism, the leading Framers of the Constitution were convinced that no "merely federal" system would suffice for the purposes of union.[13] For those purposes, the federal principle of voluntary association was inadequate; a true government of the whole was required. "Mr. Govr. Morris explained the distinction beween a *federal* and *national, supreme,* Govt.; the former being a mere compact resting on the good faith of the parties; the latter having a compleat and *compulsive* operation."[14] Accordingly, in the Virginia Plan, the leading Framers proposed "a *national* Government . . . consisting of a *supreme* Legislative, Executive & Judiciary."[15] Happily, as we may now say, they did not wholly succeed in their plan to institute "one supreme power, and one only";[16] federal elements were worked back into their national design. Had the nationalists wholly succeeded, the Preamble of the Constitution would have had to read "in order to form a perfect Union," not just a *"more* perfect" one. Had the opponents of the Constitution succeeded, the country would have remained under the radically imperfect Union provided by the Articles of Confederation. The phrase "a more perfect Union" is no grammatical solecism, but an accurate description of the compromised, compoundly federal and national system that resulted from the Convention and that Madison had the theoretical apparatus to analyze so precisely.

The Federalist's theory of federalism is not only analytically superior to our contemporary approach in explaining the American political system as originally devised, but it also better illuminates the federal-national balance of the system as it has developed historically. The Senate is again a good case in point. It has developed in some respects into a more nationally oriented body than the House, where localist tendencies are very strong. Yet why should this be so if the Senate, because of the equal suffrage of the states, is the formally federal branch of the legislature? Should that not have made the Senate primarily parochial rather than national in outlook? It could be suggested that its not having become so is but one more example of the way formal, institutional factors propose, while underlying historical and behavioral forces informally dispose in unanticipated ways. We need not have recourse to the mysterious working of such forces in

12. THE FEDERALIST No. 15, at 95.
13. 1 M. FARRAND, THE RECORDS OF THE FEDERAL CONVENTION OF 1787, at 33 (rev. ed. 1937).
14. *Id.* at 34 (emphasis in original).
15. *Id.* at 33 (emphasis in original).
16. *Id.* at 34 (remark of Gouverneur Morris).

order to explain why the Senate developed both federal and national characteristics. Using *The Federalist*'s compound theory, we can see that the Senate was formally constituted in a more compound manner than is usually appreciated. Now the leading Framers had always intended some sort of senate to balance and moderate the more immediately democratic House of Representatives; as the democratic analogue of the traditional upper or aristocratic house, it was intended to be the branch that took the longer and more systematic, as it were, the more national view. But the Connecticut Compromise (national House, federal Senate) threatened to balk that intention. The leading Framers feared that the Senators, as had been so many delegates to the Confederal Congress, would be too closely bound by state interests and views to function, as desired, on behalf of long-run national considerations. They succeeded in mitigating the federal character of the Senate by means of four subtle formal departures from the practice under the Articles of Confederation. One was the provision for per capita voting ("each Senator shall have one Vote"). The Articles had required each state's delegates to cast a single ballot as a delegation; this forced them to form, as it were, an ambassadorial judgment on behalf of the state. The constitutional per capita provision invites and enables Senators to form individual legislative judgments just as do members of the national House of Representatives.

The other departures were three closely linked provisions, all of which likewise tended to lessen the federal control of the states over the Senators. One disallowed the states the power they had under the Articles to recall their delegates at any time. Another provided for the six-year senatorial term; and the third permitted indefinite and uninterrupted eligibility for re-election. The Articles had provided that no person could serve more than three years during any six-year period, the aim being to keep the delegates on a short leash with frequent rustication, so to speak, back to the states.

It is easy to summarize the significance of all these departures. The *federal* aim of the Articles was to reduce the delegates as much as possible to the status of agents of their states. The *national* aim of the Constitution was to make the Senators, despite the federally equal suffrage of the states, more nearly into representatives in the Burkean sense, free to serve long-run national interests as the deliberative process suggested. To appreciate the effectiveness of these provisions in permitting the Senate to develop a national outlook despite its partly federal basis, think how very much more federal (like Congress under the Articles) it would have been had the state delegations been obliged to vote as a unit and had the Senators been obliged to function under the threat of state recall. By contrast, imagine that the states had not been made the electoral districts for the Senate and, as was strongly urged at the Convention, that districts had been based upon the same national population principle as the House of Representatives. How very much *less* federal—how very much less committed to the primacy of state interests and views—the Senate and all of American politics would then have become. The peculiarly mixed character of the Senate as it actually developed becomes more visible and intelligible when we understand it in the light of *The Federalist*'s theory of a compoundly federal and national constitutional basis.

Indeed, that theory of federalism can make more visible and intelligible the compound complexity of the whole American political system. It is thus especially valuable to those who treasure the federal elements in the compound and who fear that those elements are weakening, because it enables them to see more clearly what and where the sources of federal vitality are throughout the whole political system. As we have seen, these are of two fundamental kinds: everything connected with the division of governing power, and everything connected with the federal elements in the central government. The importance of the first source, the balance between state power and the enumerated powers of the central government, is understandable enough under the modern theory of federalism; indeed, that is all it comprehends. It also is that source or aspect of federalism most familiar and intelligible to students of constitutional law. Ever since *McCulloch v. Maryland*, the question of the extent of the enumerated powers has been, to use Marshall's phrase, "perpetually arising."[17] In any event, it happens to be a question that is perpetually gratifying to lawyers and the courts because it is so amenable to legal disputation and judicial determination. But *The Federalist*, as this review has argued, directs our attention to what may be called the political rather than the legal side of federalism. It emphasizes that other and neglected source of federalism, namely, the federal elements in the design of the central government itself and in its politics. Both sources of federalism, not just the one emphasized in the modern theory and in constitutional law, sustain the federal vitality of American government and political life, a vitality achieved by keeping interest, affection, power, and energy alive and well at the state level of politics in an otherwise homogenizing and centralizing age. Neither source should be neglected.

The status of the first of these two has been rendered increasingly problematic since the time of the New Deal. For decades the limiting doctrine of delegated and enumerated powers has been eroded, and the scope of national government has been vastly expanded. True, the strength of the states in the system has not been weakened to a corresponding degree. This is because the states have likewise vastly increased the scope of their activities. Although perhaps not an unmixed blessing, it means that the state is still that government which most affects citizens in their daily lives. Heedless of many learned pronouncements on their obsolescence, the states have thus stubbornly retained more of their federal vigor than might have been expected. Nonetheless, those who are concerned to preserve the federalism in the American compound remain concerned to limit the growth of national government relative to the states, as one indispensable support for that federalism. To this end, it is especially necessary to restore the moral and intellectual *bona fides* of the constitutional doctrine of enumerated powers as a crucial resource for limiting that growth.

But those concerned to preserve federalism must also devote their energies to that other support of American federalism to which *The Federalist* alerts them, namely, the federal elements in the central

---

17. 17 U.S. (4 Wheat.) 316, 405 (1819).

government. One such element now under heavy attack is the Electoral College. But the federal aspect to the Electoral College controversy has received relatively little attention: indeed, it is regarded as irrelevant to it. The argument has been that because the President is the representative of "all the people," he should be elected by them in a wholly national way, unimpeded by the interposition of the states through the Electoral College. Given the prevailing understanding of federalism, the "general" government is supposed to be purely national; from this perspective, the participation of the states in presidential selection does indeed seem to be an unjustifiable intrusion, and the potential "mischiefs" resulting from that intrusion seem insupportable. But from the perspective of *The Federalist*'s compound theory of American government, there is no reason why the President, admittedly the representative of "all the people," cannot represent them and, hence, be elected by them in a way corresponding to the American government's compoundly federal and national character.

The Presidency, especially the modern Presidency, is no doubt the most nationalizing single element in the American political system, and quite rightly so. Yet the method by which the President is elected has also operated for years in a countervailing federalizing fashion, and just as rightly so. Every Presidential election—the nominating campaigns as well as the electoral campaign itself—is a dramatic reaffirmation that the states are the basis of American political life. Nothing is more vigorously federal than this informal manifestation of federalism in political practice. But it all depends upon the formal structure of the Electoral College as originally conceived and as subsequently statutorily modified by the states. The informal federalizing effect of the Electoral College derives in the first instance from the "compound ratio" by which the states figure in the original constitutional design. Still more federalizing is the general ticket or unit-rule system (the state's entire electoral vote goes to the popular vote winner in the state) which, for nearly a century and a half, almost all the states have employed. Any removal of these federalizing elements, any change toward a purely national mode of Presidential election, would have a corresponding nationalizing effect on the spirit and practice of American politics. The nominating process—primaries and national party conventions—now is radically decentralized by force of the Electoral College's use of the states as states; the nominating process naturally takes its cues from the electing process. If the President were elected in a single national election, the same "cuing" process would continue, but in reverse.

However unproblematic such a centralizing effect might have seemed to partisans of electoral reform some years ago, it seems very problematic indeed now when circumstances are so changed. The thrust of much recent social and political criticism has been against the homogenizing and centralizing tendencies of mass society and its tendency to diminish political participation. *The Federalist* alerts us to the federal implications of the Electoral College and its potential for countervailing those tendencies. To nationalize the Presidential election, especially in this age of electronic media, is to reduce Presidential politics to a single arena with room for little participation. By preserving the federal importance of the states in the process, the Electoral College scatters the Presidential contest into fifty-one arenas (the states and the District of Columbia), with correspondingly enlarged opportunity for a vastly greater number of political participants.

The modern theory of federalism tends to blind us to such peripheral possibilities of federalism in the Presidential election process and throughout our political system. *The Federalist*'s theory is superior in clarity and comprehensiveness. The reason this can be so, despite nearly two centuries of eventful history since *The Federalist* was written, is that its political understanding was not limited to the historical period within which it was produced. Rather, it speaks to perennial political issues and, especially, to those peculiar to the genius of American politics. Publius (the pen name Hamilton, Madison, and Jay used in writing the essays) remains our most instructive political thinker. Making accessible to contemporary use his subtle understanding of federalism and of the compoundly federal and national American republic has been the intention of this review.

★★

4 American Politics, Then & Now   James Q. Wilson

In his observations of the American political system, James Q. Wilson is impressed by the argument of one observer who finds that our system has the same contradictory tendencies as a large crowd that may move either very sluggishly or very quickly. What are the causes for this sort of behavior in the political system? What can be done to restrain some of these extreme movements?

Wilson points to the handiwork of Madison and the other Framers who invented a federal system that would contain political factions and reduce the possibilities of majority tyranny. How successful was their remedy of encouraging ambition to check ambition?

The author notes the added demands that have recently been put on the political system and suggests that they have come about because it is now easier to make use of the political system. Is government in reality more accessible to the citizen? Or have these added demands clogged the established channels of access, causing increased delays and added inefficiencies in government?

One contemporary change Wilson notes in institutions such as Congress and political parties has been the "atomization" and decentralization of institutions. Political power is now more broadly dispersed within. What challenges does this pose for congressional and party leadership? What changes in legislation and party policy would you expect as a result of this "atomization"? What benefits or detriments have come as a consequence of this change?

Finally, Wilson is particularly concerned with the recent trend toward one-issue politics wherein one finds "pro-abortion" forces in opposition to "pro-life" advocates, wherein one sees "gun controllers" pitted against those who feel it their "right" to bear arms. Are there other such groups polarized along similar public policy lines? Could any of these groups be considered "veto" groups? Does an understanding of Calhoun's theory of "concurrent majority" help make clear this phenomenon? Should one expect compromise between such clashing interests? If not, how can the political system expect to bring resolution to these competing interests?

★ ★ ★

American Politics, Then & Now

James Q. Wilson

THE administration of President Carter offers an appropriate occasion for asking a question that will be raised with growing frequency as this nation approaches the bicentennial observance of the writing of the Constitution: has the American political system changed fundamentally? If no accident befalls him, Jimmy Carter will be the first Democrat in this century to serve a full term in the White House without having to lead the nation into war or out of economic disaster. Indeed, the historical rarity of the present moment is even more striking: Carter is (so far) the first Democratic President since before the Civil War to serve a full term without either war or depression and to have a Democratic majority in both houses of Congress. The Carter administration offers, in this sense, an example of a "normal" administration in the hands of what has become the nation's dominant political party.

Would the political system inherited by President Carter be recognized by its architect, James Madison? Or by the powerful Republican Senators of the late 19th century? Or even by Harry Truman? We can turn to the *Federalist Papers* for an account of what that system was supposed to be in 1787; if that seems too antiquarian a source for the restlessly contemporary modern mind, we can turn to descriptions written a generation ago by leading journalists and political scientists.

In 1948, the late John Fischer published in *Harper's* magazine an article on the "Unwritten Rules of American Politics" that was at the time, and for many years thereafter, widely recognized as the best brief analysis of the distinctive features of American politics. He drew upon the writings of John C. Calhoun, the South Carolina politician and intellectual who nearly a century before had set forth the doctrine of the "concurrent majority." In Calhoun's time, of course, that doctrine was a defense of the Southern resistance to federal legislation aimed at restricting the spread of slavery, but Fischer, aided by the writings of Peter

JAMES Q. WILSON is Shattuck Professor of Government at Harvard University and the author of, among other books, *The Investigators* and *Political Organizations*.

Drucker, found in the theory of the concurrent majority, stripped of its extremist and partisan language, an enduring and fundamental explanation of the American constitutional system.

That system was designed to preserve liberty and maintain a national union by a set of procedures meant to insure that no important decision would be reached without the concurrence of each interest vitally affected by that decision. In Congress, no important bloc would be voted down on any matter that touched its central concern. In nominating a presidential candidate, no one would be acceptable who was objectionable to any significant body of opinion within the party. In electing a President, both parties would sacrifice any interest in principle or policy to accommodate the views of the average voter and thus would almost always offer an echo, not a choice. Politics would be non-ideological, conflict would be minimized, and such policies as survived the process of interest-group bargaining would command widespread support and thus be likely to endure. All these were, to Fischer, the strengths of the system. It had costs as well—a disposition to inaction, a tendency to magnify the power of well-organized pressure groups, and a shortage of persons able to speak for the nation as a whole. But to Fischer, the strengths clearly outweighed the weaknesses, primarily because man is fallible: the very slowness of the system insured against the premature commitment to error. As Learned Hand once wrote, "The spirit of liberty is the spirit which is not too sure that it is right."

Fischer's concern for moderation, even at the price of inaction, was understandable in its time. In 1948, the Democratic party was split into three wings. Progressives (and the Communist party) were supporting Henry Wallace and Southern reactionaries were supporting J. Strom Thurmond, while beleaguered Harry Truman was struggling—as it turned out, successfully—to hold the Democratic middle.

PERSONS who believe that all this has changed point to the legislative explosion that occurred during the 1960's and early

1970's. Without benefit of a national emergency which in the past had always been necessary for the system of veto groups to be set aside, there poured forth from Congress an unprecedented wave of policy innovation. The Southern filibuster was broken and civil-rights bills became law. The caution of the House Ways and Means Committee was overcome and Medicare and Medicaid were passed. The fears of federal control of schools that for long prevented federal aid to education were set aside and such aid became a massive and growing reality. The War on Poverty, the model-cities program, and the rest of the Great Society legislation arrived, to be followed, toward the end of the 1960's, by the emergence of environmental and consumer legislation. Between 1966 and 1970, at least eighteen major consumer-protection laws and seven major air- and water-pollution laws were passed, and the activity continued well into the 1970's.

As important as the number of new programs adopted was the way in which they were adopted. The veto groups and congressional blocs that were thought to stand astride each checkpoint in the legislative process, letting nothing pass without first extracting every necessary concession, were scarcely to be found. The bill creating federal aid to education went through committee review and floor debate virtually without amendment, leading three Republicans on a House subcommittee to boycott the hearings on the bill because of the "hasty and superficial consideration" it was receiving. The original Medicare plan made provision only for paying the hospital bills of the elderly; Congress added a provision for public payment of doctors' bills as well. Congressional deliberations on the auto-safety bill of 1966 made that law, in virtually every particular, stronger than what the President had requested; when the conference committee considered the versions passed by the House and Senate, it resolved all remaining issues in favor of the tougher—that is, the more anti-industry—provision. By the end of the 1960's, the American Medical Association, long described as one of the most powerful interest groups in Washington, had been defeated and the automobile industry stood revealed, in Elizabeth Drew's phrase, as a "paper hippopotamus." Ralph Nader had become the best-known and perhaps the most powerful lobbyist in town.

II

THE opposite view is that, despite the frenzy of the 1960's, nothing of fundamental importance changed. The Carter Presidency has been functioning rather much like the Truman Presidency: unheroically, with little public enthusiasm, winning some battles and losing others. Liberal ideas of 1948, such as civil rights, national health insurance, and federal aid to education, were defeated; liberal ideas of 1976, such as national health insurance, welfare and tax revisions, and new labor laws, were likewise defeated. Though the nation was at peace in 1948 as in 1976, both Presidents were preoccupied in large measure with foreign affairs—the Marshall Plan, NATO, and international trade in the case of Truman; the Panama Canal, tension in the Middle East, and relations with Turkey in the case of Carter. Both Presidents saw Congress debate at length a bill to deregulate natural gas and neither President was able to get out of the debate exactly what he wanted. Truman vetoed a deregulation bill passed in 1950, Carter signed a compromise deregulation bill in 1978. During his first year in office, Carter won on 75 per cent of the congressional votes taken on his program, far lower than the level of support enjoyed by Eisenhower, Kennedy, or Johnson in their first or second years.

The "conservative coalition" of Republicans and Southern Democrats which has been the bane of liberal legislation was, according to the *Congressional Quarterly*, alive and well in the 95th Congress. During 1977, it appeared in about one-fourth the recorded votes in the House and Senate and won about two-thirds of the time that it appeared. Truman would not have been surprised.

The burst of legislation in the 1960's was not the result, in this skeptical view, of any profound change in American politics, but was simply a consequence of the Goldwater fiasco. The Lyndon Johnson victory in 1964 gave the Democrats so large a majority in Congress that Northern Democratic liberals acquired a control of Congress that formerly only a national crisis would produce. Northern Democrats could have passed the aid-to-education bill and come within a few votes of passing the Medicare bill even if every Republican and Southern Democrat had voted against them. Moreover, the Goldwater candidacy brought Republicans to power in parts of the South and thereby reduced the control that Southerners, by virtue of the seniority system, had once wielded in Congress. In 1962, Alabama had eight Democratic Congressmen; after 1964, only three were left.

The changes did not stop in 1964. Going into the 1966 election, Virginia may have had as much power in Congress as it had in the days of Madison and Monroe, 150 years earlier. Democrats from that state held the chairmanships of the Senate Finance Committee, the House Rules Committee, and the Senate Banking and Currency Committee. "After the election," writes Gary Orfield, "all were gone as the Old Dominion lost a century of seniority."

But with the 1970's, normalcy returned, and with it either (depending on one's political convictions) stagnation or prudence. The struggle over the energy bill was mountainous, and yet what the mountain brought forth was not even a mouse, but a Tinker Toy out of which a gifted administrator *might* be able to fashion a reasonable facsimile of a mouse. Congress has reasserted its influence over foreign affairs, in part by the enactment of five or six dozen provisions of foreign aid and other laws requiring congressional assent to presidential initiatives. Whatever vision one has of a fair and rational tax code, there seems little prospect of Congress transforming that vision into reality. Traditional porkbarrel bills, such as public works, continue to prosper in Congress; the only remarkable feature of the present day is that the President, for reasons not well understood even by leaders of his own party, has tried—with only limited success—to block some projects.

In short, once extraordinary majorities evaporate and national crises recede, it is politics as usual. Recently, Senator Edward M. Kennedy attacked Congress for being "the best money could buy" and criticized the profusion and influence of interest groups. Though Kennedy was deploring what Fischer had applauded, the categories of description were very much the same.

III

BOTH interpretations of American politics are partially correct. Congress remains able, long after the 1960's, to pass sweeping new laws almost without regard to the normal constraints of interest-group bargaining, as it did when it decided in 1978 to abolish mandatory retirement before age seventy or decided in 1973 to give absolute protection to endangered species. And Congress continues to experience great difficulty in formulating a coherent policy on matters such as taxation, energy, or school desegregation. As Anthony King has recently observed, our political system has acquired the contradictory tendencies of a human crowd—"to move either very sluggishly or with extreme speed."*

Three things account for the schizophrenia of contemporary politics: one is the greater ease with which decisions can be transferred from the private to the public sphere; a second is the "atomization," as King terms it, of political institutions; a third is a change in the governing ideas of our time. The first factor has caused the American law-making system to be in a state of permanent excitability; the second has made the outcome of any excitement difficult to predict; and the third has been the source of the energy that determines whether the system will be in its manic or depressive phase.

Madison and the other framers of the Constitution created, as everyone knows, a federal government designed to prevent the mischief of faction and the tyranny of temporary majorities by so arranging its institutions that ambition would be made to check ambition. Douglass C. North, the economic historian, has stated one consequence of the Madisonian system this way: in order to reduce the ability of interest groups to capture the government, the constitutional order attached a

high cost to utilizing the political system as compared to the marketplace for making decisions. The "entry price" for politics was high, and thus only the largest or most popular factions were able to pay it. This price was both tangible and intangible. The material cost was the great effort required to organize groups (parties, factions, lobbies) influential enough to get an issue onto the agenda of Congress and to coordinate the decision of Congress (and its many parts) and the President. The non-material cost was the widespread belief that a large range of issues—public welfare, civil rights, the regulation of economic enterprise, even for a while the building of public works—was outside the legitimate scope of federal authority.

The late E. E. Schattschneider once observed that "he who decides what politics is about runs the country." Once politics was about only a few things; today, it is about nearly everything. There has been, in North's terms, a "drastic reduction in the cost of using the political process" relative to the cost of using, for similar results, the market. That reduction has been the result of easier access to the courts (by fee-shifting and class-action suits), the greater ease of financing interest groups with foundation grants and direct-mail fund-raising, and the multiplication of government agencies and congressional staffs.

Not only have the money costs of using political strategies fallen, the ideological costs have declined as well. Until rather recently, the chief issue in any congressional argument over new policies was whether it was legitimate for the federal government to do something at all. That was the crux of the dispute over Social Security, welfare, Medicare, civil rights, selective service, foreign aid, international alliances, price and wage controls, economic regulation, and countless other departures from the past. But once the initial law is passed, the issue of legitimacy disappears, and, except in those few cases where the Supreme Court later holds the law unconstitutional, does not reemerge.

Once the "legitimacy barrier" has fallen, political conflict takes a very different form. New programs need not await the advent of a crisis or an extraordinary majority, because no program is any longer "new"—it is seen, rather, as an extension, a modification, or an enlargement of something the government is already doing. Congressmen will argue about "how much," or "where," or "what kind," but not about "whether." One consequence is that the workload of Congress will grow astronomically.

Since there is virtually nothing the government has not tried to do, there is little it cannot be asked to do. Congressmen try frantically to keep

---

* *The American Political System* (American Enterprise Institute, 1978), p. 393.

up with this growing workload by adding to their staffs, but of course a bigger staff does not produce less work, it produces more, and so the ideas, demands, and commitments presented daily to a legislator grow even faster. Moreover, Congress creates a bureaucracy of its own to keep up with the information-gathering and policy-generating capacities of the executive branch, leading to what Senator Daniel P. Moynihan has characterized as the "Iron Law of Emulation."*

This dramatic expansion of the political agenda has helped alter the distribution of political power. At one time, the legislative process was biased in favor of the opponents of any new policy. The committee system and the great powers of committee chairmen meant that the crucial calculation to be made by a proponent of a new policy was not how many congressmen were in favor of it, but which congressmen were opposed to it. The fact that the proposed policy was new and that there were few or no precedents for governmental action in that area made it easier for a Wilbur Mills, a James Eastland, or a Howard Smith to use their position on the House Ways and Means Committee, the Senate Judiciary Committee, or the House Rules Committee to block consideration of the proposal. But when the government is already doing something in the area, then there is an existing agency of government, and its associated private supporters with a stake in the matter, and at the very least the appropriations bill for that agency, and usually the legislative amendments proposed by that agency, must be considered.

Political scientists have frequently described American policy-making as "incremental." Some have used the term admiringly, because the process it describes builds consensus; others have used it critically, because that process prevents radical change and misrepresents some interests. But whatever one thinks of the concept, it is increasingly hard to believe it generally descriptive. We have brought under new regulatory machinery whole sectors of our economy; changed in one sudden blow the legality of a mandatory retirement age; rewritten (in a manner almost no one understands) the basic law governing retirement systems; banned the use of whole categories of chemicals; given to Congress a legislative veto over important parts of our foreign policy once reserved entirely for the President; adopted a vast and expensive system for financing health care; put under public auspices a large part of the American rail system; created public financing of presidential campaigns; changed the meaning of "equality of opportunity" from "fair competition" to "the achievement of racial goals"; and come close to authorizing cash grants to parents of children attending parochial schools and private colleges. These may be good ideas or they may be bad ones, but it is hard to describe them—and dozens of others like them—as "marginal" or "incremental" changes in policy.

IV

THE second change has been the atomization of certain key political institutions, notably Congress and the political parties. Congress has, to a degree, been de-institutionalized and individualized: its leadership has become weaker, power within it has been dispersed, the autonomy and resources of its individual members have been enlarged. As a result, it is no longer helpful to think of Congress as consisting of blocs, each representing an interest group and each having a potential veto over measures affecting its vital interests. This might strike some readers as a gain—vested interests can no longer so easily say no to things they oppose. But such a view neglects the price that has been paid for this: if nobody can say no and make it stick, then neither can anybody say yes and make it stick. If there are no vetoes, neither are there any imprimaturs.

The individual member of Congress has gained enormously at the expense of committee chairmen, party leaders, and interest groups. He or she now has a large personal staff and a voice in the choice of the staff members of committees. (The congressional bureaucracy is probably the fastest-growing one in Washington, with no nonsense about civil service to inhibit it. The staff in 1976 was three times larger than it was in 1956.) The seniority system no longer governs the choice of committee chairmen to the exclusion of all other considerations; in 1975, House Democrats, by secret ballot, deposed three committee chairmen and elevated in their stead more junior members. Committees no longer regularly meet behind closed doors (whereas almost half of all House committee meetings were closed to the public in 1972, only 3 per cent were by 1975). Al Ullman cannot dominate the Ways and Means Committee the way Wilbur Mills once did, it is unlikely that Robert Byrd or his successors will have the power that Lyndon Johnson did when he was Senate majority leader, and though Tip O'Neill is a stronger Speaker than Carl Albert, he is a far cry from Sam Rayburn.

Some of the enhanced autonomy and status of individual, especially junior, members of Congress was won by back-bench revolts against leadership, but much of it was given to them by leaders attempting to build their own power by doing lasting favors for the rank-and-file. When Lyndon Johnson was Senate majority leader, his stature among freshmen Senators was high in part because he adopted a practice in the 1950's of giving to

---

*See his article, "Imperial Government," in the June 1978 COMMENTARY.

each new Senator at least one major committee assignment rather than, as had once been the case, of making them wait patiently for the "Club" to admit them into the ranks of the deserving. Among the latter-day beneficiaries of this generosity were George McGovern and Walter Mondale. In 1970, with only six years' seniority, McGovern became chairman of a Select Committee on Hunger and Mondale, with only seven years of service, chairman of a Committee on School Segregation. The well-publicized hearings of these committees did not harm the political ambitions of their youthful chairmen. In decentralizing power in Congress in order to enhance (temporarily) the power of a given leader, the leader is acting much like the man who keeps his house warm in the winter by burning in his fireplace the furniture, the doors, and the walls. Soon there is nothing left to burn.

It is not just the formal apparatus of party and leadership in Congress that is weaker, but the informal and social organization as well. Not long after Fischer wrote, William White described the Senate "Club" of veteran, chiefly Southern, Senators who dominated its affairs and acted, not surprisingly, entirely in the spirit of Calhoun and the concurrent majority. Within a decade after White wrote, the "Club" was pretty much finished, the victim of deaths, retirements, defeats, and—above all—political change. In 1949, in the Congress elected when Fischer was writing, Southerners held twice as many committee chairmanships as did Northerners and Westerners combined. By 1977, the Southern committee chairman was the exception, not the rule. In the period 1947-56, Gary Orfield notes, half of *all* the Democrats in Congress were from the South; today, less than one-third are.

Individual members of Congress are far more secure in their seats than once was the case, and with increased security goes increased freedom from those organizations, be they political parties or interest groups, that once controlled the resources necessary for reelection. Between 1952 and 1974, only about 6 per cent of the incumbent representatives seeking reelection were defeated, a substantial decline from earlier in this century. Moreover, of those running for reelection, fewer face close contests. When Fischer wrote in 1948, the winner of most House contests received 55 per cent of the vote or less. By 1972, most winners received 60 per cent of the vote or more. As political scientists like David Mayhew have pointed out, safe seats have become the rule, not the exception. Barring major electoral turnovers, such as in 1964, it may be that most new entrants to Congress will come from those districts where incumbents have decided voluntarily to retire.

Campaign-finance laws will strengthen this pattern. By restricting individual donations to $1,000, they limit sharply the chances of unknown and unwealthy candidates amassing large war chests to challenge well-known incumbents. By restricting donations from special-interest groups to $5,000, they limit the extent to which money can be the basis of group influence over legislators. (Rich candidates can still finance their own campaigns without restriction.) And if public financing of congressional campaigns should become law, one can be confident Congress will see to it that this "reform," like all others it has enacted, serves the advantage of incumbents.

The individualization and decentralization of Congress that has been the result of these changes in its internal affairs has been further augmented by the general decline of the political party, the increased use of radio and television for building personal followings in election campaigns, and the emergence of campaign organizations, often designed and staffed by professional campaign consultants, that are the personal property of the candidate rather than the collective effort of the party.

ONE consequence of these changes can be seen most dramatically in the Senate. From 1900 to 1956, only 30 per cent of the major-party candidates for President or Vice President came from the United States Senate; between 1960 and 1976, 70 per cent were Senators. The Senate has become the incubator of Presidents. When parties cannot pick presidential candidates but instead meet in conventions to ratify the choices made in two dozen or more primary elections and hundreds of local community caucuses, they discover they are often choosing among Senators because of the enormous advantage these persons have in developing a national reputation. The Senate is covered by the national press in a way the House is not; skillful and ambitious Senators can preside over dramatic hearings (into auto safety, the drug industry, malnutrition, organized crime, or intelligence-gathering) that are televised. Senators have the resources (a Senator from New York, for example, has a staff budget of around $1 million a year) to develop issues and reach national constituencies with which they wish to be identified. Computers can be programmed to produce huge and precisely indexed national mailing lists useful for reaching both voters and contributors.

When Fischer wrote, presidential candidates were still picked by conventions in which party "bosses" were influential. In 1948 there were presidential primaries in only fourteen states, and in five of these unpledged delegations ran at large. The open party caucus was almost unheard of. Though the Democratic party was deeply split among its ideological factions, the extremists of the Left and the Right did not contest the primaries but organized instead as independent parties. President Truman had only nominal opposition at the 1948 convention. In 1976, there were primaries in over two dozen states, wide open local caucuses in many others, and President Ford faced serious opposition in both the primaries and the convention. In each party, the ideological divisions were obvious and wide. Party regularity was an important consideration in 1948 for convention delegate and presidential candidate alike; anybody who used such a term in 1976 would have elicited either a smile or a yawn. When compromises were made in 1948, they were made to attract the middle-of-the-road voter; when they were made in 1976, it was to appease the more militant party activists (Walter Mondale was put on the Carter ticket to soothe the liberals, Robert Dole put on the Ford ticket to help please the conservatives). That Carter, a governor with no clear record on national issues, was able to win the Democratic nomination, was right in keeping with the political style of 1948; in 1976, however, it was seen as a curiosity to be explained by the temporary triumph of image over ideology in the wake of Watergate.

All these factors have tended to make the Congress of today, in comparison with that about which Fischer wrote in 1948, a collection of individuals rather than blocs. More precisely, blocs exist, but they are typically formed by the Congressmen themselves, on the basis of personal political convictions or broad allegiances to regions or sectors of society, rather than in response to, or as an instrument of, an organized interest outside Congress. Perhaps the largest and most significant bloc today is the Democratic Study Group, an organization of liberal Democrats in the House. It has leaders, a staff, a budget, regular meetings; its influence is hard to measure, but far from trivial. There is also a Black Caucus and a Northeast-Midwest Economic Advancement Coalition. In 1948, Congressmen were more likely to organize into a "farm bloc," or a "labor bloc," or an "oil bloc." Such influences still operate, of course, but groups based on ideology or racial or ethnic identification have become more important than those based on economic interest. And Congressmen change their minds more frequently, making it harder to count in advance on their position.

More assertive and individualistic members combined with fewer sources of influence mean that more effort must be devoted to rounding up votes. In the House, Representative John Brademas, the Democratic whip, is assisted by no fewer than 35 deputy or assistant whips and spends on this vote-producing operation over $400,000 a year, more than three times as much as was spent in 1970. One assistant whip with long experience recently complained that his job is "a hell of a lot more difficult than it used to be."

The individualization of politics has meant that interest groups have had to individualize their appeal and link it directly to the electoral fortunes of individual Congressmen. Thus, the rise of "grass-roots" lobbying—the careful, often computerized mobilization of letters, mailgrams, delegations, and financial contributions from individual citizens in each legislator's district or state. When the AFL-CIO was locked in struggle with the business-oriented National Action Committee on Labor Law Reform, the two sides were estimated to have generated nearly five million pieces of mail to Congress. Mark Green, director of Ralph Nader's Congress Watch, said that grass-roots lobbying has made Washington "an absolutely different city these days." Today, he noted, "you lose bills in the districts, not in Washington."

V

BUT if key political institutions are becoming so atomized, how does any policy get passed? The explanation, I suspect, is to be found in the third change in politics—the enhanced importance of ideas and of ideology. To return to Anthony King's metaphor, what makes the difference between the sluggish and the rushing crowd is the force of a compelling idea.

The Congress of 1968 or 1978, much more than that of 1948, is susceptible to the power of ideas whenever there seems to be a strong consensus as to what the correct ideas are. Such a consensus existed in the mid-1960's about the Great Society legislation; no such consensus about these matters exists today. This helps explain, as Henry J. Aaron has noted, the changing prospects of social-welfare policies. Consumerism, ecology, campaign-finance reform, and congressional ethics are other examples of ideas with strong symbolic appeal that, so long as the consensus endures, are handled by a political process in which the advantage lies with the proponents of change.

When a consensus evaporates or a symbol loses its power, issues are handled by a process which, like that in 1948, gives the advantage to the opponents of change. But sooner or later, a scandal, a shift in the focus of media attention, or the efforts of a skilled policy entrepreneur such as Ralph Nader or John Gardner will bring a compelling new idea to the top of the political agenda, and once again action will become imperative.

I do not wish to enter the argument whether there has been an "end of ideology" in the West or whether there is a heightened degree of "ideological constraint" in the public at large. Within Congress, however, the Republican party seems to have become more consistently conservative and the Democratic party more consistently liberal. Whatever has happened in society, the principle of affiliation among legislators has become, I think, more clearly based on shared ideas, and to a degree those shared ideas conform to party labels. (More accurately, the notion of party in Congress has been infused with more ideological meaning by its members.)

The point is debatable and easily overstated, but one illustration suggests what may have happened. In 1949, the House voted on a bill to deregulate natural gas. The influence of party was scarcely detectable and, had we the data, the influence of ideology only slightly more so. The Democrats split almost evenly (49 per cent in favor, 51 per cent opposed); the Republicans were a bit more lopsided (73 per cent in favor, 27 per cent opposed). In 1977, the House voted again on a comparable though not identical bill. Now, the influence of party was almost complete: 75 per cent of the Democrats opposed it; 88 per cent of the Republicans favored it. Pietro Novola at the University of Vermont has found that ideology and partisanship were vastly more important than economic interest (whether one comes from a gas-consuming or gas-producing district) in explaining the 1977 congressional vote.

Much attention has rightly been paid to one source of politically influential ideas—the "New Class" composed of persons having high levels of education and professional occupations. This group is decidedly more liberal than other groups in society, so much so that Everett Ladd was able to conclude that by the early 1960's, a majority of the "privileged" elements in society considered themselves Democrats and voted for Democratic candidates for Congress. The New Class is responsive to, and provides support for, politicians who favor abortion on demand, environmental- and consumer-protection laws, and equal rights for women.

But every class has its counterpart class. The discussion of the New Class, and even its label, leads attention away from what is happening to other, non-liberal groups in society. Upper-middle-class white Northern Protestants, once the bastion of traditional conservatism, have not been converted into a liberal New Class, they have been split into two deeply opposed groups. Sidney Verba and his co-workers found that in the 1950's, this group was the most conservative identifiable segment of American opinion. By the 1970's, however, a profound change had occurred—one part of this group had become even more conservative, while another part had become very liberal. High-status Wasps are now the most polarized class in America, and to the extent that this class contributes disproportionately to political elites, these elites have become more polarized.

These divisions of opinion contribute powerfully to the kind of "one-issue" politics so characteristic of the present era. Pro-abortion versus pro-life; gun control versus the right to bear arms; gay rights versus traditional values; ERA versus anti-ERA; nuclear energy versus solar energy; proponents of affirmative action versus opponents of reverse discrimination—all these causes and more make life miserable for the traditional, coalition-seeking politician. Weakened institutions, individualized politics, and the rise of an educated, idea-oriented public combine to make it highly advantageous for political entrepreneurs to identify and mobilize single-issue constituencies and to enlist them, not only into electoral and legislative politics, but into court suits, referendum campaigns, and even calls for constitutional conventions.

The importance of single-issue politics is, of course, much discussed, but not without a touch of hypocrisy. Most columnists and commentators began to criticize this phenomenon only when it took directions of which they did not approve. Anti-war politics, the drive for abortion on demand, the effort to obtain gun control, and the opposition to nuclear energy are typically described by liberals as "movements" or "concerns." When the right-to-life forces or those opposing gun control get organized, however, their critics not only disapprove of their ideas, they deplore their use of "extremist" tactics.

To the extent that ideas determine whether the atomized political system will move speedily, sluggishly, or not at all, the principal task of political analysis becomes that of understanding the processes whereby certain ideas become dominant. This requires more subtle techniques for studying public opinion than any that have been routinely employed, techniques that will measure the intensity of feeling as well as its distribution and will distinguish opinions capable of providing the basis for political mobilization from those that are mere expressions of preference. And we require better knowledge about the organizations that shape opinion—the mass and elite media, the universities, and those acrónymic groups that manage to devise and implant compelling slogans.

In John Fischer's day, scholars studied big business, labor unions, medical societies, and farm groups. Today, we need to understand better how elites learn ideas in their colleges and law schools and from the magazines of opinion. How else can we explain, for example, why a generation of legislators who believed in the virtues of business regulation by independent commissions is being replaced by one seeking to deregulate many of those businesses, often over the bitter objections of the regulated industry? Or why a generation that applauded John F. Kennedy's inaugural promise to defend liberty anywhere, at any price, has become one that prefers to minimize risks of every kind, in every place?

VI

Wᴇ ᴀʀᴇ at a loss for a word or phrase to describe the new features of the political system; scholars even disagree as to whether it is all that new. Such terms as "veto-group politics" seemed most appropriate for the system that Fischer and later David Riesman described thirty years ago; that powerful insight allowed many discrete facts to be summarized in one economical statement. Today, the system is more confused and so our political vocabulary has become more prolix and less precise.

Viewed in a longer historical perspective, what we are seeing may not be all that new. The Congress in which Madison and his immediate successors sat was highly individualized. Strong, institutionalized congressional leadership did not emerge until the latter half of the 19th century; one contest for Speaker in 1856 ran to 133 ballots. Factions abounded, but national interest-group organization did not occur until the end of the 19th century. "Single-issue" politics existed, the abolition of slavery being the most conspicuous example. But in Madison's time, and for many decades thereafter, national politics was less a career than a hobby; the federal government played a minor role in human affairs; the range of issues with which Congress had to deal was small; and ideological cleavages tended to occur one at a time. Now, governing is a profession, the government plays a large role, and issues tend to pile up, one atop the other, in a network of multiple and profound ideological cleavages. Whether one describes as "fundamental" the changes in institutions and ideas that have accompanied the rise of modern government is in part a matter of style. Yet one must be impressed by the change in the dominant ethos of the times—whereas the period 1890-1920 was the great era of institution-building in voluntary associations, political parties, corporate enterprises, and congressional leadership, the last decade or so has been one that has criticized, attacked, and partially dismantled institutions.

From a broader, international perspective, one might say that the changes I have described add up to nothing of fundamental importance. The American constitutional order, with its separate executive and legislative branches and its independent judiciary, remains very different from the British system of cabinet-in-parliament. And so it does. (It is ironic to note the stirrings among British politicians who would like to see their system, which stifles the backbench member of Commons, changed into something more "American." They may suppose that they can combine the advantages of strong party government with the advantages of powerful legislative committees and more autonomous legislators, but I suspect they are wrong.)

By the standards of liberals and socialists, the American system remains far more conservative than that of European democracies. Where is our national health insurance, our comprehensive income-maintenance scheme, our government ownership of key industries? By these tests, the American system *is* conservative. But by another test it is far more activist and innovative than almost any European democracy: what other country has anything like our detailed federal regulation of business enterprise, our elaborate set of "tax expenditures," our affirmative-action programs addressed to the demands of a growing list of ethnic and racial minorities? Some rather careful distinctions must be made before one can compare how American policy-making differs from that abroad.

WHAT is more striking to me is that, since the 1930's, there has occurred in this country an extraordinary redistribution of political power without any prior redistribution of income or wealth. Those persons, of the Right as well as the Left, who are enchanted with economic explanations of political life have their work cut out for them if they insist on ignoring the powerful transformation in *ideas* that seems to lie at the heart of these changes.

★★★

5

The Cowboy Challenge: The Rise of the Southern Rim   Kirkpatrick Sale

Kirkpatrick Sale in his article points to the Nixon presidency as one of the first non-Establishment modern presidencies in which those who came into the administration held different values and served different causes from those of the Eastern Establishment. How is Sale using the term "Establishment"? How does this changeover in values compare with the change that took place following the election of Andrew Jackson, when new values, politics, and interests replaced those of the prior occupants of the White House? How important are such changes to American politics and to the political system?

Sale indicates that states of the Southern Rim share many areas of common interest. Climatic conditions, historical heritage, economic and cultural backgrounds seem to be among the more important common links. How important are these common traits for structuring regional unity?

Sale concludes by indicating the importance of the Southern Rim as a political power. What social indicators point to the growth of the Southern Rim as an economic and political power in America? What effect has the economic and population growth of this region had on the two-party system? Are there today an increased number of influential Republicans in the South and Southwest? Is the Republican party now permanently established in the Deep South? Could this region be crucial to a resurgence of the Republican party in the years to come?

★ ★ ★

THE COWBOY CHALLENGE
KIRKPATRICK SALE

The rise of the Southern Rim

In the Oval Office of the White House, shortly before two o'clock on March 13, 1973, Richard Nixon is nearing the end of a long and rambling conversation with his counsel, John Dean, about ways to deflect the growing Watergate scandals that are just beginning to threaten his administration. On Capitol Hill, L. Patrick Gray, Nixon's nominee to be head of the Federal Bureau of Investigation, is continuing his testimony to the Senate Judiciary Committee, before whom he has already disclosed damaging secrets that point suspicions directly to the White House; the day before, Nixon issued a proclamation denying permission for his staff members to appear before the various Senate committees, pulling a blanket of "executive privilege" hard around him to withstand the increasingly bitter winds of Watergate. The President is now feeling himself very much the beleaguered hero under attack from a cruel press and a manipulated public, and angrily declares at one point, "Nobody is a friend of ours," later on reflecting more plaintively, "It will remain a crisis among the upper intellectual types, the soft heads, our own, too—Republicans—and the Democrats and the rest." Dean, shrewd to detect and reflect the mood of his superior, soon joins in and begins berating with him "the press . . . the intellectuals," claiming they would never believe the Watergate burglars were acting alone, "they would have to paint it into something more sinister, more involved, part of a general plan." The President nods, seems to grow morose, and then bursts out with the idea that has been troubling him all along:

"On and on and on. No, I tell you this, it is the last gasp of our hardest opponents. They've just got to have something to squeal about it."

Dean, ever the second banana begins to chime in, "It is the only thing they have to squeal—" but Nixon, warming to his subject now, won't be interrupted.

"They are going to lie around and squeal. They are having a hard time now. They got the hell kicked out of them in the elections." Then just to make sure Dean appreciates the full dimensions of who this enemy is, Nixon enlarges: "There is a lot of Watergate around in this town, not so much our opponents, even the media, but the basic thing is the Establishment. The Establishment is dying, and so they've got to show that despite the successes we have had in foreign policy and in the election, they've got to show that it is just wrong, just because of this. They are trying to use this as the whole thing."

The basic thing is the Establishment.

Extraordinary. This is a President of the United States talking, and in the normal taxonomy of this country a President is regarded as a key part, if not the very center, of any "Establishment"—yet here is a President who plainly sees himself outside the Establishment, and, more than that, an *enemy* of that Establishment. Clearly, then, Richard Nixon is changing the usual definitions, is in fact pointing to a new conception of what the Establishment is and what its position has become in mid-century America, a conception which he no doubt had never fully articulated but which his highly developed political antennae told him was nonetheless quite real.

For Nixon, the Establishment is a distant and a foreign world, the world of New York and Boston and Newport and Grosse Pointe and Winnetka, the world of great wealth, high culture, nurtured traditions, industrial power, and political aristocracies, the world of "the soft heads" and "the media," the "liberal elite" and the "impudent snobs"—"the enemy." Nixon sees himself as standing apart from all of this, obviously a newcomer, an outsider, a challenger, representative of a newer breed of people who, no matter how many deals they make with this Establishment, no matter how many times they

KIRKPATRICK SALE *has been a writer and editor for more than 15 years, in this country and abroad. The accompanying article is from his new book,* Power Shift (Random House); © 1975 by *Kirkpatrick Sale.*

rub shoulders with it, will never be a part of that world, for they come from a new place and they hold different values and they serve variant causes. Nixon understands, if only primitively, that there is in fact a new configuration of forces in America, to which he and his Presidency are joined, that stands in opposition to the traditional Establishment and is therefore a new component to be reckoned with in the equations of national power.

Looked at in its broadest terms, the modern Establishment in America enjoyed a virtually undiminished influence from the time of its consolidation after the Civil War right down to the beginning of World War II, roughly the whole seventy-year period from 1870 to 1940. In practically every aspect of life, this country was dominated by a nexus of industrial, financial, political, academic, and cultural centers based in the Northeast, stretching from Chicago to New York, from Boston to Philadelphia, and associated with the names of Mellon, Carnegie, Rockefeller, Morgan, Ford, McCormick, Vanderbilt, and the like. It was this nexus that influenced the selection of Presidential candidates (between 1869 and 1945 only two Presidents were born outside of the Northeast), that controlled the houses of Congress, that determined American foreign policy, that set the economic priorities and directions, that more or less created the cultural and moral standards, that determined who were to be the powerful and the powerless. And such provincial areas as *did* manage to grow up at the same time—the San Francisco Bay Area, say, with its "upstart" A. P. Giannini, founder of the Bank of America, or New Orleans, prosperous through the Mississippi River traffic—were largely contained in their remoter regions and allowed to exert very little economic or political influence on a national scale.

All that began to change with the advent of World War II and its new technologies and priorities. Slowly there grew up a rival nexus, based in the Southern and Western parts of the country that stand in geographical —and to a large degree cultural, economic, and political —opposition to the Northeast, specifically in the *Southern Rim*, the broad band of America that stretches from Southern California through the Southwest and Texas, into the Deep South and down to Florida.

Here a truly competitive power base took shape, built upon the unsurpassed population migrations that began to draw millions and millions of people from the older and colder sections of the Northeast to the younger and sunnier sections of the South and Southwest . . . upon an authentic economic revolution that created the giant new postwar industries of defense, aerospace, technology, electronics, agribusiness, and oil-and-gas extraction, all of which were based primarily in the Southern Rim and which grew to rival and in some cases surpass the older industries of the Northeast . . . upon the enormous growth of the federal government and its unprecedented accumulation of wealth, the great part of which went

to develop and sustain the new areas and the new government-dependent industries, the new ports and new inland transportation systems, the new military and aerospace bases and the new water and irrigation systems . . . upon the political development of the Southern Rim and its growing influence in almost all national party organizations of whatever stripe, its decisive role in the selection of candidates of both major parties, its control over the major committees and much of the inner workings of Congress, and ultimately, from 1963 to 1974, its occupancy of the Presidency itself. Over the last thirty years, this rival nexus, moving on to the national stage and mounting a head-on challenge to the traditional Establishment, has quite simply shifted the balance of power in America away from the Northeast and toward the Southern Rim.

That this is not some arcane geographical games-playing or a form of paranoia born in Richard Nixon's mind

is easy enough to demonstrate. The evidence is abundant and rather wonderfully diverse, manifested, for example, in the takeover of the Republican Party by the new and generally conservative forces from the Southern Rim— Barry Goldwater, Ronald Reagan, Nixon himself—and the consequent displacement of Northeastern liberals, at least for the long decade between 1964 and 1974 . . . in the assaults by Southern Rim tycoons, Clint Murchison, James Ling, Nelson Bunker Hunt, Howard Hughes, and many colorful others, upon the citadels of Wall Street and the giants of Northeastern industry . . . in the shift of major-league sports franchises out of the Northeast to the South and West, and the creation of six new professional leagues by entrepreneurs of that area . . . in the succession to power in the tight and potent world of the U.S. Congress of such men, over the years, as Allan Ellender, Sam Rayburn, Richard Russell, James Eastland, Wright Patman, Wilbur Mills, Chet Holifield, John Stennis, Sam Ervin, Carl Albert, John Rhodes, Howard Baker, Joseph Montoya, every one of them from the Southern Rim . . . in the emergence of new official stock exchanges in places like Miami and Los Angeles, flourishing at a time when the New York exchanges are floundering . . . in the extraordinary rise and growth of new cities like Anaheim, San Diego, Phoenix, Albuquerque, Dallas, Houston, Memphis, Jackson,

Atlanta, Jacksonville, Orlando, stretching right across the southern part of the country, cities which have grown from sleepy cowtowns and frontier outposts into major commercial centers, among the most thriving in the land . . . in the relocation of organized crime activities out of the wizened world of the Northeast to the newly hospitable centers of Los Angeles, Las Vegas, Phoenix, New Orleans, Hot Springs, Miami Beach . . . in the extraordinary investment of $55 million by H. Ross Perot, the Texas computer executive, who single-handedly kept the stock brokerages from collapsing in 1971 . . . in the rise within the Democratic party of figures like George Wallace, Pat Brown, Jr., Lloyd Bentsen, Fred Harris, Jimmy Carter, Robert Strauss, Terry Sanford, Reubin Askew, all of them from the Southern Rim and all among the new figures reshaping that party . . . in the flight of thousands of businesses and hundreds of major corporations out of the big cities of the Northeast into the aggressive new cities of the Southern Rim, draining the Northeast of at least forty of *Fortune*'s top-ranked industrial firms in just the last ten years . . . in the development of serious cultural centers in such places as Los Angeles, Houston, Atlanta, and Miami, each with enterprises to rival those of New York's and to meet or surpass those of most of the rest of the Northeast . . . in the rising personal incomes of the people in the Southern Rim states which have been growing steadily while there has been a decline in the Northeast, and in the last decade the growth rates of the leading sunbelt metropolitan areas have been twice as high as in the leading coldbelt areas . . . and in such small facts as that the West Coast plans to build its own Statue of Liberty . . . that the Federal Reserve Board has established its first new bank in thirty-three years in Miami, Florida . . . that the national headquarters of the American Contract Bridge League is in Memphis . . . that Bergdorf Goodman, the fancy Fifth Avenue department store in New York, is owned by Carter Hawley Hale Stores of Los Angeles . . . and that Hebrew-National Kosher Foods, Inc., the most famous name in all of New York's delicatessen culture, is owned by the Riviana Corporation of Houston, Texas. . . . And that's only a start.

And the Northeast under this kind of siege? Well, it has not disappeared, nor does it give any signs of doing so: the very fact that Nixon is no longer in that Oval Office and that he has been replaced by a man from Michigan is evidence enough that considerable power still resides in the Northeast. But one can see plainly that the Establishment is *declining*, and even a presidential coup cannot disguise that reality. The large urban centers are all decaying and losing population, some like Newark and Buffalo and Detroit and Gary turning into outright sinkholes. . . .

The riches of the Northeast are flowing to other sections of the country, producing "a pronounced shift of income" over the next fifteen years toward the Southern and Western regions, according to the Census Bureau, with particularly rapid growths for manufacturing operations in the South and below-average rates for "nearly every major industry in the Middle Atlantic region . . . for the next two decades." . . . The textile firms of New York have picked up and headed for the South, the coal mines of Appalachia have been boarded up one by one, the dairy farms of New England have been deserted and left to lie fallow. . . . The railroad systems have deteriorated so rapidly, with nine major lines in bankruptcy by 1975 and others to follow, that the whole transportation infrastructure of the Northeast is facing collapse and the regional economy is seriously jeopardized. . . . The industrial importance of the Northeast is rapidly diminishing, according to the business-oriented Conference Board, citing figures to show that yankee industries accounted for 70 percent of all value added in manufacturing as recently as the late 1940s but "by 1971 this share declined to 51 percent" and was dropping with every passing year. . . . The old money markets are no longer capable of supplying the capital needs of the Northeast or of the nation, and the brokerage houses that once served as the glittering jewels of Wall Street have been so badly tarnished that they are going under at the rate of more than fifty a year. . . . And in almost every sphere the conventional stability and dominance of the Establishment is deteriorating. It is surely too soon to say from all of this, as Nixon tells it to Dean, that "the Establishment is dying," but just as surely that hyperbole is pointing toward a truth.

The idea of a "Southern Rim" in American economic and political life is not mere capriciousness, a paranoid's invention. There is a reality to this area, a climatic, historical, and cultural cohesiveness, that serves to set this broad band off from the rest of the country in many ways.

The most obvious unity to the Southern Rim is climatic, and a look at any of those weather maps that the newspapers print helps to show why. No matter what the time of year, there will probably be a dotted line running across the map from around the tip of North Carolina in the East, on out through Memphis and Oklahoma City, swerving down a bit to Albuquerque, and then up through southern Nevada and on to San Francisco. In the winter this is normally the 60-degree line—temperatures south of it running from 60 degrees on up, north of it below 60 degrees—and in the summer it is usually the 80-degree demarcation. It will vary, of course, weather being what it is, but it is remarkable how consistently the temperature line cuts this same pattern.

This seems as appropriate a way as any to start to define the Southern Rim since it is to a great degree the climate that has given it its spectacular growth. In the area below this line are to be found all of the tropical and semitropical regions of the United States: the Florida beaches, the Deep South savannas, the Louisiana lowlands, the Texas and Oklahoma plains, the Southwestern deserts, the palmy California coast. Here is the zone in which the average annual temperature is above 60 degrees, the average maximum temperature is 74 degrees; there are between 250 and 350 days of sunshine a year, and frost, if it should come, does not descend before November. This is, in short, America's sunbelt.

But there is more than climatic unity to this area. There is also a rough populational cohesion as well, for before the modern migrations this area had a fairly uniform pattern of settlement, the movement sweeping almost due west from the South, spreading a human substratum from the Carolinas to California. The earliest migrations in the eighteenth and nineteenth centuries moved almost exclusively westward from the East Coast, one broad wave sweeping southwest through Georgia and Alabama to the Gulf Coast and on up the Rio Grande, another moving due west through the Tennessee, Arkansas, and Red River valleys across the Texas plains and up against the Rockies. By the early twentieth century both of these waves had tapered off roughly in eastern New Mexico, but then came two final movements that completed the settlements, one pouring down into Florida from the Deep South states from the early 1920s on, and the other, made famous by the Okies, moving westward over the Rockies and into Southern California and the Central Valley in the later 1920s and 1930s. By the time of World War II the entire Rim area enjoyed an unusual homogeneity for "melting-pot America": it was marked not only by Southern—and overwhelmingly Southern *white*—settlement, but by the comparative absence of foreign-born immigration. And even the modern influx, though perhaps a half of it has come from the Northeast, has not changed this fixed character appreciably.

Partly as a result of these migration characteristics, partly as a result of the common heritage they imply, the Southern Rim is also marked by a rough cultural unity. The entire area encompasses almost all the regions that have historically been the principal battlegrounds of the American frontier, from the Tennessee of Davy Crockett to the Texas of Sam Houston to the Arizona of Wyatt Earp, with all that this heritage implies (which, for Frederick Jackson Turner, for example, means "perennial rebirth . . . fluidity of American life . . . new opportunities . . . simplicity . . . primitive existence . . . the meeting point between savagery and civilization"). It also encompasses almost precisely the area unique in this country for its economic dependence upon slave and subservient labor (black, brown, or red), not only the famous plantations of the South and their successors, but the ranches of Texas and the Southwest, and the fruit farms of California and Florida. The region includes all of the states of the Southern Confederacy (except Virginia), plus the two territories with greatest Con-

federate sympathy (Oklahoma and New Mexico), and that implies a cultural heritage that, of course, goes far beyond the simply military. Finally, the entire region from the Carolina coast to eastern New Mexico and from Oklahoma to Florida is the heartland of the Southern Baptist Convention and its offshoots—it is the most populous church today in every state from North Carolina to Texas—and there are additional strong Baptist representations in Arizona and Southern California as well.

Taken altogether, these characteristics of the Southern Rim define a remarkably consistent geographical area. It hardly seems an accident, in fact, that there is indeed a cartographical line that sets off this area almost precisely; the boundary line which runs along the northern hedges of North Carolina, Tennessee, Arkansas, Oklahoma, New Mexico, and Arizona, or, generally, the 37th parallel. Extend this line through Nevada and California to the Pacific, with just the slightest swing upward to embrace San Francisco, and the demarcation is complete. The land south of that line takes in all of thirteen states —North and South Carolina, Georgia, Florida, Tennessee, Alabama, Mississippi, Arkansas, Louisiana, Oklahoma, Texas, New Mexico, and Arizona—and the southern and by far the most populous parts of two more states, Nevada and California. This is the Southern Rim.

Now, traditionalists will have noted that this neat demarcation by the 37th parallel creates some divergences from normal geographical constructs. On the eastern end, for example, it excludes the state of Virginia, despite the fact that it was a part, an important part, of the Confederacy and that in its northern half it has experienced much of the same rapid growth that the true Rim areas have. Still, Virginia is simply different in its basic climate and most of its agriculture from the pattern of the Southern Rim; its historical migrations have been either due west, through the Appalachians into Kentucky and West Virginia, or dead north along the coastlines; and its population growths of recent years have almost all taken place in the Washington environs as part of a suburban belt that relates to Maryland and the North far more than to Norfolk and the South.

On the western end, the Rim demarcation includes the mid-California region from the Bay Area on the south—despite the fact that San Francisco was an old-line center of wealth, with pretensions to "old aristocracy" and the like, and though much ink has been expended trying to make a dividing line between Los Angeles and the Bay Area. The reason is simple enough: climatologically, topographically, and geologically, this region has much more in common with the south than in contrast to it (the real dividing line in California is not the Tehachapi Mountains but the Mokelumne River), and the area around San Francisco to the south (San Mateo, Santa Clara, and Alameda counties, for example) has been every bit as explosive a growth region as the southern part of the state and shares all its contemporary characteristics.

Similarly, the southern tip of Nevada is included in the territory cut by the 37th parallel, again an area that just happens to be of a piece with its southern rather than its northern neighbors: it is related by geography through the Colorado River system to Arizona and Southern California, by its mid-century patterns of growth to the spectacular boom cities like Phoenix and Los Angeles, and by its economy and culture—especially Las Vegas—to the rich world of Southern California, where most of its players come from.

The region that stands in opposition to this Southern Rim should be accorded some definition as well. The Northeast, as used here, encompasses the entire quadrant east of the Mississippi and north of the Mason-Dixon line (and its rough extension westward), taking in the fourteen states of New England and the Great Lakes: Maine, New Hampshire, Vermont, Massachusetts, Rhode Island, Connecticut, New York, New Jersey, Pennsylvania, Ohio, Michigan, Indiana, Wisconsin, and Illinois. This region, too, enjoys a certain cohesion, of climate, geography, culture, settlement, and history, but above all of economics and demography: this is the traditional manufacturing belt of America, the area that since the middle of the nineteenth century has been characterized by a band of heavy industry virtually unbroken from Chicago to Boston; and it is the land of the megalopolis, the vast urban clusters that show up on a population map as a mass of black circles again stretching almost without interval from Chicago along the Great Lakes on to Philadelphia and New York and up to Boston. There are some to be sure, who would like to divide this quadrant in half, creating some sort of "Midwest" that begins around the Pennsylvania-Ohio border—there is, alas, no evidence whatsoever that there are real distinctions between the two regions.

There is a broadly metaphorical but rather apt way of describing these rival power bases, the one of the Northeast and the other of the Southern Rim, as the *yankees* and the *cowboys*. Taken loosely, that is meant to suggest the traditional, staid, oldtime, button-down, Ivy-League, tight-lipped, patrician, New England-rooted WASP culture on the one hand, and the aggressive, flamboyant, restless, swaggering, newfangled, open-collar, can-do, Southern-rooted Baptist culture of the Southern Rim on the other; on the one hand, let us say, the type represented by David Rockefeller, Charles Percy, Edmund Muskie, James Reston, Kingman Brewster, John Lindsay, Richard Lugar, Henry Ford, Sol Linowitz, Bill Buckley, and Stephen Sondheim, and on the other the type personified by Bebe Rebozo, George Wallace, Lyndon Johnson, Billy Graham, Frank Irwin, C. Arnholt Smith, H. L. Hunt, Strom Thurmond, Sam Yorty, John Wayne, and Johnny Cash.

The terms are meant only in the loosest and most symbolic way, of course—flamboyant operators can be found in the Northeast, staid blue-bloods in the Southern Rim—but it is interesting that they even have an appropriate heritage in this very context. "Cowboy" was the epithet used by the Wall Street people who first ran up against some of the newly powerful Texas entrepreneurs, broad-rimmed hats and tooled-leather boots and all, when they started throwing their weight around in Eastern financial circles in the late 1950s and early 1960s —during the fierce battle, for example, between the Texas millionaires Clint Murchison and Sid Richardson and Pennsylvania's patrician Allen Kirby for control of the Allegheny Corporation and the New York Central Railroad in 1961. "Yankee," the invective which goes back to the days of the Civil War to describe Northerners in general, was naturally the word with which the newcomers responded, at least back home in the boardrooms and bars.

Slowly these words began to have a kind of currency, in financial circles at any rate, and then during the 1960s they came to be used by the New Left—particularly by the theoretician Carl Oglesby—in its attempt to understand and describe the workings of the "power structure" of America. From these they moved gradually into academic and journalistic circles—economist Kenneth Boulding, for example, used "the cowboy economy" to describe the period of rapacious growth after World War II, political writer Milton Viorst analyzed the Northeast as "the Yankee's America," scholar William Domhoff described a "Jewish-Cowboy" financial group behind the Democratic party. It is doubtful if Richard Nixon ever thought of the world in precisely these terms, as ably as they would have served him, but it just may be that his successor does: shortly after becoming President, Gerald Ford announced that, in settling the economic problems of America, he was not going to "act in cowboy fashion."

Let those simple terms, then, stand for the complicated process that Richard Nixon barely conceptualized that mid-March day in the Oval Office. What he was groping toward, what those labels help to delineate, is the development of a cowboy power which has risen to rival the established power, the creation of a new cowboy counterforce to contend with the old yankee hegemony—in short, *the cowboy challenge*.

This fact is of historic proportions. There have been only four major power shifts in U.S. history: the first with the consolidation of federal control at the turn of the eighteenth century, the second with the introducion of Jacksonian democracy in the early nineteenth century, the third with the expansion of Northern industrialism after the Civil War, and the fourth with the establishment of Rooseveltian welfarism in the 1930s. The rise of the Southern Rim marks a fifth.

★★★

6

The Con-Con Con: Unbalancing the Constitution   Bertram M. Gross

The specter of a constitutional convention is indeed haunting Congress, Gross explains. We have never been as close as we are now to calling a constitutional convention. Petitions have been received by Congress from states supporting budget-balancing amendments, pro-life amendments, and anti-busing amendments. Particularly popular is the prospect of a budget-balancing amendment. What effect does strong grass-roots support for an amendment have on Congress? Has the popularity of this budget-balancing movement put added pressures on Congress to pass legislation that accomplishes the same objectives that an amendment would? Could added leverage in Congress be one of the motives behind the interest to convene a convention? What benefits does an amendment have over congressional legislation? What happens to a Constitution when it becomes too burdened with amendments representing group demands and special interests?

If a convention is called, delegates must then be recruited. As Gross suggests, none of the state resolutions petitioning Congress for a convention has contained any mention or suggestion concerning delegate selection. What effect does the selection of delegates have on the types of amendments or fundamental laws that are written? Civil libertarians have expressed the concern that delegates to such a convention would be those who on previous occasions have indicated in opinion polls that they believe the Bill of Rights to be too liberal, too permissive, and too protective of the criminal element. Is the resulting document written by a convention more than the collection of values, feelings, and ideologies of the delegates who write the document? What sort of document would you expect to come from a group of delegates as described by the civil libertarians?

★ ★ ★

THE CON-CON CON

UNBALANCING THE CONSTITUTION

BERTRAM M. GROSS

"A specter is haunting Congress," writes *New York Times* columnist William Safire, in words from Karl Marx's *Communist Manifesto*, "the specter of a constitutional convention." Summoning up the same specter a few days later, conservative writer Patrick Buchanan comments: "Liberal and Tory alike blanch at the prospect of a 'People's Convention' to consider alterations in the organic document of the American union."

Safire goes on to invoke the holy name of Nobel Laureate Milton Friedman, the conservatives' beloved "Uncle Miltie." Buchanan speaks in the name of "the people," whose demand for lower prices and taxes "is being blocked by appointed bureaucrats, anointed judges and Congressional obstructionists who talk conservative rhetoric at election time and ridicule the boondocks booboisie at their Chevy Chase garden parties."

Many moderates who used liberal rhetoric at election time now go along with the pretense that cutting social services for the poor will somehow put a lid on inflation. Many liberals who used to advocate Keynesian deficits now pledge allegiance to balanced budgets—if not this year, then soon. Even some left-wingers have entered this bedroom, if not the same bed. Tom Hayden and his Campaign for Democracy have supported Gov. Jerry Brown's call for a balanced budget and a constitutional convention, just so long as a "full-employment" tag is added. This cry is echoed by John Judis, managing editor of the socialist weekly, *In These Times*, who argues that opposition to a convention discloses "an elitist view of politics." It is now clear that America is haunted by a broad spectrum of budget-balancing specters that falsify the nature of the present profit-push inflation, channel discontent along lines that help the profiteers and menace every effort to preserve or enlarge the social, economic and political rights of the American people.

As of this writing twenty-nine state legislatures have applied to Congress for a constitutional convention to propose a budget-balancing amendment. None of the state resolutions contains a word on how the delegates to a constitutional convention would be selected. It is assumed that they would be chosen in the same way as delegates to state constitutional conventions: namely, through state legislative districts. This means that all the built-in devices for underrepresentation for some groups and overrepresentation for other groups will apply to a national convention as well. Recent experience with state conventions indicates that most of the elected delegates are state legislators themselves, their associates, fund raisers and corporate lobbyists. Thus, any nationwide convention called today might be dominated by pros running a huge national con game with a stacked deck of cards. It could be a well-packed, one-House, super-legislature fully capable of advancing corporate interests behind a populist facade of protecting human rights.

Most of the state resolutions urge convention action or a constitutional amendment along the following lines: "In the absence of a national emergency the

Bertram M. Gross, distinguished professor at Hunter College and former executive secretary of the Council of Economic Advisers, has just completed a new book on basic trends in modern capitalism, entitled Friendly Fascism.

"The Con-Con Con: Unbalancing the Constitution" by Bertram M. Gross, *The Nation*, April 28, 1979. Copyright © 1979 The Nation Associates. Reprinted by permission. Illustration by Peter Steiner.

total of all appropriations made by the Congress for any fiscal year may not exceed the total of all estimated Federal revenues for that fiscal year." No matter what specific wording is suggested in the resolutions, however, the subject matter lends itself to a very large number of variations and alternatives. Two of these have already been suggested in Patrick Buchanan's proposals for a convention: (1) that the size of the balanced budget be limited to 20 percent of the gross national product, and (2) that all Federal income taxes be limited to one-third of a citizen's total income.

But if Congress calls a convention to consider budget-balancing, could the convention plunge into other subjects? Could it become a wide-open, general convention?

"No!" is the present answer of the organizers of the con-con drive. The model state resolution drafted by the National Taxpayers Union (and adopted without change in many states) provides that "this application and request be deemed null and void, rescinded and of no effect in the event that such convention not be limited to such specific and exclusive purpose." In 1974, seven lawyers appointed by the American Bar Association held that "Congress has the power to establish standards for making available to the states a limited convention when they petition for that type of convention."

But other lawyers have held that a constitutional convention would be a sovereign body and, in addition to deciding its own rules of procedure, could decide to take up any subjects it chose. It would be bound by neither the Congressional nor the state resolutions. When Charles Black of Yale Law School presented this interpretation to the California House of Delegates, the body was moved to vote down a con-con resolution ardently supported by Gov. Jerry Brown.

The Constitution itself provides no answer on either side of this question. Nor can an answer be provided by probing the debates at the 1787 constitutional convention or the presumed intentions of the Founding Fathers. The issue will be settled only if and when a convention assembles and tries to go beyond budget-balancing.

But the question of a limited versus an open convention is, in my judgment, a false issue. I have no doubt that a convention could be limited to the single issue of budget-balancing. But this issue is as broad as fiscal policy itself. It would be impossible to exclude from this subject various limitations on either spending or taxing. If this is so, then the convention could propose amendments prohibiting either spending or taxing for purposes that would undermine certain so-called "human rights"—whether the rights of employers to hire whom they choose, the rights of employees to bust a union shop, or the "right to life" of the 1-week-old embryo. Indeed, an entire Bill of Radical Right Rights could be written in fiscal policy terms. This is why the majority of labor leaders, and

many liberals and radicals, know in their hearts that a con-con could tear up vital parts of the original Bill of Rights and many other economic, social and political rights won in recent decades.

In the meantime, the con-con campaigners enjoy the best of both worlds. While on one hand they allow fears of a wide-open convention to drive Congress into initiating a budget-balancing amendment of its own, on the other they argue that a convention can be limited to the budget-balancing issue. They also support pending legislation to establish Congressional procedures for calling a convention. This legislation was earlier introduced by Senator Sam Ervin of North Carolina and passed by the Senate without opposition in 1971 and 1973. Now sponsored by Senator Jesse Helms of North Carolina and Representatives Henry Hyde and Robert McClory, both of Illinois, the proposed bill attempts to prohibit submission to the states of any convention-initiated amendment outside the subject matter set forth in the original state resolutions. Most observers feel that active consideration of this legislation would encourage the still undecided states to pass convention resolutions. If the legislatures of five more states should leap on the con-con bandwagon—say Maine, Vermont, New Hampshire, Illinois and Missouri—the convention would be mandated. No one can now safely predict whether the additional five resolutions will be obtained. My own estimate is that in the absence of more serious opposition than has yet appeared in Congress, the number thirty-four might be reached by mid-1980.

By one method of counting, that number has already been reached. In addition to the twenty-nine legislatures that have passed resolutions already, there are fifteen state resolutions calling for conventions on other subjects, such as prohibition of abortion and busing. If the seven of these states that have not passed balanced-budget resolutions are added to the twenty-nine that have, it would bring the total to thirty-six. This becomes significant in the light of former Senator Sam Ervin's argument that with no legislation to guide the convention-calling procedure, all convention resolutions should be counted: "In my opinion, if one-third of the thirty-four states wanted to amend the First Amendment, and one-third wanted to amend the Fifth Amendment and the other one-third wanted to amend the Sixth Amendment, and they asked the Congress to call the convention, setting forth no specific amendment, Congress would be obligated to call a convention." If the various right-wing con-conners should unite their now-divided forces, they might guarantee a convention call in early 1980. This might be done by model state resolutions setting forth no specific amendment; by a log-rolling understanding that a specific convention called for budget-balancing would be followed by another con-con on the next most popular subject on the conservative agenda, or by an unwritten understanding that the convention would consider prohibitions on spending or taxing for certain "undesirable" purposes.

Sparked by the con-con campaign, Congressional hearings are already underway on a budget-balancing amendment that would be passed in the usual way through Congressional initiative and ratification by the states. At the moment, there is an immense flurry of right-wing creativity on other ways of skinning the same cat. Eight proposals merit attention:

(*1*) Limiting appropriations to estimated revenues, as proposed in most of the current state resolutions;

(*2*) A more sophisticated version of the above (with a two-thirds vote in both Houses required to authorize any peacetime deficits), as proposed by an eighteen-member committee of the conservative Democratic Research Organization in the House;

(*3*) The proposal of Senator William Proxmire of Wisconsin that would require a balanced budget in any year in which the real economic growth exceeds 3 percent;

(*4*) Requiring specified annual reductions in the national debt;

(*5*) Imposing a surtax to make up for any accidental deficit, as proposed by Mississippi's Senator John Stennis;

(*6*) Milton Friedman's proposal, already supported by Republican Party leaders at their recent Tidewater conference, to limit any increase in spending to the percentage rise in the gross national product;

(*7*) Limiting total expenditures by some fixed rate of growth or a fixed percentage of the gross national product, and

(*8*) Putting a ceiling on tax revenues.

Many of the proponents of such proposals are sincerely leery of con-con. This is particularly true of members of the Congressional judiciary committees; their personal positions of influence on constitutional amendments could be weakened by a convention. But in the strange dialectics of unanticipated consequences, intentions are often self-defeating. The movement for a budget-balancing amendment in Congress also supports the con-con partisans in their efforts to line up more state legislatures. This is especially true when a previous opponent of a constitutional amendment, such as House Republican leader John Rhodes of Arizona, suddenly switches. Under his leadership the House Republican Policy Committee on March 20 endorsed an amendment to require both a balanced budget and a ceiling on Federal spending. In explaining his switch, Rhodes pointed out that the proposed amendment contains a "safety valve" to allow deficits in times of national emergency, such as depression or war. Similar safety valves, however, are suggested in most convention resolutions. The ground is therefore laid for many other politicians who would rather switch than fight to leap on the con-con bandwagon.

Another school of budget-balancers in Congress, numbering liberals as well as moderates and conservatives, holds that Congress should balance the budget itself without any constitutional amendment. "We don't need fiscal handcuffs," says Maine's Senator Edmund Muskie, chairman of the Senate Budget Committee. "We need fiscal discipline." His definition of discipline, however, comes very close to the substance of most proposed amendments.

President Carter's definition is even closer. He not only pledges a balanced budget for 1982 but also accepts the objective of bringing total Federal expenditures down to 20 percent of the gross national product. In other words, "Leave it to Jimmy." He supports this position by warning against a "restrictive" amendment, thereby leaving open his option to go

along with a "nonrestrictive" amendment. This option has been opened up by Charles Schultze, Carter's chief economic adviser. In testifying against the gimmickry of a constitutional amendment, Schultze explained some of the counter-gimmicks through which the Federal Government could quickly get a balanced budget: (*1*) raising nonbudgetary expenditures (such as Federal Housing Administration-type guarantees and Treasury loans to public or quasi-public corporations) from their present level of about $11 billion, (*2*) excluding capital expenditures (now more than $120 billion) from the operating budget, as is the practice in states with constitutional mandates for balanced budgets, (*3*) reducing Federal transfer payments to the states (now more than $90 billion a year) and (*4*) adopting regulations requiring the private sector to make certain investments. This amounts to saying that the Government could deftly slip out of any constitutional handcuffs. Therefore, no constitutional amendment would really be restrictive. With opponents like this, the constitutional amendment campaigners do not need many more friends.

The untrustworthy nature of Carter's opposition to budget-balancing amendments is borne out by a new White House campaign on the subject. The campaign's thrust is not against budget-balancing itself or even against a constitutional amendment. It is aimed at stopping con-con in state legislatures—particularly in Vermont, New Hampshire, Rhode Island, Illinois and Missouri. It also looks like a trial-run confrontation with Gov. Jerry Brown before the 1980 Presidential primaries. But the Jimmy-Jerry difference is over fiscal technique, not fiscal policy substance. In the words of White House adviser Professor Lawrence H. Tribe of Harvard Law School, White House opposition to con-con is to be coupled with "a reaffirmation of fiscal austerity." To the whole tribe of Carter's "let us do it" budget-balancers, increased spending for military and corporate handouts is still sacrosanct.

Progressive reactions to the budget-balancing campaign have been sadly divided. Some of the most steadfast libertarians still find it difficult to see the connection between civil liberties and economic rights. So long as the Bill of Rights is not directly threatened, they see the budget-balancing drive against social programs as unfortunate, but no concern of theirs. Many liberals, disillusioned with Keynesian economics, are disinclined to come to the rescue of Keynesian deficits. The gut response of many radicals is "A plague on both your houses." This is backed up by the argument that the public debt under monopoly capitalism is an inflationary factor. It is supported by the observation—factually correct but in this context politically naive—that the Federal budget could be balanced and social programs expanded at the same time, if all the waste and overkill were squeezed out. Locally, scores of progressive organizations—such as ACORN (Association of Community Organizations for Reform Now), the Ohio Public Interest Campaign and the Illinois Public Action Council—feel that their strength derives from concentrating exclusively on grass-roots issues. After all, it was at the California grass roots that Proposition 13 bloomed. What this overlooks is that the national budget-balancing campaign is a national Proposition 13 and can no longer be fought only at the local level.

Finally, many progressives are impressed by the fact that Proposition 13-style "tax revolts" have been supported by millions of working people with justified resentment against high taxes. By the same token, the national budget-balancers have an even wider appeal. With or without con-con gimmickry, they try to speak in the name not only of a taxpayer revolt but also a consumer revolt against inflation and a citizen revolt against bureaucratic red tape, inefficiency and corruption. Besides, the latest opinion polls show from 70 to 78 percent of the people in favor of a budget-balancing amendment. A poll on holding a constitutional convention would probably elicit as favorable results.

Nonetheless, a counter-campaign is stirring. Many labor unions have spoken out against budget-balancing amendments. In mid-March a group of liberal organizations formed Citizens for the Constitution to work with the White House in lobbying against con-con resolutions in the state legislatures. On March 23, victory was reported in Montana. A much broader action has been started by a committee formed by the National Emergency Civil Liberties Committee which has set up a special Committee on Human Rights and the Constitution. In addition to supporting the Equal Rights Amendment, the committee is considering constitutional amendments to prohibit gerrymandering of all legislative districts, extend to the United States Senate the "one-person, one-vote" principle already imposed by the Supreme Court on State Senates and, above all, to incorporate the basic civil, political and economic rights set forth in the two United Nations human rights covenants now gathering dust in Senate committee. Consideration will also be given to an amendment embodying the view—expressed in historic dissents by Justices Black and Douglas—that corporations should not be granted the protections given to "persons" by the Fourteenth Amendment. The committee is also exploring national legislation to make any constitutional convention a truly representative, rather than a packed, body. These proposals include: (*1*) the election of all delegates and appointment of none, (*2*) the exclusive use of House of Representatives districts for these elections, (*3*) a separate, nationwide election day, (*4*) Federal contributions for campaign expenses, (*5*) free TV and radio time for candidates, (*6*) a prohibition against any person serving as both delegate and member of Congress and (7) one vote for each delegate, as opposed to the one-vote-per-state principle at the 1787 convention. Perhaps this is the kind of convention that Tom Hayden and John Judis had in mind when they supported con-con. Proposals along these lines—each of which has enormous potential for popular support—should give pause to the big corporations now bankrolling the con-con campaign. And in the event that con-con comes into being, they could help prevent it from bringing on a national disaster.

Opposition to the other parts of the budget-balancing campaign is more complex. It requires a ringing call to all progressive people to rally round "the flag of sound money," in John Hess's words ("The Inflation Game," *The Nation*, Sept. 2, 1978). To snatch this falling flag from the budget-balancers, progressives must face up to the necessity (now at long last accepted by George Meany) of direct controls over many prices, dividends, interest rates and rents, with wage increases limited to productivity advances and catch-ups on the cost-of-living and in substandard wage areas. They must recognize the possibility that despite all his promises to the contrary, Carter may—like Richard Nixon—suddenly reverse himself and install a phony control system that will set high and leaky ceilings on prices and "zap labor" on wages. It must be clearly understood that effective price ceilings will usually squeeze profit rates, and particularly profiteering. In turn, the corporations squeezed will yell bloody murder, violate the ceilings through both direct and indirect means, create black markets and then blame the black markets on any conscientious price controllers. These problems cannot be handled by bureaucratic diligence alone. They require price monitoring at the grass-roots and high-rise levels—sometimes bolstered by boycotts, consumers' strikes, tenant strikes and depositors' strikes. A genuine sound-money campaign requires a genuine revolt by consumers, taxpayers, tenants, borrowers and citizens in general against increases in prices, taxes, rents, interest rates and military expenditures.

Finally, there is the question of a "Federal budget balanced at full employment." Here it is essential to understand that "a full-employment budget" through fiscal manipulation alone is as deceptive as the con jobs on orthodox constitutional or "leave it to us" budget-balancing. The only honest approach to a full-employment budget is a Federal guarantee based on establishing "the right to useful paid employment at fair wages for all adult Americans able and willing to work." This means bringing back from the graveyard the original Humphrey-Hawkins Full Employment Bill, strengthening it with improved provisions on the control of inflation and backing it up with Senate ratification of the United Nations human rights covenants. □

CHAPTER TWO

★ ★ ★

Civil Liberties

To many the Constitution is the Bill of Rights—those first ten amendments to the Constitution, adopted in 1791 that incorporated the most familiar civil rights and liberties. Although the Federalists were reluctant to append these amendments to the Constitution during the Constitutional Convention, James Madison successfully guided them through the House during the first Congress, after which Congress recommended twelve amendments to the states for ratification. Ten of these amendments were ratified by the requisite number of states on December 15, 1791, and have since become a very important part of the Constitution. So important have they become, in fact, that when asked to explain what is included within the Constitution, citizens will often mention 'these ten amendments before any other part of the Constitution. And there are even those on the Supreme Court of the United States who argue that the Bill of Rights *should be* considered more important than the rest of the Constitution and should be given preference to other aspects of the document. Since 1937 the Supreme Court has given more emphasis to those fundamental freedoms found in the Bill of Rights at the expense of other clauses in the Constitution. It was none other than the late Chief Justice Earl Warren who felt that the Bill of Rights should be the heart of any constitution.

Laymen and jurists alike recognize these rights as vital and important to a healthy democracy, but the meaning of these rights and liberties is often unclear. Public opinion polls have shown that because Americans do not fully appreciate the implications of these freedoms they will frequently reject them. Because the meaning of these rights is often imprecise, the Bill of Rights undergoes frequent interpretation to define its meaning. One of the best tests of these freedoms comes through the most extreme clashes of interests. A recent case, described by Carl Cohen in this chapter, involves the rights of privacy of citizens living in the heavily Jewish-populated village of Skokie, Illinois, being invaded by members of the American Nazi party, who claim they are justified in marching on the village under the unlimited right of free speech and assembly. Village residents also feel threatened by the potentially dangerous situation that might accompany such a confrontation. This case study serves as a superb measure of the limits of free speech and assembly.

Another recent test of a different aspect of the First Amendment came when a group of concerned parents agreed to the radical practice of "deprogramming" to persuade their children to disavow their unorthodox religious beliefs. In the deprogramming process, however, as Dean Kelley argues in his article on "Deprogramming and Religious Liberty," their "children"—now adults—were kidnapped, coerced, and stripped of their rights to worship and believe in the religion of their choice. This case study points to the anguish of parents seeking to control their children's religious behavior at the expense of these children of legal age giving up their rights to worship God in their own way. Such instances bring much strain to the freedom of worship guaranteed by the First Amendment.

The constitutional guarantee of "trial by jury" found in Article III as well as the Sixth and Seventh Amendments is another ill-defined aspect of the Constitution. Part of the problem here, however, is due to the difficulty of doing research on jury procedures. The jury process is protected by secrecy, making it necessary for behavioral scientists to resort to mock juries and other artificial circumstances. With the exception of a few studies of consequence, our knowledge of jury behavior is based on conjecture and a knowledge of how decision-making in a small group operates. What we do understand about trial by jury has come to us through judicial interpretations of the Constitution and Bill of Rights. Richard Harris in his article "Trial by Jury" analyzes these differences in interpretation, suggesting that the Supreme Court, in departing from earlier traditions, now concludes that twelve-member juries reaching unanimous decisions are no longer an integral part of that guarantee of trial by jury.

Press freedom may seem unique among the civil liberty guarantees of the Constitution, since the press and mass media appear at first glance to be somewhat removed from the individual citizen. But as John Stuart Mill suggests, the press is not so removed as it first appears. Indeed, the press becomes the logical extension of the freedom of thought since, he indicates, the need to protect the liberty of publishing one's opinion rests on the same premise as the need to protect the liberty of expression. The classic confrontation that occurred in 1971 between the press's protected right to publish and government's claimed need to protect national security involved the so-called Pentagon Papers. This particular case, *New York Times Company* v. *United States* (included in this chapter), poses the question whether the press continues to be one of the primary bastions against oppressive government or, on the other hand, whether government can restrict the press at will whenever it feels threatened.

A final consideration — and possibly one of the most important ones for the student of civil liberties or for anyone who holds these freedoms to be essential to a democratic society—concerns whether the state under certain circumstances can legitimately suspend any or all of these civil rights and liberties. Can it, indeed, take from the individual the ultimate civil right: the right to life itself. In the 1976 case of *Gregg* v. *Georgia*, the last selection in this chapter, the Court fully explores this question but leaves us uncertain as to how secure this liberty—the right to life—and, by extension, all liberties are for the future.

★★★

7

The Right to Be Offensive: Skokie — The Extreme Test   Carl Cohen

Should there be limits to free speech and assembly? Most jurists and students of constitutional law would argue in favor of some reasonable limits under certain circumstances. The problem comes, however, when one attempts to limit free speech and assembly in the face of a threat rather than an actual violation. Such a circumstance arose when the American Nazi party threatened to march into the village of Skokie, Illinois, whose population is 60 percent Jewish. This predominantly Jewish suburb of Chicago anticipated trouble from the beginning when the American Nazi party announced its intentions to march.

But does anticipated trouble pose a danger? Does Cohen think that the situation in Skokie is analogous to a "clear and present danger" posed when one shouts "fire" in a crowded theater? If an immediate danger existed, then the Court would have had reason to prevent the Nazis from their march. If it did not, the Nazis were acting quite within their rights. After all, given the purpose for their march, there was no better place than the Jewish-dominated suburb, nor better time than Hitler's birthday, to tell those assembled about Naziism American-style. It was reminiscent of the civil rights marches into Selma, Alabama, and Philadelphia, Mississippi, where time and place were essential to the message conveyed. Opponents of the Nazi demonstration charged, however, that the march would bring to mind the unique suffering of the Jewish people at the hands of the Nazis, causing "injury" to the Jewish residents who would recall the savage consequences of anti-Semitism. To what extent is Cohen convinced by this argument?

Because some messages are offensive to the ears or convey irrational charges, are these legitimate grounds for preventing these ideas from being made public? Whose responsibility is it to decide whether American citizens should be barred from hearing the speeches of the American Nazis or listening to the appeals from the residents of Skokie? Is it government's, the Court's, or the press's responsibility? What repercussions do you see to the freedom of speech if government assumes this responsibility?

The situation portrayed in the Cohen article is precisely the sort of situation anticipated by the Framers and those who early insisted on the passage of the Bill of Rights. Why is it so necessary to defend the rights of members of a repugnant group with as much fervor as one defends the rights of members of an accepted group?

★ ★ ★

SKOKIE—THE EXTREME TEST

CARL COHEN

"Hard cases make bad law" the saying goes. Perhaps. But good principles are rightly tested by extreme cases. The principle that "Congress shall make no law . . . abridging the freedom of speech, or of the press; or the right of the people peaceably to assemble . . ."—than which we have few better—is perennially tested by American Nazis.

The skeletal facts of the latest test are these: The National Socialist Party, under the leadership of Frank Collin, planned public demonstrations in April 1977, in the parks of suburban Chicago. The Village of Skokie, 4 miles north of the Chicago city line, blocked the demonstration within its borders by requiring the prior posting of $350,000 insurance. The Nazis persisted, announcing their intent to march without speeches aimed at any ethnic or racial groups and without distributing literature, but in uniform and with signs and swastikas. Skokie (nearly 60 percent Jewish) then won a court injunction prohibiting the Nazis from displaying their uniforms or swastikas, or disseminating literature, on the date planned. The American Civil Liberties Union, representing the Nazis in this matter, sought but did not get a stay of that injunction from the Illinois Appellate Court. The Illinois Supreme Court refused to hear the case, and the ACLU appealed to the U.S. Supreme Court for a stay of the injunction. That petition was treated by the Supreme Court as one requesting a review of all procedural issues in the case, and granted it, ordering the Illinois courts to respond.[1]

Meanwhile, three new ordinances were adopted by the Skokie Village Council, having much the same effect as the injunction at issue. The first requires a permit for any demonstration of fifty or more persons in the streets or on the sidewalks of Skokie. The second bans "political organizations" from demonstrating in "military style" uniforms. The third bans both the display of "symbols offensive to the community" and the distribution of literature that ascribes a "lack of virtue" to racially or ethnically identifiable groups. Concurrently, a small group of Jews living in Skokie, acting independently of the village and the park district, seek a separate injunction against any Nazi demonstration because of the injury it would allegedly do to them.[2]

Citizens on both sides of the controversy are outraged. Is this a hard case? The ACLU does not think so—but by defending the right of the Nazis to demonstrate it has lost some 30 percent of its Illinois membership in a matter of months. The arguments on both sides are more tangled and subtle than is commonly supposed. In the end, however, the ACLU is right: it is not Nazism that is at stake, but the freedom of speech.

Those who would block the Nazi demonstration are not insensitive to the constitutional protection of free speech. They say, in effect: "The freedom of speech—which we honor as fully as does the ACLU—is like every freedom in having limits in a good society. Defenders of free speech who retain their good sense will realize that Nazis, saying what they say in the way they say it, do exceed reasonable limits. Associating themselves with the literal annihilation of millions of Jews, they now seek to advance their views abrasively in a community populated by many of the very same people who had been tortured by Nazis. Some of these Jews, after narrow escape, have sought refuge in Skokie. We applaud the vigorous defense of controversial speech, but this is a case—given the character of these Nazis and their expressed intent—to which the constitutional protection of dissident opinion does not apply."

This general position of those who would forbid the Nazi demonstration is not sufficient as it stands. Certainly it is true that neither the First Amendment nor any sensible principle lying behind it guarantees the right to say anything, anywhere, at any time. But restrictions upon speech and assembly—especially any that would silence representatives of a political party in a public place with a public aim—must be very narrowly drawn, and face a heavy burden of justification. The task of the Nazi blockers (not "anti-Nazis" because that group surely includes most of those defending the right of Nazis to demonstrate) is to give sound argument specifying the proper limits of free speech that would be exceeded by this demonstration. Every effort to do this while preserving the basic constitutional liberties in question fails, as I shall show.

Grave danger is one limit upon speech thought reasonable by many. Justice Holmes wrote in 1919: "The question in every case is whether the words used are used in such circumstances and are of such a nature as to create a clear and present danger that they will bring

---

[1] On the narrow question of whether an injunction prohibiting the use of the swastika violated the First Amendment rights of the Nazis the Illinois Supreme Court did respond in January 1978. The injunction was struck down. The Court wrote: "The display of the swastika, as offensive to the principles of a free nation as the memories it recalls may be, is symbolic political speech intended to convey to the public the beliefs of those who display it."

[2] That private action the Supreme Court of Illinois ordered dismissed, and the appeal for rehearing has been denied. But the Anti-Defamation League of B'nai B'rith, supporting that private suit, has promised further appeal to the U.S. Supreme Court. The three village ordinances were declared unconstitutional by the Federal District Court in February; but on March 17 that court granted a forty-five-day stay of its own order, as a cooling-off period and to permit the village to appeal the ruling to the 7th Federal Circuit in Chicago. That appeal has been scheduled for late May. The stay (temporarily keeping the ordinances in force) will probably be extended until the 7th Circuit Court reaches a decision on the merits. If that court affirms the District Court (at least on the first two ordinances) the Nazis may march lawfully in late May or June—unless the U.S. Supreme Court grants a further delay.

about substantive evils that Congress has a right to prevent." [*Schenck* v. *United States*, 249 U.S. 47 at 52.] The Village of Skokie applies essentially that standard. It says that the evils of violence resulting from the demonstration are sure, the danger of them patently clear, and (were the Nazis to march) immediately present. Holmes's justly famous illustration makes the point vividly: "The most stringent protection of free speech would not protect a man in falsely shouting fire in a theatre, and causing a panic." Nazis waving swastikas in a mainly Jewish community, say the people of Skokie, are in effect shouting fire in a theatre. That irresponsible use of speech we are not obliged to permit; neither the shouter in the theatre nor the Nazi in the street is entitled to the constitutional protection of free speech.

The analogy is seriously flawed. Whoever falsely shouts fire in a theatre is certainly not entitled to free-speech protection. But the circumstances of a Nazi demonstration differ from those of the theatre in three fundamental respects.

First, the theatre audience is captive, subjected against its will to the shout and its sequel. Not so any gathering for a Nazi parade or demonstration. Those angered or offended are free to stay away, or to leave; they need have nothing to do with the affair. The panic in the theatre traps and injures those present for reasons entirely unrelated to the shout: that false alarm is not essentially speech at all; it is no different from the fraudulent ringing of an alarm bell. Of the audience any Nazi march may draw, all this simply cannot be said.

Second, the shouted warning is of such a nature that it permits no discussion. It is not the expression of an opinion but a signal for flight, giving no opportunity for reasoned reply. The Nazi demonstration may be answered with counter-demonstrations; it may be refuted, in print or by voice; then or later. Nazi demonstrators offer no threat of immediate calamity comparable to that of a false alarm in a crowded hall.

Third, the alarm in the theatre is, by hypothesis, false; we would think very differently of an honest warning. Nazi views are also false, no doubt, but being right is not a condition on which permission to demonstrate may be premised. Who should have that permission if it were? And who decide?

Some words, in some special circumstances, because of the grave danger they immediately create, cannot claim the protection of free speech. Shouting fire falsely in a theatre is one such case; a political demonstration in a park, by Nazis or anyone else, is not.

"But," rejoins the Nazi blocker, "you underestimate the seriousness of the threat this demonstration immediately creates. If the Nazis march in Skokie with swas-

Carl Cohen is an active member of the American Civil Liberties Union, having served for several years as chairman of its Michigan affiliate and as a member of its national board of directors. Mr. Cohen, who teaches philosophy at the University of Michigan, Ann Arbor, is the author of Democracy *(University of Georgia Press) and* Civil Disobedience *(Columbia University Press).*

tikas and brown shirts they will almost certainly provoke a riot. Incitement to riot is a crime. When it is deliberate, as in this case, when its violent consequences are highly probable and fully anticipated, such incitement cannot be defended as mere speech. It is conduct designed to breach the public peace, using the First Amendment as shield. Skokie has the right, even the duty, to protect itself against the threat of that despicable design."

This dangerous argument seriously misapprehends the concept of incitement to riot. The fact that a message or symbol excites an audience to furious antagonism gives no evidence whatever of criminal incitement. That crime consists in urging upon one's audience the commission of some unlawful act in a context in which it is probable that some in the audience will do what is being urged. Even then the speaker will not normally be guilty of criminal incitement unless persons in his audience do in fact engage in the unlawful conduct he urged upon them. Nothing like those conditions is present in this case. Nazi speakers shrewdly plan to urge nothing explicitly unlawful. ("Free speech for the white man" was their announced slogan for this occasion.) They urge no specific acts at all, certainly no illegal ones. In a fury directed at the Nazis, some in the Skokie audience may subsequently break the law—but those whose symbols provoked their fury cannot be legally responsible for the misconduct. In the interests of freedom, incitement must be very narrowly delineated. When overt unlawful deeds are committed as a direct consequence of agitating speech, that speech becomes part of the crime—as the planning of an actual robbery becomes part of that robbery. Persons whose inflammatory words lead immediately to the disorder they propose may be similarly culpable. But the Nazis, few of whose audience will be inclined to do anything they may urge, could never be guilty, in Skokie, of inciting to riot.

"Regarding the technical conditions for that crime you may be correct," the Nazi blocker continues, "but you are blinded by technicalities. The Nazis delight in creating fright and havoc among Jews. Recently in this country their demonstrations have several times actually resulted in riot. Nazis understand full well how maddening their symbols are to their intended victims; they plan that abrasion. It is a good principle in law that one may reasonably be held to intend the natural and expected consequences of one's acts. True, the riot will not be caused by an audience that complies with the urgings of Nazi agitators. The Nazis may thus be innocent of some narrowly defined crime of 'incitement.' They will nevertheless be guilty of engaging deliberately in conduct designed to infuriate and calculated to result in a wholesale breach of the public peace. From incitement in that more general sense we can and must protect ourselves."

This argument, having much prima facie appeal, is the one on which Skokie chiefly relies. But the village is profoundly mistaken when it assumes that speakers may be silenced because of the response expected to their words. If that were granted, no truly controversial position on an incendiary topic could be freely presented. When it could be shown that the probable reaction would be intemperate or disorderly, the advocacy of an unpopular position would have to be forbidden. Thus, tying the permissibility of controversial speech to its expected reception by an audience establishes what has been called "the heckler's veto." A society that honors freedom concretely cannot authorize that veto.

Very unpopular causes may be as freely advocated under our Constitution as those in popular favor. Aberrant political advocates, progressive or reactionary, wise or crazy, will commonly meet with an angry and unruly reception. Communists, pacifists, National Socialists —especially those on the extreme of any continuum— will be forever in need of defense. Their freedom is our interest not only because our side may one day meet similar response but because rational judgment upon any position requires that it be heard. Some lessons must be repeatedly relearned, even by those who once taught them. If the Nazis are not free to speak because their Jewish audience will be hostile, the Jews will not be free to speak when their Arab audience promises equal hostility. When demonstrations to which sufficient ire may be threatened are not allowed, the hecklers have a veto —and they have it whatever the content of their views.

The issue has been tested. A passionate message of racial hatred was delivered—also in Chicago, in 1949, by a Catholic priest under suspension—to a sizable audience in a large hall. Outside, a cordon of police struggled to control the infuriated counter-demonstrators, while Father Terminiello completed his speech. He was later convicted for creating a breach of the peace—a breach created not by him or his followers but by persons outside the lecture hall so maddened by his bigotry as to throw bottles and bricks at the windows as he spoke. Is Father Terminiello to be legally punished for speaking so? The judge in the trial court had instructed the jury that the words "breach of the peace" include speech that "stirs the public to anger, invites dispute, brings about a condition of unrest, or creates a disturbance. . . ." That, said the Supreme Court, was grave error. Justice Douglas wrote the majority opinion: "[One] function of free speech under our system of government is to invite dispute. It may indeed best serve its high purpose when it induces a condition of unrest, creates dissatisfaction with conditions as they are, or even stirs people to anger. Speech is often provocative and challenging. It may strike at prejudices and preconceptions and have profound unsettling effects as it presses for acceptance of an idea. That is why freedom of speech, though not absolute, . . . is nevertheless protected against censorship or punishment, unless shown likely to produce a clear and present danger of a serious substantive evil that rises far above public inconvenience, annoyance, or unrest." [*Terminiello* v. *City of Chicago*, 337 U.S. 1, at 4, 1949.]

The right of a racist to speak freely becomes a bulwark for all. Civil rights activists, convicted a few years later because of the tumultuous responses of their hostile audiences, had their convictions also reversed by the Supreme Court, relying on the *Terminiello* decision. Even in the most hostile territory the right to political agitation for all parties has been secured.

The case for the Nazis is stronger than that for Terminiello, whose angry opponents really did throw bricks. Nothing has been thrown at the Nazis in Skokie because they have not yet been allowed to speak there. The mere threat of disorder has served to silence political speech. An injunction based on that threat encourages continuing threats and further restrictions. Such prior restraint of speech is highly objectionable. It does not allow even for the test of the impact of that speech. In the *Pentagon Papers* case, the claim by the United States Government that publication of the papers would lead to loss of life in Southeast Asia was rightly rejected by the Supreme Court as ground for an injunction prohibiting publication in advance. Should that Court tolerate an injunction forbidding in advance a controversial demonstration on domestic public affairs?

"They should even if they won't," replies the Nazi blocker, "when that speech has a very high probability of provoking violence. We cannot know with absolute certainty what the future holds; we cannot be absolutely sure that a riot will ensue if the Nazis parade with swastikas in Skokie. But we can be confident when we predict it. Some words and symbols, by their plain meaning in known contexts, are so provocative as to cause decent and reasonable people to respond by fighting. Speech like that is rightly forbidden.

"In this, the Supreme Court is on our side. A Jehovah's Witness named Chaplinsky, convicted in New Hampshire for shouting at a policeman, when stopped from preaching in the street: 'You are a goddamned racketeer [and] a damned Fascist and the whole government of Rochester are Fascists or agents of Fascists,' claimed freedom of speech as his shield unsuccessfully. Some utterances, the Supreme Court said, are not entitled to normal protection. '[I]t is well understood that the right of free speech is not absolute at all times and under all circumstances. There are certain well-defined and narrowly limited classes of speech, the prevention and punishment of which have never been thought to raise any constitutional problem. These include the lewd and obscene, the profane, the libelous, and the insulting or "fighting words"—those which by their very utterance inflict injury or tend to incite an immediate breach of the peace.' [*Chaplinsky* v. *New Hampshire*, 315 U.S. 568, at 572, 1942.]

"That fighting words should not be protected as normal verbal controversy," the blocker concludes, "is plain good sense. In a community where live thousands of survivors of Nazi death camps, an aggressive Nazi demonstration is surely speech which, by its very utterance, inflicts injury and tends to incite an immediate breach of the peace."

The argument fails utterly. The doctrine applied—that words themselves are sometimes to be treated as equivalent to the first physical blows in a fight—is highly suspect. What words under what circumstances may be treated so must be forever disputable. Words can hurt, but there is a difference between a verbal and a physical blow that metaphor must not be allowed to blur. If the words that sometimes provoke a fight are silenced, the general uncertainty about which words may have that effect must chill all debate, hedge all robust speaking in vigorous contest. The theory that nasty words justify immediate physical retaliation is a bad one—and, in fact, it is a theory now almost universally abandoned.

Even if accepted in the extreme case, however, the application of the "fighting-words" doctrine would have to be so narrowly restricted to special circumstances as to have no bearing on a proposed demonstration by Nazis. It could apply only to utterances by one person to the face of another, being defamatory in the extreme. Political demonstrations before a general public, however despicable the views presented, are not one-to-one situations. Moreover the doctrine could apply (if ever) only after those insults were hurled and a retaliatory blow struck—clearly not the present case. Above all, the "fighting-words" doctrine, if applicable in any context, would be so only as a consequence of some personal offense, never when the cause of agitation, however bitter, is political. The gambit cannot succeed.

"Yet we all know," the Nazi blocker rejoins, "that Nazi propaganda will be exceedingly painful in this context. The expression 'fighting words' may be inexact here, but it points to the heart of the case, the real ground upon which an injunction prohibiting a Nazi demonstration in Skokie is justifiable. The Nazis may or may not begin a fight, or incite disorder, or breach the public peace—but it is certainly the case that, if they march and speak, they will do severe and irreparable harm to a substantial number of Jews—refugees from the Third Reich—now living in Skokie.

"It is not the speech as such that we ask to have enjoined, but the deliberate injury of those living their post-Holocaust lives in mutual company and refuge. By demonstrating in storm-trooper style the Nazis will inflict—and seek to inflict—direct personal pain upon those who have once already been their innocent victims. The infliction of such injury no community is obliged to permit."

Of all objections to the Nazi demonstrations this is the most serious. It is advanced not by the Village of Skokie but by a small group of Jewish survivors living there, and it relies, sensitively, upon what appears to distinguish this case from all ordinary cases of controversial speech. Consider this argument in greater detail:

(*a*) "The atrocities to which the victims of the Holocaust were subjected cannot be captured in words. For the present it may be enough to say that the mother of one of the plaintiffs in this case was murdered by the Nazis, having been thrown into a well with fifty other women while alive, and covered with gravel. To the perpetrators of this and a thousand like crimes the American Nazis give proud allegiance."

(*b*) "Upon the few surviving victims the Nazis inflicted a psychological trauma so profound as to scar their lives forever. Overwhelming anxiety, recurrent terror, paralyzing helplessness, emotional anguish—all manifested not only in mental suffering but in physical pain and disorder—flow still from those cruelties. Nazi anti-Semitism cannot pass as ordinary political controversy."

(*c*) "The Nazis' specific intent to pursue the Jews taking refuge in America—to arouse and marshal hatred of them—was plainly announced in a leaflet they distributed just prior to the planned march:

. . . we have decided to relocate in areas heavily populated by the real enemy—the Jews!

An old maxim goes: "Where one finds the most Jews, there also shall one find the most Jew-haters." With this basic truth in mind, we are now planning a number of street demonstrations and even speeches in Evanston, Skokie, Lincolnwood, North Shore, Morton Grove, etc. . . . . Our successful opposition to the Black Invasion of Southwest Chicago will now be turned on the culprits who started it all: The Jews!"

(*d*) "The survivors, if subjected now to demonstrations earlier witnessed by them personally in connection with their earlier torture, will be caused great emotional harm no matter what they do—whether they counter-demonstrate, stay in their homes, or attempt to go about their business as if nothing painful were taking place. There is remedy at law for such deliberate injury. The Illinois Supreme Court (among others) has made it clear that the intentional infliction of severe emotional distress does give a right to redress. Two conditions must be met: (*1*) 'The aggressive invasion of mental equanimity' must be 'unwarranted and unprovoked,' and (*2*) it must be calculated to cause severe emotional disturbance in the person of ordinary sensibilities, or there must be 'special knowledge or notice' of atypical sensibilities. [*Knierim* v. *Izzo*, 174 N.E. 2d, 157, at 165, 1961.] That Nazis have special knowledge of the atypical vulnerability of the Jewish survivors in Skokie is beyond question. Indeed, they planned the demonstration precisely there because that is where the Jews are. Nor is there any doubt that the first condition is also met. What provocation by the Jews warrants the Nazis' carefully planned attack upon them? What could be a clearer instance of the aggressive invasion of mental equanimity of innocent citizens? As a legal matter, as well as a moral one, the conditions of redress are surely present."

(*e*) "But may a court anticipate the need for redress by enjoining the demonstration before it takes place? Yes, it may when what the demonstrators plan to do can be shown to cause irreparable damage if allowed. 'A state has the right to curtail free speech,' an Illinois Appellate Court has written, 'when . . . it determines that such curtailment is necessary to protect the public interest. . . .' [*Jersey County Motor Co.* v. *Teamsters Local 525*, 156 N.E. 2d, 633, at 636, 1959.] The public interest at stake is evident. These survivors of Nazi terror, most of them elderly, sought sanctuary in Skokie. The invasion of that refuge would result in injury to them for which no remedy could then be purchased at any price. Citizens (to use the words of earlier court decisions) cannot expect protection from 'mere vulgarities' or 'meaningless abusive expressions' or 'trivialities and mere bad manners.' And in weighing the impact of the speech a distinction must be drawn between symptoms of emotional distress 'visible to the professional eye' and 'neurotic overreactions to trivial hurts.' Granted. Who doubts which side of that line the consequences of a Nazi demonstration in Skokie would fall?"

(*f*) "It will be said that there is no precedent for such curtailment of speech by court injunction. But no earlier set of facts is anything like these. There is no precedent for the horror of the Nazi campaign against the Jews, and there is no precedent for their publicly announced intention to prey upon their victims by calling vividly to mind the cruelties earlier done to them. 'No person,' the Illinois Supreme Court has said, 'has a right to make war on another.' [*Carpenters' Union* v. *Citizens' Committee*, 164 N.E. 393, at 401, 1928.] The Nazis make war on the Jews. They have done so, brutally, for decades; now, in Skokie, they announce their intention to do so again. There never was anything like this."

The persuasiveness of this argument depends upon its transition from the pain the Nazi demonstration may cause to the action proposed to prevent it. At issue here is not historical fact but the claim that the potenial hurt of recalling it justifies the prohibition of a political demonstration. It does not. Three points:

First. Freedoms simply do not come without cost. For the freedom of speech the cost is often substantial, and sometimes its burden must be unevenly borne. Where speech is genuinely free there must be a collective commitment to accept the consequences of that freedom. Painful and offensive utterances, some cruelly unfair, will be openly aired. Reputations will suffer, sometimes unjustly; old wounds will be opened, sometimes viciously. Our choice is between the protection of freedom with the acceptance of its costs, on the one hand, and the protection of personal sensitivities (and the alleged sensitivities of those in power) at the price of sharply restricting the public forum, on the other hand. That choice has essentially been made by the American body politic. The Nazi blocker would make another.

How great the pain will be for the Jews in Skokie is hard to say. That the public appearance of some fanatic young Nazis would reactivate all the terrors of thirty years before may be an exaggeration. Great anger will be refreshed; that may not be unhealthy. Vigorous counter-demonstrations and the expressed contempt for the Nazis by an articulate press may prove a satisfying balm. Neither pluses nor minuses can be quantified. If there is a nonmeasurable balance on the negative side—which is uncertain—that is one of the unavoidable costs of an open society.

Victims of Stalinism cannot avoid its repeated advocacy. Victims of racism may not silence a racist who teaches their genetic inferiority. Those believing organized religion to be cruel superstition have no more authority to suppress it than have religionists the authority to suppress satanic apostasy. The field of open argument—serious, angry, important argument—runs with blood from psychic wounds.

Second. Of all such costs none is so clearly entailed by the democratic process as that arising from open advocacy of a political party, however crazy or extreme. Hate them as we may, the denial that the Nazis are a party will not stand examination. On the fringe of madness they may be, but that has been said, and will be said, of every revolutionary view. We simply cannot silence a party—any party—and expect to remain free.

Third. Psychic pain, even if so great and deliberate as to be cause for redress, cannot ground the prior restraint of speech. Much of what is feared from the exercise of freedom never transpires. The constitution of an open society—not its document merely but the basic principles of its life—precludes the silencing of some out of concern for the sensibilities of others. This is not callousness but a condition of the democratic process.

Finally, the Nazi blocker must face the fact that it is not harm to some, or danger to all, or incitement to riot, or fighting words, or any such concern that chiefly motivates him. It is the evil of these Nazi views, their blatant racism and anti-Semitism, that he thinks deserves to be silenced. When other arguments have failed he comes in the end to question the principle of free speech itself, asking, in effect, whether that principle really does oblige us to protect all content, however damnable. This is his last resort:

"Some speech content—speech utterly without redeeming social value—is not and ought not be protected by the First Amendment. Hard-core obscenity, as one example, does not come under its umbr lla. Obscenity, of course, is normally associated with sexually explicit matter. But its essential, nonsexual characteristics are two: it is intolerably offensive in some settings, and it is totally worthless. Whatever may go on behind closed doors, not every form of language, or picture, or act is permitted in public places. Lewd depictions of perverted behavior, actual sexual intercourse, or other such matter is forbidden in public. Its prohibition is based on the recognition that thrusting that specific content upon an unwilling audience in a public place is a gross imposition and a cause of offense against which they (and all of us) have a right to be protected. Such matter does not contribute in any way to the political forum. It is barren of ideas, 'not in any proper sense communication of information or opinion safeguarded by the Constitution' as the Supreme Court wrote of some forms of expression not to be protected. [*Chaplinsky* v. *New Hampshire*, 315 U.S. 568, at 572, 1942.]

"Nazi garbage, although not in the same way carnal, is just like that. Citizens of a decent community have the right to be shielded against it in precisely that spirit. Indeed, the intrinsic offensiveness of lascivious acts or pictures is minor compared to that of the public thrusting of irrational racism and anti-Semitism. Its worthlessness is manifest. We contend, therefore, that in a wide but accurate sense of the term, Nazi hate-mongering is obscene. As that category is used in law, we realize, it would not here apply. But it is no stretch of language or concept to call it that, and it is no unreasonable stretch of law to prohibit its presentation on the same fundamental grounds."

All censorship comes to this in the end: some content is so very bad that it must not be heard or seen.

The root of the issue between blocker and libertarian is here exposed. We may prevent the Nazi demonstration, the blocker believes in his heart, because those views are utterly intolerable. If anything is nearly intolerable, the libertarian believes in his heart, it is that argument from badness—giving the power to silence to those who do not like what they hear. The Nazis provide a splendid illustration. Called manifestly worthless, their views in fact are laden with ideas, many of them despicable, but for that very reason highly meaningful. No segment of the community is entitled to decide for the rest of us that any ideas are so lacking in merit as to be excluded from the public forum.

Even where the matter in question has no political content, and is sexually explicit, and is known to give offense to some in the community, we protect the freedom of others to see and hear by obliging those who are offended to shield themselves by turning away, or walking away. Precisely this issue was faced by the Supreme Court in 1975, when it held invalid a city ordinance that prohibited films "in which the human male or female bare buttocks, human female bare breasts, or human bare pubic areas are shown, if such motion picture, slide, or other exhibits is visible from any public street or place." [*Erznoznik* v. *City of Jacksonville*, 422 U.S. 205, at 207, 1975.] When it is possible for a viewer or hearer to turn away, the Court concluded, his being offended when he does not do so will not serve to cancel the rights of speakers. Justice Powell:

"A State or municipality may protect individual privacy by enacting reasonable time, place, and manner regulations applicable to all speech irrespective of content. . . . But when the government, acting as censor, undertakes selectively to shield the public from some kinds of speech on the ground that they are more offensive than others, the First Amendment strictly limits its power. . . . Such selective restrictions have been upheld only when the speaker intrudes on the privacy of the home . . . or the degree of captivity makes it impractical for the unwilling viewer or auditor to avoid exposure." [p. 209.]

An earlier case—in which a young man was vindicated in his right to wear, in a courthouse, a jacket emblazoned with the words "Fuck the Draft"—is cited in support: "The ability of government, consonant with the Constitution, to shut off discourse solely to protect others from hearing it is . . . dependent upon a showing that substantial privacy interests are being invaded in an essentially intolerable manner. Any broader view of this authority would effectively empower a majority to silence dissidents simply as a matter of personal predilections." [*Cohen* v. *California*, 403 U.S. 15, at 21, 1971.]

Would the privacy rights of Skokie residents be invaded by a Nazi demonstration in an essentially intolerable manner? Surely not. Persons in their homes are entitled to protection from the intrusive noise of sound trucks blasting so as to reach them no matter what they do. But parks and streets are the common and proper place for political assembly. To some degree we cannot avoid encountering what happens in such places, but we do not have to stay; and we cannot expect to be insulated by law from all that we find intensively objectionable. Justice Powell continues:

"The plain, if at times disquieting, truth is that in our pluralistic society, constantly proliferating new and ingenious forms of expression, 'we are inescapably captive audiences for many purposes.' . . . Much that we encounter offends our aesthetic, if not our political and moral, sensibilities. Nevertheless, the Constitution does not permit government to decide which types of otherwise protected speech are sufficiently offensive to require protection for the unwilling listener or viewer. Rather, absent the narrow circumstances described above [in which exposure is impossible to avoid] the burden normally falls upon the viewer to 'avoid further bombardment of [his] sensibilities simply by averting [his] eyes.' [422 U.S. 210.] The screen of a drive-in theatre is not so obtrusive as to make it impossible for an unwilling individual to avoid exposure to it. The 'limited privacy interests of persons on the public streets cannot justify . . . censorship of otherwise protected speech on the basis of its content.' "

"Well," comes the last rejoinder from the blocker, "*is* this otherwise protected speech? By calling attention to its offensiveness and worthlessness we have shown that it, like hard-core obscenity, is not entitled to protection. Hence the legitimacy of restricting it."

But the right of the public to see the Nazis and hear what they say is at least as compelling as the right to look at bare buttocks and breasts. Nudity and sex, some hold, when enjoyed in print and pictures for themselves alone, are utterly without redeeming social value and for that reason not entitled to free-speech protection. That argument, very questionable respecting even hard-core pornography, is patently inapplicable to political matter.

Political debate—"uninhibited, robust, and wide open," in parks and streets as well as lecture halls—will rouse anger and give offense. Public offensiveness, like private distress, is an unavoidable cost of freedom. Citizens who would govern themselves have the right to hear every opinion on their public business. That the Nazis may be vicious or crazy does not cancel our need to pass judgment upon their views. Their speech is protected, as all political speech is protected, partly as a matter of their right, partly as a matter of course.

Exceptions cannot be made for nasty opinions. If the swastika is too offensive for some to tolerate today, the Star of David will be claimed equally intolerable by others tomorrow. These marchers have the same right to sing the *Horst Wessel Lied* as others have to sing the *Internationale* or *We Shall Overcome*. The answer to the argument from badness is not that the symbols complained of are not offensive but that offense of that sort cannot justify prohibiting their display in public places.

The effectiveness of public protest often depends critically upon the symbolic use of location. The Nazis would march in Skokie just because it is heavily Jewish. Think of them what we may, that is part of their political point. Civil rights demonstrators, as part of their point, often carried their moral convictions—very offensive to the segregationist majority—to the heart of Jim Crow country, to Selma, Ala., and Philadelphia, Miss. Blacks who demonstrate for fair-housing opportunity bring their protests to the heart of the suburban communities that would exclude them. If we will not protect Nazis carrying "White Power" signs in black neighborhoods, how shall we protect Black Panthers carrying "Black Power" signs in white neighborhoods?

But civil rights marchers carried the banner of decency, while the swastika is the symbol of unspeakable indecency. Yes. That judgment, however, has no bearing on the right to speak publicly. If the history of struggles to defend the freedom of thought and expression teaches anything it teaches this: that persons or parties must not be silenced because of the moral qualities their views are judged to have. Our best hope that public judgment passed upon the Nazis will prove sound rests upon the freedom of all to hear them and all to speak in reply. By presenting the extreme case, these Nazis provide an instructive test of a very good principle. □

★★

8   Deprogramming and Religious Liberty   Dean M. Kelley

The First Amendment, Kelley indicates, prohibits any interference with the freedom of religious belief—or does it? Does this amendment allow all to worship as they see fit? Does its protection only apply to advocates of established religions? Are members of cults, of sects, of bizarre religiously oriented groups deserving of this same protection? How secure are the protections of the First Amendment when advocates of a religion, as described by Kelley, must risk kidnapping, brainwashing, and physical restraint for advocating an unpopular belief? Why are some contemporary religious groups seen by many to be cultist and bizarre?

Some parents become extremely concerned when their children come under the influence of these unconventional religions. To restore their children to a semblance of "normal" behavior, some parents have resorted to "deprogramming" methods. How great a threat to civil liberties do you consider the practice of deprogramming? Can it ever be justified to preserve the sanctity of the family unit, as those concerned parents argued? Or are there limits to parental control of offspring?

Whenever two conflicting but legitimate claims are made to the courts, such as preserving parental control over the child or preserving the protections of the First Amendment, the judiciary must either choose between them or make a compromise between them. The two judges — S. Lee Vavuris and John J. Leahy—made two very different rulings on this issue. What were their decisions, and on what grounds were they justified? The difficulty here is that deprogramming as a technique to control behavior does not allow for compromise. But are there other ways to honor both of these claims without severely encroaching on either the family or the religious belief?

Kelley sees the use of deprogramming as a renewed manifestation of religious persecution. He suggests that the strange religious practices of the sects and cults are "not something new, but something old; a phenomenon sometimes labeled conversion." Furthermore, we have had earlier examples of religious persecution before today's cults were known to the public. What other religions in American history were subject to ridicule and persecution? To what extent does the judiciary reflect religious and cultural values of society and thereby act as a persecutor of religion rather than as a defender of religious liberty?

★ ★ ★

Deprogramming and Religious Liberty

Dean M. Kelley

*E*ver since the term "deprogramming" entered our national vocabulary several years ago, civil libertarians have been hard pressed to map the battlefront of this emotional controversy. Arrayed on one side are a plethora of new, high-demand "cult" religions which, dismayed observers allege, ensnare and exploit impressionable young people through "mind control" and "brainwashing." On the other side are the parents of the new converts who increasingly are resorting to deprogramming—which admittedly involves kidnapping and physical restraint—to restore their children, at great expense, to what the parents perceive as "normal." Lost in the shuffle somewhere

Dean M. Kelley is Director for Civil and Religious Liberty of the National Council of Churches, and Chairman of the ACLU Church-State Committee. Author of the book *Why Conservative Churches Are Growing*, Rev. Kelley has written for a variety of national publications; his report on the 1976 ACLU biennial Conference appeared in the Feb./March issue of *CLR*. Rev. Kelley has served for many years on the ACLU national board of directors, and he is a member of *CLR*'s editorial committee.

Illustration by Hai Knafo

is the First Amendment to the Constitution whose protection of religious freedom the new religions and their adherents claim as their own. *What is going on here?* Are civil liberties being infringed, and, if so, by whom?

Recently, the legal parameters of the issue were defined by two diametrically opposed court decisions—one in New York, and the other in California. The first case, in Queens County, New York, involved two members of the Hare Krishna movement, Ed Shapiro and Merylee Kreshour. When both Shapiro and Kreshour were forceably detained by their parents and subjected to deprogramming by a private detective named Galen Kelley, they filed a complaint with the local district attorney. As a result of a subsequent grand jury investigation, however, the complaint against the parents and the deprogrammer was thrown out, and instead the leaders of the local Krishna Temple were themselves indicted for kidnapping and unlawful detention through "mind control."

From *Civil Liberties Review*, July/August 1977, pp. 23–33. Reprinted by permission of American Civil Liberties Union Foundation.

What is the problem with deprogramming? Are civil liberties being infringed? If so, by whom?

On March 17 of this year, New York State Supreme Court Justice John J. Leahy dismissed the indictment against the Krishna leaders, criticizing it in the harshest possible terms. "The court sounds the dire caveat to prosecutorial agencies throughout the length and breadth of our great nation," wrote Judge Leahy, "that *all* of the rights of *all* our people shall be zealously protected to the full extent of the law. . . . The freedom of religion is not to be abridged because it is unconventional in its beliefs and practices, or because it is approved or disapproved of by the mainstream of society and more conventional religions."

Only a week after Judge Leahy's eloquent defense of the First Amendment, San Francisco Superior Court Judge S. Lee Vavuris rendered a decision which found for the other side in the deprogramming dilemma, the oftentimes anguished parents of cult members. The issue before Judge Vavuris was a petition to grant conservatorship—legal guardianship—over five followers of Rev. Sun Myung Moon's Unification Church to their respective parents. The petition would give the parents legal control over their children's actions even though all five were legal adults and actively claimed their right to freely assert their religious beliefs. The tactic of seeking conservatorships has been used increasingly by parents to get young converts out of the religious groups and into the supposedly salutary hands of deprogrammers.

In granting the parents' request for conservatorship on March 24, Judge Vavuris asserted that parents *do* have rights over their children after they've reached majority, but he asked from the bench that the "unprecedented" case be appealed to clarify the legal issue. "I am just a Judge sitting in the Superior Court and we have to test this case," said Vavuris. "I have researched the law, and with the exception of very few instances, there's nothing to give me a guiding light. . . . It's not a simple case. We're talking about the very essence of life here, mother, father, and children. This is the very essence of civilization . . . a child is a child even though the parent may be 90 and the child is 60." Two weeks later, a California Appeals Court ruled that the five Moon followers could not be subject to deprogramming while the case was being appealed, although all five already had, and in a later decision, the Appeals Court released the five from their parents' custody.

*O*bscured by the hue and cry of distraught parents who see their children being duped by "bogus" religions is an examination of what the process of deprogramming actually entails. It is really nothing more than a euphemism for behavior modification. The practice originated in San Diego, California, under the leadership of a man named Ted Patrick, a former (volunteer) community relations aide to Governor Ronald Reagan. The object of the deprogrammers is to restore new converts of unorthodox religious groups to society by dissuading them from their new-found beliefs. Kidnapping is the method used for these "rescues."

Deprogrammers—displaying a certain amount of uniformity—always grab the victim at a time when he is least expecting it. There are usually three or four people who stuff the victim into a car and drive him off to some hotel, motel, or private home. He can be locked up in a room for up to three weeks, though usually the deprogramming takes only a few days. The victim is deprived of sleep and food and told that he will be held until he capitulates. One such scene, related with all the drama and pathos of a B grade war

Ted Patrick said: "There's the no good son of a bitch you worship. And you call him God!"

movie, was described by Ted Patrick himself in his recent book, *Let Our Children Go*:

We hurried downstairs to the examining room where Dr. Shapiro conducted his practice, and there was Ed, a tall thin boy, his head shaven, still wearing his robes and his beads, chanting and screaming. "Get me a pair of scissors," I said. "Scissors? What for?" "First thing we're going to do is cut that knot of hair off his head."

Ed came to attention. "What? Who are you? What right do you have to go cutting my hair? I have a right to wear this. It's part of my religion. I'm a legal adult. I'm twenty years old." "Shut up and sit down," I told him. "Just shut your mouth and listen."

"I won't listen. I don't have to listen. I want to leave!" "Well, you're not going to leave. Where's those scissors?" Four of his relatives held him down and I cut off the tuft of hair they all wear on the back of their heads and I removed the beads from around his neck. As soon as we let him up, he started chanting again at the top of his voice, "Hare Krishna, Hare Krishna, Hare Hare. . ."

In the game room Dr. Shapiro had a lot of lovely and expensive art objects and souvenirs he'd collected over the years and Ed began smashing them, one by one, just ripping the place apart, chanting all the while . . . I took him by the arms and flung him into a corner up against the wall, and I said, "All right, you hatchet-head son of a bitch, you move out of there and I'll knock your goddamned head off."

I picked Ed up by the front of his robes and marched him backwards across the room, slamming him bodily against the wall. "You listen to me! You so much as wiggle your toes again, I'm gonna put my fist down your throat!" His eyes got bigger and bigger with fear. He sat down abruptly. I had a picture of Prabhupada and I tore it up in front of him and said, "There's the no good son of a bitch you worship. And you call him God!" The usual line of approach.

This "usual line of approach" has become a burgeoning business. Some deprogramming entrepreneurs are charging $10,000 to $14,000, plus expenses, for deprogrammings, even if ultimately unsuccessful. A tax-exempt foundation has been set up in Tucson, Arizona, with Joe Alexander, a protégé of Patrick, and his wife as full-time resident deprogrammers, assisted as needed by two lawyers and a psychologist. There are networks of enthusiasts for deprogramming who circulate periodic newsletters telling how the battle goes in various parts of the country, generating letters to encourage cooperative prosecutors or to discourage critics of deprogramming.

*O*n the surface, it may seem that the controversy over deprogramming is a purely personal matter, involving as it does the interaction between parent and child. But, while the origins of the issue may have been private, familial disputes, the intrusion of state agencies—the courts, local police, state legislatures—raises the problem to a much more serious level. One of the necessary elements of civil liberties issues is the violation of individual rights by the state. At first the element of state action in deprogramming was passive or covert at most: police refusing to intervene in deprogramming because it was a "family matter" or—as Patrick relates in his book—quietly cooperating with the family; prosecutors declining to prosecute admitted abductions and kidnappings; grand juries refusing to indict; or petit juries refusing to convict.

But now state action in support of deprogramming has escalated. It is no longer passive but active, no longer covert but overt. We can expect the use of

State action in deprogramming is no longer passive but active, no longer covert but overt.

court orders of guardianship, conservatorship, and writs of *habeas corpus* to deliver converts from the "clutches of the cults" to increase in the near future. Legislatures in several states are being asked to enact or to expand laws permitting conservatorships or guardianships to be granted by court order in cases of persons—of whatever age—who are not able to manage their own affairs or to protect them from "artful and designing persons," as a bill recommended by a special committee of the Vermont Legislature puts it.

Thus a parent, relative or friend could go into court and obtain an order assigning custody of an adult whose religious convictions or behavior were suspect—as the parents of the five "Moonies" did in California—for the purposes of forceably returning that person to "normal." Membership in an esoteric cult would be prima facie evidence of the need for such a court order, and even that might not be necessary. Deprogramming has already been attempted, though not under court order, on persons belonging to long-established religious bodies such as a female member of a Roman Catholic Community in Canada and a male member of the Episcopal Church of the Redeemer in Houston; people belonging to a political group like the Socialist Labor Party; and even on persons not belonging to *any* group as in the case of two girls in Denver whom Patrick was hired to bring back to the strict tutelage of their Greek Orthodox families.

So who is safe? If someone doesn't like the way you talk or act or the people with whom you associate, they can hire a deprogrammer to go after you, grab you by force, take you off to a secluded place, and work you over until you consent to act in a manner acceptable to them.

The admittedly illegal abductions of deprogramming are justified by the claim that they are necessary to prevent a worse evil, the capture of innocent, idealistic young people by the pernicious cults. Visions are conjured up of adolescents enslaved to an alien Moloch, bound to an endless round of mindless and abject servitude, obliterating from their lives the bright promise of upwardly-mobile business and professional careers. Such a picture was the defense used by Ted Patrick when he was brought to trial for kidnapping a young adherent to the New Testament Missionary Fellowship, and it worked. The argument had the remarkable effect of putting the religious group on trial, obliging it to try to justify its religious beliefs and practices. *What is going on here?*

*M*ost, if not all, of the behavior associated with the so-called cult religious movements will seem bizarre and mystifying only to those largely innocent of any knowledge of church history or, indeed, of human history. What we are seeing in these groups today is not something new, but something old; a phenomenon sometimes labeled *conversion*. Thirty or 40 years ago, similar anxieties were stirred by the Jehovah's Witnesses and their aggressive proselytizing. The Mormons were widely feared and despised in the nineteenth century, driven by state militias from one haven after another. The early Quakers were detested and persecuted for their persistent efforts to persuade others to their beliefs.

Intense and zealous movements are very frightening to the adherents of more casual and conventional faiths. They divide communities and tear families apart, creating tension, friction and turmoil.

Intense and zealous movements are frightening to adherents of more casual faiths.

Such movements are aggressive, not heeding any consideration but the propagation of the True Faith. The idea that families are—or should be—spared this kind of dissension finds little basis in history. Consider this statement from the New Testament.

Do not think that I have come to bring peace on earth; I have come not to bring peace, but a sword. For I have come to set a man against his father, and a daughter against her mother, and a daughter-in-law against her mother-in-law; and a man's foes will be those of his own household. He who loves father or mother more than me is not worthy of me; and he who loves son or daughter more than me is not worthy of me; and he who does not take up his cross and follow me is not worthy of me. (*Matthew 10:34–38*).

These words, attributed to Jesus, do not fall graciously upon the ear. People seem to have difficulty remembering them. Yet, there is no truer description of the perils of conversion, of being caught up in a new faith.

Giovanni Bernadone lived in the twelfth century, son of a successful businessman. When he sold some cloth from his father's warehouse to rebuild a ruined church, the elder Bernadone took him to the local bishop to disinherit him. At that moment, he removed all of his clothes, returned them to his father and went on his way in a monk's cloak to pursue his religious convictions. History now remembers him as St. Francis of Assisi—instead of the prosperous textile merchant he *could* have become. St. Clare's family is said to have restrained her bodily from joining the band of followers of St. Francis of Assisi. Legend has it that St. Thomas of Aquinas' family confined him in a room with a prostitute to dem-

onstrate the pleasures of secular existence as opposed to the regimen of the Dominican order he wanted to join.

Undeniably, the conversion of their children to an alien faith is a devastating experience to parents, who see it as a repudiation of all they stand for. This anguish is only heightened when the cults are portrayed as rackets, monstrous hoaxes, or alien political cabals. But these hysterical projections do not necessarily help us to understand *what is going on here*. To offer an economic or political explanation for an ostensibly religious phenomenon is to miss the direct and elemental dynamic of religious motivation, which has often proved more powerful than economic or political motivations.

*H*uman beings have an unquenchable need to make sense of their life experience in the largest conceptual framework they can conceive. This need is especially acute in adolescence when the emerging adult must find his or her own explanation that makes sense. The received family faith doesn't always accomplish that—at least not without some exploring, testing and comparing—to which we owe the expansion and modification of religious traditions. Without some effective anchorage in a system of ultimate meaning, human beings are susceptible to despair, rage, bitterness and anxiety. They become prone to the maladies of meaninglessness that are increasingly prevalent in our society. The need to fill this void of meaninglessness has been an important force in human history.

All of our great systems of ultimate meaning—religions—began as intense, high-demand movements that claimed *all* the time, energy and thoughts of the believers. Characteristically, these movements have believed that they had the

The so-called cults are the very groups which most deserve the protection of the First Amendment.

Truth, all the Truth, and that other religions were essentially false. They have required rigid discipline and unquestioning obedience from the faithful while attempting to shield them from the insidious temptations of the world, particularly those most likely to draw the new convert back into old, depraved ways—family and former friends.

People who expect new religious movements to be bland effusions of vague, diffuse amiability and good intentions are naturally not going to recognize what is going on in the groups we are witnessing today. It is precisely because such groups believe that religion is serious business, that it matters for one's eternal salvation what one believes and does in this life, that they transmit to the less fervent public an elemental quality that is both disconcerting and frightening. But these are the very groups which most benefit the people whose need for religion is acute and who are not reached by the more placid faiths. They are the very groups which most need, deserve, and test the protections of religious liberty guaranteed by the First Amendment.

To call these groups "cults" is to use a perjorative term to denigrate them without recognizing the constructive function they may be serving for present and future adherents. Many people don't realize that there is a high degree of normal turnover in the membership of these groups *without* the intervention of deprogrammers; in fact, probably to a higher degree when uncertain adherents don't feel threatened into greater solidarity with the group by deprogramming activity. Neither the groups nor the deprogrammers like to admit this natural flux of disaffection, since it suggests doubts about both the vitality of the group and the need for deprogrammers.

Part of the religious dynamic at work in these situations is the most powerful reagent in human affairs: concentrated personal attention. Adolescents who have been rather ignored by their families and peers find themselves suddenly the center of attention by attractive young people who spend hours working and talking with them to bring them into the loving circle of the group. It's interesting that the parental antidote for this so-called captivity by the religious movements is an equal and opposite dose of concentrated, protracted personal attention—deprogramming.

Young people whose parents try to dissuade them from their new religious commitments face a difficult emotional dilemma. Not wanting to argue with or hurt their parents, nor to compromise their own beliefs, the children often clam up, waiting for the storm of criticism to subside—they then are described by the parents as acting like "zombies." This type of behavior is often the catalyst which causes parents to seek the help of deprogrammers to counteract what they perceive as "brainwashing" and "mind control." But that perception—clouded as it is by strong emotion—is really a highly suppositious and elaborate explanation for behavior which seems much easier to explain without it.

*I*s it possible that this is a new set of terms used to discredit behavior which society does not approve; to make its perpetrators persons whose rights and intentions can be considered invalid? Is there such a thing as "brainwashing" at all, or is it a term we use to justify events and behavior we do not want to explain in more rational ways? Parents want to believe that some mystical or magic force must be to blame to keep them from having to think the unthinkable: that a free choice has been made for some other faith, another way of life.

Deprogrammers claim to want only to restore the free use of a young person's reason so that he or she can exercise "freedom of choice," that is, to choose freely any course *except* the religious commitment that led to the deprogramming. Reason and free choice are great goods won at high cost in human history. However, they are neither the only nor the highest goods in human experience, and indeed, have led to—or at least not prevented—much conflict and suffering.

The meaning of true liberty, especially religious liberty, is that persons must be free to subject their reason to the demands of faith if they want to do so, however bizarre and unreasonable that faith may seem to others. People must be free to live out other understandings of the good life than those accepted by conventional society if they want to do so, as long as they do not harm others or impair their rights.

Consider the many cases where deprogramming has been "successful." The result is often a person who is "depleted"—apathetic, drifting, brittle—unable to take up new interests. This condition has lasted for a year or more in some cases, unless the victim of deprogramming finds a purpose in life, as some have done, deprogramming others. Post-deprogramming denunciations of the religious group as a "hoax" should be suspect to some degree. After a person has doubly defected—once from parental values and then from the religious group—strong pressures for self-justification and the expiation of guilt are set in motion. These often take the form of insisting, "I was fooled, I was taken in, I was victimized," statements that mainly reflect the difference between being in and being out.

Of course the great criticism leveled against the new, high-demand religious movements is that they use force or coercion to gain and retain converts. If that is true, it is as illegal and repugnant as de-programming, and should be punished in a court of law where evidence is required to prove criminal conduct. Until proof is adduced, however, these charges remain mere allegations. In fact, the weight of evidence runs the other way, against those who admit using force in the physical abduction of cult members. The religious groups themselves should want to bend over backward to avoid even the appearance of taking unfair advantage of young people, but it is not the responsibility of government to compel religious groups to behave in a manner that outsiders will consider suitably decorous.

A part of religious liberty is the right of all of us to make what seem to others to be foolish choices, to be hoodwinked or to be exploited, for the sake of what seems to us to be the Truth. This is no justification for illegal activities by such groups, however, and this article is not intended as a defense or apologia for them. If they are fronts for foreign governments, then let that be investigated and proven. If they are using their tax exemption for illegal or non-religious purposes, then let that be demonstrated and the exemption revoked. But mere disputes about religious truth, about differences of religious practice such as diet, prayer, study or alms-gathering are not matters in which government is empowered to interfere.

This is not to ignore the anguish of parents who feel that their children have been taken from them. But anguish is not the only possible response to such a situation, and it has certainly been exploited and exacerbated to hysterical levels by deprogrammers who, in turn, feed off it like predators.

Let us not forget that the anguish of parents is not the only anguish involved here. Let us give equal consideration to the feelings—and rights—of young people who go about in daily dread of being physically seized and subjected to protracted spiritual gang-rape until they yield their most cherished religious commitments. *That is what's going on here.*

Let us give consideration to young people in dread of protracted, spiritual gang-rape.

That is the element that makes deprogramming the most serious violation of our religious liberty in this generation, and why it must clearly be seen as criminal. It should be prosecuted, not just as any other kidnapping, undertaken for mercenary motives would be, but even more vigorously, since it strikes at the most precious and vulnerable portion of the victim's life, religious convictions and commitments.

*O*ur nation was founded on the principle of religious freedom. After 200 years of trial and error with state-established churches in the various colonies, it really could not have been otherwise. The religious ferment in colonial America, especially during the Great Awakening of the mid-eighteenth century, familiarized the authors of our Constitution with a wide variety of zealous and evangelical sects. And it was encroachment upon this sort of fervor that the founders sought to prevent.

"Because we hold it for a fundamental and undeniable truth that religion . . . can be directed only by reason and conviction, not by force or violence," James Madison told the Virginia Assembly in 1785, "the religion of every man must be left to the conviction and conscience of every man; and it is the right of every man to exercise it as these may dictate. That right is, in its nature, an unalienable right." Is the right freely to exercise religious beliefs as one sees fit any less imperative today than in Madison's time?

One may argue, of course, that Madison had no knowledge of the alien nature of the Eastern sects emerging in our country today or of the potential to de-stroy one's free will through behavior modification. However, faiths as alien to Madison as the Krishna Consciousness Movement is to a contemporary Virginia Episcopalian certainly existed in eighteenth century America. And thus far, only deprogrammers themselves have been proven to use the mind-numbing techniques of behavior modification.

Deprogramming is a basic and fundamental violation of the constitutional guarantees to freedom of speech and association. But it is the encroachment upon the individual's religious freedom, the very right to think and to believe, that is most repugnant. Unlike many constitutional principles which have either been subject to the ebb and flow of judicial interpretation or have grown slowly from the wellspring of precedent, the right freely to exercise religious beliefs has remained close to a judicial absolute. The First Amendment is very clear.

So in the legal battle over deprogramming, Judge Leahy in New York adhered to long established tradition while Judge Vavuris in San Francisco, though understandably concerned for the grief-stricken parents, missed the point, one that has been asserted many times by the Supreme Court. Justice Douglas probably expressed it best writing for the majority in the 1944 Court decision in *U.S.* v. *Ballard*: "The Fathers of the Constitution were not unaware of the varied and extreme views of religious sects . . . They fashioned a charter of government which envisaged the widest possible toleration of conflicting views. Man's relation to his God was made no concern of the state. He was granted the right to worship as he pleased and to answer to no man for the verity of his religious views."

●

★★

9

Trial by Jury   Richard Harris

In this article, Richard Harris stresses the importance of two attributes long associated with the guarantee of trial by jury: the size *of the jury and the* unanimity *of decision. But, as Harris points out, the Supreme Court has recently begun to question whether the term "jury" really means a twelve-member panel. Does a six-member panel also qualify as a jury? Are twelve individuals deciding the guilt or innocence of an individual really superior to six persons engaged in the same process? Who would benefit from the change—the state or the accused? Was unanimity of decision an integral part of the constitutional protection of jury trial? What difference does it make if decisions are made by plurality, by majority, or through unanimity? What happens to the value of the jury as a collective body when the necessity of a unanimous decision is deemphasized?*

A concern with the jury system also highlights the role of the Supreme Court in making the Bill of Rights applicable to both federal and state laws. How is this process, known as "incorporation," exemplified in the case of Duncan v. Louisiana *that is discussed by Harris?*

In analyzing these arguments recently put forward by the Supreme Court justices, Harris discovers that the judges differ perceptibly in their confidence in the jury system. In evaluating the need for unanimous jury decisions, the justices were divided into three general positions. Which justices are in agreement in considering the legality of "near-unanimous" verdicts? Some of the justices, like Justices Powell and White, have a great deal of faith in the abilities of the jurors to carry out their duties. What does Justice White mean when he introduced the concept of the "doctrine of the conscientious juror"? Justices Douglas and Stewart, on the other hand, question the jurors' ability to weigh arguments they hear and properly deliberate decisions. Why did Douglas angrily dissent from the majority's opinion in the matter of "near-unanimous" decisions? Why did Justice Marshall also dissent in these cases? In reading the justices' opinions, one sees that a number of concepts are used to defend their views on this issue. James Madison's role in formulating the Sixth Amendment to the Constitution even becomes a consideration. How do Madison's concerns become relevant to the issue at hand?

What difference does the presence of a jury mean to the defendant? To an attorney? To the judge? It has been suggested by one student of the Court that the jury represents the only democratic element among many elitist elements in the judicial system. Would you expect the jury system, then, to act as a check on the other parts of the judicial system? If the jury were reduced in size, what additional changes would you anticipate?

★ ★ ★

Trial by Jury

Richard Harris

Trial by jury is one of liberty's oldest and most dependable safeguards. In the United States, the Constitution provides for jury trials in both civil and criminal cases, but, as with most of the other rights enumerated in that document, there are few details to show how this one should be assured in practice. On the subject of juries in criminal cases, for example, Article III says only that "trial of all crimes, except in cases of impeachment, shall be by jury . . . in the state where the said crimes shall have been committed," and the Sixth Amendment adds that the jury shall be "impartial" and chosen locally. Thousands of cases have been heard since those few words were written to decide what they mean.

One thing they didn't mean until very recently was that every citizen was Constitutionally guaranteed a jury trial in any criminal prosecution. Although state constitutions have all along provided for jury trials in criminal cases under state jurisdiction, that has largely been a matter of imitation of the federal Constitution rather than obedience to it, and up to four years ago any state could have abolished its jury system, because until the Supreme Court ruled on this point, in 1968, the Constitution was understood to offer an explicit guarantee of jury trials only to defendants in federal courts. Since the states have always been more jealous guardians of their own powers, particularly their police powers, than of their citizens' individual rights, the Bill of Rights was long interpreted, first by tradition and then by law, to apply only to federal matters. But after ratification of the Fourteenth Amendment, in 1868, there was a growing movement to interpret its key clause, "nor shall any state deprive any person of life, liberty, or property without due process of law," to mean that due process demands "incorporation" of the Bill of Rights into state as well as federal laws and procedures. That movement was fiercely resisted—chiefly by the Supreme Court—and to some extent it still is. The idea of total incorporation has never been accepted by a majority of the Court, although slowly, and often grudgingly, the Court has conceded over the years that *some* provisions in the Bill of Rights are so "fundamental" that they apply equally to the states and to the nation. The first use of this doctrine by the Court came in 1925, when it declared that freedom of speech is a fundamental personal right, and has to be protected by state governments as well as by the national government. Once the legal wall in the federal system was breached by this ruling, the fundamental doctrine was gradually expanded by succeeding Courts, most of all by the Warren Court, to apply to state cases nearly all the criminal protections in the Bill of Rights, including the Sixth Amendment right to a jury trial. This last right was extended to the states in 1968, when the Supreme Court ruled, in Duncan v. Louisiana, that they must offer anyone who is accused of committing a serious crime a trial by jury.

A jury trial is a fundamental right, the Court stated in the Duncan decision, because it offers the only Constitutional way to protect defendants "against the corrupt or overzealous prosecutor and against the compliant, biased, or eccentric judge." In 1970, the Court—now the Burger Court—went on to address itself to the question, raised in Williams v. Florida, of whether it is also fundamental for a jury to consist of twelve members, as tradition and statute had long demanded. The issue was not of "Constitutional stature," a five-member majority of the Court replied, since "the essential feature of a jury obviously lies in the interposition between the accused and his accuser of the common-sense judgment of a group of laymen," whatever their number; the size of juries, then, must be left up to the states to determine for themselves. Finally, in 1971, the Court accepted two other cases that dealt with a basic issue in jury trials of criminal cases—namely, whether the rule that verdicts must be unanimous in criminal trials is fundamental to the jury system. The principle of unanimity in jury verdicts has been traced back as far as an English trial, recorded as Anonymous Case, in 1367. Although the unanimity rule is nowhere mentioned in the Constitution, it was generally accepted, apparently without question, under English common law and in the American Colonies and the United States as an essential part of any jury trial. The specific issue of unanimity for juries in criminal trials had never been decided by the Court before, but once states were compelled by federal law to provide trials for all serious offenses, it was inevitable that the rules governing those trials would have to be clarified. The Court heard arguments on the issue in March, 1971, and then heard rearguments in January, 1972, and on May 22, 1972, handed down its decision. Four members—Chief Justice Warren E. Burger, along with Justices Byron R. White, Harry Blackmun, and William H. Rehnquist—concluded that unanimous verdicts are not required in *any* criminal trial. Four other members—Justices William O. Douglas, William J. Brennan, Jr., Potter Stewart, and Thurgood Marshall—concluded that unanimous verdicts are required in *all* criminal trials. And the last member—Justice Lewis F. Powell, Jr.—concluded that unanimous verdicts are required in federal trials but not in state trials. Because of the peculiar nature of the four-to-four standoff, Powell's view prevailed, and is now the law in this country.

At the time of the Court's ruling, two states—Louisiana and Oregon—permitted less-than-unanimous juries to convict defendants in serious but non-capital cases. Louisiana allowed as many as three dissenting jurors out of twelve, and Oregon allowed as many as two out of twelve. Both state laws were reviewed by the Court at the same time, and its decisions on them were announced together. One case, Johnson v. Louisiana, was an appeal from a decision by the Louisiana Supreme Court upholding a conviction for armed robbery by a nine-to-three jury vote. In the other case, Apodaca et al. v. Oregon, the Supreme Court reviewed the convictions of three defendants who were found guilty, respectively, of assault with a deadly weapon by an eleven-to-one vote, grand larceny by an eleven-to-one vote, and burglary by a ten-to-two vote. One of the Chief Justice's prerogatives is to decide who is to write the Court's opinion when he is a member of the majority, and in both cases Chief Justice Burger chose Justice White, the sole member of the majority in these two decisions who had not been appointed by President Nixon.

In the Johnson case, the appellant argued that a verdict of guilty by only nine of the twelve jurors clearly showed reasonable doubt on the part of the jury as a whole. And since the reasonable-doubt rule is rooted in the basic Constitutional principle of due process, it was claimed, any verdict that was not based on a finding of guilt beyond a reasonable doubt abrogated due process and thus violated the Constitution itself. Justice White disagreed. Replying that the Supreme Court had never stated that jury unanimity was an essential part of due process, he continued, "Indeed, the Court has more than once expressly said that "in criminal cases due process of law is not denied by a state law . . . which dispenses with the necessity of a jury of twelve, or unanimity in the verdict.'" The quotation was from Jordan v. Massachusetts, which was decided in 1912, and Justice White also cited Maxwell v. Dow, decided in 1900, to the same effect. He did not mention that these rulings were handed down before the incorporation doctrine began to be applied, in 1925, to extend the Bill of Rights to the states. Moreover, the two early rulings had allowed the states to dispense with juries altogether—an opinion that was flatly reversed in 1968 by Duncan v. Louisiana. But that decision had

been made after Johnson was tried, and was not retroactive, so it didn't apply to the case at hand, as the appellant had conceded in his appeal. And, for that matter, if Duncan wasn't pertinent to this case, neither was the Sixth Amendment right to a jury trial that it had applied to the states.

While Justice White agreed that due process of law requires a finding of guilt beyond a reasonable doubt before a defendant can be convicted, he saw no reason to conclude, as the appellant had, that the reasonable doubt of three jurors constitutes reasonable doubt for an entire jury. In effect, he wrote, the Court was being asked to assume that if dissenters on a jury express sincere doubts about a defendant's guilt, the jurors who are convinced of that guilt will simply ignore them, without fully debating the questions they raise or allowing themselves to be converted, and will, instead, carelessly proceed to convict the accused. Rejecting this view, Justice White set out to develop what might be called the doctrine of the conscientious juror. It is far more likely, he wrote, that when a juror presents "reasoned argument in favor of acquittal," his fellow-jurors will either answer his arguments satisfactorily or enough of them will come around to his side to prevent conviction. In practice, the Justice continued, the majority members of a jury "will cease discussion and outvote a minority only after reasoned discussion has ceased to have persuasive effect or to serve any other purpose—when a minority, that is, continues to insist upon acquittal without having persuasive reasons. . . ." At that point, he concluded, those in the majority should not be blamed for acting with improper haste; rather, the dissenter, in the words of an earlier Court opinion, "should consider whether his doubt was a reasonable one [when it made] no impression upon the minds of so many men, equally honest, equally intelligent with himself."

Justice Douglas delivered a long and angry dissent that combined the Johnson and Apodaca cases, and he disagreed with the majority on almost every point that was raised. But on none of them did he disagree as vehemently as on the subject of the way jurors actually behave in a jury room. Juries that do not have to reach a unanimous finding for a conviction, he wrote, are far less likely to "debate and deliberate as fully" as juries that do. As for the claim that there is no evidence to suggest that a majority will refuse to listen to a minority when its votes aren't needed for a conviction, he replied, "Yet human experience teaches that polite and academic conversation is no substitute for the earnest and robust argument necessary to reach unanimity." To support his view, Justice Douglas cited "The American Jury," by Harry Kalven, Jr., and Hans Zeisel, the leading work on the subject, which pointed out that in roughly one-tenth of all jury trials "the minority eventually succeeds in reversing an initial majority, and these may be cases of special importance." A likely explanation for this figure, Justice Douglas went on, was that in many courtrooms members of juries are not permitted to take notes, and since "they have imperfect memories, the forensic process of forcing jurors to defend their conflicting recollections and conclusions flushes out many nuances which otherwise would go overlooked." However, he added, in Louisiana and Oregon any "collective effort to piece together the puzzle of historical truth . . . is cut short as soon as the requisite majority is reached," and "indeed, if a necessary majority is immediately obtained, then no deliberation at all is required in these states." That may well have occurred in the Apodaca case, he suggested parenthetically, since the jury there was out for only forty-one minutes. In any event, he concluded on this point, the Court had now removed the "automatic check against hasty fact-finding by relieving jurors of the duty to hear out fully the dissenters" in a disputed case.

Justice Powell, the swing voter, chided Justice Douglas for his doubts about jurors' fidelity to the truth as they see it, and observed that "our historic dedication to jury trial" is based on "the conviction that each juror will faithfully perform his assigned duty." Passing over the fact that this historic dedication was also based, in part, on the assurance that a single juror could prevent unjust conviction by deciding that the only way to faithfully perform his assigned duty was to hold out for acquittal, Justice Powell went on to mention a couple of procedural safeguards that protect defendants against a "willfully irresponsible jury." One was that a defense lawyer has the right to use preremptory challenges and challenges for cause when prospective jurors appear unreliable. And the other was that every judge protects every defendant by reminding every jury, in his instructions to it, that the state carries the burden of proof and that each juror is obliged by oath to weigh the views of fellow-jurors. All this, he concluded, sufficiently "diminished the likelihood of miscarriage of justice."

In Apodaca et al. v. Oregon, Justice White cited the Court's refusal, in Williams v. Florida, to insist that a jury must have twelve members in support of his contention that the Oregon law maintained the essential bulwark between the state and those it accused of crimes; like the number of jurors considering a case, he argued, the old unanimity rule provided nothing of Constitutional stature and could be harmlessly dispensed with. Justice Powell agreed—in the matter of state trials, anyway—that a jury was a bulwark whether the verdict was reached by ten or by twelve out of twelve jurors. Justice Brennan, on the other hand, sharply disagreed, claiming that the premise underlying the majority's argument was unsound. Once there are enough jurors to reach a majority verdict for conviction, he wrote in his dissent, there is nothing, except perhaps common sense, at best, to restrain them from delivering it without paying much attention to the minority's views, however cogent these might be. Like Justice Douglas, Justice Brennan found the majority's opinion based on an excessive faith in human reason. "I think it simply ignores reality to imagine that most jurors in these circumstances would, or even could, fairly weigh the arguments opposing their position," he stated. In a separate dissent, Justice Stewart was even more emphatic on this point, and told the Court that it had "never before been so impervious to reality in this area." He reminded his fellow-justices on the majority side that the Court's long-standing concern about the "serious risks of jury misbehavior" had prompted a series of decisions over the years aimed at preventing juries from carelessly or willfully abusing defendants' rights. These decisions now stood in jeopardy, the Justice declared, and went on to ask a number of questions:

Why, if juries do not sometimes act out of passion and prejudice, does the Constitution [as interpreted by earlier Court decisions] require the availability of a change of venue? Why, if juries do not sometimes act improperly, does the Constitution require protection from inflammatory press coverage and . . . influence by court officers? Why, if juries must be presumed to obey all instructions from the bench, does the Constitution require that certain information must not go to the jury no matter how strong a cautionary charge accompanies it? Why, indeed, should we insist that no man can be constitutionally convicted by a jury from which members of an identifiable group to which he belongs have been systematically excluded? . . . The requirement that the verdict of the jury be unanimous, surely as important as these other constitutional requisites, preserves the jury's function in linking law with contemporary society. It provides the simple and effective method endorsed by centuies of experience and history to combat the injuries to the fair administration of justice that can be inflicted by community passion and prejudice.

The Sixth Amendment's relationship to the unanimity rule was raised in Apodaca when the petitioners contended that their convictions by less-than-unanimous juries violated the right to trial by jury under that amendment as it was applied to the states, through Duncan, by the due-process clause of the Fourteenth Amendment. This time, Justice White accepted the relevance of the Sixth Amendment, since the three cases at issue had been tried after the Duncan decision made the amendment's right to a jury trial binding on the states. But that right, he retorted to the petitioners' claim, was *all* that Duncan provided in state courts. In the Williams case, for instance, the Court stated that the size of juries was not a Constitutional issue and was up to the states; the same principle and the same reasoning the Justice said for the majority, also applied to the question of unanimity. Relegating the common-law history of the question to a long footnote, he concentrated in the body of his opinion on the legislative history of the unanimity rule in the United States. That history, he reported, was "scanty," the "most salient fact" being Representative James Madison's attempt to persuade the House to accept his version of the Sixth Amendment—including "the requisite of unanimity for conviction"—when the Bill of Rights was under debate in the First Congress. The House accepted his version, but the Senate rejected it, and a conference committee produced a compromise amendment that didn't mention unanimity or, for that matter, any of the other specific safeguards that Madison had recommended. History has left no evidence to explain why the change was made, but Justice White observed that in the Williams case the Court had considered it plausible to conclude, and had concluded, "that the deletion was intended to have some substantive effect." Since the Court was now unable "to divine 'the intent of the Framers,' " he continued, the soundest recourse was to examine "the function served by the jury in contemporary society." That function had been defined in Williams v. Florida as "the interposition between the accused and his accuser of the common-sense judgment of a group of laymen," and, in the opinion of the Court's present majority, that barrier remained unaffected by unanimity or the lack of it. Nor, Justice White insisted once more, did the reasonable-doubt principle demand a unanimous verdict, as the petitioners claimed. In proof, he cited the precedent of Johnson v. Louisiana, which was then several minutes old.

Justice Powell disputed the claim made by Justice Burger, White, Blackmun, and Rehnquist that unanimity was not essential to any kind of criminal jury trial. "In an unbroken line of cases reaching back into the late 1800s, the justices of this Court have recognized, virtually without dissent, that unanimity is one of the indispensable features of *federal* jury trial," he wrote. Reference to the First Congress's revision of Madison's proposal struck him as an ambiguous kind of justification that was assuredly "not sufficient . . . to override the unambiguous history of the common-law right." Still, he agreed that the states were not bound by the unanimity rule, since, in his view, it was not the Sixth Amendment that imposed jury trials on the states, as the other members of the Court seemed to believe, but rather the Fourteenth Amendment. And that amendment, he claimed, did not impose *all* the features of federal trials on state courts—a position that put him firmly in agreement with four members of the Court and firmly in disagreement with the four other members. One of the latter, Justice Douglas, insisted that the Sixth Amendment was wholly applicable to the states by way of the Fourteenth Amendment. And Justice Stewart agreed, on the ground that this was precisely what the Duncan decision had "squarely held." Unless the Court meant to overrule Duncan, he added, the only question left was whether the Sixth Amendment right to a jury trial carries with it the requirement of a unanimous verdict. "The answer to that question," Justice Stewart concluded, "is clearly 'yes,' as my brother Powell has cogently demonstrated in that part of his concurring opinion that reviews almost a century of Sixth Amendment adjudication."

Justice Douglas found the Court's decision "so radical a departure" from two centuries of American history and six centuries of common-law tradition that he could scarcely believe it had been made. The Court majority, he charged, had embarked on a "vast restructuring of American law," which could legally be done only by Constitutional amendment, not by the Court sitting as "a Committe of Revision." In sum, he characterized the decision as being not in the tradition of this nation's accusatorial system but "more in tradition of the Inquisition." Justice Douglas went on to point out that this decision created an obvious, and obnoxious, disparity. The Court had long and explicitly held, he explained, that the Seventh Amendment, which governs civil trials, unquestionably requires unanimous juries in civil cases tried in state courts. "After today's decision," he wrote, "a man's property may only be taken away by a unanimous jury vote, yet he can be stripped of his liberty by a lesser standard." Although the deci-

sion would apply theoretically to everyone, he added, it would "in cold reality touch mostly the lower castes in our society . . . the blacks, the Chicanos, the one-mule farmers, the agricultural workers, the off-beat students, the victims of the ghetto."

The petitioners claimed in Apodaca that since 1880 the Fourteenth Amendment had been taken to mean, in part, that jury panels must reflect a cross-section of the community. If the Court now allowed less-than-unanimous juries, they argued, it would thereby allow the exclusion of minority viewpoints as effectively as if members of minority groups were not permitted to serve on juries at all. In response, Justice White brought up the conscientious-juror theory, and said, "We simply find no proof for the notion that a majority [of jurors] will disregard its instructions and cast its votes for guilt or innocence based on prejudice rather than the evidence." Once again, Justice Stewart disagreed, and pointed out, in the Johnson case, that if one could rely on jurors to be so open-minded, the Court wouldn't have been obliged to rule again and again against "systematic discrimination in the selection of criminal-court juries." He added, "Under today's judgment, nine jurors can simply ignore the views of their fellow panel members of a different race or class." Justice Powell, for his part, vigorously supported the majority view on this issue, and stated that dissenters who held out in the face of a majority opinion were displaying their own "irrationality," against which some protection was essential.

Justice Marshall confronted this view—that dissent is unreasonable—head on. After observing that "if the jury has been selected properly and every juror is a competent and rational person, then the 'irrationality' that enters into the deliberation process is precisely the essence of the right to a jury trial," he went on to say that the fundamental feature of any jury is that it represents the community, and he argued that to "fence out a dissenting juror fences out a voice from the community, and undermines the principle on which our whole notion of the jury now rests." As a member of a racial minority, Marshall may have been especially sensitive to the problem of exclusion, but he warned that far more was at stake than the rights of minorities. "The juror whose dissenting voice is unheard may be a spokesman, not for any minority viewpoint, but simply for himself—and that, in my view, is enough," he explained. "The doubts of a single juror are . . . evidence that the government has failed to carry its burden of proving guilt beyond a reasonable doubt."

Louisiana law allows five-man juries with unanimous verdicts to convict defendants who *may* be sentenced to hard labor, twelve-man juries with a majority of at least nine to convict defendants who *must* be sentenced to hard labor, and twelve-man juries with unanimous verdicts to convict defendants who *may* be sentenced to death. According to Johnson, the appellant, this scale deprived him of the equal protection of the law guaranteed by the Fourteenth Amendment, which, all hands for once agreed, *is* binding on the states. Justice White conceded that Johnson might well have been acquitted if he had killed the person he was charged with having robbed, since three jurors doubted that he had robbed the victim in the first place, but concluded for the majority that the state law didn't violate the equal-protection clause, because there was no "invidious . . . classification" and the law served "a rational purpose." As described by the Louisiana constitution, he went on, that purpose was to "facilitate, expedite, and reduce expense in the administration of justice." Accordingly, the different kinds of juries were fully Constitutional.

In the days of the Warren Court, Justice White often spoke for the minority there against decisions asserting "new" rights for individuals in criminal prosecutions; the state had rights, too, he repeatedly emphasized—chiefly the pressing need not to be further hampered, in time and expense, by the imposition of more and more procedural safeguards upon a system that was almost at a standstill as it was. That minority viewpoint—in effect, a kind of cost-efficiency approach to justice—was now the majority viewpoint, and Justice Douglas, a holdover from the liberal majority of the Warren days, held that the Court was dangerously increasing the power of the state over its citizens by the new decision. Pointing out that the Court had allowed fewer than twelve jurors in state trials because its studies had shown "no discernible difference between the results reached by the two different-sized juries," he went on to say that experience and other studies had shown that "the less-than-unanimous jury overwhelmingly favors the states." In effect, he explained, non-unanimous juries convict defendants about twice as often as unanimous juries do. "While the statutes on their face deceptively appear to be neutral, the use of the non-unanimous jury stacks the truth-determining process against the accused," Douglas wrote. "Thus, we take one step more away from the accusatorial system that has been our proud boast." Once other state legislatures learn that they can nearly double conviction rates by means of such laws, they will undoubtedly move to enact their own, and Douglas warned that the Supreme Court's historic example of preferring to "err on the side of letting the guilty go free rather than sending the innocent to jail" had been virtually destroyed by the new decision. Then, in conclusion, he charged that a "law-and-order judicial mood" had persuaded the Court's majority to lower the barricades against tyranny, and asked, "Is the next step the elimination of the presumption of innocence?"

★★

10

New York Times Co. v. *United States*   403 U.S. 713 (1971)

This case involves the New York Times *newspaper and, in a companion suit, the* Washington Post, *and their desire to publish stolen classified documents of the Vietnam War. The multivolume documents entitled "History of U.S. Decision-Making Process on Viet Nam Policy" were popularly known as the "Pentagon Papers." They were delivered to the newspaper by Daniel Ellsberg, one of the authors and researchers. The First Amendment, as the newspaper editors read it, implied that government could not prevent publication under any circumstances. The federal government brought suit, however, against the newspapers, charging that it was not in the national interest to publish these documents. The newspaper editors decided to publish excerpts anyway, since in their judgment nothing in the documents would harm national security.*

What risks does a newspaper run when it makes a decision to declassify information? Is the best way to declassify information to publish it in a newspaper? Should the press be allowed, under the First Amendment, to print virtually whatever it wishes, or does government have a case for restraining national security information? Is a newspaper's judgment superior to government's on matters of national security? How accountable should the press be when it does print such information? Is it, as it claims, merely a neutral instrument that must print whatever comes to it, or should it assume responsibility for what it decides to print?

It was questions like these that caused a nine-member court to hand down ten opinions—nine of them written by individual justices and one collective decision. As the reader may note, a number of the justices were concerned about how quickly they were asked to respond to this controversy. Several felt that they did not have the time they needed for full deliberation. Yet what would happen to the Supreme Court as an institution if it were unable to respond so quickly?

From the excerpts quoted here, what do you observe is the Court's feeling about the First Amendment? Is the First Amendment in a "preferred position" over other clauses of the Constitution, or is it no more important to the Court than the rest of the document?

★ ★ ★

New York Times Co. v. United States

403 U.S. 713 (1971)

Per Curiam.

... The Government "thus carries a heavy burden of showing justification for the imposition of such a restraint." ...The District Court for the Southern District of New York in the New York Times case and the District Court for the District of Columbia and the Court of Appeals for the District of Columbia Circuit in the Washington Post case held that the Government had not met that burden. We agree.

Mr. Justice **Black,** with whom Mr. Justice **Douglas** joins, concurring.

... In my view it is unfortunate that some of my Brethren are apparently willing to hold that the publication of news may sometimes be enjoined. Such a holding would make a shambles of the First Amendment. ...

In seeking injunctions against these newspapers and in its presentation to the Court, the Executive Branch seems to have forgotten the essential purpose and history of the First Amendment. When the Constitution was adopted, many people strongly opposed it because the document contained no Bill of Rights to safeguard certain basic freedoms. They especially feared that the new powers granted to a central government might be interpreted to permit the government to curtail freedom of religion, press, assembly, and speech. In response to an overwhelming public clamor, James Madison offered a series of amendments to satisfy citizens that these great liberties would remain safe and beyond the power of government to abridge. ... The amendments were offered to *curtail* and *restrict* the general powers granted to the Executive, Legislative, and Judicial Branches two years before in the original Constitution. The Bill of Rights changed the original Constitution into a new charter under which no branch of government could abridge the people's freedoms of press, speech, religion, and assembly. ... Both the history and language of the First Amendment support the view that the press must be left free to publish news, whatever the source, without censorship, injunctions, or prior restraints.

... The press was to serve the governed, not the governors. The Government's power to censor the press was abolished so that the press would remain forever free to censure the Government. The press was protected so that it could bare the secrets of government and inform the people. Only a free and unrestrained press can effectively expose deception in government. And paramount among the responsibilities of a free press is the duty to prevent any part of the Government from deceiving the people and sending them off to distant lands to die of foreign fevers and foreign shot and shell. In my view, far from deserving condemnation for their courageous reporting, the New York Times, the Washington Post, and other newspapers should be commended for serving the purpose that the Founding Fathers saw so clearly.

... To find that the President has "inherent power" to halt the publication of news by resort to the courts would wipe out the First Amendment and destroy the fundamental liberty and security of the very people the Government hopes to make "secure." No one can read the history of the adoption of the First Amendment without being convinced beyond any doubt that it was injunctions like those sought here that Madison and his collaborators intended to outlaw in this Nation for all time.

The word "security" is a broad, vague generality whose contours should not be invoked to abrogate the fundamental law embodied in the First Amendment. The guarding of military and diplomatic secrets at the expense of informed representative government provides no real security for our Republic.

Mr. Justice **Douglas,** with whom Mr. Justice **Black** joins, concurring.

It should be noted at the outset that the First Amendment provides that "Congress shall make no law ... [ellipsis in the original] abridging the freedom of speech, or of the press." That leaves, in my view, no room for governmental restraint on the press.

There is, moreover, no statute barring the publication by the press of the material which the Times and the Post seek to use. . . .

The dominant purpose of the First Amendment was to prohibit the widespread practice of governmental suppression of embarrassing information. . . . The present cases will, I think, go down in history as the most dramatic illustration of that principle. . . .

Secrecy in government is fundamentally anti-democratic, perpetuating bureaucratic errors. Open debate and discussion of public issues are vital to our national health. On public questions there should be "uninhibited, robust, and wide-open debate."

Mr. Justice Brennan, concurring.

. . . So far as I can determine, never before has the United States sought to enjoin a newspaper from publishing information in its possession.

. . . But the First Amendment tolerates absolutely no prior judicial restraints of the press predicated upon surmise or conjecture that untoward consequences may result.

Mr. Justice Stewart, with whom Mr. Justice White joins, concurring.

In the absence of the governmental checks and balances present in other areas of our national life, the only effective restraint upon executive policy and power in the areas of national defense and international affairs may lie in an enlightened citizenry—in an informed and critical public opinion which alone can here protect the values of democratic government. For this reason, it is perhaps here that a press that is alert, aware, and free most vitally serves the basic purpose of the First Amendment. For without an informed and free press there cannot be an enlightened people.

. . . For when everything is classified, then nothing is classified, and the system becomes one to be disregarded by the cynical or the careless, and to be manipulated by those intent on self-protection or self-promotion. I should suppose, in short, that the hallmark of a truly effective internal security system would be the maximum possible disclosure, recognizing that secrecy can best be preserved only when credibility is truly maintained.

Mr. Justice White, with whom Mr. Justice Stewart joins, concurring.

At least in the absence of legislation by Congress, based on its own investigations and findings, I am quite unable to agree that the inherent powers of the Executive and the courts reach so far as to authorize remedies having such sweeping potential for inhibiting publications by the press. . . .

It is thus clear that Congress has addressed itself to the problems of protecting the security of the country and the national defense from unauthorized disclosure of potentially damaging information. . . . It has apparently been satisfied to rely on criminal sanctions and their deterrent effect on the responsible as well as the irresponsible press.

Mr. Justice Marshall, concurring.

It would, however, be utterly inconsistent with the concept of separation of powers for this Court to use its power of contempt to prevent behavior that Congress has specifically declined to prohibit. . . .

Even if it is determined that the Government could not in good faith bring criminal prosecutions against the New York Times and the Washington Post, it is clear that Congress has specifically rejected passing legislation that would have clearly given the President the power he seeks here and made the current activity of the newspapers unlawful. When Congress specifically declines to make conduct unlawful, it is not for this Court to redecide those issues—to overrule Congress.

Mr. Chief Justice Burger, dissenting.

. . . There is, therefore, little variation among the members of the Court in terms of resistance to prior restraints against publication. Adherence to this basic constitutional principle, however, does not make this case a simple one. In these cases, the imperative of a free and unfettered press comes into collision with another imperative, the effective functioning of a complex modern government and specifically the effective exercise of certain constitutional powers of the Executive. Only those who view the First Amendment as an absolute in all circumstances—a view I respect, but reject—can find such a case as this to be simple or easy.

These cases are not simple for another and more immediate reason. We do not know the facts of the cases. No District Judge knew all the facts. No Court of Appeals judge knew all the facts. No member of this Court knows all the facts. . . .

I suggest we are in this posture because these cases have been conducted in unseemly haste. . . .

Would it have been reasonable, since the newspaper could anticipate the government's objections to release of secret material, to give the Government an opportunity to review the entire collection and determine whether agreement could be reached on publication? . . . With such an approach—one that great newspapers have in the past practiced and stated editorially to be the duty of an honorable press—the newspapers and Government might well have narrowed the area of disagreement as to what was and was not publishable, leaving the remainder to be resolved in orderly litigation if necessary.

Mr. Justice Harlan, with whom the Chief Justice and Mr. Justice Blackmun join, dissenting.

These cases forcefully call to mind the wise admonition of Mr. Justice Holmes, dissenting in Northern Securities Co. v. United States (1904):

Great cases like hard cases make bad law. For great cases are called great, not by reason of their real importance in shaping the law of the future, but because of some accident of immediate overwhelming interest which appeals to the feelings and distorts the judgment. These immediate interests exercise a kind of hydraulic pressure which makes what previously was clear seem doubtful, and before which even well settled principles of law will bend.

With all respect, I consider that the Court has been almost irresponsibly feverish in dealing with these cases.

. . . But I think there is another and more fundamental reason why this judgment cannot stand—a reason which also furnishes an additional ground for not reinstating the judgment of the District Court in the Times litigation, set aside by the Court of Appeals. It is plain to me that the scope of the judicial function in passing upon the activities of the Executive Branch of the Government in the field of foreign affairs is very narrowly restricted. . . .

In a speech on the floor of the House of Representatives, Chief Justice John Marshall, then a member of that body, stated:

The President is the sole organ of the nation in its external relations, and its sole representative with foreign nations.

. . . [T]he very nature of executive decisions as to foreign policy is political, not judicial. Such decisions are wholly confided by our Constitution to the political departments of the government, Executive and Legislative. They are delicate, complex, and involve large elements of prophecy. They are and should be undertaken only by those directly responsible to the people whose welfare they advance or imperil. They are decisions of a kind for which the Judiciary has neither aptitude, facilities nor responsibility and which has long been held to belong in the domain of political power not subject to judicial intrusion or inquiry.

Mr. Justice **Blackmun**, dissenting.

Two federal district courts, two United States courts of appeals, and this Court—within a period of less than three weeks from inception until today—have been pressed into hurried decisions of profound constitutional issues on inadequately developed and largely assumed facts without the careful deliberation that, hopefully, should characterize the American judicial process. There has been much writing about the law and little knowledge and less digestion of the facts. . . .

The First Amendment, after all, is only one part of an entire Constitution. Article II of the great document vests in the Executive Branch primary power over the conduct of foreign affairs and places in that branch the responsibility for the Nation's safety. Each provision of the Constitution is important, and I cannot subscribe to a doctrine of unlimited absolutism for the First Amendment at the cost of downgrading other provisions. First Amendment absolutism has never commanded a majority of this Court.

★★

11

Gregg v. *Georgia*   428 U.S. 153 (1976)

This case involved Troy Gregg, who had been convicted of committing armed robbery and murdering two men who were occupants of a car in which he was riding. The jury found Gregg guilty of two counts of armed robbery and two counts of murder and returned the sentence of death. Gregg challenged the death penalty as "cruel and unusual punishment" under the Eighth and Fourteenth Amendments.

This case, like the New York Times *case, encouraged multiple opinions, as do most controversial issues. "Is the death penalty constitutional?" This was the question posed before the Court; and although it had been raised in an earlier case in 1972, it was never resolved. The Court had declared death penalties imposed in an arbitrary fashion to be unconstitutional but had not gone beyond this. Rather than do away with the death penalty altogether in 1972, most states assigned mandatory death penalties for specific crimes. Some thirty-five states, in order to avoid the charge of "arbitrariness," preserved the death penalty by passing mandatory death statutes. This was made clear by Justice White in his dissent in* Roberts *v.* Louisiana— *the companion case to* Gregg—*an excerpt of which is included in the text of the* Gregg *decision. Did the fact that so many states legislated statutes of mandatory death have any influence on the way the Court responded in* Gregg? *How might the Court have responded in* Gregg *had a majority of the states clearly opposed the death penalty?*

The Court, as it often does, resorted to searching the historical records to discover what the intention of the Framers was regarding "cruel and unusual punishment." Did the Framers ever intend the "death penalty" to be considered "cruel"? Are there difficulties in basing interpretations of the Constitution on the Founders' thoughts? Could the Founders anticipate all of the particular contemporary difficulties that need answers? How helpful is it to know the original meaning of the constitutional clauses?

★ ★ ★

Gregg v. Georgia

428 U.S. 153 (1976)

Judgment of the Court, and opinion of Mr. Justice **Stewart,** Mr. Justice **Powell,** and Mr. Justice **Stevens,** announced by Mr. Justice **Stewart.**

The issue in this case is whether the imposition of the sentence of death for the crime of murder under the law of Georgia violates the Eighth and Fourteenth Amendments. . . .

It is clear . . . that the Eight Amendment has not been regarded as a static concept. As Mr. Chief Justice Warren said, in an oft-quoted phrase, "[t]he Amendment must draw its meaning from evolving standards of decency that mark the progress of a maturing society." . . . Thus, an assessment of contemporary values concerning the infliction of a challenged sanction is relevant to the application of the Eighth Amendment. . . .

But our cases also make clear that public perceptions of standards of decency with respect to criminal sanctions are not conclusive. A penalty also must accord with "the dignity of man," which is the "basic concept underlying the Eighth Amendment." . . . This means, at least, that the punishment not be "excessive." . . . First the punishment must not involve the unnecessary and wanton infliction of pain. . . . Second, the punishment must not be grossly out of proportion to the severity of the crime. . . .

Therefore, in assessing a punishment selected by a democratically elected legislature against the constitutional measure, we presume its validity. We may not require the legislature to select the least severe penalty possible so long as the penalty selected is not cruelly inhumane or disproportionate to the crime involved. And a heavy burden rests on those who would attack the judgment of the representatives of the people.

This is true in part because the constitutional test is intertwined with an assessment of contemporary standards and the legislative judgment weighs heavily in ascertaining such standards. "[I]n a democratic society legislatures, not courts, are constituted to respond to the will and consequently the moral values of the people."

. . . We now consider specifically whether the sentence of death for the crime of murder is a per se violation of the Eighth and Fourteenth Amendments to the Constitution. We note first that history and precedent strongly support a negative answer to this question.

The imposition of the death penalty for the crime of murder has a long history of acceptance both in the United States and in England. . . .

It is apparent from the text of the Constitution itself that the existence of capital punishment was accepted by the Framers. At the time the Eighth Amendment was ratified, capital punishment was a common sanction in every State. . . .

For nearly two centuries, this Court, repeatedly and often expressly, has recognized that capital punishment is not invalid per se.

. . . Despite the continuing debate, dating back to the 19th century, over the morality and utility of capital punishment, it is now evident that a large proportion of American society continues to regard it as an appropriate and necessary criminal sanction.

The most marked indication of society's endorsement of the death penalty for murder is the legislative response to Furman.* The legislatures of at least 35 States have enacted new statutes that provide for the death penalty for at least some crimes that result in the death of another person. And the Congress of the United States, in 1974, enacted a statute providing the death penalty for aircraft piracy that results in death. . . .

The death penalty is said to serve two principal social purposes: retribution and deterrence of capital crimes by prospective offenders.

In part, capital punishment is an expression of society's moral outrage at particularly offensive conduct. This function may be unappealing to many, but it is essential in an ordered society that asks its citizens to rely on legal processes rather than self-help to vindicate their wrongs.

> The instinct for retribution is part of the nature of man, and channeling that instinct in the administration of criminal justice serves an important purpose in promoting the stability of a society governed by law. When

*Furman v. Georgia, 408 U.S. 238 (1972).

people begin to believe that organized society is unwilling or unable to impose upon criminal offenders the punishment they "deserve," then there are sown the seeds of anarchy—of self-help, vigilante justice, and lynch law.

. . . Indeed, the decision that capital punishment may be the appropriate sanction in extreme cases is an expression of the community's belief that certain crimes are themselves so grievous an affront to humanity that the only adequate response may be the penalty of death. . . .

The value of capital punishment as a deterrent of crime is a complex factual issue the resolution of which properly rests with the legislatures, which can evaluate the results of statistical studies in terms of their own local conditions and with a flexibility of approach that is not available to the court. . . .

In sum, we cannot say that the judgment of the Georgia legislature that capital punishment may be necessary in some cases is clearly wrong. Considerations of federalism, as well as respect for the ability of a legislature to evaluate, in terms of its particular state the moral consensus concerning the death penalty and its social utility as a sanction, require us to conclude, in the absence of more convincing evidence, that the infliction of death as a punishment for murder is not without justification and thus is not unconstitutionally severe.

. . . We are concerned here only with the imposition of capital punishment for the crime of murder, and when a life has been taken deliberately by the offender, we cannot say that the punishment is invariably disproportionate to the crime. It is an extreme sanction, suitable to the most extreme of crimes. . . .

For the reasons expressed in this opinion, we hold that the statutory system under which Gregg was sentenced to death does not violate the Constitution. Accordingly, the judgment of the Georgia Supreme Court is affirmed.

Mr. Justice **White,** with whom The **Chief Justice** and Mr. Justice **Rehnquist** join, concurring in the judgment.

Petitioner's argument that there is an unconstitutional amount of discretion in the system which separates those suspects who receive the death penalty from those who receive life imprisonment, a lesser penalty, or are acquitted or never charged, seems to be in final analysis an indictment of our entire system of justice. Petitioner has argued, in effect, that no matter how effective the death penalty may be as a punishment, government, created and run as it must be by humans, is inevitably incompetent to administer it. This cannot be accepted as a proposition of constitutional law. Imposition of the death penalty is surely an awesome responsibility for any system of justice and those who participate in it. Mistakes will be made and discriminations will occur which will be difficult to explain. However, one of society's most basic tasks is that of protecting the lives of its citizens and one of the most basic ways in which it achieves the task is through criminal laws against murder. I decline to interfere with the manner in which Georgia has chosen to enforce such laws on what is simply an

assertion of lack of faith in the ability of the system of justice to operate in a fundamentally fair manner.

The following opinion is excerpted from Justice White's dissent in the companion case of Roberts v. Louisiana, *wherein he gives his reasons for believing the death penalty is not cruel and unusual punishment.*

Mr. Justice **White,** with whom The **Chief Justice,** Mr. Justice **Blackmun,** and Mr. Justice **Rehnquist** join, dissenting in Roberts v. Louisiana.

I cannot say that capital punishment has been rejected by or is offensive to the prevailing attitudes and moral presuppositions in the United States or that it is always an excessively cruel or severe punishment or always a disproportionate punishment for any crime for which it might be imposed. These grounds for invalidating the death penalty are foreclosed by recent events, which this Court must accept as demonstrating that capital punishment is acceptable to the contemporary community as just punishment for at least some intentional killings.

It is apparent also that Congress and 35 state legislatures are of the view that capital punishment better serves the ends of criminal justice than would life imprisonment and that it is therefore not excessive in the sense that it serves no legitimate legislative or social ends.

. . . It also seems clear enough that death finally forecloses the possibility that a prisoner will commit further crimes, whereas life imprisonment does not. This leaves the question of general deterrence as the principal battleground: does the death penalty more effectively deter others from crime than does the threat of life imprisonment?

The debate on this subject started generations ago and is still in progress. Each side has a plethora of fact and opinion in support of its position, some of it quite old and some of it very new; but neither has yet silenced the other. I need not detail these conflicting materials, most of which are familiar sources. It is quite apparent that the relative efficacy of capital punishment and life imprisonment to deter others from crime remains a matter about which reasonable men and reasonable legislators may easily differ. . . .

It will not do to denigrate these legislative judgments as some form of vestigial savagery or as purely retributive in motivation; for they are solemn judgments, reasonably based, that imposition of the death penalty will save the lives of innocent persons. This concern for life and human values and the sincere efforts of the States to pursue them are matters of the greatest moment with which the judiciary should be most reluctant to interfere.

Mr. Justice **Brennan,** dissenting.

The fatal constitutional infirmity in the punishment of death is that it treats "members of the human race as nonhumans, as objects to be toyed with and discarded. [It is] thus inconsistent with the fundamental premise of the Clause that even the vilest criminal remains a human being possessed of common human dignity." As such it is a penalty that "subjects the individual to a fate forbidden by the principle of civilized treatment guaranteed by the [Clause]." I therefore would hold, on that ground alone, that death is today a cruel and unusual punishment prohibited by the Clause. "Justice of this kind is obviously no less shocking than the crime itself, and the new 'official' murder, far from offering redress for the offense committed against society, adds instead a second defilement to the first."

Mr. Justice **Marshall**, dissenting.

In Furman I concluded that the death penalty is constitutionally invalid for two reasons. First, the death penalty is excessive. . . . And second, the American people, fully informed as to the purpose of the death penalty and its liabilities, would in my view reject it as morally unacceptable.

. . . But if the constitutionality of the death penalty turns, as I have urged, on the opinion of an *informed* citizenry, then even the enactment of new death statutes cannot be viewed as conclusive. In Furman, I observed that the American people are largely unaware of the information critical to a judgment on the morality of the death penalty, and concluded that if they were better informed they would consider it shocking, unjust, and unacceptable. . . . A recent study, conducted after the enactment of the post-Furman statutes, has confirmed that the American people know little about the death penalty, and that the opinions of an informed public would differ significantly from those of a public unaware of the consequences and effects of the death penalty.

CHAPTER THREE

★ ★ ★

Political Socialization and Public Opinion

It is said that our government derives its power from the consent of the people. It would be very difficult for any regime to persist for long if the mass of citizens should turn hostile and demand radical change. Political revolutions throughout the world attest to this fact. But, everyday politics are also dependent upon the support of the people. Citizen attitudes ultimately affect every dimension of public life, be it the political parties, the direction of public policy, or the integrity of the Bill of Rights. By its very nature, a society persists because its members share fundamental interests, values, and beliefs. And to assure its continued stability, new members of the society are taught the "rules of the game." The term "political socialization" refers to this process by which the individual learns the political norms of society. The learning is obvious when a teacher requires students to pledge allegiance to the flag, but it goes on in numerous subtle ways every day. To the extent that it is effective, political socialization generates citizen support for our politics and government.

In "The Politics of Middle Class Children," Robert Coles explores the process of political socialization. At very early ages children develop attitudes about our political system, and it would seem that experiences immediate to their everyday lives affect those opinions deeply. Being middle-class white in a suburb, being black in the South, being Chicano in a large city, or being a poor white in Appalachia makes a real difference in a child's political outlook. And it is disconcerting to learn that not all children feel positive about our country. Class and race can affect political socialization—and adversely. Of course children do grow up. Research indicates that among adults there is some reservoir of good feeling toward the political system, even though attitudes on specific issues may vary tremendously.

Severe disillusionment about the political system can lead to alienation, as discussed by James D. Wright in "Discontented, Mistrustful, Fragmented: The Real Danger in Alienation." In recent years alienation has increased, according to the opinion polls. Childhood experiences may be partly the cause, but contemporary political events can also have a negative impact on the citizenry. The future of American democracy may be affected by this long-term trend, though Wright does not see the scenario painted by some political observers.

They see public disaffection leading to mass movements, to demagoguery, and to authoritarianism. But Wright doubts that this development will take place in America. Rather he argues that the typical result of alienation in America is nonparticipation in politics. We have been seeing a general decline in voting turnout, possible evidence for this alternative scenario. For this reason Wright fears that the "real" danger in alienation is the increased control over politics that is given to elites. Given this eventuality, the prospects grow that tragedies like Watergate and Vietnam will be repeated.

Public opinion can shape the direction of our government, if it is given the chance. Ultimately anything can be affected by the attitudes of citizens, but in the short term attitudes must be acted upon to have real meaning. Most political scientists agree that our attitudes are more important to domestic policy-making than to foreign affairs. Domestic problems simply affect our lives in a very immediate way. While true that events in the world also shape our destinies, it appears that citizens become most aware of foreign policy when it impinges upon their domestic situation.

In two articles of this chapter, the relationship of public opinion to domestic issues and to foreign policy is evaluated. In "Politics of Dead Center: The Artificial Majority," Theodore J. Lowi argues that candidates for office reflect the prevailing public mood. For example, both political parties addressed the issue of "law and order" during the 1970 campaign. Lowi says that the meaning of public opinion is distorted by the way polls are taken and by the way voter attitudes are perceived by the candidates. The politicians do not believe that voters are strongly divided on issues. For this reason, candidates offer moderation rather than serious alternatives to policy issues, to appeal to the vast majority of voters clustered in the middle. Obviously, to have impact public opinion must be defined accurately and articulated. To the extent that Lowi is correct in his diagnosis, the real impact of public opinion on domestic issues is muted by the political campaign.

The role of public opinion in foreign affairs is discussed by Jean-Francois Revel in "Reflections on Foreign Policy and Public Opinion." In his view our opinions on foreign affairs are not based on facts. Our attitudes very often have no relationship to the actual state of the world. For this reason, some scholars and diplomats fear the impact of citizens on foreign policy; they prefer diplomacy conducted by experts in secrecy. But diplomats cannot completely ignore the people. Revel doubts that public opinion exerts much influence on foreign policy in the short term, but feels it does exist over the long run. From his perspective, therefore, he also sees distortion in the communication of public opinion to government leaders.

The subjects of political socialization and public opinion are very complicated, and the writing on them is extensive. In the four articles chosen for this chapter, our goal was to present some major themes for your consideration. We have summarized the general arguments in the headnotes and the major points to be remembered.

★★

12

The Politics of Middle Class Children   Robert Coles

Political socialization is the process by which children—as well as adults— learn about politics and government. Their learning is affected by many influences. What are these sources from which children gain their political opinions? Early research on this question focused on white middle-class children, and it was determined that these children held idealized images of America. They respected the president and other authority figures; they felt that government was good and cared about the problems of the people. But as this essay by Robert Coles points out, children from "minority" groups were more disillusioned about our society. Coles' analysis shows that white children from poor backgrounds, black children, and Chicano children can be very aware of racial and class differences and of discrimination in society. What long-lasting effects might these perceptions have on the social and political integration of such minority groups in society?

It is the feeling of many political scientists that political socialization assures the loyalty of citizens to their government. What political implications may arise from the fact that minority children have less positive feelings about our society and government? How would you expect their adult "images" of the political system to be affected by these early impressions? What effects might childhood impressions have on adults' support for the political system, political participation, and feeling of patriotism?

★ ★ ★

The Politics of Middle Class Children

Robert Coles

A black child of eight, a girl who lives in southern Alabama, just above Mobile, told me in 1968 that she knew one thing for sure about who was going to be president: he'd be a white man; and as for his policies, "no matter what he said to be polite, he'd never really stand up for us." Already she knew herself to be a member of "us," as against "them."

A few miles away, a white child of nine, a boy, the son of a lawyer and plantation owner, had a rather different perspective on the presidency: "The man who's elected will be a good man; even if he's not too good before he goes to Washington, he'll probably turn out good. This is the best nation there is, so the leader has to be the best, too."

A child with keen ears who picks up exactly his father's mixture of patriotism and not easily acknowledged skepticism? Yes, but also a child who himself—by the tone of his voice and his earnestness—has come to believe in his nation's destiny, and in the office of the presidency. How about the governor? "He's better known than most governors," the boy boasts. Then he offers his source: "My daddy says that we have a better governor than they do in Louisiana or in Georgia. (He has cousins in both states.) And he says that our governor makes everyone stop and listen to him, so he's real good. He knows how to win; he won't let us be beaten by the Yankees."

Is this more sectional bombast, absorbed rather too well by a boy who now, a teenager, hasn't had the slightest inclination to develop the "cynicism" a number of students of the process of "political socialization" have repeatedly mentioned as prevalent? Or is it, more likely, the response of a child who knows what his parents really consider important, really believe in and fear? "I took my boy over to my daddy's house," the child's father recalls, "and we watched Governor Wallace standing up to those people in Washington; he told the President of the United States that he was wrong."

The boy was then four, and no doubt even were he to see a child psychoanalyst for several years he would not at nine, never mind at fifteen, recall the specific event his father and grandfather have very clearly in mind. But time and again he has heard members of his family stress how precarious they feel in relation to Yankee (federal) power, and therefore how loyal to a governor who gives the illusion of a successful defense of cherished social and political prerogatives.

Up North, in a suburb outside Boston, it is quite another story. At nine a girl speaks of America and its leaders like this: "I haven't been to Europe yet, but my parents came back last year and they were happy to be home." Then, after indicating how happy she was to have them home, she comments on the rest of the world, as opposed to her country:

> It's better to be born here. Maybe you can live good in other places, but this is the best country. We have a good government. Everyone is good in it—if he's the president, he's ahead of everyone else, and if he's a governor, that means he's also one of the people who decide what the country is going to do. There might be a war, and somebody has to send the troops by planes across the ocean. If there is a lot of trouble someplace, then the government takes care of it. I'm going to Washington next year to see all the buildings. My brother went two years ago. He really liked the trip. He came back and said he wouldn't mind being in the government; it would be cool to go on that underground railroad the senators have. He said he visited someone's office, and he was given a pencil and a postcard, and he wrote a letter to say thank you, and he got a letter back. His whole class went, and they were taken all over. They went to see some battlefields, too.

She doesn't know which battlefields, however; nor does she know which war was fought on those fields. She is one of those whom southern children of her age have already learned to identify as "Yankees," even know to fear or envy.

There are no equivalents for her, however—no name she is wont to hurl at southerners, or, for that matter, anyone else. True, she learned long ago, at about four or five, that black children, whom she sees on television but has never gone to school with, are "funny," and the single Japanese child she had as a classmate in kindergarten was "strange, because of her eyes"; but such children never come up in her remarks, and when they are brought up in the course of conversation with a visitor, she is quick to change the subject or go firmly silent. Nor is there any great amount of prejudice in her, at least of a kind which she has directly on her mind. Her drawings reveal her to be concerned with flowers, which she likes to help her mother arrange, with horses, which she loves to ride, and with stars, which she is proud to know rather a lot about.

The last interest prompts from her a bit of apologetic explanation: "My brother started being interested in the stars; my daddy gave him a telescope and a book. Then he lost interest. Then I started using the telescope, and my daddy said I shouldn't, because maybe my brother would mind, but he doesn't." And, in fact, her parents do have rather firm ideas about what boys ought to be interested in, what girls ought to find appealing. Men run for political office, she knows. Sometimes women do, but only rarely; anyway, she won't be one of them. In 1971 she thought the President was "a very good man; he has to be—otherwise he wouldn't be president." The same held for the governor and the town officials who make sure that all goes well in her neighborhood.

When the Watergate scandal began to capture more and more of her parents' attention, she listened and wondered and tried to accommodate her long-standing faith with her new knowledge: "The President made a mistake. It's too bad. You shouldn't do wrong; if you're president, it's bad for everyone when you go against the law. But the country is good. The President must feel real bad, for the mistake he made." After which she talked about *her* mistakes: she broke a valuable piece of china; she isn't doing as well in school as either her parents or her teachers feel she ought to be doing; and not least, she forgets to make her bed a lot of the time, and her mother or the maid has to remind her of that responsibility.

Then she briefly returned to President Nixon, this time with a comment not unlike those "intuitive" ones made by Australian children from New South Wales) in Professor Robert Connell's book *The Child's Construction of Politics.* "A friend of mine said she didn't believe a word the President says, because he himself doesn't believe what he says, so why should we." What did the girl herself believe? "Well, I believe my parents, but I believe my friends, too. Do you think the President's wife believes him? If he doesn't believe himself, what about her?" So much for the ambiguities of childhood, not to mention such legal and psychiatric matters as guilt, knowing deception, the nature of self-serving illusions, and political guile.

As one listens to her and others like her—advantaged children, they might be called—one wonders, again, where are to be found the symbols of political power, of pomp and circumstance, that are meant to impress, inspire, and intimidate—the

"gladiators" of Simone Weil's essay I mentioned in my first article. Of course, there is nothing very dramatic to catch hold of; unlike black children, or Appalachian children, or even the children of well-to-do southern white families, the girl I have just quoted has no vivid politically tinged memories of her own, nor any conveyed by her parents to take possession of psychologically—no governor's defiance, no sit-ins or demonstrations, no sheriff's car and a sheriff's voice, no mass funeral after a mine disaster, no experience with a welfare worker, no strike with the police there to "mediate," no sudden lay-off (not yet, at least), followed by accusations and recriminations —and drastically curbed spending.

Such unforgettable events in the lives of children very definitely help to shape their attitudes toward their nation and its political authority. The black children I have come to know in different parts of this country, even those from relatively well-off homes, say critical things about America and its leaders at an earlier age than white children do—and connect their general observations to specific experiences, vivid moments, really, in their lives. A black child of eight, in rural Mississippi or in a northern ghetto, an Indian or Chicano or Appalachian child, can sound like a disillusioned old radical: down with the system, because it's a thoroughly unjust one, for all that one hears in school—including, especially, those words quoted from the Declaration of Independence or the Constitution: that "all men are created equal," that they are "endowed by their Creator with certain unalienable rights."

The pledge of allegiance to the flag can be an occasion for boredom, at the very least, among some elementary school children; the phrase "with liberty and justice for all" simply rings hollow, or is perceived as an ironic boast meant to be uttered by others elsewhere. Here is what a *white* schoolteacher in Barbour County, Alabama, has observed over the years:

I'm no great fan of the colored: I don't have anything against them, either. I do my work, teaching the colored, and I like the children I teach, because they don't put on airs with you, the way some of our own children do—if their daddy is big and important. The uppity niggers— well, they leave this state. We won't put up with them. The good colored people, they're fine. I grew up with them. I know their children, and I try to teach them as best I can. I understand how they feel; I believe I do. I have a very bright boy, James; he told me that he didn't want to draw a picture of the American flag. I asked him why not. He said that he just wasn't interested. It's hard for them—they don't feel completely part of this country.

I had a girl once, she was quite fresh; she told me that she didn't believe a word of that salute to the flag, and she didn't believe a word of what I read to them about our history. I sent her to the principal. I was ready to have her expelled, for good. The principal said she was going to be a civil rights type one day, but by then I'd simmered down. "To tell the truth," I said, "I don't believe most of the colored children think any different than her." The principal gave me a look and said, "Yes, I can see what you mean." A lot of times I skip the salute to the flag; the children start laughing, and they forget the words, and they become restless. It's not a good way to start the day. I'd have to threaten them, if I wanted them to behave while saluting. So, we go right into our arithmetic lessons.

In contrast, among middle-class white children of our northern suburbs, who have no Confederate flag with which to divide their loyalties, the morning salute can be occasion for real emotional expression: This I believe! It is all too easy for some of us to be amused at or, more strongly, to scorn such a development in the lives of children: the roots of smug nationalism, if not outright chauvinism. But for thousands of such children, as for their parents, the flag has a great deal of meaning, and the political authority of the federal, state, and local governments is not to be impugned in any way. Among many working-class families policemen, firemen, clerks in the post office or city hall are likely to be friends, relatives, neighbors. Among upper-middle-class families, one can observe a strong sense of loyalty to a system which clearly, to them, has been friendly indeed. And the children learn to express what their parents feel and often enough say, loud and clear.

"My uncle is a sergeant in the army," the nine-year old son of a Boston factory worker told me. He went on to remind me that another uncle belongs to the Boston police department. The child has watched parades, been taken to an army base, visited an old warship, climbed the steps of a historic shrine. He has seen the flag in school and in church. He has heard his country prayed for, extolled, defended against all sort of critics. He said when he was eight, and in the third grade, that he would one day be a policeman. Other friends of his, without relatives on the force, echo the ambition. Last summer, when he was nearer to ten, he spoke of motorcycles and baseball and hockey; and when he went to the games he sang the national anthem in a strong and sure voice. Our government? It is "the best you can have." Our president? He's "good."

I pushed a little: was President Nixon in any trouble? Yes, he was, and he might have made some mistakes. Beyond that the child would not easily go. His parents had for the first time voted Republican in 1972, and were disappointed with, disgusted by, the President's behavior over Watergate. But they have been reluctant to be too critical of the President in front of their children: I don't want to make the kids feel that there's anything wrong with the *country*," the father says. There's *plenty* wrong with the President, he admits, and with the way the country is being run—and, he adds, with big business, so greedy all the time, as well as with the universities and those who go to them or teach at them; but America, he believes, is the greatest nation that ever has been—something, one has to remember, every president's speechwriters, Democratic or Republican, liberal or conservative, manage to work into just about every televised address.[1]

Only indirectly, through drawings or the use of comic exaggeration or metaphorical flights of fancy, does the boy dare show what he has been making of Watergate, news of which has, of course, come to him primarily through television. Asked to draw a picture of President Nixon, the boy laughs, says he doesn't know how to do so (he had no such trouble a year earlier), and finally manages to sketch an exceedingly small man, literally half the size of a former portrait by the same artist. Then, as he prepares to hand over the completed project, he has some second thoughts. He adds a blue sky. Then he blackens the sky. He puts earth under the man, but not, as his usual custom, grass. Then he proceeds to make two big round black circles, with what seem to be pieces of string attached to them. What are they? He is not sure: "Well, either they could be bombs, and someone could light the fuse, and they could explode and he'd get hurt, and people would be sad, or they could be balls and chains—you know, if you're going to jail."

Way across the tracks, out in part of "rich suburbia," as I hear factory workers sometimes refer to certain towns well to the north and west of Boston, there is among adults a slightly different kind of love of country—less outspoken, perhaps, less defensive, but not casual and certainly appreciative. In those towns, too, children respond quite directly and sensitively to the various messages they have learned from their parents—and to a number of low-key "spectacles": flags out on July Fourth; the deference of civil employees; pictures of father in uniform during one or another war; and perhaps most of all, conversations heard at the table. "My father hears bad news on television, and he says 'thank God we're Americans,'" says a girl of eleven. She goes on to register her mother's gentle, thoughtful qualification: "It's lucky we live where we do."

Her mother's sister, older and attracted to the cultural life only a city offers, has to live a more nervous life: "My aunt has huge locks on her doors. My mother leaves the keys right in

_____

[1] There is nothing like a political crisis, however, to cause even such a child, among others, to have grave doubts about what is happening in the world around him. The recent and continuing racial tension in Boston has prompted apprehension and con-

fusion in this white boy, who lives in South Boston, only three miles from its tragically unsettled high school The boy lashes out at important elected officials, at newspapers and television stations—repeating what he has heard, but also, once in a while, coming up with idiosyncratic and illuminating flashes of social analysis not to mention emphatic generosity:
"The people who call us bad names, like racists, don't have to send their children anywhere except where they want to; their children, a lot of them, go to private schools, even in the suburbs. It's nice and easy to give a sermon from a distance. If I was one of the black kids, I wouldn't give up. I'd keep coming here. I'd keep trying to show I can go anywhere. It's no joke being black. But it's no joke being here, with everyone telling us to behave, and do one thing and do another thing. If you've got money and influence, you can tell everyone off, and no one tells you off."
As for the black children of Roxbury who are being bused, they do indeed feel and put into words what that white child attributes to them. One black youth put it stoically, tersely:
"It's no picnic going to school in South Boston; the schools there are lousy. You take a bus ride and end up in a no good place. But we can't give in: We're fighting to get into America, and you have to get into every part of it, even the no good parts, or else they'll always be trying to keep you out, keep you out."

the car." Nevertheless, the United States of America, for the girl's aunt as well as her parents, is nowhere near collapse: "Everything is going to be all right with the country. This is the best place to live in the whole world. That's what my aunt says." The girl pauses. Now is the time to ask her what *she* has to say. But she needs no prodding; immediately she goes on:

> No place is perfect. We're in trouble now. The President and his friends, they've been caught doing bad things. It's too bad. My older brother argues with daddy; he told daddy that it's wrong to let the President get away with all he's done, while everyone else has to go to jail; and he told daddy there's a lot of trouble in the country, and no one is doing anything to stop the touble. The President, I think he's running as fast as he can from the police. I guess I would if I knew I'd done wrong. But I'd never be able to get to Egypt or Russia, so he's lucky, that President.

It is simply not altogether true, as most studies of "political socialization" conclude, that she and other children like her *only* tend to "idealize" the president, or give a totally "romanticized" kind of loyalty to the country on the basis of what they hear, or choose to hear, from their parents or teachers. Many parents do select carefully what they say in front of their children; and children are indeed encouraged by their teachers, and the books they read, to see presidents and governors and Supreme Court justices and senators as figures much larger than life. Yet in no time—at least these days—children can lay such influences aside, much to the astonishment of even parents who *don't* try to shield their children from "bad news" or "the evils of this world," two ways of putting it one hears again and again.

Black children laugh at books given them to read in school, snicker while the teacher recites historical pieties which exclude mention of so very much, and often enough challenge their own parents when they understandably try to soften or delay the realization of what it has been like and will continue to be like for black people in America. White children, too, as James Agee noticed in the 1930s, pick up the hypocrisies and banalities about them and connect what they see or hear to a larger vision—a notion of those who have a lot and those who have very little at all.

"The President checks in with the people who own the coal company," a miner's shy son aged eleven, remarked last spring in Harlan, Kentucky, where the Duke Power Company was fighting hard to prevent the United Mine Workers from becoming a spokesman of the workers. The child may well be incorrect; but one suspects that a log of the calls made by the President would show him in contact with people very much like those who are on the board of the Duke Power Company, as opposed to people like the boy's parents.

By the same token, when a child whose father happens to be on the board of a utility company or a lawyer who represents such clients, appears to overlook whatever critical remarks his or her parents have made about the United States and instead emphasizes without exception the nation's virtues, including those of its leaders, by no means is a process of psychological distortion necessarily at work. The child may

well have taken the measure of what has been heard (and overheard) and come to a conclusion: this is what they really believe, and just as important, the reason they believe what they say has to do with a whole way of life—the one we are all living. So, it is best to keep certain thoughts (in older people, called "views") to myself, lest there be trouble.

Too complicated and subtle an analysis for a child under ten, or even under fifteen? We who in this century have learned to give children credit for the most astonishing refinements of perception or feeling with respect to the nuances of family life or the ups and downs of neighborhood play for some reason are less inclined to picture those same children as canny social observers or political analysts. No one teaches young children sociology or psychology; yet they are constantly noticing who gets along with whom, and why. If in school, or even when approached by a visitor with a questionnaire (or more casually, but no less noticeably, an all too interested face and manner); those same children tighten up and say little or nothing, or come up with remarks that are platitudes, pure and simple, they may well have come up with one of their sophisticated psychological judgments—reserving for another time the expression of any controversial political asides that may have come to mind.

As for some of those children who are a little different, who get called "rebellious" or "aggressive," and sent off to guidance counselors or psychiatrists, they can occasionally help us know the thoughts of many other, more "normal" children—because someone under stress can under certain circumstances be unusually forthcoming. "My poor father is scared," says the son of a rather well-to-do businessman, the owner of large tracts of Florida land, on which work, every year, hundreds of migrant farm workers, who, believe me, are also scared.

What frightens the boy's father? His twelve-year-old namesake, who is described by his teachers as "a behavior problem"—he is, one gathers, fresh and surly at certain times—tries hard to provide an answer, almost as if whatever he comes up with will help him, too:

> I don't know, but there will be times he's sweating, and he's swearing, and he's saying he gave money to all those politicians, and they'd better do right by the growers, or they'll regret it. Then he says he's tired of living here, and maybe he should go back to Michigan where his grand-daddy was born. The other day the sheriff came by and said he didn't know if he could keep those television people out indefinitely. So, daddy got on the phone to our senator, and we're waiting. But it may cost us a lot, and we may lose. Daddy says we will either get machines to replace the migrants, or we'll go broke, what with the trouble they're beginning to cause. But I don't think he really means it. He's always threatening us with trouble ahead, my mother says, but you have to pour salt on what he says.

That same boy scoffs at what he hears his teachers say about American history; one day he blurted out in class that his father had "coolies" working for him. Another time he said we'd had to kill a lot of Indians, because they had the land, and we wanted it, and they wouldn't "bow to us, the way we wanted. " His teacher felt that she had witnessed yet another psychiatric outburst, but a number of his classmates did not. One of them, not especially a friend of his, remarked several days later, "He only said what everyone knows. I told my mother what he said, and she said it wasn't so bad, and why did they get so upset? But she told me that sometimes it's best to keep quiet, and not say a lot of things you think."

It so happens that the child's mother, speaking in front of her three sons, and without any evidence of shame or embarrassment, willingly picks up where she left off a day earlier with one of her boys:

> Yes, I feel we had to conquer Indians, or there wouldn't be the America we all know and love today, I tell my children that you ought to keep your eye on the positive, accentuate it, you know, and push aside anything negative about this country. Or else we'll sink into more trouble; and it's been good to us, very good, America has.

Her husband is also a grower. Her sons do indeed "idealize" America's political system—but when a classmate begins to stir things up a little with a few blunt comments, there is no great surprise, simply the nod of recognition and agreement. And very important, a boy demonstrates evidence of moral development, a capacity for ethical reflection, even though both at home and at school he has been given scant encouragement to regard either migrants or Indians with compassion. Both Piaget and Lawrence Kohlberg have indicated that cognitive and moral development in children have their own rhythm, tempo, and subtlety. Children ingeniously use every scrap of emotional life available to them as they develop "psychosexually," and they do likewise as they try to figure out how (and for whom) the world works. A friend's remarks, a classmate's comments, a statement heard on television can give a child surprising moral perspective and distance on himself and his heritage—though, of course, he is not necessarily thereby "liberated" from the (often countervailing) day-to-day realities of, say, class and race.[2]

---

[2] Kohlberg's work is especially helpful. Children come across, in his studies, as lively and thoughtful, as inclined to question and make critical moral judgments of various kinds, within limits set by their developing mental life.

Needless to say, as Jeb Stuart Magruder has indicated in his public remarks and his recent book (*An American Life*, Atheneum, 1974), the acquisition of moral values is very much connected to the child's moral education, obtained not only within the family (as psychiatrists often emphasize) but in the schools and, not least, informally in neighborhood play. See Kohlberg's "Moral and Religious Education and the Public Schools: A Developmental View" in Theodore Sizer, ed., *Religion and Public Education* (Houghton Mifflin, 1967).

★★★

13

Discontented, Mistrustful, Fragmented: The Real Danger in Alienation   James D. Wright

Measures of political alienation show that it has increased during the 1960s and 1970s. Alienation undermines a person's confidence in being able to shape his or her destiny; politically it reduces one's attachment to conventional institutions of democratic government. As a result, the alienated citizen may become vulnerable to the appeals of demagogic leaders, and be drawn to "proto-fascistic" movements. What is the relationship between alienation and "the politics of mass society"? To what extent did George Wallace in 1968 draw votes from groups of alienated citizens? Can we expect extremist candidates always to benefit from alienation in society?

Alienation might also lead to total withdrawal from political participation. Its causes relate to psychological conditioning during childhood and to contemporary political events—a reaction, for example, to the war in Vietnam and to the political crisis of Watergate. In this essay James D. Wright discusses the meaning of alienation, its scope within society, and its probable impact on our system. To what extent is alienation related to race, religion, class, and other social factors? Wright feels that alienation will facilitate greater control by elites over our political processes. Why is that the case? What long-lasting effects do you see if this occurs? Are there ways to reverse this trend?

Wright is concerned about increased alienation because it leads to nonparticipation in politics. But there are other scholars who are less concerned about this effect. As a counterargument, they would say that those people who do not participate in politics are generally the "have-nots"—those from the lower socioeconomic strata. Such people, they would argue, are less educated about American government and are less committed to our democratic system. Should they become involved in politics, they would violate the norms of conventional political behavior. Therefore, it is better for the political system when people who are alienated do not participate in politics. Their absence contributes to the overall stability of the regime. Can it be said that alienated persons are generally found in the lower socioeconomic strata? Is there any validity to the argument that political stability is aided when such persons withdraw from political participation?

★ ★ ★

DISCONTENTED, MISTRUSTFUL, FRAGMENTED

THE REAL DANGER IN ALIENATION

JAMES D. WRIGHT

Recent indications of general alienation, discontent and political distrust have occasioned much alarm about the "future of American democracy." As to the indicators themselves, there can be little serious disagreement. However measured, political alienation is clearly on the rise. According to the Survey Research Center (University of Michigan), for example, the proportion of the American population who feel that the government in Washington can "be trusted to do what is right only some of the time" increased from about 23 per cent in 1958 to nearly 45 per cent in 1972. To a similar question, asking whether the government is "run by a few big interests looking out for themselves," the proportion saying "yes" increased from 26 to 53 per cent in the brief period from 1964 to 1972. Seven additional indicators of political disaffection show the same pattern through the period in question. Furthermore, that period ends just before Watergate, and evidence since then from the National Opinion Research Center indicates that the trend has hardly abated. One question included in its 1973 and 1974 general social surveys asked respondents how much confidence they had in the people running the "executive branch of the government." The proportion checking "hardly any" grew from 19 to 43 per cent in the one year, and the proportion expressing a "great deal" of confidence dwindled from 30 to 14 per cent. At present, in other words, roughly nine citizens out of ten have something less than complete confidence in the American political leadership. However one chooses to measure this notion of "trust in government," the fact is that it has been in more or less steady decline since about 1964.

These signs of disillusion are indeed alarming, but what they imply about the American political future is anything but clear and may in fact be quite the reverse of the projection frequently offered. Perhaps the most common line of speculation, one having a counterpart in academic theories about "the politics of mass society," links the concept of political alienation to a series of semi-pathological traits. The alienated, it is said, are also negativistic, intolerant, politically simple-minded, authoritarian, suspicious, prone to scapegoating, dogmatic and inflexible. Apathetic and withdrawn in normal times, they are readily mobilized in times of crisis, once their alienation reaches an intolerable level and a clever demagogue appears on the scene. In this forecast, the politically discontented are a ready constituency for a mass political

James Wright is a sociologist at the University of Massachusetts, Amherst, and the author of The Dissent of the Governed: Alienation and Democracy in America (this spring from Academic Press).

movement that would directly challenge the legitimacy of the prevailing system. This movement would, of course, only reflect the ignoble predispositions of its supporters. Its initial thrust would be to "throw the rascals out," to purge the system of incumbent politicians who are seen as the proximate cause of contemporary distress. Once swept to power by a rampaging mass will, the movement would then attack the basic sources of discontent: the welfare-state apparatus would be dismantled and the welfare class abolished; the colleges and universities would be purified, the races separated, and the "old values" returned to their former place of prominence. The phraseology of these predictions is meant to evoke Fascist or proto-fascistic politics. Thus, Herbert Levine (in The Nation, August 17, 1974) explicitly links declining confidence in politicians with a presumed "culture of fascism." "Fascism," we are told, "is an expression of political anger, rooted in a perception of economic distress, and directed at irrelevant targets." As for the prospects of such a development in the United States, "it is clear that the Fascist potential has increased greatly since 1970." In a similar vein, Lewis Killian (The Impossible Revolution—Phase Two) has flatly predicted a "white national socialist (Nazi) America" by no later than 1980.

But how likely is it that these drifts in opinion will lead to some proto-fascistic development? How secure are liberal political traditions in the United States? My belief is that the course of events outlined above misrepresents the nature of the alienation trends, ignores an immense mass of contradictory evidence and therefore fails to comprehend the true "threat" of the rising discontent.

Note first that the phrase, "the politically alienated," has seriously misleading connotations. It suggests, first of all, something more than a mere statistical aggregate by implying a common political outlook or ideology, some mutual awareness of shared experiences and shared interests—in short, it assumes at least a potential basis for political mobilization. It is not so: all the available evidence strongly suggests that "the alienated" do not comprise an especially cohesive social or political group.

The politically discontented are widely dispersed in the social class structure. There are, to be sure, relatively more disenchanted and disaffected citizens in the lower social strata, but the correlation is considerably less than perfect. Data from the 1970 SRC survey on "trust in government" make the point. Among the professional, technical and managerial persons reached in that survey, approximately 40 per cent were scored as "low" in political trust. Among the skilled and semi-skilled blue-collar workers (the so-called "hard-hats"), the proportion was only fractionally higher, about 44 per cent; among the unskilled blue-collar workers, about 66 per cent. The evidence from educational attainment is approximately the same: among those with less than an eighth-grade education, about 49 per cent were scored low in political trust; for college graduates the figure was 40 per cent. This suggests that a movement based on "alienation" would have to draw more or less equally from the upper, middle, working and lower classes. Needless to say, the dispersion would raise serious problems for anyone attempting to mobilize the entire discontented group.

Much the same could be said for many other politically relevant lines of cleavage in the society—for example, region, race, religion and age. Using the same factor of "low trust," one finds the following: among nonwhites, about 61 per cent are highly distrustful; among whites in the South, the figure is about 54 per cent. The "movement" of politically alienated citizens, then, would have to draw about equally from blacks and Southern whites. There is no statistically significant difference between Protestants and Catholics in the matter of political discontent, so the "movement" would also have to appeal to both of these groups in roughly equal proportions. The difference in the level of political trust between the youngest (18 to 24) and the oldest (65-plus) groups in the sample was about 15 percentage points, the older group being the *less* trusting. Is there, then, a candidate or potential leader who could appeal strongly to blacks and Southern whites, to Protestants and Catholics, to the young and the old, to the upper-middle and the lower working classes? And even if such an unlikely person were found, someone who truly was "all things to all people," what conceivable threat could he or she pose to democratic institutions?

Given their social fragmentation, it should come as no surprise that the discontented are also politically diverse. The group is found in equal strength in the two major parties. In the 1970 data being discussed, 45 per cent of Democrats and 43 per cent of Republicans (outside the South) were scored low in political trust. A clever demagogue, bent on exploiting alienation and able to secure a major party nomination (the most obvious possibility being Wallace in 1976), would therefore immediately find that about half the intended constituency was located in the other party. It is, of course, possible that all those "other-party" alienates could be persuaded to defect, but given the tenacity of party identification in this country, the possibility seems remote.

A related problem is that, contrary to a widespread assumption, the alienated share no common political ideology. The 1968 SRC survey contains a long series of questions on political attitude that relate to such matters as the welfare state, race, and so on. These items were combined to produce a measure of "liberal-conservative ideology." Political distrust did relate to this measure of ideology, but, as before, the coincidence was not pronounced. About 48 per cent of those low in political trust scored at the conservative end of the scale, in contrast to 31 per cent of those high in trust. It is true, then, that the distrustful are somewhat more conservative than the rest of the society. At the same time, these data also show that about 52 per cent of the distrustful did not land on the conservative side of the scale, which means that the group is split nearly fifty-fifty on this broad ideological dimension. Other components of political ideology (for example, isolationism, anti-communism) showed essentially the same pattern.

Sharing no common party or common political outlook, the alienated are also not organized in any politically real sense. Almost by definition, the group is composed primarily of the unorganized and the unrepresented. There is, for example, no League of Alienated Women Voters to get out the vote on election day, no National Association for the Advancement of Alienated People to win a political hearing, no Vietnam Veterans Against Alienation to command the media's attention. The only visible exception is the Boston-based organization known as ROAR (Restore Our Alienated Rights), which has been active in the anti-bussing movement. It would be folly, of course, to infer anything about the politically disenchanted in the society from the existence or name of this organization.

One final point to be made along these lines is that the alienation which does exist in the society derives from many disparate sources. There is considerable evidence that a large portion of adult political discontent arises very early in life, as part of the normal process of political socialization in the lower and working classes. For example, David Easton and Jack Dennis have shown (in the *American Political Science Review*, March 1967) that the difference in political alienation between the working and middle classes can be observed among children as early as the third grade. In short, many of the political alienates encountered in surveys of the adult population have apparently borne their estrangement since early youth. It is not reasonable to suppose that this group has been prowling around from the age of 8 in search of some movement that would lessen its discontent. Rather, it can be expected that they will have long since made such attitudinal or behavioral adjustments as the situation requires—for example, will have decided that things could hardly be otherwise, that such is the natural or normal state of affairs, that, bad as it is, the system is probably no worse than any realistic alternative. It is not likely that this group will give much credence to some overnight savior who promises to remove all the sources of their discontent. "This," they would say, "we have heard many times before."

Not all of the current discontent, of course, can be ascribed to childhood sources. Much contemporary alienation has been occasioned by specific policy failures on the part of the political leadership—the bumbling of American policy in Vietnam, mismanagement of the economy and, most recently, the chicaneries of Watergate. But here, too, the resulting discontent has surely not been "of a piece." Some sectors of the society became frustrated and disillusioned because the government refused to withdraw American troops immediately from Vietnam; other sectors, because the government was willing to settle for something less than total victory there. Similarly, various groups differed markedly in their reactions to and interpretations of Watergate: some became more disenchanted because Nixon was not forced from office sooner; others, because he was forced from office at all. Once again, the prospects for a future alliance between these groups do not seem bright.

What we have witnessed in the last few years, then, is not the progressive disenchantment of a few malcontents residing at the social periphery, not even a trend confined to this or that specific social or political group. On the contrary, rising disaffection has touched every group in the society more or less equally. Any political movement that would capitalize on these trends, to reiterate a point already made, would be obliged to appeal simultaneously to an exceedingly broad spectrum of the population—to unskilled workers and college graduates, to the "tempestuous" young and the "recalcitrant" old, to Democrats and Republicans, Protestants and Catholics, to Southerners and non-Southerners, and so on. It cannot be emphasized too strongly how grossly implausible such a movement would seem to be. Any demagogue who relies on increasing discontent to sweep him into office is going to be severely disappointed.

Among those who might be "severely disappointed" is George Wallace, who ran for the Presidency in 1968. It is customary in conventional accounts to dwell on Wallace's successes; his popular vote, after all, marked him as the "most successful" third-party candidate since Theodore Roosevelt. What that overlooks is that nearly 90 per cent of the population *rejected* the Wallace appeal. Given that he was on the ballot in all fifty states, the 1968 Wallace vote signals the vigor, not the decay, of political intelligence in America.

Most of the themes now rampant in the commentary on rising discontent were present in the political speculation that surrounded the "meaning" of the Wallace candidacy. He was appealing directly to the sense of estrangement and despair, the growing dissatisfaction with the Tweedledum and Tweedledee offerings of the major parties, the increasing hostility to "politics as usual." His campaign, moreover, was laced with all the racist and Populist appeals that should have increased his attraction to the alienated and disaffected sectors. The "temper of the times" might also have favored his candidacy. There had been one major political assassination in the year; there had been increasingly bitter and divisive debate over American policy in Vietnam; there had been race riots in a number of major U.S. cities in the preceding summer of 1967; there had been turmoil on the campuses, rising crime, declining absolute standards of living. David English, political commentator for the London *Daily Express*, summarized in *Divided They Stand* the American scene of 1968: "Americans were almost without exception gripped by frustration, a frustration so powerful that many people feared that the nation was heading for a nervous breakdown." The times, in short, were ripe for a demagogic political movement such as Wallace represented. Yet roughly nine citizens in ten rejected his appeal.

What role, exactly, did political alienation play in the Wallace experience? What lessons can thereby be learned about the potential role of rising discontent in the immediate political future? Data from the 1968 SRC Presidential election study provide some revealing answers to these questions.

First, there was a correlation between alienation and Wallace voting in 1968; that is, the more alienated respondents were somewhat more likely to have voted for Wallace than were nonalienated respondents. Among those lowest in political trust, about 24 per cent chose Wallace as their candidate; among those highest in trust, the figure was about 3 per cent. There are, as always, two ways to read that kind of statistical evidence. First, candidates

such as Wallace do have some residual appeal to the politically discontented; but second, large majorities of even the most alienated reject such candidates in favor of more moderate alternatives. Given the facts noted earlier, one would hardly expect it to be otherwise. Even if all voters in the society had been extremely distrustful of government, it is unlikely that Wallace would have received as much as a quarter of the total popular vote. And given the extreme social and political fragmentation of the group, there is no reason to expect that it will be commonly galvanized by any other such candidate, in either the immediate or distant future. In other words, the slight preferential tendency revealed by the evidence is not sufficient to offset the pronounced party and ideological differences which exist *within* the alienated group.

In most of the commentary on the Wallace vote, the idea of alienation is linked to some presumed class-specific and region-specific appeals. The politically discontented blue-collar workers, especially those of the South, often figure as the main villains of the piece. Looking first at blue-collar workers outside the South, the data reveal that approximately 12 per cent of the *least* trusting claimed to have voted for Wallace; the comparable figure for highly alienated white-collar workers, by the way, was 11 per cent—not much difference. Among the less alienated respondents of both classes, of course, Wallace voting was somewhat lower. The major lesson to be learned from these data is that about nine-tenths of the most alienated blue-collar workers outside the South did *not* vote for Wallace. The threat of this group to established democratic institutions has apparently been exaggerated.

In the South, slightly different patterns obtain, although even here the conclusions to be drawn are about the same. There were, first, more votes for Wallace from all social classes and at all levels of political discontent. Among the most highly alienated blue-collar workers in the white South, about 43 per cent voted for Wallace, and that is about the highest level of Wallace support shown for any group in the analysis. But once again, even among highly alienated blue-collar Southern whites, well over half rejected Wallace's candidacy. Given the strong appeals which Wallace pitched at precisely this group, given the alarms in the popular press about its vengeful political intentions, it is little short of amazing that almost three-fifths of its members remained unpersuaded.

The slight tendency revealed in these data for alienated citizens to prefer a candidate such as Wallace must be weighted by a very important factor not yet considered here—the pronounced tendency of the politically discontented to participate less in politics. Several dozen academic studies of the "correlates of political alienation" confirm the conclusion that, however one defines political participation, those who are disenchanted with politics are far less likely to participate. In the 1968 election, only about half of the most alienated citizens bothered to vote, compared with nearly 85 per cent of the least alienated. (In both cases, the figures are only for those who were registered and otherwise eligible to vote.) Data from all Presidential elections since 1956 show the same pattern, and it is what one would expect. In most cases, a precondition for political participation is some confidence that one's actions might possibly make a difference, and that belief the discontented obviously lack. This means that the political preferences of disaffected groups will have far less effect than their proportionate numbers in the population would suggest, and that any "backward" impulses which they might harbor will be offset by their proclivity not to act on them. About half of any "meanness" which they exhibit never figures in the political equation. That, in any case, was undeniably true for the Wallace experience in 1968, and there is no reason to think it will be any less true under future circumstances.

The political withdrawal common among alienated citizens has received relatively little attention in popular alarmist accounts, except as an indication of their pathological response to things political. This neglect is doubly unfortunate: first, because in approximately two decades of scholarly research on political alienation and discontent, the only consistent and unambiguous finding has been that such people do not participate; and, second, because it is in this tendency that the true significance of the recent alienation trend lies.

Given what we think we know about the character and correlates of political alienation, the only reasonable prediction about short- or long-term consequences of the recent trends is that the level of political apathy will continue to rise in the society. Political participation, never remarkably high in American politics, will, I expect, sink to all-time lows through the coming decade, especially if neither major party can come up with a Presidential candidate able to rekindle popular confidence. From certain points of view, some of them quite prominent among academic theories of American democracy, decreased participation might seem a good thing; according to these theories, apathy is a sign of basic contentment with the *status quo*. My view, however, is that increased apathy would only signal a further de-democratization of a political system that is already excessively responsive to the interests of those at the top. Verba and Nie (*Participation in America*) have put the point well: the current structure of political participation in the United States, they say, only "helps those who are already better off." Any increase in mass apathy occasioned by alienation trends would strengthen that conclusion. The probable net effect of increasing discontent, then, is to intensify the existing unequal distribution of scarce social, political and economic resources in the society, to heighten still further the disparities between the higher and lower social strata, to increase that portion of democratic opinion which drops out of the basic political process. In all probability, we will *not* experience some heightened sense of mass vigilance, but on the contrary, an increased nonconcern with the comings and goings of political elites. Increased apathy, in short, will remove yet another constraint on the behavior of the political leadership; it will make another Vietnam, another Watergate, not less likely but more. The true threat of rising discontent, therefore, is not to the stability of the system but to its responsiveness and, ultimately, its justice. It is not the rise of a Wallace that we need to fear and forestall; it is another agglomeration of Nixons, Haldemans, Mitchells and related types who will be free to violate and mismanage the "public trust" because no one has retained the strength to challenge or object. Thus the situation is much akin to that noted by C. Wright Mills, discussing what he saw to be a predominant tendency among the modern democratic masses: "They lose their will for rationally considered decision and action because they do not possess the instruments for such decision and action; they lose their sense of political belonging because they do not belong; they lose their political will because they see no way to realize it." □

★★★

14

Politics of Dead Center: The Artificial Majority   Theodore J. Lowi

Elections are supposed to give the voters a choice. But as Theodore J. Lowi argues in this essay candidates avoid taking stands on specific issues in order not to alienate anyone. This political strategy reflects the candidates' perceptions that the majority is rarely divided by an issue. Thus, Lowi termed the 1970 election—and others no doubt—to be a "bore."

The candidates' perceptions are confirmed by the manner in which opinion polls are taken. Why do polls not reflect issue conflict among the voters, according to Lowi? What is the "McLuhan effect" in this context? In terms of public opinion and its measurement by surveys, what does Lowi mean by the terms "centrality," "bi-modally," and "normally distributed"? But, in reality, Lowi contends, issues do divide the electorate when very specific questions are put to the voters. It is when numerous specific issues are grouped together that the voters are found positioned together in the middle of the opinion distribution. Explain how this shift from (a) conflict on any single issue to (b) agreement on numerous issues occurs in public opinion.

For this reason, the majority's opinion as perceived by the candidates is not real but "artificial." Lowi is somewhat critical of the fact that the parties' candidates do not promote social change by raising issues for resolution. What does he mean by "strategic obfuscation"? Other scholars value the fact that our parties sustain moderation, reduce social tensions, and facilitate compromise. What do you think? From the standpoint of the political sysem, should the parties' candidates generate "productive disorder," to use Lowi's term, or should they maintain political stability? Could our parties and their candidates succeed in doing both at the same time? Which of these two alternatives is most valuable in the long run for the political system?

★ ★ ★

The Artificial Majority

Theodore J. Lowi

Mr. Lowi, a professor of political science at the University of Chicago, is the author of *At the Pleasure of the Mayor: Patronage and Power in New York City, 1898–1958* (Free Press), and *The End of Liberalism* (Norton). *The Politics of Disorder* will be forthcoming from Basic Books.

The election of 1970 was an overwhelming bore. James Reston observed in *The New York Times* that "None have come forward," and he, like many others, had in mind such leaders as Humphrey, Muskie, Stevenson, Bayh, McGovern, Tunney, Kennedy, Mondale, Hart, and House members and gubernatorial candidates too numerous to mention. On the Republican side, many candidates stuck like barnacles to their Democratic opponents, and couldn't be pried loose to give voters a clear view of the difference. Humphrey ran a virtual law-and-order campaign; Stevenson absolutely avoided distinction until late in the campaign; Tunney seemed just younger, not better.

The only excitement was the uncertainty of outcome in a few states. But if politics is to be more than a winter replacement for night baseball, mere excitement is not enough.

There was only one suprise, and it was not the stridency of Spiro Agnew. What he did was absolutely typical of Republicans, especially at the end of periods of war, when there is usually a Republican majority and a bit of panic in the air as to whether all the killing accomplished anything toward ridding the world of America's enemies. If it had not been Agnew, some other figure would have taken the lead that Nixon took during the 1950s. The surprise was the frailty of the liberals, liberal Democrats mainly, but Republican liberals as well. It was the unwillingness of these people to bring to the electorate the message that the country is in trouble; the reluctance of these usually thoughtful public men to define our problems in terms that might lead to meaningful public policies. The surprise lay in their willingness to let Agnew define the agenda and the terms of discourse. In politics, as in the courtroom, he who does that has gone a long way toward winning the debate.

Of course, it was not a matter of personal frailty. These men have all demonstrated courage upon occasion. There is something about the political system itself that explains their espousal of politics-as-usual at a time when everything else is unusual. So the question really is: what kind of electoral and party system do we have that can be impervious to social change and disorder?

Part of the answer lies in the assumption of centrality, which goes back to Locke and passes to us through a host of American historians and political scientists. It supposes that the American spirit is, as the statistician would say, "normally distributed." Americans, it is argued, think very much alike about many fundamental things. And when they disagree, they do not clash with much passion. Only a very small percentage of the population feels intensely about issues, and they are best treated as exceptions, as intellectual outsiders. Extreme disagreement means unwillingness to compromise, and that violates one of the unwritten but sacred rules of American politics. The attitudes of Americans are assumed to distribute themselves like the model given in Diagram I.

That is not necessarily a true description of Americans. It is only a model, but it is the model that political personalities carry around in their heads. They did not need to be told by Scammon and Wattenberg. They might have been surprised to learn from *The Real Majority* that the electorate had moved a bit to the right; but no one could tell the candidates, and no one tried to tell them, that the mass of voters had ceased to hover around dead center.

This assumption is reinforced by the opinion polls, but in a peculiar way. It is doubtful that the polls influence people by reporting results with which the previously uncommitted align themselves. The more likely explanation is a "McLuhan effect"—the medium is indeed the message. Polling agencies, first of all, ask only certain questions; there is simply no room for everything on the questionnaire. Often the only issues touched upon are those that have been on the agenda for some time, and it is probable that for many of these, opinion hovers around the center.

A second important factor in polling is the way in which questions are asked and responses are structured. For example, the respondent may be asked how he feels about "the law-and-order issue," and he will have to pick a single response (either

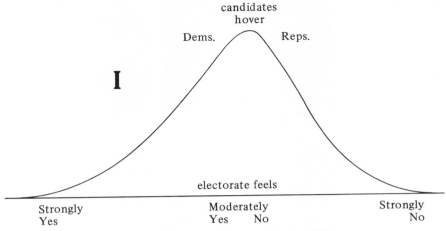

How the Electorate Looks to the Candidate

For or Against; or Strongly For, For, Against, Strongly Against—"Please check only one"). Or the question could be more specific: "Do you favor appropriating more money for the local police department?" In either case, the respondent on the usual opinion poll cannot expand on his response. Instead, he undertakes an inner dialogue, trying to balance all his plusses and minuses in order to give the interviewer his best accounting, which is really a complex response expressed in terribly simple terms. It is a "net response," a "Well, yes and no," or a "Well, I don't know," or, to be safe, a "moderate Yes" or "Maybe not."

The polling agency must then code these responses for entry on computer cards. These "net responses" have to be treated centrally, as moderate yesses and noes. At one level that is accurate; yet many of these middle-ground respondents may actually feel very intensely about certain aspects of the questions, but were given no opportunity on the questionnaire to express these intensities. The result is reaffirmation of the assumption of centrality. Reaffirmation is putting it too mildly. The polls lend Scientific Validation to the assumption of centrality.

Two most important results flow from this assumption of centrality. First, if candidates or parties believe that voters are overwhelmingly in the middle, it would be irrational of them to develop appeals and campaign strategies that were not center-oriented. Exactly the same problem arises in merchandising. Competing service stations occupy all four corners of a single intersection, where the traffic patterns are concentrated. To move slightly away from that center would be to move from the site of best exposure. Similarly, the candidates feel that, if they moved "away from center," they would be moving down the slope of the curve, where obviously there are fewer voters—if it is true that they are so distributed.

Over the years, a few major party candidates—Taft and Goldwater are the most important examples—have made a different assumption. They thought it more probable that voters were distinctly partisan and tended to distribute themselves "bi-modally," like a camel's hump, rather than in a single, central mode. In that case it would be rational to move to one or the other side of the center, as suggested in Diagram II. Only Goldwater got a Presidential nomination and the opportunity to test this theory. His defeat does not necessarily prove that there are no clearly divisive issues in the country, but it obviously convinced most candidates for all public offices that the centricity assumption was the safest.

The second result of assuming centricity is the self-fulfilling prophecy. If candidates assume that voters are moderate and centrally distributed, and if they conduct their appeals accordingly, they help bring about that very situation.

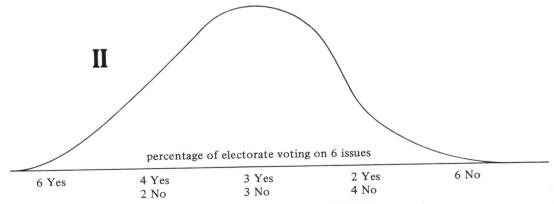

How the Electorate Actually Looks When Six (or more) Polarized Issues Are Presented Simultaneously

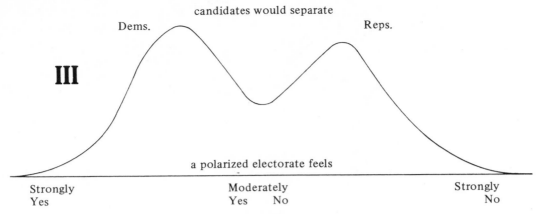

How the Electorate Actually Looks on Some Issues

This second consequence is not as simple as it sounds, because it does not happen merely because the politicians influence thousands of voters to be moderate by making moderate appeals. That may be the effect in a few cases, but more often something else happens, as we can see all too clearly in the 1970 campaigns.

Centricity prevails, first of all, because the candidates give the voters no choice but centricity. Even if the polls did not tilt the responses in favor of moderation, the candidates would. They hang together so closely around a mean that voters must vote for a middle-of-the-road position or stay home.

And even that is not the most important part of the process. How do candidates hang close together? They do it by "strategic obfuscation." In other words, they define the issues in terms so general that each candidate can virtually subsume the other. That is why the Democrats let the Agnew Republicans define the terms of discourse in 1970, why they so readily accepted "Law and Order" as the issue.

Law and Order is a generalized concept, a basket phrase that includes six, eight, even ten specific issues. Supporting this generalized form of law and order, the Democratic candidate could say, "I'm for Law and Order—with justice," as the Republicans were saying, "I'm for Law and Order—with safety." Thus they create the impression of debate, while in fact they agree to define as irrelevant to the campaign the specific issues that are part of the law-and-order basket.

At least two things follow from this. First, each voter goes through the same internal dialogue as does the respondent to an opinion poll. He has only one vote and must use it according to his own balancing of the various issues in the law-and-order package. This pulls him toward the center because, if he is to vote at all, he must vote "on net" as a Democrat or a Republican.

But a second, fascinating thing happens: the extremes are eliminated statistically! Let us say that six hard-core issues are hidden underneath the candidate's definition of law and order. Let us even propose that the electorate is polarized on all six of these, so that voter distributions on attitudes toward racial integration, student radicals, police powers and restraints, preventive detention, the Black Panthers and unilateral with-

drawal are all bi-modal, like the camel's hump, with most voters intensely for or intensely against. See then what happens when the six are treated simultaneously under the law-and-order concept, rather than one issue at a time, as in a real debate.

Diagram III is the almost inevitable result of grouping issues in one basket, because the same people are not intensely for or against all the issues. Racial questions are salient to certain voters, who will feel intensely "yes" or "no" about questions in that field. But many of these people care little one way or another about preventive detention or students. Thus only a very few highly militant types will be consistent *and* intense on all six (or eight or ten) issues.

You can be almost certain that when politicians advance conglomerate rather than specific definitions of issues they will produce, quite artificially, the impression of centrality. In effect, the Real Majority is an Artificial Majority created by artifice, and in fact combining very unlike positions. As the great political scientist E. E. Schattschneider put it thirty years ago, "Persuasion is unnecessary or secondary. Politicians take people as they find them. The politician has a technical specialty based on a profitable discovery about the behavior of numbers."

This explains the paradox of political quiescence in the midst of social disorder. When they can, politicians avoid polarized issues; when avoidance becomes impossible, they lump controversies together and thus cancel out the extremes. This is probably the controlling reason why American electoral and party politics are so stable and so isolated from the big issues of the day. It also suggests that, as the social turmoil increases, the separation between party politics and society becomes ever greater.

This pattern also suggests why there is rarely much to be gained from looking to party and electoral politics as agents of great changes. American party politics is designed to maintain the system. It maintains good things about the system, and it militates against removing bad things. And once change comes, usually through other channels, party politics adjusts and maintains the change as well. For example, a party politics all by itself would never have spread suffrage to Southern blacks;

but once the suffrage was expanded, a party politics emerged to help realize a more effective participation.

Once in a great while political parties and elections do become channels of change. Students of these critical elections, particularly V. O. Key, Dean Burnham, and Duncan MacRae, have located perhaps five national elections in 180 years that directly produced significant changes in the system. The last such "critical election" was probably 1928 (when Herbert Hoover defeated Alfred Smith), following which parties were for a brief while organized in ways relevant to making significant public policies. Students of these matters have probably been expecting another critical election for several years now, since the conditions again seem ripe. But one has not come because the polls have made politicans far more rational than they used to be, and rationality hath made cowards of them all.

It now strikes them as being safer and surer to follow the opinion pattern than to try occasionally to shape it. They fail to realize that in trying to follow opinion they are in fact shaping it—through the mechanism of the self-fulfilling prophecy.

Consequently, change will come if it does, from forces and organizations outside the party-political system. The election just held was good proof of this, for there has never been a better opportunity for candidates to embrace change. Changes come through social movements, through cumulative shifts of emphasis in education, through scientific breakthroughs, through an occasional muckraking book. Changes often come through more aristocratic channels, such as Supreme Court decisions or capitalistic advancement of important new technologies.

We need to revise our outlook toward campaigns and elections. Party and electoral politics can be understood only if accepted as the way to buy stability—Law and Order in the broadest sense. When we want a little productive disorder, we must look elsewhere. And if in large numbers we were to turn away from party politics, treating elections as the great bore they have become perhaps that would bring on a critical election, because politicians would try a little harder to get our attention.

★★

15   Reflections on Foreign Policy and Public Opinion   Jean-Francois Revel

Revel asserts that "the public mood is more solidly anchored in domestic affairs than in foreign affairs," a view supported by many observers. It is true that Americans are less interested in foreign affairs and are generally uninformed about events outside our borders. A reason for the difference between public opinion on domestic as opposed to foreign affairs, says Revel, is that public opinion on foreign policy issues is more often unrelated to the facts, thus myths persist longer.

What effect does ignorance about foreign affairs have on the public's understanding of policy-makers' efforts in international relations? As a point of illustration, Revel traces public attitudes toward the Soviet Union in the 1950s and in the 1970s. What is his argument in this regard? How does the American public view the Soviet Union today? Because public opinion can be so fickle in this area, political scientists have long wondered about the impact of citizen attitudes on foreign policy-making.

What connection does Revel see between public opinion and foreign policy? In a democracy citizen opinions should influence policy-making; however, to the extent that our views are based on misinformation, their embodiment in public policy can cause serious problems. What do you think? How closely should this nation's foreign policy follow the dictates of public opinion? Without the constraints of public opinion, what sort of limits do policy-makers operate under in the area of foreign affairs? Are these limits—if any—compatible with our democratic system?

Since this essay was written, the fact that Soviet combat troops were in Cuba was brought to the public's attention. In this light, do you think the spirit of détente and coexistence will last? Or is the American public becoming more militant in its posture toward the Soviet Union?

★ ★ ★

Reflections on Foreign Policy and Public Opinion

Jean-Francois Revel

Much more than in any other field, foreign policy in free countries often reflects collective moods which have little or nothing to do with the facts. During the fifties, for instance, when the Soviet Union was relatively weak internationally, American public opinion was strongly anti-communist and supported a very firm, assertive foreign policy. But during the seventies, when Soviet expansionism and its military buildup were stronger and more obvious than before, the American people seemed to sleepwalk into a benevolent, conciliating optimism that was oblivious to world realities.

In his conversation with Senator Moynihan in the second issue of *Public Opinion* (May-June), Dr. Kissinger correctly remarked that it is very difficult for policy makers to ignore altogether the public mood or to carry out a sort of under-cover foreign policy against the wishes of the people. It is especially hard in America, where the Congress is eager and quick to follow the wishes of the mainstream and always keeps a "club in the closet" should the President wander too far afield.

The frustration is that public moods about foreign affairs so often reflect internal, domestic trends. They

From *Public Opinion*, July/August 1978, pp. 15–17, © 1978 American Enterprise Institute. Reprinted with permission.

oscillate according to inner psychological needs, rather than to factual changes in international life. During the past five years, many fashionable Westerners have thought it their moral duty to believe in the communist determination to honor détente. Yet, the hard, external evidence during this time is that the communists were doing just the opposite of what they were saying.

While serving in government, Dr. Kissinger himself was accused or suspected of "making the world safe for communism" and of "talking like Churchill but acting like Chamberlain." As the main Western architect of the Helsinki Agreement, he often seemed to favor one-way détente and self-Finlandization. One cannot easily forget how he advised President Ford not to meet with Solzhenitsyn at the White House in 1974 for fear of irritating the Kremlin. What America got in return was never clear to me. But now that he has become a private citizen, as he illustrated in his conversation with Senator Moynihan, he has suddenly become tough and accurate again in analyzing Soviet diplomacy and Eurocommunism. Before attacking him for his shifting coloration, however, let us remember that as an actor at the State Department, Dr. Kissinger was not entirely free to speak his mind and always had to cope with the convergent pressures of Soviet blackmail and of a seemingly indifferent American public.

Harnessing Public Opinion to Public Facts

The fact that the public mood is more solidly anchored in domestic affairs than in foreign affairs is easily understandable. You cannot have a view of domestic and economic affairs totally disconnected from the facts. It may suit your peace of mind to deny that there is inflation or labor unrest, but that illusion won't survive the next bill you have to pay or the next strike of the sanitation workers. In foreign affairs, on the contrary, you may live for years with an illusion before an indisputable test clearly demonstrates its fallibility. You are able to deny or underestimate or forget a military threat until the day it materializes. France and Britain, before the war, cherished the idea that Hitler "would stop" at a certain point, and would "never launch an attack on the Western powers." It took some years of inconclusive speculations before the moment of truth came. To put it in a nutshell, wishful thinking is easier and lasts longer in foreign affairs than anywhere else. It is in that field that it is most difficult to bring public opinion into harmony with the facts. As a rule, public opinion overreacts (which is also a danger) or underreacts to major foreign events.

Accordingly, and in that sense, Senator Moynihan and Dr. Kissinger are in my view perfectly right when they assert that foreign policy should not be bent to win the short-term approval of the public. In home affairs, you cannot do without short-term approval. How can you implement a wage and price policy such as the British "social contract" without the short-term

support of the unions as well as of business? Whereas, in foreign affairs, it is true to say, in the words of Dr. Kissinger, that "what the public wants from its government is a solution to its problems," not a feeling that the government is following every fad.

Finding the Right Wave

Yet too often in history we have also had leaders who have decided that outside a handful of foreign policy makers, nobody understands world affairs and therefore foreign policy must be kept and shaped inside a very exclusive club. I am not sure Bismarck was joking when, by the end of his life, he was saying to a *London Times* reporter: "Only two men understand European affairs: an old Australian diplomat and myself. The old Australian diplomat is dead, and I am completely senile." All great diplomatic artists have a feeling that, after them, the world will be left to idiots. And while in office, they may fall into the temptation of secrecy, arguing that their job is "too complicated" to be explained. Once they have reached that point, they don't try to keep in touch with public opinion at all, which is no more possible in a democracy than to seek daily applause.

I would say that in home affairs, you have to listen to public opinion on the short waves, and in foreign affairs, you have to listen to it on the long waves. But you can never neglect it or think you can fool it altogether, even for the good of the country.

I am convinced, for instance, that the United States lost the Vietnam War on the home front not because its goals were illegitimate on a world scale perspective, but because the American people were more and more impressed that the men in office were too self-confident, were concealing more and more things from the public, were making secret decisions full of endless and terrible implications, and were practicing the gentle but unconvincing art of showing how failures are victories. Public opinion is slow to wake up about a foreign policy issue, but for that very reason equally slow to go to sleep.

If it is true to say that the citizen wants to rely upon the vague notion that "you, the government, should solve his problems," he becomes all the more balky when (rightly or wrongly) he has a feeling you don't. When he reaches that point, it's almost impossible to make him change his mind. He just wants to get rid of the whole business. Any foreign policy leader has to keep that in mind: it is during the times when public opinion is very nice to him, admiring him and believing all that he says that he is bound to make mistakes which, later, will hopelessly turn the trend against him, even if by then, he makes fewer mistakes. Quite often, a leader has to fight blindness and indifference of public opinion on the short waves, while keeping closely in touch with it on the long waves.

The Awakening Giant

Shifts in foreign policy leadership inevitably follow or

(which is better) precede shifts in the public perception of facts. I was very struck by the coincidence of the new harder lines of the Carter administration and recent polls, which were printed by *Public Opinion* in its first and second issues. Daniel Yankelovich's survey in the first issue shows a clear reversal of the American public mood, compared with the past five years. A plurality of Americans is now aware that the U.S.S.R. has used détente as a guise for more easily reaching its expansionist goals, and so the mainstream in the United States again thinks it best for the country to take an active part in world affairs. The poll in the second issue shows that, for the first time, a plurality of Americans also believes that the Soviet Union is stronger than the United States militarily. So the tougher stance of President Carter and Dr. Brzezinski, which emerged just after those surveys and after the conversation between Dr. Kissinger and Senator Moynihan, is a kind of translation of the changing tide in the public opinion. At last, there appears to be high level recognition of three main facts that were actually obvious long ago: the failure of the Soviet Union to honor the provisions of the Helsinki Agreement, Soviet imperialism in Africa, and the Soviet military buildup.

A Missing Linkage

Even so, if internationalists again outnumber isolationists and Americans are newly aware of the interdependence of countries and regions in the world, the American public does not yet seem conscious of the interdependence between economic and strategic affairs. In the surveys, they show they are still in favor of trade with the Soviet Union and the communist countries, exactly as their leaders are.

West European public opinion suffers from the same weakness. It, too, has now accepted the conclusion that détente has been a failure in two respects: in promoting human rights and in limiting the Soviet military grip on the world. But West Europeans still think that trade and business relations, capital investments, and transfers of technology should go on because they have been successful.

And indeed they have been successful—for the Soviet Union. I would say that for the Russians, the main *raison d'être* of détente was to extricate themselves from the hopeless economic quagmire of their system without reforming that system. To correct the system in order to make it more efficient would have also required a correction of the *political* system, which is the main cause of communist economic sterility. Instead, the Russians managed to import Western goods and technology and pay for them with Western borrowed money, and they borrowed at much more moderate rates than a capitalistic firm could obtain in financial markets of the West. With that aid, the Soviet Union was able to freely use other resources for its military buildup and to insure the permanence of its political

dictatorship. Without such Western aid, the country could not have taken such a huge share of its GNP for defense: 14 percent compared with some 5.2 percent by the U.S.A. Russia could not otherwise have taken that share without risking economic collapse, an aggravated scarcity of food and political unrest.

So, when we say that no matter what the Russians do in Africa or no matter what they do to Yuri Orlov, we won't "blackmail" them by refusing to "sell" them grain or technological know-how, we are throwing away the only weapon we have—short of the thermonuclear war—that they really fear. And that was the weakness of the Nixon-Kissinger duet, just as it now is the weakness of the Carter-Brzezinski-Vance-Young quartet. The "blackmailing" objection is silly. What is a negotiation if not a mutual blackmailing anyway?

I have nothing against the multinational corporations. They are purely economic organizations, and their job is not to pursue political aims. But it's a fact now that American farmers and multinational (mainly European) corporations are making highly profitable deals with the East which enable the Soviet Union to keep the totalitarian system working and to make the Red Army stronger and stronger. I would call that the multinational-communist complex—a kind of military industrial complex, but transnational.

Accepting Soviet Domination

As for the "crisis of spirit," discussed by Dr. Kissinger and Senator Moynihan, it is—like many "spiritual" crises—a rhetorical disease. Along with Third World countries, we persist in thinking of ourselves as "the right" or "conservative," while thinking of communist nations as "the left" or "progressive" societies. Why should we accept that? Why should we go on calling Western European Communist parties "the left"? Was Truman a fascist and Stalin a democrat?

Looking beyond this illusion, a deeper problem does exist in Western Europe, and that is the general acceptance of Soviet domination. Recent interviews with Chancellor Helmut Schmidt and the Premier of Belgium, Leo Tindemans, showed an alarming loss of confidence in the European capacity to resist, even by words, the Soviet pressure and a prevailing fear to stir the wrath of Leonid Brezhnev.[1] As long as we won't understand that the communist world brings nothing to the human being and takes away almost everything from him, that it is an empty box with guns outside, that our duty is to expose their inability to run their society instead of helping them to conceal it, and that they are afraid precisely of *that*, we will lose. ☑

---

[1] See Arnaud de Borchgrave in *Newsweek* (May 29, 1978); "In the original transcript, M. Schmidt had already been quite flattering about Leonid Brezhnev and his détente policy. The only criticism was in reply to my question about Soviet-Cuban adventures in Africa, which he said were clearly incompatible with détente. When I asked him whether he had made this clear to M. Brezhnev, he said, 'Yes, I did.' He changed his mind later and killed these three words. He was very anxious not to offend M. Brezhnev. He even inserted an additional sentence about M. Brezhnev's sincerity on peace and détente. He also took out a reference to the establishment of Marxist-Leninist states in Africa being a clear case of (Soviet) imperialism."

CHAPTER FOUR

★ ★ ★

Political Parties and Pressure Groups

Most political science textbooks differentiate between political parties and pressure groups. It is said that parties seek to win elective offices whereas pressure groups try to influence the incumbents in office. It is argued, moreover, that parties have larger, more diverse memberships; in contrast, pressure groups have smaller, more homogeneous memberships.

This chapter focuses on parties and pressure groups in contemporary American politics. One theme indicated by the readings, and also reflected in textbook analyses of these topics, is the perception that political party organizations are becoming weaker, while at the same time pressure groups have grown in number—and perhaps also in influence. If correct, these trends have major implications for our political system. The ostensible function of parties is to win elections, but they have other fundamental roles in American politics and government. Unlike pressure groups, which steadfastly represent their constituents' special interests, parties are seen as important to the governing process. They facilitate compromise, forge a political consensus among diverse interests, and assist decision-making in a governmental sys-

tem formalized by separation of powers and checks and balances. Certainly on occasion lobbyists find common ground for agreement, but in the absence of party organizations many observers feel that lobbying activities would lead to fragmented government, weakened political leadership, and disunity among the people.

In the essay "The Organization Man" by Ralph Whitehead, Jr., a portrait is drawn of Mayor Richard J. Daley of Chicago. His party organization remains strong, the last of the big-city political "machines" as some see it. It seems atypical of the state of political parties in most cities, in the states, and in the nation. Clearly the Democratic party of Chicago and Cook County, Illinois, has the ability to govern, to make decisions; it has the support of a large segment of the citizenry; and it has absorbed and coopted powerful interest groups in Chicago, including both business and labor. Given this fact, it may not be coincidental that its power base rests upon traditional party patronage, grass-roots precinct work, and loyalty. It does not rely upon the mass media, and it does not exploit issues that divide the electorate. Daley is no longer mayor, but the machine persists after him. One may not agree with the objectives of Daley's machine, but it clearly has all the attributes of an effective party organization.

Daley's party organization seems bent on one objective—to win and maintain power. While this would appear to be the primary goal of partisans, it is not always the case. Sometimes the political party is viewed as a vehicle by which to articulate issue positions and an ideology. In the essay "Dinosaurs & Neanderthals: The New Right vs. the GOP" by J. Brian Smith, the problems posed by ideology for a major political party are examined. Both parties have their share of political extremists; in general, Democrats are plagued by ideologues on the left, whereas the Republican party must deal with its conservative wing. Many scholars would agree with Smith's assessment that ideologues are not typically officeholders; rather, they are political activists drawn into politics for reasons of issue commitment. The GOP is being undermined, argues Smith, by the "New Right," which is more intent on promoting its ideological purity than on winning elective office. Moreover, it is not very loyal to the Republicans as a party. Serious implications can be drawn from this essay. If everybody fights for their narrow issue positions without a sense of compromise or moderation, the political parties will be severely weakened, conflict will be aggravated, and the political consensus that supports our political system will be undermined.

Apart from the dangers of ideology, a more direct threat to our parties comes from well-intentioned "reformers" who want to make them more democratic in structure. This is the lesson of "Reform Is Wrecking the U.S. Party System," by Everett Carll Ladd, Jr. Because of our culture's emphasis on individualism, there is a persistent, historical trend to allow citizens direct access to the nominating and electoral processes. Parties are seen as obstructions to full democratic participation by the citizenry. But the effect of reform has been to make the parties unrepresentative of the mass of voters. As party organization has weakened, party activities are more and more affected by political activists, rather than by elected officials. These political activists are not typical of the party's rank and file in background and issue orientation.

Parties are also supposed to facilitate decision-making in a governmental system fragmented by separation of powers, checks and balances, and federalism. Again reform has undermined this party function. Today candidates have an incentive to disavow party, to run for office as loners, and to target their appeals to narrow interests and single-issue constituencies. For these reasons, Ladd is not optimistic about the quality of American politics in the absence of strong parties. While the problems seem clear, the solutions are not so obvious. It is difficult to argue against having more democratic parties in America, where the consent of the governed is a fundamental value of the Republic.

Three articles in this chapter discuss the impact of pressure groups on our government. In the first, "The Swarming Lobbyists," this topic is given serious consideration as *Time*'s cover story. Though lobbying is not new to America, this essay suggests that the number of lobbyists has grown in recent years, as has their effectiveness. There is a relationship between the weakening of the political parties and the growth in interest groups. Lobbying exists because special interests want to influence legislation that directly affects them. It persists, the essay implies, because lobbying is functional to the operation of the law-making process. Legislators and lobbyists need each other. But one should not be misled by the title of this article, for not all segments of the society are organized for political battle. Furthermore, all pressure groups are not equally effective in advancing their cause before government. This inequality in the pressure-group system is acknowledged by many political scientists, and it is illustrated by Sanford J. Ungar's analysis on "Jewish and Arab Lobbyists."

Pressure groups are typically organized around domestic interests, but they also try to influence foreign policy when it affects the domestic society. Some interest groups, however, are seriously involved in foreign policy issues. Such is the case with Americans whose ancestors immigrated from foreign countries. Eastern European peoples are concerned about the impact of the Soviet Union on their homelands; blacks voice concern about our policy toward African nations; and the Jewish community is interested in the state of the United States–Israeli relations. This essay compares Jewish lobbyists and Arab-American lobbyists on the issue of Middle Eastern politics. Clearly this competition is unequal, for the Jewish lobbyists are very effective. Arab-Americans have fewer resources, though events in the Middle East have aided their credibility. One lesson to be gained from this analysis is that, as with domestic policy, constraints on foreign policy can be placed by an interest group

★★★

that enjoys political influence and widespread public support.

The final essay provides a novel look at the mass media. Entitled "Media Lobbyists: An Unreported Story," it analyzes a facet of lobbying not known to many Americans. We suspect that the media shape the reporting of news and political information, but rarely do we see the media portrayed as lobbyists, protective of narrow self-interests. This essay assaults the self-righteous attitude that the media exhibit toward other interest groups. It also hints that the mass media have betrayed the public's trust. For unlike any other lobby, the media have the ability to communicate their message—or simply not to communicate any message—to the people. Politicians today are dependent upon media coverage in waging their campaigns.

The six essays in this chapter address a variety of issues pertaining to the role of parties and pressure groups in our society. All are well written, relatively brief, and provocative. Parties and pressure groups are discussed together to promote an understanding of their organizational differences and to highlight how each affects the workings of politics and government.

★★★

★★★

16 The Organization Man   Ralph Whitehead, Jr.

In the late nineteenth and early twentieth centuries, many big cities in America were dominated by political "bosses" who headed political "machines." A machine tended to develop in those cities where the same political party repeatedly won the cities' elective offices establishing a relatively permanent power base. Few classic political machines survive in America today. One well-known party organization that still exists is firmly established in Chicago. For almost twenty-five years its boss was Mayor Richard J. Daley. It is he who is described as the "organization man" and discussed in this article by Ralph Whitehead, Jr. What reasons does Whitehead give for the decline of machine politics in American cities? Why does the machine survive today in this particular city?

In an era when publicity, mass communications, and glamor seem to be the mainstays of political success, Chicago's machine relies on grass-roots contact at the precinct level. How important was Mayor Daley's leadership in strengthening the machine's political base during the years he served? How easy is it for a machine to centralize power in a large city? What segments of the population supported Chicago's machine and Daley's leadership? How did the machine's electoral base change during the years Daley was in office? How important to the success of the machine was Daley's relationship to the black community?

For many Richard J. Daley personified Chicago. How did his Irish Catholic background affect his values, his political style, and the direction the machine took? Is the Chicago machine a successful governing mechanism, or is it an ineffective throwback to a bygone era?

★ ★ ★

The Organization Man

RALPH WHITEHEAD, JR.

Richard J. Daley could be a hard man to understand because he chose to express himself almost solely through an organization, Chicago's political machine. He never created an obvious or convenient body of his work, not even one as slight and as ghostwritten as other politicians so often leave: a memoir or a book on the issues, say, or some formal addresses, or a major piece of legislation. If all his public papers were gathered together, they would amount to little more than the short talks he gave at ribbon cuttings.

Daley's friends and enemies alike did try to point to the places where his personal touch might seem evident—his neighborhood, perhaps, or the Chicago skyline—but they were only clutching at conceits. Others knew him by the hard lines he chose to draw as the rest of America watched him: his cautious opposition to the Chicago civil rights campaign led by Dr. Martin Luther King, Jr., for example, or his brutal opposition to the protests at the Democratic National Convention in 1968. These cases, and the impression they create of Daley as a narrow and autocratic man, must be taken into account, of course; but his public life was too long to be measured by their evidence alone. To list him simply as the last of the big city bosses, as the headline writers did, not only is a mistake (he was not the last), but also turns a significant politician into a stock character.

Of course, the medium he chose does tend to put off quick or easy judgments. The Chicago Democratic machine is a large organization, for one thing. Through its control of patronage, the machine sponsors more than thirty-five thousand people in jobs, public and private. It is hard to know for sure what even a small fraction of them might be doing at a given time, what kindnesses or cruelties they might be performing. The pattern of their work can also be difficult to follow and comprehend. The machine is broken down into branches for each of Chicago's fifty wards, with a Democratic ward committeeman elected to run each one. The work in the wards is split again into smaller branches—the several dozen voting precincts, where anywhere from five to fifteen party workers are detailed by the machine to handle the four hundred to six hundred voters in a precinct, and through the full year, not just at campaign time. The machine is a single organization—it is commonly known as "*The* Organization" in Chicago—but it can also behave as if it were several different organizations, if only because it crosses lines of race and class and tries to hold the common support of bitter enemies.

Moreover, Mayor Daley did not build his political appeal on his personality. Unlike so many other politicians of the time, he never tried to create and project, for a mass audience, the artifact we call a public image. (He did cultivate a reputation, but he tended to groom it gradually and in detail, a single wake or phone call at a time.) He seemed to know why a majority of the voters in Chicago voted as they did. Many of them, he clearly felt, were less likely to make a consumer's judgment of the personality of a candidate than to vote according to their roots, their class, their address, or the color of their skin.

○ RALPH WHITEHEAD, JR., is completing a book on the life and politics of his native city, Chicago. He is an assistant professor of journalistic studies in the School of Humanities and Fine Arts at the University of Massachusetts.

As some voters did come to insist on making a consumer's choice at the polls, he urged them to think of the product as something other than Richard Daley, the man. Look at the record, he would say, or the party's ticket this year, or all the buildings we've put up, or all the fine things your precinct captains are doing for you, or The Organization itself—but he would never ask them to look at him. For a rough-cut man as old as he, it was a plausible approach.

Richard Daley spent the larger share of his time attending to the apparatus of The Organization. He financed it, kept up the size and the morale of its work force, and positioned it on issues in the political life of Chicago, particularly issues of race. Interestingly enough, his work on the apparatus should also be taken as the surest guide we have to the moral character of the man. The political values he honored were the right to a livelihood, security, a place to turn if you get into a jam, and a sense of continuity with the past and the future. He felt these values could survive in the city only if they were secured by the apparatus of the strong and territorial institution he led for almost twenty-five years, with its dollars and people and what in Chicago is called clout. For him, the values and the apparatus were fused, and to work on one was to work on both.

I

The Organization's boss is obliged to finance its work, usually by finding and tapping a prime source of capital. At different times, the leading backers of the machine were the utilities, the real estate boomers of the early 1920s, the legitimate wineries and breweries of the prohibition years, and the racetrack gamblers of the depression and World War II. The ten years before Richard Daley came to power were hard times for the machine. Neither of its successive leaders, Jacob Arvey and Joseph Gill, was able to finance it adequately. Mayor Daley, though, moved quickly to secure a fresh supply of capital, largely through policies of land development.

At the time, Chicago's downtown was stagnating. The investors of the fifties were turning to the cheaper land of the suburbs, and several of the major landholders and commercial interests of the city's business district, the Loop—some of the larger banks, the utilities, the department stores, and the Chicago Title and Trust Company, a major force in the land and lending markets—organized to restore its competitive standing as a business site. The repertoire of urban land policies was broadening. Public housing, slum clearance, neighborhood conservation, and other forms of urban renewal offered new means and new dollars. The proprietors of the Loop thought these public means should be used to renew, expand, and secure the downtown.

As the Mayor, Daley helped them. His reasons for doing so were complex, but it is not misleading to put them into a simplified form: his political organization was desperate for money and would fall apart without it. He saw how the renewal of the Loop could supply it, if the work was properly handled. For one thing, Mayor Daley realized that a major industry in Chicago could be the buying and the selling, the tearing down and the building up, of the city itself, provided The Organization fostered the growth through its control of eminent domain powers, zoning, public subsidies, the building codes, the property tax, and several other kinds of instruments.

Moreover, Daley knew he could establish himself as the leader of this industry. Real estate and construction are highly fragmented industries; even the giant firms hold only a tiny percentage of the total market. A public body as large as Chicago's city government was likely to be the largest single force in the marketplace, as it went about building its firehouses and police stations, its bridges and its viaducts, its curbs and its gutters, its streets and sidewalks. Of course The Organization also controlled other public agencies: the board of education, the Chicago Park District, the Metropolitan Sanitary District, the offices for Cook County, and some of the offices for the state of Illinois. All those schools, fieldhouses, pipe ways and sewage plants, court and office buildings, and miles of expressways could add even more to the machine's leverage in the industry. It was merely a matter of pulling together all these pieces of work into a larger strategy for development, as the Mayor gradually did.

Daley, then, used the renewal of the Loop to get the industry off the ground. The process created a large and steady market for land, mortgages, building supplies, construction work, bonding, and other forms of insurance. It created jobs for the skilled trades while the buildings were going up, and, after they were up, more jobs for clerks and janitors. It began to shore up the tax base. (Not for nothing was Richard J. Daley so well regarded by both the unions and business.) It took advantage of public sources of capital, through bond issues and grants by the national government. Within the political machine, there was some resistance to what the Mayor was doing; some of the ward bosses near the Loop were enraged to see their political bases torn up by the work, but progress brushed the old rogues aside. In time, the Loop was secured for private investment, just as the economy began its growth in the early sixties and more and more private dollars became available. Thus the work was taking hold: it proved itself, inspired confidence, and primed the decisions of landowners and investors. Downtown, property values began to rise. The Mayor was creating new wealth.

At the same time, the Democratic machine positioned itself to catch at least a small share of all this new money. The flow of the money varied, depending on its source in the marketplace and its destination within The Organization. The clientele for zoning help learned to befriend the leaders of the city council; the clients for tax breaks turned to the assessor's office; the building trades gladly offered campaign aid to the Mayor himself—in short, a group of what might be called profit centers began to emerge. Some worked within the law and others did not. For example, the indictments of at least six of the executives of The Organization can be traced to these arrangements. Despite the risks, though, the machine as a whole did benefit.

II

Scholars agree on reasons for the decline of Democratic big city machines—slowed-down immigration, the New Deal, and the economic growth begun in World War II—but they often neglect an added influence: the more impersonal forms of persuasion developed in the last thirty years, in politics as well as in the consumer marketplace. The political organizations in New York, Jersey City, Memphis, Kansas City, Cleveland, and, of course, Boston, home of *The Last Hurrah*, were badly hurt by this slow but sweeping change because it undercut the mainstay of the political machine: the precinct worker. Mayor Daley, however, made a conscious decision to keep up his force of precinct workers regardless of the cost.

Just as Richard Daley came to power, the advertising industry began a long campaign to undercut what it called personal selling. Its trade press and other business publications carried arguments against the value and common sense of using salespeople in the stores or on doorsteps—a sales force is susceptible to high turnover, for example, or to trade union sentiments—and tried to show how expensive this method could be, given the rising costs of labor. Far cheaper forms of persuasion were there to be used, the ad agencies said. Standardized brands and brand images made it less necessary for a buyer to seek the advice of a salesperson; impulse buying was occurring more and more; market research could gauge the likes and dislikes of consumers almost as well as salespeople could, and more cheaply; radio and TV could carry sales messages into a home at a lower cost than a door-to-door salesman could. Of course, the ad industry was running advertisements for itself here, but its evidence was sound and its figures held up.

Moreover, a number of major manufacturers were still shifting to an after-Korea peacetime economy, building a consumer market for appliances and other goods to replace the military market for hardware. Soon conventional wisdom advised them to put their sales dollars into the products of Madison Avenue. "Advertising is the finest catalytic agent to keep mass consumption abreast of mass production," said Richard Bowditch, the president of the chamber of commerce. Corporations began to freeze or even cut the size of their sales forces. In the words of E. B. Weiss, a Chicago advertising executive, a columnist for *Printer's Ink*, and the author of *The Vanishing Salesman*: "Make no mistake, we are smack in the middle of a developing era of impersonal mass selling."

Of course, some of these methods came to be used eventually in political campaigns. There, too, capital-intensive forms of persuasion began to undermine the older labor-intensive forms. They proved to be far cheaper than the political counterpart to the salesman, the precinct worker. A precinct worker could move around in a single corner of one neighborhood and talk up a candidate and help to spread the man's name around, but a sophisticated marketing strategy could turn a candidate's name into a brand and build his personality into a brand image—and for an entire city. A parallel to impulse buying also emerged as voters began to put off their final voting decision until they could consider the appeals broadcast during the last days of a campaign. Polls brought market research methods into politics. They weren't as savvy as the eye and the ear of a seasoned precinct worker, but they offered scope and efficiency, since they could measure the sentiment of an entire city in only three evenings of phone calls. Advertisements, in the mail or in newspapers, on radio or TV, could carry an appeal into a living room for pennies. The ad budget for a campaign needed to cover only thirty to forty-five days in the election season, but a precinct worker needed to be paid the year round and would be looking for a pension besides. The cost-per-thousand data alone were devastating: a precinct worker would reach perhaps 400 voters, for $7,500-a-year and up, but an advertising spot could address 250,000 voters for a few hundred dollars. The new methods were only half as good as the old, but they were twenty or thirty times cheaper. So efficiency prevailed, but not in Chicago, where Mayor Daley chose to pay the extra price.

Of course, patronage defrays the larger share of the costs of the sales force for The Organization. The government or the utilities or a friendly business firm sends a weekly paycheck to most of the precinct workers, insures their health, and sets aside money for their old age. At the same time, though, patronage salaries are often too low to reward these people for the long hours they spend in political work, in the evenings and on weekends. Many of them want a moonlighter's subsidy, and The Organization goes into its own pocket to pay for it. The workers also piece together what might be called their product line—the goods and services and favors they swap for sure votes on election day. For many of these, they turn to the government; they are the insiders, their calls get returned first, their requests go to the top of the pile, they know or can quickly learn the name of the man to see (often the man to see is a woman) for help with the police, the courts, with welfare, or streets and sanitation, water and sewers, and so on. At the same time, precinct workers provide added help, things the government doesn't do: shovel sidewalks, tune cars, or run to the store for groceries for the sick or elderly. The Organization pays for this, too. It also puts up what it calls precinct money, the small bankroll a worker carries and spends on election day and the few days before. Some of it is used to buy votes outright, for three to five dollars a vote, or to buy the liquor or the cut of meat that will be traded for a vote. (Often the liquor and the beefsteak are contributed by a friendly business.) Some of the money also buys goodwill. If a worker knows a family with six votes, he might hire the grandmother to help on election day; for a ten-dollar bill, she will make sure everybody in the house votes, and votes right. Finally, as a perquisite or as a cushion against fate, workers just like to keep a little cash around. Even the leaders of The Organization cannot say for sure how much money gets spent in its name. Very few records are kept, and they are not set down in a single place, where they can be reviewed. A conservative estimate would put the figure at $3.5 million a year.

With the money on hand, precinct workers can display their natural superiority. The work they do can be highly personal, tailored to people quite carefully and with a sense of ceremony. Their work is also open to ties of friendship and kinship, as well as loyalties based on the neighborhood, the parish, the local faith and culture. Precinct workers can acquire and store a subtle sense of the electorate as well. Few polls, no matter how skillful in design, can discover that the man in the third bungalow from the corner, there on Seventy-seventh Street, is always good for a vote for the alderman because the two of them used to play softball together on Tuesday evenings. Finally, the mere presence of these people can be an advantage. They can look and listen, adapt and manipulate, haggle and persuade. In a sense, they form a medium of a distinctive sort, as Daley appreciated. In the last week of his last campaign, while the other side was attacking him with a strong and sophisticated marketing strategy, with six different TV spots and dozens of radio commercials, Mayor Daley told the voters what he thought was at stake: "The next time you need a favor," he defied them, "go ask your television set."

III

After his first two terms as Mayor, Richard Daley shifted his base of support in the city's electorate. The change took almost ten years to complete and his strategy for it was extensive. For example, he shifted his position on a number of issues, groomed a new generation of ward bosses, and saw to the retooling of hundreds of precinct workers. Yet it seemed to be quicker and cruder than it actually was, perhaps because it was based on an explosive element in the city's life—race.

The social base for The Organization was always the oldest third of Chicago, which covered what were known for a long time as the river wards: the slums and working-class neighborhoods close to the industrial flats of the Chicago River. This was the Chicago of Jane Addams, Finley Peter Dunne, Theodore Dreiser, Upton Sinclair, Richard Wright, and Nelson Algren; it was the home of Studs Lonigan and Augie March. Here considerations of race and class and culture fused into an almost genetic affinity for the Democratic party. Still, it covered only a third of Chicago's wards, and only a third of its votes. The Democratic machine held a power of citywide and countywide scope only because it carried the votes of its natural base so overwhelmingly—85 percent wasn't uncommon. Usually this was more than enough to offset its customary losses in the outer third of the city. In these wards, the voters were white, Protestant, middle-class or better, homeowners, and suburban in their habits and values. They disdained the advice of precinct workers, if they listened to them at all. They did heed the editorial advice in the newspapers, the *Daily News* and the *Tribune*. Usually, but not always, these wards voted for Republicans. (The parties tended to split the votes in the other third of the city.) Thus, as a rule, with only a few exceptions, Chicago's noted political machine rarely enjoyed the support of more than eighteen or nineteen of the wards in the city. It rested on a narrow base.

Moreover, the racial character of that base was changing. At the end of the war, for example, only two of the river wards held black voting majorities. Eighteen years later, in 1963, as Mayor Daley campaigned for a third term, ten of those wards held black majorities and four more were transitional. In that election, the outer ring of white wards voted against him, three to two. More than half of the Daley vote was cast by blacks. The political boss of the South Side ghetto, Congressman William Dawson, read those numbers as if they were a hand full of aces. He began quietly to bet them, mainly by asking for a large piece of the insurance business that was influenced by The Organization. The Mayor put him off. Instead of conceding the changing shape of the old base, Daley began to establish a new one, in the terra incognita of the outer ring of white wards.

Publicly the Mayor began to play to the white audience on racial issues. Events helped him to define his position. The civil rights movement was emerging in Chicago at just this time. He leaned against it—in a subtle way on some occasions, a harsh way on others. He endorsed the principle of open housing but refused to advance it. He dragged his feet against a court order to build public housing in white neighborhoods and open it to both races. He subtly disavowed a school busing plan drafted by the board of education. After Chicago's fourth ghetto riot, he rebuked the superintendent of police for not ordering his men to shoot arsonists to kill, looters to maim. He fought court orders to add more blacks to the police department and the fire department. He refused to hear charges of police brutality against blacks, even though those charges were carried to him by one of his own ward leaders, Congressman Ralph Metcalfe of the Third Ward.

Quietly the Mayor made some adjustments in The Organization. Many of the Democratic bosses in the outer ring of white wards were only deadweight, since so little was customarily expected of them. After the elections of 1966, a white backlash helped the Republicans to sweep all those wards as they carried the county and the state. The Mayor saw the figures and decided it was time to bring those wards up, through some solid organizational work. In the next two years, he sacked the bosses of ten of them and moved in younger men. He gave these new men more of the sinews of war, more jobs to dispense, more money to spend. To give them something to take to their voters in the home-owning wards, he virtually froze the property tax rate after 1970. The precinct workers there became accustomed to a politics of property val-

ues: they fixed potholes in the alleys, plowed driveways, made sure the streets were clean, kept the curbs and sidewalks in repair, saw that dead trees were quickly replaced, and so on. At the same time, the character of their wards was changing, as displaced whites moved into them from the older wards. Thus the outer wards were becoming more Catholic, more Jewish, more lower-middle-class— more culturally congenial to The Organization.

As Congressman Dawson grew feeble, the Mayor limited the role of The Organization's leaders in the ghetto wards. He urged them to go into business in their home wards—into law, real estate, insurance, banking—but he refused to bring them into the more lucrative forms of political business, the citywide and countywide arrangements for legal help, bonding, accounting, construction, and the rest. He never pulled back on them logistically; they still got jobs to dispense, still got their allotment of precinct money for every campaign, because the Mayor wanted them to keep their vote count high. Yet he let them know they were to behave as tacticians, never as strategists. When William Dawson died, most of his power was buried with him, and Ralph Metcalfe, who was closest to his heir, quickly learned how little he would be allowed to say or do. The Mayor expected him to carry the Third Ward, but he would never sit down with Metcalfe and say, "Ralph, *overall*, how do you think we should be running the business?"

As the Mayor shifted his own base, he succeeded in broadening the base of The Organization as a whole. The black vote did slip, but not dramatically, and these small losses were more than offset by the gains The Organization made in the outer wards. For the first time in its history, the Democratic machine enjoyed a genuinely citywide base of support in Chicago.

Richard Daley, therefore, left his political organization in far better shape than he found it. He secured its financial base, kept its distinctive style of campaigning intact, and broadened its appeal to Chicago's electorate. Taken on his own terms, as narrow as they were, he was a successful public man.

IV

Richard Daley placed himself on the wrong side of the leading moral issues in the politics of the last decade: Vietnam, civil rights, government corruption. His position on the war can be discounted; he simply followed the line of the national government until he began to turn against the war with the concrete reasoning of a man who often stopped at two and three wakes in an evening. ("I don't like it," he told his friends. "We're getting back too many of those green bags.") On civil rights, though, his words and policies often were racist, either on their face or in their resonance. And there was little doubt as to his position on corruption in government. It was something he countenanced and even abetted.

As a result, of course, he opened himself to severe criticism. His critics regarded the issues he was wrong on as overriding issues; for them, his stand on those issues provided a complete definition of Daley's morals. If the media's portrayal of him is used as evidence, he was transformed into a grotesque—cast at different times as a king, a satrap, a hoodlum, a mandarin, a pharaoh, a suzerain, an emperor, a fascist, and Genghis Khan. At the least, he was morally discredited.

Actually, he did display a sense of political morality, albeit one of a highly specific kind. It was narrowly shaped by a particular culture and place and time—namely, the Irish Catholicism of the working-class parishes of Chicago, where he came of age politically in the 1920s and the years of the depression.

A man of Daley's background learned to think of the parish as a haven for the values of Irish Catholicism, a preserve within the city. He didn't expect those values to occur spontaneously, any more than he looked for lilac bushes to spring up in the cracks in the sidewalk. He knew, or at least sensed, the importance of the parish apparatus—the buildings, the thirty-five or forty people on the staff, the money it took to keep it all going. He regarded the apparatus not as merely a convenience, a gross means to higher ends, but as an integral part of the religion itself: the values and apparatus were fused.

Daley had a similar feeling about The Organization. It also was a preserve, but for the values of a particular strain of the Democratic party. It also was territorial, following ward and precinct lines, as the parish followed geographic boundaries. It also kept up an apparatus, with its offices around the city, and its workers getting around by phone and on foot, and the money it took to run them all. Finally, its values and its apparatus too were fused, just as they were in the parish.

This notion might seem as flawed in city politics as it did in American Catholicism. There, of course, it was a leading target of church liberals after the Vatican Council. They felt the values and the apparatus of the urban parish could indeed be distinguished, the values into content, the apparatus into form. Too often, they showed, the values of

charity and dignity were neglected or even sacrificed for the sake of the apparatus—for the building funds, the football team, or a mean-spirited campaign to keep the parish white. They didn't call for a dismantling of the forms, since they felt it was crucial that the faith be a physical presence in the city. They simply didn't want to pay too high a price for them; the forms were really at the business end of the religion and should be kept within limits. This critique in itself suggests a more reasonable critique of Daley, on terms closer to his own.

It is fair to fault him for stressing the forms as much as he did. He did lapse too often into a merely custodial role. He did make his ward bosses feel they would be judged by how well they kept the apparatus running, and by little else. He did let the business end of The Organization spring its limits. His own rhetoric did become stale, and not only because he liked, now and then, to use his version of double-talk. It let him put off the press, muddle it, and gave him more time to watch the signs before he shaped a position. Also he did get caught up too far in the mechanics of the machine, its slates and procedures and its hundred-dollar-a-plate dinners. Much of the time he sounded like little more than a general contractor.

Yet it is only fair to credit him for what he did do through those forms. He did organize small kindnesses on a large scale. He did bring the social welfare values of the Democratic party down to the doorstep, where regular people could still get at them for a job or a loan, some help or advice, or even to shake hands with the devil. Through him, those values weren't just locked into the wording of a platform document somewhere. They were a presence in Chicago, the kind of tangible presence we can all see and understand: they had addresses, phone numbers, and they'd come and knock on your door if you asked.

Of course, a lot of people in Chicago came to feel the presence was Daley's own. *He* was there personally, they seemed to think, as if he would come by to help. Hundreds of thousands of the people in his city felt they knew him; there was an understanding between them, not on everything, but on some of the more important things. They turned him to their own purposes, wove him into their own sense of things. For all his power, he let them make of him what they would. For honest souls who wish to make moral judgments about politics, the career of Richard J. Daley will everlastingly remain a conundrum.

★★★

17

Dinosaurs & Neanderthals: The New Right vs. the GOP   J. Brian Smith

In public life politicians must weigh their deeply held principles against the needs of expediency. The former demand consistency, adherence to ideology, and persistence to the end; the latter implies compromise, bargaining, and the desire to find common ground for agreement. By some definitions, a political extremist is one who would rather lose a struggle than undermine deeply held beliefs. Are our major political parties guilty of political extremism in this sense?

The major parties have recognizable ideological differences, and both have their share of members who are ideological extremists. It is generally agreed among scholars that the Republican party is the purest ideologically, and shares a homogeneity among its membership unlike that of the Democratic party. Might this be a reason why the Republicans are the minority party today? J. Brian Smith contends that the only way the Republican party will ever again win public office is to find ways to expand its constituency. Do Republican conservatives support this position, or do they insist on ideological purity? Is there disagreement on this point between the "New Right" and the "moderates" and "liberals" within the Republican party? If so, how serious are these disagreements?

By and large, leaders of the New Right, argues Smith, are not Republican politicians. If not, who are they? Typically officeholders are confronted every day with the need to bargain, compromise, and make deals. But political activists drawn into politics to simply champion causes are less willing to abandon the principles to which they have committed so much time and energy. With this attitude, can they ever become effective politicians? Should a political party repudiate established ideology and principles in order to win more votes and secure political power? Or should it maintain a commitment to principle and win or lose accordingly?

★ ★ ★

DINOSAURS & NEANDERTHALS

THE NEW RIGHT vs. THE GOP

J. BRIAN SMITH

The Republican Party could be having a good year in 1978 if all the Republican Party had to worry about were the Democrats. Incredibly, though, just when the beleaguered GOP is showing signs of health not dreamed possible two summers ago, its biggest threat comes from its own right wing.

The New Right—the "dinosaurs," as they are called within moderate Republican circles—is determined systematically to oust Republican incumbents who do not agree with them on all issues at all times. To hear its spokesmen tell it, ideologically awry Republicans are more "evil" than even the most liberal Democrats. So they raise their funds and plot their strategy, often brilliantly, in order to rid the GOP of its impure elements.

I detest the New Right and I want it understood that my emotions have nothing to do with its philosophy. On the contrary, like many other Republicans, I am frequently made proud by the party's diversity. I have often seen Maryland Rep. Robert Bauman, a conservative, save the day for the minority with his mastery of parliamentary procedure. I have also listened spellbound to the oratorical skill in hot legislative debate of the liberal Illinois Congressman, John Anderson. On both occasions I have been proud to be a Republican.

My problem with the New Right is that it will tolerate a Robert Bauman because he fits its rigid ideological specifications, but wants to stamp out a John Anderson because he does not. Indeed, Anderson, a member of the House Republican leadership, narrowly survived a bitter primary challenge this year that was organized and funded by the New Right.

Anderson is by no means the only Republican target to be found in the cross hairs of the New Right. Dozens of other Republican officeholders find themselves more threatened by Republican opposition than by anyone the Democrats seem capable of bringing forward. In Maine, where the GOP has one of its few chances to pick up a Senate seat in November, Rep. William Cohen's race against incumbent Sen. William Hathaway has been compromised by the entry of an independent right-wing candidate recruited by the New Right. He has no chance of winning; his only purpose is to prevent the election of Cohen, the owner of a moderate voting record. It matters nothing to the New Right that Cohen's Democratic opponent has probably the most liberal voting record in the U.S. Senate.

J. Brian Smith is a senior partner in a Washington firm specializing in corporate public affairs. He is currently a political consultant for a number of Republican Congressional campaigns.

Aside from actually running its people against incumbent Republicans, the New Right is balking the GOP's potential rise from the ashes with an incessant flow of negativism and intra-party bickering. Consider the following examples:

¶ Howard Baker of Tennessee, the Senate Republican Leader, agonized for several months over which position to take on the proposed Panama Canal treaties. Despite considerable pressure from the New Right, he finally announced his support. Almost instantly he received a letter signed by fourteen House Republicans who informed him that his pro-treaty stand was incompatible with his responsibilities as Floor Leader and that he ought to step down while the Senate debated the issue. The Congressmen suggested that Michigan Sen. Robert Griffin, whom Baker edged by one vote for the top leadership spot, take over the reins. Griffin, learning of the letter, advised the Republican members to mind their own business.

¶ Edward Brooke is a Republican Senator from Massachusetts, the only state to go for McGovern in 1972, as bedrock a Democratic area as one can find. Last October, Republican voters in Massachusetts and elsewhere received a letter charging that Brooke had "done a great deal to oppose conservatives" and had voted much of the time with Edward Kennedy, the Senate's "Mr. Liberal." The letter, signed by Republican Congressman Steven Symms of Idaho, solicited financial support for Brooke's right-wing primary opponent. Eight GOP Senators then lodged a formal protest with GOP National Chairman William Brock against the "cannibalism" implied by the Symms letter. Brock agreed and suggested to Republicans everywhere that "our diversity can be our greatest strength."

¶ Mary Crisp, co-chairman of the Republican National Committee, has earned the antipathy of the New Right by supporting the Equal Rights Amendment as well as by her attempts to broaden the base of the party. When, last year, she was quoted in an interview with an Ohio newspaper as disagreeing with former Governor Reagan on a minor point, she was hit with a blast from Reagan aide Lyn Nofziger that was circulated to conservatives across the country. In October, when Brock accepted an invitation to address a Republican audience in Ms. Crisp's home state of Arizona, she sent a *pro forma* request to state GOP Chairman James Colter asking for permission to introduce her boss. Colter, a rabid right-winger, lashed out at her "presumption," adding, "I fail to see why I should afford you the high profile" of introducing Brock.

Examples of New Right meddling in Republican Party rebuilding efforts are numerous. In Virginia last year, John Dalton's campaign for Governor was running smoothly until the New Right decided to put on a mail campaign attacking the record of Henry Howell, his Democratic opponent, on school busing. The letter, signed by Virginia Republican Congressman J. Kenneth Robinson, was so filled with distortions that it gave Howell a chance to decry the "smear tactics" being employed against him. Dalton, who was not consulted about the mailing, was obliged to call a press conference and apologize for the "unnecessary and counterproductive" interference from the New Right. One wishes they would go away, these dinosaurs.

The leadership of the Republican Party has been reaching out to potential new electoral constituencies as never before. One example is National Chairman Brock's campaign to attract black voters. Already this novel effort has paid impressive dividends, as when the Rev. Jesse Jackson surprised everyone by suggesting that blacks should register Republican in order to "broaden their options."

Republican candidates are wising up as well. In years past many of them were criticized for dwelling on such cerebral topics as budget deficits and balance of payments. Now, at seminars run by leading party professionals, GOP candidates are counseled to drop the old rhetoric in favor of "people issues"—the high cost of food, financing a college education and the like. It appears to be working. The party has raised more money than it can spend—not from big business (which gave more to Democrats than Republicans in the last election) but from small donors. Last year 97 percent of the contributions received by the National Republican Congressional Committee were in amounts of $100 or less.

Democrats are doing their own bit to boost the GOP. President Carter's deteriorating public approval rating has triggered speculation that he may be a one-term President. For all the talk about Thomas "Tip" O'Neill being one of the strongest Speakers in history, the Democrat-run Congress has yet to pass an energy bill. And virtually all of the serious allegations of Korean-related scandal were placed squarely at the Democratic Party doorstep.

The Democratic leadership has sniffed danger in the wind. Since November 1976, there have been six special elections for House seats, all of which had been held previously by Democrats; the Republicans won four of them. But because the New Right is committed to the defeat of ideologically objectionable Republicans as well as liberal Democrats, the GOP is approaching the November elections with less momentum than it would have had if the dinosaurs had reserved their wrath for the other party. It's not that the New Right is all that strong; in fact its strength is vastly overrated. But the negative activities are causing a drain on the spirit of a minority party weary of defeat.

Who are the people who make up the New Right? More important, why are they so determined to check the advance of the Republican Party? It's a lot easier to say who they are *not*. They are not, for example, "con-

servatives" in the traditional sense. The GOP's top leaders—Brock, Rhodes and Baker—are all considered political conservatives. Yet John Rhodes could have been speaking for all three when he complained of the New Right that "whenever I take a position which is somewhat offbeat, maybe a little unpredictable, the roof caves in."

It is similarly unfair to attribute the negative activities of the New Right to the *very* conservative elements of the GOP. California Rep. John Rousselot is a case in point. As conservative on most issues as one can be without falling off the right-hand edge of the world, Rousselot is credited with having devised a clever scheme to rescue his liberal colleague and friend, Paul McCloskey, from a bitter right-wing challenge in 1974. Back then it was considered taboo for party leaders to become involved in primary contests. Nevertheless, to save his friend, Rousselot invented a "nonpolitical" reason to bring then Vice President Gerald Ford into McCloskey's district to speak. Ford's implicit endorsement (he was used subsequently in television ads) was a key factor in McCloskey's narrow victory.

As far as elected politicians are concerned, the list of bona fide New Righters is surprisingly small. Of the fourteen Republican Governors, only New Hampshire's Meldrim Thomson, who doubles as chairman of the Conservative Caucus, fits the description of a true dinosaur. In the Senate, most of the New Right's water is carried by Jesse Helms of North Carolina, with occasional help from Strom Thurmond of South Carolina and Paul Laxalt of Nevada. In the House, the New Right derives vocal support from Illinois Rep. Philip Crane, chairman of the American Conservative Union. Currently seeking the GOP's nomination for President, Crane once told a Washington audience that the Republican Party is to him a "passing interest," one of far less importance than "The Cause." Other die-hard adherents to "The Cause" in the House are Mickey Edwards of Oklahoma, Steven Symms of Idaho, John Ashbrook of Ohio and, at various times, Robert Dornan of California and Robert Bauman of Maryland.

But these elected individuals do not represent the real threat to the Republican Party; their influence is slight beyond their own states. The real directors of the New Right, the ones who set and carry out the anti-moderate strategy, are a talented group of nonelected technocrats. Paul Weyrich of the Committee for the Survival of a Free Congress, John Dolan of the National Conservative Political Action Committee (NCPAC), Howard Phillips of the Conservative Caucus, Morton Blackwell of the Committee for Responsible Youth Politics, Lyn Nofziger and, above all, Richard Viguerie are the ones who strike fear into the hearts of many Republican incumbents who hold moderate-to-liberal voting patterns and public positions.

Viguerie is an expert in political direct mail, "one of the three or four best in the country," according to Wyatt Stewart, one-time Viguerie protégé and currently the respected director of finance for the Republican Congressional Committee. While praising his former boss as "phenomenally successful," Stewart believes that

Viguerie's recent work suggests he may be "spread too thin."

Nevertheless, under Viguerie's guidance, the five major conservative political action committees have raised and spent more than $5 million since the last national election, much of it going to defeat Republican incumbents. Reagan recently announced that his committee, Citizens for the Republic, would no longer give money to aid intra-party challenges. However, considering the tight framework of the New Right fund-raising mechanism and the fact that many of the decisions about whom to oppose are made collectively, many political commentators are skeptical about whether Reagan will do more than change the way he keeps his books.

It is true that Reagan himself has gone to great lengths since he bloodied a GOP President in the 1976 primaries to observe the "Eleventh Commandment" (Thou shalt not speak ill of a fellow Republican), but most of the politicos who gravitate toward him observe no such piety. Says Weyrich: "We are different from previous generations of conservatives. We are no longer working to preserve the status quo. We are radicals working to overturn the present power structure of this country." Howard Phillips is even more picturesque. His allegiance to the Republican Party is such that he recently registered as a Democrat in order to challenge Sen. Edward Brooke in Massachusetts. "We organize discontent," he explains, adding, "We must prove our ability to get revenge on people who go against us . . . we'll be after them if they vote the wrong way."

Why the big fuss over Republicans who vote the "wrong" way? Isn't the real political game a matter of numbers—control of, say, the Congress—and don't large numbers entail diversity of thought and opinion? The answer is that the New Right has given up on the Republican Party as a viable force in American political life. And having given up all hope of ever reaching a GOP majority, the New Right has determined to settle for ideological purity.

Says Viguerie: "I don't believe in my lifetime you will ever again be able to successfully market the word 'Republican.' You could as easily sell the Edsel or Typhoid Mary. The Republican Party is like a disabled tank on the bridge impeding the troops from crossing to the other side. You've got to take that tank and throw it in the river."

As I see it, the Republican leaders face a difficult decision with respect to the New Right. They must either persuade it that the chances for significant gains in November are good and that it must agree to restrict its fire to objectionable Democrats, or they must cut this obstruction loose once and for all. For some time the New Right has been threatening to break away from the GOP. Perhaps the GOP ought now to follow the example of Abraham Lincoln who, on learning from an aide that a resignation letter submitted to him by a Cabinet officer was the third such attempt, announced, "I guess it's about time we took him up on it."

Certainly it would be better for the Republicans if the New Right agreed to fall in line; a minority party cannot afford to lose any of its support. And, there is much positive work that the New Right *could* do for the GOP if only it would. One example is the tax cut proposal introduced by New York Congressman Jack Kemp and Delaware Sen. William Roth—just the sort of program that could help dispel the "anti-people" image that the GOP carries everywhere. Why doesn't the New Right play up the Kemp-Roth bill instead of carping incessantly about Panama, the ERA and other issues it is *against*?

The answer to that question goes to the heart of what the New Right is and how it thinks. Conciliation and a positive attitude have never been its strong suits. A recent illustration comes to mind. Soon after President Carter announced his plan to extend until Election Day the period in which citizens can register to vote, the Republican Party leadership—Baker, Brock and Rhodes—surprised the White House by endorsing the concept. Then, under the searing heat from the New Right, Baker and Brock retracted their support; only Rhodes held firm. Careful to make his support contingent on White House acceptance of several important changes in the bill, the House Republican Leader took the statesmanlike position that voter apathy at the polls is bad for the country and that Republicans ought not to fear a greater turnout.

The next issue of Ronald Reagan's newsletter carried a cartoon of Rhodes, dressed in ancient Roman garb and plunging a dagger into the body of the GOP elephant. The caption: *"Et tu, Rhodé?"*

The New Right might have blasted Rhodes's position on voter registration; it might have encouraged its readers to write him in protest. Instead, it depicted the House Republican Leader—a long-time conservative who has labored tirelessly for the party—as a *traitor*!

That tells a lot about how dinosaurs think. □

★★★

18

"Reform" Is Wrecking the U.S. Party System   Everett Carll Ladd, Jr.

Though parties seem essential to democratic government, they have been criticized in fundamental ways. The Founders of this country feared the disunity they caused; the Progressives attacked the "machines" and "bosses" they fostered; and citizens have always been ambivalent toward them. For years there has been a movement to democratize our political parties because Americans "insist on their individual rights to determine electoral outcomes."

It is difficult to argue against democratic reform in America today, yet this is the thrust of Ladd's critical essay. What does he contend has been the result of party reforms? Why has the decline in influence by elected party leaders made the parties more unrepresentative? Much of the current agitation for and against party reform has evolved from the McGovern-Fraser commission's findings. What were its recommendations?

Ladd indicates that another result of party reform is that our parties today are less competitive than they once were. This has caused, argues Ladd, a "new era of unnatural landslides." What is implied by this assertion? He contends that, within the Democratic party, reform has produced a "New Class," which tends to misrepresent the party's rank-and-file voters. How do members of this New Class differ from rank-and-file Democrats on issues? In sociological background?

Ladd argues that our parties can no longer govern because they cannot bring together the diverse segments of our population. What are the reasons for this? He prefers a strong party organization to correct these party problems and agrees with others that Mayor Richard J. Daley of Chicago was probably the "best mayor in America" because of his strong leadership and firm control of the party.

In concluding this essay, Ladd suggests several ways to protect and revitalize our major political parties. Which remedies seem most effective in strengthening our party organizations? Given the nature of our times and the force of the democratic creed in America, do you think it is realistic to try to reorganize political parties as we once knew them?

★ ★ ★

Over the last decade, efforts to democratize the parties have made them unrepresentative and unable to govern.

"REFORM" IS WRECKING THE U.S. PARTY SYSTEM

by Everett Carll Ladd Jr.

Over the 1960's and 1970's the American party system has been performing strangely, yielding novel and all too often unfortunate results. In two of the last four presidential elections, for instance—1964 and 1972—the victors were beneficiaries of some of the greatest landslides in U.S. history. But the voters did not so much confer mandates on Lyndon Johnson and Richard Nixon as declare their opponents unacceptable. There is every indication that these negative landslides had adverse consequences for the political order. Large numbers of people felt deprived of a satisfactory choice. The lack of competitiveness and the general atmosphere of negativism reduced the incentive to participate and made the campaigns a far less meaningful medium for policy debate.

We have seen over the past four presidential-nomination campaigns a series of successful and near-successful candidacies of a strongly ideological character: Goldwater in 1964, McCarthy in 1968, McGovern in 1972, and Reagan in 1976. In each case the contender enjoyed the support of only a tiny fraction of the regular party leadership and was the first choice of only a distinct minority of the rank and file of his own party. Yet two of these unrepresentative candidates managed to capture their parties' nominations, and the other two came very close indeed—and all this happened at a time when both parties were implementing a series of momentous reforms designed to make themselves more representative!

A precipitous fall in the polls

Then, in 1976, with the Republicans at their post-Watergate nadir and presidential victory available to the opposition virtually for the asking, the Democrats—the American majority party and the oldest political party in the world —brought forth a candidate who was almost completely unknown and untried in national politics. Not more than 3 or 4 percent of the electorate could even identify Jimmy Carter six months before he was nominated for the most important of all offices. It is not surprising that the Carter campaign encountered persisting doubt and skepticism on the part of the public. The voters were dissatisfied with things as they were but felt quite unsure whether they would be any better off with Carter in the White House. Partly for this reason, Carter's lead in the polls fell precipitously between July and October, and an election that had seemed destined to bring about the decisive retirement of a much-burdened incumbent became instead a near deadlock.

This series of strange electoral performances is chiefly the result of the pronounced weakening of American political parties that has taken place in recent decades—a process that by now has brought them to the point of virtual death as organizations. As a consequence of their increasing weakness, the parties are unable to perform a set of functions uniquely their own, and the whole political system has been rattled.

An American ambivalence

The enfeeblement of the parties has come to a head during the last decade, a span filled with partisan changes and experimentation that are conventionally billed as "reform." But if reform is understood to mean "the improvement or amendment of what is wrong," little of the sort has occurred. "Reform" proponents insist that the alterations have made the parties more democratic, more representative of the populace, stronger, more competitive, and generally better able to play their part in the governing process. In fact, the changes seem more to have deformed than reformed the parties. They have left the system on the whole less representative, less competitive, less able to govern.

The organizational weakness of U.S. political parties is in one sense an old story. Though Americans gave the world

Professor Ladd, who teaches political science at the University of Connecticut at Storrs, is author of Transformations of the American Party System, *soon to be issued by W.W. Norton in a second edition. This article draws on work he completed earlier this year while a visiting fellow at the Hoover Institution, Stanford University.*

its first party system, they have always been highly ambivalent about the institution. Party leaders have been seen pejoratively as "bosses" and parties themselves as no better than "necessary evils." This approach to party follows in large measure from the culture's distinctive individualism, which prompts Americans to insist on their individual rights to determine electoral outcomes, and specifically on *their* rights, rather than those of party leaders, to control the nomination process.

The reform movements of the twentieth century, however, have carried the enfeeblement of parties way beyond anything required by the culture. In the early years of this century, the Progressives took a number of critical steps in that direction, particularly through their generally successful advocacy of the idea that nominations for state and local office be controlled by voters who turn out in primaries rather than by the party organization. Over the last decade, a new burst of reform activity has picked up where the Progressives left off. It originated largely within the Democratic party, but in a less dramatic fashion it has engulfed the Republicans as well. And it has rendered the two great national parties unable to control the nominating process for the country's most important political office, that of President.

The current wave of party reform was set in motion by the tumultuous 1968 Democratic convention, which created a commission, headed first by Senator George McGovern and later by Representative Donald Fraser of Minnesota, to reform the party's system of delegate selection. The McGovern-Fraser commission regarded internal party democracy as the overriding objective and sought to promote it through a variety of measures, the most controversial of which was its recommendation of *de facto* quotas to increase the participation of previously underrepresented racial minorities, women, and young people. Nearly all the commission's proposals were subsequently adopted, and though some have been bitterly criticized in the years since, none has been abandoned in substance. Their most important effect has been that of destroying the mechanisms through which state party leaders controlled presidential nominations.

The McGovern-Fraser commission's changes required almost all delegates to be chosen through primary elections, or through caucuses or conventions open to all party adherents and committed to proportional representation for minority candidates. If a state Democratic party insisted that its central committee play a role in choosing delegates to the national convention, the number of delegates thus selected was limited to a maximum of 10 percent of the total. Proscribed was the practice whereby "certain public or party office holders are delegates to county, state, and national conventions by virtue of their official position." Use of the unit rule—under which a state's delegation votes as a bloc in the direction desired by the majority—was banned.

An unforeseen explosion

Party leaders in many states found the new caucuses and conventions so complex and unpalatable that they opted instead for presidential primaries; the rules made it easy for candidate supporters or issue enthusiasts to manipulate the proceedings and greatly weakened the position of the regular leadership. The result, quite unforeseen by most Mc-Govern-Fraser commission members, was an explosion in the number of primaries—from seventeen in 1968 to twenty-three in 1972, and subsequently to thirty in 1976. Whereas less than half of all delegates to the 1968 convention were chosen by primaries, nearly three-fourths of the 1976 delegates were selected that way.

Various counterattacks have been made by proponents of a stronger party role in the commissions that followed Mc-Govern-Fraser—but they have failed. Party control has not been revived; instead, it has continued to recede.

As the Democrats were making these dramatic changes, the Republicans were plodding in much the same direction. The low-profile Delegates and Organizations (DO) Committee was the G.O.P. counterpart to the McGovern-Fraser commission, and after the 1972 convention, the Rule 29 Committee continued the Republicans' reform efforts, paralleling the Commission on Delegate Selection and Party Structure (Mikulski commission), which was then operating within the Democratic party. While obviously the G.O.P. was not so occupied with affirmative-action measures to increase minority representation, it adopted new procedures for delegate selection that are basically the same in their anti-party thrust as those of the Democrats. And even if the Republicans had done nothing along these lines, they still would have felt the effects of reform. Many of the Democrats' changes—particularly the increased use of primaries—have been written into state law and so apply to both parties.

Reform has weakened the parties indirectly as well as directly. When nearly three-fourths of all Democratic convention delegates (and more than two-thirds of Republican delegates) are selected through primaries, for example, serious candidates have to create elaborate personal organizations to wage the costly and far-flung campaigns that are a precondition of winning. The victorious contender, once his nomination is in hand, is hardly about to disband the apparatus he put together for the primary struggle. He relies upon it and not on the party in the general election. Much attention has been devoted to the Committee to Re-elect the President, the now-disgraced instrument of the Nixon forces in 1972. Yet for all its excesses, CREEP was in many ways the prototypical contemporary electoral organization: it was formed to serve the interests of one man; it placed these above the party's; and its substantial resources enabled it to disregard the party in contesting for the presidency.

The new handicappers

Broad social changes have also helped to bring parties to the verge of organizational extinction. The populace is much more highly educated than ever, has many more sources of political information, clearly feels less dependent upon party as an active intermediary in the electoral process—and it is sharply and irreversibly more inclined to participate on an independent, nonpartisan basis.

The rise of the national press has also played a part in weakening the parties. Increasingly it has taken over important facets of the communications role that once was performed by party organizations. As journalist David Broder has observed, newsmen now serve as the principal source of information on what candidates are saying and doing. They act the part of talent scouts, conveying the judgment that some

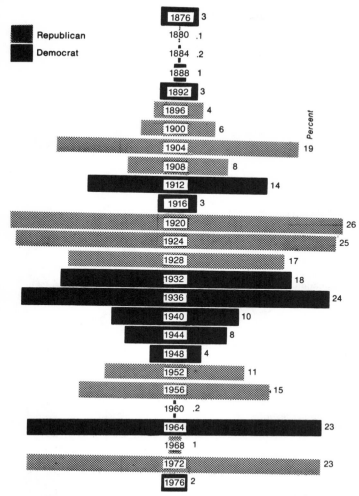

Year	Percent
1876	3
1880	.1
1884	.2
1888	1
1892	3
1896	4
1900	6
1904	19
1908	8
1912	14
1916	3
1920	26
1924	25
1928	17
1932	18
1936	24
1940	10
1944	8
1948	4
1952	11
1956	15
1960	.2
1964	23
1968	1
1972	23
1976	2

■ Republican
■ Democrat

A New Era of Unnatural Landslides

As the chart shows, margins of victory in presidential elections have tended to be pretty big since 1920. (The bars represent the percentage-point difference between the winner's and loser's shares of the popular vote.) Since 1964, however, the big wins have been "unnatural landslides," reflecting not so much the electorate's enthusiasm for the winning candidate as its antipathy toward the loser.

contenders are promising while dismissing others as of no real talent. They also operate as the race caller or handicapper, telling the public how the election contest is going. At times they function as public defenders, bent on exposing what they consider the frailties, duplicities, and sundry inadequacies of a candidate; and in some instances they even serve as assistant campaign managers, informally advising a candidate, and publicly, if indirectly, promoting his cause.

With so much going against parties, one might have hoped for a modest dose of "countercyclical policy" to bolster a deteriorating but useful institution. Just the opposite, however, has been happening. For example, federal funding of presidential campaigns, voted into law as a means of "cleaning up" national politics, has reduced the dependency of candidates on party and on the interest groups that have served as prime building blocks of party organization. A number of proposals for further electoral reform now under consideration would have a similar effect. For example, there is strong support these days for a constitutional amendment to eliminate the

electoral college and substitute direct election of the President. Whatever the proposal's overall merits, it would reduce the role of state parties by making state boundaries irrelevant to election outcomes. Candidates would become even freer to campaign without regard to the blocs, alliances, and structures that state party systems are built on.

There has been inadvertence and bad planning and just plain stupidity in all of this. But above all, the attack on political parties has come as a result of a straightforward and quite conscious pursuit of group interests. Senator McGovern for one has conceded that there are risks in "democratizing" the party, "opening it up," reducing the domination of "bosses" or "elites," and permitting "the people" to decide who the nominees will be. But he considers the risks to be worth it. "The alternative," he says, "is a closed system where you say the elite are better able to run the country than rank-and-file citizens."

The people aren't the winners

McGovern could not be more wrong in his notion that it is "rank-and-file citizens" who benefit from party "reform" and the elite who suffer; just the opposite is the case. For a century and a half, U.S. political parties, with all their faults, have been a force for extending democracy. Can there ever have been any real doubt that, were party removed from control over presidential nominations and the public invited to fend for itself in a lightly structured selection process, the winners would not be "the people"? In fact, it has been upper-middle-class groups, not the broad mass of Americans, who have confronted the party organizations, who have held them to be unresponsive to their policy perspectives, who have attacked the legitimacy of "bosses," who have urged "democratization." And it is these highly educated, well-informed, relatively prosperous groups who have primarily benefited from party "reform," for they tend to participate in more open nomination processes at a rate that far exceeds that of "rank-and-file citizens."

That party reform serves the interests of the upper-middle class can be seen in the statistics on voter turnout in primary elections. There has been much hand wringing of late about low turnout in recent general elections, but participation in them is positively robust compared with that in the primaries. In 1976, for example, in the twenty-eight states that held presidential primaries and kept statewide data on them, just 28 percent of the voting-age population went to the polls, as compared with 54 percent casting presidential ballots from those states in the November election. And there was nothing unusual about this. In the eleven state presidential primaries that were contested within both parties between 1948 and 1968, the average turnout was 39 percent, as against 69 percent in the same states' general elections. Between 1962 and 1968, the average turnout in gubernatorial and senatorial primaries in states with two-party competition was 28 percent, or less than half the 61 percent rate for the ensuing general elections.

Participation in primaries varies sharply according to socioeconomic status, with the higher-income and better-educated groups turning out in much greater proportion than other segments of the population. CBS and the New York *Times* surveyed presidential-primary voters in 1976, as did

NBC, and in state after state they found that the participants came disproportionately from the ranks of these overlapping groups: the college-trained, the professional middle class, and those with upper-middle to high income. In New York State, to cite one instance, 41 percent of the Democratic primary electorate held professional or managerial jobs and 30 percent were college graduates—proportions far above those for all New York Democrats.

And when one turns to participation in the "open" caucuses mandated by the current wave of reform, the turnout is even lower and more skewed than in the primaries. Twenty-one states held delegate-selection caucuses in 1976, and the average number of citizens who showed up represented just 1.9 percent of the voting-age population.

That the slice actually voting in the new open processes is small and demographically unrepresentative does not necessarily mean that the delegates and the nominees they select will be out of step with rank-and-file policy preferences. But the potential for a clash with mass wishes is high.

The 1976 Republican presidential contest provided a striking indication of how vulnerable the parties now are to unrepresentative candidacies. From March through June of that year, Gerald Ford consistently outdistanced Ronald Reagan in popular support among all Republicans and independents by margins of around 2 to 1. According to Louis Harris, for example, Ford led Reagan 60 percent to 40 percent in late February, 66 to 34 in late March, 67 to 33 in May, and 61 to 39 in July. Yet Ford and Reagan split the primary vote almost evenly. Democratic crossovers accounted for only a small part of the discrepancy between rank-and-file preferences as described by public-opinion polls and the actual primary vote. The main factor was simply that the primary voters were much more conservative than all Republican adherents. The choice of the broad mass of party adherents finally prevailed at the Republican convention, of course, but Ford was bruised by a long seesaw struggle that, if the rank and file of party supporters had had their way, would never have happened.

On the Democratic side, much has been made of George McGovern's success in capturing his party's 1972 nomination in spite of the fact that at no time during the long primary and preconvention struggle was he popular with the rank and file of his own party. The convention that formally nominated McGovern was strikingly unrepresentative of the policy preferences of the mass of Democrats (see the chart above). When he won the nomination, Senator McGovern declared that it was "all the more precious in that it is the gift of the most open political process in our national history." One must note that this "most open political process" produced one of the most unrepresentative outcomes in our national history.

And in 1976 things remained the same in some crucial respects. To be sure, the nominee that year was a man who had clearly established himself during the primary as a centrist popular with the party's rank and file. Yet the convention itself was as unrepresentative as it had been four years earlier. The delegates may have nominated Carter and done his bidding on the platform and related matters, but they had little in common with him or the mass of Democrats ideologically. They resembled, not the rank and file, but the New Class—the young, college-educated, professional and managerial groups who have been especially advantaged by the recent recourse to "open" selection mechanisms. They stood

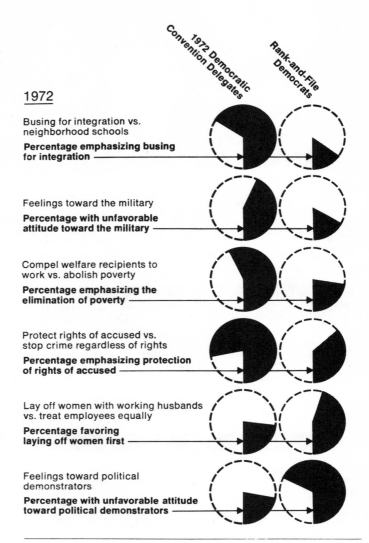

1972

Busing for integration vs. neighborhood schools
Percentage emphasizing busing for integration

Feelings toward the military
Percentage with unfavorable attitude toward the military

Compel welfare recipients to work vs. abolish poverty
Percentage emphasizing the elimination of poverty

Protect rights of accused vs. stop crime regardless of rights
Percentage emphasizing protection of rights of accused

Lay off women with working husbands vs. treat employees equally
Percentage favoring laying off women first

Feelings toward political demonstrators
Percentage with unfavorable attitude toward political demonstrators

far to the left of the rank and file, particularly on the issues of the New Liberalism—such as whether the U.S. should have a softer foreign policy vis-à-vis the Soviet Union, whether defense spending should be cut, and various social and moral questions ranging from abortion to busing.

A polarization of activists

Not only have the national parties become more open to the activists—mainly the college-educated—but the activists themselves have undergone an important transformation. For one thing, their numbers have grown by leaps and bounds, especially because of the expansion of higher education. At the same time, their attitudes have been changing. During the 1930's, 1940's, and 1950's, there was no broad ideological difference between the views of the college-educated and those of the rest of the population. Today, by contrast, there is a very considerable difference. College-trained Democrats are noticeably more liberal—especially on issues of life-style and morality—than their party's rank and file, and college-educated Republicans are consistently more conservative than their party's mass membership.

If the formal mechanisms of party had not been so abruptly dismantled, they might have provided some barrier to the

By Their Own Standards, the Reformers Have Failed

The most important objective of the Democratic "reform" movement of the last decade has been to make the party's national convention a more open and representative body. Yet the changes the reformers have instituted have had no such effect. As these charts show, the political attitudes and policy preferences of the delegates to both the 1972 convention (at left) and the 1976 convention (at right) were sharply at odds with—and greatly more liberal than—those of the party's rank and file. As those pie charts on the right demonstrate, the 1976 delegates' views were strikingly similar to those of "New Class" Democrats—young, college-trained Democrats in professional and managerial occupations. This similarity is no accident. Members of the New Class have benefited disproportionately from the new delegate-selection processes because they participate in presidential primaries and "open" caucuses at a rate far higher than that of any other part of the population. By contrast, the 1976 delegates' views were sharply different from those of older, non-college, blue-collar Democrats, who make up the party's declining, more conservative "Old Class."

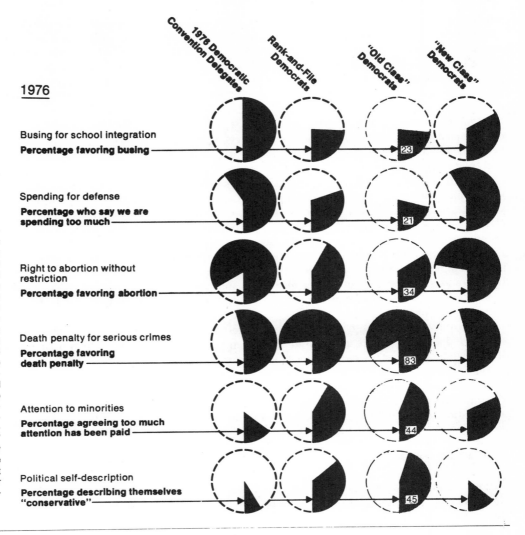

1976

1976 Democratic Convention Delegates · Rank-and-File Democrats · "Old Class" Democrats · "New Class" Democrats

Busing for school integration
Percentage favoring busing — 23

Spending for defense
Percentage who say we are spending too much — 21

Right to abortion without restriction
Percentage favoring abortion — 34

Death penalty for serious crimes
Percentage favoring death penalty — 83

Attention to minorities
Percentage agreeing too much attention has been paid — 44

Political self-description
Percentage describing themselves "conservative" — 45

---

excessive intrusion of activists representative neither in socioeconomic makeup nor in political preferences of the mass of party adherents. In 1976, for example, Gerald Ford was the choice of a large majority of Republican party leaders and elected officials around the country, just as he was the favorite of the rank and file. The leaders wanted Ford because they concluded that partisan *raison d'état* required his nomination. He was the incumbent, had not done badly, was well positioned between the main ideological camps, was accepted by a broad spectrum of the electorate, had at least a chance of winning, and almost certainly would not lose badly. If these Republican leaders had still been in charge of candidate selection, Ford would have won the nomination easily.

A promiscuous majoritarianism

It is not just by chance that the established leadership was more representative of the G.O.P. rank and file than were the activists who dominated the 1976 delegate-selection process. Party regulars—the leaders of the "organization"—have long been inclined to use what control they have over the nomination process to satisfy mass preferences as among candidates. People who spend their lives within party organizations naturally want to assure the survival and pro-

mote the growth of these enterprises, and under the American two-party system, the attainment of those goals depends on the party's success in winning a plurality of the votes in the general election. Thus party leaders and others with strong party ties tend to practice an almost promiscuous majoritarianism that rejects ideological distinctiveness and stresses representation of the tastes of the many.

When one moves outside that small slice of the population committed to party maintenance into the rest of the activist stratum, the mix of political motivations does not mesh so easily with the majoritarian ethic. Some of the activists are strongly wedded to advancing a particular program. Others articulate the claims of a single interest group. Still others may be moved by the personal virtues of a particular public figure, and so on. None of these motives is necessarily incompatible with majoritarianism: one can respond to any of them and still devoutly seek to win. But neither is there any necessary link between the activists' motivations and majoritarianism, as there is in the case of the party leaders.

The political party as a formal organization has generally produced representative nominees, not just because its leaders have a stake in winning, but also because they can do something that mass electorates cannot: *They can plan.* Even if by some stroke of fate 100 percent of a party's adherents routinely turned out in a primary, it would by no means be certain that representative nominees would result. Consider the hypothetical case of an electorate sharply polarized on ethnic lines, with one ethnic group a 60 percent majority. Add to this hypothetical situation a primary in which nominees for six different statewide offices are being selected. Given a high level of ethnic feeling, it is entirely possible that the 60 percent majority would nominate one of its own for each of the offices. The remaining 40 percent of the party's identifiers would find themselves shut out.

The situation is not really hypothetical, of course. Political parties have long confronted this sort of problem and have developed a fabled institution to meet it—the "balanced ticket." It is easy to look down on the practice of putting together a slate with "one WASP, one Jew, one black, one Italian, one Pole," or some such combination. But the balanced ticket is in fact a high and eminently sensible form of party planning. It is a response to the diversity of the electorate and an effort to put forward a group of nominees who *collectively* represent that electorate.

The public also wants good candidates as well as representative ones—individuals well suited to the complex tasks of governing. But just as party leaders no longer have the power to assure representative nominees, so are they unable to plan for competence and experience in the choice of presidential nominees. They are, of course, free to contemplate the question of who is the most able, but they cannot assure the implementation of their judgment.

Flea-market politics

Thus the U.S. has been reduced in presidential-nominee selection to a system of chaotic individualism. Each individual entrepreneur (the candidate) sets up shop and hawks his wares, i.e., himself. The buyers—the voters—do not find the same choice of merchandise in all the states, and one seller, who may attract only a small segment of all the buyers, is finally granted a monopoly. Candidates are able to win, then, because of crowded fields, low turnouts, and strategic miscalculations by their opponents—but above all because there is no one in charge. Increasingly there is no formal party mechanism in place with substantial authority to plan for the outcomes.

In August, 1950, a special committee on political parties of the American Political Science Association brought forth a report calling for a general strengthening of parties in the U.S. The stress of this report, like that of the writings of other advocates of strong parties reaching back to Woodrow Wilson, was on the role the parties play in meeting the public need "for more effective formulation of general policies and programs and for better integration of all of the far-flung activities of modern government." Few of the committee's recommendations have been acted upon positively. Today, the American party system is less able to integrate "all of the far-flung activities of modern government" than was its counterpart of a quarter century ago.

For one thing, at the national level, the presidential and the congressional parties have drifted further apart. In contrast to the situation that prevailed as recently as two decades ago, candidates for President now set up their own electoral organizations and go their own way with little regard for, or contact with, other sections of the party—including, surely, the congressional wing. Few members of the Democratic majority of the U.S. House and Senate, for example, had anything to do with the nomination of Jimmy Carter. Most congressional Democrats now take some satisfaction in the fact that one bearing their label is ensconced at the other end of Pennsylvania Avenue—but not all that much.

The American system has always provided, of course, for a formal separation of the executive and the legislature, and this in turn has made for a separation of the congressional and presidential parties quite without parallel in parliamentary systems. But in times past, the common bond of involvement in a party structure that determined presidential nominations helped to mitigate the rigid constitutional separation. That tie is gone.

Modern government is an incredibly complex instrument. It has so many different parts responsive to so many different interests that the natural centrifugal pressures are well-nigh irresistible. Party is the one acceptable counteracting centripetal force—and not only at the national level, but in the states and cities as well.

Once upon a time, many American cities were governed by parties. These "machines" surely had their venal aspects, but they were important instruments for integrating and harnessing the strong centrifugal forces at work in the modern metropolis. Not many of these "machines" have managed to survive, but one that carries on is the Democratic party of Chicago—the fabled organization of the late Richard Daley.

"The best mayor in America"

It was said of Mayor Daley's Chicago that it was almost unique in being "a city that works." Senator Daniel Patrick Moynihan of New York, recalling his days as director of the Joint Center for Urban Studies of M.I.T. and Harvard during the 1960's, when urban problems had become a major issue, points out that many urbanologists had the highest regard for Daley's accomplishments. For his own part Moynihan says Daley was "the best mayor in America." This sort of recognition reflects Daley's ability, through the vehicle of the Democratic party, to impose a little order on—and even to inspire a bit of harmony among—the diverse forces of that major city and thereby to lend some direction and coherence to its governance.

Daley's Chicago had its share of failures. But it seems incontestable that Chicago has been far better governed than, for example, New York, and the reason for this marked difference is party. For the quarter century of Daley's ascendancy Chicago had coherent party government, whereas New York has been a reformer's dream and a policy nightmare. New York City simply has not been governed; the centrifugal forces have overwhelmed the centripetal ones in its policy process.

Political parties as labels, as standards under which candidates run for office, are very much alive and well. There need be no thought of their passing. And there are many who would argue, as does one of President Carter's political aides, that "maybe we don't need parties anymore as intervening actors; maybe in the contemporary situation parties as labels are enough."

The balance of America's political experience with party "reform," however, suggests the contrary. We do need the kinds of services that only strong, autonomous party organizations can provide. By substantially removing party from nominee selection almost everywhere, we have eliminated the one institution able to practice political planning. By removing party from governance, we have aided the already strong centrifugal forces working against coherence in public policy. And even in the area of representation, where the reformers have made their proudest claims, it is at least arguable that the machinery of party achieved results superior to those of the putatively more democratic procedures that have been erected in their stead.

Protecting an endangered political species

So it is high time that the nation began rethinking public policy toward the parties. They have become an endangered species, and an all-out campaign ought to be launched to protect and revive them. Direct election of the President should not be established. It would deal too severe a blow to the already tottering state and national party systems. It is possible to take care of the problem of the "faithless elector" —and to remove any real possibility that a candidate without a plurality of the popular vote might win the presidency —within the structure of the electoral college. Federal funding of elections too much bypasses parties and encourages autonomous candidacies, and it should be ended. Looking to what are strictly intraparty decisions, the recent proposal by "strong-party" advocates on the Democrats' Winograd commission to make all Democratic governors, U.S. Senators, and Congressmen voting delegates to the national conventions by dint of their office should be revived. It is one concrete means of acknowledging and honoring the institutional aspects of party in the presidential-selection process.

The basic change that is needed, though, is simply a renewed appreciation of what useful things parties—as institutions and not just as labels—are to have around. If this should somehow come to pass, it would then be relatively easy to rebuild the parties as instruments for planning and representation within what must be recognized as a now-irreversible feature of the U.S. nominee-selection process—the widespread use of direct primaries. Restoring the organized parties to vigorous health and giving them back their central role in the presidential-selection process should be the No. 1 reform objective of the next decade.

★★★

19   The Swarming Lobbyists   *Time* Magazine

Lobbying by groups that represent special interests is as old as the nation itself, but it appears that this phenomenon has gained momentum and strength in recent years. Though lobbying carries the connotation of bribery, favors, and corruption, in fact, more subtle methods of persuasion are generally used to influence policy-makers. What are the methods used by modern-day lobbyists? Are all these methods considered to be ethical? Are all legal? Why has lobbying increased to the extent it has today? What effect have post-Watergate reforms had on this growth in lobbying?

The task of lobbying has become a much more complicated enterprise than in earlier times. What organizational changes in the Congress have complicated the nature of lobbying activities? How have the business, labor, and public interest lobbies responded to these changes? Does lobbying tend to favor conservative interests more than liberal interests? Though lobbyists are criticized for their secrecy, it would seem that they perform important functions for Congress and for our system of democratic government. What are those functions? Which interest groups are examples of public interest lobbies? In evaluating the arguments of these and other interest groups, what objective standards can be used to determine whether their interests truly serve the larger public interest?

★ ★ ★

Washington's new billion-dollar game of who can influence whom

The Swarming Lobbyists

Tax law reform. Killed.

Labor law reform. Dispatched to die in committee.

Consumer protection agency. Killed.

Hospital cost containment. Gutted.

The crude-oil tax in the energy bill. Stalled.

There is normally a complex of reasons for the failure of a major piece of legislation to emerge from Congress, and sometimes it is simply that there is no clear national consensus behind it. But in these five instances, and others like them, the force that proved decisive in blocking passage this year arose out of a dramatic new development in Washington: the startling increase in the influence of special-interest lobbyists. Partly because of this influence, President Carter has encountered serious difficulty in getting legislation through Congress; partly because of this influence, Congress itself is becoming increasingly balky and unmanageable.

The lobbyists have grown so able and strong that last week a mere handful of them was able to kill another bill, one of particular significance to them. It would have required the lobbyists to reveal who pays them, who they represent and what issues they have sought to shape.

The bill, which finally passed the House in April, came up last week before Senator Abraham Ribicoff's Governmental Affairs Committee—and was promptly consigned to either imminent death or limbo by the lobbyists. Leading the assault against it were such diverse persuaders as William Timmons, the former Capitol Hill liaison man for the Nixon and Ford Administrations, Freelancers Maurice Rosenblatt and William Bonsib, and Diane Rennert of the Association of American Publishers. In a multiple assault, they first threw their weight behind a much milder version of the bill, which was substituted for Ribicoff's stiff version. Despite telephone calls from the President, even the soft bill was then stalled indefinitely in committee, since no sponsor was willing to lead a

drive to get it approved by the full Senate. Declared triumphant Lobbyist Rennert: "It's dead, dead, dead."

There was irony in the spectacle of some of the most sophisticated generals of the vast new army of lobbyists, so skilled at casting the special interests of their clients in terms of the broader national good, now pleading so persuasively to keep their own operations secret. It was evidence of the extent to which the increasingly independent members of Congress have let the clashing voices of a multitude of special interests obscure their own sense of the broader national good.

Lobbying as such is scarcely a sin. Quite the contrary. "Without lobbying," declared three Senators (Democrats Edward Kennedy and Dick Clark, Republican Robert Stafford) in a joint statement on the lobby disclosure bill, "Government could not function. The flow of information to Congress and to every federal agency is a vital part of our democratic system. But there is a darker side to lobbying. It derives from the secrecy of lobbying and the widespread suspicion, even when totally unjustified, that secrecy breeds undue influence and corruption." Chairman Ribicoff observes that "lobbying has reached a new dimension and is more effective than ever in history. It has become a big computerized operation in which the Congress and the public are being bombarded by single-issue groups." He adds: "The Congress and the public should be aware of who's trying to influence whom and why and for what."

The Connecticut Senator's concern is justified. Lobbyists approach their jobs with more intelligence, hard work and persuasive argument than ever before. While fewer than 2,000 lobbyists are registered with Congress under a largely ignored 1946 law, their actual number has soared from about 8,000 to 15,000 over the past five years. Their mass arrival has transformed Washington's downtown K Street into a virtual hall of lobbies. New office buildings springing up west of the

White House along Pennsylvania Avenue fill up with lobbyists as soon as the painters walk out. It is estimated that lobbyists now spend $1 billion a year to influence Washington opinion, plus another $1 billion to orchestrate public opinion across the nation.

There is probably not a single major corporation that does not now employ Washington lobbyists. Ford Motor Co., which kept three representatives in the capital in the early 1960s, today maintains a full-time staff of 40 people. Among the airlines alone, 77 have their separate lobbying staffs in Washington. More than 500 corporations, including some quite small firms, operate Washington lobbies, if only for the sake of what they consider prestige. (Only 100 corporations were represented ten years ago.) Of the roughly 6,000 national trade and professional associations in the U.S., 27% are now headquartered for lobbying effect in Washington, which has overtaken New York City as a center for such groups.

Apart from business and industry, 50 labor unions maintain their separate offices in Washington, often working independently from A.F.L.-C.I.O. Chief George Meany's 300-member staff, which occupies an impressive stone and marble headquarters near the White House. Politically aware action groups also have their lobbyists in Washington, including 14 that pursue the special interests of the elderly and six that deal with air pollution. Even the Virgin Islands Gift Fashion Shop Association has a lobbyist. Large staffs are maintained by such broader public interest groups as Common Cause and the Ralph Nader organization. Grumbles House Speaker Tip O'Neill: "Everybody in America has a lobby."

Why? One major reason is obvious and ominous: the ever increasing influence of federal law and regulation over the lives of all Americans, as well as over the businesses they operate and the groups they join. The Federal Government now has rules ranging from the establishment of whisky tax rates to the placement of toilets on construction sites, from the design of atomic power plants to the milk content of ice cream, from foreign arms sales to childproof tops on aspirin bottles. A single clause tucked away in the Federal Register of regulations (this year's version has already grown to a mountainous 32,000 pages) can put a small-town manufacturer out of business or rejuvenate an industry that was on the brink of bankruptcy. The lobbyist who gets the clause removed, or puts it in, can be worth his salary for 100 lifetimes. The very magnitude of federal spending—about $565 billion this year—reflects the stakes involved as competing groups try to get what they consider their fair share, or more.

As power has been centralizing in Washington, life in this technological age has grown increasingly complex. There is no way for each member of Congress, or even each specialized federal bureaucrat, to be sure of the precise impact of his decisions. Sometimes the consequences are far from what was originally intended. The ever watchful lobbyists are eager to point out such hazards, and they serve a vital function when they do.

Yet fundamental changes in the nature of Congress have not only brought more lobbyists to Washington but have also transformed the way in which they do their work. In its rebellion against the imperial presidency of Richard Nixon, Congress has reasserted itself as at least the equal of the White House in resolving basic issues of national policy. Congress now has its own budget committees with powerful influence over spending priorities. The lawmakers have decreed that when they pass an appropriations bill, the money must be spent; it is not an option, as Nixon and other Presidents often regarded it. In the aftermath of Viet Nam, Congress asserted its control over the authority to make war and insisted on a larger role in foreign policy. And as influence flowed toward Capitol Hill, the lobbyists followed.

At the same time, Congress has also reformed its procedures. It has stripped its once autocratic committee chairmen of their almost singlehanded ability to ram through a bill—or kill it. Power has been diffused to subcommittees, where even freshman Senators and Congressmen can wield considerable influence. As the seniority system has broken down, all members have found their jobs more demanding—and many of the oldtimers have quit, complaining that Congress is "no fun any more." This, in turn, has produced a remarkable turnover in membership (more than half the Representatives have been in office fewer than six years), attracting young,

aggressive lawmakers determined to make up their own minds on all issues. Often elected from districts with no strong party preference, they listen a lot to what the folks back home are telling them, and what their constituents are saying is increasingly inspired by lobbying campaigns initiated in Washington.

While all those changes offer today's lobbyist golden opportunities, they also vastly complicate the lobbyist's job. Instead of cozying up to a few key chairmen or a powerful Speaker, the lobbyist must do tedious homework on the whims and leanings of all the legislators; he can never be certain when some relatively obscure member may prove to be the key to passing, killing or amending a bill. Lobbying now demands, as never before, highly sophisticated techniques, a mastery of both the technicalities of legislation and the complexities of the legislators' backgrounds, and painstaking effort. It is thus understandable that contemporary lobbyists relish tales of the simpler, if splashier, days in their trade.

A century ago, lobbyists could swing votes in the relatively sleepy town of Washington by applying what Congressional Correspondent Edward Winslow Martin in the 1870s called "levers of lust." Seductive "lobbyesses" were often more effective than bribes in courting key legislators. Asked Washington Journalist Ben Perley Poore: "Who could blame the Congressman for leaving the bad cooking of his hotel or boardinghouse, with an absence of all home comforts, to walk into the parlor web which the adroit spider lobbyist has cunningly woven for him?" But bribes were not ignored. By one estimate, at least $200,000 of the $7.2 million spent by the U.S. to buy Alaska in 1867 ended up in the pockets of Congressmen. Pennsylvania Republican Boss Simon Cameron, who served briefly and profitably as Lincoln's Secretary of War, summed up the financial ethics of the period: "An honest politician is one who, when bought, stays bought."

There may always be some members of Congress who can be seduced to trade their votes for bribes or women. The Korea lobby scandal is evidence of the corruption that may always endanger the delicate relationship between the lobbyist and the lobbied. Yet until the recent reforms in Congress, the modern lobbyist's most effective tactic was to concentrate on the committees where the vital decisions were made. A few decades ago, A.F.L.-C.I.O. Lobbyist Walter Mason helped labor's cause by getting Pennsylvania Republican Carroll Kearns so drunk on the nights before key meetings of the House Education and Labor Committee

that he was unable to cast his usual antilabor vote.

More recently, Railroad Lobbyist Pat Matthews cultivated a rewarding friendship with former House Ways and Means Chairman Wilbur Mills. Matthews had a network of railroad men who knew their home Congressmen intimately. Whenever the secretive Mills wanted a quick head count of the House on any issue, he flashed the word to Matthews. Within a single afternoon, back would come a surprisingly accurate count, and Mills could plot his strategy. In exchange, clauses benefiting railroads readily found their way into legislation from Mills' committee.

You can't grease it like that any more," observes Michael Cole, chief lobbyist for Common Cause. "You don't have Ways and Means wired because you're a friend of Wilbur Mills." Or, more currently, Chairman Al Ullman, whose control over Ways and Means is greatly diminished. A decade ago, the A.F.L.-C.I.O.'s skilled lobbyist Andrew Biemiller would figure that any clear labor issue had roughly 180 votes for it and the same number against it. He and his aides had only to work on about 75 Congressmen, whom they rated as "leaners," for or against them or so uncertain as to be considered "wobblies," "shaky legs" or even "bed wetters." Now Biemiller figures that only about 135 Congressmen can reliably be counted on to aid or oppose labor's position, and some 300 have to be individually assessed.

If that fuzzing of ideological lines has complicated the lobbyist's life, it has also given him fertile ground in which to cultivate votes. So too has the decrease in White House leverage on Congress. This is partly due to the relative ineffectiveness of Carter's own lobbyists on the Hill. "I like Frank Moore," says one labor lobbyist about the President's chief congressional liaison, "but he's a greenhorn. He's lost in Congress." Carter's own mild approach to Congress is also at fault. Some veterans on the Hill vividly recall Lyndon Johnson's brutal lobbying as President. "What do you do when the President gets you on the phone and eats your consummate ass out?" asks Ribicoff about L.B.J. "He told me what a lowlife bastard I was and how I'd better get right with God." When L.B.J. promised Tip O'Neill to keep the Boston Naval Shipyard open in return for a favorable vote, the Massachusetts Congressman was pleased. Yet when Carter implied similar home-state favors to a few Senators on the Panama Canal treaties, they complained loudly about unfair presidential arm twisting.

The new lobbyists in Washington have eagerly charged into the openings created by a weakened presidency and a more independent and less rigidly organized Congress. One of the most striking aspects of this new lobbying is the willingness of Big Business to join in. While corporations still somewhat squeamishly call their lobbyists "Government affairs specialists" or "Washington representatives," the fact that the heads of multibillion-dollar firms are now willing to plead their causes personally shows their awareness that Government is not going to retreat from its intrusion into their corporate lives. "Fifteen years ago, the businessman was told that politics is dirty, you shouldn't get involved," observes Albert Abrahams, chief lobbyist for the influential National Association of Realtors. "Now they know if you want to have a say, you've got to get in the pit."

The most visible symbol of the business world's new willingness to get into the trenches is the Business Roundtable, composed of nearly 200 top officers of the nation's most powerful corporations (among them: A T & T, Boeing, DuPont, General Motors, Mobil Oil, General Electric). The group's policy committee convenes monthly in New York to stake out positions on pending legislation and plot strategies to influence the outcome. Often invited to the White House, the executives get their views across to the President. While in Washington, some stay on to buttonhole legislators. Says one lobbyist: "A Congressman is impressed by the head of a corporation coming in to see him. Before, it was below a businessman's dignity to do that."

Yet some of the more aggressive new business lobbyists scoff at the Roundtable, contending that the corporate bosses flinch from a real fight out of fear of union retaliation. "The Business Roundtable is the most ineffectual lobby in Washington," contends Paul Weyrich, who heads a conservative lobby named the Committee for the Survival of a Free Congress. "They want to compromise before compromise is warranted. They never want to play hard ball." James McKevitt, a former Colorado Congressman who is the Washington counsel for the National Federation of Independent Business, is similarly scornful. Says he of the top executives: "Too many of them suck eggs with the President."

The most broadly respected business lobby is the United States Chamber of Commerce, which has far surpassed the once influential National Association of Manufacturers as a pragmatic power in Washington. As long as a decade ago, the N.A.M. was dismissed by one expert on capital powerbrokers as being lost in "a faintly fusty aura of dignity, lavender and the Union League." By contrast, the Chamber, operating out of a stately marble and limestone headquarters facing Lafayette Park, has come on strong. Embracing 2,500 local affiliates, 1,300 professional and trade associations and 68,000 corporations, it threw its weight behind 61 legislative issues last year, among them labor law reform, a consumer protection agency and public financing of congressional campaigns. It won 63% of the battles it joined—an impressive record in a Democratic Congress.

The Chamber's chief weapon, as is the case with all successful lobbies today, is the mobilizing of support at the grass-roots level. "We've never felt that we as individuals could cut much mustard at this," says Hilton ("Dixie") Davis, the Chamber's effective chief lobbyist. "It's the folks back home."

The local pressure is skillfully organized by the Chamber. Four of its lobbyists in Congress watch the progress of each bill that is worrying businessmen, then send an alert when a key legislative action is approaching. The word goes quickly to 1,200 local Congressional Action Committees with some 100,000 members. Through the Chamber's various publications, the alert soon reaches 7 million people. Thus when Washington headquarters signals an "action call"—the time for besieging members of Congress with letters, telegrams and phone calls—the membership is ready to move. The Carter bill that would have created a consumer protection agency was buried under just such an avalanche of Chamber-inspired mail early this year.

The Chamber also mans six regional offices in which some 50 operatives study the quirks and pressure points of Senators and Congressmen from their area. They pinpoint what the Chamber calls "Key Resource People," who have special local influence with a legislator. It might be a big campaign contributor, college classmate or law partner. At a critical moment, these regional staffs are told: "Get the K.R.P.s into the act." The regional offices also clip local editorials for pro-Chamber viewpoints and dispatch them to Washington. Two volumes of newspaper clippings were dumped on congressional desks with heavy impact in the Chamber's successful drive to stall passage of the labor reform bill.

Though political conservatives and Republicans are a minority in both the nation and the Congress, conservative lobbyists have lately created highly effective links with like-minded members of Congress. Liberals have long maintained such inside-outside combinations under Democratic Presidents, and still do. Labor lobbyists meet weekly with Carter's congressional aides. During the labor reform law battle, the A.F.L.-C.I.O.'s Biemiller worked out of Vice President Walter Mondale's office just off the Senate floor. But conservatives had neglected such possibilities, tending to vote their nays, accept the anticipated defeat, then share a congenial drink with their victorious opponents.

That is changing. "The belief that we can win—that's so vital," declares Chamber of Commerce President Richard Lesher. "If we stick to it, we can do it."

The key inside operator in the new conservative coalition has been Nevada Senator Paul Laxalt. Elected in 1974, he sensed that such conservative lobbies as the Right to Work Committee, with its large computerized mailing list, and a rejuvenated Senate Republican Steering Committee—unofficial counterpart to the liberals' Democratic Study Group—could combine to block passage of liberal legislation. He put that theory to work in 1975 in a coordinated conservative attack on labor's common situs picketing bill. To the astonishment of the labor lobbyists, the new combination stimulated enough grass-roots pressure to persuade President Ford to veto the bill—with a certainty that the Senate would sustain the veto. Since then, similar conservative cooperation has helped kill Carter's consumer protection agency, election day registration of voters and public financing of congressional election campaigns.

By far the most spectacular of the outside conservative lobbyists at the grass-roots level is Richard Viguerie, 44, a Houston-born specialist in mass marketing, who has compiled a detailed list of some 4 million conservative activists. Operating out of a handsome office building in McLean, Va., Viguerie and his 300 employees man two IBM computers that can break out lists of likely contributors with details of how they stand on particular issues and what they have given to which candidates or legislative drives in the past. He considers his magnetic tapes of lists so valuable that they are guarded 24 hours a day —and duplicates are kept in a secret mountain hideaway. Indeed they are valuable. His company grossed an estimated $3 million last year from the use of his tapes to stimulate mass mailings.

Viguerie figures he will send out 100 million letters this year at a cost to his clients of about 22¢ a letter. His company nets at least three of those 22 pennies. More carefully targeted mailings go first-class and include a stamped return envelope for contributions; the postage alone costs 30¢ a letter. The purpose of most Viguerie letters is to ask the recipients to send their own pleas (postcards and wording provided) to their local members of Congress to act for or against a bill—and to send a donation to cover the cost of Viguerie's mailing. Says Viguerie: "It's a self-financing lobbying system. If you can make a mailing of 3 million and break even, what a success!"

Although he lost the fight, Viguerie takes pride in having dispatched more than 2.5 million letters against the Panama Canal treaties. He estimates that he was responsible for Senate Republican Leader Howard Baker alone receiving more than 100,000 letters urging him to vote against the treaties. Baker suspected the mail did not represent sentiment in Tennessee, ordered a private poll of his state—and found that 60% of the voters favored the treaties. He not only voted for them but worked hard to enlist other Republican Senators to do the same. Viguerie concedes that many legislators pay more attention to self-generated appeals than to a flood of obviously lobbyist-inspired mail. Nonetheless, insists Viguerie, "when a Congressman gets 40,000 letters on a single issue, he ignores that at his folly."

Labor and liberal lobbyists have no similarly sophisticated computer mailing lists, although they believe they nearly matched the conservatives in inspiring mail on the labor reform law—millions of letters flowed from each side, probably the largest total outpouring of mail on any legislative issue in U.S. history. Labor drew on its decreasingly effective but still formidable network of union activists, especially retired members who have the time and zeal to respond to calls for action from the A.F.L.-C.I.O.'s headquarters. The federation has 51 state organizations and 740 local units it can muster into political action; in all, it has some 105 separate unions and 14 million members. Yet it takes at least two weeks to energize its political pressure, unlike the almost instantaneous capability of Viguerie's operation. Says Labor Lobbyist Biemiller about Viguerie's computerized propaganda, "It's a goddam scary thing."

The A.F.L.-C.I.O. produced a film about the Viguerie system, with a narrator intoning: "This is a horror film, not the usual kind featuring haunted houses, creepy creatures, ghosts or ghouls. It's going on right now—and you are the target." Viguerie loves the film, has got a copy of his own—and sends it out to conservative groups to drum up more business for himself. When opposing lobbyists argue that Viguerie's letters distort issues in an emotional way—the Panama Canal treaties were "a surrender" and "a giveaway"—he does not apologize. His view: "You have to grab an issue by the scruff of the neck."

While the conservatives are gaining in the ideological war among the lobbyists, the once influential public interest lobbies are losing ground. By arguing too self-righteously for too long on too wide a range of issues, Ralph Nader has lost his formerly considerable effectiveness on Capitol Hill. Perhaps his biggest mistake was to rush out a series of profiles of the members of Congress—sketches so full of errors and misconceptions that he lost credibility on other issues. Indiana Democratic Congressman Andy Jacobs ridicules Nader. In a formal report Jacobs filed this year on contributions, he listed among his assets: "Name-calling attacks by Ralph Nader." He rated their value as "priceless." Contends Jacobs: "Nader has become a legend in his own mind."

Common Cause still has influence, largely because its retired founder, John Gardner, retains much public respect. Its current chief lobbyist, Fred Wertheimer, has offended many Congressmen with his public scoldings when they failed to vote as he wished, but another Common Cause lobbyist, Michael Cole, 34, maintains solid connections in Congress.

It is the new breed of bright and aggressive hired guns who typify the proliferation of lobbyists in Washington. Their approach to their jobs is individualistic and shrewd, their fields of specialization varied, and their specific results often difficult to document. Yet their ubiquitous presence has transformed the city. Speaker O'Neill, who does battle with many of these independent operators, does not resent them. Says he: "Give me a guy who has the smarts. That's what lobbyists are; they're smarts."

One of the brightest newcomers is Thomas Boggs, 37, whose clients include Mars, Inc., the candy manufacturer. Since Mars advertises to children on TV, Boggs was interested to hear that the Federal Trade Commission was considering a proposal to ban all television advertising aimed at children on the ground that it is inherently deceptive. Boggs met with a group of lawyers to plan a lawsuit against the FTC regulation. Then he had a different idea: "Why don't we simply go to Congress and stop this silly law?" Boggs went to the House Appropriations Committee, where he persuaded a few Congressmen who were already angry at what they considered bureaucratic distortions of congressional intent, to add an amendment to a pending bill to finance the FTC for the next year. It stipulated that none of the money could be used to pay the salary of any FTC employee who spent his time investigating advertising aimed at children. The amendment was approved in subcommittee by a 5-to-4 vote and by the full committee, 33 to 14. When the bill reached the House floor, the amendment was deleted—but the whole FTC appropriations bill was killed too. Boggs is confident that both the bill—and his amendment—will return.

Dean Burch, former chairman of the Federal Communications Commission, has switched sides and is now a lawyer-lobbyist specializing in issues that come before his former agency. His expertise enabled him to spot a seemingly harmless bill deceptively titled the Consumers Communications Reform Act as special legislation sponsored by A T & T, which would have effectively frozen out attempts by smaller telephone companies to give A T & T more competition. A T & T had proposed the bill under the aegis of a trade group called the U.S. Independent Telephone Association and had lined up 235 House sponsors, most of them unaware of how much it favored A T & T. Burch and a few colleagues, representing small communications companies, painstakingly sought out each of the 235 sponsors and explained what the bill actually would do. A T & T's proposal died in committee. What turned it around? "We started walking the halls," said Burch.

The American Medical Association's John Zap, a onetime official at HEW, is similarly shrewd in using the practical impact of a bill to switch a vote. When Florida Democrat Paul Rogers, who heads a House subcommittee on health and the environment, proposed a tough bill to control hospital costs, Zap quickly secured statistics on just how hard the proposal would hit hospitals in Rogers' district. Rogers then modified his own bill. Contends Zap: "That was a service to him as well as ourselves. He had not realized what would happen in his district if the bill became law."

Realtor Lobbyist Abrahams found a quick way to stymie overzealous interpreters of congressional intent within the Army Corps of Engineers. Congress had decided that any project causing the diversion of navigable waters should require a federal permit. The aim was to protect wetlands, and the statute was validly used to block a jet airport in the Florida Everglades. But Abrahams discovered that the Army engineers had defined navigable as any stream that discharges water at more than 5 cu. ft. per sec. That actually meant that thousands of small ponds built in tiny streams by farmers needed a permit. Abrahams only had to point out to key Congressmen that any creek "about 3 ft. wide and 2 ft. deep" came under the law, and corrective language was passed.

Contrary to alert lobbyists who make such useful clarifications of law, the National Rifle Association is an example of a very strong lobby that can aim concentrated pressure on a single issue so as to thwart majority public opinion. Despite polls showing broad support for gun controls, N.R.A.'s regular barrages of emotional mail have persuaded nervous members of Congress to reject gun-control bills 14 times in the past ten years. When the Bureau of Alcohol, Tobacco and Firearms proposed on its own to have all new guns marked with a 14-digit identifying number—without recording the owner's name—N.R.A. Executive Director Neal Knox alerted his lobby's sharpshooters. Result: the Senate compliantly decreed that none of the bureau's 1979 appropriations could be used on any such gun regulations.

Does Congress bow too meekly to the wizardry of the direct-mail lobbyists and their magical magnetic drums of computerized lists? Too often it does. It takes a self-confident Congressman to rely on his own assessment of whether the mail truly reflects the sentiment of the voters he represents. And while it is a cardinal rule of Washington lobbyists never to mislead a member of Congress in face-to-face argument, no such niceties limit the distortions many of the lobbyists deliberately stimulate at the local level.

There are other abuses in special pleading. Some Senators have willingly lent their names and their office letterheads to big mail campaigns, conveying the false impression that the pleas are endorsed by the Senate. A House subcommittee headed by New York Congressman Benjamin Rosenthal has discovered that hundreds of corporations have been deducting their grass-roots lobbying efforts as a business expense despite clear congressional and IRS declarations that they may not do so. A few lobbyists seem to be in an unreasonable rush to cash in on the money available in the business. Two former aides of Senator Ribicoff tried to start their lobbying careers by advertising their services to help Americans working abroad lessen their tax burdens —for a fee of $200,000. Ribicoff has denounced them, and their fellow lobbyists say they violated a rule of the trade: they were not discreet.

In turn, lawmakers are at fault in their dealings with lobbyists. Many of them hold annual fund-raising cocktail parties in Washington and pressure the lobbyists to buy tickets at $50 to $500 each. Congressional stars like Howard Baker and Warren Magnuson can easily raise $50,-000 through these affairs. Democrat Lud Ashley, chairman of the House Energy Committee, held a bash in July and netted about $30,000. Lesser lawmakers barely break even, but can't seem to shake the habit of staging such parties anyway.

"It's one of the seamy sides left in lobbying," protests one of the ticket-buying victims.

There may be more serious abuses in backroom dealings between lobbyist and lawmaker, as past scandals and the Korean bribery affair suggest. Yet on balance the relationship between the governors and the governed, even when the lobbyist does represent one of the nation's many special-interest groups, is often mutually beneficial, and perhaps indispensable, to the fullest workings of democracy. The increasingly knowledgeable and competent Washington lobbyist supplies a practical knowledge vital to the writing of workable laws. He does it at no public expense—and at only the cost of being sure his own interests get the fullest of hearings. All in all, that may not be a bad bargain, but it does represent a major change in the way the Government goes about the difficult task of trying to balance competing interests against the Constitution's demand to "promote the general Welfare." ∎

★★★

20   Washington: Jewish and Arab Lobbyists   Sanford J. Ungar

Interest groups represent the views of their constituents. But not all interests are organized for the purposes of lobbying. Also, some interests are more effective in communicating their message than are others. In this essay Ungar illustrates the inequality of interest group politics. Clearly effectiveness does not depend upon size alone. Despite the fact that only 3 percent of the U.S. population is Jewish, Jewish lobbyists are very effective. What evidence points to the success of Jewish lobbyists? What factors other than size are important in establishing an effective political lobby? How do we measure a lobby's success or failure? Ungar notes that certain "assumptions" govern our relationship to Israel because of the Jewish lobbying efforts. What are they? The Arab-American community, by contrast, has never been as influential in politics, and it possesses fewer effective resources. This situation is changing, however, as the article indicates. How are the Arab lobbyists beginning to have an impact? What worldwide events have assisted the Arab lobbyists in recent years?

Although interest groups are typically organized around domestic policy concerns, this essay shows the potential strength of interest groups in foreign affairs. Given their heterogeneous backgrounds, do Americans of ethnic background become politically more active in foreign affairs when the interests of their former homeland are adversely affected by our policies? Can you recall some instances when American ethnic groups became politically active on foreign policy issues?

★ ★ ★

The voice of the Arabs is heard more clearly in the corridors of power, but their lobby is a distant second to Israel's when it comes to size, efficiency, and fire power.

WASHINGTON: Jewish and Arab Lobbyists

Sanford J. Ungar

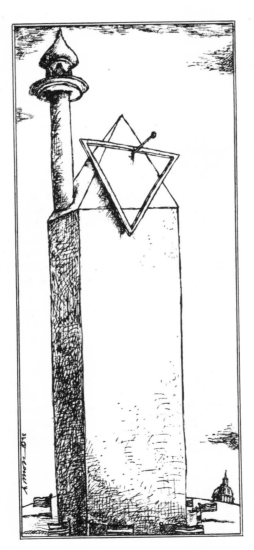

Four years ago, Fred Dutton admits, "I couldn't have stuck a pin in a map to identify the emirates." Today, he speaks of the Arabian peninsula as if the turf were as familiar to him as his own back yard, and the names of sheiks, oil ministers, and Arab princes roll off his tongue with ease. That is because Dutton—former Kennedy Administration official, onetime fund-raiser and campaign organizer for Robert Kennedy and George McGovern, liberal Democratic Washington lawyer extraordinaire—now represents the government of Saudi Arabia and its state oil company in Washington. Registered with the Justice Department under the Foreign Agents Registration Act as a provider of "legal and other services," Dutton says he spends about half of his time on the Saudi account; his fee for the first six months of 1977 was $270,490.

Other prominent Washington lawyers who draw handsome retainers from the Arab world include Democrats Clark Clifford (a former secretary of defense and frequent presidential emissary and confidant) and J. William Fulbright (a former senator from Arkansas and former chairman of the Senate Foreign Relations Committee) and Republican Linwood Holton (a former governor of Virginia).

But for those who tote up Arab and Israeli influence in the capital, the entry of Dutton into the field has special significance. He is a shrewd behind-the-scenes operator, a man who has often raised money for Democratic candidates from Jewish political activists and has long associated himself with the cause of Israel. Although his work for the Saudis largely involves drafting humdrum contracts with American corporations and briefing the ambassador from Riyadh on rudimentary matters of American politics, Dutton's involvement—and that of others like him—is bound to have an impact in the tight world of Washington policymakers. It helps put a stamp of respectability on the representation of Arab interests.

The competition for influence over U.S. policy in the Middle East is a tense one, a high-stakes Washington game that is never very far from the surface, not even in moments when peace seems about to break out between Israel and Egypt. The game has many assumptions and a few rules. One assumption is that the Israeli government really has to do very little, because the highly politicized, well-organized, and articulate American Jewish community will take care of things. On the Arab side, the converse is true: the Arab-American community is essentially docile, and the Arab nations themselves more active—with the corollary that the major oil companies, protecting their own interests, make expensive, subtle efforts on behalf of the Arabs.

Reprinted with permission from *The Atlantic*, March 1978. Copyright © 1978, by The Atlantic Monthly Company, Boston, Mass.

Another assumption is that the Departments of State and Defense have a strong pro-Arab bias, while Capitol Hill leans far in the direction of Israel; the National Security Council and White House staff can go either way.

A third assumption is that there is always extreme sensitivity, particularly in the Jewish community, to any official statement or action concerning the Arab-Israeli conflict. The Carter White House has been learning about this ever since the President's "town meeting" in Clinton, Massachusetts, last year, when he made his first public reference to the need for a "Palestinian homeland." He was inundated by expressions of protest and concern. Six and a half months later, the controversial Soviet-American joint declaration of principles for a Middle East settlement drew scores of immediate denunciations from Congress and 3500 spontaneous, differently worded telegrams to the White House for several days.

Notwithstanding these facts, one of the important rules of the game is that members of Congress who value their seats and other officials who are subject to public pressures do not complain about the efforts of the "Jewish lobby" or the "Israeli lobby." Those are code words, terms that often conjure up the specter of anti-Semitism and play into the hands of conspiracy theorists who recite the old canards about Jewish control of the media and the banks.

Yet the undeniable fact is that the American Jewish community has for years deployed an extraordinary arsenal on Israel's behalf in the capital. At the heart of the arsenal are old-line, tried-and-true organizations such as the American Jewish Committee (AJC) and the Anti-Defamation League of B'nai B'rith, which originally made their mark fighting discrimination and prejudice and only later turned to mobilizing support for Israel. Recognizing that Jews make up only about 3 percent of the U.S. population, they worked to create a secular constituency on behalf of the Jewish state. (Their success was notable; public opinion polls have consistently shown widespread popular backing for the continued existence and security of Israel.) As Hyman Bookbinder, longtime Washington representative of the AJC, recently told a CBS television interviewer, "We know that the Jewish interest cannot be pursued, cannot be protected, unless at least half of the American people and half of the American Congress believe that our concerns are appropriate concerns . . . unless we get another 48 percent added to our 3 percent—51 percent, in other words—we cannot protect our interests."

But the lion's share of the burden of protecting those interests in Washington today is assumed by the only Jewish group that is actually registered to lobby on Israel's behalf, the American Israel Public Affairs Committee (AIPAC). Started in 1954 as an outgrowth of the American Zionist Council, AIPAC has representatives of every other major Jewish organization on its board and draws on their resources at the grass roots. For more than three years, the hard-driving force of AIPAC has been Morris J. Amitay, the forty-one-year-old executive director, an intense and ingenious man who trained for his assignment during seven years as a Foreign Service officer and five years as a legislative assistant on Capitol Hill.

Amitay runs an office a few blocks from the Capitol that is widely envied and increasingly imitated. He uses an annual budget of $700,000 to create an impact that others could not achieve with millions more. AIPAC's research library is one of the best in town on the subject of the Middle East; many journalists, and even the State Department, regularly call upon it for assistance. (One of its rare commodities is a set of bound volumes containing every single statement or document on a Middle Eastern topic that has appeared in the *Congressional Record* during the past twenty-six years.) The office's printing and processing facilities are as up-to-date as any in Washington, and it also buys and gives away hundreds of copies of any newly published book that is favorable to Israel.

AIPAC monitors every piece of legislation in the United States Congress that arguably affects Israel's security and diplomatic interests. In a moment of perceived crisis, it can put a carefully researched, well-documented statement of its views on the desk of every senator and congressman and appropriate committee staff within four hours of a decision to do so. For credibility's sake, AIPAC's four lobbyists now include one Republican and one gentile. Whenever a member of Congress in a key position hires a new staff person to handle Middle Eastern questions, one of the first phone calls the staffer receives is invariably from AIPAC, offering friendly help and consultation.

Operating as he does, Amitay has become a controversial figure in his own right. (Last summer his house in the Maryland suburbs was bombed at 3 A.M., in an incident that was possibly linked to the assassination of an Israeli military attaché in 1973.) Some congressmen complain—rarely for quotation—that he has become too demanding and uncompromising in his quest for support of Israel. During the debate on last year's foreign aid bill, for example, which contained $1.785 billion in military assistance and credits for Israel, Amitay and his staff upbraided many legislators who announced they would vote against the measure because of their objections to money included in the bill to fund international institutions that lend to Vietnam, Angola, Cuba, and Uganda, among others. (When the conference report on that legislation finally did clear the House on a 229-195 vote, it was in part because of the widespread support for Israel, and White House officials called Amitay to thank him for AIPAC's crucial help on the issue.)

One young congressman who has reluctantly spoken up about AIPAC's overreach is Toby Moffett, thirty-three, Democrat of Connecticut, who is of Lebanese origin but has generally pleased his large Jewish constituency in the Hartford suburbs by voting in line with Israeli interests, despite his resistance to some aid bills and military appropriations. (He cosponsored a resolution with Senator Frank Church, Democrat of Idaho, calling attention to the plight of Jews in the Soviet Union.) "To question is in [AIPAC's] view to oppose, and that is considered traitorous," complains Moffett. "There has been an attempt to portray a perfect consensus of American Jews on every issue, and everyone knows that can't be true."

Moffett worries lest his criticism be misunderstood. "Admittedly," he says, "I'm not a Jew. I've only read about the Romans and the pogroms in czarist Russia and the Nazi Holocaust. I may not be capable of appreciating this feeling . . . but I think we'd all be better off opening a dialogue. . . . You have to resist voting for something just because it has a particular country's name on it."

At the same time, Moffett complains about the better-disguised pressures from the other side. "Oil has a whole lot to do with the Administration's [Middle Eastern] policies," he insists. "Whenever we're talking about energy policy, the State Department constantly sticks its head in the door and says, 'Oh no, we have to be nice to the Saudis.' So we can't do anything that puts a dent in OPEC." Say what he might, Moffett seems doomed to get himself into trouble. Militant Arab-American activists routinely attack him for failing to do enough to redeem his heritage, and yet his Republican opponent in 1976 meticulously exploited every remark Moffett had ever made calling for even-handedness or moderation in the Middle East; before he won his second term in the House that year, Moffett eventually had to run a newspaper advertisement headlined "LET'S SET TOBY'S RECORD STRAIGHT" and signed by eight Jewish congressmen from around the country.

Given the growing discontent with AIPAC, one might have expected the increasingly self-aware Arab-Americans to develop an effective counterforce on Capitol Hill. But that is far from the case. Unlike the Jewish members of Congress (five senators and twenty-two congressmen), the Arab-Americans have tended to regard their ethnic background as a political liability. Among them, only Senator James Abourezk, Democrat of South Dakota, has been outspoken on behalf of the Arab nations and the Palestinians—and that only after years of supporting Israel and after deciding (if not announcing) that he would not run for a second Senate term.

The five acknowledged Arab-American members of the House (there is rumored to be a sixth, but he has thus far refused to come out of the closet) rarely identify themselves that way and, apart from Moffett, seldom talk about the Middle East. They and Abourezk have never even met to discuss the issues, and the joke is told that when John P. Richardson, the newly appointed public affairs director of the National Association of Arab-Americans (NAAA), recently went calling on each of them, he had to enter their offices by the back door.

Richardson, thirty-nine, is the first official Washington lobbyist of the Arab-American community, and his initial efforts are very low-key and modest compared to those of AIPAC. He himself is not of Arab background, but became involved in the field through academic interests and then worked for years in Beirut and Washington for a group called American Near East Refugee Aid. As an outsider he has a certain advantage, because of the bitter differences in belief and emphasis among the subdivisions of the Arab-American community (mostly Lebanese or Syrians, with a growing and increasingly vocal component of Palestinians). Indeed, after a delegation of Arab-American leaders from NAAA went to see President Carter last December, they could not agree on a single spokesman to report to the press, but issued individual statements and competed with each other for attention.

The current president of the six-year-old NAAA, Joseph D. Baroody, a member of a prominent Republican family, points out that it would be impossible for his organization—a composite of some 1600 small local churches, social, cultural, and charitable groups—to focus on a single cause the way AIPAC can claim to represent Israel. "How could we ever represent everyone from Colonel [Muammar] Qaddafi of Libya to the [conservative] rulers of Saudi Arabia?" he asks.

Richardson says that his first goal on Capitol Hill is merely to supplement NAAA's general effort "to build respect for Americans of Arab background," much in the way that the Anti-Defamation League and American Jewish Committee did their best-known work years ago. From that base, the new lobbyist hopes to move on to "become a source of credible information and a valid point of view"—so that eventually a letter of protest going from Capitol Hill to the White House on behalf of Israel will not automatically obtain the signatures of seventy-six senators, as did a notorious one in 1975. As part of his own educational process, Richardson early on had lunch with Amitay.

Moffett warns that despite possible recent shifts in American attitudes toward the Middle East, the Arab-Americans will not win credibility in Washington overnight. "The American Jewish community has gained respect over the years because of its record on social issues like civil rights and the antiwar movement," he points out; "the fact is that Arab-Americans have not been progressive on social issues. Generally, when they got over here they were in a hurry to become wealthy and Republican."

Indeed, the White House is still playing by the old assumptions and rules. Relations with Arab-Americans, like those with most other ethnic groups, are assigned by Carter's political staff to the Office of Public Liaison, headed by an upstate New York politician, Midge Costanza. The Jewish community, on the other hand, takes up at least half the time of Mark Siegel, deputy to Carter's chief political adviser, Hamilton Jordan. (Siegel, once an aide to former Democratic National Chairman Robert Strauss, describes his only other major assignment as "the party.") His own views, Siegel acknowledges, are "terribly sympathetic to Israel," and he regards the Jewish organizations that are frequently in contact with him as his "constituents." All of this makes sense in a Democratic White House, he argues, given the fact that American Jews are very heavily registered as Democrats, especially in ten major urban states, and produce an estimated 90 percent turnout in most national elections. They contribute about half of the money in Democratic politics, and, as Siegel puts it, "as individuals they can articulate a policy. People will go to the synagogue and talk about F-15s" (the American fighter jets that Arab states have wanted to buy).

Recently, with Carter sometimes appearing to have separate positions on the Palestinian issue for the odd and the even days of the month, Siegel has had his hands full. Although about 75 percent of American Jewish voters are believed to have voted for Carter, many of his original supporters are now disaffected, and they bombard Siegel with complaints. The White House aide happened to be in Israel at the time of Egyptian President Anwar el-Sadat's historic visit to Jerusalem, and he is now convinced that "American Jewish opinion is more hard-line and less pluralistic than Israeli public opinion." Although there is an obvious "lag time in opinion transformation," Siegel believes that the Sadat peace initiatives are bound to have a softening effect on that American Jewish hard line.

The flurry of Egyptian-Israeli negotiations has probably already had an impact on the lives and attitudes of all of the Washington players except Amitay. Even though it has produced anything but unanimous admiration in the Arab world itself, Sadat's trip to Jerusalem, according to Richardson, "overnight changed the conventional wisdom in this country about the kind of people that Arabs are. The assumption went from irrationality to rationality."

One obvious beneficiary of the fallout has been Ashraf Ghorbal, the Egyptian ambassador, who has always enjoyed good relations in Washington but now seems to have a special status as a symbol of the prospects for Middle Eastern peace. (Ghorbal is now permitted to be sociable with his Israeli counterpart, Simcha Dinitz, and the two of them were the guests of honor at the much-gossiped-about dinner party sponsored by Barbara Walters.)

Other, more subtle shifts are in the works. On Capitol Hill, for example, the traditional role of Senators Jacob Javits, Republican of New York, and Abraham Ribicoff, Democrat of Connecticut, as spokesmen for Israel and the American Jewish community may be transferring to new actors—among them Senator Dick Stone, Democrat of Florida, who is also Jewish but prides himself on his contacts with Arab leaders both in their own countries and in Washington. (He displays prominently in his office an autographed picture and a long, discursive letter in Arabic from a Saudi prince.) A conservative on a number of foreign policy issues, Stone was disregarded by many in his party when he first arrived in Washington in 1975, but last year he became chairman of the Near Eastern and South Asian Subcommittee of the Senate Foreign Relations Committee and people began to take notice.

But Stone is not the only congressional supporter of Israel who, having traveled widely in the Arab world, seems ready to broaden his point of view. With Ghorbal's encouragement, 338 members of Congress have visited Egypt since 1973, and all but one had a personal talk with Sadat.

That fact, combined with other developments, has some of Israel's strongest American advocates running scared. A major strategic crossroads is faced by Amitay, who has shown no signs that he will let up on the pressure, even if the Egyptians and the Israelis sign a peace agreement. Some of his friends, as well as his detractors, argue that he should. If the atmosphere of confrontation eases for Israel, they suggest, AIPAC may discover more skepticism toward its alarms about Israeli security. Already there are indications that while Amitay and others continue to stimulate fervent statements of support for the Jewish state from the usual quarters, those statements are in some cases mere lip service, and true congressional sentiment, expressed privately, is a different matter.

Would a more moderate approach produce more realistic results? Abourezk claims that several of his Senate colleagues have told him confidentially that they are chafing under the pressure to renew their pro-Israeli pledges at regular intervals, and the South Dakotan says there are several possible candidates to take over his role as chief Senate spokesman for the Palestinians when he retires at the end of this year.

Leaders of the American Jewish community are worried over other trends in Washington. A more even-handed representation of Arab and Israeli interests before the U. S. government could be a good thing for all, discouraging the unfounded allegations that conspiratorial Jewish interests are somehow pulling the strings of foreign policy. And the increase in U. S. exports to Arab nations to a level of about $7.2 billion in 1977 (as compared to $1.2 billion in 1972) could actually produce economic benefits for vast numbers of Americans, regardless of their ethnic background. But if Fred Dutton and his colleagues are successful in their efforts and the Arab financial stake in this country increases substantially, alarms of an entirely different nature may be sounded. The Treasury Department keeps the exact statistics secret at the Saudis' request, but the Saudi government is believed to be the largest single holder of special Treasury notes; and the Saudis are known to have a huge investment in the securities of, among other quasi-official agencies, the Federal National Mortgage Association ("Fannie Mae"). For the moment, this is generally interpreted as a use of surplus oil revenues to shore up the weak American dollar. But what the result might be if the Middle Eastern crisis should be seriously aggravated again is anyone's guess.

Meanwhile, liberal Jewish political activists are beginning to change their minds about some old articles of faith. Worried that the recently secure 3 percent of the population could be threatened after all, they are not so sure that it is a good idea to extend the federal campaign finance reform to congressional elections (thus putting a limit on individual contributions to Senate and House races) or to abolish the electoral college (thus limiting the ability of cohesive voting blocs to throw all of the electoral votes of large states into the column of one candidate or another). They are concerned, in short, about something that has come to be called the "Arab lobby."

★★

21

Media Lobbyists: An Unreported Story   Dick Brown, Susan Antigone, Richard Gowan, Ron Duhl, and Jeremy Gaunt

Americans obtain much political information from the mass media, making the media an important ingredient of democratic government. With the protection received from the First Amendment of the Constitution, the mass media have secured especially important roles in maintaining a viable political system. Among their roles are exposing government scandals, acting as a loyal opposition to the administration in power, and articulating important political issues for the public. Without these checks on government, democratic politics would have difficulty remaining secure.

Most people do not, however, perceive the mass media as lobbyists protective of narrow, special interests. Yet this is the theme of "Media Lobbyists: An Unreported Story." These activities of the mass media are rarely known because, unlike the lobbying of other interest groups, the media are often able to control the sort of information about themselves and about events they report on. In the interest of their own survival, what sort of issues might radio, television, and newspapers have special interests in? Do all elements of the media industry share the same power and influence? How would you compare the strength of the broadcasting industry with the print medium? Are there any media biases that affect the gathering of news and its dissemination?

Legislation is being considered by Congressman Van Deerlin that would affect the media in fundamental ways. What are its major provisions and what changes to the media would be forthcoming? Unlike the newspapers, radio and television stations are required to have licenses to broadcast. Should they be licensed? Given that broadcasting is the only medium required to be licensed, does this mean that broadcasting is receiving less protection from the First Amendment than the other forms of mass media? Should broadcasters be given a license in perpetuity, or should licenses be granted every three years, as is the practice today?

★ ★ ★

Media lobbyists: an unreported story

The battle for news control is seldom in the news

Dick Brown, Susan Antigone, Richard Cowan, Ron Duhl, and Jeremy Gaunt

A quiet war of influence is being fought in Washington over the future of American television, radio, and newspapers. It is quiet not because it lacks intensity, but because the activities of lobbyists who work for the media don't make the headlines or the 6 o'clock news. Yet the lawmaking these lobbyists are influencing is every bit as vital as deliberations on energy policy or wage guidelines. At stake is who controls information and its distribution — in essence, who controls the flow of news.

Among the issues at stake in the government arena are:

❡ Cable television: Ten years from now, cable may dominate American broadcasting as network programming does today. Most of the companies now offering the service are relatively small and locally owned. But Congress is considering throwing cable competition wide open — and control of the wired empire could end up in the hands of a few corporate giants such as AT&T.

❡ Broadcast licensing: Since 1934, licenses for radio and TV stations have been granted for three-year periods. Each time broadcasters seek renewal, they are required to demonstrate their programming is in the public interest, especially when it comes to news and other public affairs shows. Under proposed legislation, licenses would be

The authors are graduate students at the American University School of Communications. This article was written in a course on media criticism directed by Adjunct Professor Nick Kotz.

granted in perpetuity — and could be revoked only for violation of technical standards.

❡ Newspapers: The independently owned daily is fast becoming a thing of the past — there are only 600 today, and they are disappearing at the rate of sixty a year. One proposal in Congress would change inheritance tax laws to make it easier for families to keep such newspapers, and another would break up the chains which are buying them. If independent papers are not protected or strengthened, control of the daily press could soon be almost totally dominated by a handful of big chains.

But while the spoils of this war of influence are great, media reports from the battlefield are sparse. The simple fact is, the American newspaper and broadcast industries are myopic when it comes to reporting on issues of concern to their own economic self-interests. As a result, few Americans know that Congress may virtually abandon regulation of the broadcast industry by rewriting laws which have stood for forty-five years. Or that legislators have a chance to help keep control of local news where it belongs — in the hands of local publishers.

And fewer still know that the same organizations which assign thousands of correspondents to cover Washington are among the most powerful at lobbying for their own interests. Because many legislators believe it is these news organizations which control their political fates, media lobbyists have leverage unlike any others'.

"They are awfully powerful," says Senator Ernest F. Hollings, Democrat of South Carolina, who is chairman of both the Senate Commerce Subcommittee on Communications and the appropriations subcommittee handling communications bills. "The average Senator...[would]...vote anything that the local broadcasters want. He's very interested in satisfying that local broadcaster because it's instrumental in his reelection."

Other legislators attest that newspaper owners, too, have enormous influence on legislation. In fact, if all the media owners had common goals, they'd seldom lose a battle. Because they differ, Washington is locked in a communications war. And who wins that war is far more than the parochial concern of the media — it is the concern of the public.

The media, like any other industry, have a right to petition government in pursuit of their own special interests. But as the controller of news they also have responsibilities to report on their own lobbying and to avoid misusing their news power as a political weapon in their own behalf.

A case in point is the current fight over the issue of children's advertising. It began when the Federal Trade Commission finally succumbed to the appeals of citizens' groups critical of television advertising aimed at young children. Many of the groups had been calling for a total ban on "kid-vid" advertising, and the FTC decided to study just what effect such ads were having, and what if anything should be done to limit them. All of those concerned — including broadcasters, cereal makers, and toy manufacturers

— would be given a chance to testify during the kid-vid inquiry.

Faced with this issue concerning the rights of impressionable, immature children, versus those of free speech and free enterprise, broadcasters had a legitimate case to present at the FTC hearings. Instead, the broadcast lobby tried to cut off funds for the hearings by pressuring members of appropriations committees in Congress. Narrowly failing in that attempt, the broadcasters along with other concerned lobbyists are now pushing legislation to restrict the authority of the FTC. If they succeed, the commission's power in the

4,500 radio and television stations and eight radio and television networks, and it's easy to see why a Senate staffer described the NAB as "one of the most influential groups around."

The NAB and another lobbying group — the National Radio Broadcasters Association — demonstrated their power late last year in forcing the Federal Communications Commission to back down on a proposed policy dealing with employe records. Concerned that some broadcasters were skirting equal opportunity requirements by manipulating job titles — for example, listing a black janitor as Vice-

Newspaper groups also have lobbyists in Washington, and like broadcasters they have been effective in mobilizing local members for massive lobbying efforts. For example, the National Newspaper Association lobbies on such issues as postal rates and regulations, wage and hour laws, reporters' shield laws, and freedom of information. Bill Mullen, NNA president, explains that "when there is an issue of importance to our members, we can generate a lot of grassroots support. Our members are close with their congressmen and are able to get through to them."

Newspapers also are represented in Washington by the American Newspaper Publishers Association and the American Society of Newspaper Editors. The ANPA has more than 1,300 member newspapers in the United States and Canada. Another group, the Independent Local Newspaper Association, seeks legislation to help family-owned newspapers resist takeover by chains such as Gannett and Knight-Ridder.

'[My congressman] knows he's got to buy them. . .so he's going to lend me an ear'

---

kid-vid issue may become nothing more than advisory.

And although the FTC did succeed in holding hearings on children's advertising, you'd have learned little about the issue by watching the network news. Aside from several brief accounts, the broadcasters ignored the hearings entirely. One independent network showed up for several hearings, but was more interested in filming Captain Kangaroo testifying than in providing adequate coverage of the advertising issue. ABC news aired a three-part series on television advertising but passed up the obvious opportunity it offered to take an in-depth look at whether children's advertising should be limited. Instead, the FTC hearings got only a brief mention in another part of the news show.

Broadcasters took their cues in the kid-vid battle from Roy Elson of the National Association of Broadcasters. Because of the savvy he gained in sixteen years as a Capitol insider — most of them as chief assistant to the late Democratic Senator Carl Hayden of Arizona — Elson often is cited as one of the most effective media lobbyists in Washington. Add to that the clout the NAB gains from a membership of

President for Sanitation Services — FCC commissioners voted to study whether broadcasters should be required to make public information on their employes' race, sex, salary, and precise job title.

The NRBA quickly issued a shrill warning to its members at 1,200 radio stations around the country of the FCC's "Big Brother" plan. The NAB, in an editorial in its *Radioactive* magazine, told its members the proposal would be "disruptive as well as ruinous to morale at practically every station in the country." Both groups urged members to contact the FCC and protest the proposal.

The very next month, the same NAB editorialist crowed about killing the FCC proposal, calling it a victory for effective lobbying pressure by hundreds of broadcasters.

Other broadcast groups, too, effectively combine the political savvy of their Washington lobbyists with the political clout of their members back home. Among them are the Daytime Broadcasters Association, which represents several hundred small radio stations, and the National Cable Television Association, which claims as members 1,600 cable owners.

In addition to these associations, the most powerful broadcast corporations have their own lobbyists. CBS, NBC, and ABC all have registered lobbyists in Washington, as do several radio networks. Even the Public Broadcasting Service and National Public Radio — which are largely funded by the Federal Government — retain lobbyists to influence Congress and the FCC. Other lobbyists represent Time Inc., *Reader's Digest*, and the Motion Picture Association of America.

While media lobbyists are becoming more sophisticated, their presence has been felt on the Hill for years. For example, as the postal system developed, daily and weekly newspapers lobbied vigorously and received favorable treatment through lower postal rates. When copyright statutes were codified in 1909, the ANPA effectively lobbied for a reduction of the maximum penalty for photographic copyright infringement from $5,000 to $200.

When Congress in 1924 considered prohibiting the labor of children under eighteen years of age, the daily newspaper industry responded with storms of protest and won exemptions which still allow carriers to begin work when they are as young as twelve years old. Although the newspapers argued it was a matter of First Amendment freedom, press critic Ben Bagdikian terms it "strictly an economic issue."

Similar lobbying by newspapers continues today. Although in some instances First Amendment freedoms actually are involved — for instance, search of newsrooms — in many others the press cloaks itself in the First Amendment while arguing for special treatment on purely economic issues. And the irony of the newspaper lobby in Washington is that it self-righteously represents freedom of the press while often ignoring press inquiries into its own activities. In a recent example, a reporter for the *Columbia Journalism Review* repeatedly called the ANPA to ask why the association had ended a program of minority scholarships. Jerry Friedheim, executive vice president and general manager of ANPA, refused to be interviewed. When the publishers meet to discuss lobbying issues, their meetings often are closed to press coverage.

Despite substantial evidence as to just how influential media lobbyists are, some legislators and many of the lobbyists themselves downplay their power. Ed James, executive editor of *Broadcasting* magazine, says the power of media lobbyists is "grossly exaggerated. They'd be the first to tell you that."

But a House staffer who deals with communications issues comments: "One of the greatest things lobbyists do up here is profess their impotence. [Actually] they take a back seat to no one. There is a whole raft of issues they've done pretty well on."

Nicholas Johnson, a former FCC commissioner and now a director of the National Citizens Committee for Broadcasting, goes one step further: "There are broadcasters, then there is everybody else," he says. "They're really in a class no one else can touch, when it comes to power. The power is the ability to defeat or elect a candidate. Unlike others who give money as a means to the end, they [broadcasters and publishers] *are* the end."

Even James admits groups such as the NAB "get the most done" when they can generate lobbying by local broadcasters, especially when those broadcasters know legislators personally. Like many who deal with communications issues, James says most media lobbying is education, not armtwisting. "Most congressmen are grossly misinformed," he says. "They are constantly voting with inadequate information. Lobbying is less a case of applying gross, Boss Tweed type of political pressure than a case of political education. There's very little of 'God damn it, if you don't do this, we're gonna turn out the guys and defeat you in the next election.'"

But despite James's assertions, there is evidence that precisely such leverage was used by newspaper lobbyists during the successful fight for the Newspaper Preservation Act, which allowed competing newspapers to merge their printing operations — an exemption to anti-trust laws which do not allow such mergers in other industries. Senator Thomas McIntyre of New Hampshire told a Chicago audience early in 1970 that "lobbying for this bill may well have set new records" in pressure tactics.

In his book *America Inc.*, Morton Mintz wrote that "some senators acknowledge privately that certain powerful publishers had given them crude ultimatums: support the bill or the publishers would oppose them the next time they were up for reelection."

Representative Lionel Van Deerlin, Democrat of California, chairman of the House Subcommittee on Communications and a former newsman, also attests to the clout of the media lobbies: "Broadcasters are the same as newspapers. There isn't anyone [in Congress] who doesn't have the feeling — however misplaced — that they can make or break you."

While Van Deerlin and others say the power to withhold or slant coverage is rarely if ever exercised, our conversation at a Washington convention showed us at least one broadcaster is willing to use that power.

The broadcaster, Joe Costello, was in town to attend a "Rally Against Over-Regulation," sponsored by the NAB, NRBA, and other broadcast groups. Costello owns and operates five radio stations in Louisiana and is remarkably candid about the power he has as a broadcaster.

"[My Representative] knows he's got to buy time on my radio station, so he's going to lend me an ear," Costello said. "We're keeping them alive back home and that's why the newspaper and radio and TV people are more effective lobbyists. That's why we don't have to come to Washington with tractors." (Also in Washington at that time were hundreds of members of the American Agricultural Movement.)

Costello said that by listening to his local broadcaster and voting on issues accordingly, a legislator can benefit where it really counts — back in his home district. "He can earn the support of 175 radio stations in the state of Louisiana by voting for something that only affects [those stations]," Costello said.

And if a legislator doesn't listen, or votes the "wrong" way, would Costello find it hard to provide the coverage he previously had?

"I think so," Costello said.

The guiding principle behind regulation of the broadcast industry has always been, "in the public interest." The Government has to regulate broadcasters, that principle says, because if it did not, they could air whatever it takes to make money and to hell with public service programs like the 6 o'clock news. To make sure broadcasters complied with public service requirements, the FCC was vested with the authority to license radio and television stations for three-year periods. The FCC has seldom revoked a license, but many media watchers say its power to do so is enough to keep broadcasters conscious of public-interest responsibilities.

With his introduction of the Communications Act of 1979 — otherwise known as "the Rewrite" — Representative Van Deerlin has thrown the public interest concept out the window, and he hopes Congress as a whole will leave it there.

"This bill is saying, in effect, that the broadcaster is no longer a public trustee," said a staffer on Van Deerlin's communications subcommittee. Since the first Communications Act was passed in 1934, she said, the number of broadcasting outlets has grown substantially and new technology such as cable and video recorders is offering the public even more options. As a result, there is no longer a scarcity of programming and no longer a need to regulate programming to ensure diversity, she said.

In short, then, Van Deerlin's bill (and to a lesser degree, bills proposed in the Senate) would throw open the broadcast industry and leave programming decisions entirely to the discretion of broadcasters. Radio would be totally deregulated immediately, and television and cable would be deregu-

ownership restrictions could allow corporations to own dozens of radio stations across the country.

Similarly, the Rewrite would open up the cable business to communications giants such as AT&T. Although the bill would require that AT&T allow other cable programmers the use of its lines, there is no doubt the Rewrite would open the door to conglomerate takeover of the cable industry. With that could come less diversity in programming and more of the same mediocre, formula shows offered by the networks today.

extinction. It is quickly being replaced by a relatively new institution — the media conglomerates which control hundreds of America's daily and weekly newspapers in virtually every major market.

The result may be that there will be only a handful of voices in the American press. Readers may be presented with less divergent ideas. As a newspaper conglomerate controls each of its subsidiaries from hundreds of miles away, it is feared communities will have less voice or input on affairs affecting their particular communities. Of equal consequence, there is the development of highly concentrated and effective lobbying groups representing the newspaper giants which have the potential of dictating their will in Congress.

The newspaper chains argue they offer the money and new technology needed to maintain and in fact improve local newspapers. They also contend that local news control is retained. But critics say these chains have lost sight of the goals of providing information and making government accountable for its actions and instead have substituted another goal — profit above all else.

'You would be amazed how members [of Congress] respond when the local publisher calls on them'

lated over the next ten years. No longer would broadcasters have to prove their programming is geared toward the needs of the community. Licenses would be granted in perpetuity — subject to revocation only for violation of technical standards. The Fairness Doctrine would be eliminated — broadcasters would no longer be required to ''seek out and broadcast contrasting points of view on controversial issues.''

Beyond programming, the Rewrite proposes sweeping changes in who can own broadcasting and cable outlets and how new station assignments are given out. Whereas in the past new assignments were made after the FCC studied the proposed programming of competing applicants, assignments would now be handled by lottery.

Current restrictions on the number of radio stations a single company can own would be eliminated, but no one could own more than one AM and FM station in the same market. Newspapers would be permitted to buy or retain ownership of broadcast stations in the markets where they publish, overturning current FCC restrictions on cross-ownership. Although the Rewrite is supposed to encourage diversity of ownership, this easing of

Naturally, media lobbyists have been busy during the four years since Van Deerlin and former Representative Louis Frey, Republican of Florida, first decided to rewrite the 1934 act. The proposed Rewrite already reflects lobbying victories for all three media — television, radio, and cable. But the real battle is raging now, as warring lobbyists seek to persuade legislators to support or fight specific portions of the bill once it reaches the full Commerce Committee and the House floor. The cable interests are fighting to keep AT&T out of their business, and small broadcasters are fighting for more stations. Most broadcast lobbyists are working to assure the deregulation they so strongly support isn't killed or diluted by legislators who don't believe, as Van Deerlin does, that marketplace forces can protect the public interest.

While Congress is considering proposals which could drastically change the broadcast industry, equally important changes are underway for American newspapers. The independent paper — long cherished as the ''Watchdog'' of American society — is threatened with

Representative Morris K. Udall, Democrat of Arizona, says he has come up with a ''stop-gap measure'' for sustaining the remaining independent newspapers by discouraging them from selling out to chains such as Gannett, Newhouse, Knight-Ridder, and Scripps-Howard. The ''answer'' is a bill introduced into the Ninety-sixth Congress which would relax inheritance tax laws for independent newspapers.

Many of the acquisitions made by chains are the result of independent publishers panicking over the thought of an heir having to pay huge chunks of money in inheritance taxes. The option to sell is further enhanced by a willingness of chains to pay up to fifty to sixty times the annual earnings of an independent newspaper. That willingness is what makes a paper's market value — and thus inheritance taxes — so high in the first place.

Under the provisions of Udall's bill, an independent publisher could establish a trust from which advance payment of estate taxes could be made. In that way, heirs to the paper would not be faced with the immediate payment of millions of dollars in taxes. The trusts would be exempt from taxes and would be available only to publishers who own and operate a single newspaper in a market.

According to Udall, the bill is gaining momentum in Congress and is being co-sponsored by about eighty members. "Some of the independent publishers have been doing their work and you would be amazed how members [of Congress] respond when the local publisher calls on them," Udall says. The publishers are "a good group of people to have on your side." The most intense lobbying, he says, is coming from the small independent dailies and weeklies. "It has really snowballed...members often come up to me and say the local publishers have talked to them. They want to know what they can do."

Udall says he does not expect intense lobbying against the bill. He says there is a "feeling of guilt" among the chains because "there is no good argument against the bill and they are so big already." In fact, Udall adds, the newspaper chains may have decided not to fight his bill so that they won't be hit with even tougher legislation.

Udall admits the bill may not succeed in stopping the growth of newspaper chains but might simply raise the cost of acquiring independent papers. "I'm not sure it's a deterrent, but it's a life preserver for the hardy souls who want an independent newspaper," he says.

While media lobbyists have been busy with the rewrite of the Communications Act and Representative Udall's inheritance tax bill, coverage of these issues has been almost non-existent. Such neglect is nothing new — while radio, television, and newspapers are quick to cover almost every other industry, they rarely cover their own.

Some of those in the media — and even some legislators who decry the lack of coverage — claim that stories about broadcast licensing or the Fairness Doctrine aren't "sexy" enough to compete for air time with reports on hydrogen bomb stories. "Nobody would listen," says Frey, former ranking Republican on the House communications subcommittee, and now a Washington lawyer for broadcasters. "Everybody would be asleep."

But broadcasters and newspapermen who have learned how to spice up stories on trade deficits and inflation should be able to do the same with stories on communications issues. Apparently they haven't tried.

But even taking into account televi-

sion's poor track record in covering itself, its neglect of the introduction of the Communications Act rewrite was a surprise. When Representative Van Deerlin stood in front of some 200 journalists, lawyers, and lobbyists on March 29, he was not just introducing a bill. Van Deerlin was talking about

'. . .don't expect to see the footsteps of media lobbyists traced on the 6 o'clock news'

the future of television — a medium viewed in 99 per cent of American homes. Yet the only television news camera to be seen at the press conference belonged to a college student from upstate New York, who was working on a documentary. There were no signs of network news correspondents, although the network lobbyists were present — attentive to Van Deerlin's intentions.

That night, not one television network news program carried mention of the bill's introduction.

With communications technology growing more complex every day, media lobbying may become even more intense. But don't expect to see the footsteps of media lobbyists traced on the 6 o'clock news.   ■

CHAPTER FIVE

★ ★ ★

Elections and Electoral Systems

America's governmental system has been called an "indirect" or "representative" democracy because the people do not make public policy themselves for the most part. Rather the people choose leaders to make decisions on their behalf. Elections are the method by which the selection of political leadership is institutionalized. In fundamental ways the electoral system affects the viability of our government. Beyond the selection of leaders, elections serve as a mechanism by which the attitudes of citizens on public issues may be communicated to government. Moreover, elections enable political leaders to govern because the electoral system gives them authority perceived to be "legitimate" by the people. And elections permit the citizenry to extract some degree of accountability from politicians; an election is the ultimate sanction to be used against officeholders who betray the public's trust.

But as they operate in reality, elections and the electoral system are imperfect, not the ideal. As the essay by Jim McClellan and David E. Anderson, "The Making of the Also-Rans," makes clear, we are severely limited in our choice of political leaders. Certain biases in the electoral system assure that Republican and Democratic candidates will

dominate the ballot, but other "minor" party candidates are less able to present their case to the people. The candidates of minor parties suffer disadvantages in the campaign process, so access to the ballot is not open to all on an equal basis. To this extent, our two-party monopoly does act as an obstacle to the communication of other policy alternatives from citizen to government.

The electoral system is imperfect also because the actual election campaign may not clearly express to political leaders the burning issues of the day. Even when campaigns appear to be closely contested and vigorous, and the opportunity would seem ripe for the discussion of policy issues, the election may in fact not signal anything too meaningful. Such was the case in 1976, argues Michael Barone in his "Nonlessons of the Campaign." It would seem that, beyond a simple yearning for change, the voters did not use the 1976 election to demand any major shift in public policy. As conducted, it emphasized personality, style, and marginal disagreements. Through our history it appears that most elections have not held great significance for American politics. So it is important to understand what factors cause the voters to choose between major party candidates for office, including the presidency.

Once elected, the political leader must govern, but all politicians face a dilemma with regard to their constituency. Though the officeholder stands for all the people in his constituency, he is aware that certain groups supported him while others opposed him. In the course of an election campaign, candidates make promises to various social groups in order to achieve a winning "coalition." From this perspective, Richard Scammon and Benjamin Wattenberg examine the political problems of President Carter. In their article "Jimmy Carter's Problem," they trace his difficulties to the fragile nature of his electoral coalition. It would seem that the South has special significance to Jimmy Carter and to his problem. Given the shift of population toward the South and Southwest, this discussion may have implications for the nature of electoral politics for many years to come.

The president and the vice-president are the only officials elected from a national constituency. The question of "legitimacy" is at the heart of the current debate over the method of election. The pros and cons of the existing Electoral College method and of the reform proposal for direct popular election are thoroughly analyzed by Thomas E. Cronin in "Choosing a President." The problem seems obvious: under existing procedures a person could be elected president without getting a majority of the popular vote. Some observers ask whether this situation would limit his ability to govern the nation in the name of the people. But reform is not so obvious; many political considerations affect this debate—for example, the impor-

tance of federalism, the impact of minority groups, and the relevance of political tradition. To date, the existing system has not been changed, but this issue is currently on the agenda of Congress. An understanding of this debate requires the student to appreciate the many complex issues that underlie reform of our electoral system.

Elections offer the voters an opportunity to "throw the rascals out of office." But this sanction does not work as effectively as one might think. In his essay "The 1978 Congressional Elections: A Renaissance for Republicans," Austin Ranney discusses one well-known election trend: in midterm elections the president's party typically loses seats in the House of Representatives. Various explanations are offered, including the notion that voters are reacting against the record of the president when they oppose his party's representatives who are up for reelection. Nonetheless, incumbents generally win reelection, for they enjoy many advantages over their challengers. It appears that the tenure of congressmen is becoming more and more secure, so much so that Ranney projected that Republicans would not do too well in the 1978 elections. Apart from gaining insights into election trends affecting the Congress, Ranney's analysis gives a perspective on the political relationship between the executive and legislative branches of government.

In the headnotes preceding each article in this chapter, you are encouraged to understand the arguments made and to speculate about the nature of our elections and electoral system. Issues are raised that have long been debated by scholars and journalists who study elections in America.

★★

22

The Making of the Also-Rans   Jim McClellan and David E. Anderson

In addition to Jimmy Carter and Gerald Ford, there were other candidates who ran for president in 1976. Who were they? Few voters were aware of them because the Democratic and Republican parties monopolized the resources needed to wage successfully a campaign for public office in America. How are minor political parties denied access to the mass media and to financial resources? By what means are they prevented from even getting a place on the ballot in many states? How serious do you think these anti-democratic biases of the electoral system are? What would you expect might happen to the electoral system if all *candidates, regardless of party, were allowed equal access to the mass media and to financial resources? How easy would it be for any one candidate to secure a majority vote among the electorate?*

Throughout American history we can think of numerous "minor" or "third" parties that ran candidates for high office, even the presidency. Do you know some of the more familiar minor parties in American history? Most political scientists agree that these minor parties serve an essential purpose in our political system. In what ways do you think minor parties enrich the democratic nature of American politics?

On the other hand, there are political scientists who worry that the presence of many candidates on the ballot would aggravate conflict, undermine political compromise, and hurt the stability of our political system. To what extent do you think these fears are warranted?

★ ★ ★

Citizens of Utah cast 241 votes for the Communist ticket, and the Mormon Tabernacle is still standing

The Making of the Also-Rans

JIM McCLELLAN and DAVID E. ANDERSON

The Presidential election is almost two months behind us, and Walter Cronkite has yet to announce even the early third-party returns. Some states have not completed the count of minor-party votes. Some never will.

Despite the slowness of the ballot tabulation, however, there are subtle reasons to suspect that Gus Hall has not been elected President of the United States. For one thing, inaugural invitations have been mailed out in envelopes bearing Jimmy Carter's return address. For another, Governor Wendell Anderson of Minnesota has modestly seen fit to appoint himself to fill the remainder of Walter Mondale's Senate term.

Still, it would be nice to see the returns. Realizing that forty million votes for Carter and thirty-eight million votes for Ford could be counted in a single night, some people might begin to wonder how many votes were cast for Hall if they couldn't be counted within two months.

It is unlikely that the delay in announcing returns for Gus Hall and the others who ran outside the Democratic and Republican Parties is the result of an extraordinary turnout for third parties. The delay is merely the final act of a political process that presupposes third parties to be unimportant and works hard to vindicate its presupposition. As Socialist Workers Party candidate Peter Camejo put it, "Before the election, Democrats and Republicans and the media waged a campaign to convince the American people that a vote for a third party would not count. To convince them further they simply didn't count the votes for most third-party candidates on election night."

Given this country's professed allegiance to democratic

and egalitarian ideals, it is disappointing that so much of the first two hundred years has been characterized by people pleading for liberties and opportunities that should have been theirs as a birthright. The problem of ensuring equal opportunities for all candidates irrespective of party affiliation is one more example.

Certainly people who do not choose to belong to the Democratic or Republican Parties have as much right to run for office as those who do. Yet independent and third-party candidates are seldom elected. In fact, they are barely tolerated. Democratic and Republican candidates by law and custom are given every possible advantage, while those who seek to oppose them have little or no access to the media, limited financial resources, and poor prospects for even being listed on the ballot.

Roger MacBride of the Libertarian Party campaigned in forty states, including Alaska (where neither Ford nor Carter cared to venture). Peter Camejo traveled 150,000 miles, crisscrossing the country twenty times, in his quest for the Presidency. Yet it is doubtful that even a quarter of those who went to the polls last November had heard of either of them, much less of the platforms they sought to publicize.

The American electorate has grown so massive it is no longer possible for a candidate to appeal directly to the voters. Conversely, most of the people never see a political candidate, and they have to depend on the communications media to see for them. If the media do not cover the campaign of a candidate, most people are left unaware of it, or if they learn about it through non-media sources they tend to discredit it since the media felt it unworthy of mention.

Television is the primary news source for a majority of the American people, and Jimmy Carter and Gerald Ford had no difficulty appealing to the voters through it. There was gavel-to-gavel coverage of the major party conven-

Jim McClellan is an instructor in history at Northern Virginia Community College. David E. Anderson is on the Washington staff of United Press International. They wrote "There Are Alternatives" in the November 1976 issue of The Progressive.

tions, which have degenerated into little more than media events anyway. Federal laws which require fair and equal treatment of all candidates by the broadcast media were overlooked so that four and one-half hours of prime time exposure could be accorded Ford and Carter. A long string of "Meet the Press," "Face the Nation," and "Issues and Answers" appearances were made by the Democratic and Republican candidates, their families, friends, and associates. The American people received a more than adequate amount of information about Miss Lillian, Susan Ford's social life, and Billy Carter's gas station.

Each night the commercial networks gave television viewers ten to fifteen minutes of Jimmy Carter and Gerald Ford. Peter Camejo received just under two minutes of evening news coverage for his entire twenty-four month campaign. Even that was a lot by third-party standards.

Eugene McCarthy's independent campaign led the non-major party candidacies in broadcast media coverage. Still, the amount of air time devoted to the former Senator is minuscule when compared to the attention given Gerald Ford and Jimmy Carter. "I can see why the media have some trouble. . .giving us time when they have all the other distractions," McCarthy explained during his "Meet the Press" interview last July. "Walter Cronkite, two or three weeks ago, spent two nights talking about the boy who had been raised by the apes. They discovered that he hadn't been; first they thought he had, then they retracted two nights later. I think it was two minutes each night. They found out the child had just watched television too much, and I thought that I might demand equal time with the ape boy at least for one night of two minutes."

The failure to obtain equal time with the Democratic and Republican candidates — or even with the ape boy — has a chilling effect on the campaigns of the minor candidates. The media do not simply reflect the credibility of a candidate; to a great extent, they create credibility. The amount of coverage and its slant determine the way the public perceives a candidate for office. By withholding coverage from third-party and independent candidates while bestowing it lavishly on the Democratic and Republican nominees, the media perpetuate major-party success at the polls and predestine independent efforts to failure.

Campaign coverage which discriminates against third parties is justified by the media on grounds that candidacies outside the major parties are not "significant." But as Aaron Orange of the Socialist Labor Party rhetorically asked the Senate Commerce Committee during its hearing on the Equal Time Doctrine a few years ago, "How can a [third-party] candidate attract the kind of following. . .that would convince the broadcasters that he is a 'significant' candidate? Isn't it a fact that in our present society one can become a 'significant' candidate only as a result of repeated exposure on the airways?" Thus, third-party candidates are not treated equally with the Democratic and Republican Party candidates because they

are considered to have no chance to win. They have no chance to win because they are not allowed to compete on equal terms with the Democratic and Republican Parties.

The Democratic and Republican preeminence with the media is paralleled by Democratic and Republican control over the ballot. The major parties write the nation's election laws and, not coincidently, are their beneficiaries. Complex and, in some cases, insurmountable legal barriers have been erected in an effort to deny third-party candidates the right to compete for office. Each election the minor parties do battle with a myriad of discriminatory laws in an effort to open up the ballot. But when the dust clears it always seems that the laws came down a bit more repressive than the time before.

The 1976 campaign, like those which preceded it, is marked by ballot "atrocity" stories — the trials and tribulations of third parties in seeking to work through a labyrinth of *Catch-22* election laws. The Libertarian Party was most successful in complying with the fifty-one separate ballot laws, winning a spot on the ballot of thirty-two states. Eugene McCarthy's name was on the ballot of twenty-nine. The rest of the nation's third parties made the ballot in less than half the states. "We had more trouble this year than ever before," said Stan Karp of the Socialist Labor Party, "and this is our twenty-third Presidential campaign."

There were the usual kinds of harassment. In Michigan, for example, several minor parties spent a year successfully complying with all the requirements of the state law for obtaining a spot on the ballot. Their success convinced the Michigan legislature that the ballot requirements must be too easy, and an entirely new set of requirements was legislated into existence. Fortunately, the State Supreme Court set aside the new law for this election. And arbitrary rulings from state officials were as bountiful and perplexing as in years past. Florida, for instance, first informed the Socialist Party that write-ins bearing the names of the Party's Presidential and Vice Presidential nominees would be counted, but at the last minute announced that it would also be necessary for voters to write in the names of all seventeen Socialist Party electors.

The successful effort of the Carter campaign to keep Eugene McCarthy's name off the ballot in New York deserves special mention. As much as $50,000 was spent, according to McCarthy, by the New York Democratic Committee in challenging the independent Presidential candidate's nominating petitions and having his name struck from the ballot. The Democratic Party feared that given a choice between Carter and McCarthy, enough voters might choose the latter to prevent Carter from carrying the state. As it turned out, Carter won New York by a narrow margin, and without the state's electoral votes the entire election would have swung to Ford. The Democratic Party may consider the money well spent, but it is a sad commentary on American politics when an election can be decided by driving a rival candidate off the ballot rather than through a successful appeal to the voters on the issues.

Ballot laws can be used to stifle radical candidacies as

well as to insulate the major parties from competition. The Communist Party collected 13,000 signatures on its petitions in Maine, several thousand more than needed to satisfy the ballot requirements. Democratic state representative Louis Jalbert, however, held a press conference to announce that there could not conceivably be 13,000 Communists in Maine, and therefore the petitions had to be invalid. The American Civil Liberties Union pointed out that it was not necessary to be a Communist to sign the Communist Party nominating petitions, but to no avail. The governor of Maine held a press conference in the state capitol to proclaim that Maine would not be allowed to become the sanctuary of American communism.

The end result was that the Communist Party was denied the right to run a slate of candidates and Maine was undoubtedly spared the embarrassment of being the first American domino to fall to communism. Much the same kind of patriotic stand by public officials was made in Utah, but the Communist Party qualified for the ballot in spite of it. "Two hundred and forty-one votes were cast by citizens of Utah for the Communist Party Presidential ticket," said Communist Party campaign chairman Simon Gerson, "and the great state of Utah is still standing, Mormon Tabernacle and all."

Money, as might be expected, was also a major problem for independent and third-party candidacies. While the Federal Government was shelling out more than $43 million for the Ford and Carter campaigns — a figure the parties have claimed is not enough — most minor parties were scratching for funds.

Third parties got none of the benefits from the new campaign financing laws and all of the hassles. "What killed us this year," said Stan Karp of the SLP, "was all the liberal reform provisions and the tons of paperwork that came with them." Independent and third-party campaigns were required to submit complicated reports on expenditures and income even though they were ineligible for public financing.

Of the third-party efforts, only Roger MacBride's campaign came close to being well financed. Campaign officials estimated that the Libertarian Party raised and spent some $1 million on local and national candidates. Jerry Eller, McCarthy's campaign manager, estimated that the former Senator had spent about $500,000; the SWP said its two-year campaign with Peter Camejo and Willie Mae Reid cost about $400,000. Unfortunately, great chunks of that money were spent not on electioneering, nor on raising issues or gaining media exposure, but on legal fees or other ballot access problems.

Jean Savage of the Camejo campaign, for example, estimated that the SWP spent "upwards of $20,000" just in its effort to gather the 150,000 petition signatures necessary for ballot status in California. That drive was complicated and compounded by footdragging state officials, and the SWP had to spend more money going into court challenging the ballot laws — a case that is still pending.

While it is impossible at this point to sort out from campaign statistics how much money was spent for the *right* to run for office as opposed to actually running, the financial drain can be surmised from the fact that McCarthy found it necessary to initiate legal challenges in twenty-seven states. The Libertarians went into court in seven states and the SWP in several others.

The discrimination directed against third parties raises a fundamental question about American elections: How much is the outcome affected by the process? The conclusion seems undeniable that to an alarming extent the process is making decisions that ought to be left to the voters.

The impact of the system's biases can be seen more readily when the discrimination is reversed. Could Carter and Ford have attracted a total of seventy-eight million votes with only a two-minute exposure on the evening news? Would MacBride, Camejo, or McCarthy have won the support of more voters with $21 million to spend or with fifteen minutes each night on network television? Would their mere inclusion in the televised debates have made their campaigns more viable and enlivened the election as a whole? If it is conceded that the outcome of the election would have been altered even a little by these shifts of resources, then it must be acknowledged that the means are shaping the end.

The political process should be neutral. It is not the function of the three commercial networks to decide for the American people which candidates are "significant" and which are not. It is not the duty of the incumbent parties to screen out potential competition and deny the electorate a broad choice of alternatives. Public funds should not be funneled to some candidates while denied to others. All candidates should be given fair and equal treatment and the voters left with the task of deciding among them.

Given the unbalanced coverage of campaigns and the firm hold of the Democratic and Republican Parties over the ballot and political pursestrings, the odds are against one of the third parties seriously challenging or replacing one of the dominant parties. The Democratic and Republican Parties have become almost as institutionalized as the Senate and the Supreme Court. It is ironic that while more and more Americans are withdrawing their allegiance from the major parties — and the polls show the number of independents at around 40 per cent and growing — the major parties have steadfastly continued to enjoy unchallengeable preeminence in American politics. It is not necessarily because they are valued and respected, but rather because of the biases built into the system. "The American parties continue to exist," as Lord Bryce noted many years ago, "because they have existed."

Probably no more than 1.5 million Americans voted for candidates other than Jimmy Carter or Gerald Ford. Of these votes, about 170,000 went to the American Independent Party's Lester Maddox, the candidate of the far Right. Roger MacBride, whose Libertarian Party appealed to both the laissez-faire Right and the civil libertarian Left, received some 175,000 votes, including an impressive 6 per cent in Alaska. Eugene McCarthy received close to three-quarters of a million votes while the rest of the minor-party vote was divided among the fragmented American Left: Hall of the Communist Party, Camejo of the SWP, Frank Zeidler of the Socialist Party, the Socialist Labor Party's Julius Levin, and People's Party candidate Margaret Wright.

A million and a half votes out of a total eighty million cast may not sound like much. But certainly it is too great a number to be so quickly and thoroughly ignored. If the portion of the electorate that voted for McCarthy and the Left candidates had registered its disapproval of the incumbent parties by gathering on the steps of the Capitol or in Lafayette Park instead of going to the polls, it would have surely won equal billing with the ape boy on the eve-

ning news. The largest antiwar demonstration, after all, attracted only a third as many people. And if the system had not worked so hard to channel people into the Democratic and Republican Parties, there would have definitely been more than a million and a half votes in the third-party column.

So, for those who might have worried that the delay in announcing third-party returns is an indication that conscientious election officials are still working frantically through mountains of uncounted minor-party votes, there is no cause for alarm. It is a lack of respect for third-party votes rather than their volume that has prolonged the count. It is unlikely that Jimmy Carter will be interrupted during his inaugural address with the message, "They've finished the count. It's Gus." ☐

★★

23 Nonlessons of the Campaign   Michael Barone

Political campaigns ideally are supposed to give the electorate an opportunity to evaluate issues, to understand the candidates' views on policy questions, and to inform office-seekers about their concerns. After every presidential election, says Michael Barone, "There is an irresistible temptation to extract lessons from what has happened." Some presidential elections, to be sure, are historic in importance, for important issues were decided by their outcomes. Which elections have presented the voters with fundamental policy choices and which therefore had long-standing impact? Do most presidential elections, throughout our history, hold tremendous significance for American politics? It would seem that the 1976 election had no such dramatic meaning. What reasons are given for Gerald Ford's defeat by Jimmy Carter? A number of factors affect the voters' choice of candidates in an election: party loyalty, issues, even personalities. Could it be said that "personality" dominated this election campaign more than policy questions? If so, why was that the case?

The 1976 election did make some headlines. It was one of very few occasions when the incumbent president lost reelection. Can you recall any other elections when the incumbent lost? It also provided the first debate since the Kennedy-Nixon debate of 1960. Who was considered to be the "winner" of that 1960 confrontation, and why? How did the 1976 debate compare with 1960 in terms of political impact? Moreover, it appears that voting turnout in the 1976 election reached the lowest point in fifty years. Could the Ford-Carter debates have been a reason for such a low voter turnout? What other factors explain voter disinterest in our presidential elections?

★ ★ ★

Nonlessons of the campaign

This year's election demonstrated that what we thought was happening was not necessarily what was going on.

By Michael Barone

After every Presidential election there is an irresistible temptation to extract lessons from what has happened. Unfortunately, such lessons can be poor guides to the future. From 30 years of post-New Deal history, commentators concluded that an incumbent President could not be ousted in the absence of a great depression; then Johnson was forced out in 1968, Nixon in 1974 (not in an election, to be sure, but by a political process) and Ford in 1976. More recently, people concluded from Edmund Muskie's unsuccessful 1972 campaign that no Democrat could enter all the primaries and survive; this year Jimmy Carter did just that, and won. Looking over the 1968 and 1972 results from the South—where Humphrey and McGovern each got about 30 percent of the votes—some concluded that in the near future no Democrat was going to carry an appreciable number of Southern states; but most of Carter's 297 electoral votes came from the South. Does this mean that there will now be a "solid South"? Not at all: Carter only ran 4 percent stronger in the South than in the nation as a whole.

And so it goes. Generals who apply the lessons of the last war too mechanically usually lose the next one. In extracting lessons from an election—this recent one included—one must avoid making universal rules out of circumstances that are peculiar to a specific time and situation. It is helpful also to write with hindsight. During this year's Presidential race, I worked for a polling firm, conducting surveys in many states in all parts of the country and with access to many others. Looking back over the 1976 campaign, I think I am able to reconstruct with substantial accuracy

Michael Barone is vice president of Peter D. Hart Research Associates, a polling firm.

what was going on—which was not necessarily what we thought was happening at the time.

(1) *Underneath all the talk of abortion and Playboy and Eastern Europe, there was a strong underlying desire for change, which worked right through Election Day for the Democrats and against Gerald Ford.* After Vietnam and Watergate, Americans felt misled and betrayed by their President. For the first time in years, surveys showed that most Americans preferred new, if untested, leadership to what they had. For example, a New York Times/CBS pre-election poll showed that voters thought the need for new ideas was greater than the value of experience—a marked departure from the traditional desire for experienced Presidential candidates. Dissatisfaction with the present also explains why the state of the nation indicator devised by Daniel Yankelovich for Time magazine was well below 50 percent during the campaign period.

Since early 1973, when the Watergate scandal broke, by margins on the order of 60 to 30 percent, voters, according to Hart Research polls, were saying that the nation is pretty seriously off on the wrong track—a sharp contrast with the past. There were only two brief exceptions: the month between the accession of Gerald Ford and his pardon of Richard Nixon and the week or so after the Mayaguez incident of 1975. Unfortunately for Gerald Ford, memory of the Nixon pardon lingered on, while the Mayaguez was quickly forgotten.

During the primary season, Jimmy Carter seemed closely attuned to the desire for change. In his standard stump speech, he emphasized that he was not a lawyer and not a member of Congress—by implication not one of those responsible for the mess we were in. Without adopting positions that would allow the press to label

him an orthodox liberal, he was able to suggest that he would make substantial changes in the way the Government works and the way leadership is exercised.

But in campaigning for the general election, instead of stressing that he stood for a new kind of leadership, Carter wrapped himself in the mantle of Franklin Roosevelt, Harry Truman, John Kennedy, and even Lyndon Johnson—a clear suggestion that he intended to be little different from what came before. Presumably Carter thought he was capitalizing on the fact that a plurality, if not a majority, of Americans consider themselves Democrats. But the more important point was that Democrats, like everyone else, were more interested in a President who would represent a break with tradition, and Gerald Ford's campaign consultants were very much aware of it.

The basic positive message of the Ford campaign was that the President had begun to produce the change Americans wanted, and the basic task of his advertising was to convince skeptical Americans. Thus, Ford's advertising stressed how much things had changed since August 1974—in effect, Ford was running against Richard Nixon as much as the Democrats were. And in October, his TV spots featured pictures of the Tall Ships—to associate him with positive feelings about the Bicentennial—and the song "I'm Feeling Good About America." The strategy was a daring one, an attempt to turn around very basic attitudes about the nation; and the polling evidence indicates that, to some extent, it worked. The numbers show voter support of Ford rising from 27 percent in July to nearly 49 percent on Election Day.

(2) *Carter's attempt to make his character a central theme almost made him a loser.* Instead of keeping public attention focused on how bad things

were. Carter insisted on focusing public attention on whether he was really as good as he said. The evidence indicates that he did this quite deliberately, beginning in the primaries, when he promised voters that he would never tell a lie, and then told them they shouldn't vote for him if he did. Naturally, the press, the political community and finally the voters themselves began scrutinizing Carter's record in Georgia and his campaign rhetoric for inconsistencies and misstatements; not surprisingly, many people felt they found some. Carter's predilection to dwell on his personal qualities was never clearer than in his granting of the disastrous Playboy interview; he had done it, he said, to help the voters understand him better.

One may commend Carter, especially after our experiences with Richard Nixon, for inviting scrutiny of his character. But as a political tactic, it was—almost—disastrous. Every gaffe he made—ethnic purity, adultery in his heart—was magnified in importance. The 1976 election is probably unique in American history as one in which the focus of attention was not on the performance of the incumbent President but rather on the character of the challenger. Carter had shifted the emphasis of the campaign from a question favorable to him (Do you want change?) to one favorable to the opposition (Is Jimmy Carter perfect?).

If Jimmy Carter's basic tactic was to test himself against the slogan "Why not the best?", the Ford campaign was sending out a far more modest message, which could be paraphrased as "You could do worse." The incumbent had set somewhat undemanding standards for himself since his initial speech as President ("a Ford, not a Lincoln"); and if he sometimes did what he had promised not to do (the pardon, running in 1976), voters and the press seemed inclined to forgive him on the ground that he was, after all, just a politician—and a nice guy. The Carter campaign didn't do much to disturb this image. Carter himself refused to mention the pardon (although Mondale did so). And the Carter forces specifically refused to use television advertisements prepared by Tony Schwartz—spots which contrasted Ford's reputation as a nice guy with his record of vetoing bills that would help people.

Until the end, the Carter TV campaign ran what I call "Salem ads" —lots of green fields and trees but little specific content. In contrast, Ford's team prepared some simple but effective negative commercials about Carter. People interviewed on the street, conspicuously including some Georgians, said they didn't know where Carter stood or that he hadn't been much of a Governor. One especially shrewd touch: The comments about Ford in the same commercials were lukewarm —enhancing the advertisements' credibility.

What finally got the public away from thinking of the election as a referendum on Carter was not anything Carter did, but the fact that the contest had become a dead heat in the public polls. People no longer had to decide whether to give their personal imprimatur to a man who was about to be elected President; rather, they had to decide whether they wanted Gerald Ford to be President for four more years or whether they wanted to take a chance on Carter. Forced finally to choose between an unsatisfactory Republican present and an uncertain Democratic future, the voters chose the Democrats—narrowly. It could have been a much larger victory.

(3) *The real winner was not Carter or Ford—but "none of the above."* The weather on election day was pleasant, and as the morning passed, the word went out that turnout was high. Not so. Turnout was at a record low. In 1976, only 53 percent of those eligible to vote actually bothered to do so—the lowest participation, with one exception, in the last 50 years. (The exception was 1948, at a time when turnout was depressed in the South by the poll tax and racial discrimination.) Of all Americans over 18, 27 percent voted for Carter, 26 percent voted for Ford, and 47 percent stayed home.

Last summer, Hart Research conducted a survey on nonvoters for the Committee for the Study of the American Electorate, which made clear that the vast majority of nonvoters fail to vote, not because of obstacles like the difficulty of registering, but because of deeply held attitudes. The overwhelming majority of nonvoters believe that their vote will never make any difference and that all politicians say one thing and do another; they believe that things are headed in the wrong direction, and will continue that way no matter who wins elections. Their nonvoting is an actual vote of no confidence in our politicians and political system.

The 1976 election results show that these negative attitudes are growing, not decreasing, in importance. Some excuse the low turnout four years ago (55 percent, compared with 61 percent in 1968) on the ground that we had an unusually large number of newly enfranchised voters that year (because of the 18-year-old vote) and because

the outcome of the election was not in doubt. Neither of these turnout-depressing factors applied this year. And in fact, comparing Census Bureau data with that of the New York Times/CBS post-election poll, even fewer voters in the 18-to-20 group turned out for this year's Presidential election than in 1972.

The low turnout for 1976 has consequences not just for this year, but possibly for a generation to come. One function of the past peak turnout years of 1940 (Roosevelt vs. Willkie), 1952 (Eisenhower vs. Stevenson) and 1960 (Kennedy vs. Nixon) was to draw into the voting stream the people in the 25-to-35 age group who were raising families and setting down roots. (Turnout is always lower among the under-25's, who are far more mobile and less attached to their communities.) Today we have a disproportionately large number of people in this key 25-to-35 age group, as a result of the high birth rates of the baby-boom years of the 1940's and early 1950's. But it is clear from the turnout figures that they are not entering the voting stream in the same numbers as did two previous generations of baby-boom people—those of World War I in 1952 and those of the 20's in 1960. This is particularly the case with young eligible voters who have never attended college—the cynical young blue-collar workers of the 70's.

And looking ahead, it is not clear when this generation will take to the polls—if ever. The most likely scenario for the 1980 election (though of course we cannot be sure) is the routine re-election of a President—an outcome without the uncertainty which has been a key ingredient in earlier peak turnout years. By 1984, it is possible that nonvoting, rather than voting, could become the norm for an increasing number of Americans—especially blue-collar workers and their families. That would reflect a population with more negative attitudes toward, and less stake in, our basic institutions. There was nothing inevitable about the high levels of participation we saw in 1940, 1952, and 1960; and it may be a long time before we see them again.

(4) *The primary system worked well, and should be retained.* Every election-year spring, there are complaints about the complexity and number of Presidential primaries. But a society which can keep track of 28 National Football League teams in six divisions with their complicated playoff schedules is capable of making sense of the results of some 31 Presidential primaries.

The primary system has a number of advantages which would be difficult to duplicate in any other Presidential-delegate selection system. First, barriers to entry are low. A Jimmy Carter or Morris Udall or Fred Harris —candidates

who have convinced a body of people who know them well that they ought to be President — can enter the primary in New Hampshire or the precinct caucuses in Iowa and, if they do well there, introduce themselves to the American people. A Carter or a Udall could not have raised the amount of money (on the

order of $10 million) needed to compete in a national primary, or even enough for a regional primary. But if he can assemble a significant constituency, then he can raise enough to carry the battle elsewhere.

The second great advantage of having a whole series of primaries is that they give us at least some insight into how candidates and their staffs handle themselves under pressure and stress.

Third, primaries are much better gauges of public opinion than are party caucuses, which tend to be made up of patronage employees or idealistic activists, neither of

whom are necessarily reflective of the general public. Democratic pros in 1967 and Republican pros in 1975 tended to underestimate opposition to their party's administration. Having a series of primaries helps us learn when the pros are wrong, as they often are.

(5) *The debates didn't determine the result.* Every one, including me, watched the debates this year with the expectation that they would do—or fail to do—what we remember the 1960 debates as having done—that is, swing the election to the Democratic challenger because he projected at least as much competence and coolness as the more experienced Republican. And when Jimmy Carter demonstrated, in the second and third debates, as much poise and expertise as Ford, and when public television's instant polls of 300 voters said Carter had "won," we assumed that the same thing was happening again.

But it wasn't, because voters weren't looking for the same mix of qualities in their President in 1976 as they had been in 1960. Back then, the quality people sought above all others was competence as measured by experience; indeed, the most experienced Presidential candidates won every election between 1936 and 1956. In 1960 Nixon was running on the slogan "Ex-

perience counts," and Kennedy had to demonstrate that he was as competent.

The voters of 1976, fresh from finding that one of the most experienced Presidents in American history was a crook, did not value experience as highly. Certainly they expected some level of competence, and both Carter and Ford seemed to meet this standard in the debate; but what voters were looking for this year was, above all else, honesty and, next, a quality that could be called responsiveness: understanding and really caring about the needs of ordinary people, being genuine.

'The contest had become a dead heat in the polls. Forced to choose between an unsatisfactory Republican present and an uncertain Democratic future, the voters chose the Democrats—narrowly. It could have been a much larger victory.'

The point here is that neither of these qualities is really tested in a debate format. So while the debates were central in 1960, because they established that Kennedy possessed the quality voters wanted, in 1976 they were not.

Certainly the debates did alter, perhaps even distort, the flow of the campaign. For several days before each debate the candidates would prepare, and afterward they would rest while their entourages proclaimed them the victors and the pundits picked over their mistakes. So during the debate periods, the only real campaigning that was done, aside from the debates themselves, was television advertising.

And it must have been advertising that was swaying people's votes. The proof is that even though Carter was generally judged the winner of the debates, it was Ford who was gaining in the polls during the period of the second and third debates — despite his mistake about Eastern Europe in the second one.* It was in October that

*This is the finding of the Harris poll and of private surveys with which I am familiar. Gallup showed Ford dropping after the second debate, then rising, with little movement in Carter's percentage. Whichever figures you rely on, it is clear that Carter, the acclaimed winner of the second and third debates, did not

Ford's negative advertisements were calling into question Carter's honesty and responsiveness — the basic qualities which voters were most looking for—and they were doing it effectively, building on Carter's earlier mistakes. Television ads are a more emotional medium than debates, and a more effective way to communicate strength or weakness of character. Indeed, this is the only good explanation for the fact that Ford's fortunes were rising through most of October and Carter's were falling.

(6) This was not a watershed or landmark election, nor is it a revival of the New-Deal coalition of the 1940's. Every time we have a close election, there is a temptation to claim that it proves more than it does. Even the most perceptive analysts fall victim. Samuel Lubell, after the 1948 election, proclaimed that

gain during this period, and that Ford, the acclaimed loser, did not lose ground.

there was a natural Democratic majority in this country; Republicans have won the majority of Presidential elections since. Kevin Phillips, writing in perceptive anticipation of the 1968 election results, predicted the emergence of a Republican majority with great strength in the South; we can be fairly confident now that that has not occurred. As for 1976, it is not the beginning of some new majority or the end of an old one; it is simply the verdict of American voters on the choice between Jimmy Carter and Gerald Ford, in this specific year.

A look at the map of states carried by the two candidates may suggest that Carter's majority, consisting of most of the South and several big Northeastern states, is a revival of the Kennedy majority or even that of Franklin D. Roosevelt in 1944. A closer look at the figures dispels these notions. Carter actually ran behind Roosevelt in every

Southern state, including Georgia; the Republicans won significant minorities in almost every one, and should not despair of winning some Southern electoral votes in a different election with different candidates. And though Carter lost most of the Midwestern states, he ran ahead of Roosevelt's showing and of Kennedy's in about half; future Democratic Presidential candidates will not write off the Midwest. Indeed, this 1976 contest proved to be extremely close in an extraordinarily large number of states, including most of the big ones.

There is a long-range tendency in American politics for the South to become more Republican and the North to become more Democratic. It is part of a movement from the regional loyalties of the Civil War period to a more homogeneous nation connected by national news media. The movement has been glacial and has proceeded at an uneven pace. As it happened

this year, both parties picked candidates from their ancestral bases (the Deep South and the Upper Midwest), where their strength has been ebbing; regional affinities and historical trends worked at cross purposes, making the election close in all parts of the country once it became close nationwide.

We are unlikely to see an enduring Democratic or Republican majority at a time when people's party ties are weakening, as clearly they are: In the last four elections, every state except Massachusetts, Arizona and the District of Columbia has voted for both Republican and Democratic candidates. So don't look for the partisan patterns of 1976 to be repeated. The primary lesson of the 1976 campaign is that many things can occur, but that it takes a lot of mistakes for a candidate to lose when the basic currents of public opinion are working in his favor. ■

★★

24

Jimmy Carter's Problem   Richard M. Scammon and Ben J. Wattenberg

There is much talk that Jimmy Carter will be a one-term president. What reasons are given to support this view? Can you see any disadvantages to the political system when a president remains in office only one term? In this essay Richard Scammon and Benjamin Wattenberg link Carter's political vulnerability to the uneasy nature of his 1976 electoral coalition. At that time it seemed that many voters were unclear as to whether Carter was a liberal or a conservative. Given his performance in office, what actions show his liberalism? His conservatism?

More important, many Southerners supported Carter because he represented their region. To what extent are Carter's origins analogous to John F. Kennedy's religion in 1960? Jimmy Carter's problem seems related to the South. Which electoral group in that region, according to the authors, was essential to Carter's victory in 1976, and why? Should President Carter become too liberal, many Southerners may oppose his reelection in 1980. On the other hand, he received many votes from traditional Democratic voters who are liberal. Which electoral groups are these?

Thus, it appears that Carter is under pressure to satisfy electoral groups with very different ideological viewpoints. Moreover, his "problem" is compounded by the fact that "there is no liberal non-South." What does this mean, and how does it pertain to Carter's problem? In light of all the events that have transpired since this article was written, do you think that Jimmy Carter's problem has gotten worse? Will his electoral coalition of 1976 survive in 1980? Is the public any clearer today as to what political ideology Carter represents? Can he in 1980 again convince the public that he is "everyman's" candidate?

This article implies that a fundamental problem faces all presidents. To the extent that a president's election is secured by making promises to various electoral groups and special interests in society, is it possible for any president to govern effectively without eventually losing much of his political base of support? Do you think, therefore, that we will be seeing numerous "one-term" presidents in the future?

★ ★ ★

Jimmy Carter's Problem

Richard M. Scammon & Ben J. Wattenberg

It is the thesis of this piece that the nature and implementation of President Carter's victory in 1976 has within it the seeds of a very great problem for him as he moves now into the second year of his term and begins, inevitably, to look ahead to his own 1980 reelection prospects.

Much of the recent talk has focused on the possibility of Carter becoming a "one-term President," on "his need for victories," the alleged ineptitude of his Georgia staff, the alienation of specific groups because of specific reasons, his attempt to "do too much," and so on. But missing from the discussion so far have been certain structural and ideological factors which may ultimately prove more troublesome to Mr. Carter than—as they say in the polling business—"all of the above."

Mr. Carter's problems are, at once, familiar and national ones, and in a more intense key, regional and peculiar ones: He won by capturing the votes of centrist switchers; he is in trouble, and may get into deeper trouble if he is perceived to be moving from the center toward the left. In his case, these not-so-unusual presidential afflictions are magnified by Carter's remarkable showing in the South in 1976.

Accordingly, it may be useful to look at that Southern regional situation first—critically important in and of itself—because it sheds light on the broader issue as well.

From *Public Opinion*, March/April 1978, pp. 3–8, © 1978 American Enterprise Institute. Reprinted with permission.

I

Why did Carter win in 1976?

It is, of course, customary after a close election for almost every group to claim that it was their specific group, their hard work, their support that "elected" the winner. When the winner in question is the President of the United States, such claims are made with particular vigor.

The aftermath of President Carter's victory has been no exception. Blacks have claimed the credit—although Gallup data show that Carter actually got a slightly lesser proportion of the black vote than did McGovern in 1972 or Humphrey in 1968. Jews have claimed the credit, although their voting percentages for Carter—73 percent according to an NBC election-day poll—were actually slightly less than in so-called "normal" years (it being understood that within the election observing trade, "normal" years have become rare enough to be called "abnormal"). Labor has claimed the credit with somewhat greater justification: They "came back" from a 1972 Republican vote to go solidly with Carter—but at a rate not really greater than pre-1972 years—and they provided him with massive financial and organizational help.

In a sense, they are *all* correct. Carter could not have won *without* their support. But that is the very nature of a close election. A close election is close. (You may quote that.) When it gets close enough our psephological favorite, the Maltese-Americans, can also claim credit for victory.

But saying "you couldn't have won *without* us" is not quite the same as saying "you won *because* of us." It may be said that the latter claim can properly be made by a group that not only provides a margin of difference, but votes *away from traditional patterns* to provide the margin of difference.

A simple analysis of recent presidental elections shows that there is one most obvious major group of voters who can lay claim to that formula for 1976. That grouping is "The South."

As the data show, in recent years "The South" had been trending steadily away from the Democrats in presidential elections—until 1976.

Democratic Percentage
of Southern* Vote in
Presidential Elections,
1960-1976

1960	50.5
1964	49.5
1968	30.9
1972	28.9
but . . .	
1976	54.1 (!)

*Eleven states of the Confederacy.

This trend has also been reflected in the electoral vote count:

Electoral Votes
Won by Democratic Presidential
Candidate in the South*, 1960-1976

1960	81
1964	81
1968	25
1972	0
but . . .	
1976	118 (!)

*Eleven states of the Confederacy.

There is another way of putting the 1976 Southern story: *Carter ran best in that area of the country where recent Democratic presidential candidates had been running worst.* That was the great paradox of the 1976 election.

There is a sub-tabulation available that is of particular relevance. The 1976 break with voting patterns in the South occurred almost exclusively among *white* Southerners. It was the sharpest break in that group in three decades. Here is a trend line for Southern white Protestants voting Democratic in recent presidential years, showing a dramatic decline—and a dramatic revival in 1976:

Southern White Protestants:
Percentage Point Deviation from the National Democratic
Presidential Vote, 1936-1976

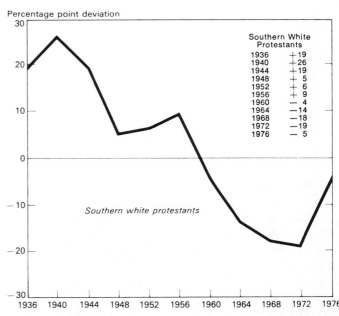

Southern White Protestants	
1936	+19
1940	+26
1944	+19
1948	+ 5
1952	+ 6
1956	+ 9
1960	− 4
1964	−14
1968	−18
1972	−19
1976	− 5

Source: Data from the following American Institute of Public Opinion surveys: *1936,* 72, 104, 150, 177; *1940,* 208, 209, 215, 219, 248; *1944,* 328, 329, 336, 337; *1948,* 430, 431, 432, 433; *1952,* 506, 507, 508, 509; *1956,* 572, 573, 574, 576; *1960,* 635, 636, 637, 638; *1964,* 697, 699, 701, 702; *1968,* 769, 770, 771, 773; *1972,* 857, 858, 859, 860; *1976,* 959, 960, 961, 962.

Note: This chart was constructed by Professor Everett Ladd and has been used in the past in his book, *Transformations of the American Party System.* Ladd determines the "percentage point deviation" by first calculating the national vote for each presidential candidate and then comparing it with the vote of a subgroup (here, Southern whites). Both the national and subgroup voting tallies are derived from Gallup surveys taken just before and after the presidential election.

The percentage of Southern blacks voting Democratic has been much higher than Southern whites—but it remained constant in 1976.

The big change came among white Southerners. Had they not switched to Carter in large numbers in 1976 he would not have won. If those switchers do not —for any reason—vote for him in 1980, it is unlikely that he will win again.

White Southerners. Aside from the fact that about half voted for Carter, enabling him to capture the South, what else do we know about them?

We know that despite all of the talk about the "New South"—a term which has a cicada-like rhythm in American politics—white Southerners are still more conservative than most voters in America. Pollster Lou Harris reported in a release last summer: "The South is easily the most conservative part of the country."

If white Southerners were the hinge of the Carter victory, and if white Southerners are more conservative than most American voters, it behooves us to ask: Was Jimmy Carter the more conservative of the presidential candidates in 1976?

The answer is no. Notwithstanding Carter's basic traditionalism (religious, ex-naval officer, small town, moral, businessman, and so on), Ford was generally seen as more conservative by the voters. A nationwide Harris poll taken in early September 1976, asked:

"How would you describe the political philosophy of (Gerald Ford, Jimmy Carter)—conservative, middle of the road, liberal or radical?"

And this was the clear response:

Political Philosophy	Ford %	Carter %
Conservative	36	17
Middle of the road	36	31
Liberal	5	26
Radical	3	4
Not sure	20	22

The most conservative part of the country voted for the more liberal candidate.

Well, then, why did so many white Southerners vote for Carter? Obviously, because he was a Southerner—and in spite of their ideological leanings. Southerners felt, with good reason, that the idea that "a Southerner couldn't be elected President" was an idea whose time had come—and gone. And so, millions of white Southerners, who in other years would likely vote for the more conservative candidate, voted for the Southern candidate.

With all that extra help, Carter managed to carry the South narrowly. Slightly more than half of the white Southerners still voted *against* him. But that was better by far than any recent Democratic candidate had done, as the tabulations above show.

So: looking to the future, we can say that if a relatively few Southern conservatives perceive Carter as a liberal in 1980 and vote conservative instead of Southern, Carter could be in serious trouble.

II

There may be a recent analogue to this tale of cross-rippling electoral tides, and it is an analogue that should be of great interest to Carter strategists.

In 1960, John F. Kennedy also won a close election when a large bloc of voters abandoned ideological and/ or party-oriented behavior to vote along the axis of an external factor. The "externality" then was not that "a *Southerner* couldn't be elected President," but that "a *Catholic* couldn't be elected President." And millions of Catholics, who would normally have voted Republican, switched to vote for Jack Kennedy in a successful attempt to smash that outrageous religious axiom of our politics.

The big question, in both the Kennedy and the Carter situations, and for election pundits generally, is this: Having once voted on an externality—Catholicism or Southernism—is a voter likely to vote that way again *once his point has been proved?* Would Catholics keep voting for a Catholic for President, against their ideological bent, even after it had been demonstrated that a Catholic *could* be elected President? Will Southerners have to prove a point about the South, again, after they proved it once in 1976?

Of course, we don't know the answer to the Southern question yet, but we have an idea about the Catholic question. John Kennedy, tragically, did not live to run for reelection in 1964. But since 1964, many Catholics have run for either President or Vice President in general elections and primaries: William Miller, Eugene McCarthy, Robert Kennedy, Edmund Muskie, Thomas Eagleton, Sargent Shriver, Jerry Brown—to name a few. *In no instance is there evidence that Catholicism became a major voting issue.*

It is as if the external issue, once settled, disappears, much as Prohibition, child labor, and free coinage of silver disappeared as issues once they were resolved.

Let us assume that the Catholic-Kennedy situation is indeed analogous to the Southern-Carter situation. With Southernism no longer a factor (as Catholicism is no longer a factor), President Carter would have to compete in 1980 along only the normal modes of voter reaction. These include: incumbency, personality, state of the nation, state of the world, record in office— *and ideology.*

Question: Under such circumstances, could Carter do well in the still-conservative white South? Surely he *could*. If the country is at peace and inflation rates are low, unemployment rates are low, and economic growth rates are high, Carter would not only carry the South, he'd sweep the nation. On the other hand, if you change the "lows" for "high" and the "high" for "lows," he might not carry Plains. But in a mixed and mottled real-world situation so common in recent years, the critical question is this: Is Carter *likely* to do as well as he needs to in the white South?

Well, he would have a good shot at it so long as he is not perceived to be wholly out of touch with mainstream Southern ideology (which remains more conservative than that of the rest of the nation).

So far—if one accepts the reportage of President Carter's administration—he has managed to maintain and even strengthen his image as a moderate. Enormous publicity is generated when black leaders denounce Carter for not spending enough. He wins more plaudits when he still says he will balance the budget. He denies federal aid for abortion. He promises the new welfare program will not hike welfare costs. He is attacked by organized labor for a variety of slights. He makes a tough-minded, vigorous defense of human rights and tough SALT proposals. And, as a result, public opinion polls show that fewer Americans regard Carter as "a liberal" than when he was elected.

On the other hand—less often reported, or less stressed for their political impact—have been a series of other acts that would, or should, or likely will, persuade more and more people that there is a "liberal" in the White House. ("Liberal," remember, is what liberal Morris Udall described in 1976 as a "worry word" when he asked the political press to please describe him as a "progressive.")

Many moderates and even more conservatives, viewing political developments through their own prisms, have noted with dismay: that Carter has signed the Panama treaties, that his welfare program ended up calling for substantially more spending, that he axed the B-1, that he condemns America's fear of communism as "inordinate" (neglecting to describe the ordinate parameter of such fear, which leads him to ask for a $10 billion increase in the defense budget), that he has taken mini-steps to recognize Cuba and Vietnam, that his energy program is widely assailed as pro-environmental and anti-production, that he backs down on SALT and human rights, that he deals the Soviets back into the Middle East, that it has become increasingly apparent this his budget will not come close to balance, that he goes public with Ralph Nader for a Consumer Protection Agency, that he allows his administration to be characterized as pro-quotas, and so on.

It could be said that these two lists are not a bad mix. Many voters' views would conform with some items in Group A and some in Group B.

But the key tactical question is this one: How vulnerable would President Carter be in his home region if he can readily be depicted as pro-Panama "giveaway," pro-quotas, pro-welfare, anti-growth, pro-Cuba, and so on. Not to put too fine a point on it, how would you like to carry that record into the South in 1980 running against a candidate who disagreed with all those positions—and perhaps had his own Southern credentials as well? (Several names come to mind.)

Well, some will say, what Carter may lose in the conservative South, he will more than make up in the liberal non-South.

But there is no liberal non-South. There is no clearer datum in modern American politics. Remember: It was Ford, not Carter, who carried the nation outside of the old confederacy, in both popular and electoral votes. And even if there were a liberal non-South, that's not how or why Carter won in 1976. Carter carried what he did outside of the South for the same reason he was able to carry the South: his opponents tried, but were not quite able to tag him as "Southern-Fried McGovern." Carter thus regained many Democratic "switchers," those voters who went to Nixon in 1972 because they found the perceived hyper-liberalism of the McGovernites unpalatable, indeed repugnant. Who were those switchers? Union men and women, Catholics, ethnics, Jews, "inner city peripherals," suburbanites and on and on. Many, many voters of all stripes; voters able in many instances to identify with a traditional muscular, bread-and-butter, pocketbook liberalism—but wholly against anything perceived as "far-out."

Looking ahead to 1980, then, it can be postulated that much of what has been advanced here about Southern votes may be wholly applicable to the non-South, albeit in lower intensity and without the special minus (from Carter's point of view) of possibly no longer having his "Southerness" as quite so potent an issue.

Public opinion polls are clear: quotas, Panama, environmentalism, Russians-in-the-Middle-East are not the issues that endear the non-Southern non-liberals to the Democratic Party or its candidate, even if he is President.

As this is written President Carter has served just a year of his first term. The issues of today will not necessarily be the issues of 1980. He has plenty of time to shift course gently, almost imperceptibly, if he feels politically threatened in the South or anywhere else for that matter.

Indeed, that may prove to be exactly what Carter tries to do—all quite properly within the general presidential rubric of "doing what's best for the country."

(After all, one of his jobs is to represent the voters, isn't it?) But there is still this question: Will he be able to make such a shift even if he wants to?

To think about that question, one must look at the nature of the presidential appointments—to those men and women who generate presidential policies and who inevitably shape the presidential image.

At the cabinet level one gets a sense of a political outlook that is, at once, technocratic and slightly left-of-center—which is about proper for a Democratic administration.

But quite a different picture emerges when one examines the sub-cabinet and sub sub-cabinet appointments. Perhaps unwittingly, perhaps wittingly, it is not moderate technocrats who most prominently populate these slots. Ideologues live there—ideologues from every one of the activist movements of the last decade. Environmentalists, consumerists, civil rights and women's activists, veterans of the peace movement have moved en masse from their ginger groups to large federal offices controlling massive budgets and armies of bureaucrats. A recent *Fortune* article names *sixty* high-level appointments made from activist groups; beneath them are a small army of their cohorts. And Senator McGovern, after a list of the Carter State Department appointees was completed late in 1976 remarked that those were the same people *he* would have picked. Senator Jackson did not make a similar statement. Columnist John Roche recently quoted a high-level State Department official saying, "I voted for Carter to get rid of Kissinger, and I got McGovern."

(This story is told: A young woman executive, formerly with the Sierra Club, now with the Department of the Interior at a salary about five times higher than the $10,000 per year she previously made, has suggested that all former Movement-niks tithe 10 percent of their salaries to their previous organizations! Imagine the public reaction if in an earlier administration a businessman recruited to government service suggested tithing back to Exxon!)

It is not the purpose of this short article either to praise or condemn the attitudes and views of those remnants of the Movement who now hold high federal office. Nor is the purpose here to suggest that all the ex-activists-now-in-government are reacting the same way to their present high eminence. Some are of the opinion that they work for the elected executive and should represent his views, some feel that ideology reigns and that it is their job to seek an outlet for their ideology.

Still, agree with them or disagree with them, a great many of these once-young ex-activists can be said to represent a general point of view. We can say several things about that point of view. It tends to be activist about the proper role of the federal government. It is often anti-establishment: anti-business, anti-defense,

anti-labor to name a few. In the age-old argument, it tends to stress equality somewhat more than liberty. It tends to be somewhat ashamed of America's role in shaping the modern world. It has a know-it-all elitist quality, probably reinforced by President Carter's insistence that all he did was hire the best people with the most merit—apparently without considering just what substantive policies these apparatchiks would be meritorious at initiating. It is a point of view not only well to the left on the American political spectrum but well to the left in the Democratic Party. It takes positions that, as perceived, tend to be "out of sync" with mainstream American attitudes—which remain opposed to quotas, a lower defense posture, ecology-overgrowth, and so on.

The President apparently feels that his activists, to use the old Washington phrase, are "on tap not on top." The theory is that the moderates can balance the activists, and one may speculate that is the reason President Carter appointed at the top rung men of moderate reputations—the Schlesingers, Strausses, Lances, Vances, and Schultzes. Ideally, these senior moderates could channel the energies and ideas of the activists into courses sympathetic to the President's own views and synergistic to his political interests.

Well, maybe. We shall see. But many veteran bureaucracy-watchers are dubious. This dubiety stems from several sources. First, in Washington, if you ever have a choice of choosing the cabinet or the sub-cabinet, pick the latter. The men and women whose names are pre-fixed with "Sec." spend a great deal of time testifying, traveling and giving speeches. Their underlings tend to make policy. Bureaucrats sense that more ideas bubble up than trickle down. Second, winning half the battles isn't nearly enough. As the bubbling-up process ensues, some—most—ideas and rhetoric (and a candidate can get hung on a phrase as well as a program) that are not in keeping with the President's views are surely screened out. No matter. Some are not. If and as they become policy or doctrine, the President must live with them and defend them—all over the country. The hardliners may win on an I.L.O. decision. Fine. But down in the ranks someone wrote a sentence for the President's Notre Dame speech about the "inordinate fear of Communism," and that may be a subject of attack even if the attackers approve of the I.L.O. position.

As this is written, President Carter is on the griddle for a number of policies that seem clearly to derive from the New Politics bias of his government-by-sub-cabinet apparatchik.

—True to that bias, his energy program was heralded as an ecology program. "The age of abundance is over," crowed the environmentalists after its promulgation last spring. True to that bias, a score and more dams were axed. In each instance, the Congress thought otherwise.

—True to that bias, ideological environmentalists within the government have recently sought to apply American ecological standards to export goods, irrespective, apparently, of the wishes of the buying countries and with scant regard for the economic chaos that might be generated in America.

—True to that bias, the government's *amicus* brief on Bakke was open to interpretation as pro-quota or at least not anti-quota: "Minority-sensitive" is the new obfuscatory phrase. The President will be politically lucky if the Nixon-dominated Court goes against his brief, bails him out, thereby mooting the issue. If it does not oblige, the President can look forward to a campaign where he is described as Jimmy Quoter.

—True to that bias, Carter seemingly dealt the Soviets a plum in the Middle East, managing in a stroke to politically unite those sympathetic to Israel with those unsympathetic to the Soviets. It was only Anwar Sadat's bold effort that was able to rectify that error.

—True to that bias, early indications show a SALT treaty destined to cause an historic Senate confrontation.

Are these chance occurrences? Will the pattern of a leftward tilt continue? Does it represent the views of "the real Carter"? Is the GOP wise enough, and unified enough, to capitalize on it? If this pattern is perceived in the Washington political community but not around the country, will a ripple effect spread the perception? Credibly? Can Carter control his apparatchiks if he wants to? Has he already begun to try? Do his State of the Union and budget messages already presage that attempt? Will his I'll-never-tell-a-lie personality, which a majority of Americans still trust ac-

cording to the polls, be enough to override these problems?

In all truth, no one knows. It is a situation without precedent. The last time the Democrats took the White House from the Republicans a very different cast of characters took over. JFK's New Frontiersmen were described as "pragmatic" and "tough." They were men very much from the center of the political spectrum.

Today it is different. The Democratic Party now has a large and militant flapping left wing, nurtured by activists who are veterans of a decade-and-a-half of civil rights, anti-war, environmental, consumerist, and feminist causes. In a party that is slightly to the left of the people on most issues, the activists are to the left of the party and the apparatchiks are often to the left of the activists. They are part of the Carter coalition, they have moved into government and no one knows what their long-range effect will be. It is fair to ask, however, "upon what meat doth this our Caesar feed?"

The circumstance being a new one, it is fair to speculate about it. How much political indigestion have the activists caused Carter so far? Considerable, the authors feel. What will happen in the future? Our speculations vary only in degree, not in kind. Mr. Scammon thinks Mr. Carter will not lose control of his government, and a majority of the apparatchiks in question will be co-opted. Mr. Wattenberg acknowledges that possibility, sees some evidence of it, hopes to see more, but remains somewhat more concerned: for him there is a recurring image of the President as the Sorcerer's Apprentice, trying desperately and honorably to gain control of what proves to be uncontrollable.   ☑

★★

25

Choosing a President   Thomas E. Cronin

To this day the president is formally elected by the Electoral College, whose members are chosen by the people of each state and the District of Columbia. The existing system is not perfect, mainly because it distorts the principle that each citizen's vote should have equal weight in electing the president. Also, the winner may conceivably have a minority of the popular votes cast. How could this happen? Do you know which presidents so far have been elected without a majority of popular votes?

To strengthen the democratic basis of the election of a president, reformers are advocating a direct popular election. How would this proposed system work? Even this approach, however, has biases, and Cronin proceeds to defend a third alternative—the National Bonus Plan. What are its major features? The difficulty in evaluating any method of presidential election is that proponents and opponents can draw upon a number of different arguments to defend their positions. What are the arguments for and against the existing Electoral College system? For and against the proposal for a direct popular election? Why does Cronin think that the National Bonus Plan incorporates the best of the Electoral College plan and of direct popular election? Do you agree? Given the arguments in this essay, which scheme of presidential election do you favor?

★ ★ ★

THOMAS E. CRONIN

CHOOSING A PRESIDENT

Every four years, political observers grumble about our electoral college system — largely because it does not assure victory to the Presidential candidate who wins a majority of the popular votes. But nothing seems to get done. The complexity of the electoral college system makes it difficult for the average voter to understand its dangers. The road to electoral college reform is littered with the wrecks of hundreds of previous efforts. And even when the disease is clear, the remedy is not. Expert scholars, journalists, politicians, and political strategists differ in their estimates of the consequences of electoral reform.

Judging from the debate in the Committee on the Judiciary in the U.S. Senate during the Ninety-fifth Congress, politicians and commentators are divided, and deadlocked, between retaining the electoral college and amending the Constitution to provide for direct popular election of the President.

This paper reviews the major current arguments for and against direct popular election of the President. It then explains the political reasons why direct popular election, which has the overwhelming support of the American public, has not been enacted in Congress. Finally, it describes a novel compromise plan that would combine some of the central features of both the electoral college system and the direct-vote plan. I present this compromise plan partly out

of advocacy, partly to widen the circle of discussion of its merits and possible flaws.

The timeliness of this analysis stems from the fact that the electoral college will undoubtedly be replaced or at least significantly altered in the near future. Many observers believe that it may take the election of another popular-vote loser to prompt the sustained action needed to amend the U.S. Constitution. Others feel that one more close election, such as those in 1960, 1968, or 1976, may be enough. Whatever change does occur will have important consequences for the health of the political system, for the quality and balance of our political parties, and for the kind of democracy we are.

Support for abolishing the electoral college system is growing. Since 1966, Gallup and Harris polls have shown a steady rise in support for a constitutional amendment in the way we elect Presidents. A constitutional amendment overwhelmingly passed the House of Representatives in 1969, but foundered due to a filibuster the next year in the Senate.

In 1977, President Jimmy Carter became the first Democratic President to support abolishing the electoral college system. Carter's March 22, 1977, statement called for "direct popular election of the President," but left it to Congress "to proceed with its work without the interruption of a new proposal."

From *The Center Magazine*, September/October 1978. Reprinted with permission from *The Center Magazine*, a publication of the Center for the Study of Democratic Institutions, Santa Barbara, California.

Carter added: "I do not recommend a constitutional amendment lightly. I think the amendment process must be reserved for an issue of overriding governmental significance. But the method by which we elect our President is such an issue." Editorial and interest-group support have also grown, although there are some unlikely coalitions for and against reform.

The Senate has been the chief obstacle in the way of electoral college reform. Birch Bayh, the Senate's leading advocate of direct popular election, conducted nine days of hearings in the conservative Judiciary Committee during 1977. He barely succeeded in getting his measure, Senate Joint Resolution 1, out of committee. Opposition came from most of the committee's Republicans and from committee chairman James O. Eastland, and Senators John McClellan and James B. Allen. The Senate did not act on Bayh's amendment, due partly to a clogged schedule of Panama Canal and labor-reform debates.

But prospects in the Senate are changing. Senators Eastland and William Scott of Virginia will retire in early 1979; Senators McClellan and Allen have died during this Congress; and Senator Edward Kennedy is slated to become the chairman of the Judiciary Committee. Senator Bayh had approximately forty-five co-sponsors for his measure this time, including active support from the majority and minority leaders as well as strong backing from President Carter and Vice-President Walter Mondale. Senators Robert Dole, Howard Baker, and Robert Byrd are supporters, as are most of the younger and more moderate members in both parties. Bayh felt, too, that this time, as opposed to 1970, he would have had the votes to overcome a filibuster. (Until 1975, it took two-thirds of the senators present to close off debate. Under the new 1975 cloture rules, if sixteen senators sign a petition, two days later the question of curtailing debate is put to a vote. If three-fifths — sixty — of the total number of senators vote for cloture, no senator may speak for more than one hour.)

The founding fathers might well be amazed to find the electoral college system still in operation. Thomas Jefferson called it a blot on our Constitution. John Roche, a contemporary historian, aptly describes it as "a jerry-rigged improvisation which has subsequently been endowed with a high theoretical content."

For a long time the Constitutional Convention in Philadelphia accepted the idea that the President should be elected by Congress. But it was feared that either Congress would dominate the President or vice versa. Election by the state legislatures was rejected because of distrust of those bodies. Only after extensive deliberations was the electoral college system agreed upon. At the time it was an ingenious and original compromise. Everyone got something: large states got electoral votes based on their population; small states got an assurance of at least three electoral votes and a contingency procedure based on the one-state, one-vote principle; those who feared the "tyranny of the majority" got an indirect method of electing Presidents; and those who feared the national legislature got a method in which the states could play a major role. Evidence suggests, however, that no one was exactly sure how well it would work.

Alexander Hamilton, writing in *The Federalist No. 68,* said the compromise was an excellent one. It was good, he noted, that the people in the states in one way or another would help choose the electors. But he seemed more impressed that the immediate election would be made by a small, capable, and judicious elite who "will be most likely to possess the information and discernment requisite to so complicated an investigation."

Others believed that once President George Washington had finished his term or terms, the electors would fail to produce majorities and the President would usually be chosen by contingency means in the House of Representatives. George Mason thought that the selection would be made in the House nineteen out of twenty times.

As compromises go, it was a gamble. The Framers expected electors to be designated by state legislatures. These electors would be distinguished citizens who would in fact, as well as in form, nominate and then elect the President and the Vice-President. The rise of national political parties changed all this. By the time of the election in 1800, electors had come, by custom, to be party agents, usually pledged in advance to vote for designated party candidates.

How does the system work today? In making their Presidential choice in November, voters technically do not vote for a candidate, but choose between slates of Presidential electors, selected by the state political parties. The slate that wins a plurality of popular votes in the state casts all the electoral votes for that state. A state has one electoral vote for each senator and representative. The District of Columbia has three votes, granted it by the Twenty-third Amendment. Thus, there are 538 votes in the electoral

The winner-take-all formula is not a part of the Constitution

college. A candidate must get at least 270 to win the Presidency.

Technically, a President is not elected on election day. The victorious slates of electors travel to their state capitols on the first Monday after the second Wednesday in December. There they cast ballots for their party's candidates, perhaps hear some speeches, and go home. The ballots are then sent from the state capitols to the U.S. Congress, where, early in January, they are formally counted by House and Senate leaders and the name of the next President is announced.

If no candidate secures a majority of the electoral votes, the decision then goes to the House. This has happened twice, once in 1800 and again in 1824. People feared it might happen in 1968 if George Wallace had received enough electoral votes to keep Richard Nixon or Hubert Humphrey from obtaining a majority. In the House, each state delegation casts a single vote. If a delegation is evenly divided, the state forfeits its vote. Further, the influence of a third-party "spoiler" candidate may be significant, because the House chooses a President from among the top *three* candidates. Consecutive ballots are taken until a candidate wins a majority of the state delegations, twenty-six.

Advocates of the direct popular system argue that everyone's vote should count equally, people should vote directly for the candidate, and the candidate who gets the most votes should win.

Perhaps the most disliked feature of our present electoral arrangements is that the electoral college method can elect a President who has fewer popular votes than the opponent. This can happen because all of a state's electoral votes are awarded to the winner of the state's popular vote, regardless of whether the winning candidate's margin is one vote or three million votes. Ironically, the major defect here — the unit-rule provision — is not a part of the Constitution. This winner-take-all, unit-rule formula is merely a state practice.

In 1824, 1876, and 1888, the popular-vote winner was the loser in the electoral college. In 1976 a shift of only about nine thousand votes in Ohio and Hawaii would have given the electoral vote to President Gerald R. Ford even though he still would have trailed Jimmy Carter by almost two million popular votes. Four other times in this century (1916, 1948, 1960, and 1968), minuscule shifts in the popular vote in a handful of states could have frustrated the popular will.

Political writer Neal Peirce says that "in the seven Presidential elections in which the leading candidate had a popular-vote lead of less than three percentage points over his closest competitor, the electoral college has elected the 'wrong man' — the popular-vote loser — in two instances, or almost thirty per cent of the time." He adds that in an election as close as that between John F. Kennedy and Nixon in 1960, there is no better than a fifty-fifty chance that the electoral vote will agree with the popular vote as to the winner.

The winner-take-all principle forces all candidates to concentrate most of their time and money in the most populous states where they have a chance to win the big blocs of electoral votes. Losing Wyoming or Alaska is not a major setback. Losing California, New York, Texas, or Ohio can be fatal.

Further, the existing system allows, even forces, the two major parties to write off one-party states as already won or lost. Neither party, for example, makes an effort in Democratic Massachusetts or Republican Kansas. That further weakens party competition and probably lowers the turnout in those and other one-party states.

Plainly, the electoral college benefits the large "swing" states at the expense of the middle-sized states. The smaller states are also advantaged by the "constant two" electoral votes. In 1976, Alaska got one electoral vote for every forty thousand popular votes, while Minnesota got one for every 194,956 popular votes.

But the fact that California cast forty-five and New York cast forty-one electoral votes to Alaska's three and Minnesota's ten overshadows all other inequalities. The eleven largest states control 272 electoral votes, more than a majority of the electoral college. The "voting power" of each individual in these large, competitive states far exceeds that of most voters elsewhere in the nation. Lawrence Longley, a political scientist, says, "A citizen voting in California in the present electoral college as apportioned in the nineteen-seventies, is found to have 2.5 times the potential for determining the outcome of the Presidential election as a citizen voting in the most disadvantaged area — the District of Columbia."

In contrast to the complexities and dangers of the electoral college system, the direct-vote method is appealing in its simplicity. It is based on a one-person, one-vote principle. It more clearly makes a President the agent of the people, not the states. Governors and senators are elected by statewide direct popular voting, and they are supposed to be agents of the states. The President should be President of the people, not President of the states.

The direct-vote plan would also do away with the present electors who occasionally have voted for persons who did not win the plurality vote in their states. This is the often-discussed "faithless elector" problem. Since our first election, fewer than a dozen electors out of almost eighteen thousand have been faithless. And these few "miscast" votes have never made a difference. Still the process seems anachronistic and potentially dangerous, and because of that, few will defend this aspect of the electoral college.

In sum, proponents of the direct vote say it is the most forthright alternative and far preferable to the present system. They contend that voters, when they are choosing a President, think of themselves as national citizens, not as residents of a particular state. The American Bar Association says the present system is "archaic, undemocratic, complex, ambiguous, indirect, and dangerous." The direct popular-vote system, it is argued, is simple, democratic, and clear-cut.

Defenders of the electoral college system are outnumbered in Congress, they are outnumbered in the general public, and they are outnumbered in the ranks of major interest groups, yet they argue with intensity and strong conviction.

First, they say we should not lightly dismiss a system that has served us well for so long. The late Alexander Bickel of Yale Law School wrote:

"We are well-served by an attachment to institutions that are often the products more of accident than of design, or that no longer answer to their original purposes and plans, but that offer us the comfort of continuity, and challenge our resilience and inventiveness in bending old arrangements to present purposes with no outward change. The English know this secret, and so does the common law that we inherited from them. We have, of course,

many institutions and arrangements that, as they function, no longer conform to the original scheme, and we have bent most of them quite effectively to the purposes of our present society, which in all respects differs enormously from the society of nearly two hundred years ago. The Supreme Court is one such institution, and the Presidency itself is another. The fact that we have used them without modifying their structures has lent stability to our society and has built strength and confidence in our people."

Advocates of the present system stress that, despite some imperfections, it works. They point out that we have not had a popular-vote loser elected by the college in ninety years. They feel that the chance of this happening is not as dangerous as the likely consequences of a move to a direct vote. They quote John F. Kennedy, who defended the electoral college, by arguing that it is not merely certain technical details of the election process that are in question, but a whole "solar system" of interrelated subtle institutions, principles, and customs. They cite Lord Falkland's epigram, "When it is not necessary to change, it is necessary not to change," and Livy's pronouncement, "The evil best known is the most tolerable."

Political scientist Austin Ranney, in testimony before the Senate Judiciary Committee, put it this way:

"It seems to me that the evil the amendment [Bayh's S.J.R. 1] seeks to prevent is unlikely to happen. What you are dealing with here, therefore, is not a very pressing problem. . . . There seems to me to be a real possibility — I cannot say certainly any more than the proponents of the amendment can say certainly that we are going to have a minority President — there seems to me a certainty that several things would happen to our political parties, to our mode of campaigning, to the kinds of candidates that might enter the whole process. So I wind up remaining to be convinced that the imminence and the size of the evil that this amendment addresses itself to are such that we ought to go ahead and risk the evils that might ensue, whatever those probabilities might be."

It was with these fears in mind that Senators Eastland, Allen, Strom Thurmond, Scott, Paul Laxalt, Orrin G. Hatch, and Malcolm Wallop opposed the direct vote of the President. These senators, in a minority report to the Senate, argued that direct election would:

☐ Cripple the party system and encourage splinter parties.

☐ Undermine the federal system.

☐ Lead to interminable recounts and challenges, and encourage electoral fraud.

☐ Necessitate national control of every aspect of the electoral process.

☐ Give undue weight to numbers, thereby reducing the influence of the small states.

☐ Encourage candidates for President who represent narrow geographical, ideological, and ethnic bases of support.

☐ Encourage simplified media-oriented campaigns and bring about drastic changes in the strategy and tactics used in campaigns for the Presidency.

Historian Arthur Schlesinger points out that the elections in 1824 and 1876, in which the popular-vote losers were elected President, had very little to do with the electoral college:

"Eighteen twenty-four is no test of the present system since that system did not exist in 1824, when there were no parties, no popular vote in six states, and no unit electoral vote in six others. In any event, it was the House of Representatives, not the electoral college, that put in Adams over Jackson. In 1876, Tilden had a majority in the electoral college; it was a rigged electoral commission that put in Hayes."

Hence, there was only one occasion in nearly two hundred years where the college system denied the popular-vote winner the Presidency. Is that reason enough to justify taking a gamble on the direct-vote method?

An additional factor has motivated groups such as the National Association for the Advancement of Colored People, the Americans for Democratic Action, and writers such as Alexander Bickel and Wallace Sayre to oppose the direct vote and back the electoral college. A 1977 statement by the A.D.A. said:

"Perhaps the only way that significant American minorities can have an impact on the political process is as the deciding factor as to which major candidate can win a given state and a given set of electoral votes. In this way, urban interests and rural, blacks, Latinos, and other minorities, the handicapped and the elderly, the young, the poor, the rich, and the middle-aged can all compete for some attention and some share of public policy. If direct election were instituted, the need for taking into account the needs and desires of minorities would no longer exist. Can-

didates would campaign for the American middle as their particular pollster describes that middle and would be beholden to no group, no cause, and no interest. These who constitute America's minorities, whether they be farmers or urban dwellers, would all suffer."

Jack Germond and Jules Witcover, two syndicated columnists, believe that with the direct vote "the weight given to small blocs of voters . . . would be far less than it is today." They suggest that blacks and Jews might especially be disadvantaged. "Jewish voters, less than three per cent of the electorate, must be given some attention now because they can tip the scales in New York or Illinois or California."

Proponents of the electoral college say that it minimizes the impact of minor parties and, because of the unit-rule provision (used by all states except Maine), encourages a politics of moderation. They also point out that under the present system, losers at party nominating conventions generally abide by their party's choice. But with a direct vote these same losers would be tempted to go after the Presidency anyway, hoping to force a runoff election. John Sears, campaign manager for Ronald Reagan in 1976, says that if the direct-vote method were in operation he would have counseled Reagan to bypass the Republican Convention altogether.

An American Enterprise Institute document says:

"The critics [of direct vote] suggest that the major parties are, on the national level, only loosely assembled aggregates of state party organizations and factional interests; such internal discipline as they possess comes primarily from their ability to make their nominations stick. They are able to do this, it is argued, primarily because winner-take-all discourages disgruntled losers and their partisans from launching a campaign on their own. Once winner-take-all is removed, say the opponents of direct election, the major parties will lose their most potent weapon for enforcing their nominating decisions."

Arthur Schlesinger also fears that tiny parties or single-issue candidates will be able to magnify their strength through the direct-vote scheme. "Anti-abortion parties, Black Power parties, anti-busing parties, anti-gun-control parties, pro-homosexual-rights parties — for that matter, Communist or fascist parties — have a dim future in the electoral college. In direct elections they could drain away enough votes, cumulative from state to state, to prevent the formation of a national majority — and to give themselves strong bargaining positions in case of a runoff."

Under the present system, the votes for these marginal parties or single-issue candidates never really get counted, although they sometimes can help one of the major parties and hurt the other. In 1976, Eugene McCarthy may have cost Jimmy Carter as many as four states. But under the direct-vote system, each vote cast for a minority party would count. Carried over from state to state, this vote might add up to five per cent, fifteen per cent or more. This, it is argued, would increase the incentives for these kinds of parties to "send a message," register their strength, flex their muscles, and cause the proliferation of splinter or third parties.

Proponents of the direct vote just as strongly argue that their plan will not undermine the two-party system. They say that we have a direct vote in the states and that the two-party system is safely intact in most of our states.

Supporters of the Bayh amendment say that the two-party system is shaped and sustained not by the electoral college and winner-take-all provision, but by the election of almost all public officials by single-member districts. Citing the writings of Maurice Duverger, they note that almost every government in the world that elects its officials from single-member districts and by plurality vote has only two major parties, while countries that use multi-member districts and proportional representation have a multitude of parties.

They point to George Wallace's effectiveness under the present system. Wallace was encouraged by the electoral college arrangements to try to carry enough states in a three-way race to enable him to force the two major candidates into a deadlock and bargain with them in the House vote. In effect, the electoral college rewards regional third parties (like Wallace's American Independent Party), while punishing third parties with a national constituency.

The Bayh direct-vote plan stipulates that a candidate must obtain at least forty per cent of the popular vote to win. To prevent that and cause a runoff, a third party would have to win more than twenty per cent of the vote while the two major parties split the rest almost evenly. Tom Wicker of *The New York Times* says, "That's no more incentive, and probably less, to a minor party than its chance, under the present system, to prevent an electoral majority and throw a Presidential election into the House."

Finally, under the direct-vote system, organizers and supporters of third parties would doubtless have to make the same calculations as to whether their efforts would take votes from the major party candidate closest to them in policy convictions. Do they really want to be a spoiler party and thereby insure the victory of the least preferred party and have it in office for the next four years?

Despite these assurances from the direct-vote advocates, there is at least the possibility that our party system will be drastically altered. We really have just a one-and-a-half-party system in the United States as it is. The Congress is now, and is likely to remain, in Democratic hands. Only the Presidency is a competitive office at the national level.

Aaron Wildavsky contends that with the direct vote we do away with the requirement that pluralities be created, state by state. This could easily undermine the remaining basis of party competition. "What is likely," says Wildavsky, "is that more and more voters will move into the primary or the majority party. Fewer and fewer voters will move into the party of the minority. The minority party, of course, will become more extreme . . . until eventually it disappears."

The current system, according to its defenders, is part of the subtle structure of federalism that, over the years, has thwarted factionalism and helped maintain liberty. They feel that to tamper with the electoral college is to tamper with federalism. The electoral college imposes a state-oriented strategy upon Presidential candidates. Each candidate must forge a coalition of supporters within each state, especially the big states. To move to a direct vote would lessen the bargaining power of state officials. Countering that argument, others as diverse in their views as Robert Dole and former Senator Mike Mansfield say that the federalism issue is phony because the electoral college encourages candidates to ignore the noncompetitive states.

"If states are abolished as voting units," writes Theodore H. White, "TV becomes absolutely dominant. Campaign strategy becomes a media effort to capture the largest share of the national 'vote market.'" Of course, television is absolutely essential in the existing arrangement. But White and some others think it will be relied upon even more. Candidates would concentrate on the easily accessible hundreds of thousands of votes in New York, Los Angeles, and Chicago. Who needs Idaho? Direct-vote advocates

The direct-vote method could produce a series of forty-one-per-cent Presidents

admit that major metropolitan areas are advantaged by the electoral college, but point out that suburbs are advantaged even more. Staff aides to Senator Bayh claim black voters would have more impact in a direct vote. The N.A.A.C.P. thinks otherwise.

The federal principle refers not only to the division of responsibilities between nation and states, but also to how we elect our national officers. The Senate, for example, is a creature of the federal principle. Political scientist Judith Best says, "If federalism is an anachronism, if cross-sectional, concurrent majorities are no longer necessary to maintain liberty, then perhaps we should abandon federalism for the national legislature as well as for the executive." She adds:

"To do one without the other, particularly to make the President the recipient of the only all-national mandate, could change our governmental solar system, could change the balance in executive-legislative relationships to the advantage of the President. The authenticity of the voice of the Congress, speaking for a concurrent majority, could be seriously undermined by a truly plebiscitary President claiming to speak most directly and clearly for the general will. The sobering experience of the Watergate era should make us reluctant to further aggrandize the Presidency."

Direct popular election would bring about demands for a uniform ballot in all states and for uniform voter qualifications. Centralization would also be needed for uniform rules governing challenges and recounts. State laws vary considerably on these matters. For example, may a defeated candidate from a national party convention obtain a ballot listing as a new-party or as an independent candidate? In 1976, Eugene McCarthy faced challenges to his access to the ballot in several states, notably New York. As it was, thirteen different candidates qualified for a place on the ballot in six or more states, but no state contained all thirteen names.

For all practical purposes, the states would have to yield a certain amount of their constitutionally granted control over the electoral process to some form of federal elections commission. Richard Smolka raises this additional point: "The question of candidates' access to the ballot — a technical question in many respects — nevertheless requires a specific definition of political party, a definition on which state laws, court decisions, and political scientists do not agree." Once Congress gets into these kinds of details, it is also likely to regulate further the Presidential primary process, the methods of voting, and hence, at least indirectly, it will influence the national conventions. One side effect of these likely new regulations will be the increased chance that even more states (there is already a trend this way) will hold state elections in non-Presidential election years. If so, the eventual effect of these changes could be a lower turnout of voters in state elections *and* in Presidential elections.

Advocates of the direct vote say that one of its virtues is simplicity. But questions of runoff elections and recounts in closely contested elections bother advocates of the present system. Political analysts warn that a recount can be a bloody, lengthy, and delayed process, as was the Wyman-Durkin 1974 recount and new election in New Hampshire. Yet Richard Scammon, an election expert, feels a national recount could be accomplished in a reasonably short time, perhaps two weeks or less, and that the recount issue is not paramount.

Neal Peirce contends that the direct vote would not undermine federalism: "The vitality of federalism rests chiefly on the constitutionally mandated system of congressional representation and the will and capacity of state and local governments to address compelling problems, not on the hocus-pocus of an eighteenth-century vote-count system."

The direct-vote method could easily produce a series of forty-one-per-cent Presidents. Abraham Lincoln was the only President with that small a vote (and he was not on the ballot in several states). Then, too, in a runoff election, the direct-vote method might enhance the chances of the person who finishes second becoming President.

At a time when confidence and trust in the national government have eroded, the direct vote would almost insure that we would have minority Presidents all of the time. We have had fifteen minority Presidents (that is, persons who won with less than fifty per cent of the vote). The current electoral college system is a two-stage process in which the popular votes are converted into electoral votes. In every election this has the effect of magnifying the vote margin of the winner, so much so that only once in the past one hundred years has a President received less than fifty-five per cent of the electoral college vote; that was Woodrow Wilson, who received fifty-two per cent.

Two scholars — Steven Brams and Peter Fishburn — have recently discussed a system called "approval voting" which might remedy part of this problem. In approval voting, citizens would vote for as many candidates as they thought worthy of the office. Under this system, which could operate along with the direct vote, several candidates might receive a majority; the one with the most votes would win office. Brams and Fishburn believe that the "legitimacy of election outcomes in the eyes of voters would certainly be enhanced if the winning candidate received the support of a majority of the electorate. This would be true even if he was the *first* choice of fewer voters than some other candidate, because this fact would not show up in the approval-voting returns."

Brams and Fishburn are not sure of all the side effects of this alternative voting scheme, but they believe fringe candidates would probably drain little support from centrist candidates because, for strategic reasons, fringe-candidate supporters would probably also tend to vote for a centrist:

"Barring unforeseen changes, it seems likely that at the same time approval voting would give some additional support to strong minority candidates like George Wallace, it would also help centrist candidates — including perhaps nominees of new parties — both in winning their party's nomination in the primaries and conventions and prevailing against more extreme candidates in the general election. Coupled with the greater opportunity it affords voters to express their preferences, and the greater likelihood it provides the winning candidate of obtaining majority support, approval voting would seem to be an overlooked reform that now deserves to be taken seriously."

A case might be made for using approval voting in party primaries, but its consequences for the two-party system in the general election pose problems. Additional centrist candidates might easily draw support away from major-party candidates and bring chaos and confusion. Brams and Fishburn do point out that these new centrists might not bring about drastic policy changes since they would not win high approval unless they were middle-of-the-road candidates. Yet they could displace the major-party candidates, and if this happened with any frequency that would probably drive the last nail into the coffin of our two-party system.

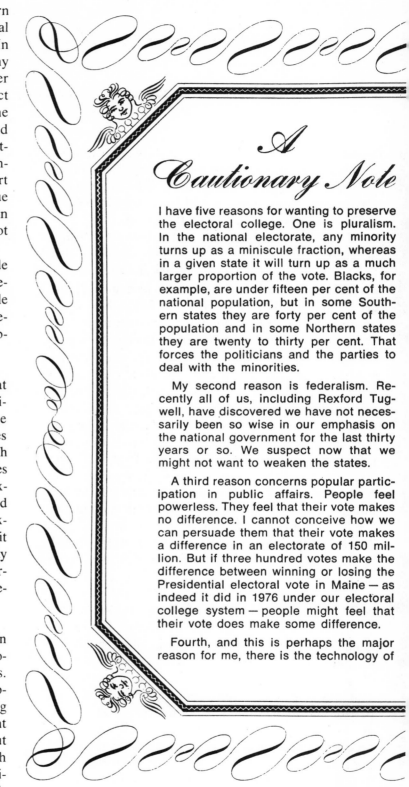

A Cautionary Note

I have five reasons for wanting to preserve the electoral college. One is pluralism. In the national electorate, any minority turns up as a miniscule fraction, whereas in a given state it will turn up as a much larger proportion of the vote. Blacks, for example, are under fifteen per cent of the national population, but in some Southern states they are forty per cent of the population and in some Northern states they are twenty to thirty per cent. That forces the politicians and the parties to deal with the minorities.

My second reason is federalism. Recently all of us, including Rexford Tugwell, have discovered we have not necessarily been so wise in our emphasis on the national government for the last thirty years or so. We suspect now that we might not want to weaken the states.

A third reason concerns popular participation in public affairs. People feel powerless. They feel that their vote makes no difference. I cannot conceive how we can persuade them that their vote makes a difference in an electorate of 150 million. But if three hundred votes make the difference between winning or losing the Presidential electoral vote in Maine — as indeed it did in 1976 under our electoral college system — people might feel that their vote does make some difference.

Fourth, and this is perhaps the major reason for me, there is the technology of political campaigning. We have been moving inexorably toward media managers and pollsters, to the denigration of both political parties and participatory politics. Campaign managers see media communication as more cost-efficient and surely more controllable than any other kind of campaign activity. In a national campaign I ran — Eugene McCarthy's in 1968 — we used to say, "You can't fire a volunteer." We felt if we did, we would rue it. To the extent that there is a premium on electoral votes — as there is in our electoral college system — you force candidates and parties to compete and organize on the local level. You force candidates to visit voters on the local level. You force candidates and parties to deal with institutional structures. If you remove that by getting rid of the electoral college, you will remove the last constraints from making national political campaigning nothing but a media campaign. Media-campaign managers will then be the most powerful people in the United States.

Fifth is the "countervailing-power" reason which Arthur Schlesinger talks about: namely, that our electoral system, by virtue of the U.S. Senate, is skewed a bit in favor of the smaller states. The electoral college slightly skews it back to the larger states, and that balances the power somewhat.

So, for these five reasons, I very much favor keeping the present system. I am not happy with the Twentieth Century Fund's proposed alternative.

CURTIS B. GANS
Director, Committee for the Study of the American Electorate, Washington, D.C.

Political scientist William Keech has noted that "a decision about which system of electing the President to prefer depends on values, on priorities among those values, and on estimates of the likely consequences of change."

There are liabilities or likely adverse effects with either the direct-vote or the electoral college system. Opponents of the direct vote have, I feel, overstated their case. The dire consequences they foresee seem exaggerated. Still they pose enough uncertainty about the repercussions of direct vote that even skeptics should consider seriously any sensible compromise.

It was with this goal in mind that the Twentieth Century Fund, a New York-based nonprofit research foundation, appointed a task force in late 1977. Its members were divided along the predictable lines with defenders of the present system taking the view that the probable consequences — some necessarily unforeseen — of shifting to a direct vote might amount to a cure worse than the disease. Others, including myself, argued the merits of the direct-vote plan. We could agree, however, on the weaknesses of both the direct-vote and electoral college procedure. We could also agree that a fair and democratic election system should maximize the likelihood that the candidate with the most popular votes would win, should encourage healthy competition through a vigorous two-party system (without unduly restricting new third parties), should promote voter participation, and should sustain the vitality of the federal system. With these values in mind, we set about to design a compromise election system. What follows is a description and discussion of what we — the twelve-person Task Force on Reform of the Presidential Election Process of the Twentieth Century Fund — devised.

Our compromise plan retains the existing 538 state-based electoral votes but adds a national pool of 102 electoral votes that would be awarded on a winner-take-all basis to the candidate who wins the most popular votes nationwide. There would thus be a combined total of 640 state and national electoral votes, and the candidate with a majority would be the winner. As a consequence, the existing federal bonus (of two electoral votes for each state and the District of Columbia) would be balanced by this national bonus given to the nationwide popular winner.

The National Bonus Plan, a reform alternative to the existing system, would virtually eliminate the major flaw in the electoral college arrangements. The new system would make it almost impossible for the popular-vote winner to lose the election, as happened in 1888, and as almost happened in 1960 and 1976.

A constitutional amendment is required to establish the National Bonus Plan. Our task force recommends other changes to be incorporated along with the national bonus feature. These changes would be for the sake of symmetry and simplicity. Under the National Bonus Plan, there is no need for the office of elector or for the electoral college. Instead, it is recommended that they be abolished so that all electoral votes — those now assigned and those proposed under the national bonus — be allocated automatically on a winner-take-all basis to the popular-vote winner in each state and in the nation as a whole. This would eliminate the "faithless-elector" problem.

In the unlikely event that no candidate receives a majority of the total electoral vote count under the National Bonus Plan, it is recommended that a runoff be held between the two candidates receiving the most popular votes. This runoff would be held within thirty days of the first national election, and the candidate who then wins a majority of electoral votes would be elected President. A reasonable alternative suggestion is made by Neal Peirce who would provide for a direct popular-vote runoff: "Given the uncertainties that would be created in the nation by a Presidential candidate field so fragmented that no candidate received an electoral vote majority in the first election, even with the 102-vote bonus for the popular-vote leader, the runoff should be as simple and direct as possible."

We also recommend a mandatory re-tally to assure that official totals are accurate. In addition, we propose that a second, independent authority or agency recheck the tallies of the vote-recording devices within a short, specified time after the first tally and that the second total be registered, even if the election is neither close nor disputed. It was felt that the use of automatic vote registering and counting procedures minimizes fraud and error and that these procedures should be extended to every precinct in the nation. An accurate national count is absolutely essential if direct election is enacted.

The National Bonus Plan and these additional correctives introduce novel features to the existing system, but they are constitutional innovations that are similar to the original balancing efforts of 1787.

These innovations should improve and simplify the fairness of the electoral process and enhance public acceptance of it without drastically restructuring the system. Retained are some of the familiar features, such as the federal principle, but eliminated or minimized are most of the problems that now plague the Presidential election process. In addition, this reform would encourage broader voter participation, enhance voter equality, and encourage party competition in all states. As against the existing system, it should:

☐ Virtually assure that the candidate with the most popular votes wins.
☐ Reduce the possibility of a deadlock and make the contingency election procedure more representative.
☐ Eliminate the so-called faithless elector.
☐ Enhance voter equality.
☐ Encourage greater voter turnout.

As against direct election it would:

☐ Avoid a proliferation of candidates and help maintain the two-party system.
☐ Preserve the federal or cross-sectional character of the Presidential election process.
☐ Lessen the likelihood of minority Presidents.
☐ Lessen the likelihood of runoff or second elections.
☐ Lessen the likelihood of regional or sectional candidates emerging as major candidates.

At one and the same time, then, this new proposal would remedy most of the problems of the electoral college system and avoid the numerous potential problems and risks that might be encouraged with direct election.

Initial reaction to the National Bonus Plan has been favorable. It has been praised as an "ingenious plan," "a notable accomplishment," a "practicable, worthy, and needed reform." Edwin M. Yoder, Jr., an editor of the Washington *Star,* says, "After many years of superficial discussion, the electoral college has at last had the thoughtful public study it deserves but rarely gets." A staff member at the White House wrote (in a personal communication to me): "It is an intriguing plan. It seems to satisfy the objections of the opponents of direct election, and yet it still would appear to accomplish the goals of that proposal. We're very interested in it. . . ." Meanwhile, Senator Birch Bayh feels strongly that his direct-vote plan is the best reform, but he has introduced the National

Bonus Plan as a proposed constitutional amendment. It is Senate Joint Resolution 123. No hearings on it have been scheduled.

There have been some objections to the National Bonus Plan. First, it is noted that smaller states such as Idaho and South Carolina might lose almost as much under this plan — in both diluted electoral vote and lessened control over state election law — as under direct popular vote.

Southern states in general have lower voting turnout and consequently would lose some voting power in the nationwide race to such states as Minnesota and Massachusetts, which have high turnout rates. On the other hand, voting turnout in the South has improved in recent years, and voter-registration reform is likely to win passage in the near future, so that turnout would increase further in that region. Also, the National Bonus Plan would, in effect, spur all states to encourage rather than discourage voter participation.

Some skeptics call the National Bonus Plan a Rube Goldberg contraption — a gimmick that is actually a direct vote in disguise. To be sure, it would achieve most of what a direct vote would achieve, but it does so in a more acceptable way. In any event, the direct-vote plan has not passed, and it consistently runs into a buzz saw of opposition. "Small state conservatives who think they might lose some advantage; blacks who believe the swing vote of big, metropolitan states would be reduced; and federal system 'traditionalists,' " is the way Neal Peirce sums up opponents of direct vote. Too many people still fear the unknown and the possible repercussions of direct popular election of Presidents.

The National Bonus Plan brings to a common position those who advocate direct election of the President and those who support the electoral college. Direct-vote advocates may be harder to win over than defenders of the college. They believe if reform can be achieved we ought to go all the way toward the simple one-person, one-vote system. Yet, Peirce, a leading advocate of direct vote (also a member of the Twentieth Century Fund task force) calls the National Bonus Plan "an innovative commendable proposal that might well break the longstanding logjam on electoral college reform." He adds that ideally he favors a simple direct-election amendment: "However, as between the existing system, with all its perils, and the National Bonus Plan, I find the National Bonus Plan infinitely preferable."

The National Bonus Plan won unanimous and strong support from the otherwise deadlocked Twentieth Century Fund task force. Its members included political strategists John Sears, Patrick Caddell, and Jill Ruckelshaus; political journalists Jules Witcover, Richard Rovere, and Neal Peirce; political scientists Heinz Eulau, Jeane Kirkpatrick, Paul Puryear, and William Keech; historian Arthur Schlesinger; and writer Stephen Hess. Five of the members have served as White House aides. At least three are Republicans. One is black. No one thought that the National Bonus Plan favored one political party at the expense of the other.

Some say we overestimate the public's insistence on one-man, one-vote. But sooner or later there is going to be another Presidential election in which one candidate wins the popular vote and yet loses the election. At that time the furor and heated emotion of the moment may cause a rush to change the system in a radical or overly simplistic way. Our compromise plan is intended to promote contemporary discussions of contending values in election policy, and to offer a reasoned alternative for such an occasion.

We welcome rigorous examination of the plan. It needs to be put under a microscope. Its potential risks and flaws should be discussed. The plan is worth examination if only because it brings this much-postponed, much-confused issue into the open at a time when reason rather than emotion can prevail.

Thomas Cronin, a former Visiting Fellow at the Center, is a Professor of Political Science at the University of Delaware. He is the author of The State of the Presidency, *co-author of* Government by the People, *and co-editor, with Rexford G. Tugwell, of* The Presidency Reappraised.

★★★

26

The 1978 Congressional Elections: A Renaissance for Republicans?   Austin Ranney

With the exception of 1934, the political party of the president has lost seats in the House of Representatives in every midterm election since the Civil War. Austin Ranney discusses this phenomenon and tries to predict the outcome for the 1978 election. Given the actual outcome for 1978, how close did Ranney come? What are the various theories that purport to explain this historical tendency? Ranney expects the Republicans to win seats in 1978, but the prospects for their winning by a large margin, he says, are not strong. Why doesn't Ranney predict an impressive victory by the Republicans in Congress? What effect might this have on the overall strength of the party? How many elections can the Republican party afford to lose before its status as a "major" party is affected? What evidence confirms the fact that, in numerous ways, the Republican party is clearly the "minority" party when compared to the Democratic party?

Clearly there is some electoral connection between the president and Congress, and some reformers wish to strengthen this relationship. They would insist that representatives serve four-year terms of office so that every four years they would have to stand for reelection along with the president. The idea is intended to facilitate cooperation between the legislative and executive branches of government. It would permit voters to judge congressmen according to their support or opposition to the president's program. Those who oppose this reform say that it would weaken our traditional "separation of powers." Do you think their assessment is correct or not?

★ ★ ★

The 1978 Congressional Elections: A Renaissance for Republicans?

Austin Ranney

With a new set of elections just over the horizon, we can expect a good deal of handwringing in coming months about the ever-shrinking status of the Republican Party and the approaching demise of our two-party system.

In past *presidential* elections, that pessimism has been badly misplaced. After all, the GOP has won four of the eight presidential sweepstakes since World War II, and their candidates have drawn a total of 270 million votes to 256 million for the Democrats. That's not bad for a "hopeless minority," and Republican presidential candidates will surely be highly competitive in 1980 and beyond.

When we look at congressional elections, however, the doomsayers may have a point. In the sixteen congressional elections since the war, Republican candidates for the House have won a total of 373 million votes to the Democrats' 421 million, and more importantly, the Republicans have won control of either chamber only twice (1946 and 1952).

In some ways, the 1976 results were the most disheartening yet for the GOP. Most Republican leaders thought the party had hit rock bottom in the "Watergate" election of 1974 when they lost a net of forty-eight House seats and five Senate seats. But there were good reasons to expect a strong comeback in 1976: most of the Democratic House gains came in districts they had not won for decades, if ever. Hence, Republican strategists were confident the party would win back most of these seats in 1976 and make a net gain

of anywhere from fifteen to thirty seats. Just to make sure, the Republican congressional and national committees put more than $3.5 million into key House races. The results were a rude shock. The Republicans defeated only two of the Democrats' first-termers and lost a net of two House seats.

The Republicans, therefore, approach the 1978 congressional elections from one of their lowest postwar ebbs. The 146 House seats they now hold are the fewest since the 1964 Johnson landslide cut them back to 140. Their current total of thirty-eight Senate seats is one better than in 1974 but four to six lower than in the Nixon years. It would seem the GOP has nowhere to go but up; yet, if they could not make headway in 1976, what hope is there for 1978?

There is at least one, maybe more: in this year's elections, the Republicans can capitalize on one of the most persistent patterns in American politics—the tendency of the President's party to lose seats in both Houses of Congress in midterm (or "off-year") elections. *This tendency has operated in House elections in every midterm election since the Civil War, with the single exception of the 1934 elections.* It has been a shade less consistent in Senate elections, but even so, the presidential party has lost Senate seats in the great majority of midterm elections. The facts for the period from 1930 to 1974 are set forth in Table 1.

In the Senate, as shown by the table, the pattern of losses for the presidential party has been more irregular than in the House. Only one-third of the sen-

From *Public Opinion*, March/April 1978, pp. 17–20, © 1978 American Enterprise Institute. Reprinted with permission.

Table 1

LOSSES BY PRESIDENT'S PARTY
IN MIDTERM ELECTIONS, 1930-1974

Election Year	Party Holding Presidency	Pres. Party Gain/Loss in House Seats	Percent Change from Two Years Earlier	Pres. Party Gain/Loss in Senate Seats	Percent Change from Two Years Earlier
1930	R	−53	−20%	− 8	−14%
1934	D	(+ 9)	(+ 3)	(+ 9)	(+15)
1938	D	−70	−21	− 7	− 9
1942	D	−50	−19	− 8	−12
1946	D	−54	−22	−11	−20
1950	D	−29	−11	− 5	− 9
1954	R	−18	− 8	− 1	− 2
1958	R	−47	−23	−13	−28
1962	D	− 5	− 2	(+ 2)	(+ 3)
1966	D	−48	−16	− 4	− 6
1970	R	−12	− 6	(+ 1)	(+ 2)
1974	R	−48	−25	− 5	−12
AVERAGE		−35	−14	− 4	− 8

Source: *Statistical Abstract of the United States, 1976* (Washington, D.C.: U.S. Bureau of the Census, 1976), Table 736, p. 461.

ators are up for reelection every two years, of course, which means that losses for the President's party may depend heavily on the number of the President's co-partisans who must face the voters. In 1978, that quirk will work against the Republicans. Although they hold only thirty-eight of the Senate's 100 seats, more than half of all the seats up for reelection this year—17 of 33—are now held by Republicans. Thus, even their minority status will not reduce their risks: they will have to expose nearly half of their incumbents to the possibility of defeat, while the Democrats must risk only a quarter of theirs.

Prospects for the Republicans may be brighter in the House. Since the Eisenhower years, it should be noted from Table 1, the number of House losses for the presidential party has been considerably smaller during the first term of an incumbent President than during the second term—a point cutting in favor of the Democrats this year—but nonetheless, looking all the way back to 1930, the average loss for the party in the White House has been a sizable thirty-five seats. Republicans believe that the anti-coattail trend may already be working in their direction: during 1977, there were four special elections to fill House seats vacated by Democrats in widely different parts of the country (Minnesota, Washington State, Georgia, and Louisiana), and the GOP won three of them. So the Republicans may be pardoned for hoping that in 1978, they will once again profit from the historical "law" that gives the party out of the White House a solid boost in midterm elections, especially in House seats.

But *is* it a law, and *will* it operate in 1978? Both questions are well worth considering, and not only for congressional politicians.

Why Does the President's Party Lose Midterm Elections?

Any search for the answer to this question might well begin by recognizing that not nearly as many people vote in congressional elections as in presidential elections. In the presidential years from 1932 to 1976, the average turnout in presidential elections was 57.6 percent of the voting-age population. In elections for the House in presidential years, turnout averaged 53.7 percent. But in off-years, turnout for House elections was only 37.6 percent. If this pattern holds—and there is no reason to suppose it will not—then we can expect a turnout in 1978 of no more than 35 to 40 percent of the voting-age population.

This small congressional electorate, moreover, differs significantly from the much larger presidential electorate. It is older, better educated, of higher socioeconomic status, more partisan and more concerned with issues. (Several of these factors favor Republican candidates, of course.)

Some political scientists believe those differences mean that presidential electorates are more likely to be swayed from their basic party preferences by such fleeting influences as a glamorous candidate or a red hot issue, while congressional electorates are more likely to stick with their parties' tickets whatever the state of the issues or personalities.[1]

But most political scientists, like most politicians, don't believe this. After all, the Democrats have had far more party identifiers than the Republicans ever since the early 1930s; yet, with the sole exception of 1934, the Democrats, like the Republicans, have lost ground in midterm elections when they held the White House and gained ground when they did not. In fact, despite their majority status, the Democrats' midterm losses in the House as the presidential party have been *greater* than the Republicans', averaging thirty-eight seats lost per election to the Republicans' thirty-one.

How can this be? Most observers believe that two basic forces are at work. One has been the tendency of past midterm elections to become essentially referenda on the incumbent President's popularity, whatever his party. If he retains most of the popularity which elected or reelected him two years earlier, his party will lose few if any seats in either house. If his popularity has dropped markedly, his party may suffer devastating setbacks. That is why congressional candidates eagerly seek close association with popular Presidents, as in 1934, 1954, and 1962, and put all the distance they can between themselves and an unpopular administration as in 1946, 1966, and 1974.

---

1 Angus Campbell, "Surge and Decline: A Study of Electoral Change," *Public Opinion Quarterly*, 24 (Fall 1960), 397-418; and Barbara Hinckley, "Interpreting House Midterm Elections: Toward a Measurement of the In-Party's 'Expected' Loss of Seats," *American Political Science Review*, 61 (September 1967), 694-700.

The second force is what political scientist Samuel Kernell calls "negative voting." This is the tendency of most voters to be more activated by candidates and policies they are against than by those they support. It means that even if most voters approve the President's general performance in office, those who disapprove are more likely to vote in midterm elections than those who approve. And the low turnout in midterm elections suggests that congressional off-year electorates have higher proportions of highly motivated "negative voters" than presidential electorates.[2]

Political scientist Edward Tufte has tried to reduce these tendencies to a mathematical formula. His study of midterm elections concludes that for every 10 percent loss in the President's approval rating between the presidential election and the ensuing midterm election (as measured by the Gallup poll), the presidential party will lose 1.3 percent of its share of the votes for the House in the midterm. And that, in turn, means that the party will lose about 2.6 percent of its share of the seats. (He also calculates that for every loss of $100 in the real disposable income per capita, there will be a reduction of 3.5 percentage points in the popular vote and a 6 point loss in the share of seats.)[3]

If Tufte's scheme worked perfectly, there might be no reason to hold elections, but it doesn't. It is highly instructive, however. The way it might be applied to 1978 is suggested by Table 2, which shows the changing approval ratings of the postwar first-term Presidents prior to their first midterm elections (I exclude Ford because he had not been elected in his own right prior to the 1974 election) and their parties' election losses.

Table 2 shows a distinct relationship (though no perfect correlation) between a first-term President's loss of popularity and his party's losses in the House in his first midterm election. Johnson lost the most popularity and the most seats, Truman the second most popularity and seats, Eisenhower third, Nixon fourth, and Kennedy the least. *It also shows that Jimmy Carter lost more popularity in his first nine months in office than any of his five predecessors.* From Carter's viewpoint, it is also ominous that the net approval of every President shown in Table 2 declined between October of his first year in office and October of his second year—and the average decline was over 15 points! At the present writing, we cannot say how Carter will fare in the polls in 1978. *If,* however, he manages to stay even and *if* presidential popularity were all that mattered, we might predict that Democratic House losses in 1978 would be in the range of 25-35 seats. An improvement in his standing would improve Democratic prospects by 10

Table 2

PRESIDENTIAL POPULARITY AND MIDTERM LOSSES IN THE HOUSE, 1950-1970

| First-Term President | Net Approval Index[a] | | | | | Pres. Party Mid-term Loss in House Seats | Per-cent Loss |
	Jan.-Feb. 1st Year	Oct. of 1st Year	Loss	Oct. of 2nd Year	Loss		
Truman (1949)	52	20	32	11	41	29	11
Eisenhower (1953)	74	45	29	44	30	18	8
Kennedy (1961)	66	65	1	40	26	5	2
Johnson (1965)	56	45	11	10	46	48	16
Nixon (1969)	54	33	21	27	27	12	6
Carter (1977)	58	24	34	?	?	?	?

a The Gallup poll asks: "Do you approve or disapprove of the way (the incumbent President) is handling his job as President?" The index is computed by subtracting the percent disapproving from the percent approving. Thus, in January-February of this year, 66 percent approved of Carter's handling of the presidency, 8 percent disapproved—and his net approval index stood at 58.

Source: American Institute of Public Opinion (Gallup Poll).

seats, while a Carter erosion on a scale similar to his predecessors could increase prospective Democratic losses to 45-60 seats. It must be emphasized that these predictions are based strictly on the "presidential popularity" theory that many political scientists have traditionally applied to congressional elections in the past.

Winds for Democratic Sails

In reality, however, several factors in addition to presidential popularity come into play in congressional elections. In fact, Republican candidates today—especially those challenging incumbent Democrats—are caught in a riptide of public attitudes, many of which tend to help Democrats return to Congress.

A quick reading of recent polls illustrates some of the problems for Republicans challenging Democratic incumbents. In the summer of 1977, George Gallup found that public affiliation with the Republican Party had sunk to the lowest point in forty years: only 20 percent of all respondents identified themselves as Republicans, 31 percent as independents, and 49 percent as Democrats. In October of 1977, Gallup found that if voters were casting their ballots then for congressional candidates, 23 percent would vote for Republicans, 51 percent for Democrats and 20 percent were undecided. In that same month, Gallup found that on the two key issues that matter most to voters, Democrats were judged better able to solve them than Republicans: on inflation by a 36 to 19 percent margin; and on unemployment by a 43 to 10 percent advantage. Thus, even though President Carter has fallen in the polls, there is

---

2 Samuel Kernell, "Presidential Popularity and Negative Voting: An Alternative Explanation of the Midterm Congressional Decline of the President's Party," *American Political Science Review*, 71 (March 1977), 44-66.

3 Edward R. Tufte, "Determinants of the Outcomes of Midterm Congressional Elections," *American Political Science Review*, 69 (September 1975), 812-826.

little evidence so far showing that his decline has rubbed off on his fellow Democrats in Congress. Indeed, a survey conducted this January by *New York Times*/CBS News found that despite the erosion of public confidence in Carter's abilities, 67 percent said that their opinion of Carter would not have any effect upon their congressional votes this fall.

There is at least one other factor that is bound to influence the 1978 elections, and we should ponder it well, for it is one of the most striking developments in postwar politics. As *Congressional Quarterly* sums it up:

> The tendency since World War II has been for incumbents to seek reelection as long as they were physically able to serve, and for nearly all of them to win. In virtually every election in recent years, more than 90 percent of all incumbents sought reelection, and more than 95 percent of those who ran won.[4]

Political scientists call this *"the incumbency factor,"* and in 1978—just as in the recent past—it should work as a powerful force for the Democrats.

The incumbency factor does not always extend to senators: in 1976, for example, only 64 percent of the incumbent senators running for reelection were successful. But it seems to have a magical effect for House members. As noted earlier, Republicans lost forty-three seats in 1974 as they struggled with the twin handicaps of Watergate and an economic slump. In 1976, they had solid hopes of recouping at least fifteen to thirty of those seats. Yet, when the votes were counted, the GOP wound up with a net *loss* of two seats and many of the Democrats who entered Congress two years earlier managed to strengthen their holds on their districts.

Several explanations have been offered for the increasing invulnerability of House incumbents: their enormous advantage in free mailings, free trips home and other forms of publicity; the fact that many of them now concentrate primarily on servicing their districts (a priority that the public at large may not appreciate but goes down well with the home folks); and the low public attention to House elections, which makes name familiarity so much more important than in higher-visibility Senate elections.

It may well be, then, that for the foreseeable future the party out of the White House will have a reasonable chance of increasing its share of Senate seats, but the only House seats it can seriously hope for are those in which incumbents have retired or have been defeated in primaries. To illustrate: over the years 1973-1977, when Republicans challenged nonincumbent

Democrats for seats previously held by Democrats, one out of every ten Republicans won; but in running against sitting Democrats only one Republican candidate out of every forty managed to win!

Republicans may draw some encouragement this year from increasing retirement rates: retirement benefits for congressmen are getting better all the time, and retirement may appear more attractive to incumbents than in the past. Preliminary reports indicate that a record number of Democratic incumbents in the House may not seek reelection this year. (As of early January, 15 Democrats had announced retirement plans, another 12 were considered possible, and more announcements were expected.) Yet, it seems clear that in 1978 and beyond, the ability of the out-party to capitalize on the President's declining popularity in midterm elections will be limited—though not eliminated—by the increasing difficulty of defeating incumbent representatives.

It should be added that 1978 will be the first midterm election in twelve years when the same party has held both the White House and the Congress. In such circumstances, if the economy were to nosedive or some other event were to shatter public confidence, it might well be that voters would forget all about incumbency and rise up to "throw the rascals out"—"negative voting" in excelsis! In 1966, for example, LBJ dropped sharply in the polls and the Democrats lost forty-seven seats in the House as well as three in the Senate. For the moment, however, no such earthshaking event looms on the '78 horizon.

In summary, members of Congress today are not as closely tied to the coattails of a President as in days past. Thus, even if President Carter were to follow past tradition and slip still further in the polls during his second year in office, it is likely that Democrats in Congress would suffer no more than a moderate electoral set-back and our modified one-party system in congressional politics would continue much as it has since 1930. Stirring together the many contrary forces, here are Austin Ranney's "guesstimates" for 1978:

Table 3

ESTIMATED DEMOCRATIC 1978 HOUSE LOSSES
WITH CHANGES
IN PRESIDENTIAL POPULARITY

If Carter's Net Approval Index in October 1978 is:	The Democrats' Losses in House Seats Should Be:
49-40	0-5
39-30	5-15
29-20	15-25
19-10	25-35
9-1	over 35

Note: Shaded area denotes Carter's net approval index as of October 1977.
Source: A clouded crystal ball.

a The Gallup poll asks: "Do you approve or disapprove of the way (the incumbent President) is handling his job as President?" The index is computed by subtracting the percent disapproving from the percent approving. Thus, in January-February of this year, 66 percent approved of Carter's handling of the presidency, 8 percent disapproved—and his net approval index stood at 58.

4 1974 *Congressional Quarterly Almanac* (Washington, D.C.: Congressional Quarterly, Inc., 1974), p. 840. See also David Mayhew, "Congressional Elections: The Case of the Vanishing Marginals," *Polity*, 6 (Spring 1974), 295-317; and Warren Lee Kostroski, "Party and Incumbency in Postwar Senate Elections," *American Political Science Review*, 67 (December 1973), 1213-1234.

CHAPTER SIX

★ ★ ★

Congress

To understand Congress, we must recognize that it is a political body that both *governs* and *represents*. The Founders, having had prior experience with a government where all power resided in the legislature, found government under the Articles of Confederation stressed representation at the expense of effective government. Not wishing to ignore either of these functions in the new government, the Framers were most careful in structuring the legislative body to assure that it would both represent as well as govern. Thus, one finds that Article I of the Constitution grants Congress specific delegated and "implied" power to enhance its ability to govern, while at the same time it creates a bicameral legislature to assure representation both for the citizens and for the states.

To make sure that each chamber of the legislature represented distinct interests, the Framers insisted that elections be held every two years to elect House members, while recruitment in the Senate was to be on a longer-term basis. The House was to reflect the changing mood of the populace. It was this chamber that James Madison described as "the grand depository of the democratic principle of the Government." But the Senate, where senators served six-year terms and were elected on a rotating basis, was to represent the steadiness and maturity missing in the House. It was to change more slowly. According to Madison, the Senate was to proceed with "more coolness, with more system, and with more wisdom" than the popular branch.

James Buckley, former senator from New York, warns in his article "On Becoming a United States Senator" that the heavy workload and the staggering number of demands placed on the contemporary Senate are creating serious problems for that body. Senators, he points out, are prevented from engaging in the adequate policy study, planning, and deliberative thought that seem necessary to preserve the very distinctiveness of this body intended by the Framers. The ability of the Senate to check and balance the House may suffer because of the heavy workload.

Although the two chambers of Congress today remain structurally distinct, the men and women who have served in both chambers do not appear that different. Since the first Congress senators and congressmen have shown remarkable similarities in terms of social class, occupation, and backgrounds. Senators since the late 1800s, for instance, have tended to come from the upper classes of society, have gravitated toward law as a profession, and have had four or more years of college.

Congressmen's attitudes toward the operation of Congress have departed radically from earlier patterns. Prior to the 1970s Congress had preferred to shut its doors to the public, relying on executive sessions to shield its operations. Today, however,

Congress is much more open to the public than it has ever been. Since 1975 only 7 percent of the standing committees in both chambers held meetings behind closed doors. Little of the legislative procedure today is barred from public scrutiny.

As a consequence of this desire for openness, there have been changes in the formal structure of Congress. For example, Juan Cameron, in his article "And They Call It the Most Important Committee in Congress," says that since 1974 such changes can be seen in the House Ways and Means Committee. This committee is no longer autocratically managed by its chairman, and as a result it no longer reflects cohesive decision-making. As the Ways and Means Committee membership has become less stabilized, a diversity of membership and member interests has replaced a similarity of interests among its members and a long-entrenched expertise. This change has made the committee more difficult to govern.

As congressman have demanded more openness in their institution and less party domination of the congressional procedures, political leaders in Congress have had to take account of this change of mood. In his description of Robert Byrd, Sanford Ungar in "The Man Who Runs the Senate" says that the ideal Senate party leader must still prove his loyalty to party, be of moderate ideological persuasion, and become a master of congressional procedure. A leader like Byrd must also realize he no longer has a cohesive party base on which to rely. As a consequence, the party leader finds he must seek a power base among individual factions in Congress, seek support from regional blocs, or even look to interest-group coalitions for needed votes. Byrd has secured support from all but the last of these.

Of all the twentieth-century changes Congress has responded to, that which has put the greatest strain on it as a governing body has been the increased workload and the general growth of the institution over the last twenty years. Indeed, Milton Gwirtzman in his article "The Bloated Branch" argues that Congress has grown so large and cumbersome that it can no longer effectively carry out its tasks. Staff increases, added specialization of the congressmen, and increased lobbying activity, he contends, have markedly slowed the process of legislation by making compromise more difficult. Without the compromise of rival interests, the political process is seriously impeded, and the very viability of the political institution is threatened.

We are, consequently, forced to ask ourselves the questions so often asked by the critics of Congress. Can this institution adapt to the needs of society and handle the demands made of it? Does it still fulfill the Framers' vision of an institution that both governs and represents? Despite the problems mentioned, Congress still considers its primary responsibility to be passage of legislation. Each year the public sees Congress pass hundreds of meaningful as well as trivial bills and resolutions. As long as the meaningful legislation predominates, we could argue that Congress continues to govern effectively. Also important to its viability is the role Congress serves as the primary check on presidential and bureaucratic power. Through its control of fiscal matters and its oversight capabilities, Congress continues as a powerful decision-making body affecting the public interest. As an institution representing society's interests, Congress is still the institution most accessible to group demands and is the most reflective of the multiplicity of interests in society. It does, indeed, remain the institution closest to the voters. Consequently, as long as the Constitution remains a viable document and Article I of that document goes unchanged, Congress will probably remain the primary "governing" and "representing" institution conceived of by the Framers.

★★

27

On Becoming a United States Senator   James L. Buckley

From James Buckley's observations as a perceptive freshman senator, one is impressed by how much strain he feels is placed on the Senate by time *and* space *problems. These are the same problems that trouble most complex institutions in society. Senators, for example, seem to have too little time to handle adequately the workload and too little space in which to operate. Time pressures encourage senators to vote without sufficiently examining the policy voted on and to accept with few questions committee versions of those bills. Congressional staff are crowded into inadequate space, and decisions about space allocations become party decisions for rewarding the loyal and faithful. Are there remedies to these two nagging concerns? Would placing Senate business on a two-year cycle, as Buckley argues, remedy the time problem? Would cutting staff remedy the space problem? Or would such cuts be impractical in view of the rising demands made of Congress?*

Buckley has other concerns that are troublesome to him: procedures that tend to limit legislative effectiveness. What are some of those procedural barriers? Would these problems be less severe for a senator with more experience? In what ways does "seniority" affect a senator's use of power and position to gain privilege in Congress?

Another difficulty Buckley notes concerns Congress's inability to reflect the mood of the country. He argues that the Senate is always ten to fifteen years out of phase with the thinking and mood of the country because the senators' lengthy tenure of office causes a "cultural" lag. Is there any way to increase the ability of Congress to reflect and represent the needs of the public and shorten this lag time without at the same time upsetting the balance of the two chambers?

Finally, Buckley ends his essay focusing on the importance of the Senate as a place to engage in public debate about the current issues of the time. What advantages do you see in using the Senate chamber in this way? Is the Senate a more deliberative assembly than the House of Representatives? Of what importance is it to have an adequately informed electorate?

★ ★ ★

THE FIRST TWO YEARS

99 — 1971 FRI — 99 — 1972 SAT

ON BECOMING A UNITED STATES SENATOR

JAMES L. BUCKLEY

On January 22, 1971, Jacob Javits, pursuant to custom, escorted me down the center aisle of the United States Senate Chamber. Vice President Agnew swore me in, and I was handed a pen with which I entered my name on the books of the Senate. I then walked a few steps to my desk on the Republican side of the aisle. I had become the Junior Senator from the State of New York. Or, as senatorial courtesy puts it, the distinguished and honorable Senator from the great State of New York.

Rarely has anyone, distinguished and honorable—or otherwise—entered the United States Senate so innocent of the mechanisms of a legislative body or of the impact of politics on the legislative process. Prior to my election I had never held public office or participated in any organized political effort other than the third-party mayoral and senatorial campaigns of the brothers Buckley.

Shortly after my election Clif White, my campaign manager and guide into the political world, organized a private dinner with a few of the senior Republican senators so that I might acquire a better feel for the life I was about to enter. I had hoped to get specific advice on how to go about the job of being an effective senator. What I got instead were affable assurances to the effect that anyone capable of winning election to the Senate would find no difficulty in getting along once in it.

From *National Review*, February 2, 1973. © 1973 National Review, Inc., 150 East 35th St., New York, NY 10016. Reprinted by permission.

I hoped to get specific advice on how to be an effective senator. What I got instead were affable assurances . . .

This was all, in its own way, reassuring; but I did not emerge from that dinner with the mother lode of hard, practical information that would help me thread my way through the complexities of the senatorial life.

The first formal business for a senator-elect is the meeting with the Sergeant at Arms and the Secretary of the Senate, who give you the basic housekeeping instructions, take from you sample signatures for franking privileges, and explain insurance and retirement benefits, as well as such perquisites as the right to a District of Columbia license plate, numbered according to one's rank in the Senate pecking order —plus one, Number One being reserved for the Vice President. (My rank was 99 because I had no prior service as a congressman or governor, which adds into the calculation of seniority. I beat out Lawton Chiles of Florida because New York has the larger population.) At that meeting I was presented with three books: *The Rules and Manual of the United States Senate*; an exegesis thereof by the chief parliamentarian, Dr. Floyd Riddick; and the *Congressional Directory* for the second session of the prior Congress. I determined to spend the next few weeks mastering the parliamentary rules, but was soon bogged down in their intricacy. I would learn to my relief that the Senate operates in a reasonably free and tolerant manner, and that much of its business is conducted not so much by the rule book as by continuing recourse to unanimous-consent agreements. Those who do know the rule book, however, are equipped, at critical moments, to take the parliamentary advantage.

New senators learn that they are expected to carry the principal burden of presiding over the Senate. For someone like me, who had never presided over any function, nor even scanned *Robert's Rules of Order*, the prospect seemed ominous. It isn't all that difficult, however, because sitting immediately in front of the Chair is one of the three parliamentarians, who whispers up the appropriate instruction. The most difficult task is to learn the identity of eighty or ninety brand new faces, together with state of origin, so that one can recognize the Senator from So-and-so without any excessive or obvious fumbling.

During this orientation period, I introduced myself to the Senate Republican leadership—to Minority Leader Hugh Scott, Minority Whip Bob Griffin, Chairman Gordon Allott of the Republican Policy Committee, and Chairman Margaret Chase Smith of the Republican Conference.

One important call was at the office of Senator Wallace Bennett, Chairman of the Republican Committee on Committees, in order to learn how committee assignments were made, and to register my preferences. The process is in fact mechanical. Once the minority vacancies on the various committees become known, the Republican members of the incoming class line up in order of seniority, and take their pick. Each senator is appointed to two major committees, and often to one or more minor ones. My own initial assignments were to Public Works, Space, and the District of Columbia.

II. *The Committee Shuffle*

It was in committee work that I first came to appreciate the enormous volume of business that courses through the Congress, and its implications. It is not unusual to find meetings or hearings involving as many as three committees or subcommittees of which one is a member scheduled for the same time, each involving business of some importance. One either spreads himself thin by putting in token appearances at each, or devotes himself to one meeting, relying on an overworked staff member to keep abreast of what is going on in the other two. I have yet to be convinced that there isn't somewhere in the bowels of the Capitol a computer programed to arrange as many conflicting appointments as possible.

The committee system constitutes a delegation of responsibility for legislative work in designated areas. It should not be assumed, however, that a given committee will be representative of the Senate as a whole. Senators naturally tend to gravitate to those committees that interest them most or whose work is most important to their particular constituencies, and a committee can become as "mission-oriented" as an executive agency. Given the broad range of viewpoints represented on each side of the aisle, the requirement that each committee have a majority and minority membership roughly comparable to that of the Senate as a whole is no guarantee that it will reflect the political spectrum in any other sense. Thus committee reports are too often "selling documents" that do not provide other senators with the kind of balanced information needed to help them reach a reasonably educated opinion regarding a particular bill's merits.

It isn't long—especially if controversial and complex legislation is being worked on—before a newcomer senses the enormous influence wielded by committee staffs. These are usually heavily loaded in favor of the majority party, in terms both of outlook and of availability to committee members. Time and again after new points are raised in committee, the staff will disappear to return the next day with what is often a significantly new or considerably refocused bit of legislation.

It can be extraordinarily difficult for committee members, even those particularly concerned with the legislation in question, to keep up with what is happening to it. There simply isn't time for a member to rethink and reconsider every interlocking provision of a complex bill each time a substantive change is made—hence the heavy reliance on staff. Furthermore, committees often work under enormous time pressures to report out particular pieces of legislation by certain deadlines which at times are set not so much by the natural rhythm of the legislative process as by political considerations.

Thus major legislation is often rushed through committee, reported out on the floor of the Senate, and put to a vote with few senators fully understanding it. It must be understood that it is virtually impossible for a senator to keep up with most—let alone all— of the significant legislation being considered by committees other than his own. I do not refer to legislation that grabs the headlines and occasions national debate: A senator has to examine such legislation in some detail if only to answer his mail and reply to reporters' questions. It is, after all, by his positions on conspicuous legislation that he establishes his political identity.

Most of the bills considered by the Senate are relatively inconspicuous—though by no means unimportant. They may involve new programs that will have an enormous impact on American society, on the states, or on the economy; programs that in time may grow into multibillion-dollar commitments. Yet many of these bills will be enacted with little real examination by most of the senators who will have to vote yea or nay on them, and with less than adequate comprehension of what the bill involves.

The average senator simply does not have sufficient legislative help to get a proper analysis of every bill that issues from the legislative mill. Too many bills are called to a vote before the ink has dried on the explanatory report. Thus, all too often a senator's vote is based simply on a summary description of the bill (which can be totally inadequate), plus whispered conversations with colleagues who may or may not have detailed information as to its content—all in the fifteen-minute period allowed for voting after the bells ring to summon him to the floor.

Technically speaking, any senator can insure that adequate time is allowed for debate of any bill. He can simply register his refusal to agree to a unanimous-consent agreement limiting the time allotted for debate. This presupposes, however, that he has had enough advance warning of the particular mischief at hand to record a timely objection to any agreement to which he is not a party. It also presupposes that he will be able to educate and energize a sufficient number of his all-too-preoccupied colleagues to assure himself of sufficient floor support to make the effort worthwhile.

I recall two cases in my own experience—although there are, unfortunately, many more—that dramatize the pressures under which the Senate operates.

In early 1971, Governor Daniel Evans of Washington suggested the need for legislation to cope with economic disasters similar to existing legislation designed to cope with natural disasters. The law he proposed would

be narrow in its focus, providing relief on a short-term, emergency basis to help communities ride out sudden economic catastrophes.

Two bills incorporating this approach were introduced, and hearings on them were held by the Public Works Committee. Several months later the Committee met in executive session to consider the legislation as revised by staff after the hearings. To the astonishment of at least some, the draft bill differed in fundamental respects from both of the measures that had been introduced. The basic concept had shifted from bringing maximum effort to bear on specific emergency situations, to an amorphous bill that would also cover areas of chronic unemployment or chronically low economic activity for which there already existed thirty or forty other federal programs. The definition of areas which could be made subject to the legislation was such that even a neighborhood could qualify for the most exotic kinds of federal help.

Nevertheless, this basically new legislation was approved in a single day by the full committee, and reported out. The legislation was then rushed to the floor of the Senate, debated before a largely empty chamber, and put to a vote—all within a day or two of the time printed copies of the bill and of the accompanying committee report had become available to senators. This legislation opened up a whole new area of federal intervention; it carried no price tag; and it was approved by senators only a few of whom had any grasp of its scope.

The second example concerned a new program of a truly sweeping nature, enacted by an overwhelming majority of senators, many of whom I am convinced had little understanding of the real issues involved. Just before the August recess in 1971, the Committee on Labor and Public Welfare reported out a measure innocuously titled "A Bill To Extend the Equal Employment Opportunity Act 1968 and Other Purposes." The "other purposes" turned out to be the inauguration of a comprehensive federal program for "child development" services designed

ultimately to embrace a very large proportion of pre-school-age children regardless of financial need. Whereas in its first year the new program would cost a mere $100 million (chickenfeed these days), the Committee report placed the figure for the second year at $2 billion—an amount significantly greater than the projected cost of all the rest of the OEO's activities. Furthermore, the report stated that the cost of the child-development program would double every two years thereafter for some time hence. Secretary Elliot Richardson, then of the Department of Health, Education, and Welfare, estimated that the annual cost of the new program would come to $20 billion before the end of the decade.

Thanks to an interested housewife who had followed the progress of the bill in committee, my office was alerted to its implications. Because of the recess, we had time to examine its horrors and I was in a position to argue on the basis of expert opinion against the child-development section. (The bill had been scheduled as the first order of business on the day Congress returned, and was voted on in the Senate the next day, "other purposes" and all.)

Senators who had happened to be on the floor to hear the debate would have learned that there was substantial controversy among professionals over the child-development section, a fact they would not have discovered from reading the report. They would have learned that a number of experts in the field questioned the need for such a vast undertaking, and, in fact, warned that permanent harm could be done to younger children placed in the impersonal "warehouse" environment of the kind of day-care facility that was apt to result from the legislation. They would have learned also that the expert opinion heard in committee was entirely one-sided, and that even among the experts who favored the program, one had remarked that its far-reaching provisions would revolutionize the concept of the family in American life.

Unfortunately, almost no one besides the sponsors of the bill and the two or three senators arguing for the elimination or modification of the child-development section were on hand to hear the debate. Thus when the time came to vote, most senators voted aye on the assumption that nothing significant was involved in the bill beyond a simple two-year extension of existing OEO

When it comes to allocating rooms and funds, senators from the larger states invariably feel short-changed.

programs. (This bill, incidentally, was later vetoed.)

This rush of business with little or no time allowed for legislative pause, thought, or deliberation brings to mind another aspect of the Senate's current way of conducting its affairs. I speak of the phenomenon of the amendment —printed or unprinted—offered from the floor with little or no notice, which can cover the range from purely technical corrections of statutory language to the most far-reaching changes in the legislation under consideration.

There is usually little check on the scope of amendments that can be offered from the floor, and no opportunity for the relevant committees and their staffs to study them so that some measure of expert analysis can be brought to bear in arguing their merits for the benefit of the Senate—always assuming other senators are on hand to hear the debate. Thus all too often, especially when the Senate is operating under unanimous agreements severely limiting the time for debate on amendments, they are apt to be adopted or rejected on the basis of their emotional or political appeal. So it was with the floor amendments that last October added $4 billion, or more than 27 per cent, to the cost of the Welfare-Social Security bill reported out by the Senate Finance Committee; with the amendments that added, in one day's time last June, almost $2 billion to the HEW-Labor appropriations bill. Surely there is a better way in which to conduct the na-

tion's vital legislative business short of the highly restrictive rules that obtain in the House.

III. *Too Much Business*

All of which brings me to certain observations about the Senate today.

At the root of most of the problems of the Senate is the enormous expansion of federal activities in recent years. A recent study by the Association of the Bar of the City of New York found that the workload of members of Congress had doubled every five years over the past several decades. The Congress, like the Federal Government itself, is simply trying to handle more business than it can digest. The results too often are waste, conflicts, inconsistencies, and superficiality.

Once upon a time Congress was in session only six or seven months a year. There is every reason to believe that during these months there was time and opportunity to think, to study, to argue, and to come to educated conclusions. As the volume of work increased, the Congress was able to cope by extending the length of its sessions. But now, as a result of the explosion of federal activity resulting from the War on Poverty and other programs of the 1960s, it is conceded that Congress is in session essentially on a year-round basis.

One consequence of these increasing demands on senators' time is that it can no longer be said of the Senate

that it is a club, exclusive or otherwise. Members once were able to spend unhurried time together, to get to know one another and develop a sense of fraternity while working toward common goals in a highly civil environment. I do not mean to suggest that all of this has disappeared. Real friendships and a sense of belonging do develop, but the sense of community which must once have existed has certainly been dissipated by the preoccupations that tend to keep senators concentrating on their own separate concerns except as their work requires them to come together. It is difficult, in fact, to come to know members of the opposition party who do not happen to serve on one's committees.

Whether the situation can be changed, only time and a differently constituted Congress will tell. But even assuming that the volume of business can be held at present levels, there remains the fact that each senator has only so many hours per day to devote to his job. A senator must be able not only to bring effective judgment to bear on his legislative duties, but also to maintain contact with his own constituency so as to find out what are the real problems people are faced with, and what are the real effects of the legislation he has helped enact.

All of this, in turn, takes adequate staff and office space. Mundane as this may seem, one quickly finds that staffing and space can become important factors in determining just how good a job he is going to be able to do.

A new senator from a state like New York quickly learns that the Senate places great emphasis on the equal sovereign dignity of each individual state; which is a polite way of saying that when it comes to allocating rooms and funds, senators from the larger states invariably feel short-changed. It should be kept in mind that the volume of work that must be handled by a senator's office depends largely on the size of his constituency. I speak of handling mail and constituent problems (the so-called case work), which have been increasing at an enormous rate as the Federal Government has become more and more intrusive into its citizens' lives.

Case work involves such things as immigration problems, chasing down Social Security checks, helping municipalities process their applications for this or that program, helping businesses thread their way through red tape—you

name it. Whereas the office workload of a senator from New York may not be sixty times as heavy as that of a senator from Alaska, it certainly involves significantly more than two or three times the volume of work. Yet when I entered the Senate in 1971, the smallest number of rooms assigned to any senator was five and the largest (California and New York), seven. As I started out with a staff of 35 and needed one room for myself, this created a degree of congestion. In like manner, my allowance for hiring staff was less than twice the allowance for the smallest state. It is of course true that each senator bears an equal legislative responsibility and needs equal facilities to keep track of legislative matters and to help him do his individual and committee work. But this doesn't explain the disparity (or lack thereof) in space and staff allowances. In my own case, for example, staff members directly involved in legislative matters are less than one-fifth of the total.

IV. *Easing the Workload*

Committee problems, time problems, space problems . . . it would seem from my description that a senator's lot is not entirely a happy one. There are, of course, compensations, not the least of which is the pervasive air of civility and mutual respect with which the business of the Senate is conducted. But even the extraordinary civility and respect that are the hallmark of the institution cannot overcome organizational and structural complexities that make a difficult job even more difficult.

What, if anything, can be done about the ever-increasing workload that is at the heart of the Senate's problems? I am not so romantic as to believe that we can dismantle the Departments of HEW and HUD in the immediate future and return most of their functions to the states and localities. Therefore another approach to restructuring the work and the flow of business in the Senate must be considered if senators are to be able to use their scarce time more effectively, and if they are to bring a maximum degree of thought to bear on legislation.

One useful approach might be to place as much of the legislative business of the Congress as possible on a two-year cycle. One year might be devoted to debate and action on bills re-

ported out of committees the prior year, and to the holding of public hearings to assemble information for committee consideration in the succeeding year. (Ideally, both of these activities, which are of a very public nature and which tend to attract headlines, would be scheduled in non-election years so that the participants would not needlessly be distracted from the business

I have not found the work frustrating because I had few illusions as to what a very junior member of the minority party would be able to accomplish on his own.

at hand. There are, however, technical difficulties with this.) The alternate years would then be available for detailed consideration in executive session of new legislative proposals without arbitrary deadlines requiring hurried, patchwork approaches to important bills, and for the important work of legislative oversight.

A system that would require committees to report out legislation one year, and to have that legislation considered on the floor the next, would allow ample time for special-interest groups, for the public at large, and for members of individual senatorial staffs to digest what it is that the senator will be asked to vote upon when the legislation reaches the floor. It would also provide a period within which amendments could be introduced sufficiently in advance of debate to enable the members of the relevant committees to study them and to give the Senate as a whole the benefit of their expert assessment.

Whether the appropriation process could also be placed on a biennial basis, I do not know; and of course, any fundamental reordering of business would have to make special provision for the handling of emergencies. But if the work of the Senate could be organized in some such manner—and I see no reason why it is necessary to enact routine legislation every year instead of every other year—then the conflicts between committee hearings and executive sessions could be eliminated or greatly reduced, the members of the Senate would have time to participate more fully in floor debate, and it ought to be possible—at least every other year—to adjourn the Congress early enough to provide senators with a

greater opportunity to return to their states to listen and to observe.

In this connection, I believe the Congress should schedule more "free" time for its members—at least a week each month—for consecutive thought, for planning, for study, for travel, for meaningful contact with their constituents. All of this is necessary if a senator or representative is to bring the best

that is in him to bear on his work as a legislator. This would also help with the problem of absenteeism, as senators would be able to schedule their out-of-town engagements during these periodic recesses.

No discussion of possible changes in the way the Senate goes about its business would be complete without further mention of the committees.

As I have already pointed out, although the Senate relies heavily on its committee system for the conduct of its business, there is no assurance that the membership of a committee will reflect the views of the Senate as a whole. Thus it will very often happen that legislation that is highly controversial in nature will be reported out unanimously, or with appended minority views that are more concerned with details of the legislation than with its basic merit. This means that in too many cases the report which accompanies a new bill is not nearly as informative as it ought to be, and fails to alert the Senate as a whole to its controversial features.

This is especially true of committees that have a tradition of trying to iron out all differences of opinion within the committee so that legislation may be reported out unanimously. This practice has a certain utility in that it results in a genuine effort within the committee to reach reasonable compromises among conflicting views. Yet I wonder if the interests of the Senate are necessarily best served by this drive to consensus; for it encourages a sense of commitment to the end product which inhibits any public expression of misgivings by individual committee members. Thus the Senate is apt to be deprived of the candid insights of those senators who are best informed about the weaknesses of the legislation in question.

It might be desirable to require that every committee report outline as objectively as possible the principal arguments for *and* against each new legislative proposal, even when the bill is in fact unanimously supported by the entire committee. I also feel that whenever a member of a committee has strong reservations about any feature of a proposed bill, he has an obligation to the Senate to spell them out in a minority view printed in the committee report.

One recommendation I will not make is that the seniority system be abolished. This does not mean that I find it in all respects to my liking, or that I will not support (as I did) such sensible proposals for restricting its application as the one recently offered by Senator Howard Baker (and adopted by the Senate Republican Conference) which affects the selection of a committee's ranking member. Rather it means that I find greater potential problems with the alternatives thus far advanced. An often overlooked fact is that the seniority system was introduced some years ago as a reform measure to minimize politicking and power plays within the Congress. The system as it operates within the Senate

today is reasonably benign; and I, as a most junior senator, have not found myself unduly abused by it. There are far more important targets, it seems to me, for a reformer's zeal.

v. *The Balance Wheel*

I have often been asked whether I find work in the Senate frustrating, and whether I have found any surprises. I have not found the work frustrating because I had few illusions as to what a very junior member of the minority party could accomplish on his own. Nor have I experienced any really major surprises, although I was not at all prepared for the enormous demands that would be made on my time, seven days a week, or for my loss of anonymity (the unsurprising result of six hundred or so thousand well-deployed dollars on television advertising during my campaign, reinforced by periodic meetings with the press since election).

Early on, I was struck by the number of extracurricular demands on a senator's time, especially one who lives as close to millions of constituents as does a senator from New York: invitations to speak which for one good reason or another cannot be declined, ceremonial visits, people with problems whom one must see and cannot refer

to staff, people in the Federal Government to get to know, and so on. The day begins to be splintered into all kinds of pieces, even before the business of legislative work begins.

One thing that in my innocence I had not anticipated was the intensely political atmosphere that prevails within the Senate, the great impact of purely political considerations on specific actions taken by individual senators. It may well be, of course, that mine was an unusual introduction to the institution, as at least a half-dozen of my colleagues were beginning to jockey for position in the presidential race within months after I had been sworn in. This had an inevitable influence on how they orchestrated their performance in the Senate. Also there was the fact that the Senate was controlled by one party and the White House by the other; and as the presidential elections approached, the political atmosphere palpably intensified.

But these unusual considerations notwithstanding, I early learned that many senators tend to cast their votes with a view toward minimizing future political controversy or embarrassment. When a senator's vote is clearly not critical to the fate of a bill, it is often deployed for future political convenience on the grounds that it "wouldn't count anyway." Thus the Senate will often cast a lopsided vote on questions on which public opinion and the real opinion within the Senate is much more evenly divided.

This protecting of political flanks seems harmless enough, but it vitiates what I have discovered to be the important educational function of the Senate. If citizens see that members of the Senate have voted overwhelmingly in favor of this or that piece of legislation, many not entirely certain of their own ground may decide that they have in fact been wrong or backward or insensitive. Yet if on such issues each member of the Senate had voted his true convictions, the breakdown might have been, say, 55 to 45 instead of 70 to 30. I can't help but wonder to what extent this form of political expediency may affect the public's perception of the issues.

There may be another reason why the opinion of the Senate—even when accurately recorded—is very often at odds with what I, at least, take to be the current mood of the American people. Without having researched the

A senator is entitled to free haircuts in a barbershop which keeps a shaving mug with his name on it.

---

point, I suspect that the Senate incorporates a cultural lag of ten or fifteen years; that it is out of phase by a period approximately equivalent to the average tenure of its membership.

A decade or so ago, the Senate was considered by some to be a backward, conservative body whose Republican-Southern Democrat coalition lay athwart progress and the will of the people. Others viewed it as a necessary brake on the rasher impulses of the House of Representatives. Today the situation is quite the reverse. The liberals in the Senate are clearly in the majority, and they do not reflect the growing public skepticism over federal initiatives; and today, for example, it is the House which tends to blow the whistle on the excessive spending approved by the Senate.

There is a reason for this cultural lag, if it indeed exists. A member of the House of Representatives is up for election every two years and studies the views of his constituency with particular care. Also, because each member of the House represents a relatively compact area, his constituency tends to be more homogeneous than a senator's and there is less of an impulse to cater to the fringe groups within it. A member of the Senate, on the other hand, represents an entire state incorporating a multitude of conflicting claims and interests. For better or worse (I suspect the latter) a senator tends to pay a disproportionate amount of attention to the loudest voices, to editorial writers and commentators, to the pressure groups. Furthermore, once in office, he tends to stay there. Thus a senator may be less sensitive than a representative to basic shifts in the underlying mood of the electorate as a whole.

I make this comment by way of observation and not of criticism. The Founding Fathers intended, after all, that the Senate be a balance wheel which would moderate the impulses of the moment. This function it in fact performs, even though at any point of time those who believe the current impulses are the correct ones may tend to impatience. The Senate, however, is not an institution to which the impatient should gravitate. It has its own pace;

and, under the present rules, it takes a little maturing on the vine of seniority to be in a position to have a large impact on the body politic.

It would be inaccurate, however, and unfair to the institution to suggest that the newest members are without the power to do more than register their 1 per cent of the Senate's total vote. The ancient tradition that stated that freshman senators were to be seen and not heard has disappeared. Somewhat to my surprise, on my initial rounds I was encouraged by the most senior members to speak out when I felt I had learned the ropes and had something to say—which was not, I hasten to say, an invitation to be brash.

In point of fact, I soon learned that there are a number of ways in which even Number 99 can make his imprint on the law of the land. If he is willing to do the necessary homework on a bill before his committee, if he attends meetings, if he presents arguments for or against specific provisions, he does have a chance to mold its final form. I have found that my own views will be given as careful a hearing as those of any other member of the committees on which I have served; again the essential courtesy of the Senate comes to the fore. It is also possible, by submitting appropriate amendments, to shape legislation after it has reached the floor.

It will also occasionally be the lot of a senator to come across an idea of such universal appeal that it will whisk through the legislative process in record time—witness two bills I introduced involving certain benefits for prisoners of war and those missing in action in Indochina. Each immediately attracted more than sixty co-sponsors, and each has since been signed into law.

Finally, there are the educational opportunities—and hence, responsibilities—which the Senate opens up to the newest of senators. These had not occurred to me when I first decided to run for office, but it did not take long for me to appreciate the skill with which some of the more liberal members were utilizing their office to reach the public. They would schedule time

on the Senate floor, often in tandem, to deliver themselves of learned or impassioned speeches to an empty chamber. Their wisdom might be wasted on the Senate air, but the exercise enabled them to alert the press that Senator So-and-so would deliver remarks on such-and-such a topic at the scheduled time. Copies of the speech would be distributed, and the gist of the senator's argument and the points he wished to make would become part of the nation's informational bloodstream. I also noted that conservative-minded senators were generally not so alert in this regard.

Whether utilized or not, the opportunity does exist for a senator to present his views on the important issues with some reasonable assurance that they will not be totally lost. Only by exploiting these opportunities for public education can he expect to help the electorate become more adequately informed on the basic issues. This in turn bears on the legislative process because, in the last analysis, public opinion dictates the outside limits of the options available to the Congress. By joining in the public debate and articulating the arguments in support of his own positions, a new senator—even one labeled "Conservative-Republican"—can contribute to the educational process which ultimately finds its reflection in national policy.

Snuff and Civility

These, then, are the random impressions of the United States Senate by one of its newest members: It is a deliberative body in which there is too little time to deliberate. It is a place where a senator is entitled to free haircuts (although he is expected to tip the barber a dollar) in a barbershop which keeps a shaving mug with his name on it. It is a place where on each desk there is a little inkwell, a wooden pen with steel nibs, and a glass bottle filled with sand with which to blot writing, and where on either side of the presiding officer's desk is a spittoon and a box of snuff.

Yet it is also a place where the rules of civility are still observed, and the rights and independence of each individual still respected. It is a place where many of the major decisions affecting the shape of our times are made; a place where even the least of its members may have a hand in making them.

It is, all in all, a good place to be. □

★★★

28

And They Call It the Most Important Committee in Congress
Juan Cameron

The Ways and Means Committee has been, since the beginning, a very important standing committee of the House. Its importance today is evident given the issues with which it deals. What issues make this committee one of the more important in the House? Since 1974, Cameron suggests, a "new order" of congressman has taken control of the House and its committees. On balance, do you feel the Ways and Means Committee has profited from this change in membership? Has it made this committee a more viable committee in Congress? Has it made Congress a more vital institution?

Cameron points to some of the staffing changes that have taken place, including the change of chairman and the addition of more congressmen to the Committee. The rather crusty autocrat Wilbur Mills was replaced by the rather passive Democrat Al Ullman. How would you characterize the political style of former Chairman Mills? Would you say the Committee was powerful and effectively governed under his leadership? What can we expect to occur when a rather powerful chairman is replaced with a decidedly weaker one on a standing committee?

The Committee increased in size from its former twenty-five members to its current number of thirty-seven. What ideological factions now exist on the Committee? Among the new members were five freshmen and some twenty members who had never served on Ways and Means before. What should one anticipate whenever a committee is so enlarged to accommodate new interests? Would you expect all the new interests to be equally represented, or would the old interests continue to dominate? Can a large diverse committee, as Ways and Means now appears to be, act as effectively as a smaller committee whose members share common interests?

There have also been structural changes to the Committee since 1974. How have the procedures of Ways and Means changed since the era of Wilbur Mills? What effect does the creation of subcommittees have on a chairman's control of the full committee? On the overall effectiveness of committee operations?

It would seem that there is a trade-off between the ideals of democratic participation—an ideal espoused by Ullman—and the requirements of governing—the prime value of Mills. Do you think that too much democracy within Congress and its committee system can undermine the viability of that institution in its ability collectively to make decisions and govern the nation?

★ ★ ★

Since the fall of Wilbur Mills, new faces and new rules have brought turmoil and disarray to the tax-writing Ways and Means Committee.

And They Call It the Most Important Committee in Congress

by Juan Cameron

Fate, helped out by that buxom stripper Fanne Foxe, was unkind to Oregon Democrat Al Ullman when it thrust him into the chairmanship of the House Ways and Means Committee last year. That is a position of great eminence, to be sure, but the timing was very bad. Ullman took over the helm of what is generally considered to be the most important committee on Capitol Hill just as the revolt against the older order by the newly elected Ninety-fourth Congress was at full tide.

That revolt took special aim at Ullman's predecessor, Wilbur Mills, whose gradually crumbling power was finally stripped away completely after his indiscreet activities with Fanne. With Mills's fall, the committee in its old form disappeared. Its membership was enlarged and liberalized. Its procedures were altered. And Ullman's powers as chairman were greatly reduced.

As a result, Ways and Means has been transformed, both in its outer manner and in its inner workings. The decorum that marked at least its public sessions has given way on occasion to sharp clashes between committee members, and between members and witnesses. The committee used to forge a bipartisan consensus in secret. Now, politically polarized, it often takes important decisions in controversial matters such as energy and tax reform in open sessions, before reaching internal agreement. Says Bill Frenzel, a moderate Republican from Minnesota: "We have gone in a single year from the tyranny of one-man rule to a state of anarchy. We can't reach a conclusion on anything."

Ullman's ability to cope with the anarchy has not been helped by his passive manner in the chair. A Democratic colleague voices a common criticism that "Al wants to be an umpire and scorekeeper, rather than someone who forcefully guides the committee and tries to bring some discipline to its work."

The fiscal time bomb

With his leadership ability still in question, he has been forced to face the prospect of some painful decisions about taxes. The most difficult decisions will be concerned with how and from whom to raise the new revenues that Ullman believes will be necessary this year and in the future as well. Especially pressing is the need to find new financing for Social Security programs, whose costs have far outrun the revenue produced by the payroll tax. "This is a fiscal time bomb," agrees Barber Conable, the committee's second-ranking Republican.

Social Security benefits were raised by 58 percent from 1970 to 1976, and were linked to the consumer price index. Partly as a consequence, the program's deficits have been growing rapidly despite continual increases in the payroll tax. The deficit of the Social Security Trust Fund, $5.4 billion this year, will grow to $11.4 billion by 1982, at which time the fund will be broke unless new revenues are provided.

President Ford recently proposed a further increase of $4.4 billion in the Social Security tax next year, but Ullman and many of his colleagues feel that far-reaching changes are needed to keep the system solvent over the longer haul. "The payroll tax has reached the end of the line," Ullman says. "It has become too heavy a burden." He adds that he "was shocked at my own Social Security payment last year."

In two decades, the payroll tax has changed from a minor to a major tax burden. Its current $72-billion yield is almost double the yield of the corporate income tax and more than half that of the individual income tax. Half of all wage earners (those earning $15,000 or less) now pay more in Social Security than in income taxes.

A Westerner's distrust

Ullman has similar misgivings about the long-run ability of the corporate and personal income tax system to meet future needs for government revenue. He is not optimistic that the growth of federal spending, which has increased by $100 billion in the past two years, can be slowed down very much.

The resulting deficits he sees looming ahead worry him as the chairman of the principal congressional committee charged with raising revenue. As a Westerner, too, he shares that region's distrust of high interest rates. In the last couple of years high interest rates have hurt Oregon's large lumber industry, which is dependent on a strong construction industry, a matter of special political concern to Ullman.

In a period of constrained federal spending, there is a strong temptation to raid the tax structure, substituting "tax expenditures" for budget expenditures. "Tax expenditures," as officially defined, are revenue losses resulting from "exceptions to the 'normal structure' of the individual and corporate income tax" (i.e., all forms of tax relief except reductions in rates). President Ford's latest budget calls for $1.4 billion in tax expenditures to promote construction of electric-utility facilities, wider ownership of common stock, and investment in high-unemployment areas.

The revenue loss from such measures is already very large. Tax expenditures have grown by about $30 billion in the past five years. All of the deductions, exemptions, allowances, credits, deferrals, etc. in the entire tax code currently amount to $92 billion a year.

Once tax revenues are given away, recouping is difficult. Efforts to restore even temporary tax reductions meet with rough resistance. If the economic advance continues, Ullman will probably ask his committee to eliminate the tax reductions passed last year, but he is not optimistic about his chances of succeeding.

Economic arguments aside, members of Congress feel strong political pressure, especially from middle-income taxpayers, pinched by inflation as well as rising taxes. Ullman himself is concerned about growing tax evasion among middle-class people, who "feel they don't have the tax shelters available to corporations and high-income groups." Higher tax rates could bring on a taxpayer revolt, he fears.

The tilted system

Nor does the chairman expect any large results from the efforts of tax-reform-minded members of Ways and Means to raise additional revenues by eliminating some of the tax relief voted in the past. And the reformers themselves do not display much confidence these days. Last year, Illinois Democrat Abner Mikva, one of the Ways and Means committee's ablest members, was in the thick of the fight to close some corporate tax preferences. As justification, he points to the dramatic shift in the tax burden from corporations to individuals. Ten years ago the corporate tax brought in 60 percent as much rev-

enue as the individual income tax. Today it brings in only one-third as much as the individual tax. "Can we say we have a fair tax structure when the system has been tilted like that?" But Mikva and like-minded colleagues were sobered by the lobbying pressures that the real-estate industry and large corporations mounted last year to defeat moves to take away some of their tax breaks.

For every tax loophole that is closed, Ullman observes, a new one is usually opened up. Last year, the House voted to close up a number of tax shelters used by businesses and individuals, but at the same time it voted new or additional tax breaks for, among other things, child-care expenses, retirement income, and alimony payments. For every $3 in revenue gained by taking away old tax breaks, the House gave out roughly $2 in new tax breaks.

One vote for VAT

Ullman feels that a basic restructuring of the tax code is required to meet the needs of Social Security, provide funds for a national health-insurance program (minimum cost: $10 billion to $15 billion a year), and help narrow federal budget deficits. While the income tax would remain the backbone of the tax system, he sees a need to supplement it with something quite like a value-added tax—a tax levied on business transactions. The idea of a value-added tax, widely used in Western Europe, has been put forward by a number of American economists in recent years, and for a time President Nixon showed some interest in the idea. (See "The Brewing Interest in VAT," by Henry C. Wallich, FORTUNE, April, 1971.)

As a sweetener to business, Ullman suggests that his new tax might make it possible to mitigate the double taxation of corporate profits by lightening the tax on dividends in some way. "The sticking point," he adds, is that such proposals involve "very substantial revenue losses," which only a new tax of some kind could make up.

Ullman's idea of a bold restructuring of the tax system is certain to face stiff opposition in his committee. There is a strong resistance to new tax ideas— a venerable saying has it that any old tax is a good one, any new tax is a bad one. In the past, proposals for a value-added tax have been criticized on the grounds of its regressivity, even though the tax could be fashioned to include a

system of refundable credits to families below a certain income level. And tax reformers tend to feel that advocating a value-added tax is a cop-out in the struggle to increase revenues through reform of the existing income-tax structure.

Steadiness in safe seats

A very serious practical obstacle to any bold restructuring of the tax system is the condition of the Ways and Means Committee itself. In its present form, at least, it is incapable of coherent action on major tax issues.

The committee has lost the cohesiveness it once had. It used to be that Congressmen served an average of fourteen years before going on the committee. Long seniority meant that the members held safe seats, which helped insulate them from the political winds of the moment. It also meant that Ways and Means members were more conservative than the general run of the House.

Last year the committee was expanded from twenty-five members to its present thirty-seven. The twelve Democratic holdovers were joined by thirteen new members, only two of whom might be classified as conservative. In an unheard-of break with tradition, five freshmen, all strongly in favor of "tax reform," were included among those thirteen newcomers. (Two of the five, however, Mikva and Andrew Jacobs of Indiana, regained seats they had previously lost, and so were freshmen in a technical sense only.) At the same time, the Republicans included seven new members in their twelve-man bloc. That made a total of twenty Ways and Means members who were new to the committee's work.

The addition of the thirteen new Democratic members was aimed directly at liberalizing the committee outlook and weakening the control of the chairman. Moreover, the committee was ordered to set up subcommittees—there had not been any in the preceding sixteen years. This step has weakened Ullman's control over proposed legislation, as well as over the staff (which, to serve the six new subcommittees, has increased from fourteen professionals to thirty-nine). Some other steps taken by the House leadership were also, as Ullman puts it, aimed at "dismembering" the powers of the chairman.

The new faces and the structural changes have destroyed the discipline of the committee and its ability to reach a consensus. At one extreme is an aggressive group of seven reform-minded Democrats who have used the liberalized procedures of the committee to push for reforms of the tax laws. At the other extreme is a united group of twelve Republicans. They form a solid bloc that invariably opposes the Democratic majority. Representative Conable says that "When Ullman asks us for votes, our answer is usually no because we're given little input. He could get a better deal from us if he felt less pressure from the reformers on the committee."

Proxies in his pocket

The Republicans have found allies in the six conservative southern Democrats, who often refuse to go along with the chairman. Joe Waggonner of Louisiana, a shrewd tactician who enjoys the role of spokesman for the conservative South, has emerged as the leader of the Southerners on the committee, and a key contact for White House lobbyists. When he takes a position against his Democratic colleagues, he usually has twelve Republican proxies in his pocket. On controversial issues when business lobbying has been intense, this Republican-southern Democratic group has usually been able to pick up swing votes from the middle-of-the-road Democrats to form a majority within the committee.

The expectation of last year that the new Ways and Means Committee, with its twenty-five to twelve Democratic majority, could accomplish a major reform of the nation's tax structure has been deflated by the nearly even split between conservatives and reformers. Even when the Democrats are able to halt defections among the moderates, the majority is too thin to enable Ullman to take major tax proposals to the floor of the House and expect them to pass.

The split on policy has created new tensions among committee members. The ranking Republican, Herman Schneebeli of Pennsylvania, complains that the newcomers to the committee, whom he describes as "belligerent intruders," have destroyed its old decorum. He was aghast when a demonstration took place in the committee's cavernous hearing room during the contest over tax credits for child care. Things like that were not supposed to happen at Ways and Means hearings.

"It became a joke"

The new liberal members feel they have livened things up. Representative Fortney Stark, a California Democrat, says, "This committee operated in secret for so long and played it so safe, it became a joke. We've opened up the place to some meaningful dialogue. This is the only way we are going to regain respect."

Newcomers have cleared away some of the staid customs and stale thought that had permeated the committee. Some of the liberal members have hired their own staff tax experts because they felt the committee's staff was not partisan enough. Stark is suspicious of some Mills holdovers on the staff. "If you go to sleep for a moment," he says, "they'll put something over on you."

Liberals have also formed close alliances with public-interest lobbyists. Robert Brandon, who is with the Naderite "Tax Reform Research Group," has in effect become an auxiliary staff member to reformers such as Representative William Green of Pennsylvania. Another ally of the liberals is Thomas Field, who heads an organization called "Taxation with Representation." Brandon, Field, and a few others like them have become a small but potent offset to the corporate world's highly paid tax lobbyists, whose ranks include four former high Treasury officials and three former Commissioners of Internal Revenue.

Besides bringing a new tax-reform-oriented viewpoint to the committee's work, Field has organized mass mailings to generate grass-roots pressures by reformers outside Washington. Representative Waggonner grumbles that if "a member does something these folks don't like, they'll call his hometown paper to publicize it."

Sometimes the new "meaningful" dialogue hardly seems to constitute any kind of improvement. When Stark called Secretary Simon a "liar" (for presenting as a Treasury study material that Stark says was cribbed from studies by General Electric and Chase Manhattan Bank), a hush fell over the stunned committee. (Earlier on the same issue, Stark had lectured Simon on the "big difference between chicken salad and chicken shit." He felt that Simon's testimony fell in the latter category.) Boiling with rage, Simon told Ullman that he would not appear again before the committee while Stark sat on it.

Simon had to relent on that threat. But the Treasury's once close relationships with Ways and Means have grown more distant in the past couple of years. In particular, the important input of that department in writing tax law has dwindled. The loss of close ties with the Treasury has seriously weakened the committee's effectiveness.

The missing member

The older members of Ways and Means invariably express regret at the loss of Wilbur Mills's participation in the work of the committee. They recall his ability to cite passages from the Internal Revenue Code from memory, and his ability to erect a philosophical tent in which all members found a place.

These days Mills's seat in the committee room is usually vacant. He seldom participates in committee work. When a vote is taken—225 were logged last year—he frequently leaves the hearing room and turns over his proxy to Representative Waggonner. Other members have found it difficult to engage Mills in talk about committee business. When approached in the cloakroom off the floor of the House, he often turns the conversation to his work with Alcoholics Anonymous. One Congressman says, "Like most reformed alcoholics, he will point out which members drink too much, and which members he feels are in danger of becoming drunks."

About the only reminder of Mills's former eminence is the oil portrait of him that hangs on the left side of the committee dais. By tradition, the new chairman's picture should hang there now, but Ullman has let the fallen chairman's portrait remain in its place.

Trembling prices

When Mills fell, no one replaced him in power and influence over legislation. His role was uniquely large. After he decided to seek his party's presidential nomination in 1972, Representative Sam Gibbons of Florida asked him, "Why do you want to run for President and give up your grip on the country?"

No chairman of Ways and Means could wield that kind of power today. For one thing, the committee itself has been weakened. In the past year it lost jurisdiction over revenue sharing and Medicaid. And the committee's Democratic majority lost its authority to appoint Representatives to other committees—this power was shifted to the Democratic Steering and Policy Committee.

Even so, Ways and Means still has very wide jurisdiction. Its most recent annual report still opens with a reminder to readers that in terms of amounts of money involved and impact on the national economy, the committee is without peer. The report's historical note is fond of repeating year after year the comment of a member in 1865: "All springs of wealth and labor are more or less influenced by the action of this committee." When the chairman of Ways and Means proposes a tax bill, the passage continues, the "price of every article we use trembles." The report notes that from the committee's membership over the years have come seven Presidents, seven Vice Presidents, three Associate Justices of the Supreme Court and one Chief Justice, twenty-one Speakers of the House, and thirty Cabinet officers, including twelve Secretaries of the Treasury.

Despite all the erosions of power in recent years, seats on the committee are still eagerly sought after in the House. Democrat Otis Pike of New York, for example, gave up a senior seat on the Armed Services Committee to take a more junior slot on Ways and Means.

The committee's grip on the sharp instrument of taxation is the principal source of its power. The White House, the Treasury, and the Senate Finance Committee, all have an important say in tax writing, but it is the Ways and Means Committee that principally exercises the constitutional power to "lay and collect taxes." Through its power to set tariffs, the committee also has a large say in trade policy. Its jurisdiction over federal spending is nearly as large as that of the Appropriations Committee. It controls the Social Security, welfare, Medicare, and unemployment-insurance programs, whose combined annual outlays exceed $120 billion.

Bills for friends back home

Beyond having a voice in national affairs, each committee member is in a position to favor friends and campaign contributors back home. A useful device for this purpose has been the institution known until recently as "members' bills" and now cosmetically called "technical and minor bills." These measures used to be reported by the committee directly to the floor of the House, where they usually passed without debate.

The committee's new open style plus new procedures and safeguards have made it more difficult to get away with some of the outrageous measures that went through in the past. Even so, the closing days of the first session of the present Congress saw the committee considering members' bills to give tax breaks to cigar makers, small brewers, fishing-tackle makers, cemetery operators, and a Texas-based outfit called the Confederate Air Force Flying Museum —not to mention an amendment (tacked onto a major tax bill) favoring Dallas businessman H. Ross Perot.

As in the case of Perot, who gave $27,400 to a dozen Ways and Means members in 1974, there is often a direct connection between the beneficiary of such special legislation and a sponsoring member's campaign funds. Ten of Perot's beneficiaries voted for the amendment that would have provided him a tax rebate of some $15 million if Albert Hunt of the *Wall Street Journal* had not exposed the matter. Eventually, the amendment was killed on the floor of the House.

Undemocratic but advantageous

Quite apart from members' bills, the chairman of Ways and Means has been considered one of the most influential members of Congress, and, for that matter, in the whole federal establishment. Since the chairman controls what the committee will take up, he has a large say in the fate of an Administration's legislative proposals. As a result, he has been usually courted by Presidents, who were often required to make major concessions to win his support.

In the Mills era, the chairman wielded his power in an autocratic manner. The committee was a tidy, closed shop, and that seemed to suit the House just fine. Its undemocratic and secretive operation had the advantage of shielding the House from pressures to give away tax revenues, or from having to vote in public on sensitive tax breaks for powerful constituents.

The committee did hold public hearings on proposed legislation. But when the time came to work up a draft of a bill, the action moved behind closed doors. Besides members of Ways and Means, only the staff and invited government officials were in attendance. Except for a few lobbyists who had close contacts with committee members, neither the public nor the rest of Congress had much idea of what the committee was up to.

The fermenting process

Few votes were taken in these executive sessions, and no record of the deliberations was available except to committee members themselves. The committee report issued after the drafting was finished was the only written record of the reasoning behind the committee's actions. And often it was available only a short time before the committee's legislation came to the floor for a vote.

Under Mills the committee took a cautious approach to legislation. Representative Schneebeli recalls that Mills's practice when moving into a new area of legislation was to let the issue "ferment in public, then draw back if he sensed opposition before he returned to it." This approach, Schneebeli observes, was the reason "things were so peaceful up here."

The lopsided votes by the Ways and Means Committee enabled Mills to bring a tax bill to the floor on a take-it-or-leave-it basis. Tax legislation was presented under a "closed rule" that permitted no floor amendments except those offered by the committee itself. The vote to recommit—send the bill back to the committee—was the only test of controversial aspects of new legislation. During his long tenure as chairman, Mills lost only three important bills on the floor of the House.

Defending the new style

By the early 1970's, however, the committee's autocratic way of operating began to come under increasing attack. Mills was challenged on the floor over some of those members' bills, and eventually lost to a coalition of reformers. Not long afterward the House required the committee to open its meetings to the public and to take recorded votes rather than informal polls. In another procedural reform, the Democrats dented the closed-rule procedure; they allowed committee members who wanted a floor vote on an issue to appeal over the chairman's head to the House Democratic caucus. And then, in late 1974, came the revolt: the toppling of Wilbur Mills and the moves to broaden the membership of the committee and pare down its power.

While he is aware of the disarray in his committee, Ullman defends the new, democratic style, even though it gobbles up time and frustrates his aims. "The day is gone when a chairman can wrap up a neat little package in his back room," he says. "The open hearings and open markups, in which all members, not just a few, have a say, is the way this committee must work."

It is not working very well, however, and some members blame the chairman for that. He is faulted for his decision to take on energy legislation when there was no consensus in the committee or in the House for his tax-oriented approach (Ullman built his bill around a sharp increase in the gasoline tax.) Others complain that he doesn't know how to count noses, and doesn't have a feel for the sensitivities of committee members. The outspoken Stark says Ullman is always trying to make deals with the Republicans and Southerners, and ends up being double-crossed.

Ullman, who is a proud man and something of a loner, is sensitive to the inevitable comparisons with Mills. Not long ago, a Democratic freshman Congressman observed that Mills had better luck than Ullman at pushing legislation through. Ullman replied: "If you follow the Mills philosophy, you'd wait until the controversy had run its course and then you'd try to do something. But I haven't done that. I don't worry about being defeated on the floor."

That is a creditable attitude, certainly. But the fact remains that Mills was regarded as an effective chairman and Ullman—so far at least—is not. Some old-timers feel that Ullman's defeats have damaged the committee's prestige.

There will be some departures

Privately, Ullman may find some consolation in the thought that things are bound to be different next year. Different won't necessarily mean better, but he can at least hope. In any event, there will be some new faces on the committee. Two senior members, Democrat Phil Landrum of Georgia and Republican Schneebeli, have announced they will not seek reelection to Congress this year. There is doubt that Mills, though he is showing signs of life again, can retain his seat. And several of the new liberal members of the committee will have difficulty in retaining theirs. William Green plans to run for the Senate. With the committee so closely balanced, the change of

even a few members could turn victories into defeats, and vice versa.

A new President—or Gerald Ford free of election-year temptations and backed by a strong mandate—could make an enormous difference to the committee's effectiveness. Certainly the split between a Democratic Congress and a weak Republican President has greatly contributed to the paralysis that has marked Ways and Means, and indeed the entire Congress, in the past year.

With that situation resolved or at least alleviated after November, and with significant changes in the membership of the committee, Ways and Means may be able to make headway toward resolving some of the serious tax issues confronting it. Perhaps the committee might even be able to get on with the task of drastically reforming the nation's overgrown, gummed up, unfair tax code. Even Wilbur Mills never made much progress in that direction, but it is not clear that he really tried.

★★

29

The Man Who Runs the Senate—Bobby Byrd: An Upstart Comes to Power

Sanford J. Ungar

Senator Robert Byrd is no newcomer to party leadership. He has served as secretary to the Senate Democratic Conference and as party whip, and is currently serving as Senate majority leader to the 96th Congress. Sanford Ungar, writing about Byrd when he was party whip, spends much time describing and analyzing the leadership style Robert Byrd has developed. What has made Byrd a more effective party leader than Senator Edward Kennedy? What enabled him to defeat Kennedy for the position of Democratic party whip? What distinguishes his leadership style from that of the late Lyndon Johnson, when he was in the party leadership of the Senate? How is Byrd different from former Senator Mike Mansfield, when he was the majority leader? How has Byrd adapted his approach to those independently minded senators elected since 1974 who feel less tied to party and more tied to their constituencies? Has Byrd also proven to be an effective party leader outside the Senate, or is his style of leadership effective only within the chamber?

Because a party leader must spend so much time with the membership of the Senate and with the problems of the chamber, do you suppose this might be detrimental to the party leader's relationship to his home state? Must the party leader choose party or institutional interests over his state's interests, or is there a way to handle them all? How has Robert Byrd resolved this problem? Ungar argues that Byrd's ideological position on issues has changed over time. How have his views changed? Is there a need to moderate one's ideological position when gaining a leadership position within a political party?

★ ★ ★

THE MAN WHO RUNS THE SENATE

Bobby Byrd: An upstart comes to power

by Sanford J. Ungar

Robert Byrd, a little-known, fiddle-playing West Virginian, is the Senate's Democratic whip, probably its next majority leader, and just possibly a favorite son at the 1976 Democratic Convention. Says he: "I believe that a big man can make a small job important." Some of his colleagues think Byrd also proves the converse: that a big job can help a small man to grow.

"**B**obby Byrd is a member of the early morning health club," says the master of ceremonies. "Every morning, early, he gets up, calls Mike Mansfield, and asks him, 'How's your health?'"

The occasion is a luncheon "roasting" in honor of Robert Carlyle Byrd, fifty-seven, junior senator from West Virginia, and the Democratic whip of the Senate. It is given by the P. T. Barnum Tent of the Circus Saints & Sinners Club of America—one of those slick and seamy Washington events where nearly everyone is called a "VIP," the food is inedible, and the true aficionados arrive early to watch a striptease show over pre-lunch cocktails

before the more worldly political hoopla begins. Byrd, the fall guy for the day, does not ordinarily travel in these hell-raising stag circles. He has a standing rule against attending downtown (off Capitol Hill) lunches and, in fact, proclaims himself to have "no time to socialize" at all; there is too much work for that. During twenty-three years in Washington, he has been to one football game (to crown the queen at half time), three baseball games (two of them in one day, a doubleheader), and one movie (he found it dull and left in the middle). He does watch television now and then, however, and once protested on the Senate floor when *Gunsmoke,* a favorite of his, was canceled.

But such are the responsibilities of power and acceptance on the national scene that Byrd has reluctantly agreed to be feted by the Saints & Sinners, to try to enjoy himself. Business on the Senate floor makes him unavoidably but conveniently late—it would hardly do if a statesman soon to speak at a national Baptist convention in Atlantic City appeared at a striptease. Once on hand, in a vast ballroom of the Shoreham Hotel, he sits through interminable introductions of other people, some very unfunny skits about moonshine liquor in "West By-God Virginia," and a nightclub comic whose routine consists largely of imitating drunken men coming home late at night to their angry wives. Given his turn, Byrd allows as how the affair "is an honor for a country boy from the hills and hollows of West Virginia," and he announces that the $500 charitable contribution in his name which is part of the day's honors will go to the family of a police officer recently killed in Beckley, West Virginia. He surprises many people in the audience by telling a few off-color jokes himself. Then the usually dour Senator picks up his most reliable prop, his fiddle, and plunks out "Rye Whiskey," complete with hoots and lyrics. That brings the house down, so he plays another, "Goin' Up Cripple Creek," which he dedicates to Mike Mansfield.

Byrd's lusting after Mike Mansfield's job as majority leader has become one of the central factors and favorite jokes of Democratic politics in the Senate. It is all "an exaggerated assumption," says he; "I don't have the consuming desire that people attribute to me"—although, "if the position were to open up, I would be compelled to run for it. I believe in advancing forward, moving up." For the moment, Byrd insists, he is content to work under Mansfield, whom he names without a trace of hesitation as the colleague he most respects: "I admire his patience, his fairness and his honorableness, his integrity. . . . This may appear to be self-serving, but that is how I feel."

The relationship, by all accounts and appearances, works very well indeed. Mansfield plays the senior statesman, the venerated elder from Montana who makes broad policy pronouncements and worries about the future of the republic, while Byrd runs the Senate. Through a series of procedural changes he has initiated or supervised during the past few years, including a shortening of the Senate's "morning hour" and of the speeches that may be given during it, Byrd controls the floor and, most of the time, who may have it and how it may be used. (One rule, which has other senators depending upon him and their aides detesting him, bans all senatorial staff from the chamber except when the man they work for is speaking.) He hammers out the "consent agreements" that keep the Senate running smoothly and efficiently—and, some argue, without its old charm and unpredictability—and he stays on the floor most of the time to be sure that the agreements are carried out. In a word, he is probably as powerful as anyone in the legislative branch, because of the access he controls and the shrewdness with which he uses it.

Most senators in both parties seem to feel that Byrd performs his tasks fairly, although he has been known to pull a few fast ones on liberal Democrats he considered to be advocating extreme positions and on Republicans he suspected of exploiting procedure for partisan advantage. During the recent debate over how to solve the disputed New Hampshire Senate election, for example, he said he would happily go along with a GOP sug-

gestion to have the proceedings televised, but on the strict condition that the Republicans agree to set a time limit on the debate. The Republicans, who wanted to filibuster until the Democrats agreed to send the whole issue back to New Hampshire for a new election, quickly backed out.

"This never would have happened if Lyndon Johnson were still with us," said an aide to one liberal Democratic senator when three conservative southern members of the party repeatedly foiled attempts by the Democratic leadership to invoke cloture and cut off debate on the dispute over how to settle the New Hampshire election deadlock this summer. Sooner or later Johnson would have forced a resolution of the issue, whether by discipline or backroom deal. Indeed, there could be no greater contrast between the Johnson style of Senate leadership—in which arms were twisted and egos bruised if necessary to work out compromises and pass critical legislation—and the soft, easygoing Mansfield style, which places full confidence in the ability of the Senate eventually to "work its will." The question is how Byrd will handle the majority leadership if he succeeds to it. "There are advantages to both [the Mansfield and Johnson] styles," he says diplomatically; "but if I had to choose between the two, I prefer the Mansfield approach . . . You have to remember, you have a different Senate now from when Mr. Johnson was the leader. He was in a position to utilize discipline more than it can be used now, and there is no longer a very cohesive southern bloc." That cohesiveness was one of the key constants in Johnson's formula for working his will on the Senate. One important difference is that the Democrats today have a far larger, more unwieldy, and somewhat less pragmatic majority in the Senate than in the Johnson days of the 1950s; a growing number of senators are inclined to vote their conscience on this matter or that. But many senators suspect that Byrd would try to assert greater authority over his troops than he is prepared to admit.

Byrd is an enigmatic man, churlish and angry one moment, and coming on with a sly, foxy smile the next. He is capable of alternating rote recitation of political boiler plate and florid eighteenth-century rhetoric with frank and insightful political analyses. He is discouraged by Gerald Ford's attacks on Congress, and believes that while they may win points for the President in the short run, they will ultimately backfire. "Mr. Ford knows how the system works. He is as partisan as any of us," he complains; "I think he has a mistaken impression that he can follow the approach that Mr. Truman followed. But circumstances are a lot different now than when Mr. Truman was President, and Mr. Ford is not Mr. Truman."

Robert Byrd came to Congress as a conservative.

Sanford J. Ungar is *The Atlantic*'s Washington editor.

Many of his early attitudes and some of the premises he holds to today were developed while he was coming of age as a poor white boy in West Virginia, struggling for a meager existence during the Depression. At first he did not go to Sunday school, because he was embarrassed that he had no socks to wear. For many of those years he earned only $50 a month, even after he had a wife to support (the Byrds were married in 1937). The Byrd family's first refrigerator was not even an icebox, but half an orange crate nailed outside the kitchen window; there was no car, and when the Byrds wanted to go somewhere they borrowed one from his father-in-law, a coal miner.

Byrd's manner is taut, and he is notorious on Capitol Hill for being tough with his staff; even on the night before a holiday, they may wait for him to dismiss them before going home. Sometimes his penchant for hard work goes to extremes: when his trusted secretary Ethel Low is away, for example, Byrd himself opens all the office mail. His personal life is spartan. He takes no vacations, rarely touches alcoholic beverages, and is most comfortable in the company of his wife, Erma, two daughters and sons-in-law, and six grandchildren, who are all close at hand in the Virginia suburbs of the capital. There he relaxes with a cigar or the fiddle; often he plays a tune before going to sleep at night. He has very few close friends, in Washington or West Virginia. The senator from whom he has sought advice in recent years is John Pastore of Rhode Island. Asked whom he really trusts and feels he can confide in, he answers only, "My wife."

Few people knew or cared much about Bobby Byrd (for decades "Senator Byrd" meant Harry Flood Byrd of Virginia) until he achieved a dragon slayer's reputation in January, 1971, by defeating the incumbent Democratic whip, none other than Edward M. Kennedy of Massachusetts. The feat was popularly portrayed at the time as an overnight coup, a blow at Kennedy while he was still suffering the effects of the Chappaquiddick scandal. Byrd will not discuss the subject, but he probably does have an old antipathy to the Kennedy family. He supported Hubert Humphrey over John Kennedy in the crucial West Virginia Democratic primary in 1960 (although he was really a Lyndon Johnson man, and went to the convention that year as a Johnson-committed delegate), and had some nasty quarrels on the Senate floor with Robert Kennedy. He clearly would not favor the nomination of Teddy Kennedy in 1976, and says bluntly, "If the pollsters and media would leave [Kennedy] alone, he would keep on being a good senator." He does not like fashionable, sophisticated liberals, whether as members of dynasties or as individuals.

Actually, Byrd's 1971 coup was long in the making. In the course of four years, as secretary of the Senate Democratic Conference, a previously meaningless job in itself, Byrd came to function as Mansfield's de facto right-hand man, doing the routine chores that did not interest Kennedy. While Byrd's better-known colleagues were off at cocktail parties and other ruinous pursuits ("I despise cocktail parties," he says; "you just stand around and waste time"), he would stay late at night in the office of the Senate parliamentarian, mastering the intricacies of the Senate rules. Now he knows those rules better than any of his peers, and can make the rules do whatever is needed by him, his friends, or his party.

"I believe that a big man can make a small job important," says Byrd in one of his favorite bits of armchair philosophy. Some of his colleagues believe that while he is a good example of that maxim, he is also living proof of the converse principle, that a big job can help a small man to grow. During his early days in the Senate—he was elected with the 1958 crop of Democrats who profited from President Eisenhower's decline in popularity—Byrd took mostly easy, conservative positions. He railed against welfare cheaters and voted against major civil rights legislation, including the 1964 law; he came to have an unbroken record as a hawk on the Vietnam war and related international issues. He denounced student protesters and, as a member of the Appropriations Committee, took his turn worshipping at the altar of J. Edgar Hoover, even after the FBI director's performance had begun to slip. But by the time his senior colleague from West Virginia, Jennings Randolph, an old-time New Dealer, nominated him for whip when the Democratic caucus convened in 1971, Byrd had metamorphosed into a moderate and had enough progressive votes on his record—including support for open housing and gun control—to be acceptable across the spectrum.

The transformation has continued and intensified. Although he is still regarded more as an institutional creature than as a creative thinker on substantive issues, Byrd has taken several steps leftward into the Democratic mainstream. He talks about the danger that we in the United States will "overextend ourselves" in the world, and he urges a careful review of all of the nation's international commitments, treaties, and alliances. Once a vehement anticommunist, he now supports the resumption of diplomatic relations with Cuba, and he accepted an invitation to visit China this summer. (He was invited once before, but turned down the opportunity because it would have meant being away while the Senate was in session.) This year he supported an extension of the Voting Rights Act of 1965, though he opposed it twice in the past.

Named to the Senate Judiciary Committee in 1969, he put a sharp, young—and liberal—aide onto the committee staff in 1971 and then used that vantage point to build a part of his new image.

Byrd rarely attended the long Judiciary Committee hearings in the spring of 1972 on the nomination of Richard Kleindienst as Attorney General, but he authorized his Judiciary Committee aide, Tom Hart, to work closely with assistants to Edward Kennedy, of all people, in turning up new ammunition for the anti-Kleindienst effort, especially details of the suspect dealings between the Nixon Administration and the International Telephone and Telegraph Corporation. Every night Byrd met with Hart to review the latest developments, and he may be one of the few people in Washington who has read the entire 1751-page Kleindienst hearing record. Finally, although he declared Kleindienst to be an able lawyer, and "a man of remarkable charm and ingratiating personality," he took the Senate floor to say that he would vote against the nomination because "important questions remain unanswered and . . . uneasy doubts remain which cannot be explained away." Byrd was one of only nineteen senators to vote against Kleindienst in the end, but the onetime "law and order" hardliner from the West Virginia hills was becoming a leader of Democrats who saw battle lines drawn with the Nixon Administration over issues of legal and political ethics—issues that later came under the wide Watergate umbrella.

Even before L. Patrick Gray III, acting director of the FBI for a year, was nominated by Nixon as permanent director of the agency, Byrd declared that Gray would be unacceptable to him. He obtained copies of secret Watergate-related depositions from Washington *Post* reporters, talked personally on the telephone with airline pilots who disapproved of Gray's controversial handling of a hijack case (FBI agents shot out the tires of the plane), and relentlessly cross-examined the acting director before the Judiciary Committee. Eventually, it was Byrd who extracted from Gray the damaging admission that John W. Dean III, Nixon's White House counsel, had "probably" lied to the FBI during the early stages of the Watergate investigation. That statement led Dean to begin talking with prosecutors in order to protect himself, which in turn helped break the case open. In May of 1973, Senator William Proxmire (Democrat of Wisconsin), ordinarily no great admirer of his party's whip, declared that Robert Byrd was "the unsung hero" of the Watergate investigation then gathering force.

When Clarence M. Kelley was named FBI director in the summer of 1973, Byrd spent an entire day quizzing him and asked the only tough questions of the hearings, zeroing in on the issue of whether FBI practices violated civil rights. He negotiated a promise of independence for the Watergate special prosecutor and demanded close scrutiny of Gerald Ford and Nelson Rockefeller, the first two Vice Presidents named under the terms of the Twenty-Fifth Amendment.

Byrd's switch—his new role as a man concerned about civil liberties and a Watergate warrior—was

a subject of great curiosity and some wonderment on Capitol Hill. For his own part, he insists that it is the issues and the circumstances which have changed more than his own position; but one long-time Byrd-watcher says, "He realizes where the tide is going, and he will drift with it to compile a public record that is more defensible and acceptable" than his old narrowly conservative posture. Another suggests simply, "It was inevitable: he went national."

Byrd still keeps the faith on some points of conservative orthodoxy, denouncing busing, for example, not only on policy grounds, but also because "it is a waste of money—buying buses and burning all that gasoline." The slightest mention of repression by the South Korean government sets him off on a tirade: "If we want to talk about repression, let's talk about India. We have to look out for our own interests sometimes; we can't tell everyone what kind of government to have. . . . As long as a government is pro-United States and the country is important to our long-range national interests, we have got to look out for Uncle Sam first." He frets about "over-liberal" social theorists, and is delighted that the "libertarian" justices on the Supreme Court have been balanced out by Nixon appointees. (During his period of flirtation and friendship with the Nixon Administration, he himself was considered for a Supreme Court slot.)

The result of all this is a jagged, if well-mapped, course through the middle. Byrd has his own conception of where the American people stand ideologically—somewhere just right of center—and if he has his way, he will steer the Democratic party there. He is increasingly asserting himself as a national spokesman for the party, appearing on Sunday network television interview programs at the drop of a hat. He is said to be looking for a good speechwriter who can take on the Republican Administration.

"Don't forget 1924," says a devoted Byrd follower who takes a visiting stranger aside after the Senator has addressed a luncheon of the Parkersburg (West Virginia) Rotary Club. "The Democratic Convention was dead-locked and there seemed to be no way out. Finally, on the ninth day and the hundred-and-third ballot, they turned to a West Virginia boy, John W. Davis."

That is one way of looking at the events of 1924. John W. Davis had been a member of Congress, Solicitor General of the United States, counsel for the American Red Cross, an adviser to President Woodrow Wilson at the Versailles peace conference, ambassador to Great Britain, and a Wall Street lawyer who represented, among others, the House of Morgan before he became the compromise presidential nominee of the hopelessly divided Democratic party in the race against Calvin Coolidge. But he was born in Clarksburg, West

Virginia, and practiced law there for several years before being elected to the state's House of Delegates in 1899 and going on to greater fame and fortune.

Robert Byrd started in the West Virginia House of Delegates too, but his background was rather more humble than that of Davis. He was brought to the state from North Carolina when he was a year old, after his mother had died in a flu epidemic, to be raised in coalfields country by an impoverished aunt and uncle who adopted him. (His real name is Cornelius Calvin Sale, Jr., a fact he learned when he was sixteen. When his brother, Clyde Sale, wrote to him from North Carolina on the occasion of his victory over Edward Kennedy in 1971, he learned for the first time that his true birthdate was November 20, 1917, two months earlier than he had always believed and than is listed in *Who's Who*.) He worked as a garbage collector, a gas station attendant, a butcher, and, during World War II, a welder in the shipyards of Baltimore and Tampa; it was only on his election to Congress in 1952, at the age of thirty-five, that he gave up his grocery store in Sophia, a tiny town in Raleigh County. His law degree took ten years to earn in night school, first at George Washington University and then at American University, while he was a member of the House and, later, the Senate.

But the analogy between Byrd and Davis, however flawed, is picking up steam in West Virginia. Davis' nomination came in Madison Square Garden in New York, which is under consideration as a possible site for the 1976 Democratic Convention. Then, as now, the party, although thought to attract the loyalties of a majority of the public, was torn asunder by factional disputes, even in the aftermath of shameful Republican scandals. Calvin Coolidge, like Gerald Ford, was a man who had succeeded to the presidency but had never been elected to it. Davis was all over the map ideologically, and while he began his career as a conservative (supporting the "Red Raids" of Attorney General A. Mitchell Palmer, for example), he took increasingly liberal, populist-sounding positions; as *The Saturday Evening Post* saw it at the time, he represented the "respectable medium" among Democrats. Curiously, Davis and Byrd both had political problems concerning their attitude toward the Ku Klux Klan, Davis for failing to denounce it with sufficient vigor, and Byrd for having been a member in his youth ("a 100 percent mistake," he now acknowledges). "Fifty years have passed since West Virginia's only major party candidate for President" was nominated, noted Representative Ken Hechler, a liberal downstate congressman, in a small-town newspaper column last year. Since Davis was from the north of West Virginia, Hechler said,

. . . the time for a good and strong candidate [for President] from the southern part of the state is now here. In recent years, Senator Byrd has broadened his base of appeal. There was once a time when only certain elements in the political spectrum would accord him enthusiastic support. Now he attracts supporters from all those who are tired of deviousness, dishonesty and deceit in politics and who yearn for a return to traditional virtues which are practiced instead of merely preached.

Byrd, for his own part, plays it cool and coy. "I feel that I can do any job that the American people wish to assign me. I would not reject the nomination, although I am not actively seeking it," he says. He insists that he has no favorite in the field of declared and undeclared candidates, and, while he was lukewarm about George McGovern in 1972, sees nobody "among the current aspirants" whom he could not support or, for that matter, run with as a vice presidential candidate—including George Wallace of Alabama. He hopes for an open convention that will produce "a moderate ticket, not too far out in any direction." And although he considers the prospects unlikely, he says it is "not inconceivable that the convention could turn to me." He would be ready, and thinks that West Virginia law would permit him to run for re-election to the Senate and national office at the same time, just as Lyndon Johnson did in Texas in 1960.

Bobby Byrd no longer maintains a home in the state, and rarely even spends a night within its borders. Yet he is putting West Virginia, long the brunt of jokes, back on the map. The state has two fewer elected representatives in Washington now than it did fifteen years ago, but when one of them is Byrd, that hardly seems to matter. He is clearly West Virginia's favorite son, and traveling with him to his native state makes it easy to understand why.

As soon as the door of the Piedmont Airlines plane closes at Washington National Airport, Byrd is back in his element, among the people of West Virginia. "I feel good when I meet the people down here," he confides. "They're home folks. . . . They accept me, when I hug them or shake their hands." He does a lot of hugging and touching during his hectic one-day visits, whether in the aisles of the airplane, among a crowd at a shopping center, or with people he encounters in the street. His rule of procedure is simply stated: "I may not know them, but they know me. If they look at me, I stop and talk." The talk may be about arthritis, the price of gasoline, or the weather, but it hardly ever stops. He puts his arm around a young man washing the walls at the Kanawha County Airport in Charleston and huddles in a confidential conversation with him. He squeezes the shoulder of a policeman driving him to the airport in Huntington and asks, "How're you gettin' along in your work? Do you like your work?" A security guard shouts out, "Hey, Senator

Byrd, will you have a spot in the Cabinet for me?" and the Senator beams knowingly. "Where're you from?" he asks a man who reaches out to him in the plane. "Oak Hill." "Oak Hill? Be sure to say hello to my friend Shirley Donnelly" (a minister). "Sure thing, Senator, I'll call him in the morning."

At the Parkersburg Rotary Club, a bastion of Republican conservatism in an area along the Ohio border where both parties are strong, Byrd talks about crime—or, as he is more inclined to pronounce it in West Virginia, "crahm." It is a tough law-and-order talk that could be straight out of the late 1960s:

> I think the proliferation of crime all across our country can be largely attributed to one fact: there is so little punishment for it. Fewer and fewer criminals pay any penalty for crimes they commit. Retribution is so slow as to be almost nonexistent in an overwhelming majority of criminal situations. The old adage that crime does not pay is no longer true in case after case. . . . The best way—and perhaps the only way—to halt the crime wave that has been getting worse and worse . . . is to lock up the criminals. . . . I say that it is better to build more prisons and hire more jailers than it is to allow American cities to deteriorate further into jungles in which no one is safe. It may not be popular to say so, but some people belong in jail, and the quicker we recognize that fact and put them there the better off our society will be.

"Bob shouldn't be talking like that," says one old friend of his privately after the meeting. "That stuff is easy, and everybody knows it. He should be talking about the great issues of the day—the energy crisis, the economy . . ." Those issues are the ones the reporters at the luncheon ask him about afterwards, and he gives his stock reply: that the Democrats in Congress have better answers than President Ford, and once given time to develop and pass their programs, they will show the country the way out of its problems. On the whole, the Rotary appearance is a happy one for the Senator. Only one thing nags at him: an old friend said, in his introduction, that Byrd has a 95 percent attendance record in the Senate; "actually it is just over 96 percent."

Byrd visits a real estate office that has pictures of him from the early days of his political career, and a photographic studio that is making new portraits of him for a museum soon to be started up in Parkersburg; then he embarks on a long drive to Huntington with Chester Airhart, the Democratic sheriff of Wood County, and his principal deputy for tax collection. Until his recent retirement and entry into politics, the sheriff was for many years the FBI resident agent in Parkersburg, and Byrd chats with him about how much crime has increased in the area—80 percent in a year. Airhart is proud of the county's newly opened "correctional center," but reinforces the Senator's view that "we haven't figured out any way to correct them yet." The deputy is a wizened character who, as Byrd notes later, "knows a little bit about West Virginia politics." The conversation focuses on the gubernatorial race in 1976 and the chances of Jay Rockefeller (John D. IV, the Democrat and adopted West Virginian in the Rockefeller family, who lost on his last try). The primary, potentially a divisive one, is another fight that Byrd will sit out, accepting the voters' verdict on who should join him on the Democratic ticket. He could accept Rockefeller, even though that ambitious young man was once found in the unfortunate situation of having contributed money to a Byrd opponent in the primary. (The Senator, who beat that opponent with 89 percent of the vote, says he doesn't even remember the man's name.)

In Huntington, Byrd joins in on-the-air festivities inaugurating a new transmission tower for WOWK-TV. He is in no mood for small talk with the station officials before the ceremony, and looks stiff and out of place in the midst of falling balloons as he pulls the switch to activate the new tower; but later he enjoys the taping of a half-hour "newsmaker" interview with two reporters, an easy, unaggressive encounter in which the Senator has plenty of opportunity both to play the statesman on national issues and to boast about all that he has done for West Virginia. He has no compunction about saying that he will "use whatever influence I can bring to bear," as chairman of the Senate Appropriations subcommittee which approves the budget for the Department of the Interior, to have an experimental coal gasification plant located in the state.

Byrd's power base in West Virginia, like his position in Washington, is strictly a one-man operation. Whereas the state's other senator, Jennings Randolph, is the favorite of the United Mine Workers and other unions, and Republicans like Governor Arch Moore are entrenched with the state's business community, Byrd keeps his distance from both. "Bob Byrd's strength is in the people who come down from the hollows to vote for him. Some of them only vote when he is running," says his press secretary, John Guiniven. The resilience of that power base has never really been tested, because since he first entered Congress in 1952, Byrd has never faced a tough election fight.

En route to the airport for the flight back to Washington, Byrd lights up one of his favorite big fat cigars; but when there is no time to finish it, he stubs it out and slips what is left of it back into his briefcase. On the plane, he gives the stewardess his autograph and talks resignedly about how little power he feels the leaders of the Senate really have: "It's frustrating, you know. People expect too much . . . What power do I have? Or Mike Mansfield? We can have some input into legislative policy, but you're still just one senator, and there are ninety-nine others with their own ideas about how things ought to work . . . Now the President, he speaks for the executive branch; he has real power."

When Joseph R. Biden, Jr. was elected to the Senate from Delaware in 1972, and at thirty became the youngest member of that august body, he had a great deal of help from some prominent and established fellow Democrats. Statewide mailings went out from Washington, carrying the pictures and signatures of celebrities like Teddy Kennedy, Birch Bayh, and others, exhorting the voters to "send Joe Biden" down to join them. Some politicians spoke in Delaware on his behalf, and there was an appearance in the conservative area below the Chesapeake and Delaware Canal by one Robert C. Byrd. Barely six weeks after the election, Biden's wife and young daughter were killed in a traffic accident in Wilmington (his two sons survived). Although the funeral was a small, private matter, a public memorial service was held in a suburban Catholic church, and Biden let it be known through an aide that he would welcome the attendance of any of his new colleagues who had helped him in the campaign and could break away from their holiday schedules. Only one came— Bobby Byrd. He drove up from Washington on a cold, miserable, rainy night and sat unobtrusively in the back row of the church. After the service, according to one man who observed the scene closely, Byrd stood in line for seventeen minutes for the opportunity to shake Biden's hand and say a few words of condolence. Then he left for the two-and-a-half-hour drive back to Washington.

When Biden came to Washington to interview people for his staff, he had the use of the Whip's ornate, chandeliered office in the Capitol. Along with Walter Huddleston of Kentucky and a few other members of that year's class of freshman Democratic senators, he was looked after by Byrd and treated to occasional homemade political science lectures, relating, among other things, that the Senate is made up of "work horses and show horses." Regardless of their political philosophies, Byrd treated them much the way the late Richard Russell of Georgia had once treated him (from his deathbed, Russell cast the proxy that won Byrd the whip's job in 1971), and once they became his protégés, they found it much easier to obtain extra office space and other amenities.

Was the Byrd who was so sensitive to Biden in time of tragedy, and beyond, the one who is often mocked for doing and saying the expedient thing in order to enhance his own power? Or the one who without fanfare sent the daughter of the owner of his favorite Chinese restaurant through college after her mother died? Or some of each?

Officially, Mike Mansfield still intends to run for re-election to the Senate in 1976, and to continue for at least another two years as majority leader. If he does not, there are those who say that Lloyd Bentsen of Texas might make a run, that Edmund Muskie of Maine, or Alan Cranston of California, could attract substantial liberal support, or that good old Hubert Humphrey of Minnesota might want to return to the leadership and the limelight. As far as Byrd is concerned, any one of these men could make a fine whip; but there is little doubt in his mind or that of anyone else who carefully counts votes in the Senate that he could beat all of them for the top spot with one hand tied behind his back. Even should Mansfield stay in the Senate, say the people behind the scenes, if a way could be found to guarantee him continued use of his limousine, he would gladly step down in Byrd's favor. The upstart from West Virginia is probably already working on a way to arrange that, just in case. □

★★★

30

The Bloated Branch   Milton S. Gwirtzman

Milton Gwirtzman complains that even though the number of congressmen and senators has not increased beyond the current 535 for decades, personal and committee staffs have grown tremendously, becoming too large and unwieldy. Since 1954, for example, staff in the House and Senate has increased from 4,500 to 16,000 people. Are there other measures we could use to measure growth? Does this increase make Congress too large an institution? Is there an optimum size for a legislative body beyond which inefficiencies become a part of its operation? Gwirtzman thinks that this expansion reflects the operation of "Parkinson's Laws." In what ways may he be correct? Has the increase in staff members who act as "caseworkers" improved the congressman's ability to serve the ordinary constituent? Has the increased staff permitted Congress to better exercise its "oversight" function over executive agencies? Is there any relationship between the growth of legislative staff and the growth of public demands on Congress?

The author suggests that the power of the individual congressman is actually measured by the number of staff positions he controls. But how much power do individual staff members have in the legislative process? Is there a danger in the elected official losing control of decision-making when he must delegate much of the workload to his staff?

A large staff, Gwirtzman argues, is something most congressmen favor since it can, as much as anything, assure their reelection. What can a large staff do for the congressman's image and reputation? How important is "boffo" in this context? Has the enlarged staff encouraged a closer relationship between congressmen and the public, or do large staffs impede this relationship? What problems are posed for the institution as a whole when there are so many appointed staff members? How much does the institution benefit by the additional information gathered by personal and committee staffs? What reform does Gwirtzman advocate to limit growth in Congress?

★ ★ ★

The Bloated Branch

By Milton S. Gwirtzman

Though the President is Commander in Chief, Congress is his commander; and, God willing, he shall obey. He and his minions shall learn that this is not a Government of kings and satraps, but a Government of the people; and that Congress is the people.
—Representative THADDEUS STEVENS, January, 1867.

Members of Congress still rank in public esteem just ahead of skunks.
—Representative LLOYD MEEDS, August, 1974.

After decades of playing second fiddle to powerful and sometimes glamorous Presidents, the United States Congress once again seems to have taken the initiative. Stung by the excesses of President Johnson's Vietnam policies and Richard Nixon's campaign tactics, encouraged by the ascendance of a new President who was one of its own for 25 years, the Senate and the House of Representatives are warming up for battle, readier to influence Federal policy than at any time since Thad Stevens and his colleagues tried to run the Government themselves and impeached a President who stood in their way. Congress has repealed resolutions that gave the President the power to make war on his own initiative, passed legislation forbidding him to impound funds without its consent, set up its own budget office to match the White House program for program and computer for computer in deciding how Federal money should be spent and has dusted off its power to withhold confirmation of Presidential appointees to force changes in Administration policies.

Whether Congress will be able to use this new muscle to give the country the laws and direction it needs is very much in doubt. Searching questions have been raised about the strength of its present leadership, the rigidity of its seniority system, the power of hidebound committee chairmen (despite retirements, their average age is still 66) and the intrinsic difficulty of getting 535 independently elected powers, who often speak for clashing interests, to agree on vitally needed programs. But aggravating each of these handicaps is the little-recognized fact that Congress may simply have become too large and cumbersome, and its expansion by now may well be out of control.

The House and Senate had combined staffs of 4,500 people and an operating budget of $42-million in 1954. Today they have 16,000 employees and a budget of $328-million. When I first came to work on Capitol Hill in the late nineteen-fifties, Senators and their staffs worked in a single office building, House members in two. The operations of Congress now take up five buildings and are spilling over into adjacent hotels and apartments. Recently, a sixth office building has been commissioned, at a cost of $84-million, and an acquisition plan has been ordered for even more real estate. The number of constituents, that is, the country's population, has increased, too, but Congress's staff and budget spending have grown well over 15 times faster. At the rate of growth established over the past 10 years, the United States Congress will cost more than a billion dollars a year to operate by 1984.

Until World War II, the average Congressman's staff consisted of little more than a secretary and

Milton S. Gwirtzman, now a Washington lawyer, was a legislative assistant in the United States Senate from 1959 to 1964.

a clerk. In 1946, each member was given an administrative assistant, who was supposed to handle Government problems for constituents, leaving Congressmen free to concentrate on more solemn duties. This function is now performed by so-called "caseworkers," stationed in Washington and in field offices in the state or district. (Senators have as many as six such offices.) Administrative assistants now act as political lieutenants and exercise general supervision over office staffs, often aided by office managers, who in turn direct secretarial supervisors, who in their turn tell the secretaries what to do.

Members of the House are currently allowed 16 full-time employees for their personal staffs—not a startling number, but as many as Senators had 15 years ago. Senators now have empires. The late Senator James Duff of Pennsylvania had 17 employees; his successor, Richard Schweiker, has 47. In the mid-nineteen-fifties, the offices of the two Senators from California employed 40 people between them; their current successors have 118. When Senator Sam Ervin of North Carolina first came to Washington in 1954, he had an office staff of seven; when he retires this year, he will leave 10 times as many, spread between his personal office and 18 committees and subcommittees.

A glance at job titles listed in last year's Senate phone directory shows how elaborate the empires have become. The office of Gaylord Nelson of Wisconsin, with a staff of 42, has a legislative director, three legislative assistants, three legislative correspondents and three secretaries. Alan Cranston of California has a media secretary, who in turn has two assistants. Vance Hartke of Indiana employs a "communications director," who supervises five "communications analysts." John Tunney of California has a "local-issue director," a "local-issue coordinator," two office managers, a secretarial supervisor and a mail supervisor.

Only George Aiken of Vermont, with Yankee frugality, has kept his office small. Twenty years ago, seven people worked for Aiken. Now there are nine, including his wife who serves—without pay —as his administrative assistant and press secretary. And he never did open a field office, feeling, as he said last summer, that "a home office will get you in more trouble than it will help, particularly if the manager gets the idea that he or she wants to run against you."

Legislators from other countries are astounded by the size of the Congressional establishment. Members of Parliament and the French National Assembly have no staff at all. If they need a secretary, they hire one out of their own pocket or ring up the typist pool. For serving constituents, they rely on the party organizations in their districts. Members of the West German Bundestag get $800 per month for clerk hire, compared with $16,000 a month for a member of the House.

An even greater explosion has taken place in the Congressional committees. The Senate Committee on the Judiciary, which listed 15 employees when I first came in contact with the Senate, now has 177. The Committee on Labor and Public Welfare, which had 14, has 97. The Committee on Interstate and Foreign Commerce has swollen from 10 to 72 staffers, spread over five suites of offices. All told, Congress now spends $50-million a year for the committee operations alone.

In its earlier years, Congress used to form a new committee to handle each new crisis. To raise money for his Army, President Lincoln had to negotiate with the Joint Committee on the Conduct of the War. Crises passed, but the committees

often kept going. Bitter fights between them over power and jurisdiction made it increasingly difficult for Congress to move. The Legislative Reorganization Act of 1946 eliminated 47 standing committees, paring the total down to 34 (19 in the House, 15 in the Senate) and prohibiting creation of more except by special legislation. But virtually all the committees abolished by that act have been reborn, as subcommittees of the allowed committees. The Senate now has 147 subcommittees, the House 133. They include such vital instruments of national policy as the Special Subcommittee on the Freight Car Shortage, the Subcommittee on Small Business Problems in Smaller Towns and Urban Areas, and the Select Committee on Parking. In the House, especially, subcommittees have proliferated in obvious attempts to give chairmanships and patronage to as many Congressmen as possible. The House Committee on Education and Labor has a Special Subcommittee on Labor, a General Subcommittee on Labor and a Select Subcommittee on Labor, each headed by a member with close ties to the union movement.

The expansion of Congress has changed the neighborhood around the Capitol from a quiet, if seedy, residential environ into one of the prime growth areas of Washington—a noisy, traffic-choked enclave into which have come private office buildings, headquarters of executive agencies and even a subway station. Capitol Hill literally swarms with police. With almost 1,000 uniformed members, the Capitol Police—Congress's own force —is the 25th largest police force in the United States, ranking just behind San Diego, Calif., a city of 700,000. A Senator for whom I worked in the early sixties had a policeman on his patronage roll whom we nicknamed "No Bullets" Murphy, because he didn't know how to use his gun and carried no cartridges in his belt. He was typical of the Capitol Police of the time—patronage employees, many of them college students. Today the Capitol Police is almost exclusively a career, professional force, with its own training program, communications center, fingerprint identification unit and surveillance capability. It is hoping to build its own headquarters.

Why Congress has expanded so fast has almost nothing to do with its increased workload. Like other bureaucrats, Congress brings more work upon itself as it multiplies its number of workers, in keeping with Parkinson's law that "work increases to fill the time and staff available to do it." I suppose the fundamental reason is that the ability of Congress to spend money on itself is one of the few powers of the Government that is neither checked nor balanced in our Constitution. Budget requests from the executive agencies are first pared by the Office of Management and Budget in the White House and then reviewed by several Congressional committees. But Congress alone decides how much to appropriate for its own operations, and each chamber accepts the other's decision without question.

Members of Congress do not come to Washington with the intention of building empires. Their initial concern is to serve their constituents. As they become more secure in their jobs and begin to absorb Washington's political value system, they see that to make a mark for themselves, they are going to have to carve out an area of expertise. This can be done most comfortably through one of the committees to which they are assigned. A legislator with a few years of seniority tries to dream up an area, within his committee's jurisdiction, that has sufficient public interest to

From *The New York Times Magazine*, November 10, 1974. © 1974 by The New York Times Company. Reprinted by permission.

justify a subcommittee of his own. (The environmental movement was a fortuitous happening for this purpose; Congress has nine new subcommittees dealing with this subject.) If he waits long enough, coöperates with the leadership, carries his share of committee work and has a good word put in for him with the committee chairman, he will eventually get what he wants. If he happens to be on the Senate Judiciary Committee, he must perform an additional ritual of having a few drinks with the chairman, James Eastland of Mississippi. In the spring of 1973, Senator John Tunney, the most junior Democrat on the committee and the only one without a subcommittee of his own, was seen entering Eastland's office at 9 in the morning. He emerged an hour later, somewhat unsteady, but as the new chairman of the Subcommittee on Representation of Citizens' Interest.

Among the more senior members of Congress, power is measured by the number of staff positions one controls. Republicans fight Democrats for a larger share of committee staff positions, under the banner of "protecting the interests of the minority." When Senators on the new Budget Committee met, the first thing they undertook was granting each other one new professional staff member. All government agencies like to add employees but only Congress can do so with such abandon.

It should also be noted that each member of Congress is engaged in a genteel but constant competition for public attention. For most, the rivalry is with local and state officials for space in the hometown media. For many Senators and the more prominent Representatives, there is an additional competition: with each other for the wire-service story or the snippet of tape on network television news that will give them national prominence. When a Senator goes home at night, his briefcase bulges with ideas from his staff for bills, speeches and investigations that will serve this purpose. Alan Novak, a Washington entrepreneur who used to work for Edward Kennedy, once borrowed from vaudeville to describe the process. He called it looking for a "boffo." A boffo is something a legislator can do that is sufficiently interesting to the media that it will be played heavily for several days. With so many Senators trying for boffos, even Novak's old boss, who is as newsworthy as anyone on Capitol Hill, finds them hard to come by. This does not stop scores of staffers from trying their best.

And their best is very good. The quality of Congressional staffs has increased impressively in recent years. I remember going into the office of the late Senator Thomas Dodd of Connecticut one day, and having to tiptoe past an elderly gentleman asleep at his desk. They called him the "Judge"; he was an old friend of the Senator's, and he was not to be disturbed. There are still a generous number of loafers and hacks around Capitol Hill, but the pace is set by young ambitious professionals, in their 20's and 30's, engaged in the endless quest of boffos for their bosses. They are there because the pay is good, the fringe benefits sensational,* the work interesting and the chance to wield real power, as always, irresistible. Most of them leave after a few years—Congressional experience is a valuable credential for a job in a law firm or a university—but there are always plenty of applicants to take their places.

One would think that with larger staff support, Congress could write more laws. It doesn't. The number of bills enacted last year was exactly the same (257) as 10 years earlier, when its budget and staff were less than one-third their present size. One might also think the influence of outside pressure groups would decline because Congressmen would not have to depend on them so much. Instead, the lobbying industry has grown even faster than the Congress. Registrations under the Federal Lobbying Act have doubled in recent years, and this represents just the tip of the iceberg, since that act is enforced as strictly as the rule barring football fans from bringing liquor into the stadium, and has about as many violators. More importantly the traditional lobbyists (those representing special-interest groups and the executive agencies) have been joined in recent years by the public-interest lobbyists — Ralph Nader, Common Cause, the environmental organizations and the like. By skillfully employing many of the same techniques as their adversaries in the private sector —supplying drafts of legislation, information, arguments and generating pressures from back home — these groups have become a powerful force.

The confluence of increased staffs and more intensive lobbying is slowing down the legislative process instead of speeding it up. It has always been easier to block a measure than to pass one. Each stage of the legislative process—the subcommittee, full committee, the House floor and conference committee—is a separate hurdle. Each must be cleared before Congress adjourns. With a better balanced array of interests knocking on their doors, Congressmen and Senators find it harder to agree. They become locked into inflexible positions, which they defend with the help of their larger staffs. Throughout this year, for example, the Senate has been trying to pass the Consumer Protection Bill, which would create a new Federal agency to do what Ralph Nader now does, and give it important legal powers that even Nader doesn't have. A handful of Senators, responding to fierce pressures from business organizations, have filibustered, and four attempts to muster a sufficient majority to end the filibuster have failed. In earlier days, a Lyndon Johnson could have called opposing Senators together and cajoled them into a compromise, perhaps one which weakened certain features of the bill in return for an end to the filibuster. Today, even Johnson, with all his powers of persuasion, could not accomplish this. Were the Senators favoring the bill to accept such an accommodation, they would be considered cop-outs by the powerful proconsumer lobbies, which have effective ways to communicate their displeasure to the folks back home. Important legislation, such as national health insurance and national land-use programs, have been deadlocked by similar clashes of interest. Thus, as Congress becomes more sensitive to more interests, it is losing its ability to meet the needs of the country at large. This is one of the reasons why only 15 per cent of the public expressed faith in Congress as an institution.

One would think, too, that with more professional assistance, Congress would be better able to exercise its oversight function, to check the excesses and right the wrongs of the Federal bureaucracy. It is true that there are more investigations, and more frequent responses to Administration actions. Where the issue is highly visible and the political risks small, larger staffs allow the Congress to move with lightning speed in holding hearings and drafting corrective legislation. Within three weeks after President Ford and the General Services Administration announced arrangements with Mr. Nixon for the disposition of Presidential tapes and "transition" money, Congress had moved to set the agreements aside. But in matters that really count, Congressional oversight is still too weak. Take the defense program, whose claims on the Federal budget have starved urgent domestic programs for a generation. Former Senator Paul Douglas of Illinois once expressed the frustration of a legislator who tries conscientiously to review the budget requests of the Defense Department (whose outlays today are larger than at the height of the Vietnam war). Analyzing a budget section titled "New Clothing Procurement," he came across the following item: *Underwear: $90-million.* "How in the name of God," Douglas asked, "can we possibly know whether $90-million is too much or too little for underwear?" And if you think underwear for the United States armed forces is complicated, try the ABM or MIRV missiles systems.

With a couple of hundred cost accountants on the staff of the Appropriations committees, perhaps Congress could make an informed decision. But even that would not dispose of the biggest impediment to adequate review, the fact that to most members of Congress, the military budget has as much to do with jobs and prosperity as with national security. Let's suppose that Congress's new Office of Technological Assessment, designed to give the legislators the capability for reviewing technical and scientific aspects of Administration programs, had been in operation back in 1964 when Defense Secretary Robert McNamara announced he might phase out the Boston Navy Yard. Even if Congress's technological assessors had concurred in the wisdom of the plan, would this have stopped House Speaker John McCormack from telling two successive Presidents—as he did—that if they wanted his cooperation they had better keep the yard open? Not as long as hundreds of his constituents worked there.

Indeed, the gravest surrender of Congressional authority —the series of resolutions by which the President was given unrestricted power in advance to make war in various parts of the world—resulted not from lack of information but from failure of nerve. Even if the staff of the Senate Foreign Relations Committee had been large enough to have had an observer at the Gulf of Tonkin, to dispute the Administration's version of what happened there in 1964, the Tonkin resolution would still have passed. How many members of Congress would have risked the political consequences of inhibiting a then-popular President from doing what he and his generals said was necessary to meet the Communist menace? (Only 2 of the 535 did.) "Unless the United States moves quickly," said John Foster Dulles in testimony in behalf of a Middle East resolution in 1957, "it is our definite belief that this area is very likely to be lost. . . . If Congress is not willing to trust the President to the extent he asks, we can't win this battle."

Finally, it is argued that with the Government's widening influence on our daily lives, Congressmen need help so they can be ombudsmen for their constituents. Instead of dealing with bureaucracy directly, increasing numbers of citizens are asking their legislators to run interference for them, encouraged by the way Congressmen advertise their ability to "get things done for constituents." Members of Congress can't do as much as they would like us to think. One of my jobs as a Senate aide was to write the Defense Department on behalf of local firms bidding on defense contracts I composed eloquent letters for my boss's signature about the superiority of the firm's product, its importance to the national security and the severe unemployment in the community. Invariably I would be referred to the hard realities of the Armed Services Procurement Regulations, which directed the contract to someone else. In a moment of rare candor, a high-level procurement officer told me what we were doing wrong. "If a Senator sends me a letter, I reply that we will give the matter thorough consideration, and I throw it in the wastebasket. I know he's just going through the motions. If he calls me up, I say, 'Yes, Senator, of course, Senator; I'll certainly do everything I can.' When he hangs up, I call him a son of a bitch for taking up my time and go about my business. I learned a long time ago that when one of these guys *really* wants something, he'll come down here himself and pound on my desk until he gets it."

Members of Congress don't have time to pound on the desk of every bureaucrat who is giving a constituent a hard

*The highest paid administrative assistants receive $37,000 per year, just slightly less than an Assistant Secretary of Defense. In the numerous amenity rooms in the basement of the House and Senate office buildings, staffers can buy a hot, four-course lunch for $1.50, get a haircut (men's) for $1.25, a shoeshine for a quarter, have their pictures framed and packages wrapped for nothing. Ticket agents are on hand to help them with travel reservations and the Internal Revenue Service has personnel available year round to help them with their taxes, without charge. Those who stay for 20 years are eligible for the most liberal retirement plan in the Federal Government.

time. If a Social Security check is lost, or an extra bed is needed in a veterans' hospital, a standard Congressional inquiry usually works. If the matter is more complicated, it is fairly certain to be covered in the detailed regulations which govern the administration of every Federal program and which are rarely bent, even after a request from the Hill. When a Congressional office receives a plea for intervention, it normally sends what is called a "buckslip" to the appropriate agency. In 90 per cent of the instances, Congressional caseworkers admit, the agency sends back a letter stating why the exception is impossible. This is forwarded to the constituent with a covering letter indicating that the Representative has done his best. In line with another of Parkinson's laws, "Officials make up work for each other," this ombudsman function has spawned larger Congressional liaison staffs in the executive departments. In 1971, the Department of Defense had more than 300 people and a budget of $4.4-million devoted primarily to filling Congressional requests.

Thus, the principal result of Congress's ombudsman role has been the creation of a class of constituents who are preferred from the standpoint of expedition. Those who know enough to use their Congressmen may not get a better shake, but they do get a faster one. This means that while the bureaucrats are answering the buckslips, the problems of the great majority of the population remain on the bottom of the pile.

The rise of the Congressional empires has made legislators busier than ever. Senators, and the more prominent members of the House, have come to resemble members of the Cabinet: They have only a casual connection with most of what is done in their name. On any morning on Capitol Hill, the typical Senator has four or five of his committees holding hearings at the same

time. He ignores some, shuttles between the others. He gets a quick oral briefing from the staff on arrival, stays to ask a few questions, leaves to keep other appointments. In the afternoon, he races between more appointments, more meetings, and roll-call votes on the Senate floor. As a result, important legislation rarely gets a full hearing. Votes are cast on scanty knowledge. The time for useful discussion is minimal, for reflection, almost nil. Privately, Senators admit the current pace is frenetic. They know that many of the subcommittees are being run by the staffs, and they don't like it. They are willing to accept all these drawbacks in return for the chance to participate in as many important issues as possible.

They know also that the rise of the Congressional empires has given them an important headstart in winning re-elections. A Senator from a middle-sized state like Connecticut or Iowa has almost $400,000 a year in public funds to spend on his personal staff. With a moderate amount of seniority, he controls another $200,000 in committee salaries. The first duty of a Congressional employe, as anyone who has worked there will testify, is to do one's job in a way that makes the boss look as good as possible. Personal staffs can participate in re-election campaigns. While committee staffs are prohibited from doing so, there is nothing to prevent them from giving priority to requests from the boss's constituents or working on issues which appeal to the people at home. Many of them do just that.

There is thus some merit in the charge that the new Campaign Financing Act, while admirable in other ways, is, in the words of Representative William Armstrong of Colorado, a "sweetheart incumbent bill . . . which will make it harder than ever to defeat an incumbent." Under the new law, both a Representative and his challenger can spend

up to $168,000 (including expenses of fund raising), first in the primary and again in the general election. At this point, the challenger's allowable spending stops. But he faces an incumbent who has had, *each year*, almost a quarter of a million dollars in public funds for staff and office expenses, a major portion of which is used to help the home folks and keep his name in front of them in a favorable way.

Congress could easily reduce its working force, with no loss in power and probably an increase in effectiveness. It is futile to expect this will happen. The best that can be hoped is for further expansion to be avoided. No one wants legislators to do anything rash, such as write their own speeches or stop trying to get publicity. They should, however, hold their own operations up to the same standards of economy as everyone else is being forced to.

They could begin by scrapping plans for further physical expansion, including construction of the third office building for the Senate. More space will just bring pressure for more staff, which will bring pressure for more space. If quarters are tight, existing employees will concentrate on important projects.

Congress should set a fixed budget ceiling for itself. Then it should direct the General Accounting Office to investigate Congressional operations — as it does with executive agencies — to uncover waste and duplication, and to recommend which subcommittees are effective enough to stay in business. A new Legislative Reorganization Act might provide, for example, that each committee consolidate all its subcommittees that lack authority to write legislation into a single unit that would both oversee the implementation of existing laws and investigate wrong-doing in the country for the purpose of recommending new ones.

One might also recommend that the power to appoint staffs be spread more evenly among committee members, instead of being concentrated in the chairman. (Unfortunately, the House, in its recent consideration of committee reform, went in the opposite direction. To give more staff to the Republican minority, it tripled the number of professional employees on committee staffs. It turned down the proposal to abolish the old Un-American Activities Committee, and it created a new committee, dedicated to problems of the aging, a subject on which 21 other House subcommittees already have jurisdiction.)

If Congress forced bureaucracies to be more responsive to all our citizens, it could cut down its load of casework. People should have a simple way of challenging arbitrary bureaucratic decisions in informal courts of the small-claims type, where they could receive money damages, if justified, for errors and delays beyond a specified period. Then, perhaps, they could get action from the Federal Government without having to appeal to their Congressmen. The Internal Revenue Service, because it deals with such a delicate subject, has been far ahead of most Federal agencies in reaching out to citizens. Call a toll-free number, and you can discuss your tax problems with an expert, without revealing your name. Replies to letter writers must be prepared within five days. I.R.S. personnel appear on radio talk shows and keep offices open on Saturdays, to increase their availability. Congress has the power to lean on more agencies to follow the lead of the I.R.S.

In issues of defense and foreign policy, what Congress needs most is a greater quality of skepticism and independence. It cannot hope to have all the facts and intelligence available to the executive, and indeed it does not need them.

It needs only enough information to ask the right questions, and to reject the stock answers. Congressmen have a good deal of common sense about the kind of influence America should exert around the world; witness their reaction to our bungling in Chile and in Cyprus. What they all too often lack is the courage to follow their best instincts in evaluating the pleas of alarmist generals and persuasive diplomats.

Unless Congress can curb its own phenomenal growth, its renewed quest for authority will yield only further conflict and public mistrust. In the end, its real strength and stature will be determined by the quality of each member. If he wants his staff to lead him, it will oblige. If he wants to keep shuffling bureaucratic paper, he will have plenty of opportunities to do so. If his main concern is to expand his staff and enhance his reputation, we shall continue to have a Congress whose members are respected by their individual constituencies, but whose standing as a body is debased.

The American people expect a higher standard of performance from Congress in the postwar, post-Watergate era. In addition to honesty and independence, they want timely, forceful action in those areas where the performance of government can improve their lives and preserve their liberties. The critical issue before the Congress is not whether it has enough authority. Within the boundaries of the Constitution, it has always had as much power as it has been willing to use. If our legislators can suppress the all-too-human desire to build empires or monuments to themselves, perhaps they can still use the power they have reclaimed to produce a few more boffos for the country.■

CHAPTER SEVEN

★ ★ ★

The Presidency

Not too long ago political science defended the use of power by strong activist presidents such as Lincoln, Wilson, Franklin D. Roosevelt, and Truman. It was held that strong presidential power was needed to counterbalance Congress and its inherent conservatism. Moreover, presidents were seen as the vital force behind noble causes, whether civil rights, social welfare, or international relations. We almost forgot the meaning of separation of powers and checks and balances, but then Vietnam and Watergate occurred. In the aftermath of these events, academics have reassessed their long-standing assumptions about presidential power. The emphasis today is on restraint and on the need for Congress to reassert itself. These themes are indicated by most readings chosen for this chapter; they are a sign of the times. But apart from our concern with institutional issues—the president's powers, his advisory system, his bureaucratic isolation, and the like—a new research thrust has focused on the president as a person. While it is true that political scientists were aware that presidents varied greatly in style and in performance, there was little attempt to fashion a coherent theory to explain the critical psychological variables that account for their behavior. Today, having been disillusioned by presidents who seemingly acted capriciously and, at times, even maliciously, we are concerned about the "character" of the nation's most powerful elected leader. The presidency is still respected for its importance to our system of government, but clearly some of the halo has been eroded in recent years.

These themes are best expressed in the first two articles: "Flouting the Constitution" by Louis Fisher and "Presidential War" by Arthur Schlesinger, Jr. The first article studies four issues to determine the extent of abuse by the president. Fisher calls for a return to legal principles and our adherence to the meaning of our Constitution. Though not explicit, this discussion hints at a major reason for the expansion of presidential powers beyond permissible limits. In the name of honorable purposes, we have permitted the Constitution to be distorted and manipulated. Lest we look for a conspiracy, it would seem that Congress lacked the capability or willingness to make effective public policy. Thus, it permitted the president to expand his authority in a number of areas. Fisher studies these four issues: (1) delegations of statutory authority to the president, (2) the veto power, (3) delegation of government reorganization authority to the president, and (4) violations of the Antideficiency Act. In light of the arguments in this essay, it would seem that a return to the separation of powers principle will be only partly accomplished by constraining the president. The Congress must fulfill its responsibilities also.

The essay by Arthur Schlesinger, Jr. focuses on what is perhaps the major issue of concern to academics, the president's ability to make war without a congressional "declaration." Again, this is no impromptu circumstance; it has been evolving over many years. In the nineteenth century Congress permitted the president latitude to make war, but Schlesinger argues that President Nixon, and to a lesser extent President Johnson, distorted historical precedent in a fundamental way. Nixon assumed the "inherent" right to make war at his own discretion. This article was written in 1973, so it gives us a keen perspective on the intensity of feeling by some academics toward Nixon's conduct of the war in Vietnam. According to Schlesinger, Nixon violated both "written" and "unwritten" checks on his powers as commander-in-chief. The essay dramatizes the scope of a president's warmaking power, and the weaknesses of counterbalances in the government. Ultimately, Schlesinger's analysis was correct, for Nixon was driven from power by public opinion, the media, the courts, and by outspoken legislators in Congress. Nixon's contempt for the "unwritten" checks on his authority eventually undermined his position, but the process was slow.

Two more articles study bureaucratic politics from the perspective of the presidency. The arguments indicate that institutional arrangements are narrowing his perspective, undermining his support base among the people, and limiting his ability to govern the nation effectively. In "Jimmy Carter's Ruling Class," Roger Morris looks at the cabinet. In Schlesinger's view, one of the "unwritten" checks on a president is his strong, independently minded advisers. But such persons are few and far between, if Morris's analysis is correct. In general, he feels that cabinet and middle-management personnel are wealthy organization men with political connections. Furthermore, presidents of both political parties tend to select the same type of individuals to serve in their administrations. For this reason, Morris argues that President Carter does not get meaningful advice—or conflicting opinions —from his top decision-makers. Rather than focus on the sociological backgrounds of top-level administrators, Thomas E. Cronin in "The Swelling of the Presidency" speaks to another dimension of the president's advisory system. He counts more and more advisers, and more and

more employees who work directly for the president. Moreover, the cabinet is losing influence to the Executive Office of the President. Rather than highlighting the political biases that result when certain types of individuals are recruited into government service, Cronin sees a system attribute which undermines the president. A large staff gives rise to the president's insulation; bureaucratic infighting results; control over government is weakened; and the principle of "accountability" is destroyed. These problems are very contemporary in origin, for the Executive Office of the President was established during the administration of Franklin D. Roosevelt. Before him, presidents had very small personal staffs.

The last reading involves the Watergate scandal during the administration of Richard M. Nixon. Included here are excerpts from the Supreme Court decision in the case of *United States* v. *Nixon*. In trying to determine the extent of criminal activities in the Watergate scandal, the Special Senate Watergate Committee subpoenaed certain records and tapes of White House conversations. President Nixon refused to comply on the grounds of "executive privilege," but the Supreme Court ruled against him. No doubt a major reason for Nixon's eventual resignation was the Court's role in revealing the facts to the American people. The Court's opinion was written by Chief Justice Burger, whom President Nixon had appointed. This issue symbolizes the role of the Supreme Court as a check and balance to the president's authority, and it can be fiercely independent in that capacity.

The articles in this chapter were selected to highlight issues of direct relevance to the contemporary presidency. All reflect upon the powers of that high office, and indicate that a serious reevaluation of the presidency in light of Watergate and Vietnam is being undertaken by political science. For each reading, headnotes are provided to guide your analysis of the arguments made by the authors. This subject demands intellectual dialogue, for we are calling into question many traditional assumptions about the role of the presidency in our political system.

★★

31

Flouting the Constitution   Louis Fisher

"What's the Constitution between friends?" With this statement Fisher alludes to the political pressures that undermine the integrity of our Constitution. In this article he analyzes four powers of government to determine whether the Constitution was violated by their use. The first power that poses potential difficulty for the Constitution is Congress's willingness to delegate authority to the president. The problem with such a transfer of power from the Congress to the executive is that there are no available standards or objectives to guide the transfer. Why does Fisher disapprove of trying to ascertain legislative intent for delegations of authority by reading such materials as the legislative hearings and committee records? What overall effect does this accumulation of power by the president have on the political system? A second power he considers is the presidential veto, and he traces its use from the beginning of the Republic. It has been used by presidents for both "constitutional" and "political" reasons. How did Gerald Ford use the veto power? Does Fisher think that Ford abused this power?

In 1905 Congress enacted an Antideficiency Act designed to prevent agencies of government from spending more money than was appropriated to them during the fiscal year. How has the president misused this particular act? The last issue raised pertains to the president's ability to initiate government reorganization unless stopped by either the House or Senate. This power was temporarily rescinded by Congress in 1973, but President Carter wished to regain it. During the debates of 1977, what arguments were made in favor of giving this authority to President Carter? What are Fisher's objections to giving this power to the president?

The author argues for a return to constitutional principles. But the essay suggests that very often powers are given to the president because Congress is unable to exercise them effectively. Would a return to strict legal principles severely limit our ability to govern the nation? Or do you think recent events have prompted Congress to recognize its responsibilities in the governing process? What advantages and disadvantages do you see from returning to the original separation of powers doctrine?

★ ★ ★

LOUIS FISHER

Flouting the Constitution

During debate on the first budget resolution for fiscal 1978, the U.S. House of Representatives considered an amendment which would have eliminated the recent pay increases for the executive and judicial branches. To Congressman Bob Eckhardt (D.-Texas) this seemed a flagrant effort to violate the constitutional language that prohibits diminution of compensation to judges. Eckhardt took the floor with some discomfort, explaining that "I know that when I enter the well I am always subject to somebody saying, 'You are bringing up the darned Constitution again.' "

Eckhardt's experience recalls a celebrated incident that involved President Grover Cleveland, who was once asked by a Tammany politician to support a certain bill. He refused, on the ground that the legislation was unconstitutional. His explanation brought forth from the politician this bewildered response: "What's the Constitution between friends?"

This nonchalant attitude about the Constitution has been a disturbing element of recent decades. In 1964 Lyndon Johnson was able to enlist the support of almost every member of Congress behind the Gulf of Tonkin Resolution. His later use of the Resolution, particularly as a "functional equivalent" to a declaration of war, was interpreted by many dismayed legislators as a violation of congressional intent. But Johnson did not misread the statutory language, which represented a blanket and careless abdication of authority that had been vested in Congress by the Constitution.

Several years later, in 1969, the Senate Foreign Relations Committee publicly apologized for its part in this episode. It admitted that Congress, in adopting the Resolution, had "committed the error of making a personal judgment as to how President Lyndon Johnson would implement the resolution when it had a responsibility to make an institutional judgment. . . ." Congress had improperly set aside the Constitution to accommodate political needs. The proper course, said the Committee, would have been to ask whether it was appropriate under the Constitution to grant such authority to any President.

These examples illustrate a duplexity that runs throughout the American system of government. They echo Faust's lament: "Two souls dwell, alas, in my breast. The one wants to separate from the other." Our constitutional system is under constant stress from forces struggling for control. Statutory and constitutional restrictions are erected to keep

From *The Center Magazine*, November/December 1977. Reprinted with permission from *The Center Magazine*, a publication of the Center for the Study of Democratic Institutions, Santa Barbara, California.

governmental actions within legal bounds. In sharp competition is the drive for political power that tests those boundaries, stretches them to satisfy momentary needs, and sometimes succeeds in doing what law forbids.

Unfortunately, a large element of the citizenry (and Congress) wants to look the other way. They cringe from any serious debate on constitutional issues. The mere mention of a "legal" dimension seems to stifle further discussion. Not only students but professional colleagues are intimidated by legal questions. Why this is so I have never fully understood. Perhaps the technical presentation of court decisions presents a barrier, and yet federal judges usually write with a flair, lucidity, and intelligibility that is rarely matched by offerings of the scholarly journals.

Part of the resistance comes from the habit of associating political events with the real world, while consigning legal matters to the remote and ethereal. This is a puzzling attitude, for constitutional and legal questions have their roots in tangible and concrete injuries. Someone suffers and seeks relief. Convictions and deeply held feelings cause plaintiffs to take their grievances to the courts, often after being rebuffed by Congress and the executive branch. Great questions of constitutional law, Henry Steele Commager has written, are great "not because they are complicated legal or technical questions, but because they embody issues of high policy, of public good, or morality."

This paper reviews the record of four constitutional issues of current importance that have been distorted and twisted by political pressures and practices: delegation of stabilization powers to Richard Nixon, the question of Gerald Ford's "unconstitutional" use of the veto power, continued violations of the Antideficiency Act, and the grant of reorganization authority to Jimmy Carter.

❦

Not since 1935, in the two National Recovery Act cases, has the Supreme Court struck down a delegation of power to the executive branch because of inadequate legislative guidelines. Statutory language has been sanctioned even when it has been vague and ill-defined, such as general guidelines of "excessive profits," "reasonable rates," "unjust discrimination," and "in the public interest." This kind of language is tolerated by the courts not because the language is specific, which is far from the case, but

because Congress supplies standards of due process to guide officials in administering the statute. Agencies are required to give notice and a hearing prior to issuing a rule or regulation. Also, findings of fact are supplied for the record; procedures exist for appeal. The Administrative Procedure Act establishes various standards for agency rule-making in order to guarantee fairness and equitable treatment. Through such procedural standards Congress tries to eliminate or minimize the opportunity for executive caprice and arbitrariness.

Still, there is an uneasy feeling that Congress has handed over to executive officials too much of its legislative power. The current potential for delegation is measured by the broadness of the Economic Stabilization Act of 1970, which authorized the President "to issue such orders and regulations as he may deem appropriate to stabilize prices, rents, wages, and salaries at levels not less than those prevailing on May 25, 1970." The remaining sections of the Act failed to provide for procedural safeguards, e.g., giving notice prior to issuing orders, providing a hearing for affected parties, and establishing machinery for judicial review.

In view of President Nixon's public opposition to wage-price controls, it was evident that Democratic members of Congress were trying to embarrass him and create an election-year issue. Each time the expiration date of the Act grew near, Congress extended it. Nixon's refusal to use the authority permitted legislators to chastise him for inaction in dealing with economic problems. Then, on August 15, 1971, he stunned Congress by placing a ninety-day freeze on all prices, rents, wages, and salaries. In part he based his action on the authority given him in the Economic Stabilization Act. Congress had passed a domestic equivalent to the Gulf of Tonkin Resolution.

Private parties appealed to the courts to have the Act struck down as an invalid delegation of legislative power. In one of the principal cases, *Amalgamated Meat Cutters,* a circuit court upheld the legislation by noting that some of the legislative guidelines had been included in committee reports and the legislative history of the Act: "Whether legislative purposes are to be obtained from committee reports, or are set forth in a separate section of the text of the law, is largely a matter of drafting style."

It is more than that, however. Agencies are bound by law. They are not necessarily bound by nonstatutory controls. In 1975, the U.S. Navy ignored language that Congress had placed in a conference report on an appropriations bill. LTV Aerospace Corporation attempted to have the General Accounting Office declare the Navy's action as null and void, on the ground that directives placed in a conference report were binding on an agency. After months of study, the Comptroller General ruled that such directives had legal force only when some ambiguity in the language of a public law requires recourse to the legislative history. Otherwise, agencies follow nonstatutory controls for political — not legal — reasons. Agencies may ignore nonstatutory controls, said the Comptroller General, but only "at the peril of strained relations with the Congress." To be legally binding, the directive to the Navy would have to appear in a public law.

It is evident from these examples that more explicit standards for administrative action must come from Congress, not the courts. Political accountability and democratic values depend on the establishment of clear guidelines for administrators. Also, vague statutes make it difficult to conduct program evaluation, for how can Congress — assisted by the G.A.O. and other staff support — determine whether programs are being carried out effectively unless the original legislative goals are clearly stated?

Congress is presently considering the Administrative Rulemaking Reform Act as one remedy for excessive or uncertain delegation. The legislation would permit Congress to review (and reject) agency regulations. In order to determine the fairness and reasonableness of a regulation, members and their staffs would have to study the entire hearing record that supports it. There is no indication that Congress intends to do that. If not, on what would members base their decision to disapprove a regulation — on hunches and political pressures?

If Congress believes that agencies are departing from legislative intent, it would be better to draft statutes in more explicit fashion. Only a few agencies appear to present a problem. Let Congress focus on remedial legislation for those agencies instead of passing an omnibus bill for the entire government. The pending bill would permit Congress to pass judgment on regulations issued by most of the agencies; it might also encourage Congress to legislate with even fewer guidelines in the future. Advocates for vague delegation could always argue that Congress would be in a position to review regulations to make sure that they square with congressional intent. But if the statute is vague, and if the legislative history supplies inadequate or conflicting standards, who is to say that the agency is departing from the legislative

purpose? The "will of Congress" could degenerate into after-the-fact judgments by a few legislators and staffers as to what Congress meant in the first place.

❦

There is general agreement that the President may exercise his veto to protect his office from legislative encroachment. Use of the veto for other purposes has produced periodic waves of hysteria. As recently as the Administration of Gerald Ford, critics claimed that he had used the veto unconstitutionally. Edward Pessen, a professor of history at Baruch College, wrote an article for *The Nation* in 1975 in which he concluded that the veto power as exercised by Ford, Nixon, Johnson, and almost all the Presidents since Andrew Jackson was "utterly at odds" with the intentions of the framers. According to Pessen, the veto was to be rarely exercised. James Madison and Alexander Hamilton, he said, believed that the veto should be used for limited purposes: "protection of the integrity of the Presidential office and rejection of flagrantly unconstitutional legislation."

Charles L. Black, Jr., a professor of law at Yale University, also insisted that Ford had misused the veto. That power was to be applied "only rarely, and certainly not as a means of systematic policy control over the legislative branch, on matters constitutionally indifferent and not menacing the President's independence." Early use of the veto, by Black's reckoning, was invoked mainly to protect the integrity of the President's office.

Two basic propositions are advanced in these critiques: the veto should be used sparingly; it should be used primarily to protect the President's office. Neither assertion survives much scrutiny.

As to the frequency of vetoes, Hamilton and James Wilson at the Philadelphia Convention tried to support an absolute veto on the ground that there was little danger the veto would be "too much exercised." Not a single state voted for their proposal; ten states voted against. That certainly suggests that delegates did not anticipate vetoes on rare occasions.

More important, the framers could not have anticipated the vast range of activity to be drawn within the compass of the federal government, the outpouring of legislation that resulted, and the great mass of private bills. On a single day in 1886 President Cleveland received nearly 240 private bills granting new pensions for veterans, increasing their benefits, or restoring old names to the list. Many of these bills were so indefensible that a veto was im-

perative. Congress adopted the practice of keeping separate lists of public and private bills. While congressional votes to override vetoes of public bills are taken on a regular basis, Congress often concedes, without a vote, vetoes of private bills.

Nor did the framers foresee the emergence of party politics, the potential for different parties to control Congress and the White House, and the encouragement that would give to vetoes. Congress behaved in ways to invite vetoes, such as passing hundreds of measures in the closing days of a session.

Congress devised still other techniques to enhance its power. A favorite device consisted of tacking non-germane amendments ("riders") onto appropriations bills. Since appropriations were necessary for the operation of the government, members hoped to gain "safe passage" for a legislative idea that probably would not have survived the journey on its own merits. Rutherford B. Hayes was steadfast in fighting against this tactic, which he regarded as a coercive measure designed to strip him of the veto power. After a series of vetoes he was able to prevail, but future Presidents continued to receive omnibus bills that were an amalgam of disparate elements. All of these factors help explain the growth of Presidential vetoes.

What of the second proposition: that vetoes should be used primarily to protect the President's office? Justice Byron White, in a 1976 decision, claimed that the veto's principal aim was not "another check against poor legislation" but rather to protect the Executive against legislative encroachments. Some delegates at the Philadelphia Convention, including Elbridge Gerry, did regard the veto primarily as an instrument to defend the executive branch and not the general interest. But Madison viewed the power in more generous terms. The veto was available "to restrain the legislature from encroaching on the other coordinate departments, or on the rights of the people at large; or from passing laws unwise in their prin-

ciples, or incorrect in their form. . . ." Hamilton, in *Federalist 73*, defended the veto as necessary to protect the President but also to furnish "an additional security against the enaction of improper laws. It establishes a salutary check upon the legislative body, calculated to guard the community against the effects of faction, precipitancy, or of any impulse unfriendly to the public good, which may happen to influence a majority of that body." The veto would protect not only the Executive but also the community from the passage of "bad laws, through haste, inadvertence, or design." This larger view of Madison and Hamilton has carried the day.

It is interesting that Ford's critics placed such heavy emphasis on the use of the veto to protect the President's office. The historical record is quite to the contrary. George Washington vetoed two bills — the first on constitutional grounds (an apportionment bill) and the second because he thought the bill so carelessly drafted and so unwise in substance that it should not become law. Neither bill affected the President's office. Professor Black suggested that the second bill, involving the military, "may have been seen as a dangerous weakening of the country's military force, connected with the Commander-in-Chief's power, so that the veto may well be thought to fall within the category of defense of the Presidential office." This supposition rests on too many mays. The evidence is straightforward: Washington thought it was a bad bill.

John Adams and Thomas Jefferson did not use the veto power. The next President, James Madison, relied on it five times for regular (as opposed to pocket) vetoes. Four were for constitutional reasons (involving trials in district courts, internal improvements, and two on church-state separation), while one bill (regarding the national bank) seemed to Madison too poorly designed to accomplish its purpose. Professor Black states that Madison vetoed the bank bill because it failed to provide adequately for circulating money in time of war: "Perhaps, without stretching too much, such a veto may (like Washington's second veto) be connected with protection of the President's role as Commander-in-Chief, and with the effective execution of that power." Again, too many perhapses, mays, and stretches.

During this initial period of twenty-eight years, covering four Presidents and seven administrations, there were seven regular vetoes, five of them for constitutional reasons. Only one affected the independence of the Executive: the district courts bill, which Madison vetoed in part because he thought it usurped his appointment power.

Ironically, the critics of the Ford Administration were borrowing unwittingly from Whig theories of the nineteenth century. Increased use of the veto by Presidents Andrew Jackson and John Tyler had produced three basic complaints: (1) since the veto was rarely overridden, it amounted to an absolute veto, contrary to the framers' intent; (2) the veto was originally granted to bolster a weak Executive, who was now able to defend himself by other means; and (3) the veto's limited purpose (to defend the Constitution) had been ignored by Presidents. Efforts were made to reduce the vote needed for an override from a two-thirds majority to a simple majority, but all such proposals failed.

During this period a number of Chief Executives recorded their positions on the veto power. In 1841 President William Henry Harrison recommended a restrained use of the veto, for it was "preposterous" to believe that the President could better understand the wishes of the people than their own representatives. He conceded that Presidents were more independent of sectional pulls, however, and might have to veto legislation of a strongly local nature. Vetoes were justified in protecting the Constitution from violation, defending the people from hasty legislation, and preserving the rights of minorities from the effects of combination.

Harrison's successor, John Tyler, exercised the veto too frequently for his opponents in Congress. A resolution was introduced to impeach him. Among the grounds was this: "I charge him with the high crime and misdemeanor of withholding his assent to laws undispensable [*sic*] to the just operations of government, which involved no constitutional difficulty on his part."

The Democratic Party held to a less restricted view of the veto power. President James Polk, in a detailed analysis in 1848, denied that the obligations of the President were "in any degree lessened by the prevalence of views different from his own in one or both Houses of Congress." It was not merely hasty and inconsiderate legislation that the President was required to check. If Congress, after full deliberation, agreed to measures which the President regarded as "subversive of the Constitution or of the vital interests of the country, it is his solemn duty to stand in the breach and resist them." The Democratic platforms of 1844, 1848, 1852, and 1856 placed the Party "decidedly opposed" to taking from the President the qualified veto power by which he was able to suspend the passage of bills that could not command the approval of two-thirds of each House. The veto power, claimed the platforms, had saved the Ameri-

can people from the "corrupt and tyrannical domination" of the U.S. Bank and the "corrupting system of general interest improvements."

Zachary Taylor, who followed Polk into the White House, adhered to the Whig interpretation. He viewed the veto as "an extreme measure, to be resorted to only in extraordinary cases, as where it may become necessary to defend the Executive against the encroachment of the legislative power or to prevent hasty and inconsiderate or unconstitutional legislation." The personal opinion of the President "ought not to control the action of Congress upon questions of domestic policy; nor ought his opinion and objections to be interposed when questions of constitutional power have been settled by the various departments of government and acquiesced in by the people." On such subjects as the tariff, the currency, and internal improvements "the will of the people as expressed through their representatives in Congress ought to be . . . carried out and respected by the Executive." In essence, that was the position of Democrats who criticized Ford's veto record. How chagrined they would have been to know that they walked in the footsteps of Zachary Taylor!

❧

One of the most frustrating tasks for Congress is to hold agencies to the amount appropriated by Congress. The principle seems simple enough. The Constitution states, "No money shall be drawn from the Treasury but in consequence of appropriations made by law." Agencies ran out of money for a variety of reasons and had to draw on surpluses or transfer funds from other accounts. The situation deteriorated to such an extent that in 1870 Congress passed legislation to prohibit executive departments from spending in a fiscal year any sum in excess of appropriations for that year; nor could any department involve the government in any contract for the future payment of money in excess of such appropriations. To the reader these prohibitions may seem terribly esoteric and technical, but if agencies are free to obligate beyond what Congress has appropriated, the constitutional process is turned on its head.

The thrust of the 1870 law was undermined when agencies ran out of money before the end of the fiscal year. True, they had not over-obligated but neither could they carry out the laws for the full year. Congress could do little else but pass supplemental appropriations to tide the agencies over. The next step was the Antideficiency Act of 1905 which tried to force agencies to spread their funds evenly over the course of a year. The Act required monthly or other allotments to prevent "undue expenditures in one portion of the year that may require deficiency or additional appropriations to complete the service of the fiscal year. . . ." The Act also provided that any person violating the procedure shall be summarily removed from office and may also be punished by a fine or by imprisonment. Those sanctions are still in law, but neither punishment has ever been invoked. The Act was rewritten in 1906, 1950, and 1974. Deficiencies still continue.

From 1963 through 1973, executive agencies committed 278 violations of the Antideficiency Act, totaling $188 million. The Defense Department committed 216 of those violations, representing a dollar value of $165 million. A massive violation was a $110 million deficiency by the Navy. Defense Secretary Melvin Laird had informed Congress in 1972 that the Navy over-obligated and overspent in the "Military Personnel, Navy" account. The House Appropriations Committee discovered that certain individuals had made willful adjustments to accounting records in an effort to conceal the infraction. Laird did not find evidence of willfulness. The violations were caused, he said, "by mismanagement, poor judgment, inadequate or non-observance of procedures and controls, and personnel turbulence associated with the Southeast Asia conflict." He believed that the corrective actions taken by the Navy, together with actions he directed, were adequate to prevent future violations. Departmental controls, as spelled out in a Pentagon directive on deficiencies, "are considered adequate and no change is contemplated."

To believe that the Defense Department has adequate control over deficiencies, you would have to ignore its record of repeated violations. You would also have to overlook a remarkable deficiency that surfaced last year. On November 5, 1976, the G.A.O.

reported to Congress on over-obligations by the U.S. Army totaling $205 million in three appropriations. The largest deficiency was $150.1 million for the "Procurement of Equipment and Missiles, Army" account. In addition, the Army was preparing violation reports on two other appropriations and was investigating the possibility of eight more violations. The Army had dug such a hole for itself that it had to stop payment on about 1,200 contracts involving some nine hundred contractors.

Deficiencies used to be more visible. Congress would act separately on deficiency requests from the agencies, appropriating whatever amounts were necessary in a deficiency bill. But the practice for a number of years has been to add such amounts in a supplemental appropriations bill. It is not possible to isolate the funds being appropriated to cover a deficiency. Even close students of the budget process cannot determine the extent to which the Antideficiency Act is being violated each year, the reasons for the violations, and the disciplinary and administrative actions taken to discourage future violations.

❧

The President's authority to reorganize the executive branch, after lapsing in 1973, was revived in 1977 at the request of President Carter. Congressman Jack Brooks (D.-Texas) mounted a major constitutional challenge, claiming that Congress should vote affirmatively on a reorganization plan instead of letting it become law after sixty days without a veto by either House, but the one-House veto prevailed. The constitutional issue was not prominent during Senate action and was raised only haphazardly during House consideration. One has the impression that neither House wanted to think through the constitutional implications with any thoroughness.

The Justice Department, having objected to previous legislative vetoes on the ground that they trespassed upon the President, made an exception for reorganization authority. Attorney General Griffin Bell argued that the decision to present a plan lay solely with the President. This freedom not to act was treated as an equivalent to a Presidential veto. Judging from the executive branch's record on reorganization authority, it appears that the Justice Department can construct whatever argument is necessary to obtain this power for the President. In 1938, President Franklin D. Roosevelt told Congress that the only permissible instrument was a joint resolution, which must be presented to the President for his signature or veto. The next year the Administration acquiesced in a concurrent resolution (which is not presented) and went along with a one-House veto in 1949. Presidents who wanted reorganization authority had to accept the legislative conditions that accompanied it. Harvey C. Mansfield cut through the constitutional complications by making this astute observation about the legality of reorganization authority: "There the question has rested, 'no tickee, no washee.' "

The debate on the 1977 reorganization legislation was not distinguished for its analytic rigor. Attorney General Bell claimed that the reorganization statute "does not affect the rights of citizens or subject them to any greater governmental authority than before. It deals only with the internal organization of the executive branch, a matter in which the President has a peculiar interest and special responsibility." That statement is so unrealistic it does not merit a rebuttal. The House Committee on Government Operations, when it reported the bill, acknowledged the substantive impact of reorganization on the people. It added a new congressional intention that "appropriate means should be provided by the President for citizen advice and participation in executive reorganization. This intention recognizes the vital role that citizens and the public (those ultimately most affected) should play in government reorganization. . . ." But if the issue is so "vital," why shouldn't Congress go on record by an affirmative vote?

For many members of Congress it was sufficient that Jimmy Carter had promised during the 1976 campaign to reorganize the federal government. To deny him that authority, they reasoned, would torpedo a solemn pledge made to the American people. Still, a campaign promise cannot relieve legislators of the responsibility for deciding whether a delegation of authority is constitutional or prudent. Members also used other arguments to evade the constitutional question. They said that the issue was already in the courts and would be resolved there. But the courts might not be able to decide the matter, or might decide it in a manner unsatisfactory to Congress. We cannot accept literally the injunction of Charles Evans Hughes: "We are under a Constitution, but the Constitution is what the judges say it is. . . ." The Court is a coequal, not superior, branch. If Congress concludes that proposed legislation is unconstitutional, it should not act. If the President receives legislation that he thinks is unconstitutional, he should veto it. Frequently the courts will defer to practices adopted by the political branches. In 1903,

prior to the famous Myers decision, the Supreme Court upheld the President's removal power. It based its ruling largely on the "universal practice of the government for over a century. . . ."

Members have a duty to express their own views regarding the constitutionality of their actions. They take an oath of office upon joining Congress. They solemnly swear (or affirm) to support and defend the Constitution of the United States against all enemies, foreign and domestic; to bear true faith and allegiance to the same; to take this obligation freely, without any mental reservation or purpose of evasion, and to well and faithfully discharge the duties of the office on which they are about to enter. This duty cannot be set aside lightly by legislators who say they are not lawyers, or, if lawyers, not constitutional experts. To swear to defend a document, and then claim ignorance of its contents, is an empty exercise.

❦

The American Constitution is designed in part to protect individual liberties. That requires the consent, and the understanding, of the governed. All too often the people shy away from constitutional issues as technical and abstract, preferring to leave those matters to legislators, executive officials, the courts, and academics. Then legislators let matters slip past them to the courts. That is an unhealthy sign for a democratic society. A dependence on the people, Madison counseled in *Federalist 51*, is the primary control on the government. They depend, in turn, on legislators who are willing to prepare themselves for the major issues and act with confidence as a coequal branch. This is no time, after Watergate and the bicentennial celebrations, for Congress to defer to the Presidents or to the courts.

Members of Congress can take heart in the words of someone whose entire experience with the federal government lay outside the legislative branch. Robert H. Jackson, Attorney General under Franklin Roosevelt and later a Justice of the Supreme Court, offered a perspective that should encourage us to hold fast to basic principles: "With all its defects, delays, and inconveniences, men have discovered no technique for long preserving free government except that the Executive be under the law, and that the law be made by parliamentary deliberations."

Louis Fisher, a research specialist in the government division of the Congressional Research Service, is the author of President and Congress.

★★

32

Presidential War   Arthur Schlesinger, Jr.

Scholars have long recognized the power of a president as commander-in-chief. Consequently, the importance of this essay, "Presidential War," may be overlooked at first glance. And yet it was the presidential wars of Lyndon Johnson and Richard Nixon that contributed to academia's and the public's disillusionment with Vietnam. Did Presidents Johnson and Nixon invent the concept of "presidential war"? Or has it been with us from the beginning of the Republic? Many academics, including Schlesinger, have long defended presidential war powers, but in the wake of Vietnam many of them felt a need to reassess these powers. Did Richard Nixon's violation of the "written" and "unwritten" checks on presidential power also encourage such a reassessment of these powers? What were these "unwritten" checks that were violated? How did he violate them?

Although the Founders gave Congress the power to "declare" war (rather than "make" war), the expectation was that presidents would "make" war only when threats to the very life of the nation existed. In terms of this aspect of war powers, Schlesinger argues that those "presidential wars" engaged in by Presidents Abraham Lincoln, Franklin Roosevelt, Harry Truman, and John Kennedy were therefore "legal." What actions did these four presidents take, and why does Schlesinger consider them to be legal? Contrary to historic precedent, Nixon claimed "inherent" powers as commander-in-chief, even though no crisis threatened the existence of the nation. On what grounds did Nixon defend his invasion of Cambodia in 1970?

At the conclusion of this essay, Schlesinger ponders ways to restrain presidential warmaking. One of the primary ways to do this, he feels, is for Congress to reassert itself. Why doesn't he think the War Powers Act is an effective mechanism for regaining legislative authority over warmaking? Another possibility is impeachment. Did Schlesinger think it would be used against Nixon? Ultimately, he thinks that the president can be restrained by mobilizing the various "unwritten" checks. Will these "unwritten" checks really restrain a strong executive? Have you seen any evidence that the president is any weaker today as commander-in-chief than he was during the Vietnam war years?

★ ★ ★

Presidential war:

"See if you can fix any limit to his power"

By Arthur Schlesinger Jr.

Allow the President to invade a neighboring nation, whenever he shall deem it necessary to repel an invasion, and you allow him to do so, whenever he may choose to say he deems it necessary for such purpose—and you allow him to make war at pleasure. Study to see if you can fix any limit to his power in this respect. . . . If, today, he should choose to say he thinks it necessary to invade Canada, to prevent the British from invading us, how could you stop him? You may say to him, "I see no probability of the British invading us" but he will say to you "be silent; I see it, if you don't."

—ABRAHAM LINCOLN to W. H. HERNDON, Feb. 15, 1848

"Study to see if you can fix *any limit* to his power"—when he thus advised his friend Herndon, Congressman Lincoln of course had President Polk in mind. Yet by contemporary standards Polk would be in the clear. He had meticulously observed the constitutional forms: he had asked Congress to declare war against Mexico, and Congress had done so. But the situation Lincoln imagined a century and a quarter ago has now come much closer to the fact. For war at Presidential pleasure, nourished by the crises of the 20th century, waged by a series of activist Presidents and removed from processes of Congressional consent, has by 1973 made the American President on issues of war and peace the most absolute monarch (with the possible exception of Mao Tse-tung of China) among the great powers of the world.

President Nixon did not invent Presidential war, nor did President Johnson. In their conceptions of Presidential authority, they drew on theories evolved long before they entered the White House and defended in general terms by many political scientists and historians, this writer among them. But they went further than any of their predecessors in claiming the unlimited right of the American chief executive to commit American forces to combat on his own unilateral will; and President Nixon has gone further in this respect than President Johnson.

In 1970, without the consent of Congress, without even consultation or notification, President Nixon ordered the American ground invasion of Cambodia. In 1971, again without consent or consultation, he ordered an American aerial invasion of Laos. In December, 1972, exhilarated by what he doubtless saw as an overwhelming vote of personal confidence in the 1972 election, he renewed and intensified the bombing of North Vietnam, carrying it now to such murderous extremes as to make his predecessor seem in retrospect a model of sobriety and restraint—all this again on

Arthur Schlesinger Jr. is Albert Schweitzer Professor of the Humanities at the City University of New York.

his personal say-so. And so assured and confirmed does President Nixon now evidently feel in the unilateral exercise of such powers that he does not bother any longer (as he did for a moment in 1970) to argue the constitutional issue. If he should now choose to say he thinks it necessary to invade North Vietnam in order to prevent the North Vietnamese from attacking American troops, how can anyone stop him? Congress might see no threat in North Vietnam to the security of the United States, but: "Be silent; I see it, if you don't."

How have we reached this point? For throughout American history Presidents have acknowledged restraints, written and unwritten, on their unilateral power to bring the nation into war. The written restraints are to be found in the Constitution; the unwritten restraints in the nature of the democratic process. Why, after nearly two centuries of independence, should there now seem to be no visible checks on the personal power of an American President to send troops into combat?

This was plainly not the idea of the Constitution. The provision in Article I, Section 8, conferring on Congress the power to declare war was carefully and specifically designed to deny the American President what Blackstone had assigned the British King—"the sole prerogative of making war and peace." As Lincoln went on to say in his letter to Herndon, it was this power of kings to involve their people in wars that "our [Constitutional] Convention understood to be the most oppressive of all Kingly oppressions; and they resolved to so frame the Constitution that *no one man* should hold the power of bringing this oppression upon us. But your view destroys the whole matter, and places our President where Kings have always stood."

How did we get from Lincoln's no-one-man doctrine to the position propounded by President Johnson in 1966: "There are many, many who can recommend, advise, and sometimes a few of them consent. But there is only one that has been chosen by the American people to decide"? The process of placing our Presidents where kings had always stood has been gradual. In the early 19th century most Presidents respected the role of Congress in decisions of war and peace against sovereign states. Even a President like Jackson, otherwise so dedicated to enlarging the executive power, referred the recognition of the Republic of Texas to Congress as a question "probably leading to war" and therefore a proper subject for "previous understanding with that body by whom war can alone be declared and by whom all the provisions for sustaining its perils must be furnished." Polk may have presented Congress with a *fait accompli* when he provoked a Mexican attack on American forces in disputed territory, but he did not claim that his authority as Commander in Chief allowed him to wage war against Mexico without Congressional authorization (cf., President Nixon explaining why such authorization was not required for his invasion of Cambodia; he was only meeting his "responsibility as Commander in Chief of our armed forces to take the action I

consider necessary to defend the security of our American men").

In the course of the 19th century, however, the Congressional power to declare war began to ebb in two opposite directions—in cases where the threat seemed too trivial to require Congressional consent and in cases where the threat seemed too urgent to permit Congressional consent. Thus, many 19th-century Presidents found themselves confronted by minor situations that called for forcible response but appeared beneath the dignity of formal Congressional declaration or authorization—police actions in defense of American honor, lives, law or property against roving groups of Indians, slave traders, smugglers, pirates, frontier ruffians or foreign brigands. So the habit developed of the limited executive employment of military force without reference to Congress. Then in the early 20th century McKinley and Theodore Roosevelt began to commit military force without Congressional authorization not only against private groups but against sovereign states—McKinley in China, T.R. in the Caribbean. Since Congress agreed with most of these uses of force, it acquiesced in initiatives that soon began to accumulate as formidable precedents.

As far as cases where the threat seemed too urgent to permit the delay involved in summoning Congressmen and Senators from far corners of a sprawling nation, this was a possibility that the framers of the Constitution themselves had envisaged. Madison had thus persuaded the Constitutional Convention to give Congress the power not to "make" but to "declare" war in order to leave the executive "the power to repel sudden attacks." Given the hazards and unpredictabilities of life, no sensible person wanted to put the American President into a constitutional straitjacket. No one wrote more eloquently about the virtues of strict construction than Jefferson. Yet Jefferson, who was at bottom a realist, also wrote: "To lose our country by a scrupulous adherence to written law, would be to lose the law itself, with life, liberty, property and all those who are enjoying them with us; thus absurdly sacrificing the ends to the means. . . . The line of discrimination between cases may be difficult; but the good officer is bound to draw it at his own peril, and throw himself on the justice of his country and the rectitude of his motives." In other words, when the life of the nation is at stake, Presidents might be compelled to take extraconstitutional or unconstitutional action. But, in doing so, they were placing themselves and their reputations under the judgment of history. They must not believe, or pretend to the nation, that they were simply executing the Constitution.

So when Lincoln in the most dreadful crisis of American history took a series of actions of dubious legality in the 10 weeks after the attack on Fort Sumter, he fully recognized what he was doing and subsequently explained to Congress that these measures, "whether strictly legal or not, were ventured upon under what appeared to be a popular

From *The New York Times Magazine*, January 7, 1973. © 1973 by The New York Times Company. Reprinted by permission.

The President has become, on issues of war and peace, the most absolute monarch among the great powers—"with the possible exception of China's Mao Tse-tung."

demand and a public necessity; trusting then as now that Congress would readily ratify them." Though he derived his authority to take such actions from his constitutional role as Commander in Chief, he was always conscious of the distinction between what was constitutionally normal and what might be justified only by a most extraordinary emergency. "I felt that measures, otherwise unconstitutional," he wrote in 1864, "might become lawful by becoming indispensable to the preservation of the Constitution, through the preservation of the nation."

So, too, when Franklin Roosevelt in our second most acute national crisis took a series of actions designed to enable England to survive against Hitler, he obtained in the case of the destroyer deal not only a favorable interpretation of a Congressional statute but the private approval of the Republican candidate for President. In the case of lend-lease, he went to Congress. In the case of his North Atlantic "shoot-at-sight" policy, though the threat to the United States from Nazi Germany could be persuasively deemed somewhat greater than that emanating 30 years later from Cambodia or Laos, and though his commitment of American forces was far more conditional, Roosevelt did not claim in the Nixon style that he was merely meeting his responsibility as Commander in Chief. Knowing that Congress, which would renew Selective Service by a single vote in the House, would hardly approve an undeclared naval war in the North Atlantic, Roosevelt in effect, like Jefferson and Lincoln, did what he thought was necessary to save the life of the nation and, proclaiming an "unlimited national emergency," threw himself upon the justice of his country and the rectitude of his motives. Since the Second World War there have been only two emergencies requiring immediate response. In the first, Harry Truman, confronted by the North Korean invasion of South Korea, secured a mandate from the

United Nations; in the second, John Kennedy, confronted by Soviet nuclear missiles in Cuba, secured a mandate from the Organization of American States.

Only Presidents Johnson and Nixon have made the claim that inherent Presidential authority, unaccompanied by emergencies threatening the life of the nation, unaccompanied by the authorization of Congress or of an international organization, permits a President to order troops into combat at his unilateral pleasure. President Johnson, it is true, liked to tease Congress by flourishing the Tonkin Gulf Resolution. But he did not really believe, as he said in an unguarded moment, that "the resolution was necessary to do what we did and what we're doing." President Nixon has abandoned even that constitutional fig leaf. William Rehnquist, then in the Department of Justice and later elevated to the Supreme Court as what President Nixon hilariously called a strict-constructionist appointee, said on behalf of his benefactor that the invasion of Cambodia was no more than "a valid exercise of his constitutional authority as Commander in Chief to secure the safety of American forces." One somehow doubts that if Brezhnev used the identical proposition to justify the invasion of a neutral country by the Red Army, it would be received with entire satisfaction in Washington. Today President Nixon has equipped himself with so expansive a theory of the powers of the Commander in Chief, and so elastic a theory of defensive war, that he can freely, on his own initiative, without a national emergency, as a routine employment of Presidential power, go to war against any country containing any troops that might in any conceivable circumstance be used in an attack on American forces. Hence the new cogency of Lincoln's old question: "Study to see if you can fix *any limits* to his power in this respect."

In short, President Nixon has effectively liquidated the 11th paragraph of Article I,

Section 8 of the Constitution. He has thereby removed the most solemn written check on Presidential war. He has sought to establish as a normal Presidential power what previous Presidents had regarded as power justified only by extreme emergencies and to be used only at their own peril. He does not, like Lincoln, confess to doubts about the legality of his course, or, like Franklin Roosevelt, seek to involve Congress when such involvement would not threaten the life of the nation. Nor has his accomplishment been limited to the exclusion of Congress from its constitutional role in the matter of war and peace. For he has also taken a series of unprecedented steps to liquidate the unwritten as well as the written checks on the Presidential war power.

WHAT are these unwritten checks? The first is the role of the President himself. President Nixon has progressively withdrawn from public scrutiny. He was an invisible candidate in the 1972 campaign, and he promises to be an invisible President in his second term—invisible on all but carefully staged occasions. Franklin Roosevelt used to hold press conferences twice a week; President Nixon holds them hardly at all and has virtually succeeded in destroying them as a regular means of public information. As William V. Shannon of The Times has written, he "has come as close to abolishing direct contact with reporters as he can." Even on matters of the highest significance he declines to expose himself to questioning by the press. Consider, for example, the Indochina peace negotiation. Does anyone suppose that if this had taken place in the previous Administration President Johnson would have trotted out Walt Rostow to discuss it with the media? Can anyone imagine Presidents Kennedy or Eisenhower or Truman dodging their personal responsibility in such momentous matters? Does anyone recall Franklin Roosevelt, returning from a wartime summit, asking Harry Hopkins or Admiral Leahy to explain it all to the press? Yet we have acquiesced so long in the Nixon withdrawal from Presidential responsibility that virtually no surprise is expressed when on such occasions he

repeatedly retreats behind Dr. Kissinger (who, for his part, is permitted to undergo searching interrogation by Oriana Fallaci, but not by the Senate Foreign Relations Committee). Moreover, President Nixon, by flinching from press conferences, not only deprives the American people of opinions and information to which they are surely entitled from their President but deprives himself of an important means of learning the concerns and anxieties of the nation. Obviously, he simply does not recognize much in the way of Presidential accountability to the people. As he recently put it: "The average American is just like the child in the family." And, presumably, father knows best.

A second check on Presidential war-making has often come from the executive establishment. Genuinely strong Presidents are not afraid to surround themselves with genuinely strong men and on occasion cannot escape the chore of listening to them. Historically, the Cabinet, for example, has generally contained men with their own views and their own constituencies—men with whom the President must in some sense come to terms. Lincoln had to deal with Seward, Chase, Stanton and Welles; Wilson with Bryan, McAdoo, Baker, Daniels and Houston; Roosevelt with Stimson, Hull, Wallace, Ickes, Biddle and Morgenthau; Truman with Marshall, Acheson, Byrnes, Vinson, Harriman, Forrestal and Patterson. But who in President Nixon's Cabinet will talk back to him—assuming, that is, they could get past the palace janissaries and into the Oval Office? The fate of those who have tried to talk back in the past is doubtless instructive: Where are Messrs. Hickel, Romney, Laird and Peterson now? In his first term, President Nixon kept his Cabinet at arm's length; and in his second term he has put together what, with one or two exceptions, is the most anonymous Cabinet within memory, a Cabinet of clerks, of compliant and faceless men who stand for nothing, have no independent national position and are guaranteed not to defy Presidential whim. Most alarming of all in connection with Presidential war has been the deletion, so far as high policy is concerned, of the Department of State. In short, President Nixon, instead of exposing himself to the temper-

ing influence of a serious exchange of views within the Government, has organized his executive establishment in a way to eliminate as far as humanly possible internal question or challenge about his foreign policy. And to complete his insulation from debate, the President does not even tell most of his associates what he intends to do.

A third check in the past has come from the media of opinion—from the newspapers and, in more recent years, from television. With all its manifest imperfections, the American press has played an indispensable role through our history in keeping government honest. President Nixon, however, not only hides himself from the press and television, except on elaborately controlled occasions, but has launched a well-orchestrated campaign to weaken the mass media as sources of information and criticism.

He has tried a variety of methods — prior restraint on the publication of news; Vice-Presidential denunciations of erring newspapers and reporters; proposals to condition the renewal of television licenses on the elimination of anti-Administration material from network programs; subpoenas to compel reporters to surrender raw notes; even jailing newspapermen who decline to betray confidential sources to grand juries—this last a practice which would not be constitutional had it not been for the Nixon appointments to the Supreme Court.

The Nixon Administration has tried to justify such actions by complaining that it has been the target of exceptional persecution by the media. Why it should suppose this is hard to fathom. Not only has 80 per cent of the press backed Mr. Nixon in two elections, but the Presidency has supreme resources of its own in the field of communications, and no previous President has used them more systematically. In his relationship to the media, President Nixon can hardly be described as a pitiful, helpless giant. No President enjoys criticism, but mature Presidents recognize that, however distasteful a free press may on occasion be, it is, as Tocqueville said long ago, "the chief democratic instrument of freedom" and that in the long run government itself benefits from a healthy adversary relationship. But this is clearly not President

Nixon's view. If his Administration has its way, the American press and television will become as compliant and as faceless as the President's own Cabinet.

Still another check on Presidential war has been a President's concern for public opinion. Here again, President Nixon differs sharply from his predecessors. He explained his peculiar idea of the role of public opinion in a democracy last Oct. 12 when he scolded what he termed "the so-called opinion leaders of this country" for not responding to "the necessity to stand by the President of the United States when he makes a terribly difficult, potentially unpopular decision." It is hard to imagine an idea that would have more astounded the framers of the American Constitution. Indeed, who before President Nixon would have defined the obligation, "the necessity," of American citizens, in peacetime and outside the Government, as that of automatically approving whatever a President wants to do? In the past it was naively supposed that the American system would work best when American citizens spoke their minds and consciences.

I F President Nixon dismisses public opinion in the United States as disobedient and refractory when it dares dissent from the President, he is even more scornful of what in the past has served as another check on Presidential war—that is, the opinion of foreign nations. The authors of "The Federalist" emphasized the indispensability of "an attention to the judgment of other nations. . . . In doubtful cases, particularly where the national councils may be warped by some strong passion or momentary interest, the presumed or known opinion of the impartial world may be the best guide that can be followed. What has not America lost by her want of character with foreign nations; and how many errors and follies would she not have avoided, if the justice and propriety of her measures had, in every instance, been previously tried by the light in which they would probably appear to the unbiased part of mankind?" President Nixon's attitude could not be

"Most alarming of all . . . has been the deletion, so far as high policy is concerned, of the State Department."

more different. It is concisely revealed by the studied contempt with which he has treated the United Nations. Only recently, he made it perfectly clear that he regards the post of United States Ambassador to the United Nations as less important than that of chairman of the Republican National Committee; at least one supposes that he thought he was promoting, not demoting, George Bush.

I began by suggesting that on issues of war and peace the American President is very likely the most absolute monarch in the world of great powers. The Soviet Union is in other respects a dictatorship, but, before Brezhnev makes a new move in foreign affairs, he must touch base with a diversity of forces in the Government and the party. It would be hard to name anyone with whom President Nixon touched base before he invaded Cambodia or resumed the obliteration of North Vietnam. Moreover, in other countries, dictatorships as well as democracies, failure in foreign policy can lead to political oblivion: Anthony Eden could not survive Suez, and in time the Cuban missile crisis did in Khrushchev. But Nixon, his tenure assured by the rigidity of the quadrennial election, will be running things in the United States until January, 1977.

With checks both written and unwritten inoperative, with Congress impotent, the executive establishment feeble and subservient, press and television intimidated, national opinion disdained, foreign opinion rejected, the fear of dismissal eliminated, our President is free to indulge his most private resentments and rages in the conduct of foreign affairs, and to do so without a word of accounting to Congress and the American people. Thus, on Dec. 18 he began the heaviest bombing of the whole ghastly war, but had not, by the time this article went to press, nearly a fortnight later, personally vouchsafed any

form of explanation to the nation or to the world. Unidentified White House officials did say, however, to The New York Times, that the President intended the terror to convey to Hanoi "the extent of his anger over what the officials say he regards as an 11th-hour reneging on peace terms believed to be settled." Historians will have to settle the point as to which side started reneging first, though strong evidence suggests that it was the Americans. But we will all have to suffer the consequences of a President whose policy, in the curt summation of that sober Scotsman, Mr. Reston of The Times, has become that of "war by tantrum."

Four more years? Is the American democracy really unable to fix any limits to the President's power to make war? The first line of defense must be the United States Congress, whose abdication over the years has contributed so much to the trouble we are in. The Senate passed a so-called War Powers Bill in April, 1972, but Vietnam was specifically exempted from its operations. In any case, though its objective is admirable, the bill itself is both unduly rigid and unduly permissive. Had it been on the statute book in past years, it would have prevented Roosevelt from protecting the British lifeline in the North Atlantic in 1941, and it would not have prevented Johnson from escalating the war in Vietnam. Given the power of any President to dominate the scene with his own version of a *casus belli*, the War Powers Bill, if it is ever enacted, would be more likely to become a means of inducing formal Congressional approval of warlike Presidential acts than of preventing such acts.

Congress must find another route to end American involvement in Indochina. But does Congress really possess the courage to assert those rights the loss of which has been such a constant and tedious theme of Congressional lamentation and self - pity? Perhaps it will at long last make a determined effort to reclaim its constitutional authority. The issue here is not (as some opponents of the war mistakenly suppose) the question of formal declaration of war. Even in the 18th century, as Hamilton wrote in "The Federalist," the ceremony

of formal declaration "has of late fallen into disuse." A decade after the adoption of the Constitution, Congress without a declaration but by legislative action brought the United States into naval war with France. As Chief Justice Marshall put it in deciding a case that arose out of the war: "The Congress may authorize general hostilities . . . or partial war." But, whether the hostilities be general or limited, war was considered to require Congressional authorization, and this is the issue today. It has been

two-thirds vote of the Senate is required for conviction, with the Chief Justice presiding over the trial. If it seems unlikely that a President elected with more than 60 per cent of the vote should find himself in such a plight, one has only to reflect on the fate of the three other Presidents this century who also took more than 60 per cent—Harding, Franklin Roosevelt and Johnson, all of whom were in serious political trouble a year or two after their triumphs. Still, at this point, impeachment hardly seems a

"President Johnson liked to tease Congress by flourishing the Tonkin Gulf Resolution. . . . President Nixon has abandoned even that constitutional fig leaf."

argued that Congress has implicitly authorized the Indochina war by voting appropriations in support of the war, and that argument is not without plausibility. But it is within the power of Congress to counter and cancel that argument by asserting a conflicting claim of authority.

Moreover, Congress can cut off funds for the continued prosecution of the war. But will even this restrain the President? Mr. Nixon has shown in other contexts his indifference to Congressional action. He has, for example, refused to expend funds appropriated by Congress for duly-enacted legislation. Senator Ervin recently estimated that Presidential impoundment has now reached the staggering sum of $12.7-billion. In his state of postelection euphoria, as well as in his righteous wrath over the refusal of the North Vietnamese to roll over and cry uncle, President Nixon might conceivably ignore end-the-war legislation. He might even, I suppose, try to use impounded funds to continue the war.

Should this happen, the constitutional remedy would be impeachment. Certainly such conduct would represent a considerably more serious transgression than poor Andrew Johnson's defiance of a law—the Tenure-of-Office Act — which the Supreme Court itself eventually found to be unconstitutional. The House would have to adopt an impeachment resolution; a

usable remedy or a probable outcome.

The inability to control Presidential war is now revealed as the great failure of the Constitution. That failure has not brought disaster to the nation through most of our history because most of our Presidents have been reasonably sensitive, in Justice Robert H. Jackson's great phrase, "to the political judgments of their contemporaries and to the moral judgments of history." When they have not been particularly responsive to the Constitution, the unwritten checks—above all, the power of opinion—have made them so. If no structural solution is now visible, the best hope is to reinvigorate the unwritten checks. Not only must Congress assert itself, but newspapers and television, governors and mayors, Mr. Nixon's "so-called opinion leaders" and plain citizens must demand an end to Presidential war. Where, for example, are all those virtuous conservative pillars of business and the bar who have spent most of their adult lives wailing about the Constitution? Where are they when what is threatened is not their money but the peace of the world? Where are they when the Constitution really needs them? Perhaps President Nixon is right, and in the end Americans are just like children in the family. Or perhaps Lincoln was right when he said: "No man is good enough to govern another man without that other's consent." ∎

★★

33

Jimmy Carter's Ruling Class   Roger Morris

When he campaigned for the presidency, Jimmy Carter tried to convince the public that he was an "outsider" to Washington. As such, he would be free of established interests and, therefore, better able to serve the vast majority of Americans. But as president, it appears that Carter has come to rely upon a number of Washington "insiders." This is the theme of "Jimmy Carter's Ruling Class" by Roger Morris. Morris provides a character portrait of President Carter's cabinet. As a group, what socioeconomic interests seem to be represented among cabinet members? Five of the Carter cabinet members come from the previous Democratic administration of Lyndon Johnson. Who are they? Could you consider them to be "organization men"? If they are, what values seem to characterize these persons who seek power through bureaucratic organizations?

Do the same characteristics that dominate cabinet members also characterize Carter's "middle management"? Among this group of administrators, Morris is impressed by the absence of "anybody with an outspoken and independent cast of mind." Under this presumption, how would Morris explain the behavior of Andrew Young, who was appointed United Nations ambassador by Carter? It is noted that Carter's cabinet resembles those of Republican presidents, for example, Nixon's. This is one reason, Morris feels, why public policy does not change much even though presidents do change. Why is that the case?

Morris observes that over time the qualities of cabinet leadership have "shifted steadily from qualities of intellect or representative politics to the weight of money." Of what importance is this assertion, if true? Is American government today dominated by a "ruling class" compared to earlier periods in our history? If so, could this have an effect on public policy?

★ ★ ★

JIMMY CARTER'S RULING CLASS

The shared ethic of the Carter Cabinet is an
accommodation with the interest of the wealthy

by Roger Morris

*I can tell you that there is a major and
fundamental issue taking shape in this election year. That issue is the division between the "insiders" and the "outsiders."
. . . The people of this country know from
bitter experience that we are not going to
get these changes merely by shifting around
the same group of insiders. . . . The insiders
have had their chance and they have not
delivered. And their time has run out. The
time has come for the great majority of
Americans—those who have for too long
been on the outside looking in—to have a
President who will turn the government of
this country inside out.* —Jimmy Carter
February 17, 1976

A POLITICAL RIDDLE for our time:
What body of Jimmy Carter's "outsiders" has eleven heads, about seventy cumulative years on the public
payroll, some thirty corporate directorships,
and an average 1976 income of $211,000?

Answer: the Cabinet of the United States.
(You know, the one you got on that promise
to turn the government "inside out.")

Class, as everyone knows, is one of those
dirty, forbidden words in the American political vernacular, and never more obscene than
when prefaced by *ruling.* Twentieth-century
education and cynicism aside, polls and politicians testify that we continue overwhelmingly to believe the U.S. is a "government of

the people, by the people, and for the people."
We are a country that has always exercised
and tolerated privilege more easily than we
could discuss it. And nothing is so congenial
to a ruling class as this sort of rhetorical refusal to have one.

But now, however, there is a general awareness that what happened in Washington last
January was something less than a born-again
American revolution of the obscure and the excluded. From the Cabinet through the hundreds of policy positions below in the federal
bureaucracy, Jimmy Carter has installed or
kept on a more than slightly used regime of
established figures. They turn out to be patrons and protégés who have been governing
us for some time, if not directly from the
Potomac, then from corporate headquarters,
venerable law firms, university viceroyalties,
or the special-interest niches of Congress and
local government.

All that was apparently familiar enough,
even congenial. The *New York Times, Newsweek,* and *Time* took it easily in stride. No
indignant mobs marched on the White House.
Yet you don't have to be Karl Marx to discover that this "new" regime is dominated in
every precinct by people with shared values
and characteristics, with similar advantages
and interests to preserve, whose lives are lived
to much the same purpose, who see themselves as distinct from other groups, who
delegate and eventually pass on their power
to people strikingly like themselves. By most
definitions, those people constitute a kind of
political, social, and economic class. Given
their considerable power in Jimmy Carter's
Washington, it's a ruling one.

*Roger Morris, a grad-
uate of Harvard and
former member of the
National Security Coun-
cil and various Senate
staffs, is now a writer
living in northern New*
*Mexico. He is the au-
thor of the forthcom-
ing* Uncertain Great-
ness: Henry Kissinger
and American Foreign
Policy.

The distinction is only partly a matter of income. It is true that while the Carter Cabinet averaged $211,000 last year, not counting certain dividends and stock options, 86 percent of American families made less than $25,000. And although the median income for the rest of us is less than $14,000, the median for the roughly 300 top Washington officials under Jimmy Carter is around $40,000. But rulers do not become relatively wealthy merely because they govern. Many still take a hefty cut in pay with their first Treasury check. Moreover, they seldom come by Washington power merely because they are rich compared with the vast majority of their countrymen. Far fatter cats never become government officials, and, what's more, may not want to.

Nor are we necessarily stalking here the sinister commissions and collusions of multinational businesses on three continents, or some intricate Rockefeller revenge, or homey plots hatched in Plains. An identifiable group ends up running the country mostly because it has run it before. In that obliging world, as Richard Nixon never quite learned, conspiracies are rarely required.

No, we are governed under Jimmy Carter, as often before, by a particular species of the rich and powerful who got to be both almost incidentally because of the similar texture and warp of their adult lives. To understand their endurance in power, to fathom some of the mysteries of their government, and thus to appreciate our own plight a bit better, we just may have to start regarding them as what they seem so clearly to be—our ruling class, newly restored to health and office by a properly appreciative populist peanut farmer. Seeing Jimmy Carter as the agent of a ruling class *redux* should explain a good deal of what will—and will not—happen to us over the next eight years.

Eminent Americans

In all societies . . . two classes of people appear—a class that rules and a class that is ruled.
—Gaetano Mosca, *The Ruling Class*, 1896

CONSIDER FIRST some unvarnished brief lives of that extremely well-heeled Carter Cabinet. What matters are the marks of quality and vision and class that seldom seep through standard puff biographies or inane Congressional confirmations. Five of the secretaries come by direct primogeniture from the Johnson Administration with suitable exiles in between.

Secretary of State Cyrus Vance: Patrician schooling, marriage, and apprenticeship in a prestigious New York law firm lifted him as an LBJ protégé into the Kennedy regime, where his careful organization loyalty and lack of independent opinion enabled him to become an important but obscure policy-maker on the war and other failures. Afterward, the same values helped make him a successful corporate lawyer and pliant director of the Rockefeller Foundation, Pan Am, IBM, and the *New York Times* in the Nixon interregnum. At sixty his life is marked by no cause, issue, or question save his own advancement and acceptability.

Secretary of Defense Harold Brown: A child physics prodigy, he became house scientist, then administrator, of the military-industrial complex. At fifty he has spent nearly twenty years on government payrolls, working on laboratory development of nuclear weapons and then advocating Vietnam bombing as LBJ's Secretary of the Air Force. As President of Cal Tech during the Nixon years, he courted vast government contracts for the school. He sat on the boards of several companies (including IBM with Vance), and worked part time for the Republicans on the SALT delegation. Reputedly brilliant, he has never served any master but the larger military establishment, and never audibly questions the orthodoxy of the moment.

Secretary of the Treasury W. Michael Blumenthal: From an impoverished refugee childhood in Shanghai, he worked his way to a Ph.D., and with Princeton contacts rose in the Kennedy-Johnson regimes by handling esoteric trade issues. At the Kennedy Round in the 1960s, he efficiently and quietly negotiated widespread exploitation of the Third World by U.S. and European corporations. Offered the presidency of Bendix International, he revived the firm during the Nixon years and became a millionaire. By all accounts the sharpest mind in the Cabinet, he lives an adult life dedicated without pause or other pretense to personal gain and wealth and, for him anyway at fifty-one, the increasingly profitable status quo.

Secretary of Health, Education, and Welfare Joseph Califano: Of the two main types of Washington lawyer, the heavy and jowled and the squash-court svelte, he belongs at forty-six to the first, after a twenty-year glide that began with Harvard law, a New York legal practice, and an early job as assistant to Vance in the Pentagon. With Vance's and McNamara's patronage, he became LBJ's legislative counsel, stoutly defending the war, hiding its cost, and finally graduating into the upper reaches of Democratic party organizational politics and a lucrative Washington law practice with Edward Bennett Williams. Representing Coca-Cola, drug and chemical companies, and other wealthy clients, he made more than $500,000 in 1976.

Secretary of Housing and Urban Development Patricia Harris: A "twofer," as *Newsweek* called her, she is a woman and black (two for one for symbol-minded institutions) with, by her own modest count, twenty-nine honorary degrees and forty memberships and seats on the boards of Chase Manhattan, IBM, Scott Paper, and the National Bank of Washington, the last at the time of Tony Boyle's plunder of the United Mine Workers' pension fund. After various jobs in the government, including LBJ's Ambassador to Luxembourg, and teaching at Howard University Law, she makes, at fifty-three, more than $100,000 a year from a Washington law practice and real estate and stock holdings, and some $40,000 in corporate director's fees. "I didn't stop being the white man's nigger to become a black man's nigger," she once said in refusing the demands of protesting Howard students, who questioned both ends of the statement.

Three more are officially advertised as newcomers to power, but the resemblances in careers and clients make, as Sherlock Holmes would say, an "interesting coincidence."

Secretary of Commerce Juanita Kreps: Almost as serviceable as Patricia Harris in such matters, she is the corporate public-relations dream for the female director. She sat on eight boards, including RJ Reynolds tobacco, the New York Stock Exchange, Eastman Kodak, and Western Electric, eking out her $40,000 academic salaries as a vice-president at Duke and lecturer at the University of North Carolina with $61,150 in director's fees (and no visible dispute with any of the business practices she ostensibly oversees). A competent but unremarkable economics teacher, she soon went into administration at Duke, and lives her life, with her banking professor husband, in a careful, unbroken ascent through academic bureaucracy, tame government consultancies, mounting stock dividends, and, of course, those directorships, which certify her, at fifty-six, as a "safe" woman for the biggest board of all in the White House.

Secretary of Labor Ray Marshall: The low-income academic in the Cabinet, he made only $75,000 last year, including $40,000 at the University of Texas and $30,000 as a consultant, with a house and ranch worth at least $150,000. He is a bright, widely published labor economist with memberships in several nonprofit organizations promoting employment and improved labor relations. But his career has never left the smooth groove of academic politics lubricated by government money. From 1970 he ran a center at Texas with a steady stream of Labor Department subsidies (and no obstreperous research or projects to threaten it). He served the Johnson and Nixon regimes on some nine consulting panels with scarcely a ripple. Reputedly an indifferent chairman of the University of Texas economics department (now come to manage Labor's unruly domains), his résumé and colleagues portray him as intent on that ultimate featherbedding: high government office.

Attorney General Griffin Bell: What can one say about an obscure boy from Americus, Georgia, who ends up at fifty-eight with: (a) an income of $155,000 a year; (b) large investments in Coca-Cola (one of his law clients as well as Califano's) and the National Bank of Georgia (the one Budget Director Bert Lance ran and which loaned money to Jimmy Carter); (c) the praise of both segregationists and middle-class blacks after a shady political accommodation with racism; (d) an obscure record on the federal appeals bench; and (e) the highest position at the Justice Department? You could say he knows the name of the game, and was ready to play it to the top when his fellow Georgian (and game player) took him to Washington.

The remaining three Cabinet members, politicians all, fulfill the time-honored ruling-class tradition of providing certain special interests with secretaries they can come to think of as their own. But even if these secretaries are "specialists" in that sense, their lives have the same recognizable contours.

Secretary of Transportation Brock Adams: The storybook achiever's résumé. A Phi Beta Kappa, Adams earned a scholarship to Harvard Law School and eventual partnership in a prestigious Seattle firm. After Kennedy appointed him U.S. Attorney for western Washington, he won six straight Congressional terms from Seattle with chairmanships of key committees and subcommittees, wholesome memberships in everything from the Civic Unity Committee to the local tennis club, and a net worth, at fifty, of more than $150,000. What the résumé doesn't show is how one goes along to get along so impressively. In Congress he was the unswerving representative of the Boeing Corporation, and the intimate friend of the airlines, railroads, and trucking industry.

Secretary of the Interior Cecil Andrus: Presumably the representative of the nation's poor, he made only $42,000 as governor of Idaho, and, with mining shares and other assets, he is worth, at forty-six, only about $108,000, the Cabinet poverty level. An insurance man with one year of college and memberships in such organizations as the VFW and Ducks Unlimited, he adds a more plebeian touch. But as the first Democratic governor of Idaho in twenty-four years, his conservative economic policies pleased big business while token environmental measures blunted the popular agitation on that issue and still opened the state to big mines and developers. (Note: The ruling class tends to prefer Western politicians for Interior, and, like all liberal institutions, occasionally lowers admission standards to fill the quota.)

Secretary of Agriculture Bob Bergland: He worked and then inherited a $500,000 farm in northern Minnesota, meanwhile rising through the Farmers' Union and state farm bureaucracies, was an assistant administrator in the Agriculture Department from 1961 to 1968, and, after one losing run, won a Democratic Congressional seat in 1970. During the 1970 campaign (though casualties in his district were among the highest in the state), he discreetly ignored the Vietnam war for fear of alienating powerful farm organizations and agribusiness support. In Congress he was the quiet go-between for Southern agricultural interests and the Northern market combines. For the past twenty of his forty-nine years he has variously served, and been enriched by, a government-backed monopoly system victimizing consumers and small farmers alike, to whose class, in any case, he has long since ceased to belong.

The list could go on among the most senior Carter appointees. There is the powerful Bert Lance, the Director of Management and Budget, whose background and girth exude the ubiquitous banking-corporate ethic and business politics in Atlanta to match; or the National Security Adviser, Zbigniew Brzezinski, house academic with a career marked by discreet government consultation, prolix orthodox writings, and corporate patronage.

An apparent exception is Vice-President Walter Mondale, the former Democratic Senator from Minnesota. A bright liberal raised by the state's machine (that it was liberal obscured in some quarters that it was, and is, indeed a machine), Mondale brought to the Carter regime a cynical wit, which endeared him to press and colleagues alike, and an often remarkable record of defending awkward causes, from busing to migrant labor to a national child-care plan. But behind the intelligence, humor, and conscience was another Mondale. He has also been, successively, the loyal young party lawyer in middle-class Minneapolis-St. Paul; the loyal appointed state attorney general; the loyal appointed Senator who backed his President's war until 1970 and supported those admirable issues that did not affect his largely white, affluent Minnesota constituency while nimbly dodging questions about topics such as abortion, which were closer to home. Now he is Carter's more conspicuous but equally loyal Vice-President, his presence at high-level meetings noticed more than the Administration's cutback on a dozen key reforms, from welfare to energy to health care, to which Mondale was ostensibly committed a year ago.

A S THESE PROFILES suggest, there are several characteristics that cut across the lives of our rulers, and entitle them to class membership. Though suitably discreet, the common devotion of these people, the protoplasm of their power, is money. The incumbent President and Cabinet are unimaginable in or near high office without money and the distinctions earned by acquiring it either for themselves or for others. No other comparable or unrelated attainment marks their ascent; no other achievement singles them out so clearly from the crowd of fellow citizens of otherwise identical merit. Amid the hardscrabble of Plains, after all, Carter's own peanut fortune makes him a veritable J. Pierpont Morgan. As the Cabinet portfolios attest, the monetary rewards of ruling-class membership are similarly remarkable. Those who pass back and forth through government can customarily count on their market value doubling or even tripling when they return carrying profits and prestige to the private sector—witness the handsome sinecures of the former Nixon-Ford officials as well as the lucrative interludes of Vance, Blumenthal, or Harris between the Johnson and Carter regimes.

The deeper point about the ruling class is not so much that its members have money as that they accept, respect, admire, and serve it as the overriding social-political value—that they understand its unchallenged centrality in American life and government. The bribe and the bought campaign may be nearly extinct in American politics, but the force of money as social cachet, and as the primary national interest at home and abroad, remains supreme. The ethic of their advance is thus still very much a basic accommodation with money, and an inexhaustible tolerance for the demands of careers nurtured by money power. They may gain no more themselves, it is true, than the ever-perishable authority of hired hands. And in that sense, within the larger governance of money, they are often more nearly a *presiding* than a ruling class, hostage to the organizations and mores that propel them to the top, knowing that the system that giveth also taketh away. For all that, however, it is a hallmark of our rulers that the quiet omnipotence of money is rarely acknowledged. So powerful, so pervasive, it is the god no one need audibly profess, the ethos so vulgar yet pivotal that it is downright gauche to mention it.

But in that, it should be stated quickly, Carter's senior officials are scarcely different from their Republican predecessors. Remember the exciting and varied Nixon Cabinet of 1969? William Rogers (a corporate lawyer) at State, David Kennedy (a banker) at Treasury, Rep. Melvin Laird at Defense, John Volpe (a construction magnate and state governor) at Transportation, and so on, not to mention a carefully turned-out Rockefeller retainer and academic politician named Henry Kissinger. Ironically, what most distinguishes Jimmy Carter's "outsiders" from that GOP regime of privilege and power is that present Cabinet members are individually and collectively far wealthier.

Much of this is apparent even on the surface of the Carter Cabinet biographies. Sometimes less visible is the structure of their power, the rules by which they flourish and govern, and suffer a certain melancholy along with the perquisites. For all the differences in time and place, there is a decided modern bureaucratic orthodoxy and conformity to their progress, and, most revealing, in their obvious sense of themselves (or lack of it). Without notable exception, they are a group of organizational aspirants and dependents, their lives defined and their careers thrust onward by the institutional perch of the moment in government, law firm, university, corporation. They are uniformly undistinguished outside an organizational setting, outside the expectations and rewards it gives them. That they have survived and prospered so well in their oligarchies of American life marks them plainly.

Within the class, they have been political, and politic, in the rudimentary sense of those words. They have obviously learned whose boots wanted licking, and when and how. Like all those of attained rank they have been intent on appearances, if only because a safe reputation is the modern substitute not merely for noble birth, but for talent as well. To the degree intellect plays a part—and as a threat to conformity it's a risky possession—it is usually an advertisement, and one in which no one reads the fine print. So last January it was far more important, as Washington gossip noted, that Zbigniew Brzezinski was a protégé of David Rockefeller's and a guest at Averell Harriman's Georgetown house than that he was the author of an unbroken succession of misguided, mediocre books. Like their predecessors for the past three decades, the ranking advisers to Jimmy Carter are hardly the best and the brightest from among a large and generously gifted population. (Indeed, counting their collective debacles from the LBJ era as well as the pedestrian quality of their other performances, they may even be worse and duller than usual.) They are just the most available, and often the least exceptionable, from among a class of institutional survivors. And once more the connecting thread of money is crucial if also paradoxical. In many ways, these people are precisely the opposite of the classic capitalist. In place of boldness, risk, and innovation, they prize routine, safety, and acceptability.

Middle management

SO BY THE TRADITIONS of the class, there are three main categories among our rulers. The most numerous, of course, are the organization men whose parent institutions cluster geographically or financially around Washington. Then there are the few customary President's men, separated from the others perhaps by their narrower local base around the candidate, but practiced in business, state government, or simply the campaign in the same class rules. Finally, there are the politicians, if not in the wider

sense that Sam Rayburn meant when he made that oracular remark to Lyndon Johnson in the early 1960s that he'd feel better if those fellows Rusk, Bundy, and McNamara had just once "run for sheriff."

For most of Carter's proconsuls, the national watershed was not Watergate but Vietnam. All of them were clearly in the ready pool of potential rulers regardless of Richard Nixon's fate, and would have succeeded sooner or later in a Democratic regime. It was the war and its selective wreckage of reputations that cleared away the lodged mandarinate of the 1960s. The departure of the Bundys and Rostows made room for Vance and Brown and Brzezinski; the tarnish on Kennedy and Johnson domestic policies similarly opened the way to second-rank aspirants such as Harris, Califano, and Marshall; electoral casualties of the war years were replaced in office or on key committees by people like Bergland and Adams. Never mind that many of the successors were equally culpable for the folly and deception and waste of it all. They were relatively obscure in a politics of the conspicuous.

The most important mark of the ruling class, then, is this sameness of values. Yet the point is somehow frequently missed. Thus critics look for some more precise cabal in the Trilateral Commission, the agency of U.S., European, and Japanese multinational corporations built by David Rockefeller on Brzezinski's concept, and including in its ranks Carter, Mondale, Vance, Brown, Blumenthal, U.N. Ambassador Andrew Young, and several lesser officials. But if the commission displays a certain embarrassing elitism, a preference for far-flung profits, and even a benign distaste for unruly democracies, it is because Vance et al. came to it with long-demonstrated fealty to that ethos. The American "trilateralists" were simply doing what came naturally from their own lives and ambitions by joining such a group. They and *Time* magazine can thus honestly dismiss the conspiracy talk as kooky, while behaving in office much as their like-minded peers on the commission would hope.

The same chicken-and-egg problem clouds the ultimate political coup of the ruling class —its members' selection for office by the President. But again such people do not somehow conspire to be picked, nor does a scheming politician, even one so shrewd as Jimmy Carter, gather them to his purposes by pre-arranged plan. It is true that Vance, Brzezinski, and others early volunteered to advise Carter, and that the candidate knew some of them from the trilateral meetings. Maneuver and calculation obviously played a role on all sides. But mostly they are there sitting in Carter's Cabinet room, much as they sat at the Trilateral Commission, or at other committees and showplaces, because of the largely tacit understanding, crucial to all ruling classes, that they should be. The political essence and peril here, like that of royal marriages, is inbreeding. Having aspired to the ruling class and played the game themselves, striving politicians such as Johnson or Carter summon such people because they are expected to, because they are indeed "successful," and because their very mode of success makes them politically known, experienced, and reliable. They were "good managers," Carter announced of his new Cabinet, wishing as always to be little more himself, and knowing that it was not the meek (read outsiders), but rather the organization men, who would inherit the earth.

A ruling group is a ruling group so long as it can nominate its successors. The Party is not concerned with perpetuating its blood but with perpetuating itself. Who wields power is not important provided that the hierarchical structure remains always the same.
— George Orwell, *1984*

POLITICAL THEORISTS have long been fascinated by the capacity of ruling classes to rejuvenate themselves. Ingrown aristocracies soon peter out on the congenital indifference or idiocy of their offspring (witness some of our oldest allies). But the modern political and economic elites of the industrial state have generally been able to replenish themselves from the lower estates, and our own ruling class is an apt example, drawing to its subordinate offices such a heavy transfusion of younger candidate members. The acolytes come from the educational and general civil-rights opportunities opened by the affluence and reforms of the past quarter-century, particularly the post-Sputnik panic that put dependable, ambitious middle-class kids on fast tracks. More immediately, they flock to Carter's sub-Cabinet and bureaucratic offices from the junior seats of law firms, the middle levels of business, some foundation sinecures of corporate money, and, notably, from the Democratic Congressional staffs—which always provided some recruits, but in the swollen bureaucratic growth of the Congress in the past eight years now form one of the largest pools.

The new people are absorbed by the same ethic of advance and reward that spurred their elders, and are shielded from obstreperous rivals by the same ostracism—deliberate or self-inflicted—which keeps the ranks free of Vietnam dissenters, unassimilated minorities, or anybody with an outspoken and independent cast of mind. The tolerable mobility of American life saves the ruling class not only from revolution, but from itself.

Read after the repetitious biographies of their Cabinet superiors, the résumés of the vast majority of middle-level Carter appointees are a bad dose of *déjà lu*. Of the eleven deputy secretaries, not one comes from a broader spectrum of American life. Drawn predominantly from corporate law, business, and Congressional bureaucracies, they are people who, like their patrons, live at the most remote reaches of income and social contact. The names, degrees, and positions stretch on by the dozens, almost invariably tied to financial or bureaucratic tests—this firm or that center, this vice-presidency or that fellowship, all within respectable confines, their leisurely sequence testifying to the holder's understanding of the requirements of such credentials.

In the welter of such cases, three examples are representative. Thus the Dartmouth alumni magazine proudly announces the appointment of Richard Beattie, class of '61, to supervise 350 lawyers as HEW's deputy general counsel. Beattie is moving from his comfortable home in Rye, New York, and a Manhattan partnership at Simpson, Thacher and Bartlett (Vance's old firm), where he specialized in corporate finance. He has been a trustee of one corporation providing legal services for the poor and on the legal-assistance committee of the New York bar. His qualifications, or motivation, for governing at HEW are not clear from the résumé—or are they? Bert Carp is the well-thought-of assistant director of the White House Domestic Council, a key policy-making job. He is a lawyer who comes to the regime from the Carter campaign staff and before that from Mondale's Senate staff. Almost his entire experience and qualification is in his plodding years of service as Capitol Hill bureaucrat and, of course, his allegiance to Mondale. He has patiently hung on, and it is paying off. Anthony Lake (Harvard class of '61) is the State Department director of policy planning. After working and rising as a foreign-service officer under Henry Cabot Lodge, Nicholas Katzenbach, and Henry Kissinger, he resigned over the 1970 invasion of Cambodia. In a series of jobs for the 1972 Muskie campaign, the Council on Foreign Relations, and the Carnegie Endowment, he criticized Nixon's foreign policy, but never his former or future Democratic employers. Privately he disdained the grasping and isolation of the foreign-affairs elite, and publicly he cultivated and served them. At Vance's urging, he worked on the campaign and the transition, and succeeded to his place in the State Department. At thirty-eight, he has spent most of his adult life in Washington, in quest of the job he now has.

Patronage is the lifeblood of such candidate members. In a tiny universe where murmured opinions among the older men spur and sink careers, one does not readily ask larger questions about the character and quality of lives. As for the patronage itself, it can be generously bipartisan once basic issues of reliability are settled. For instance, it was Joseph Califano who gave us Alexander Haig, by recommending Haig to Kissinger in 1969 on the strength of Haig's work for Califano at the Pentagon. Haig went on to play a critical role in the Vietnam policy of 1969-72, and of course was Richard Nixon's loyal chief of staff in the last year of the regime.

But then the Carter Administration has benefited from the ruling class's bipartisanship, too. In addition to Haig, who is now NATO Supreme Commander, the Administration has rehired at the White House, State Department, and Pentagon more than a dozen key "non-career" officials who worked prominently for the Nixon regime. At the National Security Council Staff, for example, the apparently noncontroversial fields of intelligence and international economics are under the same men who did the job for Kissinger for eight years.

Polite obscurity

In general, the powerful and the influential in our society shape the laws and have a great influence on the legislature or the Congress. This creates a reluctance to change because the powerful and the influential have carved out for themselves or have inherited a privileged position in society, of wealth or social prominence or higher education or opportunity for the future. —Jimmy Carter, May 4, 1974

HAVING THE SAME PEOPLE in policy positions, or at least the same kind of people, helps answer the quadrennial public puzzle as to why elections don't seem to change government policy all that much. Certainly there are tactical differences within the ruling class, bitter personal rivalries (what boardroom hasn't seen them?), and old alignments of Right and Left. But along with their blanketing ethic and patron-

age renewal, the other distinguishing feature of our governors is their instinctive aversion to certain issues and policies.

Not surprisingly, there is a club ordinance against genuinely controlling corporate power (and not just those corporations whose boards bequeathed us Cabinet officers). Thus the Administration speaks boldly on South Africa, but is silent about the petty apartheid of U.S. firms in that country, such as Coca-Cola or General Motors, or for that matter, the discrimination and exploitation by other U.S. corporations in every other region of the world. When the house radical, Andrew Young, speaks of black "liberation" in South Africa, it is in a speech extolling the virtues of corporate profit-sharing with blacks in Atlanta. Presumably, the deeper foreign-policy message is that Fascism is bad for business. Another taboo subject is America's own apartheid, the still rampant residential segregation which mocks school desegregation and a generation of legal progress. The Carter regime, after its leader's brief brush with "ethnic purity," can attack the hidden disgrace no more than its predecessors, shrinking from the vast money, popular prejudice, and governmental complicity that underlie it.

The essence of the ruling class is obscurity —its social obscurity from the rest of the country, and the political obscurity of its own responsibility for government. Sealed off by its comparative wealth and security, preoccupied with its own demanding ethic, it is the most serious casualty of what Archibald MacLeish called the divorce between "knowing and feeling," between the relentless rain of statistics or information about the problems of the nation and the capacity to feel or experience the human reality. The problem is too fundamental. What indeed does Califano or Bell, so lately absorbed in Coca-Cola's corporate tribulations, know of babies stuffed into garbage cans in the Bronx? To command Washington bureaucracies of legendary recalcitrance, Jimmy Carter hired a Cabinet and sub-Cabinet of bureaucratic survivors whose principal distinction has been their tractability. To deal with national problems of want and inequity comes a Democratic regime of the relatively rich and insular. But simple as the connection is, public discussion of the results is still rare, perhaps because it would shatter the most sustaining myths of our electoral democracy. Consider the Urban League's reluctant, almost incredulous reaction this summer to the all too evident observation by Vernon Jordan that the Carter Administration had done so much less than its leader had promised for black Americans. What exactly did the worldly members of the league expect, one might ask, of rulers who reside in spirit and place on the other side of that racial *cordon sanitaire* partitioning every major American city?

The elite's concern with class politics, the aversion to controversy or public failure as career obstacles, the cultivated habits of manipulation, only build on this sharp, strangely accepted segregation of rulers and ruled in America. The product is a chronic furtiveness which can be amazingly similar across the outward differences of party and circumstance. Having worked for both, I can testify that the preparation for a press conference—the studied shaving of answers, the nervous sarcasm about press and public—is largely the same for Henry Kissinger in the West Basement of the Nixon White House as for Walter Mondale in the Senate Office Building.

The quintessential issue for the ruling class is energy. Policy begins by ruling out any breakup of the monopoly that controls the principal fuels, and proceeds by promulgating a series of marginal but endlessly debatable controls. For some forty years, such programs have been the fetish, and authentic public control the anathema of the ruling class. But if the charade continues in foreign and domestic economic matters, there is a new, perhaps ultimately more disturbing, set of issues emerging. By the limits of its temperament and intellect, not to mention experience, the ruling class is visibly at sea when confronted by questions such as abortion or the rights of homosexuals. Thus Mondale's revealing admission—after walking out on a recent speech in California when heckled by homosexuals —that he did not feel "comfortable" with such people. A generation that has conditioned itself to such self-serving conformity in so many ways may be able to deal with poverty, much as a foundation executive charts a selling campaign in the slums. But when the issue cuts across and deep through the old categories to expose questions of values, the ruling class is by definition in trouble.

The policy evasions can long survive, however, because Mondale can walk away from the hecklers, and the larger Washington government to which he returns is as "uncomfortable" with them as he. By a kind of old-boy formalism—a combination of medieval personal homage and a certain modern procedural deference—the ruling class makes its peace with the rest of Congress and the press, both with their own oligarchies to protect, and both still satisfied to put form and prerogative over substance.

How did we come to be ruled by the ersatz expertise of people who are adept only at the rules of their confined world? Like the rest of us, most American historians are loath to talk in unpatriotic class terms. But it is clear that between the age of Jefferson and the settlement of the frontier a century later, the balance of government shifted steadily from qualities of intellect or representative politics to the weight of money. The turning point probably came, however, with the erection of a modern interventionist government in the Thirties and Forties, making the Washington bureaucracies an often caricatured replica of large economic organizations, and fastening on the taxpayer (as on the shareholder and consumer) the management of the organization's wards, who by definition were bred to manage little more than their own rise. The ruling class owes much of its status to the bigness of government and to the myth of competence in institutional politics, neither of which seems likely to change in our lifetime. What is worse about the present regime, as distinct from its Republican forerunners, is that there has been so much pretense—and so much apparent public credulity—that it is something else. In fact, the Carter Administration has not only restored to office the predictable succession of Johnson exiles, but also taken on many of the younger public-interest advocates in consumerism, auto saftey, or environmental affairs who had gathered in Washington opposition over the past several years. After nearly a year, the effect has been to disarm public lobbies and to corrupt once antibureaucratic elements, with no appreciable effect on government policy. A ruling class prefers nothing so much, after all, as to rule.

Programs of a political nature are important end products of social quality that can be effective only if the underlying structure of social values is right. The social values are right only if the individual values are right. —Robert M. Pirsig
Zen and the Art of Motorcycle Maintenance

HAVING EMBRACED lives as scenarios, our rulers seem to have pinned the fate of the rest of us to that dubious philosophy. Not that the country was ever an Eden misled; some of the most confining and antidemocratic impulses of the ruling class—its reverence for money, its inertia, its worship of empty credentials and advertisements—grow from cultural flaws that are truly national. Yet whether their values are derived or imposed, our governors project an unflattering image of America. Beyond a Washington regime in ceaseless jockeying, we have become a people similarly craven for means without regard for the ends —for the *use* of technology and bureaucracy to generate more of both, without asking, any more than our rulers pause to ask about their lives and system, about the quality or meaning of it all. Missing most of all from the ruling class—and perhaps the absence is essential to its serenity, if not its survival—is a sense of themselves beyond the résumé entry of the moment, a genuine seriousness of commitment beyond self. And that is missing, too, in the nation they govern.

There is, of course, inevitable pathos and melancholy in such a life. That is why, as a final trait, our rulers are a class with so much palpable privilege and so comparatively little visible *élan*.

Seen at close range, our rulers are neither particularly impressive in their power nor contemptible for its misplacement. They are, as one might expect from their sociology, generally ordinary creatures, often ensnared in the system and in a sense forlornly unwilling victims of it as much as the citizenry over whom they preside. The toll is frequently most awful on families. There was a moment in 1975, for example, when two of Henry Kissinger's most senior State Department aides could be found anxiously visiting the same adolescent ward of a Washington psychiatric hospital, their children in some part the casualties of too many years of maneuver and ambition.

The attrition of the "use" philosophy on its practitioners is relentless, from the loaded briefing books prepared late at night to the deadening interagency meetings and the dinners with Xerox-copy superiors and spouses. Many of the junior men of the Carter regime, such as Anthony Lake in the State Department, now sadly find themselves enduring all that, much as they did under Johnson or Nixon, and with questions that can never be answered. We have long been held fast by such mores, but seldom with more false sentiment and sheer misrepresentation than under this Jimmy Carter regime of "outsiders." There may come a moment when the nation demands more authentic leadership than our shallow leaders can muster, more courage than organization men have left. But we seem destined for some time to go on knowing far more than we feel—and wondering in willing naiveté why government does not represent us.

Like most ruling classes, ours is probably entrenched until, by degeneration, it drives itself from power. At least in that sense, 1984 is not only the date of the next probable shuffle of offices; it is a state of the Union that is already here. □

★★

34 The Swelling of the Presidency   Thomas E. Cronin

This essay by Thomas Cronin focuses on the Executive Office of the President. As the title indicates, the number of employees working in the Executive Office of the President has grown significantly in recent years. Though this article was written during President Nixon's second term, the pattern of growth has not changed since then. Are the problems raised here contemporary in origin, or were they evident earlier? Cronin finds it curious that a significant increase in the president's staff occurred during Nixon's term, even though Nixon claimed to be a conservative and to be management-minded. Does bureaucratic growth, therefore, occur despite presidential efforts and ideology?

Cronin shares the concern of other political scientists about these circumstances in the executive branch. What adverse consequences can you see in the uncontrolled growth of presidential staff? With this excessive growth has the presidential staff gained increased influence at the expense of the cabinet? What are the reasons for the growth? Have Cronin's observations remained intact since Carter's election? Do you find the current Executive Office troubled by excessive growth? The analogy has been made that, just as the monarch had his court, the president now has his staff. To what extent is this analogy appropriate to President Carter's relationship to his White House staff?

★ ★ ★

THE SWELLING OF THE PRESIDENCY

BY THOMAS E. CRONIN

The number of government employees working directly under the President of the United States has grown an alarming 20 per cent in the last four years, and now approaches the size of the State Department's domestic bureaucracy. A White House watcher weighs the consequences of the burgeoning "Presidential Establishment."

he advent of Richard Nixon's second term in the White House is marked by an uncommon amount of concern, in Congress and elsewhere, about the expansion of presidential power and manpower. Even the President himself is ostensibly among those who are troubled. Soon after his re-election, Mr. Nixon announced that he was planning to pare back the presidential staff. And in recent days, the President has said he is taking action to cut the presidential workforce in half and to "substantially" reduce the number of organizations that now come under the White House. Mr. Nixon's

Thomas E. Cronin, a visiting fellow at the Center for the Study of Democratic Institutions in Santa Barbara, is coauthor and editor of The Presidential Advisory System *and author of* The State of the Presidency, *to be published this year.*

announcements have no doubt been prompted in part by a desire to add drama and an aura of change to the commencement of his second term. But he also seems genuinely worried that the presidency may have grown so large and top-heavy that it now weakens rather than strengthens his ability to manage the federal government. His fears are justified.

The presidency has, in fact, grown a full 20 per cent in the last four years alone in terms of the number of people who are employed directly under the President. It has swelled to the point where it is now only a little short of the State Department's sprawling domestic bureaucracy in size.

This burgeoning growth of the presidency has, in the process, made the traditional civics textbook picture of the executive branch of our government nearly obsolete. According to this view, the executive branch is more or less neatly divided into Cabinet departments and their secretaries, agencies and their heads, and the President. A more contemporary view takes note of a few prominent presidential aides and refers to them as the "White House staff." But neither view adequately recognizes the large and growing coterie that surrounds the President and is made up of dozens of assistants, hundreds of presidential advisers, and thousands of members of an institutional amalgam called the Executive Office of the President. While the men and women in these categories all fall directly under the President in the organizational charts, there is no generally used term for their common terrain. But it has swelled so much in size and scope in recent years, and has become such an important part of the federal government, that it deserves its own designation. Most apt perhaps is the Presidential Establishment.

The Presidential Establishment today embraces more than twenty support staffs (the White House Office, National Security Council, and Office of Management and Budget, etc.) and advisory offices (Council of Economic Advisers, Office of Science and Technology, and Office of Telecommunications Policy, etc.). It has spawned a

vast proliferation of ranks and titles to go with its proliferation of functions (Counsel to the President, Assistant to the President, Special Counselor, Special Assistant, Special Consultant, Director, Staff Director, etc.). "The White House now has enough people with fancy titles to populate a Gilbert and Sullivan comic opera," Congressman Morris Udall has reasonably enough observed.

There are no official figures on the size of the Presidential Establishment, and standard body counts vary widely depending on who is and who is not included in the count, but by one frequently used reckoning, between five and six thousand people work for the President of the United States. Payroll and maintenance costs for this staff run between $100 million and $150 million a year. (These figures include the Office of Economic Opportunity (OEO), which is an Executive Office agency and employs two thousand people, but not the roughly fifteen thousand-man Central Intelligence Agency, although that, too, is directly responsible to the Chief Executive.) These "White House" workers have long since outgrown the White House itself and now occupy not only two wings of the executive mansion but three nearby high-rise office buildings as well.

The expansion of the Presidential Establishment, it should be emphasized, is by no means only a phenomenon of the Nixon years. The number of employees under the President has been growing steadily since the early 1900s when only a few dozen people served in the White House entourage, at a cost of less than a few hundred thousand dollars annually. Congress's research arm, the Congressional Research Service, has compiled a count that underlines in particular the accelerated increase in the last two decades. This compilation shows that between 1954 and 1971 the number of presidential advisers has grown from 25 to 45, the White House staff from 266 to 600, and the Executive Office staff from 1,175 to 5,395.

But if the growth of the Presidential Establishment antedates the current administration, it is curious at least that one of the largest expansions ever, in both relative and absolute terms, has taken place during the first term of a conservative, management-minded President who has often voiced his objection to any expansion of the federal government and its bureaucracy.

Under President Nixon, in fact, there has been an almost systematic bureaucratization of the Presidential Establishment, in which more new councils and offices have been established, more specialization and division of labor and layers of staffing have been added, than at any time except during World War II. Among the major Nixonian additions are the Council on Environmental Quality, Council on International Economic Policy, Domestic Council, and Office of Consumer Affairs.

The numbers in the White House

The expansion of the White House has made the traditional textbook picture of the executive branch nearly obsolete.

entourage may have decreased somewhat since November when the President announced his intention to make certain staff cuts. They may shrink still more if, as expected, the OEO is shifted from White House supervision to Cabinet control, mainly under the Department of Health, Education, and Welfare. Also, in the months ahead, the President will probably offer specific legislative proposals, as he has done before, to reprogram or repackage the upper reaches of the executive.

Even so, any diminution of the Presidential Establishment has so far been more apparent than real, or more incidental than substantial. Some aides, such as former presidential counselor Robert Finch, who have wanted to leave anyway, have done so. Others, serving as scapegoats on the altar of Watergate, are also departing.

In addition, the President has officially removed a number of trusted domestic-policy staff assistants from the White House rolls and dispersed them to key sub-Cabinet posts across the span of government. But this dispersal can be viewed as not so much reducing as creating yet another expansion—a virtual setting up of White House outposts (or little White Houses?) throughout the Cabinet departments. The aides that are being sent forth are notable for their intimacy with the President, and they will surely maintain direct links to the White House, even though these links do not appear on the official organizational charts.

Then, too, one of the most important of the President's recent shifts of ex-

ecutive branch members involves an unequivocal addition to the Presidential Establishment. This is the formal setting up of a second office—with space and a staff in the White House —for Treasury Secretary George Shultz as chairman of yet another new presidential body, the Council on Economic Policy. This move makes Shultz a member of a White House inner cabinet. He will now be over-secretary of economic affairs alongside Henry Kissinger, over-secretary for national security affairs, and John Ehrlichman, over-secretary for domestic affairs.

In other words, however the names and numbers have changed recently or may be shifted about in the near future, the Presidential Establishment does not seem to be declining in terms of function, power, or prerogative; in fact, it may be continuing to grow as rapidly as ever.

Does it matter? A number of political analysts have argued recently that it does, and I agree with them. Perhaps the most disturbing aspect of the expansion of the Presidential Establishment is that it has become a powerful inner sanctum of government, isolated from traditional, constitutional checks and balances. It is common practice today for anonymous, unelected, and unratified aides to negotiate sensitive international commitments by means of executive agreements that are free from congressional oversight. Other aides in the Presidential Establishment wield fiscal authority over billions of dollars in funds that Congress has appropriated, yet the President refuses to spend, or that Congress has assigned to one purpose and the administration routinely redirects to another—all with no semblance of public scrutiny. Such exercises of power pose an important, perhaps vital, question of governmental philosophy: Should a political system that has made a virtue of periodic electoral accountability accord an ever-increasing policy-making role to White House counselors who neither are confirmed by the U.S. Senate nor, because of the doctrine of "executive privilege," are subject to questioning by Congress?

Another disquieting aspect of the growth of the Presidential Establishment is that the increase of its powers has been largely at the expense of the traditional sources of executive power and policy-making—the Cabinet members and their departments. When I asked a former Kennedy-Johnson Cabinet member a while ago what he would like to do if he ever returned to government, he said he would rather be a presidential assistant than a Cabinet member. And this is an increasingly familiar assessment of the relative influence of the two levels of the executive branch. The Presidential Estab-

lishment has become, in effect, a whole layer of government between the President and the Cabinet, and it often stands above the Cabinet in terms of influence with the President. In spite of the exalted position that Cabinet members hold in textbooks and protocol, a number of Cabinet members in recent administrations have complained that they could not even get the President's ear except through an assistant. In his book *Who Owns America?*, former Secretary of the Interior Walter Hickel recounts his combat with a dozen different presidential functionaries and tells how he needed clearance from them before he could get to talk to the President, or how he frequently had to deal with the assistants themselves because the President was "too busy." During an earlier administration, President Eisenhower's chief assistant, Sherman Adams, was said to have told two Cabinet members who could not resolve a matter of mutual concern: "Either make up your mind or else tell me and I will do it. We must not bother the President with this. He is trying to keep the world from war." Several of President Kennedy's Cabinet members regularly battled with White House aides who blocked them from seeing the President. And McGeorge Bundy, as Kennedy's chief assistant for national security affairs, simply sidestepped the State Department in one major area of department communications. He had all important incoming State Department cables transmitted simultaneously to his office in the White House, part of an absorption of traditional State Department functions that visibly continues to this day with presidential assistant Henry Kissinger. Indeed, we recently witnessed the bizarre and telling spectacle of Secretary of State William Rogers insisting that he *did* have a role in making foreign policy.

In a speech in 1971, Sen. Ernest Hollings of South Carolina plaintively noted the lowering of Cabinet status. "It used to be," he said, "that if I had a problem with food stamps, I went to see the Secretary of Agriculture, whose department had jurisdiction over that problem. Not anymore. Now, if I want to learn the policy, I must go to the White House to consult John Price [a special assistant]. If I want the latest on textiles, I won't get it from the Secretary of Commerce, who has the authority and responsibility. No, I am forced to go to the White House and see Mr. Peter Flanigan. I shouldn't feel too badly. Secretary Stans [Maurice Stans, then Secretary of Commerce] has to do the same thing."

If Cabinet members individually have been downgraded in influence, the Cabinet itself as a council of govern-

THE PRESIDENTIAL ESTABLISHMENT

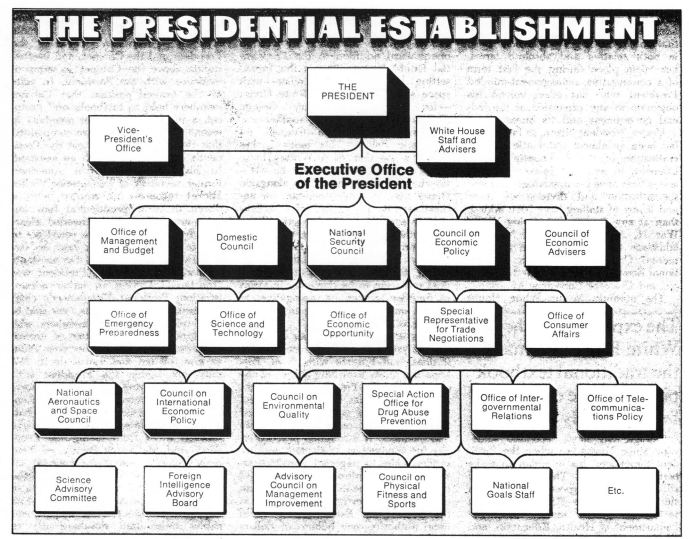

ment has become somewhat of a relic, replaced by more specialized comminglings that as often as not are presided over by White House staffers. The Cabinet's decline has taken place over several administrations. John Kennedy started out his term declaring his intentions of using the Cabinet as a major policy-making body, but his change of mind was swift, as his Postmaster General, J. Edward Day, has noted. "After the first two or three meetings," Day has written, "one had the distinct impression that the President felt that decisions on major matters were not made—or even influenced—at Cabinet sessions, and that discussion there was a waste of time . . . . When members spoke up to suggest or to discuss major administration policy, the President would listen with thinly disguised impatience and then postpone or otherwise bypass the question."

Lyndon Johnson was equally disenchanted with the Cabinet as a body and charateristically held Cabinet sessions only when articles appeared in the press talking about how the Cabinet was withering away. Under Nixon, the Cabinet is almost never convened at all.

Not only has the Presidential Establishment taken over many policy-making functions from the Cabinet and its members, it has also absorbed some of the operational functions. White House aides often feel they should handle any matters that they regard as ineptly administered, and they tend to intervene in internal departmental operations at lower and lower levels. They often feel underemployed, too, and so are inclined to reach out into the departments to find work and exercise authority for themselves.

The result is a continuous undercutting of Cabinet departments—and the cost is heavy. These intrusions can cripple the capacity of Cabinet officials to present policy alternatives, and they diminish self-confidence, morale, and initiative within the departments. George Ball, a former undersecretary of state, noted the effects on the State Department: "Able men, with proper pride in their professional skills, will not long tolerate such votes of no-confidence, so it should be no surprise that they are leaving the career service, and making way for mediocrity with the result that, as time goes on, it may be hopelessly

difficult to restore the Department. . . ."

The irony of this accretion of numbers and functions to the Presidential Establishment is that the presidency is finding itself increasingly afflicted with the very ills of the traditional departments that the expansions were often intended to remedy. The presidency has become a large, complex bureaucracy itself, rapidly acquiring many dubious characteristics of large bureaucracies in the process: layering, overspecialization, communication gaps, interoffice rivalries, inadequate coordination, and an impulse to become consumed with short-term, urgent operational concerns at the expense of thinking systematically about the consequences of varying sets of policies and priorities and about important long-range problems. It takes so much of the President's time to deal with the members of his own bureaucracy that it is little wonder he has little time to hear counsel from Cabinet officials.

Another toll of the burgeoning Presidential Establishment is that White House aides, in assuming more and more responsibility for the management of government programs, inevitably lose the detachment and objectivity that is so essential for evaluating new ideas. Can a lieutenant vigorously engaged in implementing the presidential will admit the possibility that what the President wants is wrong or not working? Yet a President is increasingly dependent on the judgment of these same staff members, since he seldom sees his Cabinet members.

Why has the presidency grown bigger and bigger? There is no single villain or systematically organized conspiracy promoting this expansion. A variety of factors is at work. The most significant is the expansion of the role of the presidency itself—an expansion that for the most part has taken place during national emergencies. The reason for this is that the public and Congress in recent decades have both tended to look to the President for the decisive responses that were needed in those emergencies. The Great Depression and World War II in particular brought sizable increases in presidential staffs. And once in place, many stayed on, even after the emergencies that brought them had faded. Smaller

---

Even a partial listing of specializations that have been grafted onto the White House forms a veritable index of American society.

national crises have occasioned expansion in the White House entourage, too. After the Russians successfully orbited *Sputnik* in 1957, President Eisenhower added several science advisers. After the Bay of Pigs, President Kennedy enlarged his national security staff.

Considerable growth in the Presidential Establishment, especially in the post-World War II years, stems directly from the belief that critical societal problems require that wise men be assigned to the White House to alert the President to appropriate solutions and to serve as the agents for implementing these solutions. Congress has frequently acted on the basis of this belief, legislating the creation of the National Security Council, the Council of Economic Advisers, and the Council on Environmental Quality, among others. Congress has also increased the chores of the presidency by making it a statutory responsibility for the President to prepare more and more reports associated with what are regarded as critical social areas—annual economic and manpower reports, a biennial report on national growth, etc. Most recently, President Nixon responded to a number of troublesome

problems that defy easy relegation to any one department—problems like international trade and drug abuse—by setting up special offices in the Executive Office with sweeping authority and sizable staffs. Once established, these units rarely get dislodged. And an era of permanent crisis ensures a continuing accumulation of such bodies.

Another reason for the growth of the Presidential Establishment is that occupants of the White House frequently distrust members of the permanent government. Nixon aides, for example, have viewed most civil servants not only as Democratic but as wholly unsympathetic to such objectives of the Nixon administration as decentralization, revenue sharing, and the curtailment of several Great Society programs. Departmental bureaucracies are viewed from the White House as independent, unresponsive, unfamiliar, and inaccessible. They are suspected again and again of placing their own, congressional, or special-interest priorities ahead of those communicated to them from the White House. Even the President's own Cabinet members soon become viewed in the same light; one of the strengths of Cabinet members, namely their capacity to make a compelling case for their programs, has proved to be their chief liability with Presidents.

Presidents may want this type of advocacy initially, but they soon grow weary and wary of it. Not long ago, one White House aide accused a former Labor Secretary of trying to "out-Meany Meany." Efforts by former Interior Secretary Hickel to advance certain environmental programs and by departing Housing and Urban Development Secretary George Romney to promote innovative housing construction methods not only were unwelcome but after a while were viewed with considerable displeasure and suspicion at the White House.

Hickel writes poignantly of coming to this recognition during his final meeting with President Nixon, in the course of which the President frequently referred to him as an "adversary." "Initially," writes Hickel, "I considered that a compliment because, to me, an adversary is a valuable asset. It was only after the President had used the term many times and with a disapproving inflection that I realized he considered an adversary an enemy. I could not understand why he would consider me an enemy."

Not only have recent Presidents been suspicious about the depth of the loyalty of those in their Cabinets, but they also invariably become concerned about the possibility that sensitive administration secrets may leak out through the departmental bureaucracies, and this is another reason why Presidents have come to rely more on

their own personal groups, such as task forces and advisory commissions.

Still another reason that more and more portfolios have been given to the presidency is that new federal programs frequently concern more than one federal agency, and it seems reasonable that someone at a higher level is required to fashion a consistent policy and to reconcile conflicts. Attempts by Cabinet members themselves to solve sensitive jurisdictional questions frequently result in bitter squabbling. At times, too, Cabinet members themselves have recommended that these multi-departmental issues be settled at the White House. Sometimes new presidential appointees insist that new offices for program coordination be assigned directly under the President. Ironically, such was the plea of George McGovern, for example, when President Kennedy offered him the post of director of the Food-for-Peace program in 1961. McGovern attacked the buildup of the Presidential Establishment in his campaign against Nixon, but back in 1961 he wanted visibility (and no doubt celebrity status) and he successfully argued against his being located outside the White House—either in the State or Agriculture departments. President Kennedy and his then campaign manager Robert Kennedy felt indebted to McGovern because of his efforts in assisting the Kennedy presidential campaign in South Dakota. Accordingly, McGovern was granted not only a berth in the Executive Office of the President but also the much-coveted title of special assistant to the President.

The Presidential Establishment has also been enlarged by the representation of interest groups within its fold. Even a partial listing of staff specializations that have been grafted onto the White House in recent years reveals how interest-group brokerage has become added to the more traditional staff activities of counseling and administration. These specializations form a veritable index of American society:

Budget and management, national security, economics, congressional matters, science and technology, drug abuse prevention, telecommunications, consumers, national goals, intergovernmental relations, environment, domestic policy, international economics, military affairs, civil rights, disarmament, labor relations, District of Columbia, cultural affairs, education, foreign trade and tariffs, past Presidents, the aged, health and nutrition, physical fitness, volunteerism, intellectuals, blacks, youth, women, "the Jewish community," Wall Street, governors, mayors, "ethnics," regulatory agencies and related industry, state party chairmen, Mexican-Americans.

It is as if interest groups and professions no longer settle for lobbying Congress, or having one of their number appointed to departmental advisory boards or sub-Cabinet positions. It now appears essential to "have your own man right there in the White House." Once this foothold is established, of course, interest groups can play upon the potential political backlash that could arise should their representation be discontinued.

One of the more disturbing elements in the growth of the Presidential Establishment is the development, particularly under the current administration, of a huge public-relations apparatus. More than 100 presidential aides are now engaged in various forms of press-agentry or public relations, busily selling and reselling the President. This activity is devoted to the particular occupant of the White House, but inevitably it affects the presidency itself, by projecting or reinforcing images of the presidency that are almost imperial in their suggestions of omnipotence and omniscience. Thus the public-relations apparatus not only has directly enlarged the presidential workforce but has expanded public expectations about the presidency at the same time.

Last, but by no means least, Congress, which has grown increasingly critical of the burgeoning power of the presidency, must take some blame itself for the expansion of the White House. Divided within itself and ill-equipped, or simply disinclined to make some of the nation's toughest political decisions in recent decades, Congress has abdicated more and more authority to the presidency. The fact that the recent massive bombing of North Vietnam was ordered by the President without even a pretense of consultation with Congress buried what little was left of the semblance of that body's war-making power. Another recent instance of Congress's tendency to surrender authority to the presidency, an extraordinary instance, was the passage by the House (though not the Senate) of a grant to the President that would give him the right to determine which programs are to be cut whenever the budget goes beyond a $250 billion ceiling limit—a bill which, in effect, would hand over to the President some of Congress's long-cherished "power of the purse."

What can be done to bring the Presidential Establishment back down to size? What can be done to bring it to a size that both lightens the heavy accumulation of functions that it has absorbed and allows the Presidential Establishment to perform its most important functions more effectively and wisely?

First, Congress should curb its own impulse to establish new presidential agencies and to ask for yet additional reports and studies from the President. In the past Congress has been a too willing partner in the enlargement of the presidency. If Congress genuinely wants a leaner presidency, it should ask more of itself. For instance, it could well make better use of its own General Accounting Office and Congressional Research Service for chores that are now often assigned to the President.

Congress should also establish in each of its houses special committees on Executive Office operations. Most congressional committees are organized to deal with areas such as labor, agriculture, armed services, or education, paralleling the organization of the Cabinet. What we need now are committees designed explicitly to oversee the White House. No longer can the task of overseeing presidential operations be dispersed among dozens of committees and subcommittees, each of which can look at only small segments of the Presidential Establishment.

Some will complain that adding yet another committee to the already overburdened congressional system is just like adding another council to the overstuffed Presidential Establishment. But the central importance of what the presidency does (and does not do) must rank among the most critical tasks of the contemporary Congress. As things are organized now, the presidency escapes with grievously inadequate scrutiny. Equally important, Congress needs these committees to help protect itself from its own tendency to relinquish to the presidency its diminishing resources and prerogatives. Since Truman, Presidents have had staffs to oversee Congress; it is time Congress reciprocated.

Similar efforts to let the salutary light of public attention shine more brightly on the presidency should be inaugurated by the serious journals and newspapers of the nation. For too long, publishers and editors have believed that covering the presidency means assigning a reporter to the White House press corps. Unfortunately, however, those who follow the President around on his travels are rarely in a position to do investigative reporting on what is going on inside the Presidential Establishment. Covering the Executive Office of the President requires more than a President watcher; it needs a specialist who understands the arcane language and highly complex practices that have grown up in the Presidential Establishment.

Finally, it is time to reverse the downgrading of the Cabinet. President Nixon ostensibly moved in this direction with his designation several days ago of three Cabinet heads—HEW's Caspar W. Weinberger, Agriculture's Earl L. Butz, and HUD's James T. Lynn—as, in effect, super-secretaries of "human resources," "natural resources," and "community development" respectively. The move was expressly made in the name of Cabinet consolidation, plans for which Mr. Nixon put forward in 1971 but which Congress has so far spurned.

The three men will hold onto their Cabinet posts, but they have been given White House offices as well—as presidential counselors—and so it may be that the most direct effect of the appointments is a further expansion of the Presidential Establishment, rather than a counter-bolstering of the Cabinet. But if the move does, in fact, lead to Cabinet consolidation under broader divisions, it will be a step in the right direction.

Reducing the present number of departments would strengthen the hand of Cabinet members vis-à-vis special interests, and might enable them to serve as advisers, as well as advocates, to the President. Cabinet consolidation would also have another very desirable effect: it would be a move toward reducing the accumulation of power within the Presidential Establishment. For much of the power of budget directors and other senior White House aides comes from their roles as penultimate referees of interdepartmental jurisdictional disputes. Under consolidated departments, a small number of strengthened Cabinet officers with closer ties to the President would resolve these conflicts instead. With fewer but broader Cabinet departments, there would be less need for many of the interest-group brokers and special councils that now constitute so much of the excessive baggage in the overburdened presidency.

Meantime, the presidency remains sorely overburdened—with both functions and functionaries—and needs very much to be cut back in both. Certainly, the number of presidential workers can and should be reduced. Harry Truman put it best, perhaps, when he said with characteristic succinctness: "I do not like this present trend toward a huge White House staff . . . . Mostly these aides get in each other's way." But while the number of functionaries is the most tangible and dramatic measure of the White House's expansion, its increasing absorption of governmental functions is more profoundly disturbing. The current White House occupant may regard cutting down (or transferring) a number of his staff members as a way of mollifying critics who charge that the American presidency has grown too big and bloated, but it is yet another thing to reduce the President's authority or his accumulated prerogatives. As the nation's number-one critic of the swelling of government, President Nixon will, it is hoped, move—or will continue to move if he has truly already started—to substantially deflate this swelling in one of the areas where it most needs to be deflated—at home, in the White House. □

★★★

35

United States v. Nixon   418 U.S. 683 (1974)

In 1974 the investigation of the Watergate scandal reached a legal climax. The Special Senate Watergate Committee had subpoenaed certain presidential records and tapes of White House conversations. President Nixon refused to comply with the request on the grounds of "executive privilege," a concept that grants the president and his aides and subordinates the privilege to refuse testimony before Congress. When are presidents most likely to claim this privilege? Would you expect a weak or a strong president to use it most often?

Executive privilege has been defended on the grounds that the separation of powers assures the autonomy of the executive branch of government. The Supreme Court in this case tried to determine how far the principle of executive privilege extended in law. The opinion was delivered by Nixon-appointee Chief Justice Warren Burger. Why was the case of Marbury v. Madison *cited in this opinion? Did the Supreme Court admit to the legality of executive privilege in general? For what reason did the Supreme Court disallow its use in this particular case?*

In this decision Justice Rehnquist refused to sit in judgment because he had worked closely with Richard Nixon as attorney general. Do you think the other three justices who were appointed by Nixon also should have refused to decide this issue because of potential conflict of interest? President Nixon clearly lost the decision since the Court voted 8–0 against him. Can it be said that this was a landmark decision of importance to the entire political system? Did it fundamentally weaken the office of president—or simply the political position of Richard Nixon?

★ ★ ★

United States v. Nixon

418 U.S. 683 (1974)

Mr. Chief Justice **Burger** delivered the opinion of the Court.

In the performance of assigned constitutional duties each branch of the Government must initially interpret the Constitution, and the interpretation of its powers by any branch is due great respect from the others. The President's counsel, as we have noted, reads the Constitution as providing an absolute privilege of confidentiality for all Presidential communications. Many decisions of this Court, however, have unequivocally reaffirmed the holding of Marbury v. Madison (1803) that "[i]t is emphatically the province and duty of the judicial department to say what the law is."

. . . We therefore reaffirm that it is the province and duty of this Court "to say what the law is" with respect to the claim of privilege presented in this case.

. . . Whatever the nature of the privilege of confidentiality of Presidential communications in the exercise of Art. II powers, the privilege can be said to derive from the supremacy of each branch within its own assigned area of constitutional duties. Certain powers and privileges flow from the nature of enumerated powers; the protection of the confidentiality of Presidential communications has similar constitutional underpinnings.

The second ground asserted by the President's counsel in support of the claim of absolute privilege rests on the doctrine of separation of powers. Here it is argued that the independence of the Executive Branch within its own sphere . . . insulates a President from a judicial subpoena in an ongoing criminal prosecution, and thereby protects confidential Presidential communications.

However, neither the doctrine of separation of powers, nor the need for confidentiality of high-level communications, without more, can sustain an absolute, unqualified Presidential privilege of immunity from judicial process under all circumstances. . . .

The impediment that an absolute, unqualified privilege would place in the way of the primary constitutional duty of the Judicial Branch to do justice in criminal prosecutions would plainly conflict with the function of the courts under Art. III. . . . To read the Art. II powers of the President as providing an absolute privilege as against a subpoena essential to enforcement of criminal statutes on no more than a generalized claim of the public interest in confidentiality of nonmilitary and nondiplomatic discussions would upset the constitutional balance of "a workable government" and gravely impair the role of the courts under Art. III. . . .

The expectation of a President to the confidentiality of his conversations and correspondence, like the claim of confidentiality of judicial deliberations, for example, has all the values to which we accord deference for the privacy of all citizens and added to those values the necessity for protection of the public interest in candid, objective, and even blunt or harsh opinions in Presidential decision making. A President and those who assist him must be free to explore alternatives in the process of shaping policies and making decisions and to do so in a way many would be unwilling to express except privately. These are the considerations justifying a presumptive privilege for Presidential communications. The privilege is fundamental to the operation of government and inextricably rooted in the separation of powers under the Constitution.

. . . Nowhere in the Constitution, as we have noted earlier, is there any explicit reference to a privilege of confidentiality, yet to the extent this interest relates to the effective discharge of a President's powers, it is constitutionally based. . . .

In this case we must weigh the importance of the general privilege of confidentiality of Presidential communications in performance of his responsibilities against the inroads of such a privilege on the fair administration of criminal justice. The interest in preserving confidentiality is weighty indeed and entitled to great respect. However, we cannot conclude that advisers will be moved to temper the candor of their remarks by the infrequent occasions of disclosure because of the possibility that such conversations will be called for in the context of a criminal prosecution.

. . . A President's acknowledged need for confidentiality in the communications of his office is general in nature, whereas the constitutional need for production of relevant evidence in a criminal proceeding is specific and central to the fair adjudication of a particular criminal case in the administration of justice. Without access to specific facts a criminal prosecution may be totally frustrated. The President's broad interest in confidentiality of communications will not be vitiated by disclosure of a limited number of conversations preliminarily shown to have some bearing on the pending criminal cases.

We conclude that when the ground for asserting privilege as to subpoenaed materials sought for use in a criminal trial is based only on the generalized interest in confidentiality, it cannot prevail over the fundamental demands of due process of law in the fair administration of criminal justice. The generalized assertion of privilege must yield to the demonstrated, specific need for evidence in a pending criminal trial.

. . . Mr. Chief Justice Marshall sitting as a trial judge in the Burr case was extraordinarily careful to point out that "[i]n no case of this kind would a court be required to proceed against the president as against an ordinary individual." Marshall's statement cannot be read to mean in any sense that a President is above the law, but relates to the singularly unique role under Art. II of a President's communications and activities, related to the performance of duties under that Article. Moreover, a President's communications and activities encompass a vastly wider range of sensitive material than would be true of any "ordinary individual." It is therefore necessary in the public interest to afford Presidential confidentiality the greatest protection consistent with the fair administration of justice.

Mr. Justice **Rehnquist** took no part in the consideration or decision of these cases.

CHAPTER EIGHT

★ ★ ★

The Bureaucracy

Government employees would rather be called civil servants, administrators, managers, or public servants—rather than bureaucrats. To many people "bureaucrat" is a derogatory term. In the eyes of some people the bureaucracy wastes money, is inefficient, and unresponsive to the needs of the citizenry. Under our system of government the bureaucracy is supposed to be supervised by our elected officials, such as the president, but, experience shows that too often agencies enjoy such independence that they may safely ignore the wishes of elected officials, even the president.

In his essay "Down the Bureaucracy," Matthew P. Dumont discusses reasons why the federal bureaucracy is less effective than it ought to be. However, rather than condemn individuals in government service, he sees the system as the problem. That is, bureaucrats are constrained to do things for the survival of their agency, in spite of the impact of their actions on the general public. The problem is that the formal organizational structure and chain of command say little about how an agency really works. Rather, powerful informal "norms" of conduct set the tone for bureaucratic operations. The outlook for improved government efficiency is not so good, so this essay seems to be particularly pessimistic.

The president is expected to be the "chief executive," charged with carrying out the laws. But much political science research supports the view that many agencies of government enjoy much

autonomy and discretion. One reason for bureaucratic independence is the so-called "subgovernment" that exists in government administration. It is an alliance composed of three: (1) the congressmen on committees with jurisdiction over a given program; (2) the executive agency that carries out that program; and (3) the "clientele" group in society that receives benefits from that program. In this arrangement each party supports each other so that the program continues and is expanded. Its workings are noted in two articles in this chapter.

Resistance by subgovernments is a major reason why presidents cannot reorganize the federal bureaucracy. This problem is analyzed by Rochelle Jones and Peter Woll in "Carter vs. the Bureaucrats: The Interest Vested in Chaos." In the tradition of Theodore Roosevelt, Herbert Hoover, Franklin D. Roosevelt, and Richard Nixon, President Carter campaigned on the need to reorganize government. Like the others, it appears that he will not be very successful. Reform upsets the traditional power relationships among legislators, agencies, and interest groups. Even top administrators chosen by the president become protective of their agencies' jurisdictions and prerogatives. From this perspective, the notion that authority runs down from the president to his bureaucracy must be called into question. Some agencies—for example, the FBI under Director J. Edgar Hoover—become so politically independent as to be virtually untouchable by a president.

The notion of a subgovernment suggests that a relatively small interest group has great influence over public policy. Many political scientists argue that well-organized small groups have greater impact in our bureaucracy than they do in Congress, where political competition and public access is greater. Such a view gains credence when the Federal Reserve System is evaluated. Congressman Henry Reuss does this in "Federal Reserve: A Private Club for Public Policy." Its members tend to be bankers, but they make monetary policy that can affect us all. Its deliberations are made in secrecy, so the public has no real opportunity to influence its decision-making. Defenders of the Federal Reserve System argue that such independence is needed to insulate the agency from gross political influences. On the other hand, critics say that its actions may hinder the country's economic health, in which case it cannot be held accountable. Since there are a number of "independent" commissions, agencies, and corporations in government, this question of whether agencies should be apart from the president's direct control is a major one for our consideration.

When subgovernments are found in certain policy areas, it may indicate that private interests dominate at the expense of the public welfare. Notwithstanding the fact that some programs are advanced in the name of the public interest, however, behind every program are administrators, legislators, and interest groups who steadfastly see that "public interest" only in terms of their own narrow definition. So programs ostensibly established for noble purposes can have serious adverse, but unintended, consequences for society as a whole. This is a major reason why there is a movement today against bureaucratic controls and in favor of government "deregulation." Agencies become committed to their own version of the "public interest" when implementing programs, and their actions sometimes run counter to legislative intent and public opinion. Such is the theme of Steven Rattner's article "Regulating the Regulators." Until recently, most government regulation was related to business competition, to licensure, to price controls in such industries as transportation and communications. But within the past decade it has been extended into areas of health and safety, a reflection of our concern for occupational hazards and environmental quality. These new regulatory activities were promoted for humanitarian reasons—and some benefits have been derived—but high social costs have been added to the burden of the citizen as taxpayer and consumer. Given the reaction to overregulation, Rattner observes that federal agencies have tried to soften the burden of their regulations. What this highlights is the fact that bureaucrats also want to survive, as well as prosper; thus administrators do adapt their programs in the face of hostile social pressures.

Finally, one would think that an answer to the problems of subgovernments and overregulation would be to permit the president the power to appoint more policy-makers in administrative agencies so as to assure their loyalty to him and to influence public opinion. But the solution is not so obvious, because many people do not wish to see politics affect the "professional" conduct of government. They recall the sordid days when waste, inefficiency, and partisanship under the "patronage" system dominated government in America at many levels. This problem is at the heart of Roger Morris's analysis in "Diplomatic Spoils." He is concerned that many ambassadors are unqualified because they were appointed by the president for political reasons. Even career diplomats who are made ambassadors very often have only mediocre credentials for their positions. Though Morris studies the appointments made by President Carter, much the same could be said about those made by his predecessors. To the extent that politics does affect top-level appointments, any control the president gains over the bureaucracy is gotten at a price—the suspicion of many citizens that government administrators lack the competence and integrity to carry out faithfully their official responsibilities.

A common theme seems to run through all five articles in this chapter—a discontent with existing bureaucratic procedures. After you read these selections, judge whether these criticisms are too severe. Can you think of a well-managed governmental agency, one that is responsible to the public and accountable to the chief executive?

★★★

36

Down the Bureaucracy!   Matthew P. Dumont

A bureaucracy is a form of social organization by which the tasks of many individuals may be coordinated in such a way that a larger purpose or goal is achieved. Government means bureaucracy today, and this essay takes a critical look at the workings of bureaucracy. As Dumont points out, it appears that bureaucracy as a system of human behavior contains within it the seeds of its own inefficiency. Civil servants appear to be guided in their behavior by an unwritten code of conduct that results in waste and ineffectiveness. What does Dumont mean by the concept "Eichmannism"? What are the five "norms" that he discusses? How are they manifested by on-the-job behavior? Is this an inevitable consequence of bureaucracy, or are there ways to counter these inefficiencies and wastes?

One reason for the persistence of government programs regardless of their effectiveness is the fact that most agencies are supported by their own political "constituency." What examples of this agency-constituency linkage are given by Dumont? Dumont argues further that these "norms" lodge real power in the hands of middle managers rather than top administrators or the public. Why is this the case? Why do top administrators have difficulty in controlling the organization? What effects can you expect when the power to control is given to middle management?

The tone of this essay is certainly pessimistic about government bureaucracy, and Dumont calls for "change agents" to infiltrate the system in order to enhance its productivity and creativity. He calls the existing bureaucracy "homeostatic," "self-serving," and "elitist." What arguments does he make to support these accusations? Evaluate this article in light of your own experiences with a government bureaucracy. Would you say it was generally effective in its administration of programs? A part of the public's ambivalence toward government rests upon society's traditional faith in private institutions and free enterprise to solve problems and to provide the good life. Do you think Dumont's analysis applies to any bureaucracy—private as well as public—or is it more indicative of governmental administration?

★ ★ ★

Comment . . .

Matthew P. Dumont

Down the Bureaucracy!

There has been a certain tension among the people of our federal city lately. I am not talking about the black population of the district, which becomes visible to the rest of the world only when its rage boils over. I am referring to the public servants who ooze across the Maryland and Virginia lines each day to manipulate the machinery of government.

It has never been a particularly gleeful population, but in the last year or so it has developed a kind of mass involutional melancholia, a peculiar mixture of depression, anxiety and senescence.

As in similarly depressed communities, the young, the healthy and those with good job prospects have tended to migrate. Among those who have departed are a large proportion of that scarce supply of idealistic and pragmatic people who try to work for social change "within the system." They are leaving because they feel unwanted and ineffectual. Let me describe what they are turning their backs on.

Washington is a malaria swamp covered over with buildings of neofascist design and ringed with military bases.

Do you remember Rastignac shaking his fist at Paris from Goriot's grave site? Washington is a city made for fists to be shaken at. Shaken at, not bloodied on. Federal buildings are especially constructed to be impervious to blood. You can rush headlong into a marble balustrade smearing brains and blood and bile three yards wide. But as the lady does on television, with a smile and a few whisks of a damp cloth, the wonderful material will come up as clean and white and sparkling as before.

Some people have tried burning themselves into the concrete. That doesn't work either.

And, as you might have guessed, all that urine on the Pentagon was gone within minutes after the armies of the night retreated.

No, you may, individually or en masse, descend upon the Federal Triangle. You may try to impale and exsanguinate yourselves, flay, crucify and castrate yourselves. You may scream shrill cries or sing "Alice's Restaurant" or chant "Om," but it won't help. The buildings were made to last forever and to forever remain shining and white, the summer sun glaring off their walls, stunning the passersby.

Inside, one might spend eternity hearing the sounds of his own footsteps in the corridors of these buildings and never see his sun-cast shadow. If you took all the corridors in all of the federal buildings in Washington and laid them end to end, and inclined one end slightly and started a billiard ball rolling down, by the time it reached the lower end, the ball would have attained such a velocity that it would hurtle on through space while approaching an infinite mass and thereby destroy the universe. This is not likely to happen because such coordination is unheard of among federal agencies. But we will get to that later.

Off the corridors are offices and conference rooms. (There is also a core of mail chutes, telephone lines, elevator shafts, sewer pipes, trash cans and black people, but these are all invisible.) The offices have desks—wooden ones for important people and steel ones for unimportant people. (Otherwise, the distinction is impossible to make unless you could monitor their telephone calls to each other and determine the relative hierarchy depending on whose secretary manages to keep the other party waiting before putting her boss on.)

The offices also contain file cabinets that are filled with paper. The paper is mainly memos—the way people in the federal government communicate to one another. When communication is not necessary, memos "for the record" are written and filed. It has been estimated that the approximate cost in labor and supplies for the typing of a memo is 36¢. The cost in professional time for its preparation is incalculable.

The conference rooms are for conferences. A conference is for the purpose of sharing information among a group of federal officials who have already been apprised of the information to be shared, individually, by memo. Coffee and cigarettes are consumed. By prior arrangement, each participant is, in turn, interrupted by his secretary for an urgent phone call. After the conference additional memos are exchanged.

But let me describe the people who work in the federal government because some mythology must be laid to rest.

They are good people, which is to say that they are no less good than anyone else, which is to say that we are all pretty much cut from the same material and most of it is pretty rotten. I do not wish to be cavalier about the problem of evil, but I will ask you to accept as a premise for this thesis that the differences between the "best of us" and the "worst of us" are no greater than the differences *within* each of us at varying times.

I have been and will be more sober and precise about this issue in other writings, but what I am attempting to convey is a conviction that the great evils of mankind, the genocides and holy wars, the monstrous exploitations and negligences and injustices of societies have less to do with the malice of individuals than with unexamined and unquestioned institutional practices.

I am talking about the Eichmannism —a syndrome wherein individual motives, consciences or goals become irrelevant in the context of organizational behaviors. This can be seen in pure culture in the federal government. There are a host of written rules for behavior for the federal civil servants, but these are rarely salient. It is the unwritten rules, tacit but ever present, subtle but overwhelming, unarticulated but commanding, that determine the behavior of the men and women who buzz out their lives in the spaces defined by the United States government.

These rules are few in number. Rule number one is to *maintain your tenure*. This is at the same time the most significant and the easiest rule to abide by. If you desire to keep a job for several decades and retire from it with an adequate pension, and if you have the capacity to appear at once occupied and inconspicuous, then you can be satisfied as a "fed."

Appearing occupied means walking briskly at all times. It means looking down at your desk rather than up into the distance when thinking. It means always having papers in your hands. Above all, it means, when asked how things are, responding "very hectic" rather than "terrific" or "lousy."

Being inconspicuous means that your competence in appearing occupied should be expressed quietly and without affect. The most intolerable behavior in a civil servant is psychotic behavior. Being psychotic in the federal government is looking people directly in the eye for a moment too long. It is walking around on a weekday without a tie. It is kissing a girl in an elevator. (It doesn't matter whether she is a wife, mistress, secretary or daughter.) It is writing a memo that is excessively detailed, or refusing to write memos. It is laughing too loud or too long at a conference. It is taking a clandestine gulp of wine in a locker room rather than ordering two martinis over lunch. (This explains why there are more suspensions for alcoholism among lower level workers than higher level ones.)

In short, there is no more sensitive indicator of deviant behavior than personnel records of the federal government.

This does not mean that federal officials never vary their behavior. Currently, for example, it is modish to sport sideburns and a moustache. The specter of thousands of civil servants looking like Che Guevara may seem exciting, but it has no more significance than cuffless trousers.

You may or may not wish to follow the fashions, but do not initiate them. In general, follow a golden mean of behavior, that is, do what most people seem to be doing. Do it quietly. And if you are not sure how to behave, take annual leave.

The second rule of behavior in the government, and clearly related to the sustenance of your own tenure, is to *keep the boss from getting embarrassed.* That is the single, most important standard of competence for a federal official. The man who runs interference effectively, who can anticipate and obviate impertinent, urgent or obvious demands from the boss's boss, or from the press, or from the public, or from Congress, will be treasured and rewarded. This is so pervasive a desideratum in a civil servant that the distinction between line and staff activities becomes thin and artificial in the face of it. Your primary function in the hierarchy (after the protection of your own tenure) is the protection of your superior's tenure rather than the fulfillment of assigned responsibilities. (Obvious exceptions to this rule are J. Edgar Hoover and certain elements

in the Department of Defense, who, like physicians and priests, respond to a higher authority.)

The third unwritten rule of federal behavior is to *make sure that all appropriated funds are spent by the end of the fiscal year.* Much of the paper that stuffs the orifices of executive desks has to do with justifications for requests for more money. For money to be returned after such justifications are approved is to imply that the requester, his supervisor and Congress itself were improvident in their demands on the taxpayer's money. It would be like a bum asking for a handout for a cup of coffee. A passerby offers a quarter and the bum returns 15¢ saying, "Coffee is only a dime, schmuck."

Contract hustlers, who abound in Washington, known that their halcyon days are in late spring when agencies are frequently panicked at the realization that they have not exhausted their operating funds and may be in the black by the fiscal year's end. Agencies that administer grant-in-aid programs celebrate end-of-fiscal-year parties with Dionysian abandon when instead of having a surplus of funds they cannot pay all of their obligations.

The only effective way to evaluate a federal program is the rapidity with which money is spent. Federal agencies, no less than purveyors of situation comedies, cigarettes and medical care, are dominated by a marketplace mentality which assumes that you have a good product if the demand exceeds the supply.

The fourth unwritten rule of behavior in government is to *keep the program alive.* It is not appropriate to question the original purposes of the program. Nor is it appropriate to ask if the program has any consonance with its original purposes. It is certainly not appropriate to assume that its purposes have been served. It is only appropriate to assume that once a program has been legislated, funded and staffed it must endure. An unstated and probably unconscious blessing of immortality is bestowed upon the titles that clutter organizational charts in federal agencies.

Congress, with its control of funds, is perceived as a nurturant breast with a supply of vital fluids that may at any time run dry and thus starve the program to death. Such a matter must be looked upon with intense ambivalence, a state of mind associated with schizophrenia in the hostile-dependent offspring. And, indeed, Congress is perceived by federal executives with a mixture of adulation and rage, and, indeed, federal programming is schizophrenic.

Like the schizophrenic, federal programs have the capacity to assume pseudomorphic identities, having the outline and form of order and direction and vitality but actually being flat, autistic and encrusted with inorganic matter. Like the schizophrenic, federal programs develop a primitive narcissism that is independent of feedback from the environment other than the provision of life-sustaining funds.

Even programs that are conceived with some imagination as relatively bold and aggressive attempts to institutionalize change, such as Model Cities or Comprehensive Community Mental Health Centers or Community Action Programs, become so preoccupied with survival that compromises in the face of real or imagined criticism from Congress very quickly blunt whatever cutting edges the program may have had.

The fifth and final unwritten rule of federal behavior is to *maintain a stable and well-circumscribed constituency.* With so great a concern for survival in the government, it is necessary to have friends outside of it. One's equity within an agency and a program's equity in Congress are a function of equity with vested interests outside. The most visible and articulate vestedness is best to cultivate. Every agency and every department knows this, as does every successful executive. The constituency not only represents survival credits but has the quality of a significant reference group. The values, purposes and rewards of the federal agent must mesh with those of his program's constituents.

It is easy to see how this works between the Defense Department and the military-industrial complex; between Agriculture and the large, industrialized farming interests; between Labor and the unions; between Commerce and big business. It is obvious that the regulatory commissions of government have a friendly, symbiotic relationship with the organizations they were meant to monitor. It is less clear, however, that the good guys in government, the liberals who run the "social programs," have their exclusive constituents as well. The constituents of welfare programs are not welfare recipients, but social workers. The constituents of educational programs are not students, but educators. The constituents of health programs are the providers of health care, not their consumers. The mental health programs of the government are sensitive to the perturbations of mental health professionals and social scientists, not so much to the walking wounded.

In the latter case, for example, to suggest that nonprofessionals should have something to say about the expenditure of millions of research, training and service dollars is to threaten a constituency. And a threatened one is an unfriendly one, which is not good for the program in Congress or for the job possibilities of the executive in the marketplace. As long as the constituency is stable and circumscribed, credits can be counted.

These, then, are the rules of behavior for functionaries in the federal bureaucracy. If they sound familiar, they should. They are not by any means unique to this system. With minor alterations, they serve as the uncodified code of conduct in any organization. They are what sustained every arch-bureaucrat from Pilate to Eichmann. They explain in large part why the United States government is such a swollen beast, incapable of responding to the unmet needs of so many people.

But only in part. One other feature of the Washington scene must be described before we can say we know enough of it to elaborate a strategy of assault. This has to do with power.

There is a lot of nonsense about power in the government. One sees a black Chrysler with a vinyl top speeding by. A liveried chauffeur, determined and grim, operates the vehicle. In the rear, a gooseneck, high-intensity lamp arched over his shoulder, sits a man studying the *Washington Post*. One is tempted to say, "There goes a man of power."

It is a vain temptation. Power in the government does not reside within gray eminences in black Chryslers. It is a soft, pluralistic business shared by a large number of middle managers. Organizational charts in federal agencies read as if there is a rigid line of authority and control from the top down. It would appear that the secretary of each department with his designated assistants and deputies would control the behavior of the entire establishment. In fact, there is a huge permanent government that watches with covert bemusement as the political appointees at the top come and go, attempting in their turn to control the behavior of the agencies "responsible to them."

This does not mean that there is not a good deal of respect and deference paid by middle managers to their superiors. But, as in many organizations, this deference can have an empty and superficial quality to it that amounts to mockery. In most hospitals, for example, it is not the doctors who determine what happens to patients, but nurses.

Nurses may appear as subordinate to physicians as slaves to their masters, but as soon as the doctor has left the ward the nurse does what she wants to do anyway.

Similarly, in federal agencies, it is the great army of middlemanagers that controls the show. There is not even the built-in accountability of a dead patient for the boss to see.

Power in the government resides less in position and funds than it does in information, which is the medium of exchange. The flow of information is controlled not at the top, but at the middle. There is very little horizontal flow between agencies because of the constant competition for funds, and all vertical flow must be mediated by the GS 14 to GS 17 bureaucrats who make up the permanent government.

This concentration of power in the middle, controlled by masses of managers who subscribe to the unwritten code of behavior described above, is the reason why the national government is essentially unresponsive. It does not respond to the top or the bottom; it does not respond to ideology. It is a great, indestructible mollusk that absorbs kicks and taunts and seductions and does nothing but grow.

But it's worse than that. The government is righteous. The people who man the bastions of the executive branch (like the rest of us) have the capacity to invest their jobs with their personal identities. Because it is theirs, their function must be defended. Their roles become, in the language of psychiatry, ego-syntonic. Their sense of personal integrity, their consciences, their self-esteem begin to grow into the positions they hold. It is as if their very identities partake of the same definition as their organizationally defined function.

Can you imagine trying to fight a revolution against a huge, righteous marshmallow? Even if you had enough troops not to be suffocated by it, the best you can hope for is to eat it. And, as you all know, you become what you eat. And that is the point. For a revolution to be meaningful it must take into account the nature of organizational life. It must assume that the ideologically pure and the ideologically impure are subject to the same Eichmannesque forces. If a revolution harbors the illusion that a reign of terror will purify a bureaucracy of scoundrels and exploiters, it will fail. It matters little whether bureaucrats are Royalist or Republican, Czarist or Bolshevik, Conservative or Liberal, or what have you. It is the built-in forces of life in a

bureaucracy that result in the bureaucracy being so indifferent to suffering and aspiration.

Does this mean that radical change is not possible? No. It means that intelligence and planning must be used, as well as rhetoric, songs, threats, uniforms and all the other trappings of a "movement." The intelligence and planning might orient themselves around a concept of nonalienated revolution that relies on a strategy of guerrilla administration.

This is not meant to be an exclusive strategy. Social change, radical and otherwise, has to be a pluralistic phenomenon. It needs to allow for foxes as well as hedgehogs. This represents one attempt, then, to approach the Great White Marshmallow in such a way that victories are neither impossible nor terrible.

Assuming that power in the federal government is controlled by a vast cadre of middle managers who are essentially homeostatic, and assuming the softness and purposelessness of the system in which they operate, it is conceivable that a critical mass of change agents working within that system may be effective in achieving increasingly significant ad hoc successes.

This requires a group of people who are prepared to work as civil servants but who have little or no concern with the five unwritten rules of behavior of such service. Specifically, their investment in their own jobs carries a very limited liability. The ultimate sanction, being fired, is no sanction at all. Either because they command credentials which will afford them the security they need wherever they work or because they emerge from a generation that has not been tainted by the depression and so have fewer security needs, they are not afraid of being fired.

While they may like the boss, and one may hope they do, they do not see themselves as primarily concerned with saving him from embarrassment.

Spending the program money by the end of the fiscal year and the related rule—keeping the program alive—are significant to them only insofar as the program's purposes mesh with their social consciences, and then only insofar as the program is demonstrating some fealty to those purposes.

Most important, however, is that this critical mass of change agents *not* abide by the rule of maintaining a stable and circumscribed constituency. This is at the same time a liberating principle of behavior and a major strategy of change. It is precisely by broadening the base of the constituencies of federal programs that they will become more responsible to the needs of more people.

This network of communication and collaboration shares as its purpose the frustration of the bureaucracy. But it is the homeostatic, self-serving and elitist aspects of bureaucratic life that are to be frustrated. And this can only be accomplished through the creative tension that emerges from a constant appreciation of unmet needs.

The network of change agents represents a built-in amplifier of those needs either because the agents are, themselves, among the poor, the colored and the young or because they are advocates of them.

It is not critical that the guerrilla administrators who compromise this network be in a position to command funds or program directions. They must simply have access to information, which, you recall, is the medium of exchange in government.

This network, in order to avoid the same traps as the bureaucracy it is meant to frustrate, should never become solidified or rigidified in structure and function. It may have the form of a floating crap game whose location and participation are fluid and changing, but whose purposes and activities are constant. The contacts should remain informal, nonhierarchical and task-oriented. The tasks chosen should be finite, specific, salient and feasible. The makeup of each task force is an ad hoc, self-selected clustering of individuals whose skills or location or access to information suggests their roles. This network of change agents becomes a reference group, but not a brotherhood. There need not be a preoccupation with loyalty, cordiality or steadfastness. They do not even have to be friendly.

This is a rather dry and unromantic strategy of social change. It does not stir one's heart or glands. Where is the image of Parnell pulling his cap low on his forehead as he points his gallant band to the General Post Office? Or Lenin approaching the borders of a trembling Russia in a sealed train? Or Fidel or Che? Or Spartacus, or Mao? Where are the clasped hands and the eyes squinting into a distant line of troops? Where are the songs, the flags, the legends? Where is the courage? Where is the glory?

Such a revolutionary force has nothing of the triumphal arch in it. Nor has it anything of the gallows. It lives without the hope of victory or the fear of defeat. It will yearn for saints and despair of scoundrels, but it will see as its eternal mission the subversion of those systems that force both saints and scoundrels into a common, faceless repression of the human spirit.

Matthew T. Dumont is Assistant Commissioner for Drug Rehabilitation in the Massachusetts Department of Mental Health.

---

37   Carter vs. the Bureaucrats: The Interest Vested in Chaos   Rochelle Jones and Peter Woll

Complaints that the federal bureaucracy is wasteful, inefficient, and bloated have been heard again and again. But it is very difficult to reorganize the structure of government in order to improve its operations. Throughout the twentieth century various presidents proposed reform, without much success. What were some of these reorganization efforts by contemporary presidents? When was the Executive Office of the President established? And who recommended creating four super-departments?

Like his predecessors, Jimmy Carter promised reform; like them also, he has not been very successful. Jones and Woll indicate how the agencies, congressmen, and interest groups all have vested interests in bureaucratic "chaos." In what ways do they benefit under the existing bureaucratic system? How can change ever be successful as long as those responsible for change are profiting from the status quo? How can reform be made more advantageous than the status quo? Members of the administration are often powerful spokesmen of vested interests in society. Which members of Jimmy Carter's cabinet have the strongest political connections to clientele groups? This essay clearly portrays President Carter's frustration in trying to promote reform. As the authors point out, on occasion modest changes do occur, and they point to the successful establishment of the Departments of Housing and Urban Development and of Transportation. How is this to be explained?

Jones and Woll do not give much attention to public opinion, and it seems that one reason why reorganization fails is that the citizenry cannot be easily mobilized behind the president. Do you think this evaluation is correct? If the public insists on reorganization, how effective might their pressures be? Do you think public pressure might be the only way to force through structural changes to neutralize vested interests?

★ ★ ★

CARTER vs. THE BUREAUCRATS

THE INTEREST VESTED IN CHAOS

ROCHELLE JONES and PETER WOLL

"I think that it is generally agreed that there should be a systematic reorganization and reassembling of its [the government's] parts so as to secure greater efficiency and effect considerable savings in expense."
—President Woodrow Wilson, 1914

"For many years we have all known that the executive and administrative departments of the Government in Washington are a higgledy-piggledy patchwork of duplicative responsibilities and overlapping powers."
—President Franklin Roosevelt, 1937

"The time has come to match our structure to our purposes—to look with fresh eye, and to organize the Government by conscious, comprehensive design to meet the new needs of a new era." —President Richard Nixon, 1971

"It's time for us to take a new look at our government, to eliminate waste, to release our civil servants from bureaucratic chaos, to provide tough management. . . ."
—Presidential nominee Carter, 1976

A lot of people who thought last November that a vote for Carter was a vote to clean up the mess in Washington are in for a disappointment.

As Presidential nominee, Carter campaigned on a platform of government reorganization, attacking the bloat and waste in the federal bureaucracy and pledging to reduce the number of executive branch agencies from 1,900 to 200. An electorate, disenchanted with grandiose federal programs and the large-scale bureaucracies that administer them, saw in him a political outsider whose very lack of ties to Washington would enable him to take on the federal bureaucrats and win.

But it is one thing for a Presidential nominee to promise reorganization and quite another for a President to carry it out. Such attempts are bound to unite the Washington political establishment against the President, even while it superficially supports his goals.

The opposition is not based on disagreement with President Carter's premises; the waste and inefficiency created by a hodgepodge of government agencies are too well documented. The federal bureaucracy consists of eleven Cabinet departments, forty-four independent agencies and some 1,240 advisory boards, committees, commissions and councils, with more added annually. In fact, President Carter has already established four new advisory bodies—the Commission on Mental Health, the U.S. Circuit Judiciary Nomination Commission, the Committee on Selection of the Director of the Federal Bureau of Investigation and the Advisory Board on Ambassadorial Appointments.

Rochelle Jones is a free-lance writer, and author of The Other Generation, *to be published this summer by Prentice-Hall. Peter Woll is professor of politics at Brandeis University and author of* The American Bureaucracy (*W.W. Norton*).

There are some 228 separate health programs, 156 separate income security and social service programs and eighty-three separate housing programs. Functionally similar programs are scattered throughout the various Cabinet departments. Education, for instance, is nominally the responsibility of the Department of Health, Education and Welfare, but the Department of Agriculture operates its own graduate school and the Department of Defense oversees a far-flung school system for the children of military personnel abroad. The regulations issued by federal agencies and programs fill 60,000 pages of fine print a year in the *Federal Register* and the paperwork they stipulate is so extensive that the state of Maryland not long ago declined a $60,000 HEW grant because it would cost at least that much to apply.

Thus, everyone agrees in the abstract that government reorganization would be desirable, but while the electorate perceives it as relief from an overburdening government, politicians, political appointees and top career civil servants see it as a threat to power and status. They are for reorganization—but of somebody else's program or agency.

Every American President in this century has taken office pledging wholesale reorganization of the federal bureaucracy, and each of them has had to settle for piecemeal reform at best. Meanwhile, the bureaucracy has continued to grow.

Theodore Roosevelt established the pattern in 1905 when he appointed the Keep Commission, the first Presidential commission on government organization, to study the efficiency of the Cabinet departments. Its recommendations, like those of its successors, were defeated by Congress and a recalcitrant Cabinet. (It was William McAdoo who, as Secretary of the Treasury in the Wilson administration, reportedly "kicked like a steer" at even the suggestion that health services and the building of post offices be taken away from his department.)

During the 1930s public concern over the how and why of government organization reached its peak. Congress succumbed to this pressure long enough to pass the Economy Act of 1932, which permitted the President to reorganize the executive branch unless his proposals were vetoed by either branch of Congress within sixty days. It was the first in a series of such acts, enacted over the next twenty years, culminating in the Reorganization Act of 1949. Hoover submitted a sweeping reorganization plan to Congress in late 1932, but his recommendations were rejected by a heavily Democratic House of Representatives.

The Presidential election that year had been dominated by two issues: government organization and the economy. Franklin Roosevelt joined the issues by calling for a reorganization of the government so that federal expenditures could be reduced and the budget balanced. He promised to secure in advance the cooperation of potential Cabinet appointees and at his first press conference as President named reorganization as one of his top priorities.

However, he waited until the end of his first term to appoint his Committee on Administrative Management popularly called the Brownlow Committee. Roosevelt by then saw reorganization through the eyes of the President, who is always responsible for, but never fully in control of, the bureaucracy. At one point, for example, he learned from a newspaper story that the Navy planned to undertake a $2 billion shipbuilding program. Roosevelt, recalling the incident, said, "Here I am, the Commander in Chief of the Navy having to read about that for the first time in the press. Do you know what I said to that? . . . I said: 'Jesus Chr-rist!' "

The Brownlow Committee made recommendations designed to insure Presidential control of the bureaucracy. Roosevelt then waited until after his landslide re-election and the election of an overwhelmingly Democratic Congress in 1937 to ask for authority to implement the recommendations. Even so, his request met tough opposition. Secretary of Interior Harold Ickes wrote, "I do not believe that I have seen so much hysteria over any proposed piece of legislation since the World War and the attempt of President Wilson to force the ratification of the League of Nations." Congress finally approved a narrowly circumscribed version of Roosevelt's original request. Roosevelt's only real achievement under the act was the creation of the Executive Office of the President, including the Bureau of the Budget.

Richard Nixon, the most anti-bureaucratic of Presidents, tried the most sweeping reforms. He proposed merging a number of existing Cabinet departments into four super departments—Community Development, Natural Resources, Human Resources and Economic Affairs. The proposal was thoroughly logical but totally impractical, given the political reality. After some cursory Congressional hearings, the proposals were forgotten—even by Nixon.

He was more successful in reorganizing the Executive Office of the President. After a tough struggle with Congress, he abolished the Bureau of the Budget, which had operated by statute, and created in its place the Office of Management and Budget, which operated under Presidential directive. He created the Domestic Council and other staff agencies, hoping that a new Presidential bureaucracy would counterbalance and control the existing bureaucracy. But he lost touch with his own organization as it expanded, and in the end both bureaucracies were beyond his control. In fact, the Washington bureaucracy grew the most under Nixon, the President who most desired to control it. Between 1969 and 1972 there was a net increase of eighty agencies, many of them in the Presidential bureaucracy.

That being the capsule history of bureaucratic reform, one may expect Mr. Carter to find that Congress will fight to preserve the status quo and the bureaucrats—career civil servants and Cabinet officers—will oppose any diminution of their authority. Congress and the federal bureaucracy have established a highly effective relationship in this area. Bureaucrats intent on resisting attempts to dismantle agencies and programs under their control find allies on Capitol Hill among the chairmen of Congressional committees and subcommittees that control their authorizations and appropriations. The civil servants obviously need the Congressmen to keep their agencies and programs alive and funded. The Congressmen, less obviously, need the civil servants whose expert knowledge of their areas helps to build the Congressmen's legislative reputations. Each needs the other to survive in Washington. The result is exemplified in the career of Rep. Jamie Whitten (D., Miss.), chairman of the House Appropriations Subcommittee on Agriculture. Whitten has been called the Permanent Secretary of Agriculture, a nickname earned by his long-time advocacy of funds for farm programs sponsored by the department. In turn, the civil servants who run Agriculture, administration after administration, provide Whitten with inside information that helps him to maintain his reputation among fellow Congressmen as an expert on agriculture policy.

Virtually every Cabinet department and administrative agency of any consequence is backed by powerful members of Congress. For example, Sen. Warren Magnuson (D., Wash.), chairman of the Commerce Committee, permitted the transfer of the Federal Aviation Administration into the Department of Transportation only on condition that the FAA retain its separate identity. Even the smaller, more obscure agencies have loyal supporters. The American Battle Monuments Commission was criticized on national television earlier this year by a Congressman who felt that its mere existence demonstrated the need for government reorganization. But when representatives of the commission appeared before a House Appropriations Subcommittee a few days later to make their annual request for funds, the chairman, Rep. Edward Boland (D., Mass.), had nothing but praise for the efficiency and quality of the commission's work.

Congressmen have strong incentives to preserve, even tacitly to encourage, the present hodgepodge of overlapping jurisdictions among agencies and departments. The wider the responsibility is diffused throughout the executive branch, the greater the number of Congressional committees and subcommittees that can legitimately claim jurisdiction. Then, when an issue like energy captures national attention, nearly every Congressman has an opportunity to be personally involved. During the first nine months of the 94th Congress, energy-related hearings were held by twelve committees and twenty-five subcommittees in the Senate and seventeen committees and thirty-five subcommittees in the House of Representatives. The Federal Energy Administration alone testified at forty-six Senate hearings, fifty-eight House hearings and eight joint Congressional hearings in 1975.

In addition to the support of Congressmen, the federal bureaucracy can count on the support of Congressional staff, particularly committee staff. The tremendous growth in staff—a 44.2 percent increase between 1970 and 1975—has created a Congressional bureaucracy which often has a vested interest in supporting its counterparts in the federal bureaucracy. When the FEA was due to expire in 1976, the eighteen staff members of the Energy and Power Subcommittee of the House Interstate and Foreign Commerce Committee automatically backed its extension. Their jobs depended largely on the continuation of the FEA.

Some reorganization is possible if the power structure of existing Congressional committees is not threatened. The creation of both the Departments of Housing and Urban Development and of Transportation, for instance, left the committee systems intact. However, former Undersecretary of the Interior John Whitaker recently stated that Congressional jurisdictional disputes blocked the creation of a unified energy department in the Nixon administration. For similar reasons, President Carter's proposed Department of Energy is likely to win quicker approval in the Senate than in the House. Senate committees were reorganized this year and jurisdiction over energy was consolidated in the Energy and Natural Resources Committee. Its chairman, Sen. Henry Jackson (D., Wash.), has enthusiastically endorsed the new department. Jurisdiction in the House remains scattered through numerous committees.

The federal bureaucracy does not always need to turn to its Congressional allies for support. Cabinet officials and federal bureaucrats are often capable of opposing on their own Presidential interference in their departments. Over the years the Cabinet departments have evolved their own special views on policy which reflect a blend of special and bureaucratic interests, and these positions are jealously guarded against Presidential encroachment. J. Edgar Hoover is the paradigm of bureaucratic resistance. The FBI was untouchable while Hoover was alive, and remains so to a large extent today because of his influence. Most bureaucrats, however, prefer to work quietly behind the scenes. Public resistance and outright opposition are usually left to Cabinet secretaries.

Most Cabinet officials, in fact, are chosen with the concurrence of groups having a special interest in the departments they will head. That is particularly true at departments like Labor, Agriculture and Commerce that serve a well-defined constituency. Peter Brennan, for instance, was head of the New York State Building and Construction Trades Council before he became Secretary of Labor. Such Cabinet officials represent first the interests of their departments and the groups their departments serve; the interests of the President and the public at large come second.

Even when Presidents attempt to circumvent the special-interest groups by making an "outside" appointment, they soon find their appointees adopting the viewpoint of the department. Walter J. Hickel, a millionaire with close ties to the oil industry, seemed an unlikely environmentalist when he was tapped for the post of Secretary of the Interior by Nixon. In fact, as Governor of Alaska he had favored the economic development of public lands in the state. Hickel, however, compiled an outstanding record on conservation issues at the Interior Department. President Carter clearly sought the approval of the

vested interests—labor, business, conservation, agriculture—served by the departments when he picked his Cabinet officials. In many instances he selected people who already had an ingrained interest in protecting their departments because they were part of the establishment served by the department. Secretary of Defense Harold Brown was Secretary of the Air Force in the Johnson administration. Secretary of Health, Education and Welfare Joseph Califano created many of its programs as Lyndon Johnson's deputy and alter ego for domestic affairs. Secretary of Transportation Brock Adams represented for twelve years a Congressional District in which Boeing Aircraft is the major employer. Secretary of the Treasury Michael Blumenthal was chairman of the board, president and chief executive officer of the Bendix Corporation. Others in the Cabinet, including some of the fresh faces promised by Carter, have strong ties to their constituencies. Secretary of the Interior Cecil Andrus, when Governor of Idaho, fought alongside conservationists to preserve the scenic and wild rivers of that state. Secretary of Agriculture Bob Bergland is a farmer and former member of the House Agriculture Committee. Secretary of Commerce Juanita Kreps was a member of the Board of Governors of the New York Stock Exchange, Inc., and served on the board of directors of several corporations, including the J.C. Penney Company.

Moreover, President Carter has promised to give his Cabinet officials unprecedented autonomy in running their departments. He has repeatedly said his Cabinet secretaries will not be dictated to by White House staff. In the Carter administration the Cabinet has not only the incentive to resist any reorganization but also a power base from which to do so.

And, in fact, several Cabinet secretaries have already begun to preserve and protect their departments from Presidential tampering. Brown said shortly after his nomination that he could not envision reducing the defense budget by the $5 billion promised by Carter during the campaign. Califano has stated that he did not become Secretary of the Department of Health, Education and Welfare to preside over its dismemberment. While Andrus reluctantly agreed to relinquish to the proposed Energy Department the authority to establish production goals for gas, oil and coal produced under federal leases, he refused to cede Interior's power to lease the land in the first place.

Under President Carter paper reorganizations of the executive branch and cosmetic reforms of the federal bureaucracy may be possible, as they have been in the past. But substantive changes are as unlikely now as they were seventy-two years ago when Theodore Roosevelt resolved to improve the government's efficiency. The real power in Washington, as President after President has discovered to his dismay, is not located in the Oval Office. It is held by the politicians and their aides, the top career civil servants and the political appointees. The arms of this political establishment will continue to support and protect one another, held together by a network of mutual self-interest, professional ties, and a shared belief that "this is the way it's done in Washington." □

★★★

38   Federal Reserve: A Private Club for Public Policy   Henry S. Reuss

The Federal Reserve System controls the nation's monetary policy. It is not directly accountable to the president, nor is it entirely accountable to Congress. In this essay the Federal Reserve is described as a "private club," and Congressman Reuss goes on to criticize its basis of authority, its composition, its isolation within government, and its manner of secrecy. What evidence does Reuss provide to substantiate the idea that the Federal Reserve is a "private club"? For each criticism a reform is proposed by the congressman. What reasoning lies behind each of his reform proposals? How might these reforms affect the "independence" of this agency? Do you understand the difference between "monetary" policy and "fiscal" policy? The latter is not typically under the control of the Federal Reserve.

Opponents of Congressman Reuss's reforms would argue that the independence of the Federal Reserve is required to insulate the agency from gross political pressures. Given your understanding of the arguments in this essay, do you think there are valid reasons for insulating certain agencies from the president's leadership? What is the overall effect of insulating certain agencies? How do such agencies remain accountable to the policymakers and voters when they are so insulated? Can a democratic system afford to allow such isolation of an agency so vital to economic stability? Congressman Reuss would point to policy issues when the Federal Reserve stood against the wishes of the president and Congress. On what policies has there been conflict between this agency and the president and Congress?

★ ★ ★

FEDERAL RESERVE

A Private Club for Public Policy

REP. HENRY S. REUSS

Washington

In these days of government in the sunshine, it would be hard to imagine the following scene: A board of twelve men meets behind closed doors once a month to decide the nation's fiscal policy. Seven of them have been chosen by the President, five by representatives of banking and big business. At this particular meeting they review the nation's economic condition and decide that what's needed is a hike in taxes and a cut in federal spending. The next morning, their decisions are quietly put into effect. Thirty days later, they issue a summary of the meeting telling the country what they did.

Fiscal policy, fortunately for the nation, is not really made that way. Taxing and spending decisions are debated thoroughly, in a healthy tug of war between the executive and legislative branches. But we allow *monetary* policy to be shaped in a way that closely fits the scene just described.

The decisions made in secret each month by the twelve-man Federal Open Market Committee (FOMC), the Federal Reserve System's controlling arm on monetary policy, have enormous influence. They affect jobs, prices, economic growth, profits, interest rates, capital investment, the flow of money between the United States and other countries. When the FOMC decides to tighten or loosen the money supply, the Fed's traders promptly move into the open market. They quietly buy up government securities from the banks, thereby giving the banks more money which they can lend out; or they sell government securities to the banks, sopping up the banks' reserves and making it tougher for their customers—corporations, small businesses, consumers—to get credit.

Open market policy is a powerful tool. Actions by the Federal Reserve can induce slowdowns in the economy. The recessions of 1966-67, 1969-70 and 1974-75 were caused in part by deliberate Fed decisions to pull in the reins. If the Fed miscalculates, the slowdown may be deeper, larger and longer than intended. Or the Fed can pump things up. In the weeks before the 1972 election, it went on a monetary binge. The money supply ballooned, and the future looked rosy by November. Unfortunately, the Fed's generosity helped overheat the economy and contributed to later double-digit inflation and unemployment.

Rep. Henry Reuss (D., Wis.) is Chairman of the House Committee on Banking, Currency and Housing and a member of the Joint Economic Committee. He is the author of The Critical Decade: An Economic Policy for America and the Free World (McGraw-Hill).

Since the public has such a large stake in its decisions, reform of the Fed to make it more responsive to Americans at large should have high priority. Reform could well start with changing the way members of the FOMC are selected. The decisions of the FOMC are clearly public, not private, decisions. Yet they are made not only in secret but in substantial part by people who have been privately, not publicly, selected.

The FOMC's twelve voting members consist of the seven members of the Federal Reserve Board, who have been appointed by the President and confirmed by the Senate, plus five presidents of the Federal Reserve Banks. There are twelve such Banks, and their presidents take turns as voting members. These Bank presidents are chosen by the Boards of Directors of the twelve Banks—two-thirds of whom have been selected by banks that are members of the Federal Reserve System. They do not necessarily represent a public viewpoint, yet they make public monetary policy, and affect the regulation of the banks to whom they owe their positions. Nowhere else in the federal government do we allow essentially private persons to make governmental decisions of such monumental importance.

Letting Federal Reserve Bank presidents make monetary policy is more than just unwise; I am firmly convinced that it is unconstitutional. The Constitution (Article II, Section 2) says that only "officers of the United States" may make governmental decisions. The Federal Election Commission had to be reconstituted recently to comply with a Supreme Court ruling. The Court held the FEC unconstitutional because its members, who were making governmental decisions, had not been appointed by the President and confirmed by the Senate as the Constitution requires. Surely, the same logic must apply to the FOMC.

A second, badly needed change is in the make-up of the boards of directors of the Reserve Banks. These boards have broad public responsibilities. Nominating the Bank presidents is their most important single function, but their influence extends to other aspects of the Fed's responsibilities. In recent years the Fed has been given increased regulatory responsibility. It must enforce such laws as the Consumer Credit Protection Act, the Equal Credit Opportunity Act, and the Bank Holding Company Act. Thus it is startling to see the Reserve Banks almost completely dominated by banking and commercial interests.

It would be hard to find, anywhere in government, as white, male, upper-class and exclusive a group as the board members of these Reserve Banks. Some 108 persons serve on the boards at a given time (twelve Banks with nine board members each). That group includes no family-sized farmers—though farmers are among the most constant users of credit. There are only two blacks—though the viewpoint blacks would bring to economic policy making could be quite different from the view of the comfortable majority. Incredibly, not one of the 108 directors is a woman, though women are increasingly to be found in the top directorates of private industry. In the sixty-three-year history of the Fed, there have been no women and only four minority members among the 1,088 persons who have served on the boards.

The way the boards are selected gives some clue to why they are so exclusive. Three "Class A" directors are chosen by the Fed's member banks, and are bankers. Three "Class B" directors are also elected by the banks, and must be persons "actively engaged in commerce, agriculture, or some other industrial pursuit." In five of the twelve Districts, nominations for the Class A and Class B directors are actually channeled through state bankers' associations, the lobby for the industry.

The three "Class C" directors are supposed to be representative of a broader public. In fact, they represent the same narrow interests as the others: twenty-nine of the thirty-six current Class C directors are executives or directors of corporations, mostly large. Members of consumer organizations or labor unions are never chosen for these posts. An extensive study by the staff of the House Banking Committee recently concluded that the directors are "representative of a small elite group which dominates much of the economic life of this nation."

The study also found a pervasive pattern of clubbiness in the way the Fed consistently dips into the same pools —the same companies, the same universities, the same bank holding companies—to fill directorships. The system is replete with interlocks. Many of the bankers on the boards are also directors of the biggest corporations.

One must also wonder about the conflict of interest of board members when it comes to Federal Reserve regulation of bank holding companies. Twenty-five of the present 108 directors serve, or have served, as officers or directors of these very holding companies. How objective are they likely to be? At the Minneapolis Fed, even the three Class C "public" directors were all former directors of First Bank System, Inc., the nation's twelfth largest multi-bank holding company, or one of its affiliates.

The Federal Reserve Reform Act was before Congress this year. It would have increased the Reserve Banks' board membership from nine to twelve by adding three more public members and provided that directors be selected without discrimination and with consideration given to women, minorities, consumers and labor. The bill passed the House last May, 279 to 85, but got lost in the Senate's adjournment rush in September. It will be up for consideration again next year. Meanwhile, there is some reason to hope that the Fed has seen the light, and that the thirty-six appointments to be made by the end of 1976 will be less one-sided than in the past.

A third need is to end the isolation of the Federal Reserve from the rest of economic policy making in the government. The Fed is supposed to have a large measure of independence, enough to shelter it from shifting political winds. To that end members of the Board of Governors have fourteen-year terms. But the Fed should not be so independent that, as Prof. James Tobin of Yale University said, it always "has the last word" and can offset the basic economic policies and priorities arrived at by the President and the Congress.

When Congress voted a tax increase to cool off the overheating economy during the war in Vietnam (mid-1968), and the President signed it, the Fed offset the will of Congress by loosening up on the money supply. Inflation actually accelerated. Such actions raise a basic question: with fiscal and monetary policy pulling in opposite directions, how is one to pinpoint responsibility for the nation's economic performance?

Certainly, there should be more coordination between fiscal and monetary policy. Prof. Milton Friedman of the University of Chicago, conservative in monetary matters, said in Banking Committee hearings on January 22, 1976, that fiscal and monetary policy "ought to be conducted in concert. . . . I do not share the view of those people who say you should have a nonpolitical monetary policy any more than you should have a nonpolitical fiscal policy." The Federal Reserve Reform Act, mentioned above, seeks to coordinate fiscal and monetary policy.

A fourth need is to require the Federal Reserve to be more open with Congress and the public about its policies. A good start was made in the 94th Congress: it brought the chairman of the Fed before Congress every three months for a dialogue on the targets of money supply and long-term interest rates. Paul Volcker, president of the New York Federal Reserve Bank, said recently that the hearings have proved a useful exercise in "practical monetarism"; the FOMC has had to justify its decisions more clearly in its own mind. Chairman Burns himself has acknowledged that the increased public dialogue has been "most helpful."

This exchange of views should be expanded. There is no reason why the Fed should not tell Congress and the people what *results* it expects to achieve with its stated targets—what rate of inflation, what rate of unemployment, what rate of economic growth, what level of interest rates. The Fed has batteries of economists making those projections; the public, which pays for such research, is certainly entitled to know what the projections are, and how they were arrived at.

Fed officials have complained that, if it were required to divulge its projections, the staff would become so gun shy that it could not do honest economic work. In fact, it would be doing nothing more than the Council of Economic Advisers does every January in its projections on taxing and spending policy.

Even within its present limitations, the Fed's testimony could be sharpened to give the public a better reading on monetary performance. Chairman Burns has made his target of growth in the money supply so wide (most recently 4.5 to 7 per cent for the most narrowly defined money supply—cash and checking accounts) that its meaning is considerably diminished. There is a great deal of difference, in the effect on the economy, between 4.5 and 7 per cent.

Those of us who have been pressing for changes in the Fed are sometimes accused of wishing to "politicize" the System, thus compromising its vaunted "independence." The argument for "independence" usually goes like this: the decisions the Fed makes are highly complex; sometimes unpopular decisions require a long-range viewpoint; nonbankers, nonbusinessmen, and certainly politicians, should not have too much say. That line of reasoning has a certain appeal. It could also apply to decisions involving commitment of troops abroad, regulation of the airlines, taxation or health insurance. Is monetary policy any more complex than decisions in those areas? Yet no one argues that such decisions should be exempt from public scrutiny.

Reform of the Fed, like tax reform or any other change that challenges entrenched interests, is long in coming. Reform too often is an orphan, with powerful enemies. We have seen this in the 94th Congress. Comprehensive reforms were proposed that would have opened up the Federal Reserve to the revealing light of public opinion. But there was no lobby for such reforms. Consumer groups and public-interest organizations favored the changes, but found it hard to interest their constituents in issues that are remote from most people's view. The Fed and its powerful friends in the financial community had no such trouble. The American Bankers Association vowed its "total opposition" to *any* reform.

We must stop thinking of the Fed as simply a "bankers' bank." It is not just a bank. It is a government agency, and our laws should treat it as such. ☐

★★

39 Regulating the Regulators   Steven Rattner

The following article focuses on a broad-based movement in today's society— articulated by academics and politicians as well as by businessmen—that overregulation by government is not achieving its purposes but rather is imposing tremendous social costs on all the people. A leader of this new movement is Charles Louis Schultze, and his role in getting regulatory reforms is highlighted by Rattner. What is Schultze's political background?

Support for regulatory reform is promoted by liberals as well as by conservatives, and both Senator Edward M. Kennedy and President Jimmy Carter favor legislation to achieve such reform. What are some of the negative effects of overregulation, according to the critics? There are, of course, defenders of the existing regulations too. What arguments are made in defense of existing government regulations? As Rattner points out there has been a shift in government regulatory policy from the "economic regulation" of the early 1900s to an emphasis on controls of "health and safety." How do these objectives differ, and why is this new emphasis particularly upsetting to the critics of overregulation? In this context, what does OSHA stand for? And how has its regulatory activities given ammunition to the critics of overregulation? In an effort to lessen the burdens of regulation in the face of mounting criticism, government agencies are trying new tactics and strategies. What is the "bubble concept" as used by EPA, for example? Much of the current discussion centers on evaluating the advantages of regulations versus the disadvantages. In this regard, what are the issues and problems involved in trying to implement "cost-benefit" analysis to solve this dilemma?

It would seem that the debate concerning overregulation has occurred because of the unanticipated consequences of some government regulations. That is, while it is easy to see the direct danger to individuals who work with toxic chemicals, it is not easy to see effects on society of regulating various activities. Do you think that overregulation contributes to our inflation rate, lower productivity, and slowed pace of economic growth? Is government regulation becoming excessive? To what extent is the argument of columnist James J. Kilpatrick valid? He suggests that government regulations be confined to matters seriously affecting people's health and safety. Or do you think that when the government tries to force us to wear auto seat-belts we prefer not to wear, the government really knows what is best for us?

★ ★ ★

Government regulations are being blamed for an array of ills — especially for boosting inflation. Can they be cut without harming the public?

REGULATING THE REGULATORS

By Steven Rattner

Charlie Schultze has impeccable liberal credentials. Over the years, the 54-year-old, gravelly-voiced economist has advised an array of solidly Democratic candidates, such as Senator Edmund S. Muskie. He was budget director in the days of the Great Society. In the interstices surrounding his time in Government, he was a senior fellow at the Brookings Institution, a think tank of liberal repute. And at the moment, he is the chairman of the Council of Economic Advisers in the latest administration of liberal pretensions.

But today, Charles Louis Schultze is at the cutting edge — some would call him the

Steven Rattner is a Times reporter based in Washington.

leader — of a bitterly controversial movement to overhaul the nation's system of Government regulation, a cause with a decidedly illiberal aura. His 1976 Godkin Lectures at Harvard University are a modern classic, the "Das Kapital" of the regulatory-reform movement. From his current pulpit, he ardently preaches regulatory reform; in Congressional testimony, in speeches and interviews, he repeats the Schultze refrain: "By now, regulation almost parallels the taxing and spending powers of Government in terms of its influence and importance in the life of the nation. Finding ways to improve how it goes about regulating is the most important managerial task now facing the Government."

Mr. Schultze was an early convert to a campaign that is now gaining awesome momentum. Suddenly, all the world seems to be against Government overregulation. Today there are 56 Federal regulatory agencies, with a combined budget of $6 billion, double the budget of five years ago. Together, regulatory agencies influence virtually every facet of the national life and economy. They control the price of milk, the kind of car you can buy and the upholstery you can put on a sofa. Government regulation is

being regarded by increasing numbers of people as an often unwarranted interference in their private lives, and over-regulation is being blamed for a vast collection of public economic and noneconomic ills: reducing the number of jobs available, adding to the international-trade deficit, stifling enterprise and cutting the productivity of workers. Most of all, the critics say, it adds to the inflation rate, increasing the cost of products ranging from airline tickets to coal to cat litter. Conservatives, long opposed to regulation, are saying "I told you so," and many liberals, in something of a shift, are contending that they've been complaining about Government regulation for years.

Commissions and centers are studying regulation; review groups, councils and task forces in Government are trying to improve it. Hardly a day goes by that businessmen aren't inveighing against Government regulation, and they are now being joined even by some regulators. For his part, President Carter has concluded that regulatory reform is an important and appealing issue and has made it a principal tenet of his Administraton. "Regulation has a large and increasing impact on the economy," he said in a recent message to Congress. "If we are to continue our progress, we must insure that regulation gives Americans their money's worth." Even a liberal such as Senator Edward M. Kennedy of Massachusetts has gotten into the act by proposing his own regulatory-reform legislation, which essentially complements the President's.

Legislators, always sensitive to aggrieved constituents, are rushing to get on the bandwagon. Before even taking his seat in January in the House of Representatives, one newly elected Democrat from Westchester, Peter Peyser, announced the "Monkey Wrench Award" for the agency issuing the most nonsensical regulation. A spate of bills aimed at improving the efficiency of regulation — including one from the Administration — has been introduced in Congress, no doubt reflecting the public mood. One poll, by Opinion Research Corporation of Princeton, found that only 50 percent of those questioned in 1977 felt that Government regulation was a good way of making business responsive to their needs, down from the 60 percent in 1973.

Opponents of regulation, eager to press their case, offer controversial allegations of damage inflicted by overregulation. One day, the Dow Chemical Company will be contending that Federal regulation now costs it $268 million, up 54 percent in a single year.

Another day, there will be a study by George Sternlieb of Rutgers University that regulation adds $9,844 to the cost of the average house. Or, it will be pointed out that car prices are $600 higher due to design changes mandated by Federal regulation. In perhaps the most disputed study, economist Murray Weidenbaum of Washington University contends that, all told, the annual bill now exceeds $100 billion, close to the nation's yearly expenditures on defense.

"In large measure, the costs of Government regulation show up in higher prices of the goods and services that consumers buy," says Mr. Weidenbaum. "These higher prices represent the hidden tax imposed by Government regulation." Barry P. Bosworth, director of the Council on Wage and Price Stability, pegs regulation's contribution to higher prices at between three-quarters and one and a half percent each year.

The intensity of this reform movement has produced an equally intense reaction from the defenders of regulation. They argue that various Federal, state and local regulations have, over the years, provided many obvious and enormous public benefits and protections, from simple fire regulations to more complex clean-water or clean-air regulations; and they assert that the money saved by the regulations often exceeds the cost. The White House Council on Environmental Quality maintains, for example, that $13.1 billion was spent to meet Federal air-pollution standards last year but $22 billion was saved in damages prevented. The proregulation forces contend, too, that in some cases, such as the saving of human life through control of cancer-causing chemicals, the value cannot be measured in terms of monetary cost. These people accuse the regulation reformers of trying to dismantle several decades of progressive social policy. "We should recall that a business community that attacked regulation as 'creeping socialism' in the 1950's today attacks 'over-regulation' and 'big Government,'" said Mark Green, director of Congresswatch, a Ralph Nader group. "The words are different but the melody lingers on — to roll back the consumer and environmental advances of past years."

But the advocates of regulatory reform concede that the vast majority of Americans have come to demand clean air, unpolluted water, a safe workplace and wholesome food, the costs of those achievements notwithstanding. What does not enjoy such wide support, they argue, is the way these goals are pursued.

☐

The Rudd (Iowa) Public Library was nearly required to install facilities for the handicapped even though no handicapped person lived in the town and the cost of the remodeling could have exceeded the library's entire budget for a year.

☐

Government regulation is, of course, as old as the Constitution itself which gave to Congress the right to regulate interstate commerce. The first significant regulatory efforts were not made, however, until the creation of the Interstate Commerce Commission in 1887. Every schoolchild recalls the circumstances — the predatory pricing and anti-competitive business practices of the Robber Barons. Today, few would dispute the validity of the original purpose behind the creation of the I.C.C. and other early agencies with related purposes, such as the Federal Trade Commission. The second burst of regulatory fever erupted in the 1930's in response to the Depression and as part of the New Deal. Those troubled times produced a shift in the American attitude about the responsibility of business to society and the propriety of greater public involvement — through Government — in the affairs of business. And welfare state begat welfare regulation in the guise of a broad array of new regulatory agencies, ranging from the Federal Communications Commission to the Civil Aeronautics Board.

Most of these early agencies were engaged in "economic regulation" — the control of prices, market access and related business practices. The creation of the C.A.B. in 1938, for example, brought the controls over pricing and route structure that economists now decry as being in nobody's interest. Like the I.C.C., most of these agencies were originally created to combat very genuine problems. But as the problems were gradually eradicated, many of the agencies became moribund or began to protect the businesses they were supposed to be monitoring. The Federal Communications Commission, for example, was expending much of its effort until recently toward protecting the monopoly of the American Telephone and Telegraph Company.

The most dramatic efforts to dismantle these unwanted agencies have been taken by Alfred E. Kahn, former chairman of the C.A.B. and now the President's chief inflation fighter. From his C.A.B. perch, Mr. Kahn labored energetically to permit the airlines to serve the cities they chose at prices arrived at through competition. Along the way, Mr. Kahn won legislation providing for the abolition of the C.A.B. in 1985.

Progress on loosening economic regulation has helped turn attention to another form of regulation, far more controversial and with substantially higher stakes for most Americans. Now, the debate is chiefly over "health and safety" — a clean environment, effective drugs and the like. As with the agencies engaged in economic regulation, the "health and safety" agencies were created in response to very real problems. Against this backdrop, passage of most of the legislation was not only logical, but desirable. Government would at last take unto itself the responsibility for protecting workers that private industry seemed unable to assume. The failure of business in the 1960's to protect the safety and health of its workers was as much responsible for the creation of the Occupational Safety and Health Administration (OSHA), for example, as the predatory practices of the railroads which led to the formation of the I.C.C. in the 19th century.

Most of the new agencies, including OSHA, enjoyed broad public support in those heady days of the late 1960's and early 1970's. Anything and everything could be regulated in the name of the public interest. Regulators waded in with heavy hands, and adopted many sweeping regulations. But for a variety of reasons the public support began to wane. The agencies had trouble implementing the regulations efficiently. The high cost, often initially ignored, began to be apparent. Frequently well-intentioned efforts to correct obvious defects began to accelerate into efforts to eliminate trivial abuses, or to eliminate abuses that affected a small portion of the population. Sulfur-dioxide air pollution affects a great segment of the population, for example, and has engendered widespread fears; on the other hand, ozone, a more recent concern of the Environmental Protection Agency, affects a much smaller number of people, those who are serious asthmatics. In some cases, the cures were worse than the disease, and the backlash that resulted was the beginning of today's revisionist groundswell.

□

In Maryland, a state law requires hospitals to keep hot water in patients' rooms at no less than 110 degrees while a Federal regulation requires that it be kept at no more than 110 degrees.

□

Consider OSHA, which is a graphic example of the problem. One of its first acts, as directed by Congress, was to adopt more than 30,000 safety standards that industry groups had developed over a couple of decades. It decreed, for example, that tanks intended for storage of inflammable liquids must have fireproof linings — suggesting that industry must be ordered to do something that seemed patently obvious; that exactly seven rivets (not six or eight) must be used in boilers, for no explicit reasons of safety; that if a tree falls in the street, someone must be assigned to direct traffic around it — again, something utterly obvious.

In its early years, OSHA was plagued by mismanagement and spent much of its time trying to implement or defend such rules as those dictating, with great specificity, the shape, size and placement of exit signs. The effect of blindly adopting 30,000 regulations, without question, and then enforcing them inefficiently or without any great sense of priority was to alienate further the businessmen whose cooperation OSHA desperately needed. "Because the standards were so absurd, a lot of people just said, 'Come and get me,'" said Philip J. Harter, a Washington attorney who has worked extensively with OSHA. "The standards have huge gaps in them; a lot aren't applicable, and to the extent that they are design-oriented, they inhibited technical development. But in fairness, industry was in part hoist with its own petard. It had the voluntary standards but it wasn't enforcing them."

The charge that Federal-agency overzealousness has led to ham-handed regulation without any regard for costs has also been made against OSHA. Three months of hearings on a new cancer policy has produced a 250,000-page record — the largest ever compiled. Critics complained that the proposed new policy could cost industry as much as $36 billion annually. On the same point, a United States Circuit Court has voided the way OSHA proposed specifically to control emissions of benzene, a cancer-causing chemical, because "OSHA disclaimed any obligation to balance these costs against expected benefits."

Some of the first signs of the regulatory revolt came not from the economists but from consumers. In 1973, a law passed by Congress required that all new cars be equipped with an interlock that prevented the car from being started without seat belts being fastened. In 1975, under pressure from a rebellious public, Congress recanted. Similarly, when the Food and Drug Administration took action, to restrict the use of saccharin, Congress quickly rebelled. Many citizens were screaming that they would not give up saccharin, even if it were cancer-causing. A similar scenario is already being sketched out over the issue of nitrates, food preservatives, used in bacon, for example, which are known to cause cancer but for which there are no known, reasonably inexpensive substitutes.

In addition to offending consumer sensibilities, regulation has come to grate on some liberal nerves as well in its tendency to impose costs and requirements that large companies have the resources to meet but which often pose formidable hurdles for smaller firms. In the case of the automobile fuel-efficiency standards, for example, General Motors will be able to meet the standards with relative ease, while Chrysler may not be able to meet them at all.

□

There are more than 4,400 different types of Government forms (not including tax and banking forms) that require 143 million man-hours a year to fill out.

□

The news of the regulatory revolt has not escaped the notice of the regulators, particularly the new breed of agency heads that arrived with the Carter Administration. Sensitive to the politics and even to the economics of regulatory reform, they have begun to modernize their agencies and bring new efficiencies. As a consequence, regulators are now finding that they must become more moderate, more effective and more eloquent. That includes the people at OSHA, which is an arm of the Department of Labor. One morning not too long ago, reporters were invited to the Labor Department's sleek, modern auditorium for a "media event," meaning, in Washington parlance, an effort to generate favorable publicity. The princiapl speaker was Dr. Eula Bingham, the head of OSHA.

"When I came here I didn't come just to let the agency run the way it had," she reflected recently in her office. "I knew that I had to revise and rewrite a number of standards. I was hostile to the idea that you had to have a fire extinguisher so many inches off the ground. That's not what safety is all about." The revision of the safety standards, in which, for example, 25 pages of national fire-protection rules were replaced by a single paragraph, earned Dr. Bingham high marks among the reformers. Likewise her drastic cut in paper-work requirements of 50 percent, and her organizational changes, have brought vitality if not total efficiency to the agency. She has even won praise from James J. Kilpatrick, the conservative columnist, who noted approvingly that the same week that Dr. Bingham repealed the 928 nit-picking regulations, she imposed the heaviest civil fines in the agency's history on N.L. Industries, a chemical conglomerate, for exposing workers to lead.

"This is precisely the kind of thing that OSHA should have been doing all along," Mr. Kilpatrick wrote. "If the agency will confine itself to serious matters of employee health and safety and leave the shape of toilet seats alone, employers, employees, and taxpayers will all benefit. Hooray for Dr. Bingham!"

In inflation-conscious Washington, all Dr. Bingham's efforts have not been met with universal approval. She is, in some ways, a 1960's regulator thrust into the 1970's antiregulation fervor. But there is "no doubt about the fact that we're going to keep on coming out with health and safety standards," she said. "People expect it. We want cost-effective regulations. We don't want to put out ridiculous regulations, but I do not expect us to stop putting out regulations altogether."

The economists would agree. Indeed, almost as often as it is criticized for overregulation, OSHA is criticized for not regulating enough — by economists as well as others. Since OSHA's creation, 2,500 carcinogens or suspected carcinogens have been identified in the workplace, yet the agency has fully controlled exposure to only 22 of them. The economists side with Mr. Kilpatrick — that OSHA's problem is priorities, that it must not just deal with the most important hazards first, but it must deal with them in a balanced way that will eliminate the hazard as a significant threat but without imposing overwhelming costs and provoking unnecessary acrimony.

The most difficult problem is in the area of carcinogens. The inflexibility of OSHA's present approach and the anticipated costs startle not only industry but also much of the Carter Administration. Under the agency's proposed general carcinogen standard, exposure to any chemical found to be a carcinogen would have to be automatically reduced to the "lowest feasible level." A company protesting a new rule would be given a hearing but there would be little opportunity for presenting all the ramifications or for reaching some form of flexible compromise. The standing joke even among other regulators has become that "what OSHA is doing is enough to give cancer prevention a bad name."

A half-decade ago, a proposal like the carcinogen standard might have slid easily through the regulatory process. But in today's climate, the reaction has been quite the opposite. The standard has been delayed and is almost certain to be drastically modified, if not scrapped. Meanwhile, the controversy over the carcinogen standard has led to the creation of the Regulatory Council, a voluntary association of regulatory agency heads. As one its first tasks, the Regulatory Council undertook the development of a cancer policy that could be employed governmentwide. The formation of the Regulatory Council and its work on cancer reflected the fear of other regulators that the backlash from OSHA's earlier mismanagement would ultimately impede the Government's ability to help prevent people from getting cancer.

"Public patience is a shared resource all regulators chew away at," said Donald Kennedy, the highly regarded head of the Food and Drug Administration, who recently submitted his resignation. "We need to husband it." At the head of the new Council is another highly regarded regulator, Douglas M. Costle, the administrator of the Environmental Protection Agency, which has earned a reputation for high-quality analysis. Prodded a bit by Government economists, the E.P.A. has begun to experiment with new regulatory techniques that the White House would like to see extended to other agencies. One, called the "bubble concept," leans heavily on the notion that regulation is most efficient when it allows flexibility-performance standards rather than what are called specification standards. Instead of the present practice of setting individual limits on every type of air pollutant, for example, the bubble concept treats a plant as if it were a giant bubble and regulates only the total emissions coming out at the top. That allows businesses to spew a little more of one pollutant in return for tightening down further on another. Business would search out the cheapest mix.

Initiatives such as the bubble concept and the Regulatory Council represent actions taken voluntarily by the regulators, either because they genuinely believe in the need for regulatory reform or because they believe voluntary actions could stave off more substantive changes by the White House or by the Congress. Indeed, the White House — even the Domestic Policy Staff which is widely thought of as liberal — has been in the forefront of the battle to improve regulation, particularly through the person of Charles Schultze.

Mr. Schultze's principal involvement in the regulatory process has been through the creation of the Regulatory Analysis Review Group, ostensibly an interagency body but in reality a small cluster of White House economists. The group has hammered away at proposed regulations that they think are going to be particularly costly. Should all subway stations be required to be remodeled to allow use by the handicapped, even if the bill amounts to $9 billion? The answer was no, so the cost of that regulation was trimmed by 30 percent. Should new strip-mining rules for coal operators be issued that could add 10 percent to the price of coal? The economists say the cost was trimmed by as much as $1 billion without substantial ecological harm. Should environmental requirements for building new industrial facilities in clean-air areas be so tough that few could be built? That bill was changed to reduce the cost to business by $20 million.

☐

To retain the flameproof quality of children's sleepwear, the garments should be washed in detergent with phosphates. New York and other states have banned phosphates for environmental reasons.

☐

Like so much else in Washington, regulatory reform moves slowly. Charles Schultze and his allies have been unable, or reluctant, to do much more than use their powers of persuasion on recalcitrant agencies. Only one issue has been taken directly to the President by the economists — that of cotton-dust controls they regarded as too expensive. In that case, OSHA, arguing that cotton workers badly needed better protection, prevailed over the economists.

Assuming that the amount of regulation the economy can bear is limited, how can we be sure of getting the most efficient mix? Under the present system, there is no way to balance the cost of controlling the quantity of an individual pollutant from one source versus the cost of controlling it from another source. An even tougher question would involve trading off one hazard against another. For example, OSHA might be speeding ahead on regulating some cancer-causing substance which might cost $1 million in compliance costs for each life saved. But over at E.P.A., there might be a way of saving lives at half the cost. The problem is that on the regulatory front, there is not an effective equivalent of the Office of Management and Budget, whose job it is to assess the relative merit of various programs, across agency lines.

Whether the regulatory revolt will ultimately be able to respond to these questions is in doubt. To be sure, the very difficulty of compiling accurate numbers makes the challenge forbidding. One of the hottest regulatory issues today is cost-benefit analysis, the contention by economists that the costs of complying with a regulation can be measured in terms of the expected benefits, the lives saved and the like. Cost-benefit analysis does not require a value to be put on human life, as many suspect, but it does allow the cost of saving lives by various regulations to be assessed.

Not all agree with the cost-benefit concept. "Cost-benefit analysis of health and safety regulation is today about as neutral a concept as literacy tests in the old South," said Mark Green. "Because business regulates control and exaggerates its costs, and because benefits are often unmeasurable and generational, anyone who urges that all regulations pass a mathematical cost-benefit test wants not analysis but paralysis."

Such response is not unusual. Each slight movement by the economists to modify regulation engenders a more intense reaction from old-school regulators. Recently, the Administration offered a much-heralded bill to reform the regulatory process. It would require regulators to choose the least expensive path or explain why they couldn't, and it would centralize responsibility to insure efficient regulatory procedures. But the bill has been greatly watered down during the internal review process and faces further dilution on Capitol Hill.

Meanwhile, the proponents of regulatory overhaul plug away, maintaining that society can have as much regulation as it is willing to pay for — but that it must also understand how much it will cost and that it should be accomplished in the least expensive way. "There are some libertarians who want to do away with regulation; I call them right-wing kooks," says Murray Weidenbaum. "It's not the ends, it's the means that are at issue: How to attain objectives." ■

★★

40

Diplomatic Spoils: The Washington Bureaucracy Abroad   Roger Morris

Appointments to government offices often were made on the basis of political connections. While this practice has been largely eliminated in hiring the majority of federal employees who are under civil service, it still affects top-level appointments—such as ambassadors. Though President Carter stated that diplomats should be qualified for their positions, his record of appointments is not much better than that of his predecessors. What political factors affect a president's appointment of ambassadors? Which seem to be most important?

Roger Morris argues that America's diplomats are not very competent or skillful, and that our ability to conduct foreign relations suffers accordingly. He contends that even the career diplomats from the foreign service have only mediocre records. Why is that the case? Does this indicate that we need to look at our methods of recruiting foreign service personnel more carefully? What changes might be needed to recruit the sort of foreign service officer who would be more successful? What are the lasting effects on the quality of government if the people appointed are mediocre?

The tension between the needs of politics and the requirements of professionalism is clearly shown in this essay. Perhaps we are fortunate with regard to our ambassadors, since, as Morris contends, they are not generally very powerful or influential persons. Why is the position of ambassador not thought to be very important? Is patronage to be blamed? Give this issue serious attention, for the president very often makes political calculations when he appoints his cabinet, bureau heads, and the Supreme Court—as well as ambassadors. Should a president consider politics and qualifications when making these high-level appointments? Or should competence be the only criterion?

★ ★ ★

DIPLOMATIC SPOILS

The Washington bureaucracy abroad   by Roger Morris

"When I go into an embassy in South America or Central America or Europe and see sitting as our ambassador, our representative there, a fat, bloated, ignorant, rich major contributor to a Presidential campaign who can't even speak the language of the country in which he serves, and knows less about our own country and our consciousness and our ideals and our motivation, it's an insult to me and to the people of America and to the people of that country."—Jimmy Carter, November 23, 1975.

QUESTION: *"Can you name one such fat, ignorant, bloated ambassador who can't speak the language?"*

CARTER: *"No, I wouldn't want to name any."*

QUESTION: *"Can you name one, though?"*

CARTER: *"The point I make is that—whether they are actually fat or thin—that they are appointed because there are political interrelationships and not because of quality."*

—CBS's "Face the Nation," March 14, 1976

THE SCENE NOW SHIFTS forward to midsummer 1977 and the State Department's ornate, antique-laden Benjamin Franklin Room overlooking the Potomac, a ceremonial eighth-floor penthouse where senior diplomats of the new Carter Administration are gathered for the swearing-in of an ambassador. Richard Moose, the new Deputy Undersecretary of State for Administration, former aide to Dean Rusk, Walt Rostow, Henry Kissinger, J. William Fulbright, and John Sparkman, is there to administer the oath to his old friend and patron, Lawrence S. Eagleburger, lately Moose's predecessor as Deputy Undersecretary, former aide to Rusk, Rostow, Kissinger, Nicholas Katzenbach, and Melvin Laird, and now President Carter's Ambassador to Yugoslavia.

"As I look around this room, I see such a marvelous collection of faces and persons," Moose tells the assembly. "It's almost as though, in the words of Claude Rains from *Casablanca,* someone had sent word out to round up the usual suspects." Everyone laughs, of course. The quip becomes a "One-liner of the Month" among rhapsodic ambassadorial biographies in the *Newsletter* of the Department of State. For the rest of us, however, it is no joke.

Despite that vivid campaign rhetoric about the physiognomy and other qualifications of our diplomats, the Carter Administration in its first year and a half has indeed rounded up most of the usual suspects to fill its ambassadorial jobs. Figuratively and literally, American embassies still seat an ample quota of the "fat, bloated, and ignorant," whose money speaks the old diplomatic *lingua franca* of political patronage, sometimes with a Georgian accent. Yet even more common in the President's diplomatic appointments has been his feckless resort to career bureaucrats, whose brand of ambassadorial nepotism and "political interrelationships" turn out to be no less insidious for being obscure or professional. Like most of his predecessors, Jimmy Carter has chosen to represent us to the world with a largely banal collection of friends, careerists, and adaptable holdovers who owe much of their eminence to the dubious men and methods Carter was elected to replace. Like their predecessors in turn, some of those ambassadors become relatively harmless satraps in the trivial, forgotten outposts of the diplomatic service. But too many others, atop embassies with serious business, are just weak enough to preserve the worst habits of foreign policy, while strong enough in their weakness to

Roger Morris, a graduate of Harvard who worked in the State Department and on the National Security Council under two administrations, is now a writer living in northern New Mexico. He is the author of Uncertain Greatness: Henry Kissinger and American Foreign Policy *(Harper & Row).*

undermine reform. As Carter the candidate seemed to recognize more clearly before he acquired his own ambassadorial corps, it is indeed an "insult," at home as well as abroad.

Business as usual

THE AMBASSADORS occupy one of the dusty corners of the Carter government. No David Marstons or Bert Lances have disturbed the customary public indifference to our man in Canberra. Nor do ambassadorships, as we shall see, usually attract the zealous or the powerminded.

The saving irony is that, in most cases, ambassadors don't matter all that much. The "dirty little secret" of both career and noncareer envoys—discovered by some ruefully too late—is the banality and common power-

lessness of the job. Their requisite incompetence places most at the mercy of their own staff. The Washington-centered system of policy forces the envoys to take orders from relatively junior desk officers or upstart White House and Pentagon staff men in any event. Moreover, the ambassador is prey to the savage bureaucratic feudalism of foreign policy, in which the competing baronies of CIA, Agriculture, Defense, Treasury, and even Commerce or Labor may wield more power than the State Department, and thus more than the ambassador in his own post. The Carter regime has already gone through the quadrennial exercise that begins with a Presidential cable announcing that U.S. ambassadors are in charge of everyone in their embassies, including the CIA, and ends with a secret cable from the CIA Director (by the separate cable lines the CIA has to every mission) telling his people to ignore the first order whenever they must.

The surpassing ceremonial force of the office, the trips to Washington with visiting heads of state, the false deference of more powerful bureaucrats—these are enough to satisfy the sort of people who get the job in most cases.

Still, new diplomatic appointments were something of an embarrassment in the first year of the Administration. Having vowed to select envoys (like U.S. Attorneys) on the basis of merit, the White House soon found certain discreet embassies for willing if not so able political retainers—"second-rate fat cats," as one career diplomat described them. The manner and ease with which this patronage occurred gives a revealing glimpse into the style and substance of the Carter regime.

Early in February, 1977, with some piety and flourish ("a 'first' for the nation," declared one official announcement), the President convened a blue-ribbon "Advisory Board on Ambassadorial Appointments." In the words of the Executive Order creating it, the board's task was to review "the qualifications of individuals for an ambassadorial post for which noncareer individuals are being considered," or, more plainly, to screen the sort of chubby, monolingual contributors Carter found so offensive under the Republicans. Behind the press releases and executive prose, however, the committee would be like most of its kind: ritually assembled for political window dressing. Its twenty members included the obligatory sampling of docile politicians, academics, women, and minorities with sufficiently little experience in the bureaucratic thicket into which they were being led. And it placed them alongside authorities such as Dean Rusk, Averell Harriman, and William Scranton, who were impaneled because they knew the territory only too well. Rusk, for example, would

ZEVI BLUM

be chairman of the board's subcommittee on ambassadorships in the Middle East and Asia, presumably on the basis of the success of his own policies in those regions as Secretary of State.

Staffed solely by the State Department, the board was also carefully fed and trained to the role by its bureaucratic handlers. In the omnipresent loose-leaf briefing books that clutter the meeting tables of such "citizens' panels," the department's "country reports" depicted international issues and the needs of American diplomacy in the empty vernacular of government handouts. The lists of ambassadorial candidates before the group had been duly run through government computers, and were composed almost entirely in accord with White House or Congressional patronage. In any case, the practical authority of the board was limited to passing on to Carter and Vance—with neither comment nor ranking—three to five of the prescribed names for each post.

The board met five times during 1977 and once more last January, its deliberations stamped "secret" and its decisions based, like the Politburo's, on what an attendant staff official earnestly called "unanimous consensus." Out of this none too subtle laundering came five ambassadorial nominations that drew immediate fire from the American Foreign Service Association (AFSA), a loose guild of career officers that has been the vehicle for the diplomatic bureaucracy's increasingly public opposition to the most egregious examples of the old embassy spoils system. Thus, for Australia the board duly endorsed, Carter nominated—and the AFSA, on grounds of "professional standards," testified against— Philip Henry Alston, Jr., an Atlanta lawyer and Carter backer, whose credentials for the post apparently lay somewhere among his lucrative legal practice, directorships in various local businesses, or the presidency of the University of Georgia Alumni Association. The AFSA similarly opposed: Anne Cox Chambers, assigned to Brussels by way of Miss Porter's School, the Atlanta Junior League and Peachtree Garden Club, the chairmanship of Atlanta Newspapers and Cox Broadcasting Corporation, and generous support for the right Presidential candidate; Marvin L. Warner, an Alabaman turned Ohio real estate and savings-and-loan magnate who dabbled in Jewish philanthropies, thoroughbreds, the New York Yankees, the Tampa Buccaneers, and Democratic politicians, and who now is U.S. Ambassador to Switzerland; William B. Schwartz, Jr., another well-heeled real estate investor and Atlantan whom a grateful President sent to oversee a sleek embassy and occasion-

ally restive natives in the Bahamas; and Milton A. Wolf, Cleveland's prosperous "Builder of the Year" in 1964, Sen. John Glenn's valuable supporter in 1974, Carter's efficient Ohio fund-raiser in 1976, and this year's U.S. Ambassador to Austria.

"Those five were too much," said one Foreign Service officer speaking for the AFSA, adding with unintended irony, "Noncareer ambassadors should be there because they have something special not found in the Service." By the same logic, AFSA might have gone on to dispute other Carter nominees.

As it was, however, the AFSA's testimony against the original five was politely taken and promptly ignored by the Senate Foreign Relations Committee. The confirmations skimmed through, and the disgruntled career men, in the manner of their trade, retired with a certain weary and cynical resignation at having made the point for the record.

B
Y THE END OF 1977, even the would-be bureaucratic critics, along with the Congress and press, had come to feel that Carter's ambassadorial patronage was nonetheless more professional than usual. Of sixty-five new envoys named over the year, only twenty-three were noncareer, making a slightly lower proportion of political appointees than under any recent Administration. There was also general approval of many of the selections. The *New York Times* and *Washington Post*, echoed by appreciative Senators, pronounced "admirable" the appointments of Kingman Brewster, former president of Yale, to London, Robert Goheen of Princeton to New Delhi, UAW head Leonard Woodcock to Peking, and the seventy-four-year-old former Senate Majority Leader, Mike Mansfield, to Tokyo. Other, less notable appointees came similarly certified and praised from litmus careers in business, educational bureaucracies, foundations, journalism, or past government service. Their political loyalties ran, if not to Carter personally, at least to the Democratic party and its previous regimes. Richard N. Gardner, Columbia law professor and early loser in the scramble among Carter campaign advisers for the more important Washington jobs, was sent to Rome with his socially prominent Italian wife. A former assistant to Walt Rostow and academic administrator, W. Howard Wriggins, heads the embassy in Sri Lanka. Louis A. Lerner, a suburban publisher, art collector, and political supporter, went discreetly to Norway; Rodney O. Kennedy-Minott, an instructor in American history and a California loyalist, was given Sweden. Like the

"The 'dirty little secret' of both career and noncareer envoys . . . is the banality and common powerlessness of the job."

advisory board who vouchsafed them, these ambassadors included too a suitable sprinkling of women and minorities. And in accordance with tradition, the Carter Administration duly matched the latter to what it no doubt saw as postings of appropriate color and culture. To troublesome Algeria, for instance, went Ulric St. Clair Haynes, Jr., black vice-president of Cummins Engine and onetime aide to Mc-George Bundy in the Johnson White House. Two Spanish-surname academics and a Mexican-born former governor of Arizona were named to deal with tyrannical Latin regimes in Nicaragua, Honduras, and Argentina. Two other similarly chosen appointees—both foundation functionaries, erstwhile government consultants, and blacks—were dispatched to Kenya and Cameroon.

Without exception, these more agreeable non-career ambassadors were the well-burnished products of organizations close to government in either geography or ethos, and usually both. Even the academics were more often noted for their bureaucratic status in some administrative hierarchy rather than for professional distinction as scholars or teachers. And as a group, the shared cachet and domestication of these other political appointees gave them ready, uncontested entry compared

with the realtors, lawyers, and heiresses of relatively vulgar pedigree. No one would ask about the deeper importance of such credentials for the job at hand. Are the realities of running Yale or Princeton—the years spent placating trustees and faculty, grubbing for money in the corporate and legislative countinghouses —so much better preparation than negotiating land deals in Atlanta or campaign money-grubbing in Cincinnati? Does climbing the ladder of a listless union hierarchy, or presiding for fifteen years with gentlemanly torpor and abdication over the U.S. Senate, naturally make for more gifted diplomats than owning a business or raising thoroughbreds and peach trees? Are ambassadors so much better schooled in the monotonous ranks of the Ford Foundation than in the local law firm and savings-and-loan? Among establishment institutions in which prestige, self-esteem, and pensions have much to do with pretense and myth, some questions are best unanswered—and some ambassadorial nepotism entirely proper.

Least of all did the Carter appointments occasion serious discussion of diplomacy itself and the considerable demands on its practitioners—subjects for which busy Congressional committees and reporters, not to mention new Presidents, never seem to have time. Students

ZEVI BLUM

of the art from Machiavelli to Henry Kissinger have agreed that the ambassadorial job, properly done, requires extraordinary breadth. The competent envoy begins with a detailed knowledge of the history, language, culture, and politics of his hosts, not only to understand and interpret them, but also to escape a dangerous dependence on his own underlings or the home office. He should also be an avid, critical observer with a sense of his own ignorance, and a shrewd operator, with the intellectual courage, bureaucratic irreverence, and political independence to tell his government what it may not want to hear about the world, or about itself. Even skipping the more rigorous job description, it is clear that only a handful of the Carter ambassadors could meet a genuine test of fitness. Intellectual distinction in the subjects of their mission, a demonstrated talent for digging beneath the surface, most of all political and bureaucratic independence—singly the qualities are in scant supply, and almost nowhere in combination among the score of spoils men and their Establishment betters whom Jimmy Carter rewarded with political ambassadorships.

What seems more unsettling and even less recognized, however, is that records and qualifications are hardly more impressive among the career officers the new President appointed in such apparently reassuring numbers.

Records of questionable judgment

IN THE DEPARTMENT's *Newsletter*, as in any corporate magazine, the newly appointed career envoys hover—in standard promotion-photo pose—over the spare official biographies that list, without unseemly elaboration, the successive dates and titles of the bureaucratic ascent to ambassador. As with comparable rises to power at General Motors or Gulf or Yale, the announcement spares the public the in-house realities of how and why it happened, the connections between the bland faces and resumés and the flesh-and-blood world of policy. Some, of course, are competent and devoted civil servants, their careers untainted by dubious patronage or disastrous diplomacy. But too many of Carter's Foreign Service appointments have histories that should have given someone pause.

Throughout the ambassadorships of the new Administration are men recommended or raised to prominence by the intimate patronage of the figure whose foreign policy Jimmy Carter campaigned so vocally against: Henry Kissinger. Elliot Richardson and Gerard C. Smith, both early and close Kissinger allies in the savage bureaucratic wars of the first Nixon Administration, are ambassadors-at-large, with Smith (also a onetime Rusk protégé) assigned to the ominous nuclear nonproliferation negotiations in Geneva. To Iran, Carter named William H. Sullivan, Kissinger's principal State Department aide, supporter and public apologist during the final bloody years of negotiation and terror bombing in Indochina. Lawrence Eagleburger, perhaps Kissinger's closest assistant over his eight years and an ardent Nixon and Ford supporter, sits in Belgrade. John Holdridge, for years Kissinger's chief aide for Asian affairs, is now Carter's envoy to Singapore. Arthur A. Hartman represents the new Administration in Paris; appointed an Assistant Secretary by Kissinger, he is thus an adherent of Nixon-Ford policies on Eurocommunism, including CIA interference in Italy and Portugal. Kissinger's major department aide and spokesman for African policy during the Angolan intervention, William E. Schaufele, Jr., was nominated by Carter to be Ambassador to Greece. One of Kissinger's most partisan advisers and Rusk's press secretary during all those years of official candor on the Vietnam war, Robert McCloskey, was rewarded as the envoy to the Netherlands and subsequently to Greece. Robert Anderson, Kissinger's own press spokesman and, like McCloskey, noted for his work in public information, is now our man in Morocco. With the exception perhaps of Richardson, who was the Republican lieutenant governor of Massachusetts before being appointed Nixon's Undersecretary of State, all of these men were relatively junior and minor bureaucrats who ascended well beyond the normal levitation for their devotion to the extraordinary methods and policies of the Kissinger era. "The most distinguished alumni of HKU," as one official put it.

But they are by no means the only new ambassadors with records of questionable judgment. The Carter career appointments go on to read like a veritable roll call from most of the major foreign policy debacles, notorious and obscure, over the past fifteen years. From the Dominican invasion of 1965 comes Ambassador W. Tapley Bennett, Jr., now envoy to NATO. William J. Jorden, Walt Rostow's aide for Vietnam, is Ambassador to Panama. Another key official on Vietnam, Robert H. Miller, who was one of Rusk's State Department desk officers, is in Malaysia. William G. Bowdler, the Administration's initial Ambassador to South Africa, was Rostow's aide for Latin America during major CIA interventions in Brazil, Chile, Bolivia, and elsewhere: Harry Shlauderman, deputy chief of the mission in

". . . too many of Carter's Foreign Service appointments have histories that should have given someone pause."

Chile during the Nixon subversion of the Allende regime, and later accused by some of dissimulation before Congressional committees, is in Peru. To Malta, Carter nominated Lowell Bruce Laingen, another erstwhile desk officer. Laingen was a principal voice in U.S. policy toward the Pakistani dictatorship in 1971, when the State Department ignored the murder of thousands and the exodus of 10 million in what later became Bangladesh. Two former African Bureau officials, David Newsom (who as Nixon's Assistant Secretary for Africa presided over much official U.S. indifference toward starvation in Biafra) and Herman J. Cohen (who as a desk officer with Newsom condoned silent support of a genocidal regime in Burundi) were named Carter's Ambassadors to the Philippines and Senegal, respectively. Newsom, who had been Kissinger's Ambassador to Indonesia, where he was a strong advocate of more aid for the Jakarta junta and less talk about human rights, practiced the same cliency in Manila. And this spring, having ascended to foreign service seniority on a trail of disastrous policies, Newsom was routinely appointed Undersecretary of State for Political Affairs, the third-ranking office in the department and the zenith of career officialdom.

The list might continue through other Kissinger protégés, other retainers to Rostow or Rusk, other desk officers discreetly husbanding disasters, other diplomats who have lied to, if not for, their country. In his first year in office, Jimmy Carter spent his ambassadorial appointments not only to pay off political friends or to enlist the usual quota of Establishment notables, but more largely to promote bureaucrats who participated in foreign policies that the Democratic Party—and most vocally Carter himself—found reprehensible in previous Administrations.

E MBASSIES WERE dispatched in 1977 largely as they have been over the past thirty years—by one of Washington's most durable old-boy networks. The names of the ambassadorial chosen wind through a ritual maze of interoffice nominations and clearances among the State Department's regional bureaus, the office of the Deputy Undersecretary for Management, and the Director General of the Foreign Service. All are bastions of seniority in which surviving bureaucrats patronize and serve other bureaucrats who patronize and serve them—and quash those who don't. Like Britain's Indian Army (though with less éclat), the American diplomatic corps promotes not from the top—

and only inadvertently on merit—but rather from deep within, at the median of talent and power, where the seasoned civil servant has reached his level of incompetence and passes on the same privilege to others of compatible tastes. Our ambassadors thus have a way of emerging mostly from the patronage of stalled desk or personnel officers, of superannuated assistant secretaries, of "administrators" who long ago in their careers were deemed unable to handle the greater demands of political or economic reporting in the Foreign Service's intellectual caste system. This protocol is, incidentally, similar to that which guides the recruitment of new officers in the State Department. The Board of Examiners of the Foreign Service, the certifying body for fresh talent, tends to be a final sinecure for failed officers on their way to slightly premature though pension-prosperous retirement. For both the renewal of the corps and the selection of those who will hold its crowning offices, the American Foreign Service has for a long time relied on the judgment and favor of its career derelicts.

The system at least explains how bureaucrats manage to outlive their constitutionally elected or appointed leaders, with some understandable confusion about whose men they are. So having risen according to their ardor for the policies of the time, the Kissinger-bred bureaucrats were well placed for promotion to embassies.

No "advisory board" was thought necessary under Carter to varnish this process, which is only faintly understood outside the State Department, and never seriously questioned. Nominees who have not run afoul of the Foreign Service's cautious patronage are passed on—one choice per post—to the Secretary of State and the President, who may, at least theoretically, challenge the bureaucracy's consensus. But when the Secretary is himself a docile, dependent, organizational creature, when the President seems without stomach or insight to question his underlings on such procedures, when the White House staff is similarly inert or ignorant, the bureaucratic distillation is the *de facto* power of appointment. And so it has been in the Carter Administration.

The ostensible check on all this is the Senate confirmation process. Yet failing a major public storm over the appointment beforehand, Senatorial consent to ambassadorial nominations is a polite farce. The same anesthetic State Department biographies that accompany the recommended names to the White House also go to Capitol Hill, where a Senate Foreign Relations Committee staff with its own share of co-option, seniority, and sloth seldom looks further. For example, it makes for speed and congeniality in the discharge of constitutional duty that there has been a growing interchange of personnel between the committee and the State Department.

Even should the staff acquire a sudden infusion of independence, however, there is always that final fail-safe of bureaucratic government: the Congress itself. There are scores of untold Washington stories about the shocking carelessness of Senators questioning ambassadorial nominees. The confirmation fraud is now so much a part of the city's routine that journalists rarely cover any but the three to four most prominent State Department hearings each year, and the vast majority of confirmations simply disappear into the unread, often unpublished transcripts of the committee. Nor is there a second chance. Barring national scandal—which is itself unlikely, in part because of the weaknesses of Congressional oversight and confirmation—envoys are almost never called back before the committee to answer basic questions of competence and performance. For the beneficiaries of these practices—the Ambassadors Extraordinary and Plenipotentiaries—and for the younger officers looking on, the lessons are plain. Conformity as well as judgment iron out the wrinkles in one's career, and the Foreign Service takes care of its own.

Comfort, boredom, and authority

MOST OF THE ambassadorial reality—the limousine life, the office politics, the vacant self-importance—is today more than ever the stuff of a Durrell parody or even Terry Thomas in a slightly seedy linen suit. Yet the costs, like Richard Moose's joke, are not funny. If the majority of embassies represent only the usual malaise and lost opportunity, some ambassadors *do* affect policy. Theirs is the power in which caution, vagueness, and parochialism become strengths—not to make policy so much as to unmake it. Set against change or reform, allied with the normal sluggishness of unruly government, and playing on political neuroses at home, the ambassador may do what the conventions of his organization allow him to do best and most safely: to delay, to evade, to do nothing, to outlast—and to do it, like their Terry Thomas forerunners too long in the East, while mistaking the interests of their clients and their mission for the national interest. Thus the Carter arms-supply policy, a "reform" announced by the President with char-

acteristic pretense and naiveté, has been promptly made a mockery by the importunings of embassies from Saudi Arabia to Chile. In the Philippines, Zaire, Nicaragua, Indonesia, and a half-dozen other countries, discreetly insubordinate ambassadors have maintained a public and secret flow of various forms of U.S. aid despite unrelieved human rights abuses.

But the system is never so purposeful or consistent as conspiracy-minded critics think. Ambassadors in their strength and weakness are random forces in the politics of foreign policy and in the genteel chaos of bureaucratic oligarchy; those with the most power to get the job for themselves or others are often the most powerless once they have it.

UNLIKE THE MILITARY, the diplomat is not the spoilt child of historians," wrote a retired ambassador, jaded at last in his memoirs. Yet the problem with American envoys is less bad history than merely no attention at all. No Senator or Congressman probes the shady cul-de-sac in which they are appointed and function. No editors and reporters find titillation in their banal though sometimes fateful politics. No Foreign Service insurgents testify against their colleagues, demanding the same professional scrutiny of "professionals" as of political hacks. No Benjamin Franklins or even Anatoly Dobrynins, men or women of authentic power at home and a knowledge of the game, rush to fill the embassies. The indifference is chronic. Congress has little taste for the political risks of genuine opposition to foreign policy, much less the arcane rites of bureaucracy. The press, as so often, does not understand—or does not want to understand—how it all works. And typically, the issues that agitate the diplomatic bureaucrats, as company people everywhere, are promotion, salaries, pensions, and the next slot.

So the Carter diplomatic appointees are likely to serve out their three to four years in varying comfort, boredom, and authority. The occasional question (or colorful campaign rhetoric) directed to obese contributors will continue to obscure the far more serious issue of bureaucratic patronage and inbred incompetence. Presidents whose main talent is running for office will go on appointing envoys in ignorance or acceptance. Reflecting the scarce virtues and dull vices of organization America, Jimmy Carter's ambassadors unextraordinary may not represent to the world and ourselves the America we want to be. But their collective mediocrity is an emblem of the country we are.   □

"Ambassadors in their strength and weakness are random forces in the politics of foreign policy and in the genteel chaos of bureaucratic oligarchy . . ."

CHAPTER NINE

★ ★ ★

The Supreme Court

Over the last two decades Americans have become increasingly aware of the important role the judiciary has played in confronting some of society's most pressing social and political questions. During those activist Warren years from 1953 through 1969, one saw a vigorous Supreme Court dedicated to defending civil rights and liberties regardless of social consequences. Questions of prayer and Bible reading in the public schools and questions of reapportionment and expanded criminal rights filled the dockets of the Warren Court. One might go so far as to say, as one political analyst has done, that the Warren Court believed instinctively that each social wrong deserved a legal remedy. And although decisions of the present Burger Court would never be characterized in the same way as those of the Warren Court, it too has broken new ground in handling issues such as the right to privacy and questions related to life (abortion rights) and death (capital punishment).

As one sees both activist and more restrained courts become more and more involved with such issues, one becomes concerned about the potential power of the Court. After all, the institution that has authority to interpret the law becomes in essence the law-giver. Since the Court deals with very controversial issues, such as abortion, capital punishment, and obscenity, one should ask whether the Court is the best institution to have absolute authority to interpret law. Is this unelected, unrepresentative body, whose membership is composed basically of white, middle-class, law-school trained, male political appointees, who are remote and insulated from the public, the best institution to remedy social ills? Are the judges who often lack the resources, capacities, and time for decision-making the best political actors to resolve these complex issues? These are the questions that Peter Rusthoven raises in his article on "The Courts as Sociologists."

The justices, although they do not face regular elections as do other political policy-makers, need some contact with the electorate. Since the Court has no way to enforce its own decisions, its impact depends largely on public confidence and support. If the Court loses this support and its decisions go unheeded by a majority of the public and policy-makers, institutional viability becomes of serious concern. This delicate relationship between the public and the Supreme Court is dealt with by Seth Kupferberg in his article "Don't Blame the Court."

Just as vital as public support is to the influence of Court decisions are the so-called "rules of the game," which have an important impact on the results of the "game" itself. In other words, the way decisions are made can largely determine the decision. The deliberative procedures, the type of briefs, and the time limits imposed on argument before the Court can all affect the Court's decision. Fully appreciating this, Nina Totenberg in her article "Behind the Marble, Beneath the Robes," goes into some detail about the formal procedures of the Court.

★★

An adequate analysis of decision-making of the Supreme Court must include the role of personality and its influence on political decisions. Of all the justices who have served on the High Court, those who seem to have been the most important are the chief justices. While some chief justices like Waite, Fuller, and White are barely remembered, one cannot think of the Supreme Court as an institution without recalling the names of Marshall, Taft, Hughes, and Warren. It is not that these chief justices control more votes than the others, or serve longer terms on the Court, but they are potentially a more persuasive influence on decision-making. It is the chief justice, for example, who decides who is to write the Court's opinion when he is in the majority, and he is also responsible for setting the pace of the Court, establishing the environment for decision-making, and determining the future direction of the Court.

The present Court largely owes its color, successes, and failures to its chief justice—Warren E. Burger. When Burger became chief justice in 1969, Court analysts fully expected that the Burger Court under his leadership might reverse and undermine the major social advances made during the Warren years. That did not happen. Some of the Warren decisions were reinterpreted and the scope of others limited, but no major decision was reversed. In addition, Burger went his own direction and led the Court into some areas of civil liberties barely touched upon by the Warren Court, including abortion and privacy. Yet Burger has not appeared as formidable as he might have liked to appear. He has had difficulty bringing cohesion to the Court. He has not been able to cement the so-called "Nixon bloc" on the Court—Justices Rehnquist, Blackmun, Powell, and Burger—into a controlling faction. In two of the important cases decided by the Burger Court, those involving capital punishment and the Pentagon Papers, all nine justices wrote separate opinions. It is this sometimes successful, sometimes unsuccessful, chief justice that Nathan Lewin is particularly concerned with in his article "A Peculiar Sense of Justice."

The Court as an institution has managed to survive all of its chief justices—from Jay to Burger—despite the fact that a number of them have changed the Court's direction, tailored its style, and set its mood, causing controversy with each change. The Court today remains an institution cloaked in myth and tradition. As one of the most powerful political institutions in government, it has made important contributions to stabilizing democratic government.

★★

★★

41

The Courts as Sociologists   Peter J. Rusthoven

As the Supreme Court has become more and more involved with social problems, members of the Court have begun to sound like amateur sociologists. But as Peter Rusthoven argues, the justices are "pseudo-sociologists" rather than social scientists. The difference between the judge as "pseudo-sociologist" and the social scientists, of course, is that the judge has no training, has scant familiarity with the social sciences, and has no basis on which to evaluate significant scientific discovery. Consequently, Rusthoven contends, the Court's unsupported observations of society are often of questionable validity. Consider, if you will, the difference between the Court—in the name of the Constitution—making such invalid observations and a citizen making the same observations. Are the judges misusing the authority of the Constitution to rationalize their own political beliefs about social conditions? Are there dangers to society, to the Court, and to the federal system in allowing the Court, in such a fashion, to mandate policies in the name of the Constitution to deal with social problems? Are there protections from such judicial tyranny? What will happen to alternative policies, offered by other institutions, that fail to win Court approval and constitutional sanction?

The Court today, Rusthoven observes, focuses its attention on the importance of individual rights, while at the same time insisting that the best protection for these rights is through the formalities of law. The Supreme Court has relied heavily on the provisions of the Fourteenth Amendment in dealing with individual rights. Which recent Supreme Court cases best illustrate this reliance? What was the Court's legal reasoning in each of these cases? As a consequence of the Court's focus, interest groups—including the old, the young, the blacks, the whites, the gays, and the handicapped—have demanded and received legal remedies from the Courts. What effect has this increase in demands had on the Court? Have those broad, ill-defined clauses of the Constitution that grant "equal protection" and "due process" enabled the Court, as Rusthoven claims, to expand further its control over a wider area of social concerns?

★ ★ ★

*Through imaginative reading of the Constitution, the
judiciary in recent years has assumed a powerful
role in our society. Today's courts see themselves
as the best instrument to redress society's ills*

The Courts as Sociologists

PETER J. RUSTHOVEN

*In 1974, the Equal Employment Opportunity Commission
selected Thomas Hadfield, a white applicant, to be its Philadelphia District Office Director. George Rogers, a black
whose application had been rejected, brought suit in federal
court, charging that the EEOC—the Federal Government's anti-discrimination agency—had itself been guilty
of race discrimination in making the selection. The court
found that Hadfield was better qualified than Rogers; that
the selection officer—herself black—had made her choice
primarily on that basis; and that the hiring decision had
been approved by superiors who had no knowledge of either
applicant's race.*

*However, the selection officer also stated that because the
three other EEOC directorships in the area were filled by
blacks, she had thought that choosing a white "would reflect a racial balance." Despite Hadfield's superior qualifications, and despite the fact that the selection officer's concern
for "racial balance" was found by the court to have been
"never more than a make-weight" in the selection process,
the court concluded that Rogers had been the victim of
illegal discrimination. Accordingly, it awarded him back
pay at the level of the director's job from the date Hadfield took office, which pay was to continue until the next
opening in the Philadelphia area was filled, or until Rogers
himself accepted another position with equal or better pay.*

*On March 20, 1974, a juvenile began yelling at a sales-
woman in a downtown Boston department store, calling her,
to quote from a subsequent account of the incident, a
" 'f------ a------' and the like." When a female security guard
approached, the juvenile "continued his tirade, calling her,
among other things, a 'f------ a------' and a 'f------ pig.' "
When asked to leave, the youngster "gestured by raising
the third finger of his hand, symbolizing what he was
verbally expressing." The juvenile was finally removed from
the store, but managed to return and resume his previous
behavior. All told, his activities went on for some forty
minutes, and were witnessed by more than a hundred shop-
pers. The juvenile was tried and convicted of being a disorderly person; on appeal, however, the state Supreme Court
overturned the conviction, holding that it had violated the
defendant's right to "freedom of expression" under the First
Amendment to the United States Constitution.*

THESE INCIDENTS are not the whimsical constructs
of a spoof of current tendencies in American law.
Both are actual cases decided last year—the first, *Rogers* v.
Equal Employment Opportunity Commission, by the United
States District Court for the District of Columbia, and the
second, *Commonwealth* v. *A Juvenile*, by the Supreme
Judicial Court of Massachusetts. While they are somewhat
extreme examples, neither would greatly surprise the vast
majority of the nation's lawyers and judges. Indeed, the
reasoning and the results of *Rogers* and *A Juvenile* are
sufficiently within the present mainstream of American
judicial thinking that many legal professionals, particularly
on the bench, would contend that both decisions were
eminently correct.

Since at least the mid-1960s, conservatives have been
disturbed by developments in the nation's courts. Ten years
ago, the major cause for concern was a series of innovative
decisions by the Supreme Court, especially on the constitutionality of criminal procedure. It seriously worried many
Americans that the routine conviction of an unquestionably guilty criminal could not stand if, for example, the
suspect had given a wholly voluntary confession without
the police's informing him of his right to an attorney before
questioning. The then-Chief Justice, Earl Warren, was often
blamed, and his impeachment was implored by a thousand John Birch Society billboards. Most of the disgruntled, however, sought other remedies, and the promise
to appoint judges sensitive to the "victim's rights" as well
as the criminal's became part of Richard Nixon's successful campaign for the Presidency. More recently, public displeasure with the judiciary has centered on court-ordered
busing to achieve "racial balance," a story that does not
need retelling here.

The public's most common charges are that courts are
exercising too sweeping a power (often usurping the legitimate functions of the legislative and executive branches in
the process) and, specifically, that liberal judges are using

---

*Mr. Rusthoven is an Indianapolis attorney and a monthly
columnist for* The Alternative. *A graduate of the Harvard
Law School, he was a member of the board of editors of
the* Harvard Law Review *from 1974 to 1976.*

From *National Review*, December 10, 1976. © 1976 National Review, Inc., 150 East
35th St., New York, NY 10016. Reprinted by permission.

their office to impose results that accord with their political and social views. Although some of the Warren Court's constitutional cases present harder questions than many lay critics would admit, there is much to be said for these complaints.

BUT EXCESSIVE power and political bias are not, I believe, the most significant of the problems with the judiciary. These problems are largely reflections of a more serious, philosophical difficulty: an increasing number of judges hold the belief that law and the courts are the most appropriate and effective means of redressing the perceived ills of our society. An examination of a representative sampling of recent decisions shows that this belief transcends the rights of criminal defendants or the forced juggling of black/white pupil ratios.

The courts' most flexible and widely used tool is the Fourteenth Amendment, which holds that no state shall "deprive any person of life, liberty, or property, without due process of law; nor deny to any person within its jurisdiction the equal protection of the laws." Passed just after the Civil War, the Amendment has in recent years been stretched to a degree undreamt of by its authors. The "due process" and "equal protection" clauses have provided a foothold for judicial supervision of almost every imaginable activity.

The case primarily responsible for encouraging the wide use of the due-process clause was *Goldberg* v. *Kelly*, in which the Supreme Court decided that the Constitution requires the punctilious observance of certain procedures before an individual can be removed from the welfare rolls.

KELLY WAS A New York welfare recipient whom the city eventually deemed ineligible for benefits. Although he had the right to request a post-termination review, he instead brought suit, contending that the procedures themselves were unfair. The Supreme Court's decision, both in its sociological commentary and in its legal definition, is a paradigmatic illustration of the "activist" judicial philosophy. Welfare, the majority opined, represents part of the "Nation's basic commitment . . . to foster the dignity and well-being of all persons within its borders," and serves to "bring within reach of the poor the same opportunities that are available to others to participate meaningfully in the life of the community." Moreover, the Court said, "welfare guards against the societal malaise that may flow from a widespread sense of unjustified frustration and insecurity." Moving on to points of law, the *Goldberg* decision concluded not only that welfare benefits, since they "are a matter of statutory entitlement for persons qualified to receive them," are a *property right* deserving of constitutional protection, but also that welfare is so important a right that it cannot be taken away without a *pre*-termination evidentiary hearing, complete with right to counsel and adversary procedures.

Goldberg is very easily criticized on practical grounds. Given the history of welfare in New York, most citizens would probably accept the city's decision that someone is ineligible without the holding of a semi-trial. But beyond this, one is struck by the ease with which the Court tosses off sociological observations of sweeping generality

and at least doubtful validity. How could a majority of the unquestionably intelligent men who sat on the nation's highest bench in 1970 conclude that welfare has fostered dignity and well-being and provided opportunities for meaningful participation—much less that it has served as an effective guard against "societal malaise"? What is more surprising, however, is that the Court felt perfectly at home, first, discussing and "deciding" such issues, and, second, making that "decision" the basis for its explicit legal conclusions. Those legal conclusions themselves provide an excellent example of the mode of decision-making that has become typical in today's courts: a heavy emphasis on the rhetoric of "rights," plus an overweening faith in the well-nigh universal value of procedural formalities.

THUS, WELFARE—or more precisely, the continuation of benefits after the government has challenged eligibility—is styled a "right," a term most of us reserve for aspects of human freedom more stirring than the chance to remain on the dole. In holding that an about-to-be-terminated welfare recipient has a right to counsel at his hearing, the *Goldberg* decision quotes from an earlier case (*Powell* v. *Alabama*, 1932) that held that an indigent defendant is entitled to state-appointed counsel if the charge against him carries the death sentence. As United States Court of Appeals Judge Henry J. Friendly, one of the nation's most respected jurists, commented in a recent article ("Some Kind of Hearing," *University of Pennsylvania Law Review*): "Apparently no difference was perceived between a capital case and the suspension of a welfare allowance."

Goldberg v. *Kelly* has become a "seminal case." It has sparked, as Judge Friendly puts it, a veritable "due-process explosion" in which "the hearing requirement [has been carried] from one new area of government action to another"; the trend "has been to say, 'If there, why not here?'" Consider just the following case, last year's *Pope* v. *Chew*, which, although its result is not as disturbing as *Goldberg*'s, illustrates well how innovative interpretation of the due-process clause has affected the lower federal courts.

Pope v. *Chew* involved a convicted murderer who had been pardoned in 1962 after serving 26 years of a life sentence (and he was serving a life sentence only because the governor had commuted a death sentence). The pardon was conditional upon, among other things, Pope's never again being convicted of a criminal offense; if he were, the pardon would then become "null and void." In 1973, Pope was convicted, after a full-scale trial, of possession and sale of heroin, and the then-governor, on recommendation of the parole board, revoked the pardon. Seemingly a perfectly straightforward act—but wait. Pope sued in federal court, contending the revocation was unfair; and the United States Court of Appeals for the Fourth Circuit agreed, holding that he had been deprived of "liberty" without due process of law. Since two previous, less serious infractions by Pope had not cost him his pardon, the court decided that the governor's action was, despite the express language of the operative document, a "discretionary act." Moreover, said the court, Pope in any event had a "right" to "plead for further tolerance." Accordingly, the authorities could not force Pope to resume serving his life sentence without a hearing.

Thus, before Virginia can reincarcerate a man who has violated the terms of its act of executive grace, it is put to the expense of what promises to be a singularly silly judicial proceeding—what, after all, can Pope possibly "show" at his hearing? On a nationwide scale, the expense that results from decisions like this is clearly significant. As Judge Friendly observes, "It should be recognized that procedural requirements entail the expenditure of limited resources, that at some point the benefit to individuals from an additional safeguard is substantially outweighed by the cost of providing such protection, and that the expense of protecting those likely to be found undeserving will probably come out of the pockets of the deserving." But what is more significant is the reappearance in *Pope* v. *Chew* of the factors noted in *Goldberg* v. *Kelly*—the rhetoric of "rights" and the excessive veneration of procedural formalities, combining to yield a social "solution" set forth in the name of the Constitution.

AT PRESENT the due-process clause seems infinitely elastic. The most significant recent Supreme Court decision is *Goss* v. *Lopez*, which holds that public-school students have a constitutional right to notice and a hearing before they may be suspended. There is no telling where, if anywhere, it will all end.

Judicial developments in other areas are equally illustrative of the judiciary's perception that law, especially the sort of "law" it mandates, provides the best approach to a variety of social difficulties. What is both disturbing and highly revelatory here, as in the due-process cases, is that the courts often see fit to impose, under the ostensible aegis of the Constitution, and in difficult and controversial areas, their own notions of reform.

Consider the Fourteenth Amendment's "equal protection" clause, which in essence prohibits a state from discriminating among different groups of citizens. As an extreme example, it would prohibit different penalties for Irish and Italian thieves. The recent use of the equal-protection clause is, however, of a subtler strain, and is surprisingly extensive in its scope.

The Supreme Court, for example, has voided duration-of-residency requirements for receipt of welfare benefits (*Shapiro* v. *Thompson*), and for voting in state elections (*Dunn* v. *Blumstein*), in decisions that also have "right to travel" overtones. In some instances, lower courts have invalidated at-large schemes for the election of city officials, claiming that such systems "dilute" the black vote—e.g., by making it impossible for a predominantly black district to elect its "own" representative to a city council. This has happened in cities as large as Dallas (*Lipscomb* v. *Wise*), and as small as Albany, Georgia (*Paige* v. *Gray*). Another court has held that equal protection means that a city cannot experiment with single-sex public high schools (*Vorcheimer* v. *School District of Philadelphia*). And one federal panel has even found that the Constitution demands that girls be permitted to play Little League baseball, at least if a municipality is materially supporting the League's program (*Fortin* v. *Darlington Little League, Inc.*). This last decision begins by stating, "This case concerns the right of a girl to play Little League baseball"; throughout, the opinion rather cloyingly refers to the young female plaintiff by her nickname, "Pookie." What is more important, however, is that even though Congress had already amended the Little League charter by inserting "young `people" in place of "boys," the court still felt obligated to place the sexual integration of Little League baseball on a constitutional footing.

LIKE MOST interested citizens, I have opinions on residency requirements for voting, on at-large *versus* district election schemes, on co-education for adolescents, and even on the merits of mixing the sexes on a scaled-down baseball diamond. These are issues of widely varying importance, to be sure, and my views on them vary in intensity of passion. But I believe that the document penned by Madison and his colleagues at Philadelphia, even as subsequently amended, makes at most a highly attenuated and inferential contribution to these various debates, and often does not speak to the issue at all. It is a feature of the federal system they forged that it permits states and municipalities to adopt different answers to the issues posed by collective civilized existence. It is a distressing commentary on today's courts that they seem more willing than at any time in our history to impose their own views on these questions, and to label their prescriptions constitutional.

What I believe is finally revealed by the cases I have mentioned, and by others too numerous to recount, is that our judiciary seems no longer to share the Founding Fathers' confidence that the survival of our secular moral order depended less on governmental institutions—even those they were so carefully crafting—than on the ethical character of the citizens who would inherit the fruits of their labor. Most of our judges are reasonable, intelligent, earnest men, deserving of our respect; their efforts, including many with which I fundamentally disagree, can be faulted for neither insincerity nor bad faith. What those efforts can be faulted for, however, is their attempt to forge a role for the judiciary which doesn't suit it and in which even its best efforts must fail, with ill consequences to the society as a whole. The very attempt itself raises doubts about the health of that society; as the late Learned Hand noted in *The Spirit of Liberty* (1960), "Constitutions must not degenerate into vade-mecums or codes; when they begin to do so, it is a sign of a community unsure of itself and seeking protection against its own misgivings."

ALMOST TWO hundred years ago, Alexander Hamilton wrote in Federalist No. 78, employing a phrase made famous in our day by the late Professor Alexander M. Bickel, that the judiciary would prove "the least dangerous" branch of the newly established Federal Government. To be sure, Hamilton, along with Madison and Jay, was using *The Federalist* to sell the Constitution to a somewhat balky populace and was not inclined to emphasize latent difficulties in the product of the 1787 Convention. But it is unfortunate that reasonable men today cannot adopt Hamilton's assessment with the same confidence that he displayed. Human nature is of course imperfect, and defective judicial decisions will doubtless be with us for the duration of the Republic. But until cases like *Rogers*, *A Juvenile*, and *Goldberg* become rarities, rather than expressions of a prevailing judicial philosophy, the "least dangerous" branch will bear careful watching.   □

★★★

42

Don't Blame the Court   Seth Kupferberg

To survive as a viable institution, the Supreme Court needs public support. Yet, as Seth Kupferberg observes in this article, the Court seems to protect only segments of the populace in any given decision. It has been known to defend the poor, the weak, and the friendless, but it has also on other occasions supported the rich, the middle class, and the suburbanite. Can a Court that extends "more favored" treatment to segments of society ever hope to win overall support from the entire policy? Are there ways, do you think to predict which social groups the Supreme Court will protect, or does this depend exclusively on the individual Court, its membership, its ideology, and its approach to law? Some critics no longer see the Supreme Court as supportive of civil rights, the poor, and the feminist organizations. What decisions handed down by the Burger Court would warrant this contention? What interests does the Burger Court seem to support?

Kupferberg suggests further that both liberals and conservatives prefer judicial remedies over any other to effect social change. Although liberals have somewhat changed their views of the Supreme Court's role in fostering social change, both liberals and conservatives favor the "activist" Court as long as the Court will use its political power to protect them and their causes. But liberals become outraged if judicial policy appears to support only the conservatives, while conservatives react in similar fashion if liberals appear to gain the Court's favor at their expense. What effect might this "love-hate" attitude of liberals and conservatives have on the overall support for the Court? Should liberals and conservatives once again consider appealing to the Congress, in addition to the courts, as an alternative source of social change? Why do you think any group would turn to the Supreme Court to remedy a grievance rather than petition the Congress or the president?

★ ★ ★

Don't Blame the Court

by Seth Kupferberg

There's an idea abroad that the Supreme Court is no longer a friend of greater freedom or democracy. Civil rights groups, feminist organizations, anti-poverty activists—all the people who only recently looked on the Supreme Court as the protector of their interests—now regard it as a blockade in the path to needed social change.

This is a fairly recent development. In the fifties and sixties, the Supreme Court usually took the side of the class of people one pioneering Court opinion called "the poor, the ignorant, the numerically weak, the friendless, and the powerless"—those who had customarily been shut off from society's benefits. The Court ordered the states to desegregate their schools,

Seth Kupferberg is a second-year student at Harvard Law School.

helping to spark one of the great changes of American history. After Congress passed the Civil Rights Act of 1964, the Court became the chief guardian of the rights of women. It protected people accused of committing crimes from overbearing or unscrupulous police. It overruled attempts to stamp out civil rights and antiwar protests. It helped preserve the natural environment and people's privacy. And by imposing the one-man-one-vote rule, the Court brought about reapportionment that gave more clout to racial minorities, poor people, and the working class.

All this began to change when Richard Nixon appointed three Associate Justices and a Chief Justice to the Court. Nixon had promised during the 1968 campaign to change the Court's makeup: he wanted "strict constructionists," not liberal activists. As Nixon promised, a change soon became apparent in the Court's decisions.

Instead of insisting that disadvantaged voting districts have the same rights as privileged ones, the Burger Court said states could give more money to rich school districts than to poor ones. After outlawing hiring criteria that tended to exclude blacks and women, the Burger Court moved toward ruling out only specifically intentional discrimination. The Court said suburbs didn't have to help cities integrate their schools. It dashed liberal hopes by ruling that capital punishment is not inherently cruel or unusual. It let local communities outlaw movies they considered obscene. It cut back on protections for accused people and for workers who observe a Saturday Sabbath, and it restricted union leafleters' access to public places.

Most recently, the Court ruled that the government isn't required to pay for abortions—just the kind of situation, in which poor people are effectively deprived of a nominal right, that might have struck the Warren Court as a denial of equal protection of the law.

Each Burger Court decision has provoked a liberal outcry greater than the last. To listen to the protests, including some from dissenting holdover Justices, each one all but doomed the Constitution. In fact, the complaints bring forth memories of the New Deal, when liberals were accustomed to throwing up their hands at the Court's determination to thwart any progressive reform.

But there's an important difference between these times and those. The fact is that the Burger Court hasn't been a major factor in obstructing social change—at most, it has refused to push change forward. What's more, the Court is a strange rock for liberals, supposedly committed to the people's sovereignty and to democratic decision-making, to lean on for salvation.

Dispossessed and Discontented

From the beginning, the Supreme Court has been unpopular with the dispossessed and discontented. Andrew Jackson denounced the Court when it declared the Bank of the

United States constitutional, and he refused to abide by a decision protecting Indians' rights. Lincoln, in his First Inaugural, said that if Supreme Court decisions were immune to challenge, "the people will have ceased to be their own rulers."

In the 1890s the Supreme Court set off another onslaught of complaints when it declared that federal income taxes were unconstitutional. It also restricted laws designed to curb the power of large corporations—for example, it modified state laws that let commissions establish utility rates and overturned minimum-wage, child-labor, and maximum-hour laws. And the Court limited antitrust laws' application to big business, using them instead to outlaw strikes by fledgling labor unions. No wonder the American Federation of Labor developed an antipathy to courts so strong that it opposed any ongoing government interference with employment until well into the New Deal.

The last great wave of protest against a conservative Supreme Court crested with Franklin Roosevelt's attempt in 1937 to increase its size. For three years the Court had been overturning major New Deal programs— the National Recovery Act, laws establishing moratoriums on debts and permitting cities to declare bankruptcy, the New York Minimum Wage Law for Women. Roosevelt's solicitor general, Robert Jackson (later a Supreme Court justice himself), expressed the tenor of the times when he wrote that "never in its entire history can the Supreme Court be said to have for a single hour been representative of anything except the relatively conservative forces of its day."

Most of these pre-1970 quarrels with the Supreme Court sprang from the frustration people felt after seeing laws go through Congress or state legislatures and then be invalidated by nine unelected men responsible to nobody. There was usually no recourse from the Court's decision; no matter how impressive a majority reformers might pile up, the Court was always free to countermand the people's verdict.

In a Liberal Direction

Today, the situation is radically different. Most of the Burger Court's illiberal decisions have involved a *refusal* to overturn laws, not an insistence on doing that. What liberals now seem to want is a Supreme Court that will, in effect, legislate—as long as it legislates in a liberal direction.

Thus, liberals who are outraged when their appeals to the Supreme Court's sense of justice fail are in a strange position. They are implying that an appointed, elite body—rather than the popularly chosen Congress and President, or the states' governors and legislatures—is the proper avenue of reform.

Through most of American history, the Supreme Court has been the protector of precisely the kind of people liberals love to raise the cudgel against: small groups that feared the people's will. Slaveholders, creditors, large corporations—all hoped that the judiciary would preempt policies that, because of their popular support, had gotten legislative backing. That's why popular leaders from Jefferson to Roosevelt attacked Supreme Courts that overruled laws and resisted change.

Now, all of that has been reversed. The Constitution is invoked by liberals, seeking social change, in an attempt to render politics unnecessary. Why is it that today's democrats, believers in increased equality and greater civil liberties, want to bypass democratic means? What liberal wants his liberation by judicial fiat?

One answer sometimes given is that ordinary political processes can get stuck. Liberal law professors sometimes cite the abortion issue as a good example—a vocal passionate minority has stopped the popular will from being heeded in the legislatures, so that only the courts can get the country moving in the right direction. Like many liberal attacks on Right-to-Lifers, though, this one is uncomfortably reminiscent of conservative attacks on antiwar protests a few years back. Then, too, an emotional, single-minded, and uncivil minority helped stop something that at first had most Americans' support. To say that this means the protests were a distortion of democracy would be to say that only a head count of feelings and beliefs should be considered, not their importance to those who hold them.

True, there are cases where politics gets stuck and the courts have to step in. It would've been a bad joke to tell disenfranchised Southern blacks to get their legislatures to abolish segregated schools. But women, feminists, and liberals all have votes already; they aren't beaten up for organizing, or lynched for holding rallies. Instead of moaning about a hostile Supreme Court, they should be politicking to get a friendly Congress elected. If leafleting and letter-writing can stop abortions, they can also start them again.

So far, all the Burger Court has done is to refuse to find the political meanings in the laws and the Constitution that liberals see in them. This is the kind of behavior by the Court that past generations of American liberals used to fervently hope for, because they felt secure in their ability to persuade the people and thus control the legislative process. Today's liberals ought to feel the same security. They should remember that the way to political and social change is through politics and society, no less than through the courts. ■

★★

43

Behind the Marble, Beneath the Robes   Nina Totenberg

Without question, the Supreme Court and the federal judiciary compose our least accountable branch of government. Secrecy of the Supreme Court procedures, Nina Totenberg argues, is without peer in the political system. Congress, for example, over the last ten years has all but done away with its closed sessions, but the Court has remained as closed to the public as it was in the eighteenth century. In what ways does secrecy pervade the operations of the Supreme Court? What consequences for the democratic system would you expect if all our political institutions were as protective of their internal processes as is the Court?

Although the Court only hears about 170 cases a year, Totenberg suggests it is deceiving to judge its influence on this basis. Those 4,800 cases a year that the Court refuses to hear are equally important, for they are also "decided" by the High Court, since the decisions of the lower courts automatically stand. Does the authority of the Court to choose which cases are reviewed allow for certain issues to be consistently ignored? How important is the makeup of the Court in deciding which issues are ignored and which are given full review? Totenberg indicates that on the Burger Court the liberal judges have an "unwritten agreement" not to review lower court rulings that would assure a loss for liberals. Can such agreements prevent certain questions from being reviewed?

How important to the Court is the role of the chief justice? Totenberg indicates that Burger has violated tradition in using his power to assign opinions. Thus Justices Brennan and Stewart are rarely allowed to write opinions to important cases. What effect might this have on the way opinions are written?

Differences of opinion prevail on most Courts at most times. Oliver Wendell Holmes once suggested in commenting on the environment of the Court: "We are very quiet here, but it is the quiet of a storm center." Totenberg's focus on the capital punishment cases gives the reader some idea of the differences of opinion that can divide the justices when a controversial issue comes before them. What difference does it make whether decisions are decided by a five-to-four margin or by a nine-to-zero vote? What might you expect the public's reaction to be toward a decision decided by a narrow margin?

★　★　★

Behind the marble, beneath the robes

By Nina Totenberg

WASHINGTON. It was Saturday, and the United States Supreme Court, like the rest of Washington's public buildings, looked lonely and deserted. But inside, five of the Justices were hard at work. A sixth had interrupted his routine to visit with a friend from out of town. The fire in the Justice's chambers crackled warmly as the two men talked. The visitor ventured the opinion that the Court's biggest case of that year would be a capital-punishment decision and asked if the Justice had made up his mind yet. The Justice didn't answer. The visitor, suddenly aware that he had asked an improper question, started to apologize. But his voice caught in his throat at the sight of his old friend. The Justice was slumped ashen-faced in his chair, eyes closed; his words seemed almost a whisper. "My God, all those lives."

The visitor was dismayed. He quickly changed the subject. But the moment of good cheer was gone. The Justice was preoccupied.

There is probably no more secret society in America than the Supreme Court. Its nine Justices are among the most powerful, yet least visible, men in the United States. It is unheard-of for a Justice to reveal anything specific about the Court's case work; law clerks, too, are sworn to secrecy. The Court's written decisions are supposed to speak for themselves. It is the least accountable branch of Government, and in the common understanding, its Justices are robed symbols of seriousness, wisdom and the majesty of the law.

And yet to those who are familiar with the Court's daily functioning, the Justices are also people—nine men who work terribly hard and are sometimes very smart, men who constantly fight to overcome their own prejudices and backgrounds, men who sometimes win that battle and sometimes lose it, men who agonize, strain and manipulate to reach joint conclusions, and sometimes change their minds. "Judicial decision-making," wrote a former Supreme Court law clerk in a recent Harvard Law Review, "involves, at bottom, a choice between competing values by fallible, pragmatic and at times nonrational men engaged in a highly complex process in a very human setting."

What follows is an attempt to lift the Court's curtain of secrecy a bit so that the Justices and their work may be better understood. It does not pretend to be a definitive picture; rather, it is one reporter's attempt to put together in one place information gleaned from scores of interviews with Supreme Court law clerks, friends of the Justices, law professors,

Nina Totenberg covers legal affairs for National Public Radio and is a special contributor to New Times magazine.

attorneys who practice regularly before the Court, and the Justices themselves. All of the facts reported here have been obtained from or verified by at least two of these sources.

The basic event in the Court's decision-making process is a weekly conference, usually scheduled for Wednesday afternoon and all day Friday, at which cases are discussed. On Friday, the Justices arrive punctually at 9:30 A.M. Some, like William H. Rehnquist and Potter Stewart, are "night people" who look solemn-faced as they fight the morning doldrums. Others, like Justice William J. Brennan Jr., who rises each morning at 5:30, are cheerful and wide awake.

In the center of the oak-paneled room is a massive mahogany table, surrounded by nine high-backed chairs and about 25 carts. The carts, wheeled in from each Justice's office before the conference, are loaded with briefs, transcripts, memos from clerks, notebooks — everything the Justice thinks he will need for every case that may come up during the exhausting all-day session. The Justices pour themselves coffee from a silver urn. Then they shake hands, as has been the custom since 1888, and sit down to do battle.

The first function of the conference might be called deciding to decide. Each year roughly 5,000 cases come before the Court. The Justices sift through these cases and decide which ones are worthy of their full consideration. Last year, for example, the Justices agreed to hear only 170 cases.

Copies of each case go to every Justice. Justice Brennan is the only one of the nine men who reads virtually all the petitions asking for review. Three other Justices share this chore to varying extents with their three law

clerks and have their clerks write summarizing memos. Still others—the four Nixon appointees plus Justice Bryon R. White—have in recent years created a rotating pool of their law clerks to write summary memos. Each Justice then makes an independent, tentative judgment as to whether the case provides a substantial Federal question that is ready to be resolved by the nation's highest court. If a Justice thinks a case presents a substantial Federal question, he asks that it be put on the conference list for discussion. With the exception of a small fraction of cases that fall into a technical legal category, no case is put on the conference list unless at least one Justice requests that it be considered. The vast majority of cases, having aroused no Justice's interest, automatically go on what is known as "the dead list" and are denied further consideration.

Once on the conference list, a case faces an even bigger hurdle, for it takes the votes of four Justices to grant it review. The votes to grant review are not always routine or trivial, and the arguing over them may turn out to be highly significant, as it was when the Court was asked to rule on whether President Nixon could refuse to release his tapes to those investigating his subordinates. When the case came to the Court, the legal question was whether the Justices should leapfrog the appeals process to expedite a crucial question. Justice Stewart is reported to have argued forcefully that it was up to the judiciary to settle quickly an issue that was so terribly paralyzing the other institutions of Government and so deeply affecting the national well-being. Stewart was joined by Justices Lewis F. Powell Jr. and William O. Douglas, and soon they had won over two more of their colleagues, leaving Chief Justice Warren E. Burger, Justice

Harry A. Blackmun and Justice White to dissent, in a vote that until now had been kept secret. (Justice Rehnquist had disqualified himself from the case.) This procedural vote, coming when it did, was pivotal in forcing the rapid resolution of Watergate and the impeachment process.

Occasionally, when there are not enough votes to grant review, one Justice will write a dissent from the refusal to hear the case. And here the game gets really interesting, for it is not unusual for the dissent to be so persuasive that the other Justices change their minds. The briefs in a case are often so poor that the Justice's dissent provides the only available serious presentation of the case.

For example, in 1968 the Justices voted not to hear the case of Representative Adam Clayton Powell, who claimed he had been unconstitutionally barred from his seat in Congress. Powell had lost his case in the lower courts, and there were strong feelings on the Supreme Court that to grant review of the case might involve the Court in a potentially serious clash with Congress. But Justice Douglas disagreed and wrote a dissent that persuaded the Court to take the case. The Douglas dissent, of course, has never been made public (as it would have been had the Court held to its original position) for seven months later, the Justices overruled the lower court by a vote of 7 to 1.

This kind of persuasive dissent is not seen much these days at the Court. According to Court sources, the liberal Justices have an "unwritten agreement" to try to keep many cases out of the hands of the Court so long as the conservatives have the five-vote majority needed to carry a decision. Thus, for example, if an important First Amendment case comes up on appeal, the liberals will vote not to hear it—even if it involves what they consider a horrendous lower-court decision—for fear a conservative majority would result in a Supreme Court decision restricting First Amendment rights. It is better to save final resolution of the issue for another day and a more liberal Court, they reason.

In any event, once the Court agrees to hear a case, it is scheduled for oral arguments some months later. In the interim, lawyers for both sides file lengthy written briefs—usually 60 to 80 pages long—arguing the case. Sometimes as many as 10 or 20 other "friend of the court" briefs are filed by other parties who claim an interest in the case.

Finally, the day for oral argument comes. Each side generally has a half-hour to make its points. The Justices pepper the attorneys with questions. Oral argument is like verbal fencing; at its best, it can be a lawyer's virtuoso performance.

At the end of the week, the following Friday, the case is back in conference, this time to be decided tentatively. Beginning with the Chief Justice and then in order of seniority, each Justice voices his views. They argue, cajole, persuade and finally they vote, this time with the junior Justice going first. Depending on the personalities and mood of the Justices, the conversation can get quite heated. It is said that in the days when Felix Frankfurter and Hugo Black were on the Court, the guards stationed outside the conference room could hear the Justices yelling at each other. The Burger Court, at least on the surface, is more civilized.

Nobody except the Justices is permitted in the conference room. All the notes are taken by the Justices themselves. The Chief Justice, if he is on the majority side, assigns a Justice to write the opinion. The dissenters usually agree among themselves who will write their opinion. Then the negotiating begins. The Court has a tradition that up to the moment when an opinion is announced in public, any Justice can change his mind, and occasionally it takes less than an hour for a majority arranged in the conference to fall apart. "You can leave that conference room thinking you are to write the majority opinion, and one hour later and one telephone call later you can be converting it into the minority opinion," explains one Justice.

Some capital-punishment cases illustrate how the Court wrestles over a single subject in the face of shifting issues and events. In 1969, the Court had agreed to hear *Maxwell v. Bishop*, which presented a test of two key capital-punishment issues. The first question involved "split-verdict," as opposed to "single-verdict," trials. In a single-verdict trial, the jury hears the evidence, then retires to determine both guilt and punishment. The defendant in the Maxwell case contended that this one-step system forced him to choose between his right not to incriminate himself and his chance to explain his actions before he was sentenced. He asserted that in capital cases the Constitution required a split-verdict system under which the jury would first determine guilt and then return to hear the defendant's evidence in mitigation—insanity or intoxication, for example—before passing sentence. Defendant Maxwell's second argument was that he had been denied due process of law when the jurors condemned him to die without having been given detailed standards to guide them in their decision.

The Supreme Court heard the case and, according to Court sources, voted 6 to 3 to require a split-verdict system. Standardless discretion for juries was upheld. But the split-verdict requirement would have knocked out death sentences in all but six states and required massive resentencings. The six-man majority included Chief Justice Earl Warren, the conservative Justice John Harlan, and liberal Justices Abe Fortas, Thurgood Marshall, Brennan and Douglas. Justices Stewart, White and Black dissented. Justice Douglas was assigned to write the opinion. But he couldn't hold onto the majority. Later in the year, Fortas was forced to resign from the Court, leaving the case at a 5-to-3 vote. Then Justice Harlan said he wanted to write a concurring opinion, that he was not in complete agreement with the reasoning of the majority. In the process of writing his concurring opinion, Harlan changed his mind, deciding that the Constitution did not require split trials.

The Court then found itself locked in a 4-4 tie and ordered the case reargued the following year, when it would have a full nine-man court. The next year, however, Chief Justice Burger replaced Warren, and Blackmun replaced Fortas. Since Blackmun had served previously on a lower court that ruled on the Maxwell case, he was disqualified from ruling on it again. So the Justices washed out the Maxwell case and took another set of cases that presented the same issues. The new cases, known as *McGautha v. California*, were finally decided in the spring of 1971. The High Court, by the same numerical vote of 6 to 3, this time rejected both the split-verdict and the standards arguments. And Justice John Harlan wrote the opinion.

Once the Court had disposed of these two issues, the problem the Justices faced was whether to grant a case testing the ultimate constitutionality of capital punishment in light of the Eighth Amendment prohibition against cruel and unusual punishment.

In 1969, when they had voted to require split verdicts, the Justices had tentatively decided not to accept any more death cases for review. Warren, Black and Harlan firmly believed that the death penalty was constitutional. The majority who wanted split verdicts reasoned that they would make imposition of the death penalty as fair as possible and then leave the ultimate question of cruel and unusual punishment to be decided by another Court far, far in the future. By 1971, there were 600 people on death row, and the split-verdict ruling, as finally decided, would not require massive resentencings. The Justices were divided on the issue of whether to grant review of the ultimate capital-punishment question.

Justice Thurgood Marshall, at the time, voiced the private opinion that he was the only vote on the Court for total abolition of the death penalty. And Justice Douglas proposed that the Court hear a rape case in which the death penalty was imposed. He reasoned that the Court could forbid capital punishment in cases where nobody was killed and the Court opinion at the same time could make clear that the death penalty was permissible in murder cases. But the Justices finally decided to grant review of a series of murder cases in which the death penalty was imposed. The Court was finally going to try to decide the ultimate question.

On June 29, 1972, the High Court ruled 5 to 4 that capital punishment as then administered in the United States was unconstitutionally cruel and unusual punishment. Surprisingly, Justices White and Stewart, who had consistently voted to oppose a split-verdict requirement, this time voted against the death penalty. And their reasoning was that it was imposed so arbitrarily as to be capricious. Of course, split verdicts and standards for imposition of the death penalty might have mitigated the arbitrary nature of the death penalty as it came to be administered. But, as a former Supreme Court law clerk observes, "the Court doesn't sit as a legislature—with a clean slate to write on. A legislature can do pretty much what it wants; but the Court has to take cases as they come up, and this sometimes forces the Justices to do things they wouldn't do if they had been able to choose the order in which issues arose."

The Court has reversed itself midstream on other issues as well. For example, in the 1967-68 term, the Court heard *Shapiro v. Thompson*, which tested the constitutionality of state residence requirements for welfare recipients. The Justices originally voted to uphold residence requirements, but the dissenting opinion changed a number of minds. The Court eventually struck down state residence requirements as unconstitutional.

Another big switch occurred in *Time Inc. v. Hill*, in which Hill claimed that magazine photos of the Broadway play "Desperate Hours," used to depict his family's ordeal at the hands of criminals, violated his constitutional rights. Hill was represented by attorney Richard Nixon, and the case pitted the right to privacy against freedom of the press. Initially, the Justices sided with Nixon, for the right to privacy. Justice Fortas, the man Nixon would later help push off the Court, was assigned to write the opinion. Justice Hugo Black, when he saw Fortas's opinion, said it was the worst First Amendment opinion he had seen in a dozen years. Indeed, Black was so outraged that he said it would take him all summer to write his dissent, that it would be the greatest dissent of his life. Black knew full well that no opinion is ever issued without its dissent and that any case not completed in a term is reargued the following year. Indeed, the Court did order the case reargued the following year. By then, Black had changed enough minds, and the case came out the opposite way, with Fortas writing the dissent.

The shifts in votes are usually what most people assume them to be—changes of mind that result from the ongoing efforts of the Justices to apply their best judgment and knowledge of the law to their best understanding of subtle or ambiguous facts. But Court insiders say that judicial minds are sometimes changed for less elevated reasons. Most recently such criticism has focused on Chief Justice Burger.

Critics of Burger cite his voting behavior in the Court's first big busing case—the 1971 Charlotte, N. C., case—in which he wrote the Court's unanimous decision ordering extensive busing to desegregate Southern schools. The first vote in conference was said to have been 6 to 3 against busing. In an unusual move, each Justice went back to his chambers and drafted an opinion. Justice Harlan's was said to have been the toughest pro-busing opinion. Then several Justices had second thoughts and switched their votes. Soon the vote was 6 to 3 for busing, with Burger, Blackmun and Black dissenting. Eventually, the three capitulated — Black being the last holdout. And Burger, who had envisioned himself writing the opinion against busing, ended up writing the opinion for it and incorporating much of the language from the drafts of the more liberal Justices.

Some who know the Chief Justice well contend that he changed his vote for personal and political reasons rather than reasons of legal judgment. At the time, they speculate, Burger did not wish to be a part of a small minority if that stance would cause people to think of him as an automatic supporter of positions favored by then-President Nixon. Critics point to other examples of Burger's fighting hard in conference to get a conservative position upheld, only to switch to the other side when he saw he had lost. This occurred, they say, in the Court's unanimous ruling in 1972 that the Government could not wiretap domestic radicals without first obtaining a court-approved warrant—a stunning rebuff to the Nixon Administration. In that case, Burger and Blackmun are said to have originally supported the view that no warrant was necessary, though they eventually switched their votes. And in the abortion case, Burger is said to have fought doggedly for the position that states have the right to prohibit abortions. But when it became clear that a majority would vote the other way, he voted with it.

Burger has attracted further criticism in legal circles and, according to sources close to the Court, generated hostility among the other Justices because of the ways he has chosen to assign opinions. The power to assign the writing of opinions is tremendously important, since the choice of an author often determines whether the opinion will be written on narrow or broad grounds, whether it will be cautious or sweeping. The assignments may also be made with an eye to enhancing the eventual impact of the decision — such as the national security wiretapping case, when Justice Douglas assigned the opinion to Lewis Powell. Powell, as a lawyer, had spoken out publicly for the Government's right to conduct warrantless wiretapping of domestic radicals. Thus, his judicial opinion to the contrary was perhaps doubly respected. Similarly, it was generally thought inside the Court that Chief Justice Burger would assign the Detroit busing opinion to Justice Stewart, who provided the swing vote giving the conservatives their first majority on busing. But Burger assigned the case to himself.

The cases assigned to each Justice frequently determine whether that Justice feels happy and satisfied in his job. It is said that one of the ways Chief Justice Warren exerted such tremendous leadership over the Court was that he assigned the most tedious and difficult opinions to himself and tried to assign to other Justices the opinions he knew would interest them.

Burger's assignments, however, have been criticized for the way they reflect personal or political conflict with other Justices. Law clerks and law professors say that his assignments have resulted in "the complete emasculation of Brennan and Stewart." And it does appear that remarkably few "juicy" opinions—those that arise from big, controversial cases—are being assigned to them. There is perhaps some explanation for Brennan's getting fewer important opinions than he used to. He tends to be more in the liberal minority these days and agreed with Burger in only 45 per cent of the cases decided in the last term. But Stewart agreed with Burger 77 per cent of the time and he was assigned virtually nothing of major public importance. Indeed, a quick scanning of the record indicates that last term Burger assigned the most important cases to himself or to the two most junior Justices, Powell and Rehnquist, and to a lesser extent, to White.

Burger's critics also charge that he has used his traditional power to assign opinions in ways that could be interpreted as tactical. The abortion case, for example, was first decided in the 1971-72 Court term. The vote was 5 to 2, with Burger and White dissenting. (The vacancies resulting from the health-related resignations of Justices Black and Harlan had not been filled). Burger, in disregard of tradition, assigned the opinion instead of letting the senior Justice in the majority—in this case, Douglas—do it. And he assigned the opinion to his old friend Blackmun, the most conservative Justice in the majority. Burger did this, his critics speculate, in the hope that Blackmun would write a very narrow opinion or perhaps even change his mind. Then, they assert, Burger persuaded Blackmun that the case should not be decided at all, that it should be reargued before a full, nine-man Court the following year, when the vacancies were filled, a practice the court had followed on similar occasions.

Blackmun agreed, and since the feelings of the man who is writing the opinion carry great weight, the full Court went along with the suggestion that the case should be reargued. But when Burger saw that the majority would hold and that Powell was joining it to make the majority 6 to 3, the Chief Justice changed his vote. The public saw only the final decision: 7 to 2, with Burger in favor of more liberal abortion laws and White and Rehnquist the only dissenters.

The abortion case was the most flagrant example—so flagrant that it provoked Justice Douglas to write an internal protest memo—but according to those familiar with the Court's operations, it was not the first time Burger assigned a majority opinion when he was in the minority. Some Justices thought the assignments, which are posted a few days after the Friday conferences, were "just mistakes — inefficiency," and since voting in these early deliberations may be tentative, and since the only records are those kept by the Justices themselves, the votes may in fact be subject to different interpretations. But others saw the apparently mistaken assignments as a part of a deliberate attempt by Burger to usurp traditional powers. Some Justices even believe that the Chief Justice has on occasion cast "phony votes" in conference—voting with the majority so that he can assign the opinion and then dissenting from it when it is finally written.

Certainly other Courts and Chief Justices have had their personality difficulties. The late constitutional scholar Alexander Bickel, who was a law clerk when Fred Vinson was Chief Justice, once described that Court as "nine scorpions in a bottle." But Vinson, whatever his shortcomings, was never accused of so serious a break with tradition as assigning opinions when he was in the minority. Burger, for his part, vehemently denies the critical allegations, calling them "utter absurdity." He has told friends that anyone who says he ever made a mistaken assignment is "either stupid or lying." However, these serious allegations about Burger began with the Justices themselves, not their clerks.

Writing any sort of Supreme Court opinion—important or routine—is a long and arduous process. Each Justice runs his chambers differently. One Justice likens the Court to "nine separate law firms." But each Justice has only three law clerks to assist him. Daniel J. Meador, who clerked for Justice Hugo Black in 1954, described in The Alabama Law Review the process of writing an opinion:

"When 'the Judge,' as his clerks called him, is assigned a case for an opinion, he dives into reading the record and all the briefs. He absolutely masters the facts and the arguments. Then he moves into the relevant literature—cases, statutes, treatises and law reviews. The clerks often read along with him or dig out additional material and feed it to him. The issues will be discussed intermittently. After a while, Black will feel that he is ready to do a first draft.... The draft is then turned over to the clerks, and with all the confidence of youth, they work it over. Then the fun begins. The . . . clerks and Black gather around his large desk and start through the draft, word by word, line by line. This may go on for hours. When the Judge has an opinion in the mill, he does not drop it for anything else. The discussion often . . . last[s] until midnight. Often revisions result; sometimes a clerk can get a word or comma accepted, but the substance and decision are never anything but Black's alone."

The Justices take their obligation to research opinions so seriously that in one area of law—obscenity—the result has led to a lot of snickering both on and off the bench. Since 1957, the Court has tried repeatedly to define obscenity. The subject has become so familiar at the Supreme Court building that a screening room has been set up in the basement for the Justices and their clerks to watch the dirty movies submitted as exhibits in obscenity cases. Justice Douglas never goes to the dirty movies because he thinks all expression —obscene or not—is protected by the First Amendment. And Chief Justice Burger rarely, if ever, goes because he is offended by the stuff. But everyone else shows up from time to time.

Justice Blackmun watches in what clerks describe as "a

near-catatonic state." Justice Marshall usually laughs his way through it all, occasionally nudging a colleague and wisecracking. Justice White rocks back and forth in a straight-backed chair; on leaving, he has been heard to mutter about "filth." Justice Powell, the aristocratic Virginian, was appalled by the first film he saw, "Without a Stitch,"

'To write a Court opinion, you have to sew a big enough umbrella for five guys to get under, and that can require some pretty fancy sewing.'

---

which is quite mild by today's popular standards. Justice Brennan has gotten used to porn, though it is said that it took him more than a decade to overcome his upbringing on the subject. The late Justice Harlan used dutifully to attend the Court's porno flicks even though he was virtually blind; Justice Stewart would sit next to Harlan and narrate for him, explaining what was going on in each scene. Once every few minutes, Harlan would exclaim in his proper way, "By George, extraordinary!"

The dirty movies have provided some of the Court's most funny, and most private, moments. For example, there was the time that the movie began with a psychiatrist telling the audience about the sad life of a nymphomaniac named Laura. The psychiatrist's voice continued to narrate while the film showed Laura engaged in various sexual feats. At the end, the psychiatrist came back on the screen. By this time Justice Marshall was already out of his seat and walking toward the door. The psychiatrist lamented that Laura "is still not cured." Marshall, hand on the door knob, declared, "And neither are you." Then he opened the door, adding, "But I am," and walked out.

Most Justices begin their work on cases during the three-month summer vacation that Congressmen annually

complain about. Justice Powell, for example, reads through all the briefs in cases that have already been scheduled for argument in the coming term. He then dictates a lengthy memo on each case. In addition, he picks out 15 to 18 cases he thinks will be particularly important and has his clerks do extra research on them. Each case is assigned to a clerk. Then, during the Court term, shortly before the case is to be argued, Powell sits down with the clerk in charge of the case, and they discuss the issues presented.

Once Powell is assigned an opinion, either he or his clerk roughs out a draft opinion. Who does the first draft depends on what the workload is in the office at the time. The opinion then goes back and forth between the Justice and his clerk like a shuttlecock, being worked and reworked, drafted and redrafted, until both are satisfied. Then the opinion is given to a second clerk, who goes over it like an editor, looking for mistakes, poor reasoning, unclear writing. Then the opinion is sent to the print shop the Court maintains inside the building. Then the third Powell clerk reads the opinion, acting as an editor-proofreader.

Once the opinion is written so that a Justice is satisfied with it, it is circulated to the other Justices. "You wait for the join memos from the people who voted with you and pray," one Justice says. And then the memos begin to fly.

"It can be very difficult to get one Court opinion, even if people agree with the judgment," explains one Justice. "To write a Court opinion you have to sew a big enough umbrella for five guys to get under, and that can require some pretty fancy sewing." It's even harder to write a unanimous opinion, as evidenced in the Nixon tapes case.

By the time the tapes case was argued before the Court last July 9, the Justices had all done vast research on the issues at hand. Many had written lengthy memorandums on every conceivable position. Moreover, the Justices had completed all their work for the term and could devote full time to this single case.

When the historic case went to conference, there was only one vote. According to Court sources, the Justices were in immediate agreement on all

the basic issues. The Chief Justice assigned himself the opinion and received memorandums from each of his colleagues.

However, when Burger circulated his first opinion draft, it met with a wholly negative response. For unknown reasons—some relating to its technical execution and some to its substance— the other Justices were completely dissatisfied with the opinion. The job then became one of getting Burger to accept language drafted by other Justices —principally Powell and Stewart. But the other Justices —sometimes alone and sometimes in groups of two or three—produced new opinions almost every day.

By a process of erosion, they finally got Burger to incorporate their language. The section that Burger is reported to have held to most strenuously, and successfully, acknowledges for the first time that there is a presumption of executive privilege in the Constitution.

Negotiations in less important cases can be as tortured and involved. "You know, you work your brains out and you finally circulate something," remarks one Justice. "Then one guy sends you a note saying, 'I'll be happy to join with you in *Smith v. Jones* if you'll take out that paragraph on the top of page 5.' And then you get a note from someone else saying he'll be happy to join you if you strengthen that paragraph at the top of page 5." Or more frequently, one Justice requests a change, and another Justice objects to it when he sees the new draft of the opinion.

In either event, negotiations then begin in earnest. Justice White is said to be a master at working the telephone. But some Justices feel it is improper to lobby their colleagues. And it is not unusual for a Justice to dispatch his clerks to "feel out the territory" among the clerks from another Justice's chambers.

What happens when minor differences cannot be reconciled? As one former law clerk put it: "That's when you fudge it, and then the law professors complain that the Court doesn't write clear opinions. Or else you leave out the point altogether. And then the law professors complain that there is a step missing in the Court's logic."

Sometimes, notes one Justice, an opinion is circulated and someone has "a whole new concept he wants in, and if you've got only a five-man

majority, you have to listen to all suggestions very seriously or you might lose the whole thing." (That problem was illustrated in Justice Blackmun's maiden opinion, *Wyman v. James*. He was severely criticized by many legal scholars because his opinion equated welfare with charity. In fact, this whole notion wasn't Blackmun's at all and was put in at the insistence of another Justice.)

Each time a new draft of an opinion is circulated, all changes are marked in the margin with a black line. By the time a decision is announced, it has sometimes undergone as many as 10 drafts in a Justice's chambers and 17 or 18 more to satisfy other Justices. Each Justice writes between 13 and 18 opinions each year, plus nearly as many dissenting and concurring opinions. In addition, each Justice must review those thousands of cases that are appealed to the High Court each year in hopes of a hearing. So it is no wonder that most Justices work six or seven days a week, that Justice Brennan begins his work day with a walk at dawn, or that Justice Rehnquist closes his briefcase each night at about midnight.

Is the Court's workload too great for nine human beings to handle properly? Some believe that it is, and in fact the four Nixon appointees to the Court, led by Chief Justice Burger, have protested lustily that the Court is overworked. A number of committees, one appointed by Burger, have recommended changes in the Court's structure to limit the number of cases the Court must review.

But it is noteworthy that four of the more senior Justices — Douglas, Marshall, Brennan and Stewart—have spoken out against these proposals for change. Indeed, some Justices even object to Burger's hiring of additional administrative staff for the Court. They fear that enlarging the staff may make the Court into another Government bureaucracy. And if the alternative is for the Justices to cope with a superhuman workload, they declare, that is what the Justices will have to do. "Sure, it's hard and exhausting," remarks one Justice, "but we weren't put here because we're lightweights." Indeed, the Justices are deceptively ordinary looking people. As the late Justice Oliver Wendell Holmes once observed, "We are very quiet here, but it is the quiet of a storm center." ∎

★★

44

A Peculiar Sense of Justice   Nathan Lewin

The relationship of the chief justice to his associates on the Court and to the public gives us some indication of how the Court operates in general. To those around him, Nathan Lewin indicates, Warren Burger appears brusque, stern, and regal. Burger himself has put some distance between the Court and the public by insisting that much of the pomp and circumstance that traditionally had been part of the Court over the past years continue. Court procedures have also been emphasized. In what ways have the procedures of the former Warren Court been formalized by Chief Justice Burger?

Burger has also been involved in restoring the Court building to its original luster, making it a suitable location to house the highest court. How would you expect this sort of elitist bearing on the part of the chief justice to affect the process of justice? Lewin indicates that the Burger Court may be thought to dispense a "peculiar sense of justice." What does that mean in the context of Burger's attitudes toward criminal law and procedure? What does it mean as it relates to religious freedom? Would Burger have been in agreement with Justice Felix Frankfurter regarding the rights of criminal defendants?

Burger, Lewin suggests, has spent more time than any other chief justice in developing his own position. He has been instrumental, for example, in initiating the Supreme Court Historical Society to preserve Court history and in molding the Judicial Conference of the United States into a strong lobbying and policy-shaping institution. He has personally become a strong and effective lobbyist and spokesman for the Court before the Congress. In addition, he has been a fierce advocate of judicial reform and is concerned with the excessive demands made on the Court. What impact does such personal advocacy by the chief justice have on the Court, on the role of chief justice, and on the separation of powers? Is such advocacy consistent with the "regal" tone that Burger has established for the Supreme Court?

We are reminded in this essay that presidents and congressmen have long been advocates of their own causes, but they operate within a framework that is relatively open to the scrutiny of public and press. Judges like Burger, on the other hand, insist on having the right of personal advocacy but refuse to subject themselves to a similar open framework of operation. Can the democratic system long tolerate the Court to continue personal advocacy without insisting that judicial operations be opened to scrutiny? What would be the impact of such open decision-making? If this could be achieved, how would one make such changes in Court procedures?

★ ★ ★

When Warren Burger speaks, felons quake
and the faithful praise the Lord

A Peculiar Sense of Justice

by Nathan Lewin

WHEN Warren Burger came before the Senate for confirmation as Chief Justice in June 1969, the late Everett Dirksen said of him that "he looks like a Chief Justice, he speaks like a Chief Justice, and he acts like a Chief Justice." Appearance and impression probably expedited the Senate's approval (which was granted in less than three weeks), but the nominee was far from a closed book to the Congress. Burger had served for more than 13 years on the United States Court of Appeals for the District of Columbia —a unique federal appellate court because it then had jurisdiction over all serious criminal offenses committed in Washington, D. C. A separate local court system has, by this date, been given the exclusive authority to try local crimes. But when Warren Burger was judge, every armed robbery, serious assault, or auto theft committed in the nation's capital was tried in a United States district court, and appeals would be taken to the court on which the future Chief Justice sat. The Senate knew where he stood, particularly on the law-and-order controversies that had engulfed the Warren Court and had become issues in the presidential campaign of 1968. Senator Strom Thurmond observed thankfully that the nominee did not show "excessive concern for the rights of criminals," and only three senators opposed his nomination.

In the seven terms of the Court since he was sworn in as Chief Justice, Warren Burger has continued to look, speak, and act like a Chief Justice. He presides over Court sessions like a stern schoolmaster, with an air that is both regal and solemn. In this respect, Burger reminds an observer of his predecessor, Earl Warren, who also seemed taller and more erect than the eight Associate Justices who surrounded him and who was able, with silver hair and judicious demeanor like Burger's, to command respect from all in the courtroom.

Warren Burger has taken more pains than did Earl Warren, however, to improve the Court's appearance so as to make it look, speak, and act like the highest judicial body in the land. The Supreme Court Building has been given a thorough overhaul. The Justices' chambers have been enlarged to take up virtually the whole first floor; the Justices' bench has been reshaped to eliminate the row of privileged correspondents that separated the Court from the advocates who appeared before it; the courtroom's lofty ceiling has finally been repainted and regilded; and the previously bare halls have been stocked with Supreme Court memorabilia and exhibits to inspire and educate visiting tourists. There is almost no part of the physical plant that has escaped the improver's touch. The public cafeteria has been modernized and augmented with a snack bar; the Court clerk's office has been moved, reorganized, and expanded; and even the underutilized fourth-floor library—surely one of the world's most silent retreats—is now undergoing renovation and rearrangement. All that remains secure are the oversize public lavatories and the enormous telephone booths with sliding wood-and-glass doors, hidden away at the rear of the building's ground floor.

There was a good-natured flabbiness to the procedures of Earl Warren's Court that is not tolerated in Warren Burger's. Time was wasted by the old Court on ceremony that was meaningless to anyone but the participants. Earl Warren enjoyed greeting new members of the Supreme Court bar who were sponsored for admission by senators or congressmen or other elder attorneys, and between five and fifty minutes might be spent during each of the Court's public sessions on this courtly practice. Soon after Chief Justice Burger took over, the routine was changed, and most lawyers now receive their licenses by mail.

Nathan Lewin is a Washington lawyer and adjunct professor of constitutional law at Georgetown University. He was law clerk to Justice John M. Harlan of the Supreme Court and served as Assistant to the Solicitor General and Deputy Assistant Attorney General in the Kennedy and Johnson administrations.

The Warren Court also frittered away its time in public announcements of decisions and dissents by the individual Justices. Since there is no advance word that any particular case will be decided on any particular day, the announcement of results in open court is made to the audience that has fortuitously shown up on that occasion to hear whatever the Court may have to say. The Warren Court's Justices appeared to enjoy debating with each other—sometimes with sharp extemporaneous exchange—to this accidental conglomeration of listeners. Chief Justice Burger instituted the practice of perfunctory oral announcements, which leaves the press with the job of reading, and trying to comprehend, the Court's decisions. To make the rulings understandable, however, the Burger Court begins each published decision with a brief explanatory summary, called a "syllabus," prepared by the official Court reporter for the edification of the unlearned and impatient. And the Court's past is studied, analyzed, and publicized under the auspices of the Supreme Court Historical Society—a body that owes its existence to the organizational talents of the present Chief Justice.

WARREN BURGER has also taken much more seriously than his predecessor his role as Chief Justice of the *United States*. In 1970, he initiated an annual "State of the Judiciary" message, which he delivers to the American Bar Association's convention each spring. These reports now consist principally of a catalog of administrative accomplishments—such as statistics proving that the efficiency of the federal courts has been improved by new management techniques attributable to the Institute for Court Management, which Burger proposed and developed—and exhortations for legislation that will enable the courts to do even better. Last year, for example, the Chief Justice urged that laws assigning special three-judge courts for certain cases and granting immediate appeal to the Supreme Court be amended to reduce the burden on the lower courts and on the Supreme Court. By the end of 1976, the requested changes had been made. Other amendments he has suggested—among which is the perennial request for more federal judges—are slower in coming, but the Chief Justice is not reluctant to let his views on these subjects be known. He has loudly stated his support for various proposals that would establish an intermediate federal appellate court immediately below the Supreme Court, and he has vigorously advocated that the federal courts be relieved of having to hear cases where the only federal interest is that they involve citizens of different states.

The Chief Justice's judicial philosophy is related to these organizational interests. Since he believes that the courts are overworked, he is unwilling to expand their jurisdiction into new areas or to enlarge, beyond what is absolutely necessary, the number of groups that may demand the aid of a court. Lawyers' concepts such as "standing" or "ripeness" or "mootness" are invoked to limit or deny access to the judicial system. The single dominant chord struck by the Burger Court in recent years has been the diminished availability of courts, and the American Civil Liberties Union's overriding objection to the record of the Burger Court pertains to this aspect of its work.

With a few exceptions, however, the decisions closing the doors of federal courts to litigants who might raise new questions of individual liberty have not been written by Chief Justice Burger. It is hard to know how influential he has been in moving the rest of the Court in that direction—although his administrative pronouncements disclose that the goal of reduced access is one he would gladly embrace. His judicial opinions have left a particular impression in three other areas. In two of those areas he differs markedly from his predecessor, while in the third their views are closer than might initially be believed.

The most important area of disagreement is criminal law and procedure, where the opinions of Burger and Warren as to the Supreme Court's duty are as opposite as opinions can be. It was unpleasant business to represent the government in a criminal case that came before the Warren Court. The Chief Justice would glower from the bench whenever it appeared during oral argument that a policeman or prosecutor had cut a corner, and he would then mercilessly interrogate the government lawyer. Archibald Cox, who was in that position many times during his tenure as Solicitor General in the Kennedy administration, has recalled "Chief Justice Warren's persistent questions, 'Is that fair?' or 'Is that what America stands for?' "

Chief Justice Burger's view is that the means of investigating and prosecuting crime are less important than the ends of apprehending and jailing criminals. In late March of this year, to the surprise of those attending Court on an otherwise ordinary Wednesday, Burger departed from the routine announcement procedure to read extensively from his dissenting opinion in an Iowa case. The question on which the case turned was whether a suspect in the murder of a ten-year-old girl had voluntarily spoken to the police and directed them to his victim's body when he was questioned during a ride he took in police custody from Davenport to Des Moines. The suspect had been given the warnings required by the Supreme Court decision in *Miranda* v. *Arizona*, and he had consulted a lawyer appointed for him. The lawyer had told him not to answer any questions during the ride back to Des Moines and had received an assurance from the police that there would be no interrogation.

Five Justices on the Court (including Justice Powell, with whom Burger agrees between 80 and 85 percent of the time) concluded that the police officers were questioning the suspect during the ride in violation of their agreement, and that the answers obtained were involuntary under the *Miranda* rule. They said that any information obtained as a result of the interrogation, including testimony concerning the finding of the body, could not be offered in evidence. The Chief Justice delivered a passionate dissent, which began: "The result reached by the Court in this case ought to be intolerable in any society which purports to call itself an organized society."

These fighting words led some observers who were present in the courtroom to ascribe greater significance to the majority's ruling than it deserved. The next day's headlines in several major national newspapers made it appear as if the Court had considered repudiating the *Miranda* rules and had, by one slim vote, refused to do so. In fact, the *Miranda* rules were not themselves under attack. What Chief Justice

> ## "There was a good-natured flabbiness to the procedures of Earl Warren's Court that is not tolerated in Warren Burger's."

Burger did challenge on this occasion, as he had vociferously done twice before, was the "exclusionary rule," under which any evidence that is obtained by police misconduct may not be used in a criminal trial.

THE basic issue of legal and constitutional policy here is open to question. If the police violate a suspect's constitutional rights and as a result of that violation obtain evidence that is truthful and reliable, should the evidence be usable against the suspect? On one side of the argument is the proposition that all evidence relating to an accused's guilt or innocence should be considered, no matter how it has been obtained. Benjamin Cardozo, no mean liberal, supported that position while he was a judge on New York State's highest court. If illegally obtained evidence were not usable, he said, it would mean that "the criminal is to go free because the constable has blundered."

On the other side, however, stands Felix Frankfurter's classic observation that "the history of liberty has largely been the history of observance of procedural safeguards." Applying this principle, Frankfurter believed that the "civilized conduct of criminal trials" and "a decent regard for the duty of courts as agencies of justice and custodians of liberty" should forbid judges from sending people to jail for having committed crimes when evidence used against them has been obtained in violation of law. And in a more practical vein, judges have come to recognize that the best way to keep police from overstepping constitutional bounds is to deprive them of the incentive to do so. If a police officer is told that the evidence he gets by violating a constitutional right can never be of any use (and may, in fact, make successful prosecution of a suspect even more difficult), he will have little motive to take unlawful action.

While he was still a judge on the federal court of appeals, Burger repeatedly expressed the view that the almost exclusive objective of the criminal law in an "organized society" should be to convict the guilty and acquit the innocent. When judges concentrate on procedural technicalities, he said, they substitute for the issue of guilt or innocence "myriad rules, subrules, variations, and exceptions which even the most alert and sophisticated lawyers and judges are taxed to follow." He questioned whether the "adversary system," which pits courtroom advocates of extreme positions against each other, did not put "all the emphasis on techniques, devices, mechanisms," and thus result in "a society incapable of defending itself—the impotent society."

A SECOND subject on which Chief Justice Burger disagrees with his predecessor and on which he undertook to speak for the Court until his views were overridden by a Court majority is the subject of religious freedom. Early in his tenure he wrote an opinion in a case challenging the constitutionality of churches' property-tax exemptions, in which he developed the concept of "benevolent neutrality" toward religion. In a later case involving the constitutional right of the Old Order Amish to be excused from compulsory post-elementary schooling, he applied the theory of benevolent neutrality to require an exception for the small minority sect. The Amish, he noted, are law-abiding and self-sustaining. In language that would do any liberal proud, he said: "There can be no assumption that today's majority is 'right' and the Amish and others like them are 'wrong.' A way of life that is odd or even erratic but interferes with no rights or interests of others is not to be condemned because it is different."

Aid-to-parochial-school cases present a different aspect of the problem of religious minorities. Although there are dangers in permitting government assistance to religious schools, the financial burden of the devout—who must pay school taxes while at the same time bearing tuition costs for their children's education at religious schools—cannot be ignored. The Chief Justice, speaking for a Court majority, rejected the first plans, which provided for direct state payments to private schools or teachers, but he sympathized with the position of religious minorities and would have allowed financial aid given as "child benefits" if payments or tax credits went directly to the parents.

Earl Warren, on the other hand, was a strict separationist in the Religion Clause area, and he gave short shrift to the needs of religious minorities. In upholding the constitutionality of "Sunday laws," the former Chief Justice rejected the arguments of Sabbath-observers whose religious convictions might force them to surrender their livelihoods.

In the third area, where religious morality and crime coalesce, the views of Burger and Warren are not fundamentally different. Chief Justice Burger is known for his 1973 opinions setting new standards for the prosecution of those producing or selling obscenity. Earl Warren had no more sympathy for individuals "in the business of purveying textual or graphic matter openly advertised to appeal to the erotic interest of their customers." A more liberal general philosophy regarding the reach of the First Amendment's protection for free speech impelled the former Chief Justice to join reluctantly, on occasion, with findings that a particular work could not be banned. But one suspects that if Earl Warren could have had his way, he would have locked up the pornographers with the same zeal that Warren Burger has shown. ◉

CHAPTER TEN

★ ★ ★

Public Policy: Domestic

Public policy can be defined in a number of ways. Very simply it can be said that public policy is that which governments choose to do or choose not to do. More precisely, we might think of public policy as any rules, decisions, or decrees coming from any decision-maker that allocate deprivations or rewards to society or its members. This definition has the advantage of calling attention to some of the more important components of policy, including *goals*—defined as those ends which are to be achieved; *proposals* and *plans*, which include the means to achieve those goals; *programs*, which are the means finally authorized to obtain the goals; *decisions*, which include those actions to obtain and implement the programs and goals; and the *effects*, which include the overall impact of the program. These are the components, then, that should be considered whenever assessing the importance of any particular policy to the political system.

When one contemplates welfare policy, its structure and underlying assumptions become very important in determining policy substance and content as well as determining the policy's later acceptance by the electorate. A. Dale Tussing in his article "The Dual Welfare System" gives a fascinating account of this phenomenon, indicating how the welfare *programs* written for the poor differ so strikingly from those *programs* assisting the "non-poor." The two programs differ, however, not so much in content as they do in legitimacy and social acceptability. Assumptions policy-makers have made about the poor and about poverty in America, for example, have decidedly influenced their policy *proposals* for the poor just as the policy-makers' ideas about the social needs of the non-poor have influenced their policy *goals* and plans for them. In addition, the impact of these two programs is also distinct in relationship to their respective clientele. *Programs* for the nearly 14 million poor seem to stimulate continued poverty and bring increased degradation to the poor, while *programs* such as social security for the non-poor seem to bring a needed element of security to them. One begins to sense, then, how some policy *decisions* can have a decided negative and even coercive effect on particular segments of society, whereas other policy *decisions* appear supportive to other groups and interests. One political scientists feels *all* policy has a coercive element to it, and he even goes so far as to define policy as "deliberate coercion."

As society's attitude toward the poor has affected welfare policy, so society's attitudes toward blacks have had an influence on educational policy. Maurice deG. Ford in his article "Courts, Bussing and White Flight" indicates how policy *decisions* to integrate the schools are tied closely to attitudes toward general social integration. Successes and failures of integration in the schools are directly linked, he argues, to how forcefully political institutions like the courts encourage or discourage social integration. The federal courts have been in a position to do both, and Ford indicates that the Supreme Court's current reluctance to stand firmly behind the principles of *Brown* v. *Board of Education* has had the effect of discouraging general integration in the schools.

Policy can also bring definition to constitutional principles. Susan Schiefelbein in her article "Alaska: The Great Land War," for example, indicates how clashes between preservationists and developers over the control of the Alaskan environment have brought new meaning to the principles of federalism. Because we have never clearly answered some of the more pressing questions of federal-state relationships, controversies such as those between the developers and conservationists can bring a redefinition to this relationship. We still do not know, for example, to what extent a state such as Alaska is bound to follow national guidelines in determining its own development, or how much control state residents have over their own state. Alaskan congressional, state, and local leaders unitedly support the industrial development of their state, feeling Washington political leaders should not interfere with their *goals*. Conservationists, supported by a majority of the congressional leadership and the president, think differently. Their goal is an environmental policy that would prevent industry from having a controlling influence over the entire state. Until the Court, the president, or Congress finally supports such a *program*, similar clashes of interest are inevitable in the future.

Social policy can also have unanticipated results and wide-ranging *effects* on even the most un-assuming citizen. A policy such as legalized abortion, for instance, first articulated by the Supreme Court in *Roe* v. *Wade* (found in this chapter), raises crucial social, political, and ethical questions for everyone. These questions are such that even the judges of the High Court are reluctant to answer them. The judges' difficulty is compounded by their utter refusal to answer the primary *question* on which all the answers to the other questions really depend, namely, "When does life begin"? While few would blame the Court for its refusal, it nevertheless makes it necessary for the Court to decide the abortion decision on the basis of auxiliary concerns, such as concerns of privacy, of convenience, and of the state's concern for the "living." Legalized abortion has had far-reaching *effects*. One of the reasons the percentage of population growth has decreased since 1973, for example, is because unwanted births, many of them aborted, have been significantly reduced. Family life has also been affected by the decision. The decrease in available adoptable children, the decrease in the number of teenage marriages, and the reduction in the rates of infant and maternal mortality are all partly due to the Court's decision in *Roe* v. *Wade*.

Concerns about abortion policy have remained intense on both sides of the issue since the Court's decision in 1973. Those favoring abortion and those opposed to it have had significant influence on the political process. Ellen McCormack's challenge in 1976 to the Democratic party when she ran in the Massachusetts primary is illustrative. She ran on the single issue of "anti-abortion" and yet still received 24,903 votes, which was a solid 3.4 percent of the votes cast. The turmoil and intense reactions to abortion policy well illustrate what a valuable index policy in general can be to analysts of society.

Regardless of what type of policy one considers or what focus it has, the policy-maker and citizen alike are guaranteed that, once passed and applied, public policy will more than likely have a lasting *effect* on the political process and system.

★★★

45

The Dual Welfare System: Anxiety and Discontent   A. Dale Tussing
in the American Economy

Tussing describes in detail how the belief in individualism seems to reject the welfare state out of hand. Important to this belief is the confidence put in the contributing members of society who are job holders. Those who are not workers in the marketplace are labeled "non-contributors." How can public policy avoid such attitudes ingrained in society? Would you predict that a successful policy could be devised to aid the poor under such conditions?

In looking at the two welfare systems—one for the poor and one for the non-poor—Tussing discovers five major differences between the two. These include the amount of money involved in the programs, camouflage of the programs, the degree of intervention into personal and family life by government, the level of government involved in administering the program, and the intent and side-effects of the programs. Would you predict success for the poverty programs if they were written in exactly the same fashion as programs for the non-poor? Would you predict failure for the programs for the non-poor if policy-makers structured them in the same way they currently devise programs for the poor? Or would you see little or no change at all despite the restructuring of the programs given the social biases against the poor? How do we name programs for the non-poor to avoid the stigma of welfarism? In what ways are state and local governments involved in administering welfare programs for the poor? Do welfare programs for the poor invade their personal privacy and freedoms, as Tussing argues?

Tussing charges that having separate programs for the poor has separated their interests from the interests of the rest of society. Has this had its repercussions? Has this been a reason for creating inferior programs for the poor and encouraging hostility between the poor and non-poor? How could we go about integrating the interests of the poor with those of the non-poor? Would integration of the interests solve most of the difficulties of the poor? Would the non-poor contributor who supports the government through tax payments then feel that he is on "welfare" and no better than the person who is unemployed and not a financial contributor to society?

★ ★ ★

Anxiety
and
Discontent
in the
American
Economy

The Dual Welfare System

A. Dale Tussing

The differences between poor people's and regular welfare programs are systematic and significant. They mean minimal survival for poor people, and reasonable comfort for non-poor; they mean degradation for poor people, and dignity for non-poor; and most important, they imply continued poverty and dependence for many poor, and continued security and apparent self-reliance for the non-poor.

Two welfare systems exist simultaneously in this country. One is well known. It is explicit, poorly funded, stigmatized and stigmatizing, and is directed at the poor. The other, practically unknown, is implicit, literally invisible, is nonstigmatized and nonstigmatizing, and provides vast but unacknowledged benefits to the non-poor—whether working class, middle class or well to do.

Despite the attention given to programs for the poor, they are dwarfed by the programs for the non-poor. As Gordon Tullock has observed, "Almost all standard discussions of redistribution imply that it is normally from the rich to the poor. Some such redistribution does indeed go on, but it is a trivial phenomenon compared to the redistribution within the middle class. I find the concentration of discussion of redistribution upon the very minor phenomenon of redistribution from the wealthy to the poor and the general ignoring of the major phenomenon—redistribution back and forth within the middle class. . . remarkable."

The legitimacy of one's income and, especially, one's position in the overall distribution of income, are central preoccupations in America. No welfare programs are inherently legitimate in the United States, where the dominant ideology of individualism still appears to reject the welfare state in principle (while applying it in practice—a conflict of some significance). In the view of many people, job-holders are members of and contributors to society; non-job-holders are not. Job-holding legitimates one's political role, as well. In local, state and national politics, more is heard today about "taxpayers" than about "citizens."

Other socially legitimate sources of income exist, but their legitimacy traces directly or indirectly to someone's job. For instance, one can *save* out of one's earnings to provide for one's own retirement, either with a bank or some formal pension scheme. Similarly, one can provide through savings or insurance for an income while sick, or for one's family when one is "no longer there." Virtually all private provisions of this sort are automatically legitimate.

When a recently urbanized and industrialized America found that it could no longer rely on the old, traditional, nongovernmental forms of income protection and maintenance (the extended family, the community and systems of obligation) and had to create a governmental welfare apparatus, a major problem was that American ideology opposed such welfare devices in principle. If both the need for welfare programs *and* the ideology were to be satisfied, either the ideology would have to change, or the *form* and *name* of welfare programs

---

> ## "Public charity," or the welfare system for the poor, has been constructed to be illegitimate.

---

would have to be carefully designed to make them seem to fit the ideology. In particular, they would have to have (or seem to have) a productivity basis.

Two systems were created. Clair Wilcox has labeled the explicit transfer parts of them "social insurance" and "public charity." "Social insurance," the heart of the welfare system for the non-poor, has been constructed to be legitimate, to protect the integrity and dignity of the people involved. To a large extent, this legitimacy is provided by some form of camouflage—by protective nomenclature such as "parity," "compensation" and even "social insurance"; by the paraphernalia of private programs, such as Social Security account numbers; and by burying welfare programs in tax laws.

"Public charity," or the welfare system for the poor, has been constructed to be illegitimate. Thus it too leaves the ideology intact. The illegitimacy of poor people's welfare is multifold. There is, first, the illegitimacy of dependency—living off the incomes of others. Second, there is the separate illegitimacy of apparent idleness, and the usual association with sin. And third, there is the inherent illegitimacy of government spending, financed by taxation. Most welfare programs for non-poor people either do not take the form of government spending (tax relief to some increases others' taxes, but most people do not consider a loophole comparable with an expenditure item), or use earmarked payroll taxes and segregated trust funds, and are thought of, and officially treated as, generically different from spending out of the general revenues of government.

Three examples illustrate the importance of the *form* of a program, and the association of form (rather than content) with legitimacy.

In 1968, Wilbur Cohen, then Secretary of Health, Education and Welfare, advocated a program of "income insurance," as preferable to a guaranteed income, negative income taxes and similar schemes, to cover unemployment as well as more chronic poverty. Cohen pointed to the greater acceptance of Social Security and other programs financed by payroll taxes and with separate trust funds. He argued that the poverty gap could be closed in America—that there were no "economic" reasons that we couldn't afford to redistribute income to eliminate poverty altogether—that the only barriers were "psychological."

In New York State, union members on strike have been eligible to draw public assistance checks. In one upstate city, a prominent labor leader, an outspoken foreign-policy hawk and vehement critic of public assis-

tance recipients, found his membership receiving benefits, and was asked for a justification, both in light of his general antipathy for public assistance, and in light of the argument that public assistance was created to help the poor survive, not to underwrite strikes. His response was that his union members had for years been taxpaying members of the community, and were now only drawing on a fraction of what they had paid in. By contrast, he argued, regular welfare recipients were *less* entitled to public assistance, since they had not (he said) been taxpayers. He was in effect converting the program into a contributory one—for his members, but not for the poor. In both cases, changed perceptions converted a welfare program to a contributory basis, and thereby made it legitimate.

The third example concerns the Brannan Plan, which provides for farm products to be sold for whatever prices they bring in the market while farmers' incomes are supplemented by government checks. Farmers opposed this plan, despite its general superiority to the price-support programs (no storage costs, lower food prices) because a subsidy through the market was less explicit and therefore more legitimate than a direct cash transfer. Opponents used words like "socialism" to describe the Brannan Plan. More revealing still, some said they "didn't need charity." Only when farm surpluses turned into shortages in 1973 was a Brannan Plan-type program seen by farmers as preferable.

Social Security—a Closer Look

Legitimacy of welfare programs for the non-poor is provided by some form of camouflage, and acceptability requires changing the form, not the content, of welfare programs. The classic case of a legitimate welfare program is Old-Age and Survivors and Disability Insurance under Social Security. Social Security has existed for more than 35 years, and has covered millions of beneficiaries. And yet it is almost uniformly misunderstood. Its protective camouflage consists in part of widespread mythology.

The details of the Old-Age and Survivors and Disability Programs are as follows: effective 1974 (but subject to change), there is an employee tax of 5.85 percent on the first $12,000 of payroll income, and an identical tax paid by the employer. Economists believe that the employer share is passed on to the employee, in the form of a lower wage rate, so that it is fair to say that there is a tax of 11.70 percent on the first $12,000 of payroll income. There is a rough relationship between the amount a worker pays in, and the amount to which he is entitled, but only a rough one. Each person is given an account number, and a record is kept of his tax contributions. Each year's benefits (approximately $40 billion annually in the early 1970s) are paid from that year's tax contributions. In addition, there has typically been a small surplus, so that over the years a balance has built up in the Old-Age and Survivors and Disability Insurance trust funds of about $45 billion (as of 1972).

Many people conclude from these details that the Old-Age and Survivors and Disability Insurance system is not a welfare program at all, but is merely a compulsory pension or compulsory saving scheme. As recently as June 1971, NBC newsman David Brinkley, commenting

---

Friedman has called Social Security "the poor man's welfare payment to the middle class."

---

on a news item which stated that Social Security was the largest program of government payments to persons, said, "Social Security is not a government payment to individuals. It is just the government giving the people's own savings back to them."

A second, somewhat more subtle myth, often appears in the conservative press—that Social Security is inefficient, and that individuals could do better by saving on their own through banks and other investments than through a government program. The argument runs as follows: if a man were to "tax" himself at current Social Security payroll tax rates (employer and employee shares combined) and to deposit the proceeds in a savings account, and at age 65 were to stop paying and start drawing a "pension," he would do better (on the average—age of death is, of course, unknown) than under present Social Security benefits.

The argument contains a serious conceptual error: it misunderstands the nature of Social Security by comparing present benefit levels and present tax rates. Yet no one will spend a lifetime paying present tax rates, and then retire and receive present benefit levels. The fact is that tax rates have been rising throughout the existence of Social Security, and that benefit levels have been rising even faster. The fact is also that Social Security payments are, on the average, well over four times the amount paid in by each taxpayer (counting employer and employee shares, and interest) rather than slightly less than he could earn from a bank on the same payments.

How is it possible for a trust-funded program to pay out over four times as much to each beneficiary as he paid during his working life? Three things make this possible: a rising population and work force, which means that more people will always be currently paying taxes than will be receiving benefits; a rising aggregate income level; and rising tax rates. Could a private pension program do the same—relying on growth in the number of clients, and paying out more to each retired person than what he has paid in, together with earned interest? Obviously not. Only a government unit can be completely confident of its ability to continue growing, as only a government has the power to tax.

Social Security is not, then, essentially a scheme by which individuals pay into a fund, from which they later withdraw. Instead, it is a scheme by which those who are now employed are taxed to pay benefits to those who are now unemployed. It is a transfer at this time rather than across time. It is a welfare program, not a savings program.

The resemblence between Social Security and private, funded pension programs is illusory in other ways, too. In a funded pension program, the more you pay in, other things being equal, the more you get. The later in life you enter the program, other things being equal, the less you get. And your eligibility is not typically affected by your eligibility for other pension benefits. None of this is necessarily true with Social Security. As Professor Milton Friedman has written,

> . . . the relationship between individual contributions (that is, payroll taxes) and benefits is extremely tenuous. Millions of people who pay taxes will never receive any benefits attributable to those taxes because they will not have paid for enough quarters to qualify, or because they receive payments in their capacity as spouse. Persons who pay vastly different sums over their working lives may receive identically the same benefits. Two men or two women who pay precisely the same taxes at the same time may end up receiving different benefits because one is married and the other is single.

Because private pension programs are a form of individual saving, in which beneficiaries receive what they have paid in, together with interest, but less administration costs, private pension programs *do* save for their members, and in fact, acquire massive amounts of stocks and bonds. Over the years, Old-Age and Survivors and Disability Insurance members have paid in more in payroll taxes than have been paid out to beneficiaries, and by 1972 the Social Security Trust Funds had acquired $45 billion in U.S. government securities. Since both own billions in assets, ownership of Treasury securities makes Social Security resemble a funded pension program in still another way. But that ownership actually reflects another *dis*similarity.

These trust funds' ownership of over $45 billion worth of U.S. government securities in 1972 meant that one agency of the federal government (the U.S. Treasury) owed money to another agency (the Social Security Trust Funds). (The other dozen trust funds—most of which, like Railroad Retirement, Medicare and Unemployment Compensation, are linked to welfare programs along the lines of Social Security—owned an additional $40 billion in U.S. government securities.) Since almost every year, receipts exceed payments, the assets of these trust funds continue to grow, though they are far lower than would be necessary to place the system on the same actuarial footing as a private insurance company.

To the extent that Social Security taxes exceed benefit payments, and the excess is "lent" to the U.S. Treasury, Social Security taxes are actually being used to finance expenditures on defense, interior, agriculture, foreign affairs and the rest of the budget. The "lending" is merely a bookkeeping entry. The earmarking of these taxes turns out to be less than perfect—present about $2 billion a year. The point is not that Social Security taxpayers are being bilked, their money being siphoned off into the Treasury. They receive over four times, on the average, what they have paid in—hardly a bilking. The point is, instead, that the Social Security system is not a segregated, quasi-private, compulsory insurance scheme, but rather a government welfare program, fully integrated in fact if not in form with the other functions of the government.

This fact makes it all the more important that Old-Age and Survivors and Disability Insurance payroll taxes are America's most regressive major tax—exempting interest, profit, rent, capital gains, and all payroll income over $12,000, and with no allowance for number of dependents. Moreover, the higher one's income, the larger the ratio of the benefits received to the taxes paid. Friedman has called Social Security "the poor man's welfare payment to the middle class."

Differences Between the Systems

There are five major differences between the welfare programs for the non-poor, and those for the poor. They are: the amounts of money involved; the camouflage, or lack of it, in making the programs appear to be something else; the level of government—federal, state and local—involved in administering the program; varying incentive and distributional side-effects of the programs; and the degree of intervention into personal and family life.

Levels of Support

Both in the aggregate and on a per-person basis, the welfare system for the non-poor provides more liberally than that for the poor. Side-by-side comparisons are hazardous, because coverage from program to program varies according to circumstances (for example, age, number of children and so forth) because the specifications of welfare for the poor and non-poor are different, because there are state-to-state differences in a number of programs, and because some recipients have dual coverage. Nonetheless, the following comparisons are revealing. In March 1973, the average unemployment compensation recipient received $256.76 per month; the average family receiving General Assistance (including,

among others, families of those unemployed persons who are ineligible for unemployment compensation) received $114.15. The average retired worker received $164.30 from Old-Age Assistance under Social Security, while the average recipient of Old-Age Assistance under public assistance received $78.65. On the whole, the excess of non-poor over poor welfare programs seems to be in the 20 to 30 percent range for most programs, though some items go up to 100 percent or more.

Most non-poor Americans would probably be willing to agree that poor people are poor because of circumstances rather than lack of merit.

There are interesting differences even within public assistance. The amount per person averaged as follows in March 1973: Aid to the Blind—$110.10; Aid to the Permanently and Totally Disabled—$106.55; Old-Age Assistance—$78.65; General Assistance—$68.81; and Aid to Families with Dependent Children—$54.20. (As of 1974, benefits for aged, blind and disabled are the same.)

Far more dramatic differences than these exist. In Mississippi the average monthly Aid to Families with Dependent Children payment per recipient was only $14.39. In that same state, a corporate farm, Eastland, Inc., owned by the family of a U.S. senator, received over $250,000 annually in various farm subsidies.

Our welfare systems do not distribute benefits on the basis of need. Rather, they distribute benefits on the basis of legitimacy. Poor people are viewed as less legitimate than non-poor people, and among the poor, those who are disabled, blind and old are seen as more legitimate than those in the General Assistance or Aid to Families with Dependent Children categories—both heavily dominated by minority group members, including ghetto mothers and their children, and even including small numbers of unemployed men.

Implied here is a social judgment that—rhetoric to the contrary notwithstanding—America's poor are poor because they *should* be poor. This judgment takes the following form. Most non-poor Americans would probably be willing to agree that poor people are poor because of circumstances rather than lack of merit, except that to do so would also imply that they themselves were comfortable, affluent or rich because of circumstances rather than because of merit. Poor people are not necessarily thought to be inferior. Rather, non-poor people are thought to be superior. The success/failure, deserving/undeserving distinctions lead us to create categories of assistance which on the surface appear to be functional, but which on deeper examination prove to be moral and ideological rationalizations. Poverty reflects inadequate performance; and high levels of welfare support for the poor would be tantamount to rewarding sin.

Concealment of the Welfare Nature of the Program

By and large, welfare programs for the poor are obvious, open and clearly labeled, and those for the non-poor are either concealed (in tax laws, for instance) and ill understood, or are clothed in protective language and procedures (such as "parity," "social security" and "unemployment insurance," for instance, or both ("tax relief," for instance).

If his programs are called "relief," "welfare," "assistance," "charity" or the like, he is surely poor; but if they are called "parity," "insurance," "compensation" or "compulsory saving," he is surely a member of the large majority of non-poor.

Whether a person is poor or not can often be determined by the names of his welfare programs. If his programs are called "relief," "welfare," "assistance," "charity" or the like, he is surely poor; but if they are called "parity," "insurance," "compensation" or "compulsory saving," he is surely a member of the large majority of non-poor persons who do not even think of themselves as receiving welfare payments.

The degree of concealment in turn influences the level of support, in a number of ways. First, welfare programs for the poor, being more noticed, are more in the public eye. Concealed and camouflaged programs are more likely to escape the wrath of taxpayers' groups. The deductibility of interest on home mortgages and of property taxes, known as "tax expenditure" items, cost the federal government $2.4 billion and $2.7 billion, respectively, in 1971. These tax deductions for home owners serve as a massive "rent supplement" for homebuyers. Either, if acknowledged as such, would be the largest single housing program in the federal government. Together they are more than quadruple the size of all programs combined for housing poor people—including public housing, rent supplements, assistance in purchase of homes and all others. Yet they are all but unknown, except as computations on one's income tax return. According to U.S. Treasury figures, 85 percent of the benefits from these provisions go to taxpayers with over $10,000 of adjusted gross income, while less than .01 percent go to those with adjusted gross incomes of $3,000 or less.

In the eyes of many Americans, the openness of poor people's welfare reinforces the sense that the poor are undeserving. Poor people are viewed as idle and dependent (characteristics often attributed to even the most hard-working and independent); and the publicity given to public assistance and to public assistance recipients is likely to (and often is calculated to) reinforce this impression.

This difference in concealment permits taxpayers to demand and legislators to provide differential levels of support without being conscious of discriminating. Those who have convinced themselves that they are wholly independent and self-reliant, in spite of vast camouflaged welfare programs, will not feel they have provided less generously for poor people. In their opinion, they have provided only for poor people.

The degradation and humiliation involved in some poor people's programs, and the sense of failure in life which is instilled in those who accept poor people's welfare, makes poor people strive mightily to "stay off welfare." This is undoubtedly a major reason that the majority of those legally eligible for public assistance do not receive it at all. The number who decline to claim special tax deductions and other tax preferences in order to preserve their dignity is by contrast surely quite small.

The techniques used for concealment of welfare programs for the non-poor often provide for automatic increases in amount as the years go by. This is especially true of "tax expenditures," which require no annual appropriations, but only that the same tax structure remain intact with higher and higher levels of income.

Level of Government

The third difference between welfare for the poor and welfare for the non-poor concerns the level of government involved. Welfare programs for the non-poor tend to be federally financed and federally administered, with decisions on eligibility and on levels of support made nationally, with but two exceptions (unemployment compensation and workmen's compensation), and those exceptions involve federal-state partnerships. Programs for the poor, on the other hand, while they may be partially or almost totally supported by federal funds, are characteristically administered as local programs, primarily by county welfare departments (or as state programs in those states where welfare departments are state operated). Even the War on Poverty efforts of the Office of Economic Opportunity and such related programs as Model Cities are tied to local government and local politics.

There is one important and revealing exception to this statement. In 1969, President Nixon proposed a major revamping of the public assistance system, including federal administration and a federally determined minimum payment level, for all four federally aided groups—families with dependent children, the aged, the blind and the disabled.

For nearly four years the Congress labored, and in 1972 it completed its work. The major changes were all rejected, and a bill was passed which made few departures. The most significant of these was the federalization, effective 1974, of a combined program, called Supplementary Security Income, replacing three federally aided state and local programs: Old-Age Assistance, Aid to the Blind and Aid to the Permanently and Totally Disabled. Benefit levels in the new Supplementary Security Income program are, however, lower than those of a number of states in the antecedent Old-Age Assistance, Aid to the Blind and Aid to the Permanently and Totally Disabled programs. Since states are permitted to supplement the federal payments (making the federal benefit the floor or minimum payment), and since a number of states are expected to do so in order not to reduce payments, even the 1972 legislation does not fully federalize assistance to these groups. Benefit levels still depend on state decisions, and state taxes are still involved.

The public assistance system is now left with three levels of federalization: the new, semi-federalized Supplementary Security Income program, for the most "deserving" poor—the aged, blind and disabled; the federally aided program, Aid to Families with Dependent Children, with eligibility and support-level decisions made by the states, and with state and local administration—viewed by many people as the "ghetto mother" program; finally, there is no federal contribution at all for General Assistance, which covers the least socially legitimate of all dependent poor, unemployed single and childless married persons, and unemployed fathers. It is clear that the degree of federalization, like level of support, depends on legitimacy or worthiness. All three of these degrees of federalization are in contrast to the complete federal control, administration and financing of such regular, mainstream welfare programs as Old-Age and Survivors and Disability Insurance under Social Security.

With these partial exceptions, the rule consistently applies: programs for the non-poor are federal; programs for the poor are state and/or local. This fact increases the exposure of poor people's welfare (not only because these programs are subject to local decisions, closer to home and easier to see, but because poor people's welfare legislation will be debated and acted upon on at least two and probably three levels of government, when the Congress, the state legislature, and the local council or board of supervisors passes on public assistance, housing, food and other programs). Poor people's welfare is limited, simply because it is tied to inelastic local and state revenue sources, such as the property tax, while the regular welfare system can provide vast benefits, since it is tied to the overproductive federal tax system.

Local and state administration of poor people's welfare means control over the size of the population of the poor in given areas. Just as many cities, counties and states compete with one another to attract and keep industry and high-income population, so also do they (with less fanfare, of course) compete to discourage or drive away low-income population. Before Department of Agriculture reforms prompted by the Poor People's March and Resurrection City, hundreds of counties, primarily in the South, refused to participate in surplus food distribution, and a few openly stated their motive: to drive away once-needed farm workers, tenant farmers and sharecroppers, made unnecessary when technology affected agriculture. Competition to get rid of poor people is not limited to the South. A city councilman in a northern city, commenting on the council's recent negative vote on a public housing issue, was quoted as saying that the majority would be delighted to build more public housing for the city's poor, except that construction of public housing would merely attract more poor people to the community. Suburbs have steadfastly refused (with, since 1971, Supreme Court approval) to provide public housing. And, despite the fact that residence requirements for public assistance were declared unconstitutional in 1969, states continue to adopt them and enforce them.

This direction of thought has some apparent logic. In most cases, poor people's welfare programs will require state and/or local tax money; and even where they don't, taxes paid by poor people will not cover the costs of their public education, police, fire and other services. However one feels about the morality of trying to drive away people for purely economic gain, no amount of local competition to get rid of them will reduce the national total of poor people; it just affects their geographic distribution. In fact, there is good reason to believe that these policies increase the amount of poverty. Since they reduce the mobility of poor people, such people are unlikely to be able to leave unpromising regions to move to growing and prosperous ones. At the same time, low levels of services and support to poor people trap them into poverty's vicious circle.

Incentive and Distributional Side-Effects

Poor people's welfare programs discourage poor people from becoming self-supporting, from being thrifty and from maintaining a regular family life. The regular welfare system frequently provides nothing to those with the greatest need, and then provides increasing benefits as need declines. The best-known disincentives to the poor are in the public assistance program, particularly in Aid to Families with Dependent Children. The manner in which most recipients are covered provides that every dollar they earn reduces their assistance check by a dollar. If a family is entitled to $150 per month, and the family earns nothing, it will get a check for $150; if it earns $50, it will get a check for $100; and so forth. This means that, in effect, there is a "tax" of 100 percent on earned income. Since businessmen with marginal tax rates of far less complain of the disincentive effects of taxation, it should hardly be surprising that the motivation of someone with a tax rate of 100 percent should be affected adversely.

In some poor people's welfare programs, the effective marginal tax rate may even exceed 100 percent. This is true wherever a food-stamp, public housing, medical care or other program has a fixed eligibility threshold—an income level above which families or individuals become ineligible to participate in the program. A family may find that any further increases in its income will force it to leave public housing, and pay a rent increase which exceeds the pay increase; force it off food stamps, increasing the grocery budget by more than the pay increase; and force it out of other programs as well.

The Work Incentive program for certain Aid to Families with Dependent Children parents reduces the effective tax rate from 100 percent to 66.67 percent. President Nixon's proposed welfare reforms would have reduced the rate to 50 percent. These lower rates still remain high enough to discourage effort. While recent research indicates that this kind of disincentive is less potent than was once thought, it nonetheless constitutes an added burden on the poor, a "sandbagging" of those who need no such handicaps.

There are other kinds of disincentives in poor people's welfare. The best known is the incentive to break up the family. In a majority of states, Aid to Families with Dependent Children, the largest public assistance program, is available only where there are no employable, unemployed adults in the household. In practice, this has meant that virtually all such families are headed by husbandless mothers. Chronically unemployed husbands often must desert their families in order for the families to become eligible for assistance.

Mainly because of their concealment, many mainstream welfare programs provide in ways which are inversely related to need. The most glaring examples are found in welfare programs buried in the tax laws. The general proposition is: the dollar value to the taxpayer of any item which reduces his taxable income, whether it is a deductible expense, a dependents' exemption or an exclusion (nontaxable income item), is equal to the size of that item multiplied by the marginal tax rate applicable to that taxpayer. A $100 deduction for someone in the 25 percent marginal tax bracket is "worth" $25.00. With a progressive income tax, the dollar value of any given deduction, exemption or exclusion rises as income rises.

The simplest example of the inverse relation to need is the extra dependents' exemption allowed those over 65. The extra $750 exemption is worth nothing to the person whose taxable income is so low that he pays no taxes; it is worth $105 (14 percent of $750) to a person in the 14 percent bracket, a person with up to $1,000 taxable income; and it is worth $325 to a person in the highest, 70 percent bracket, for families with over $200,000 in taxable income. The added exemption is worth the least to those with the most need, and the most to those with the least need.

Even though the amount of this extra dependents' exemption is the same for all people, its value to the taxpayer rises as income rises. This effect is aggravated whenever the amount of the deduction or exclusion itself rises with income.

The "income-splitting" provision (husband-wife joint tax returns) also provides benefits which increase with income. The effect of the joint return provision is to double the size of each tax bracket. The 14 percent rate applies to 0-$500 for single persons and 0-$1,000 for married couples filing jointly. The 15 percent bracket is $501-$1,000 for single persons, and $1,001-$2,000 on the joint return, and so on. The greatest benefit comes at the highest end of the income scale, because the brackets are much wider (for example, $100,000-$200,000). People with high incomes are, in effect, paid thousands of dollars to be married (which helps explain why many rich persons are well known for having wife after wife, or husband after husband—they formalize their affairs, for tax reasons). As incomes decline, so do the tax advantages of being married. And when the family is so poor as to qualify for public assistance, they instead are paid to break up!

There are ways to design income tax provisions, using credits instead of exemptions, and using such devices as disappearing deductions, to avoid making their benefits inverse to need. The regressive effects that are found in U.S. law are not inherent in progressive taxes. The regressive effects are a by-product of the concealment of these implicit welfare programs. Can anyone believe that the American people would permit Congress to establish an explicit old-age pension which paid nothing to those with zero income or only Social Security or public assistance income, paid $105 to a person with $1,000 in income, and $525 to someone with over $200,000 a year? The same question might be asked of farm programs, which also pay inversely to the size of the farm operation, and hence presumably inversely to need.

Intervention into Personal and Family Life

A final distinction between the regular or non-poor welfare system and that for poor people is the degree of intervention into personal and family life. Programs for the non-poor make little or no intrusion into sensitive family decisions; programs for the poor exact, as the price of assistance, an element of control and a surrender of autonomy.

Control over the family's budget is control over important family decisions. Whenever someone can tell you what to buy, he is really telling you how to live. The poor people's welfare system does so in two ways: by providing goods instead of money (public housing, medical care, uplifting symphony concerts for ghetto kids and so forth), and by controlling the use of money transfers (through vouchers, such as food stamps, or through close administrative supervision, as in Aid to Families with Dependent Children).

Who can doubt that some mothers, faced with the choice between required employment out of the home, and having another baby in order to continue to have pre-school children, will choose the latter?

Another way that poor people's welfare weakens autonomy is that people change behavior and family characteristics to become or stay eligible. Can anyone doubt that one reason that there are so many husbandless mothers who head poor families is that the government has for years paid husbandless mothers? Can anyone doubt that some poor people have children because most states do not provide assistance for childless single or married people, no matter how impoverished? President Nixon's family assistance reform proposals would correct the first but not the second of these. It would reduce assistance by a crucial $500 a year for mothers who did not work, unless they had pre-school-age children. Who can doubt that some mothers, faced with the choice between required employment out of the home, and having another baby in order to continue to have pre-school children, will choose the latter? Such choices are not coldly calculated. Rather, the government subtly influences such decisions by determining the environment and reward system in which decisions are made. In precisely the manner described by former Selective Service Director Lewis Hershey, in his famous "channelling" memorandum, just as college students were led to think that becoming engineers or clergymen was their own decision, so poor people are led to think that having children or breaking up a home is theirs.

A third invasion of personal privacy is that various bureaucrats in the poor people's welfare system actually monitor the behavior of their "clients." Public assistance caseworkers, public housing tenant-relations officers and social workers in a variety of agencies view their role as anything from mere advisor and family friend through parent- or husband-surrogate to warden. Mothers have had assistance checks held up because they were seen in bars. Families have been evicted from

housing because of delinquent children. Families have been denied surplus food because they owned a television set.

By contrast, the use of Social Security or Unemployment Compensation checks is never monitored. Though families get a dependent's exemption in the income tax for each minor child, no one checks to make sure the family spends at least as much as the exemption on the child. Home buyers who have drunken orgies will not have their F.H.A. loan insurance revoked, Farmers may spend their farm surplus money as they please.

This double standard makes liars and cheaters out of the stronger poor people, and psychologically dependent grown-up children of the weaker ones. Neither characteristic is conducive to personal development. Moneylessness is only one side of chronic poverty, and the larger and more difficult problem is powerlessness. While some poor people's welfare programs attack this powerlessness, a great many of them aggravate it. An important consequence of stunting independence and reinforcing dependence is to keep many poor people poor.

The differences between poor people's and regular welfare programs are systematic and significant. They mean minimal survival for poor people, and reasonable comfort for non-poor; they mean degradation for poor people, and dignity for non-poor; and most important, they imply continued poverty and dependence for many poor, and continued security and apparent self-reliance for the non-poor.

America's dual welfare system is unique in the world, at least in degree. In other developed countries, while there is persistent debate between the advocates of "universal" and of "selective" social welfare programs, the former win out far more frequently than they do in the United States, where virtually every welfare, health, housing and employment program is designed specifically either for the poor or the non-poor.

We have noted the harmful effects of this dual approach. Separate programs for the poor are typically inferior; they involve demoralizing stigmata; and they tend to be built on assumptions which attribute poverty to defects in the poor. Their structures tend, whether accidentally or not, to inhibit economic and personal development among the poor.

Worse than all of these is the fact that the segregation of social welfare programs has separated, or seemed to separate, the interests of the poor from the interests of the rest of society. This separation helps account for a mutual hostility between the poor and lower-income non-poor, notably the working class, which has been enormously destructive to the interests of both. It is hard to believe that much progress can be made against poverty in America as long as this separation and hostility persist.□

★★★

46

Courts, Bussing and White Flight   Maurice deG. Ford

While racial integration is certainly important from a broad social perspective, Ford suggests that social-class integration is more relevant to improved educational standards. Would it be easier to integrate schools socially than it has been to integrate schools racially? Are schools and the courts better equipped to encourage social-class integration than they have been to encourage racial integration? This very question was raised by James Coleman, whose original report—"Equality of Educational Opportunity"—studied the effects of racial integration on learning. What were the findings of the Coleman Report? Since his first report Coleman has issued a second one that highlights the fact that forced school integration produces "white flight" from the inner city schools. What are major findings of this second report?

Ford refers to two Supreme Court cases decided since 1973 that seem to put the Court in a position of discouraging racial integration. In the Rodriguez v. San Antonio School District *and* Bradley v. Milliken *cases, the Court ruled against certain aspects of forced integration. Of what specific importance were the findings of these two cases? Can social change take place without court action? How instrumental are the courts in establishing racial and social-class integration?*

In writing about the Coleman Report II, Ford seems to agree with James Coleman's criticism of judicial decisions. In particular he is critical of the Court's using research data as a basis for structuring policy. But if valid research is not used, what is the option? Is it preferable to draw conclusions about social issues without the benefits of social data?

Ford seems to feel that excellence of education would be a major incentive to parents to participate and willingly cooperate in integration plans in the city. Is this a superior approach to forced busing? Why does Coleman favor the "Louisville Plan" to integrate schools? What might be the political consequences in choosing excellence in education to forced busing? Would this be sufficient incentive? How would blacks react to it? If we reduce our commitment to forced busing as a tool to racially integrate schools, what serious consequences could you expect to society's objective to promote racial equality and harmony?

★ ★ ★

Courts, Bussing and White Flight

Maurice deG. Ford

Cambridge, Mass.
Prof. James Coleman, principal author of the famous 1966 Coleman Report, *Equality of Educational Opportunity*, is in the news again. He is cited in the press as having changed his position on integration and court-ordered bussing. "A Scholar Who Inspired It Says Bussing Backfired," runs the front-page headline in a recent edition of *The National Observer*. Referring to the "loss" of Dr. Coleman, Nathaniel Jones, general counsel for the NAACP, laments that "the academic sector is just not reliable" as a civil rights ally.

A careful reading of a recent interview with Dr. Coleman suggests that, contrary to the headlines, he has really not "retreated" or grown that much more conservative on "forced bussing." But this does not really alter the issue, which is people's perceptions of what Coleman has been saying rather than what he actually said.

My purpose here is to present a more balanced coverage of the latest revised social science study, which we might call Coleman Report II. Just released, it is a preliminary report on the new study that he is doing for the Urban Institute on the effects of desegregation. His main conclusion, according to the extended interview published in *The National Observer*, is that an extensive "white flight" from the twenty largest school districts in the country is causing resegregation. There is some white outward migration also from the smaller school districts, but the problem is less severe. Asked what accounts for the difference, Coleman replies, "I'd say it has to do with the degree of security that parents have about their children in the two situations. In large cities, where the system often seems out of control, there's a much greater feeling of inability to have any impact on the schools, a feeling that schools cannot maintain order, and a feeling that the schools cannot protect the child." He believes, according to *The National Observer* inter-

view, that "it's not entirely lower-class blacks that middle-class whites are fleeing. They are fleeing a school system that they see as too large, as unmanageable, as unresponsive, to find a smaller more responsive system."

Dr. Coleman is discouraged about the immediate effects of court-ordered bussing in large, particularly Northern, urban school districts. But contrary to the headlines he insists that he is not retreating from his former position. Anyone familiar with the findings of *Equality of Educational Opportunity* would have to agree with him. In that report, Dr. Coleman emphasized that *"per pupil expenditure, books in the library, and a host of other facilities and curricular measures show virtually no relation to achievement if the 'social' environment of the school—the educational backgrounds of other students and teachers—is held constant."* (Coleman's italics.) What was most important for meaningful racial integration and educational improvement was social class integration. And by "social class integration" Coleman meant not necessarily rich kids with poor kids, but kids from family and home atmospheres conducive to learning (even if the father was a church-mouse-poor minister) going to school with kids from educationally more impoverished home environments. The hope, based on the realization that children learn best from other children, was that some of the "culture" and constructive attitudes toward learning of the more advantaged "middle-class" kids would "rub off" on those less fortunate.

Civil rights attorneys and others who read the Coleman Report used its findings to buttress the case for metropolitan (that is, urban center plus suburbs) desegregation. For in a society where the central cities—such as Newark, Cleveland, Detroit, Oakland, Philadelphia—were becoming increasingly poor and black and ringed by comparatively affluent white suburbs, a metropolitan solution was clearly necessary. Attempts were made to correct the economic and racial disparities between the central cities and their surrounding suburbs

---

Maurice Ford, a tutor at Dunster House at Harvard College, is at work on a book entitled "Southie Is My Home Town."

through the courts. But by identical 5-to-4 votes the Supreme Court twice thwarted these attempts to have the findings of the Coleman Report influence constitutional law. In 1973, in *Rodriguez* v. *San Antonio School District*, the Burger Court, with the four Nixon appointees—Burger, Blackmun, Powell and Rehnquist—joined by Justice Potter Stewart in the majority, held that, where educational expenditures were concerned, a federal district judge was powerless to eliminate financial disparities between the central city and its suburbs.

And just a year ago, the day after it handed down its decision in the Nixon "tapes" case, the same majority of the Court voted against metropolitan desegregation in the Detroit case. Federal district Judge Roth, who died just before the Supreme Court overturned his verdict, had ruled that the only way the Detroit public schools, which were becoming overwhelmingly black, could be desegregated was to involve the suburbs in a metropolitan remedy. In this he was backed by the Sixth Circuit Court of Appeals. But the Burger Court, perhaps conscious of pressures in Congress for a constitutional amendment banning forced bussing, said nay in *Bradley* v. *Milliken*.

Taken together, the Supreme Court's *Rodriguez* and *Bradley* decisions have tied the hands of federal judges. Many believe that if he had been allowed to do so, Judge W. Arthur Garrity would have compelled Boston's white suburbs to join with the central city to bring about equal educational opportunity. But after the Detroit decision he felt unable to do so. While a metropolitan school district may be larger than Coleman would like, a metropolitan solution would have brought about the social class integration that he still feels is indispensable.

In his *National Observer* interview Dr. Coleman says in detail why he feels that having a majority of middle-class children in each classroom is so crucial:

> The theory is that children who themselves may be undisciplined, coming into classrooms that are highly disciplined, would take on the characteristics of their classmates, and be governed by the norms of the classrooms. So that the middle-class values would come to govern the integrated classrooms. In that situation, both white and black children would learn. What sometimes happens, however, is that characteristics of the lower-class black classroom, namely a high degree of disorder, came to take over and constitute the values and characteristics of the classroom in the integrated schools. It's very much a function of the proportions of lower-class pupils in the classroom.

One may, of course, quarrel with the "middle-class norms" that Coleman espouses, and many blacks and educational theorists, notably Jonathan Kozol and John Holt, do quarrel with them. One may also wonder how social class integration can take place in the largest cities, and thus produce the educational climate Coleman desires, without some sort of metropolitan solution. He does not seem to have squarely faced this issue.

However, like Robert Coles before him, who tried to explain why the integration of lower-class Roxbury and lower-class South Boston would be a disaster, Coleman is not surprised by the tumult which has developed in Boston, that "Athens" of ethnic islands:

> Boston is a peculiar kind of metropolitan area, with a large proportion of the metropolitan area outside the central city, including most middle-class whites. The desegregation order was, of course [after *Rodriguez* and *Bradley*], limited to Boston proper, which meant that it involved primarily lower-class communities with strong ethnic ties, whites and blacks. Now under those circumstances, with most of the higher-achieving middle-class schools in the suburbs, one could hardly expect integration to have beneficial effects on achievement.

As an example of a solution which he hopes will work, Coleman points to the Louisville Plan. There a federal judge, distinguishing the pattern of segregation in Louisville from that in Detroit (as, was recently also done with respect to the Wilmington, Del., public schools), has gotten around *Bradley* v. *Milliken* and ordered a metropolitan remedy. Under the Louisville Plan, children will attend neighborhood schools part of the time and be bussed to an integrated school (in surrounding Jefferson County) three days a week. Coleman believes that desegregation which follows this pattern will "reduce fears that lead to white flight."

Another hope for achieving integration, according to Coleman, lies in especially innovative and thoughtful educational programs—excellence at the end of the bus ride. "I think there has to be an incentive," he says, "either in government money and assistance or attractive programs.... What you need are positive inducements for families to keep their children in integrated schools. You can't create integration by court edict. In the larger cities, certainly, it's a very temporary matter." No one seems to agree with Coleman on this more fervently than Judge Garrity in Boston. He has involved twenty colleges and universities, as well as twenty business organizations in the metropolitan Boston area, to work with the Boston School Committee in creating a Magnet School Program, which he calls the "magic" of his desegregation order. (See Ford: "The Schools: Detente in Boston," *The Nation*, May 3.) If this partnership is able to overcome political obstacles and work, it may make the Boston public school system second to none.

A final intriguing aspect of Coleman's interview in *The National Observer* is his discussion of the courts' use of social science evidence, such as the 1966 Coleman Report, in arriving at desegregation decisions. He emphasizes that there should be a strict separation between redressing constitutional grievances and writing social science opinion into the law of the land:

> The evidence in my [1966] report is not relevant in any way to the question properly before the courts. The question is whether school systems have acted in a way that deprives students of their constitutional rights. That's a legal question, not a question of achievement levels. I think the courts were wrong to consider the report in any way. It's appropriate for school boards to consider such evidence but not courts....
> Consider what would have happened if the report had said that segregated classrooms improved pupil performance. Would the courts have been justified in order-

ing bussing to create racial imbalance? Of course not. Courts are taking a very precarious path when they make research results about the achievement consequences of school integration a basis for reorganizing a school system. That's not their function, in my view.

Nor does it seem to be the view of many judges. Very few courts, somewhat contrary to Coleman's fears, have in fact rested their desegregation decisions on the findings of his report. That report, and its methodology, have been enormously controversial, spurring now almost a decade of academic debate. David Cohen and Michael Garet summarize the controversy in a recent article, "Reforming Educational Policy with Applied Social Research" in the *Harvard Educational Review:*

> The last decade, then, has seen a spectacular display of methodological fireworks about school effects. As a result, something more is now understood about how schooling affects achievement, income and other outcomes. Still more is understood about how to analyze these issues. But methodological sophistication has not in the least reduced stubstantive disagreement over the meaning of research results. Quite the contrary. It has refined technical issues, pressed them to higher levels and made at least some people more self-conscious about what the issues imply. This is an advance in knowledge. It is not, however, an advance which has produced any noticeable convergence, either in the sort of questions being asked, in the techniques with which answers are provided, or in the answers themselves.

Despite my disagreement with the result reached, perhaps Justice Lewis Powell was right, in his majority opinion in the *Rodriguez* case, not to rest the Supreme Court's decisions about the need for financial equalization of educational expenditures on the social science evidence presented in the briefs. With so many experts in disagreement, it would have been presumptuous for the Court, he felt, to attempt to wrest the

"truth" from the contending academic factions and proclaim it as constitutional law.

James Coleman seems correct to me, at the present time, in emphasizing that desegregation decisions must continue to be made, quite apart from reports like his own. He seems also correct in his skepticism about expecting instant positive results from court-ordered bussing. The task before the courts, North and South, ever since *Brown* v. *Board of Education*, has been to bring about desegregation (which is preliminary to, and quite different from, integration). The emphasis is on the elimination of a stigma. The courts cannot afford to turn back from this task, particularly given the tentative and conflicted state of our social science knowledge. Coleman emphasizes that courts must continue to march forward and undo the discrimination which official action has brought about.

Very few civil rights advocates are surprised that test scores do not substantially improve, or racial attitudes markedly change, during an initial period of desegregation such as is now taking place in Boston. Indeed, given the level of violence and tension in schools like South Boston High and Hyde Park High, it would be a miracle if test scores did not go down and stereotyped attitudes did not become more fixed in these initial stages. The hope is not so much for the present. It is, after all, only the first step, albeit a step which must be made. The hope is that, perhaps twelve years from now, when the present turmoil has subsided, black and white kindergarten children and first-graders will begin to go to school together in peace and begin to learn to love and respect each other and to appreciate each other's diverse talents and contributions. Only then may those test scores start to improve. Yet, as Coleman rightly summarizes, given the box into which the *Rodriguez* and *Bradley* decisions have put federal district court judges, it seems illusory that much progress can be made toward achieving a truly integrated society until some way is found to attract the middle class—both white and black—back into our urban public schools.

★★

47

Alaska: The Great Land War   Susan Schiefelbein

Whenever federal interests clash with state interests, serious constitutional questions are bound to arise. In the power relationship, is the federal government ever in danger of losing a battle to the state? What sort of leverage does the federal government maintain over state government? Alaska is the focal point of a controversy involving environmental concerns and economic development. What are the arguments on each side of this question? What persons and groups favor the protectionist viewpoint as opposed to the position for economic development? Congressman Don Young of Alaska was incensed when the federal government declared some 56 million acres of Alaska to be "national monuments" and Secretary of the Interior Cecil Andrus set aside an additional 50 million acres, which prevented important mining interests from working the land. Congressman Young abruptly charged Washington with "colonial rule" of Alaska. Do his charges have any validity? What role did President Carter play in the controversy? What similarities and differences do you see in the relationship between Washington and Alaska and that of "colonial rule" elsewhere?

Independence and isolation have given Alaska an unsual relationship to Washington. On which side of the issue are most residents of Alaska? Only since the Alaskan pipeline installation have social relationships among Alaskan natives begun to change. Similar social and physical ills now plague the towns and cities of Alaska that long have troubled those in the "Lower Forty-eight." How did life in Fairbanks, Alaska, change with the building of the oil pipeline? How would you suggest Washington should handle this isolation and independence in order to govern more easily? Can Alaska continue to preserve this strong sense of states' rights as long as the federal government demands control over 60 percent of its land? How does this federal-state relationship differ from that of Nevada, Utah, and Idaho, where federal ownership of land exceeds even that of Alaska? Are these states—as in Alaska—very defensive of states' rights?

Schiefelbein indicates that wherever wildlife and land must be protected from industry and industrial profits, with only a few exceptions, the preservationists usually have the more difficult time proving the worth of their cases to the policy-makers. Why is this the case? Is the American public more concerned about economic development than with environmental issues? Where else might the preservationists go to present their case if the political system will not favorably respond?

★ ★ ★

ALASKA
THE GREAT LAND WAR

by Susan Schiefelbein

Just below the Arctic Ocean, an awesome expanse of earth sweeps across five time zones: Alakshak, the great country, the land we call Alaska. Its northern lights shimmer over endless stretches of ice—one of the glaciers here is larger than all Holland—and yet its boundaries also embrace sand dunes and desert and a dense rain forest. Its three million lakes and ten thousand streams brim with rainbow trout, Arctic grayling, and five kinds of salmon. Bald eagles and falcons ride the winds; below them wander the last great herds of caribou in the Americas. Valleys store oil, gold, and a dozen other precious minerals. McKinley, the highest mountain on the continent, presides over this domain, its craggy face a testimony to its native name—Denali, the Great One. No wonder Alaskan natives need only one word—gar-rundi—to express both "life" and "land." For here the two are entwined.

TODAY, ALASKA FACES an uncertain future. The time has come to decide how much of its wilderness should be commercially exploited and how much should be preserved—and the dilemma has touched off a national debate. The issue first made headlines last year when the House passed legislation that would prohibit development on an Alaskan landmass the size of California. Although the bill never reached a Senate vote, the fact that congressmen have vowed to reintroduce it this session has fueled opponents' and proponents' fervor. Lobbyists are snatching for Alaska's acres as though they were stashed in a bin at a rummage sale—environmentalists want as much land as possible preserved and developers want it left open for extracting its resources. Senators have accused colleagues in Congress of sabotaging bills, spreading propaganda, and stooping to Watergate tactics; some have even threatened to oust the Secretary of the Interior for supporting a conservationist bill. In Alaska, a newspaper has suggested that environmentalists are in collusion with Arabs in a plot to lock up North Slope oil, and a state legislator has proposed that fires be set in the national parks.

For the moment, Alaska rests safely, the lands in question declared as monuments by President Carter in an effort to keep all hands off them until congressmen address the issue this year. Influential senators and the President himself say the congressional deliberations to come will be the most significant environmental debate of the century; for what legislators decide will in large part determine whether Alaska is wisely developed and its beauties preserved, or whether Lilliputian special-interest groups will carve this ancient giant into a crosshatch of land claims, squandering its wealth and disfiguring its face for all ages hence.

On one side of the coming debate stand those who cherish Alaska for its vast store of wealth—an estimated 12-49 billion barrels of oil (the U.S. consumes about 6 billion a year); 29-132 trillion cubic feet of gas; 130 billion tons of coal; and profitable amounts of 16 of the 18 minerals the Department of Defense calls "critical" to national security. The people who oppose such preservation efforts as last year's bill (H.R. 39) want to develop such riches to the fullest. Their numbers include the entire Alaskan congressional delegation (Senators Ted Stevens and Mike Gravel, and Representative Don Young); the oil, mining, and timber industries; and a great many of the Alaskans themselves.

On the other side are those who believe that the unspoiled wilderness is itself a precious resource that should be preserved. Leading spokesmen for this group include Representative Morris Udall (D-Arizona), who introduced last year's House bill; Representative John Seiberling (D-Ohio), who shepherded the bill through the subcommittee; Secretary of the Interior Cecil Andrus, who orchestrated the administration's monuments declaration; and most conservation groups—especially the Alaska Coalition, which is made up of more than two dozen environmental organizations that have banded together for the Alaskan wilderness battle. They contend first, that industry has plenty of resources to exploit in areas outside the parks they have proposed, on state acreage and nonrestricted federal land. They also feel that oil and minerals—which, due to the nature of Alaskan ore deposits, would almost all require open-pit or strip mining—are not always the land's most valuable assets. "There are those who think that the only worth to the land is an extractable resource," says Andrus. "But some people are willing to consider living resources. To those who say 'oil is where you find it,' I say, caribou are where you find them, too. And unlike the oil, we know exactly where the caribou are."

Unfortunately, the issue is more complicated than even these two seemingly deadlocked positions suggest. The bill introduced last year was crammed with all the details that must be considered when a state has not been fully settled—or, in Alaska's case, not even fully civilized. Future railway lines, provisions for sewer facilities, the rights of those who hunt for most of their food, the right of bush planes to penetrate the otherwise impenetrable wilderness—all are causes for contention between the developers and the preservationists. The complexities, however, must not obscure the fundamental issue: How much of America's last and largest wilderness will we sacrifice for present profit, and how much can we afford to protect in its natural state?

THE LEGISLATIVE HISTORY of the Alaskan lands battle started more than a century ago, when the words *energy shortage* and *environmentalism* were not even in·the common vocabulary. In 1867, when Seward purchased his "folly" from the czar, the Russian treaty specified how the United States was to treat the "uncivilized"—that is, the natives who had lived in Alaska since their ancestors crossed the Asian land bridge—but it never actually discussed the land rights of these people. The United States followed this lead, assuming ownership of a territory despite the fact that its native people, unlike the American Indians, had never been conquered, bought out, or even conned out of their lands. Native land rights were once again ignored when Congress granted Alaska statehood in 1958.

When the federal government grants statehood, it gives some land to the new state government and keeps some for itself, with its largest shares being in Nevada (where the United States owns 87 percent of the land), Utah (66 percent), and Idaho (63 percent). Although Alaska stands fourth in this line—with 60 percent of its land federally owned—its size is so awesome that the "leftovers" given to the state translate into a whopping 104 million acres, nearly five times the acreage granted to any other state. The state was also granted all navigable waters and its coastline, rich with oil and longer than the entire coastline of the lower 48 states.

These lands, though, were not divvied up all at once. The federal government proceeded to pick its acres at leisure, setting aside parks and national forests as the need arose. The state was given 25 years in which to choose any lands not previously claimed by the nation. Hoping to acquire land best suited for settlement and mineral exploitation, the state also made its choices slowly. In the first decade of statehood, Alaska selected only 26 million acres of the 104 million acres it had been granted.

Then, in 1968, came the impetus that forced all sides to cease their sluggishness on the lands problem. Atlantic Richfield struck black gold on the North Slope, some ten billion barrels of it. In short order, the natives, who had been claiming an aboriginal right to the entire state, filed suit, and a half dozen oil companies realized that the pipeline they had planned would trespass across native land if the natives won a sizable land settlement. Congress responded by passing the Native Claims Settlement Act, in 1971, which granted 44 million acres and $1 billion to Alaskan natives and, not coincidentally, cleared the way for the pipeline.

AT THIS POINT, one more group joined the now burgeoning cast of characters in the play for Alaskan land. Environmentalists eyed the huge statehood grant, the huge native grant, and the huge corporate oil and mineral claims, and they began to fear that Alaska's wilderness would be exploited without forethought, that scenic values would be destroyed in the rush to make the last frontier our next Detroit.

To allay environmentalist fears, Congress included a special section—"17D(2)"—in the Native Claims Act that was intended to give some order to the confusion of land grabs. The section required that Congress examine up to 80 million acres of Alaska's lands for inclusion in the nation's park system. Section D2 had one hitch: Its temporary freeze preventing the state from claiming the rest of its land would end on December 18, 1978; if Congress was going to preserve any of the lands permanently, it would have to act before then.

D2 created an uproar. The fury in the state was only partially caused by the number of acres set aside; with or without D2, after all, the federal government would eventually own 60 percent of the state. Alaskans fumed instead over what the government was planning to *do* with those lands.

Unowned land in Alaska has always been overseen by the federal government; but it has been overseen with very little restriction by the Bureau of Land Management, an agency so pro-industry that Andrus has labeled it the "Bureau of Livestock and Mining." BLM land is open to the public for logging, road-building, hunting, mining, fishing, cattle grazing, and hydroelectric development. One of the four federal ownership classifications, national forest, is also open to "multi-use"—an official euphemism, some say, for multi-abuse. At the time of D2, the BLM and the Forest Service managed 90 percent of Alaska.

> **'Alaskans feel that they can dance around a bonfire refusing conservation and the issue will go away,' says Udall. It won't; he is reintroducing a bill this year.**

The reason why state and development interests found D2 troublesome was that the 80 million acres set aside were to be considered for inclusion in the three other, more restrictive classifications—wild and scenic river; wildlife habitat; and national park—in which almost no development can take place. Any of these classifications can be made still more restrictive by giving them a "wilderness overlay," which prohibits even the building of roads and permanent structures.

Thus the pro-development interests were especially outraged when, early in 1977, Congressman Udall introduced H.R. 39, which was even stricter than the authors of D2 had envisioned. The bill put aside 121 million acres in the strict classifications, about half of which were also given a wilderness overlay. The legislation passed the House.

But when the bill reached the Senate, it hit a snag. Although the House had reviewed the bill thoroughly and conducted thousands of hearings, industry sympathizers felt they had not had their day in court.

While Udall claimed that 70 percent of Alaska's mineral wealth lay outside his proposed parks, as well as 95.5 percent of the favorable oil and gas deposits and all of the coal, developers saw the statistics differently. They contended that while *most* of the deposits were outside boundaries, they felt the *best* ones were inside. Worse, they said, Udall's estimates were based only on *known* deposits—and Alaska has not yet been fully explored.

Udall, of course, had an answer for these objections: "If you want a final resource analysis," he said, "drill up the whole state. We didn't know everything there was to know about the Grand Canyon, either, but we knew enough to be justified in setting it aside." Seiberling, for his part, felt that the problem had little to do with whether most resources were outside proposed parks. "The problem," he said, "is that developers don't want 95 percent of the resources; they want them all. The selfishness of the industries involved in this issue would blow your mind."

Andrus also argued against the industry lobby. To those developers who claimed that preservation would devastate Alaska's economy, he pointed out that southeast Alaska's biggest employer, the fishing industry, would stand only to benefit if streams and spawning beds were protected; and he emphasized that Alaska's tourism—which is expected to burgeon if a bill passes—brought in $150 million just last year. And as for the industry claim that an area the size of California was being "locked up" in parks, Andrus pointed out that the land left open to exploitation would be *twice* the size of California. Finally, Andrus stressed, preserves could be opened for exploitation in the future if the need arises.

But the bill's opponents found postponed extraction almost as objectionable as no extraction. Said Alaskan Congressman Don Young: "What will happen if there's a war or a world shortage of resources? They'll go in and tear up the wilderness for copper and bauxite. There will be no controls and they will destroy the fish and pollute the air. A bill like H.R. 39 could be the worst environmental bill in history."

Environmentalists, however, were not worried by Young's dire predictions; nor, for that matter, was the administration—which, represented by Interior Secretary Andrus, had submitted a lands proposal that was very much in the conservationist spirit of H.R. 39. Nevertheless, in the end, the string of haphazard events that surrounded the bill's Senate stay led to a far different conclusion than Udall, Seiberling, or Andrus had hoped for. First, Alaskan Senator Mike Gravel threatened to filibuster any Alaskan lands bill that was brought to the Senate floor. He even arrived at the Senate one day prepared to read the entire two-volume biography of Gerald Ford, boasting to the press that he could "bring the Senate to its knees on the subject." He did not attend any of the subcommittee meetings at which the Senate bill was drafted. Despite the antipathy of some Senators and heckling in the press (which has been a thorn in his side ever since he nominated himself for Vice President in 1972 and, on another occasion, proposed that a domed metropolis be built at the base of Mt. McKinley), he stood firm on his filibuster plan. "Where the survival of the state of Alaska is at stake, I feel morally justified." His popularity in Alaska soared.

Alaska's Republican Senator, Ted Stevens—the minority whip, who was recently critically injured in a plane crash—did push the bill along, despite the fact that he considered H.R. 39 "an abortion" and Congressman John Seiberling a "dilettante." He readily admitted that his eagerness to pass a bill stemmed only from the fact that Andrus had publicly warned that the administration would declare the land as monuments if Congress failed to meet its December deadline. Stevens thus attended virtually every meeting of the Senate Interior Committee, although some observers say that his bickering did more to delay the bill than to push it forward. Editorialists went so far as to say that the great conservation record of Senator Henry Jackson, who chaired the committee, was in danger of being shattered, so amenable was he to Stevens's suggestions. The bill that finally was reported was considered, by some, to be a chaotic mess of land divisions. Seiberling described the Senate plan as "unacceptable." Andrus called it "less than desirable." No compromise was made, and the bill was never brought to a vote.

The lands proposal did not evaporate in total ignominy, however. The President, as Andrus had urged him, declared some 56 million acres as national monuments—which gives them virtually the same protection as parks. And Andrus has used his own power to set an additional 50 million acres aside for three years, making them ineligible for state, native, and mining claims. Both actions are revocable by Congress—which is exactly what Andrus had intended: "I am not superimposing my personal beliefs over Congress. But on December 18, the land would have been unprotected, and I wasn't going to let the rape, ruin, and run boys exploit it before Congress could act again."

However temporary these designations may be, they do not suit the state. Alaskan Congressman Young insisted—in a flood of angry comments about "bearded backpackers" and environmental "zee-lotts"—that the state was being subjected to colonial rule from Washington. "We'll do something," he said. "We'll get rid of the Secretary of the Interior in two years." Gravel called the executive declaration an "abuse of power" by which he is "horrified." And while Stevens at least prefers the President's action to a bill as strong as H.R. 39—he says he can undo what the President does, but not what Congress legislates—he promised that if an environmental bill ever does pass, he would use his Senate vote as a mechanism for revenge. "I don't get mad anymore," he said; "I get even. The rest of the country would never get over it."

NEITHER UDALL nor Seiberling is worried about the Alaska delegation's accusations or their tactical plans for the coming years. Both hope to reintroduce a proposal this session. "There is a feeling in Alaska," Udall reflected recently, "that they can dance around a bonfire refusing to accept any land conservation proposal and the whole thing will go away. But every major land bill of this

---

Stevens has pledged that if an environmental bill passes, he will in the future use his Senate vote for revenge. 'I don't get mad any more,' he says; 'I get even.'

---

kind has taken more than one Congress. I worked my tail off for eight years on the strip-mining bill; so be it with this one.

"And I want tickets to next year's filibuster," he concluded serenely. "Because it's going to have to last 20 months. We'll see if Senator Gravel can succeed in tying up the Senate that long for his selfish reason."

HOWEVER HEATED the debates, the issue looks a bit cut-and-dried in the colorless corridors of Washington. Maps, statistical graphs, and postcard-pretty photos lie piled on desk tops, and it seems that one need only look at the figures objectively to make a cold but rational decision. While bureaucrats draw their boundaries across government maps, the concept of sacrificing profits to preserve birds, glaciers, and caribou seems like silly sentimentality.

But it isn't that way at all when viewed from the heights of a mountain in Alaska, where the wilderness stretches out before you to eternity. The most frustrating experience in a visit to Alaska, in fact, is the difficulty one has absorbing its magnificence. The land is more than primitive; it is primordial, one of the last corners of earth that remains the way it was in the days before man was even created. Every time the eye moves it comes upon another spectacle. The pageantry of the landscape, brilliantly colorful in the clear air—the awesomeness of the distances and heights—are so overwhelming that one has the desperate impulse to wear blinders so that the beauties can be appreciated one by one.

Which of these panoramas have created the deadlocks in land decisions? One of the areas most bitterly disputed is the Arctic National Wildlife range. About 60 miles east of Prudhoe Bay, the area overlies the eastward extension of the geologic structure now producing the prodigious amounts of

North Slope oil. Energy czar James Schlesinger's staff claims that the area is one of the largest potential onshore petroleum fields in America.

But this range is also the winter home of the great, galloping Porcupine caribou herd. Each year 120,000 of these magnificent beasts migrate between the Arctic Wildlife range and its extension in Canada—a distance equivalent to a round trip between Washington, D.C. and Chicago—requiring millions of acres for feeding on the tundra's sparse vegetation. The Canadians, hopeful that Americans would share in the responsibility of guarding the herd, have already prohibited a gas pipeline across their share of the grounds, knowing that some 250,000 animals in the only other arctic herd have died in the past seven years, a loss that some zoologists say was caused in part by the construction of the Alaskan pipeline.

The Tongass rain forest in southeast Alaska is another legislative battleground. The region erupts with dark mountains that loom from fjords whose silver waters serve as reflecting pools for the rugged terrain at their edges. One of the first areas settled by Caucasians, the land is dotted with historic remains of the early Indian cultures, the Russian period, and the Klondike gold rush. Environmentalists say these lands should not serve as an open pit for copper miners who wish to extract a mineral that is already a drag on the market.

The Noatak River has posed another conflict. The river drains the largest undeveloped and unpolluted watershed in the nation; the United Nations has declared it an International Biome Reserve—a river qualified to give scientists the opportunity to study a water system that is entirely untouched by man. If one stream feeding into it becomes polluted, the reserve's worth to scientists disappears.

The remaining conflicts are too extensive to catalog here, but descriptions of the areas in question read like letters from Shangri-la. They include the Yukon Delta, which is the breeding ground for most of the swans, ducks, geese, and other waterfowl that eventually migrate throughout North America; the Wrangells, the most expansive stretch of glaciers in the nation; and the Gates of the Arctic, awesome, needlelike granite peaks that stand at the doorway to the Yukon.

But in the end, oil and minerals, caribou and eagles, mountains and glaciers and tundra are really not the most important considerations in the Alaska issue. More important is the effect the decision will have on the people involved—in Alaska and the nation, now and in the future.

How do Americans feel? Of the 2,000 individuals who testified on H.R. 39—a greater number of people than has testified on any legislation since the civil-rights bill of 1964—the overwhelming majority supported conservation of Alaska, with an intensity that, as John Seiberling described it, was stunningly philosophic, sometimes almost biblical.

But despite the fact that testifiers came from all age-groups and hundreds of occupations, many Alaskans dismiss the outcome of the hearings, due mostly to their conviction that anyone who would support conservation in Alaska must be a bearded berry-picker—that old hippies never died, they just faded into environmentalists.

One might think that Alaskans—the people who have actually seen the wilderness—would be the first to protect it from developers. Not so. While they appreciate the scenic beauties of the bush, many residents came to Alaska to share in the singular experience of building a state. Despite the low ratio of people to land—the population of the city of Buffalo, living in a state twice the size of Texas—most Alaskans live in towns. And the atmosphere in those towns is fiercely independent; they want to do things on their own—construct more roads, more rails, more buildings—conquer the wilderness. Anchorage is a displaced boomtown from the Old West, complete with saloons that still erupt with brawls.

Contributing to this frontier spirit is the fact that Alaskan towns must be self-sufficient; they are cut off not only from the rest of the nation but from each other as well. Only 3,062 miles of road have been paved in the entire state—17 percent of the paved mileage of Connecticut. Three-quarters of the post offices can be reached only by air. Teenagers don't ask to use the family car—they want the family bush-plane.

As a result of this isolation, a camaraderie has grown up among Alaskans, a "them against us" spirit reflected even in the everyday speech. The rest of the country is referred to as "the lower 48" or "the United States." A non-Alaskan—whether from Chicago or Tokyo—is an "outsider." When the telephone company finally managed, in the not-so-distant past, to bypass operator assistance in calls from Alaska to the rest of the nation, newspaper ads read, "Now you can dial America direct." Alaskan humor, too, is touched by the same sort of independent spirit. A favorite Klondike prank entails covering hard moose droppings with gold paint, then sending the package off to outsiders as a gift of "gold nuggets."

As the prank suggests, Alaskans tend to think of outsiders as ignorant when it comes to the Alaskan lifestyle—and they resent what they consider to be an "uneducated" intrusion into their state. "We voted for statehood because we thought we'd get some rights and not be run out of Washington like we were a territory," says John Miscovich, a gold-miner at Flat who is planning a 25-square-mile open-pit mine with four major corporations. Miscovich adds that environmentalists he has spoken to are "sly foxes who can't be trusted"; and as for their precautions—well, if his claims were on federal ground, he'd have to be replanting his exploration sites "so some moose wouldn't trip over them." Walter Magnusen, another rough-hewn miner, who once found a single nugget worth $400,000, claims, "There are already lands set aside for

---

Fairbanks now has the singular distinction of being the most polluted city in the United States.

---

birds. It's okay to draw those section lines as long as they show the birds where the boundaries are."

There are Alaskans, of course, who think differently. One poll, for example, revealed that 61 percent of the people questioned supported a "wilderness concept." Says gold-miner John Fullerton, "I don't think preservation of some lands would be so bad, but I hesitate to say anything. I'm always looking over my shoulder to see who is coming into the room." His comment underlined a remark Udall once made—"You're not part of Anchorage society if you support a preservationist bill."

That society is led, as well as recorded, by the *Anchorage Times*, the most widely read paper in the state. The *Times* is flamboyantly antipreservationist, and its editorial philosophy frequently slips off the opinion pages and into the headlines, a habit that may at least partially explain why many Alaskans are so misinformed about last year's legislation. John Seiberling, for example, describes a press conference arranged for him when he went to Anchorage to conduct hearings last year. The *Anchorage Times* reporter wasn't there, but afterward, he approached Seiberling, apologized for being late, and proceeded to ask the congressman if it were true that he wasn't interested in the opinion of Alaskans. Seiberling says he answered, "If all we were doing was taking a poll of Americans, 400,000 Alaskans wouldn't count for much next to the population of the rest of the nation. But it's obvious that we're interested in Alaskans by the very fact that I'm here in Anchorage to conduct hearings." The next day the *Times* headline read: *400,000 Alaskans Don't Count.*

If one wonders how Alaskans could be influenced by such distortions of fact, it is all the more puzzling to discover that the truth about the biggest development project yet to hit the state—the construction of the Alaskan pipeline—has been all but forgotten. That story may hold the key to the issues surrounding the great Alaskan lands lockup.

On September 10, 1969, Alaska opened bidding to North Slope oil land; by the end of the day the state had taken in nearly $1 billion in cash. Construction of a pipeline started a few years later. Personal income in Alaska rose quickly by 20 percent; unemployment went down by 3 percent. The field is capable of **producing some 10,000 barrels of oil a day, compared to the average 11 barrels pumped by a well in the lower 48, and the oil is now gushing to West Coast buyers. It would appear that everyone has what he wanted.**

But what happened to the state in the years of pipeline construction? In 1974, the year that pipeline work began—three years before any oil was piped—construction workers were responsible for 177 spills. Creeks were filled with mudslides. In one "incident," on a day when government environmental supervisors were off duty, pipeline workers rechanneled 2,300 feet of the Dietrich River to make room for a road. When the federal overseers returned, they were shocked to find a river that suddenly had an "appalling resemblance" to a ditch. "The new channel," their report read, "is straight and fishless; destruction is total and permanent." One supervisor added, "These guys are in a hurry. They have a lot more money than they do time."

INDUSTRY, HOWEVER, claims that it spent most of that money—millions of dollars—protecting, not destroying, the Alaskan environment. But no sum they could spend could change the pipeline's effects on the Alaskan people.

Shortly after construction was begun, 16,000 workers descended on a state that at the time was prepared to support only its 200,000 residents. Alaska was hit by the worst inflation in the nation. Auto theft, larceny, juvenile arrests, and prostitution soared. In Fairbanks, which served as headquarters for pipeline employees, 8,000 more vehicles were registered in 1974 than the year before; and concurrently, inhabitants' blood levels of toxic exhaust substances rose to nearly twice the amount the federal government says is safe. Today, ice fog—the frozen version of smog—is getting dangerously severe as pollution intensifies. Fairbanks, which now produces 10 times more pollution per capita than Los Angeles, has gained the singular distinction of being the most polluted city in the nation. All to exploit an oilfield that will be dry in 25 years.

The experience is a sobering one; and it is difficult to understand why so many Alaskans have already forgotten it. "Every Alaskan should be taken on a tour of Appalachia," says John Seiberling. "It still stands as the great symbol for what happens when an industry comes into an area, uses it, abuses it, then leaves it. Appalachia is the symbol of poverty. We don't want to repeat that error in Alaska."

Some Alaskans have accused preservationist congressmen of trying to pay for past environmental sins with Alaskan penance. It may not be a bad idea. "Suppose that a century ago," says Udall, "Abe Lincoln sent you West, that he said, 'Go, bring me 100 million acres to preserve.' What would you have picked? Jackson Hole? The Grand Tetons? All of Arizona? Before they burned the land, before they chopped the timber? What would you pick if you could turn the clock back, see the tall grasses blowing on the prairies in Kansas; see the Rockies looming; see the land the way God made it? If we save parts of Alaska, people can have that experience."

As Udall's vision and the pipeline debacle suggest, there are deeper questions at the heart of the Alaskan problem than how much land to develop and how much to preserve. First, what is progress? If it is a studied march toward a mechanized, profitable, but undesirable and uninhabitable world, some of us may wish to fall out of the parade. And even more important, to whom does Alaska belong? Is it the property of the people who live there? Is it the property of industries that pay taxes on the resources they withdraw? Is it the property of the state, of the nation? Or is it a property that belongs to the past and should be willed to the future? Perhaps the *Anchorage Times* headline wasn't all wrong. Perhaps 400,000 Alaskans don't count—not any more than the rest of us, not any more than the generations who will follow us. ◉

★★

48

Roe et al. **v.** *Wade, District Attorney of Dallas County*   410 U.S. 113 (1973)

Jane Roe, then pregnant and single, challenged the constitutionality of the Texas criminal abortion law that would have prevented her from receiving an abortion for any reason other than to save her life. The Supreme Court struck a compromise in its decision and agreed with both Ms. Roe and the state. To do this, the judges divided the pregnancy into three stages, suggesting that in the first trimester a decision as to whether to abort or not should rest with the woman and her physician. The Court ruled that during the second trimester the state might regulate abortion procedures to assure maternal health. In the final trimester of pregnancy, the state could regulate or even prevent abortion from occurring.

Justice Rehnquist in his dissent thought such a division of the pregnancy smacked of judicial legislation and that it prevented the Court from carrying out its designed function: to search for the intent of the drafters of the Fourteenth Amendment. Is pregnancy legally divisible? What interests might such a division of pregnancy serve?

In deciding Roe *v.* Wade, *several of the justices, including Justice Blackmun who delivered the majority opinion, tried to weigh and balance the interests involved. For Blackmun the important interests were the right to privacy and the state's interest in the potentiality of life. What interests did Justice White weigh in his dissent? From White's choices of the values to balance, can you anticipate his conclusion? Can the Court reasonably weigh values in any meaningful way? Is this a superior way to decide a case than to look for the intent of the Founders?*

★ ★ ★

Roe et al. v. Wade, District Attorney of Dallas County

410 U.S. 113 (1973)

Mr. Justice **Blackmun** delivered the opinion of the Court.

We forthwith acknowledge our awareness of the sensitive and emotional nature of the abortion controversy, of the vigorous opposing views, even among physicians, and of the deep and seemingly absolute convictions that the subject inspires. One's philosophy, one's experiences, one's exposure to the raw edges of human existence, one's religious training, one's attitudes toward life and family and their values, and the moral standards one establishes and seeks to observe, are all likely to influence and to color one's thinking and conclusions about abortion.

In addition, population growth, pollution, poverty, and racial overtones tend to complicate and not to simplify the problem.

Our task, of course, is to resolve the issue by constitutional measurement, free of emotion and of predilection. We seek earnestly to do this, and, because we do, we have inquired into, and in this opinion place some emphasis upon, medical and medical-legal history and what that history reveals about man's attitudes toward the abortion procedure over the centuries. . . .

But when, as here, pregnancy is a significant fact in the litigation, the normal 266-day human gestation period is so short that the pregnancy will come to term before the usual appellate process is complete. If that termination makes a case moot, pregnancy litigation seldom will survive much beyond the trial stage, and appellate review will be effectively denied. Our law should not be that rigid. Pregnancy often comes more than once to the same woman, and in the general population, if man is to survive, it will always be with us. Pregnancy provides a classic justification for a conclusion of nonmootness.

. . . [W]e feel it desirable briefly to survey, in several aspects, the history of abortion, for such insight as that history may afford us, and then to examine the state purposes and interests behind the criminal abortion laws.

It perhaps is not generally appreciated that the restrictive criminal abortion laws in effect in a majority of States today are of relatively recent vintage. Those laws, generally proscribing abortion or its attempt at any time during pregnancy except when necessary to preserve the pregnant woman's life, are not of ancient or even of common-law origin. Instead, they derive from statutory changes effected, for the most part, in the latter half of the 19th century. . . .

In this country, the law in effect in all but a few States until mid-19th century was the pre-existing English common law. Connecticut, the first State to enact abortion legislation, adopted in 1821 that part of Lord Ellenborough's Act that related to a woman "quick with child." The death penalty was not imposed. Abortion before quickening was made a crime in that State only in 1860. . . .

Gradually in the middle and late 19th century the quickening distinction disappeared from the statutory law of most States and the degree of the offense and the penalties were increased. By the end of the 1950's, a large majority of the jurisdictions banned abortion, however and whenever performed, unless done to save or preserve the life of the mother. The exceptions, Alabama and the District of Columbia, permitted abortion to preserve the mother's health. . . .

It is thus apparent that at common law, at the time of the adoption of our Constitution, and throughout the major portion of the 19th century, abortion was viewed with less disfavor than under most American statutes currently in effect. . . .

Three reasons have been advanced to explain historically the enactment of criminal abortion laws in the 19th century and to justify their continued existence.

It has been argued occasionally that these laws were the product of a Victorian social concern to discourage illicit sexual conduct. . . .

A second reason is concerned with abortion as a medical procedure. When most criminal abortion laws were first enacted, the procedure was a hazardous one for the woman. . . . Thus, it has been argued that a State's real concern in enacting a criminal abortion law was to protect the pregnant woman, that is, to restrain her from submitting to a procedure that placed her life in serious jeopardy. . . .

The third reason is the State's interest—some phrase it in terms of duty—in protecting prenatal life. Some of the argument for this justification rests on the theory that a new human life is present from the moment of conception. The State's interest and general obligation to protect life then extends, it is argued, to prenatal life. Only when the life of the pregnant mother herself is at stake, balanced against the life she carries within her, should the interest of the embryo or fetus not prevail. . . .

The Constitution does not explicitly mention any right of privacy. In a line of decisions, however, . . . the Court has recognized that a right of personal privacy, or a guarantee of certain areas or zones of privacy, does exist under the Constitution. . . .

This right of privacy, whether it be founded in the Fourteenth Amendment's concept of personal liberty and restrictions upon state action, as we feel it is, or, as the District Court determined, in the Ninth Amendment's reservation of rights to the people, is broad enough to encompass a woman's decision whether or not to terminate her pregnancy. . . . Maternity, or additional offspring, may force upon the woman a distressful life and future. Psychological harm may be imminent. Mental and physical health may be taxed by child care. There is also the distress, for all concerned, associated with the unwanted child, and there is the problem of bringing a child into a family already unable, psychologically and otherwise, to care for it. In other cases, as in this one, the additional difficulties and continuing stigma of unwed motherhood may be involved. All these are factors the woman and her responsible physician necessarily will consider in consultation.

. . . As noted above, a State may properly assert important interests in safeguarding health, in maintaining medical standards, and in protecting potential life. At some point in pregnancy, these respective interests become sufficiently compelling to sustain regulation of the factors that govern the abortion decision. The privacy right involved, therefore, cannot be said to be absolute. . . .

We, therefore, conclude that the right of personal privacy includes the abortion decision, but that this right is not unqualified and must be considered against important state interests in regulation. . . .

The Constitution does not define "person" in so many words. Section 1 of the Fourteenth Amendment contains three references to "person." The first, in defining "citizens," speaks of "persons born or naturalized in the United States." The word also appears both in the Due Process Clause and in the Equal Protection Clause. . . . But in nearly all these instances, the use of the word is such that it has application only postnatally. None indicates, with any assurance, that it has any possible prenatal application.

All this, together with our observation, **supra**, that throughout the major portion of the 19th century prevailing legal abortion practices were far freer than they are today, persuades us that the word "person," as used in the Fourteenth Amendment, does not include the unborn. . . .

Texas urges that, apart from the Fourteenth Amendment, life begins at conception and is present throughout pregnancy, and that, therefore, the State has a compelling interest in protecting that life from and after conception. We need not resolve the difficult question of when life begins. When those trained in the respective disciplines of medicine, philosophy, and theology are unable to arrive at any consensus, the judiciary, at this point in the development of man's knowledge, is not in a position to speculate as to the answer.

It should be sufficient to note briefly the wide divergency of thinking on this most sensitive and difficult question. There has always been strong support for the view that life does not begin until live birth. . . . Physicians and their scientific colleagues have regarded that event [quickening] with less interest and have tended to focus either upon conception, upon live birth, or upon the interim point at which the fetus becomes "viable," that is, potentially able to live outside the mother's womb, albeit with artificial aid. Viability is usually placed at about seven months (28 weeks) but may occur earlier, even at 24 weeks. . . .

In areas other than criminal abortion, the law has been reluctant to endorse any theory that life, as we recognize it, begins before live birth or to accord legal rights to the unborn except in narrowly defined situations and except when the rights are contingent upon live birth. . . . In short, the unborn have never been recognized in the law as persons in the whole sense.

. . . It follows that, from and after this point, a State may regulate the abortion procedure to the extent that the regulation reasonably relates to the preservation and protection of maternal health. . . .

With respect to the State's important and legitimate interest in potential life, the "compelling" point is at viability. This is so because the fetus then presumably has the capability of meaningful life outside the mother's womb. . . .

To summarize and to repeat: . . .

(a) For the state prior to approximately the end of the first trimester, the abortion decision and its effectuation must be left to the medical judgment of the pregnant woman's attending physician.

(b) For the stage subsequent to approximately the end of the first trimester, the State, in promoting its interest in the health of the mother, may, if it chooses, regulate the abortion procedure in ways that are reasonably related to maternal health.

(c) For the stage subsequent to viability, the State in promoting its interest in the potentiality of human life may, if it chooses, regulate, and even proscribe, abortion except where it is necessary, in appropriate medical judgment, for the preservation of the life or health of the mother.

. . . The decision leaves the State free to place increasing restrictions on abortion as the period of pregnancy lengthens, so long as those restrictions are tailored to the recognized state interest.

Mr. Justice **Rehnquist,** dissenting.

The Court's opinion decides that a State may impose virtually no restriction on the performance of abortions during the first trimester of pregnancy.

. . . I have difficulty in concluding, as the Court does, that the right of "privacy" is involved in this case. Texas, by the statute here challenged, bars the performance of a medical abortion by a licensed physician on a plaintiff such as Roe. A transaction resulting in an operation such as this is not "private" in the ordinary usage of the word. Nor is the "privacy" that the Court finds here even a distant relative of the freedom from searches and seizures protected by the Fourth Amendment to the Constitution, which the Court has referred to as embodying a right to privacy. . . .

If the Court means by the term "privacy" no more than that the claim of a person to be free from unwanted state regulation of consensual transactions may be a form of "liberty" protected by the Fourteenth Amendment, there is no doubt that similar claims have been upheld in our earlier decisions on the basis of that liberty.

. . . The decision here to break pregnancy into three distinct terms and to outline the permissible restrictions the State may impose in each one, for example, partakes more of judicial legislation than it does of a determination of the intent of the drafters of the Fourteenth Amendment.

The fact that a majority of the States reflecting, after all, the majority sentiment in those States, have had restrictions on abortions for at least a century is a strong indication, it seems to me, that the asserted right to an abortion is not "so rooted in the traditions and conscience of our people as to be ranked as fundamental."

Mr. Justice **Douglas** concurring.

The Ninth Amendment obviously does not create federally enforceable rights. It merely says, "The enumeration in the Constitution, of certain rights, shall not be construed to deny or disparage others retained by the people." But a catalogue of these rights includes customary, traditional, and time-honored rights, amenities, privileges, and immunities that come within the sweep of "the Blessings of Liberty" mentioned in the preamble to the Constitution. Many of them, in my view, come within the meaning of the term "liberty" as used in the Fourteenth Amendment.

First is the autonomous control over the development and expression of one's intellect, interests, tastes, and personality.

These are rights protected by the First Amendment and, in my view, they are absolute, permitting of no exceptions. . . .

Second is freedom of choice in the basic decisions of one's life respecting marriage, divorce, procreation, contraception, and the education and upbringing of children.

These rights, unlike those protected by the First Amendment are subject to some control by the police power. . . .

Third is the freedom to care for one's health and person, freedom from bodily restraint or compulsion, freedom to walk, stroll, or loaf.

These rights, though fundamental, are likewise subject to regulation on a showing of "compelling state interest." . . .

The Georgia statute is at war with the clear message of these cases—that a woman is free to make the basic decision whether to bear an unwanted child. Elaborate argument is hardly necessary to demonstrate that childbirth may deprive a woman of her preferred lifestyle and force upon her a radically different and undesired future.

. . . [I]t is difficult to perceive any overriding public necessity which might attach precisely at the moment of conception. As Mr. Justice Clark has said:

> To say that life is present at conception is to give recognition to the potential, rather than the actual. The unfertilized egg has life, and if fertilized, it takes on human proportions. But the law deals in reality, not obscurity—the known rather than the unknown. When sperm meets egg life may eventually form, but quite often it does not. The law does not deal in speculation. The phenomenon of life takes time to develop, and until it is actually present, it cannot be destroyed. Its interruption prior to formation would hardly be homicide, and as we have seen, society does not regard it as such. The rites of Baptism are not performed and death certificates are not required when a miscarriage occurs. No prosecutor has ever returned a murder indictment charging the taking of the life of a fetus. This would not be the case if the fetus constituted human life.

Mr. Justice **White,** with whom Mr. Justice **Rehnquist** joins, dissenting.

I find nothing in the language or history of the Constitution to support the Court's judgment. The Court simply fashions and announces a new constitutional right for pregnant mothers and, with scarcely any reason or authority for its action, invests that right with sufficient substance to override most existing state abortion statutes. The upshot is that the people and the legislatures of the 50 States are constitutionally disentitled to weigh the relative importance of the continued existence and development of the fetus, on the other hand, against a spectrum of possible impacts on the mother, on the other hand. As an exercise of raw judicial power, the Court perhaps has authority to do what it does today; but in my view its judgment is an improvident and extravagant exercise of the power of judicial review that the Constitution extends to this Court.

The Court apparently values the convenience of the pregnant mother more than the continued existence and development of the life or potential life that she carries. Whether or not I might agree with that marshaling of values, I can in no event join the Court's judgment because I find no constitutional warrant for imposing such an order of priorities on the people and legislatures of the States. In a sensitive area such as this, involving as it does issues over which reasonable men may easily and heatedly differ, I cannot accept the Court's exercise of its clear power of choice by interposing a constitutional barrier to state efforts to protect human life and by investing mothers and doctors with the constitutionally protected right to exterminate it. This issue, for the most part, should be left with the people and to the political processes the people have devised to govern their affairs.

CHAPTER ELEVEN

* * *

Public Policy: Foreign

A nation's foreign policy states the terms of its relationship to other countries in the world. As such, it is partly a response to the actions of other nations. But it is also affected by the domestic society—its political, economic, and cultural influences. No public policy can remain static in the face of changing societal conditions, but many observers see an "elitist" bias in the process of making our foreign policy. That is, the people do not typically have great impact but rather much discretion is permitted the president, his advisers, and experts within government. In addition to the elitist nature of diplomacy, a degree of stability affects foreign policy because the parameters of action are somewhat limited by the "national interest." It is said, minimally, that every country wants to survive, and preferably as an independent nation. Beyond that aspect of the national interest, a country may want to extend its sphere of influence in order to prosper and develop, or simply to dominate other nations. We can easily perceive "imperialistic" gestures when a nation uses military force against other nations, but there are other forms of penetration that are more subtle. Dominating other countries by economic means is one such example.

Americans do not generally perceive our foreign policy as being imperialistic, though some people will admit that President Theodore Roosevelt's attitudes toward Latin America were a bit heavy handed. On the whole, we prefer to see American foreign policy motivated by honorable, just goals. In his essay "Empire Begins at Home," Walter LaFeber uses the term "interventionist" to characterize our foreign policy over two centuries. We intervened in the affairs of other nations, he says, because American leaders believed the national interest required such action. Though some scholars feel that the United States developed during the nineteenth century in an era of relative peace and security, LaFeber argues that a number of threats to our security were countered by our leadership. From this perspective certainly, it seems that "realism"—not idealism—dominated American foreign policy early in our history. So-called realists in foreign affairs see power as the basis of international relations; the objective is to stabilize power relations among nations. They would argue that moral considerations should not be permitted to undermine vital national interests. By implication, moreover, this essay shows that American interventionism is bipartisan in origin. Presidents of both political parties, whether Polk, or McKinley, intervened in the affairs of other nations to assure our security. LaFeber identifies four eras in the twentieth century when the tactics of interventionism changed, though typically we used military or economic sanctions. This essay highlights the perception that diplomacy, and its objectives, are long term in nature, and not subject to great policy variations in the short run. In this light, it is not strange to find that LaFeber sees Presidents Ford and Carter in the same diplomatic tradition.

If LaFeber's argument is correct, it would seem that the experience of Vietnam did not affect our diplomatic posture very much. However, it may not be coincidental that "economic" rather than military intervention by the United States came in the post-Vietnam era. Nonetheless, our experience in Vietnam deeply affected many people, including members of academia, and these critics feel that American foreign policy must be reevaluated fundamentally. They sense that the United States can no longer be the world's policeman, a theme expressed by T. D. Allman in "America's Innocence Abroad" and by Lewis H. Lapham in "America's Foreign Policy: A Rake's Progress."

Allman's viewpoint may be difficult for some Americans to accept. He doubts that we can fundamentally change events in the world in line with our expectations. He feels that there are limits to our influence. He suggests that very often international problems resolve themselves without our involvement. Not only may this position be contrary to that of some citizens, but it is also not the view of Henry Kissinger, the subject of Allman's analysis. He suggests that Kissinger, in the face of diplomatic problems, had the urge to act, to bring order to the world. This propensity to act is related, says Allman, to our perception that events are "caused" rather than that they simply occur. If they are caused, we feel we can alter their outcomes if only the proper application of American influence is used. But Allman doubts our capability. Recent Presidents—Johnson, Nixon, Carter— were all afflicted with the desire to act, so obviously they would not agree with Allman's assessment. But Allman's view reinforces the argument made by LaFeber; both see action and intervention as keystones to American foreign policy.

Lapham writes an essay critical of American diplomacy, but from a different perspective. He uses the parody of a "rich man" to describe our foreign policy. Clearly, a paramount fact about America is our economic wealth and military power. As Lapham indicates, however, the world of 1945 is no longer. But though the world order is changing, our attitudes toward diplomacy still reflect the biases and values of a "rich man." Thus he is analyzing what seems to be a blind spot in our ability to comprehend the world and affects our ability to act with a sense of proportion. His analogy is effective, for he raises questions that demand serious inquiry. Do we overestimate our importance as an actor in international relations? Are we really ignorant about other countries and international events? Do we squander our resources? Are we excessive in our drive toward national security? Lapham does not relate our foreign policy failures to any president or to any political party. It is our condition of wealth that gives rise to mistaken perceptions of the world and to diplomatic blunders.

The final essay in this chapter departs from the themes of the three preceding articles. This essay, "Cyrus Vance Plays It Cool," by Bernard Gwertzman focuses on the background, style, and objectives of a key foreign policy decision-maker, the secretary of state. It is a character portrait, and through it we gain insight into the subtle influences that underlie the effectiveness of top policy-makers. The preceding articles viewed diplomacy from broad conceptual and historical perspectives. This analysis looks at one participant in the policy-making process. Gwertzman suggests that subtle diplomatic maneuvers can shape the eventual outcome of foreign policy initiatives, for instance the SALT agreement with the Soviet Union and the Israeli-Egyptian peace treaty. The picture that emerges is one of an effective, confident secretary of state, who has impact on the nation's conduct of diplomacy.

These articles were chosen because they address foreign policy from both historical and contemporary perspectives. They indicate the concern of some persons today that the United States is ineffective in diplomacy. One article certainly suggests that we can have impact when key decision-makers have a sense of history and purpose. Questions presented in the headnotes will guide your reading of these essays, but you are also encouraged to ponder the serious questions raised by these authors. In a world where nations are becoming more and more interdependent, foreign policy looms more important as a factor that can strengthen or undermine a nation's viability, as well as the standard of living of its citizenry.

★★

49

Empire Begins at Home   Walter LaFeber

The theme of this article by Walter LaFeber is that American foreign policy historically has been "interventionist." While the tactics of intervention have varied, making use of military, cultural, and economic means, one objective has remained constant, namely, to ensure our security in the international arena. American intervention into other countries has usually occurred because our policy-makers believed that the "national interest" required such action. Is this sufficient justification for such intervention? LaFeber argues that during the nineteenth century, leaders only intervened out of a concern for the nation's independence and security. What specific "interventionist" acts by our government took place in the nineteenth century? Were they all justified in terms of the national interest? Are there other criteria we should use in assessing the worth of intervention? Can an understanding of the nineteenth-century acts of intervention aid us in interpreting twentieth-century behavior in foreign affairs? How?

LaFeber documents four periods of intervention during the twentieth century. Has the pattern of intervention been different in this century than in the last? What areas of the world have been affected? To what extent have they been affected? What important comparisons does LaFeber make between the 1920s and the 1970s? How valid are his comparisons? He also looks at the period following World War II and compares this to the turn of the century. What common attributes does he see here? LaFeber sees the period we are living through as a "New New Era," one in which President Carter seems to be fashioning foreign policy in the same diplomatic tradition as Nixon and Kissinger. What evidence supports his argument? What effect have President Carter's concerns for human rights had on foreign policy? Are moral concerns such as human rights consistent with a foreign policy protective of our "national interest"?

★ ★ ★

Empire Begins At Home

WALTER LaFEBER

A cult of personality has shaped American historical writing ("if Roosevelt had only lived. . ."), political conversations and best-seller lists. It is well to recall, therefore, that certain major forces have been common in the American experience regardless of who held power, and that structure has determined foreign policy choices. Since its birth, for example, the United States has been an interventionist power. At the same moment in 1775 that the Founding Fathers edged toward the treasonous discussions about independence, they ordered a ragtag army to march north and conquer Canada.

Intervention may be defined as the interference of one state in another state's affairs for the purpose of forcing the latter to act according to certain wishes of the former. Using that perspective, American history can be viewed not only through the prisms of the vanishing frontier, evolving democracy and immense resources that created "a people of plenty" but through a persistent policy of interference that has shaped the lives of other peoples. From their beginnings, Americans sought both independence and a security that could be gained only through acquiring what the Founders called "empire." That process has employed various means, but it has been unrelenting as the United States intervened in a continental, then global, arena.

Recent interventionist policies, particularly those developed since the early 1970s, are new in degree but not in kind. They utilize military, cultural and especially economic, powers that have deep historical roots. The most striking insight into the present is provided by American diplomacy in the 1920s, but the roots go deeper.

Walter LaFeber, Noll Professor of history at Cornell University, is the author of The New Empire *(Cornell University Press) and* America, Russia and the Cold War *(John Wiley).*

In the eighteenth and nineteenth centuries, U.S. diplomacy rested on the premise that the nation's future security depended on limiting the security of others. Between 1803 and the Civil War, the United States used various tactics to acquire its continental territory. It supplied an anti-French revolution in Santo Domingo, whose success compelled Napoleon to sell Louisiana; fomented in Spanish East Florida a revolution whose smooth operation would have made the C.I.A. envious and which led to American annexation of the territory; invaded militarily the remainder of Spanish Florida, then used the invasion as leverage to force Spain to sell the rest of its continental claims to the United States, and declared war against Mexico in 1846 in order to seize one-third of that nation for the use of American merchants and farmers.

Across the Pacific, meanwhile, U.S. officials, missionaries and businessmen cooperated with the British and French empires in opening China to Western prayers and products. Historians have generously labeled Washington's approach as "jackal diplomacy," but the victim was not dead and this jackal often attacked before the larger animals arrived. The Chinese, at least, made no distinction among the predators. Anti-foreign rebellions targeted Americans as well as Europeans. After President William McKinley landed troops in Peking to protect Americans—and also preserve their Chinese markets against Russian and German threats—China declared war against the United States. Back home, troops completed a 300-year effort to contain and/or eradicate the Native American population. The justifications—that is, the white desire for resources and a racism encapsulated in Theodore Roosevelt's remark that Indians were only "a few degrees less meaningless, squalid, and ferocious than . . . wild beasts"—were then applied between 1893 and 1903 to Hawaiians, Spaniards and Filipinos who tried to stop the United States from seizing hegemony in the Caribbean and naval bases in the Pacific.

This record is outlined not to demonstrate that American interventionism has been any more bloody or morally reprehensible than the acts of other imperial powers. It does demonstrate that twentieth-century United States power emerged out of 300 years of constant intervention in the affairs of other peoples; that the interventionism occurred on a number of levels—covert, military, missionary and economic, and that when either Woodrow Wilson or Jimmy Carter declared war against sin, their own nation's historical record indicated that the war would be an uphill fight.

In the National Interest

Most important, Americans intervened because they believed their national interest, at times their existence, was at stake. John Kennedy once remarked that since American development before 1900 was easy and relatively painless, we should be tolerant of newly emerging nations who fight for survival in a more difficult world. His advice was good, but his history questionable, notwithstanding that Kennedy followed research findings of distinguished historians who have argued that the United States indeed reached maturity rather easily through an era of "free security." When, however, Presidents moved forces into Louisiana, Florida, Texas or northern Mexico, they did so partly from fears of foreign invasion into the United States or the establishment of a great power such as England on another American boundary. Throughout the late eighteenth and nineteenth centuries, officials, merchants and farmers constantly argued that unless they found new lands and resources, the political system would collapse. Southerners believed that to such an extent that they tried to form their own expanding empire in 1861 after the Republicans threatened to contain them (and prevent pro-slavery intervention in the Caribbean and Central America).

Throughout their history, Americans have intervened not simply out of perverseness, misperception, misplaced values or the false belief—whose falsity does not make it less beloved by experts on international affairs—that "political vacuums" always entice "great powers." (Even as a minor power the United States intervened in areas, such as Canada and the Caribbean, that were not political vacuums.) Americans interfered in the affairs of other peoples because they saw their national (and individual) interests in jeopardy. The era between 1750 and 1900 saw little free security, but a great deal of intervention to seize resources and territory in the hope that some security could be found. That hope has persistently diminished. In 1760 Benjamin Franklin argued that England's intervention in Canada would assure colonial allegiance and security; in 1846 President James Polk argued that intervening in Mexico would assure the security of Americans in all sections of the country; in 1898 the McKinley Administration argued that intervening in the Philippine revolution would help secure U.S. interests in Asia, and since 1945 many have argued that creating a strike force that could effectively intervene anywhere—including Southeast Asia and the Middle East—is necessary for American security. But as Reinhold Niebuhr observed nearly thirty years ago, the irony of American history is that as our power has grown to a degree infinitely greater than it was in the time of Franklin or McKinley, our security is infinitely less.

The motivations for, and the instruments of, American intervention during the twentieth century, therefore, are present throughout much of our history. The degree of the power and the areas in which it has been employed since 1900, however, are new. That twentieth-century history can be surveyed by dividing it into four eras.

The Four Eras

The first, lasting through World War I, was marked by military intervention in the surrounding neighborhood. Justified by Theodore Roosevelt's "corollary" to the Monroe Doctrine that the United States could act as a policeman who insured peace and the containment of revolution in much of Latin America, American troops marched into Cuba, Panama, Santo Domingo, Nicaragua, Haiti and Mexico. In one sense, the use of soldiers in Europe during 1917-18 was an aberration, given traditional American military abstention from the Continent. In another respect, however, Wilson's deployment of force in France —and especially in Russia when he tried simultaneously to reopen the Eastern Front and undermine the Soviet regime—developed naturally out of the experience in Latin America. (Latin America has often been used as the laboratory in which U.S. policies have been tested and developed before they have been applied globally.) According to such early "realists" as Roosevelt,

Capt. Alfred Thayer Mahan and Lewis Einstein, wisely used military force made the wheels of evolution and Western civilization go 'round. Wilson extended that belief to conclude that U.S. intervention in 1917 would also propel him into the peace discussions that would reconstruct a shattered Europe. At Versailles, however, Wilson learned the limits of American influence. The Senate rejected his compromises, and the more perceptive officials searched for better methods of exerting United States power.

The second period—1920 until the outbreak of World War II—became known for a time as the New Era. It was new not because the United States quit using force in Latin America but because of the paramount economic power the nation built through loans and trade arrangements with the declining European powers. Washington officials used this weapon to preserve business opportunities throughout the world, including the revolutionary areas of Russia, Mexico and China. As *The Atlantic Monthly* preached in 1928, "The work that religion, government, and war have failed in must be done by business." American self-interest was again the motivation: "The prosperity of the United States largely depends upon the economic settlements which may be made in Europe," Secretary of State Charles Evans Hughes declared in 1921. With that insight, Hughes and other officials used American economic dominance to force England to the gold standard, pressure France to accept German reconstruction, seduce the Russians back to an acceptance of capitalistic investments and maneuver the Japanese and Western Europeans into accepting naval disarmament plans.

By 1929, Republicans congratulated themselves for building with economic intervention what Wilson and the Europeans had almost destroyed with force. They also applauded themselves for another reason: reconstruction had been accomplished through the private banking sector, and particularly the great central banks, which did not have to be overly sensitive to the vagaries of democratic politics. To rephrase the thought, the bankers worked outside the control of Congress, the American people, and—at critical moments—the Executive itself. This occurred largely by design. The Senate's action in 1919-20, the doubts cast on the usefulness of public

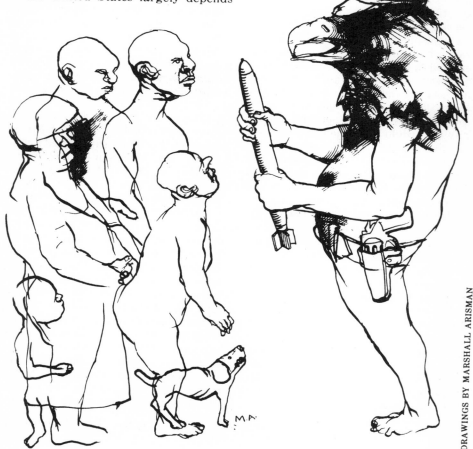

DRAWINGS BY MARSHALL ARISMAN

opinion by Walter Lippmann and others, a new Foreign Service corps that was as ideologically prejudiced as it was elitist, and the just-established Council on Foreign Relations—all combined to assure that the global economic interventionism of the New Era was as insulated as possible from the scrutiny of democratic processes.

This system began to self-destruct in 1929, but by 1939 it re-emerged transformed. Such New Deal measures as the Export-Import Bank, the Reciprocal Trade Agreements Program and direct deals between the Administration and a besieged China brought the Government in line with the New Era's system without changing either the motives or objectives of that system. Resembling officials of the 1920s, leading New Dealers believed that economic intervention, not military, could save the situation. That situation, however, was already critically ill because of such economic intervention. The Soviet Union, then Japan, then Germany declared themselves independent of the dollar. With more subtlety, England and France also declared their independence. The New Era-New Deal interventionism finally failed because American officials and businessmen alike confused the supposed values of an international marketplace with international stability. As a result, the Congress that had been bypassed (sometimes willingly) by bankers and bureaucrats found itself voting for war measures in 1938-39.

World War II to Vietnam

During the third period, lasting roughly from 1939 until the early 1970s, American leaders reacted to the supposed historical lessons of the New Era by stressing that superior armed force had to be combined with the nation's incomparable economic power to create postwar order and contain Soviet expansion. Harry Truman observed that the military commitment of the Truman Doctrine and the Marshall Plan's economic commitment were "two halves of the same walnut."

The military soon became much the greater half of American foreign policy. Between 1945 and the 1970s, the United States carried out an average of one major military intervention each eighteen months. By another count, it used armed force or the threat of it 215 times between 1945 and 1975. American officials justified this in the name of a "realism" that was based historically on the experience of a European balance of power that had seldom worked,

and that assumed the possibility of managing armed force in a rational, limited fashion. Realist interventionism included the use of covert activities (as in Iran and Guatemala), and economic influence (as in multinational lending agencies) that Theodore Roosevelt's generation had not been able to employ on such a scale. But in important respects, post-1945 interventions were only T.R.'s and Wilson's interventionism extended globally. Both justified using force in the name of a higher, Western morality that became not a restraint but a rationalization for moving as far as your power allowed (for example, Roosevelt and Mahan earlier and John Foster Dulles later). Both used similar devices to blunt controls on their acts by Congress and democratic procedures (T.R.'s executive agreements earlier, the imperial Presidency later). Both argued that the interventionism was defensive and not offensive (Roosevelt's and Wilson's "policeman" earlier, "containment" later). And both generations believed that through pragmatism and elite leadership they could fine-tune and closely control power. Interventionism, however, developed its own momentum. As a Defense Department official warned during an early debate over whether United States intervention in Vietnam could be limited, "One cannot go over Niagara Falls in a barrel only slightly."

The failures of Vietnam policy, a declining dollar and the criminal acts of an imperial Presidency brought the third period to an end in the early 1970s. The importance of this era is not that it ended in tragedy but that it is an aberration in American history. While sharing common traits with the 1900-to-1920 years, the post-1945 era was also marked by the American attempt to use military power to reshape global affairs, not merely those in the Caribbean and Western Europe. By the mid-1950s a resurgent Europe and Third World were already fighting that attempt, and by the mid-1970s, Americans encountered a new cold war—one in which they could no longer control the decentralizing forces that had first appeared two decades earlier.

The danger is that whether they are debating alternatives for their military budgets, SALT II, or energy sources, Americans who matured between 1945 and 1970 will assume the era was a norm rather than an aberration. The danger is less one of a Munich syndrome or, for younger generations, a Vietnam syndrome, than that an American-Century syndrome which devel-

oped after World War II will shape future policy debates.

A New New Era

The United States entered a fourth period in the 1970s that is resembling the New Era of the 1920s rather than the earlier and later years of military realism. Richard Nixon and Henry Kissinger tried to adjust to the realities by transforming the instruments of intervention from overt military weapons to the weapons of massive arms sales, C.I.A. activities, and trade. The Carter Administration has preserved these tools and has added human rights. The question about such a use of human rights is not whether individual rights should be preserved but whether they are best preserved through public crusades, and whether such crusades are only a more acceptable form of intervention. As a State Department official recently testified, the United States has opposed forty-eight loans from international financial bodies to fifteen countries that violate human rights, and has told other nations that if they brought up loan projects we would oppose them. Given American power in these agencies, such a position usually dooms the projects.

Some Americans continue to use the rhetoric of 1945 to 1970, especially as Presidential primaries approach. George Bush, who advertises himself as a Republican moderate, has said that Carter should have intervened to save the Shah Mohammed Riza Pahlevi: "It is not intervention in another country's affairs for the United States to support friendly governments facing revolution. That's not meddling, that's supporting." Bush's approach, however, is less characteristic of American policy in the post-1973 years than Kissinger and Carter's quieter use of dollars, American markets, arms aid and U.S. technology to maintain some control over both Allies and the détente process with Russia and China. The means are changing but the objectives remain the same. Those objectives are reminiscent of Charlie Chaplin's advice when a fellow actor asked him how to play the next scene: "Behind me and a little to the right."

The Kissinger-Carter approach attempts to retool the diplomacy of the 1920s. The analogy is especially striking since the 1970s, resembling the 1920-29 era all too closely, has also witnessed the development of private banking power to a point where it may be beyond the control of the major capitalist governments. Since 1973, these banks have handled the recycling of OPEC balances, and in the process—in the words of a recent Organization for Economic Cooperation and Development report—"effectively make the crucial decisions regarding access to liquidity and the financing of payments imbalances" for a host of less-developed nations. And again as in the 1920s, these decisions are made outside the public's view. As Robert Keohane remarked, "the unstated premise" in this new economic policy is "that democratic politics must adjust to capitalist economics, rather than vice versa."

Such readjustment could continue even after defaults by a number of countries create a banking crisis that once again requires massive governmental intervention to preserve the order needed by a modified state capitalism. The question will not be whether the state should intervene at home and overseas—the New Deal settled that on both counts. Nor will it be whether the state should intervene at all; nothing in their past, or in a future that holds shortages of raw materials and energy, indicates that Americans will be reluctant to intervene forcefully in other nations' affairs.

The most interesting question is by which process will such interventions be determined. Who will decide the tactical issues and who, if anyone, will be able to hold the decision makers responsible? For although the first three eras of twentieth-century interventionism differed in some respects, they shared three common characteristics: the interventions were undertaken on the assumptions that they were required by tangible American interests and could be controlled; they ultimately got out of control and created crises both at home and abroad, and a struggle then ensued to make future interventions more politically responsible and accountable. Those struggles, from the democratic perspective, were never very successful. In preparing for the next one it should be remembered that American intervention abroad has both begun and ended at home. In history as in architecture, after all, structures are studied so persons can change them. □

★★★

50   America's Innocence Abroad   T. D. Allman

Although many feel we possess almost unlimited authority and power in the international arena, there are limits to American power in diplomacy. T. D. Allman argues in this essay that our "innocence" in foreign affairs results from our inability to appreciate these limits. Do Americans have a need to intervene in world affairs to bring order to international relations, as Allman contends? Is the behavior of former Secretary of State Henry Kissinger in his personal diplomacy missions understandable unless one accepts the fact that Americans do indeed have this need?

Allman suggests that very often international events are simply beyond our reach and influence. Moreover, he believes that situations unaffected by American diplomacy ultimately work to our advantage. What evidence does he give for his assertion? He admits that his perception is contrary to America's style of diplomacy, for he argues that "America's relations with the external world have remained ensnared in that misapprehension of causality." Does this explanation make sense in the context of the rest of his argument? Does President Carter's support for human rights fit within our diplomatic tradition? Does Carter believe that international problems can be corrected through proper application of American power? What examples does Allman cite in response to these questions? Allman argues that America is effective in the world community not so much because of what we try to do but because of what we stand for: "American freedom, American influence, and American technology still can enthrall so much of the world." Can it be the case that our life-style and degree of progress affect other nations in ways fundamentally more important than our overt attempts to influence them by power and politics?

★ ★ ★

AMERICA'S INNOCENCE ABROAD

I**T WAS YET** another of those moments when all that seemed to stand between Henry Kissinger and world order was the naive incompetence of his own subordinates. The subject that day was Portugal. It was mid-1974, and surely that subtle aloofness in the receptionist's manner as Stuart N. Scott, American Ambassador to Lisbon, was led into the Secretary of State's office, was an omen.

At first, the Secretary listened impassively as Ambassador Scott propounded his heretical thesis that the Portuguese revolution must be treated as something other than a gratuitous affront to Henry Kissinger's personal need for strategic orderliness. But his patience disintegrated as Ambassador Scott plunged into American foreign-policy apostasy. The only possible way to stop the Communists in Portugal, Scott warned, was for America and its entire diplomatic, military, and intelligence establishment to do absolutely nothing at all.

If the U.S. government kept the CIA on the leash, if it did not dabble in assassination in Lisbon and secession in the Azores, the Ambassador emphasized, then democratic forces would win the first free elections in half a century, and the country would remain a faithful U.S. ally. But to do what America, what Kissinger himself, had done in Chile and Greece and Indochina, Scott warned, would not only drive Portugal out of the NATO alliance, it would create "the greatest self-fulfilling prophecy in history," and turn Portugal into the Cuba of Western Europe overnight.

As the Secretary replied, the venom was diluted with despair at the widening discrepancy between America's decadent softness and the undiminished tumescence of his own genius. Did not the Ambassador understand that the entire southern flank of NATO was crumbling? Could he not grasp that France was a can of worms, Italy a basket case, Archbishop Makarios a Red—that America's only reliable allies were the Greek colonels? The Communists were sure to win the Italian elections. Now the Communists were subverting Portugal too, and all the U.S. Ambassador could propose was that America behave like some pitiful, helpless giant.

A few months later, a similar scene was enacted in the same office. This time the muddlehead called on the carpet was Mario Soares, the socialist leader of Portugal. Like Scott, Soares explained that if America minded its own business, his Socialist party would defeat the Communists. Again the Secretary's bitterness was moderated by contempt. "You will be the Kerensky of Portugal," he announced. It was then that Kissinger made up his mind. Not only must the Portuguese Communists go. Soares must go too. As the first step, that dunderhead U.S. Ambassador must be sent packing as well.

So Ambassador Scott was fired publicly for rank incompetence, and driven from the State Department in disgrace. In early 1975, Kissinger's hand-picked choice as Ambassador, Frank C. Carlucci, arrived in Lisbon. Throughout that city of eighteenth-century buildings and twenty-first-century wall posters, the Communists, with relish, and the Democrats, in dismay, waited for the dirty tricks, for the

A foreign policy of bungling arrogance and misguided altruism

by T. D. Allman

T.D. Allman, a contributing editor of Harper's, *is Director of Urban Research of the Third Century America project at the University of California at Berkeley.*

ultimatums from the U.S. Embassy, for the civil war to begin. Carlucci's instructions were explicit. Do for Portugal what two of Kissinger's favorite Ambassadors, John G. Dean and Henry J. Tasca, had done for Cambodia and Greece. Forget the carrot. Use the stick. Rid the Portuguese of their silly notion that democracy was anything other than a code word for strategic surrender. Get Portugal back on the team.

Yet soon both Kissinger and Alvaro Cunhal, the Portuguese Communist leader, found themselves grievously disappointed by Ambassador Carlucci. Truth to tell, his cables could have been written by Ambassador Scott. Don't do a thing, Carlucci urged Kissinger, just sit tight. Meddle, the new Ambassador added, and NATO soon would have its first Communist member.

Carlucci's job—perhaps Portuguese democracy too—was saved by the Old Boy network. Carlucci had been Donald Rumsfeld's roommate, and Rumsfeld was Jerry Ford's fair-haired boy. Confronted by his own Ambassador's insubordinate refusal to destabilize an allied government, Henry Kissinger averted his eyes from Portugal the way a famous surgeon turns his back on a patient who is about to die.

"When Henry found Jerry wouldn't let him fire Frank," a high official later commented, "he did what he did when Indochina went down the tube. Henry's number-one priority was to preserve his own reputation, to make sure others took the blame."

A renaissance of democracy

I RECENTLY RETURNED to Southern Europe after an absence of two years or more. Back then, in those melodramatic days of shuttle diplomacy and tape erasures, the conventional wisdom had held that Watergate and the Indochina defeat, to say nothing of such acts of Congressional impudence as the scrutiny of the Central Intelligence Agency's budget, were imperiling the future of freedom itself. To practice democracy, so the official argument ran, was to subvert it, by endangering the entire U.S. security system from which our freedoms derived. And when Portuguese, Spaniards, Italians, Greeks, Turks, and even Americans, too, exercised their prerogative not only to criticize Dr. Kissinger, but to remove from power those leaders upon whom he had conferred his confidence, the Secretary had tried to bring the world to its senses by convoking an emotional press conference in Austria.

The years after 1974, however, were not kind to the doctrine of "linkage"—the strategic axiom that any threat to Henry Kissinger's wishes anywhere in the world was a threat to Western civilization. The Portuguese overthrew Caetano, the Greeks brought down Papadopoulos, and Richard Nixon was turned out of the White House. "Peace and prosperity are impossible without a major American role," President Nixon warned only a few years ago. Yet since then America's capacity to play a major role in Southern Europe had eroded to the vanishing point.

I packed my suitcase with trepidation. Surely by now the Kerensky of Portugal would be about to be eaten alive by its Lenin, and with Franco no longer in Spain to defend traditional American values, a dictatorship of the proletariat was inevitable. With the CIA unable to pass black bags stuffed with lire to the Christian Democrats, surely red flags would soon fly over Rome too. In Greece the moans of collectivization would echo off the marble pillars of the Acropolis, and from their bases in Cyprus the Soviets would smile as Turkish commissars tortured liberal democrats.

Instead I found a pattern of peace, a modicum of social progress, a veritable renaissance of democracy—all combined with far less U.S. intervention in its allies' internal affairs than at any time since the beginning of the Cold War. For the first time since the promulgation of the Truman Doctrine, freedom of speech, press, and political association is respected by every U.S. ally in Europe. In spite of the periodic pronouncements in Washington on the dangers of free political choice, more than a dozen national elections have been held in Southern Europe, from Portugal to Turkey, since 1974. Parties committed not just to human rights, but to the U.S. alliance, have won them all.

In Turkey—where Congress was accused of endangering U.S. strategy by suspending military aid—anti-Communist parties have formed the government following two successive national elections. In Greece—where Kissinger believed the colonels were the only alternative to anti-American chaos—supporters of the conservative prime minister, Constantine Caramanlis, won 220 out of 300 seats in free parliamentary elections. In Spain—where King Juan Carlos was so ill-advised as to legalize the Communist party—moderate liberals and socialists have reaped the harvest of democratization.

But it was in Italy where Kissinger's Spenglerian alarums of doom were proved silliest of all, where that most cherished notion of the Kissinger claque in the media, bureaucracy, and think tanks was laid bare in all its fatuous absurdity. Whatever Kissinger's manifold insensitivities elsewhere, his apologists always claimed, his intuitive comprehension of his native continent was a marvel of clairvoyance. In the end, Henry Kissinger revealed that he possessed the same understanding of Italy as he did of Cambodia or Angola.

From 1974 to the summer of 1976, the impending Communist victory in Italy was bandied about as proof of the irresponsibility of the Secretary's critics. Just when what was needed to save Italy was the same kind of hardheaded, open-ended, interagency interventionism that had characterized the American success story in Chile, here were Congress and the press emasculating America's capacity to defend its vital national interests. With the Lockheed and CIA scandals inhibiting U.S. involvement, the impending Communist victory, months before the Italians went to the polls, was elevated from the realm of the putative to the status of geopolitical immutability.

"I give the rest of Western Europe three to five years," one person on a first-name basis with the Secretary of State announced a month before the June 1976 Italian elections. "All my Italian friends have bought farms in Nebraska."

Happily enough for Giovanni Agnelli and Sophia Loren, if not for the analytical powers of the U.S. government, this new domino theory of Eurocommunism was unsubstantiated by events. The Italian elite was spared a future of covered-dish church socials and Italy's Communists did what they have done in every election for a generation: they came in second. The amazing thing—considering the bankruptcy of the Christian Democrats' policies—was not that the Italian Communists did so well, but that they did not do even better.

The Italian election posed a fundamental question about the entire ethos of U.S. foreign policy. "We cannot let a country go Communist, simply because of the irresponsibility of its people," Henry Kissinger had declared, propounding the essence of his foreign policy during Richard Nixon's first term. But even after the Nixon Presidency disintegrated, the voters of Southern Europe showed themselves to be considerably more responsible than those who presumed to tutor them. Even when they were not bribed into doing it by the CIA, or browbeaten into doing it by the State Department, or blackmailed into doing it by the Pentagon, might America's unruly, ungrateful allies nonetheless possess some small capacity to act in their own self-interest? Could it be that the cause of American security, even of

plain old anti-Communism, was best served when the American cop was not patrolling the block? In the years since Kissinger dismissed Ambassador Scott for suggesting that the Portuguese voters were capable of making an intelligent choice, Soares's Socialist party has routed the Communists in two national elections, in a Presidential election, and in nationwide municipal elections.

During 1975, the year the American intelligence community was on the defensive at home and Portugal's political future hung in the balance, Ambassador Carlucci restored U.S. prestige in Portugal, retained the Azores bases, kept the Soviets out of Portugal, and kept Portugal inside the NATO alliance. He achieved all this not merely by ignoring Dr. Kissinger's instructions, but by defying the entire interventionist premise of U.S. foreign policy since World War II—by pursuing what might be called a policy of masterful indolence. As Alvaro Cunhal made speeches about the menace of U.S. subversion, Carlucci reduced the U.S. Embassy staff. When the pro-Communist leader of the fifth provisional government, Vasco dos Santos Gonçalves, accused him of fomenting a right-wing coup, Carlucci, with studied conspicuousness, busied himself building a new embassy tennis court. "Carlucci was something new for us," remarked Vasco Correira Guedes, a Portuguese historian and political commentator, "an American diplomat capable of diplomacy."

While restraint paid off in Portugal, interventionist orthodoxy nonetheless prevailed at the opposite end of Southern Europe. No back-talking bureaucratic bunglers stood in Henry Kissinger's way in Cyprus and Greece, and thus two high-ranking U.S. officials, Rodger P. Davies, the U.S. Ambassador to Cyprus, and Richard Welch, the CIA station chief in Athens, found their missions ended somewhat differently from those of Ambassadors Scott and Carlucci. Ambassador Davies, a strong advocate of arms shipments to the Athens junta, was murdered in Nicosia in 1974 by outraged Greek Cypriot nationalists. Mr. Welch was gunned down near Athens in 1975 by Greeks similarly piqued by U.S. support of the dictatorship there. If the esteem the United States now enjoys in Portugal is understandable, the least that can be said of these two crimes is that the motives were understandable too.

"Makarios is a very big man for such a small island," Kissinger once remarked when the archbishop, like Soares, had the temerity to disagree with U.S. policy. Thereafter Dr. Kissinger behaved like a very petty man for the Secretary of State of such an immense

> "Even after the Nixon Presidency disintegrated, the voters of Southern Europe showed themselves to be considerably more responsible than those who presumed to tutor them."

country. In 1974 agents of the Greek junta—using U.S. guns and ammunition and led by U.S.-trained Greek officers—mounted a harebrained coup against Makarios and the entire delicate balance keeping Greeks and Turks from each others' throats. The coup no doubt would have collapsed in hours, and peace been restored, had not the American Secretary of State perceived in the crisis yet another brilliant opportunity to manifest his credibility to Congress and the Soviets by conjuring up yet another reactionary client regime in the eastern Mediterranean.

In the ensuing tragicomedy of American statesmanship, Kissinger's gratuitous meddling transformed Cyprus from a tourist paradise into a partitioned island of barbed wire and refugees. He also achieved a feat of diplomatic prestidigitation previously considered impossible by managing to make America simultaneously the most hated country in both Greece and Turkey.

If the lessons of Portugal were never learned, the lessons of Cyprus were soon forgotten. "The United States cannot pursue a policy of selective reliability," Kissinger sniffed, as he parachuted munitions on Phnom Penh and unleashed his brief, disastrous vendetta against Angola. It was left to Jerry Ford, however, to mouth in all its mindlessness the essential U.S. strategic doctrine that failure everywhere was the consequence of America's failure to intervene, that every success must be credited to the manic little gnomes at Langley and the National Security Council.

"We have been successful in Portugal, where a year ago it looked like there was a very great possibility that the Communists would take over in Portugal. It didn't happen," Ford rejoindered, when his critics dared to suggest that all the CIA's clandestine operations and all of Henry's pyrotechnics often did more harm than good. "We have a democracy in Portugal today."

Ambassador Carlucci had no comment, and Mario Soares laughed all the way to the ballot box.

A LL AMERICANS must understand that, because of its strength, its history, and its concern for human dignity, this nation occupies a special place in the world."

Though they resemble them closely, those were not Jimmy Carter's words when he announced his worldwide crusade for human rights, and sent Rosalynn and Andy Young off to hold tent revivals in Africa and Latin America. They come from a speech Richard Nixon made just before he invaded Cambodia.

Times have changed, but the rhetorical continuity of American foreign policy reveals an overlooked truth. From the age of manifest destiny to the era of détente, America's relations with the external world have remained ensnared in that misapprehension of causality psychiatrists say explains both the benign and pathological variants of clinical schizophrenia. Whether the victim of the disorder imagines he is General Patton or Albert Schweitzer, the defect of ratiocination is the same: the patient cannot distinguish between his inner needs and the outer world, between the limits of reality and the infinity of his own volition.

No doubt Jimmy Carter's affliction is less malign than the Nixon-Kissinger psychosis. But beneath the new policy lie the old symptoms. Just as once it was supposed that smart bombs could erect a viable South Vietnam, so now it is believed that American good intentions will cause Bantu and Boer to love one another. In a nation supposedly instructed in its limitations by its recent failures, Jimmy Carter in a matter of months has demonstrated how little America has learned. Recycling the moral absolutism of John Foster Dulles, the rhetoric of John F. Kennedy, the ethnocentrism of Lyndon Johnson, and the global pretentiousness of Richard Nixon into a bright new foreign-policy package, Carter has not so much dispelled the old illusions as made them newly fashionable.

We were the world's gendarme then. We will be its itinerant moralist now. So where once we ostracized evil, now we hasten to open embassies in Havana and Hanoi lest even those we formerly harassed be denied access to our goodness. The President's conviction that it is morally right to recognize Peking is matched only by his sense of moral obligation toward Taiwan. He detests the arms trade and believes in Saudi Arabia's right to have a modern army. He loathes torture and loves the shah. Shall we give the Panamanians the canal, or keep it for ourselves? Our President has devised a treaty that purports to do both.

In Algiers some years ago, I found myself in a café, composing a list of that tiny, deprived minority of states it was the daily business of U.S. diplomacy neither to defend nor to destroy—countries with which, for one reason or another, we in fact had no diplomatic relations at all: the Vatican and Cuba. China and Andorra. Mongolia and the Maldives. Albania and Bhutan. At that time, both Syria and Cambodia. Iraq, Liechtenstein, and Algeria itself, which, even though it then had no U.S. Ambassador, no CIA station chief, no military attachés, no AID mission, and no glossy brochures from the U.S. Information Service, nonetheless seemed content enough to sell us oil and buy back our technology. I had spent a month in Algeria, managing somehow to survive without the protection and guidance of an official U.S. mission.

What is more, Algeria had demonstrated a truly unexpected capacity to get along without one either. It had won its independence without American aid. It was retaining its independence without American help. Of course Algeria did do all sorts of disreputable, un-American things. It disagreed with U.S. policy in the Mideast and Indochina. It rounded up political prisoners, censored the local press, and rigged the local elections. But then so did the governments of neighboring Tunisia and Morocco—which were just chockablock with busy American officials with just enough time in their crowded calendars to inform a visiting journalist how indispensable the U.S. presence was to American security, and to world peace and progress. It suddenly occurred to me what the watch merchants of Vaduz and the cadres of Shanghai, the pearl divers of Gan and the scarlet-robed cardinals of the papal Curia, all had in common, besides no American Ambassador to invite to their cocktail parties: unlike our allies and adversaries, they were causing the United States of America no trouble.

Until recently the Horn of Africa caused us no trouble, and we made no trouble for the Horn. For decades, however, we did lavish money, expertise, and weapons systems on neighboring Ethiopia. Our Peace Corps volunteers taught its unemployed intellectuals to read Marcuse and wear their hair like Angela Davis. Our FBI agents pitched in by teaching Haile Selassie's secret police a thing or two. The Pentagon transformed the Imperial Ethiopian Armed Forces into yet another bulwark against the menace of geopolitical instability. Meanwhile we had no diplomatic relations at all with Somalia, in spite of its vital strategic position astride the Horn. Ethiopia, like all dutiful client states, cost us much money, and in return gave our Ambassadors and CIA agents and AID officials that international treasure beyond all price, the illusion of influence.

Somalia, in contrast, cost us nothing and was more valuable to the Pentagon than the Azores bases and the Greek junta combined. For without that fabled Soviet naval base at Berbera, what would our base at Asmara have spied upon? Without the growing Soviet threat on the Horn, how could Congress have been talked into paying for Diego Garcia? Today the results in Somalia and Ethiopia are the same as they earlier were in Portugal and Cyprus. The Ethiopians detest us as much as the Cypriots do. But while the Ethiopians parade around their prefeudal villages proclaiming the dictatorship of the proletariat, the rulers of Somalia now are as eager to go on television with Barbara Walters as is Dr. Castro.

Not too long ago, however, when he was asked where American diplomacy might take the offensive, Jimmy Carter singled out Somalia. So the fate of Ethiopia now stalks that hitherto unmolested and untraumatized country too, thanks to the continuing importance of being earnest in our foreign policy. One wonders what diplomatic horrors will erupt when we finally have full-scale embassies in Havana and Peking. Cuba is only ninety miles off our shores, and China does have one-quarter of the world's population. Are the risks of diplomatic relations really worth it?

Trop de zèle

SOUTHERN AFRICA and the Mideast afford the types of problems American statesmen traditionally have been unable to understand, let alone solve. It would hardly become an American foreign policy, after all, if it were based on the un-American premise that some problems surpass the capacities even of the Brookings Institution and the National Security Council to solve. But external reality, if not the wish-fulfillment apparatus in Washington, indicates that another Mideast war may be inevitable whatever we do, and that not even American know-how and virtue can spare Africa the historical consequences of centuries of racism and unequal development.

In foreign policy, success has many parents. When the next Arab-Israeli war breaks out, or the negotiations in Africa break down, Arab and Israeli, black and white, no doubt will concur that failure is America's bastard child. And the genealogy may well be warranted, for Jimmy Carter is the true heir to Woodrow Wilson and Richard Helms. What unites his human-rights policy with the Fourteen Points and the CIA's fascination with mind-control drugs is that traditional American delusion that, if only America can devise the right political or chemical formula, then the world will stop being what it is, and become what we wish it to be. Medical science to date nonetheless has had little success curing those who imagine themselves to be Napoleon Bonaparte by putting them in command of great armies. Like so many of the ills Amer-

> **"Kissinger achieved a feat previously considered impossible by managing to make America simultaneously the most hated country in both Greece and Turkey."**

ica's global activism is supposed to cure, the malady afflicting our own foreign-policy perception may have no remedy, and the only treatment may be merely palliative.

"Surtout, pas trop de zèle," Talleyrand was fond of telling his diplomats and secret agents. If the American millennian impulse cannot be exorcised, that maxim nonetheless may provide the best guidance for coping with a zealous world and with our own zealous instincts. No doubt shutting down all our embassies and CIA stations might cause us nearly as much trouble as keeping them open does. But it would add a sense of proportion and a structure of priority to the conduct of U.S. foreign policy if we stopped, every now and then, to consider how seldom what we do, or do not do, really decides whether we succeed or fail —that is, whether reality winds up corresponding to our wishes or not.

IN RECENT YEARS we have "lost" Indochina and Ethiopia and Angola. We have "kept" Portugal and the Philippines and Morocco. We also have "won back" Egypt and Chile, at least in the sense that Moscow has lost them. What is clear in retrospect is that all these geopolitical alterations may well have occurred whatever policy the United States did or did not pursue, and that, in total, these changes have affected our lives, and the security of our country, far less, one way or another, than most persons could have imagined at the time. What held true in the past no doubt will be equally true of the future. Democracy in Greece and Spain and Portugal, to say nothing of India, broke out quite independent of Henry Kissinger's distrust of it, or Jimmy Carter's faith in it. While no reverse causality operates either, it hardly would be astonishing to see a tsunami of repression sweep the world now that America has enunciated its fine new foreign-policy principles.

To return to Southern Europe, indeed, is not so much to find the answers being asked for in Washington as to be instructed yet again in the irrelevancy of America's questions.

Can the Eurocommunists really be counted on to be independent of Moscow? We forget that Communists already rule four Southern European countries, and that if the averages in Yugoslavia, Albania, Rumania, and Bulgaria hold true, at least three out of four Eurocommunist governments will cause Moscow far more trouble than our NATO allies ever do. But aren't the Eurocommunists only pretending to believe in human rights? Won't they kill off democracy even if they don't follow Soviet orders? The real question is whether any government or ideology—no matter what it does —can convert Italy, for example, into a functioning nation-state. I should be much more astonished to see the Italian Communists succeed, should they eventually gain power, where Garibaldi and Mussolini failed, than to see them stab the "historic compromise" in the back. Similar questions pose themselves in Greece, where, under democracy and dictatorship alike, socioeconomic power remains in the hands of a small plutocracy. Mario Soares is finding inflation a far more formidable adversary than the Portuguese Communists, and in Spain the economic miracle was in trouble even before Franco died. Under military or civilian rule, inside or outside NATO, there seem no solutions at all to Turkey's problems.

It is instructive that, no matter how many times it is born again, U.S. policy so seldom addresses itself to those kinds of questions. Indeed the real question in Southern Europe today, and practically everywhere else, is one that neither Henry Kissinger nor Jimmy Carter has ever asked. Why is it that in spite of our global pretensions, in spite of our unceasing activism on every continent for thirty years, in spite of our serene faith that it is the destiny of the world to become like us, the American Dream has come true in so few places?

In spite of all our bungling arrogance and all our misguided altruism, the extraordinary thing is not that we so often make ourselves seem foolish and contemptible, it is that American freedom, American affluence, and American technology still can enthrall so much of the world. In both Lisbon and Istanbul, this takes the form of two immense, costly, and useless suspension bridges spanning the Tagus and the Bosporus. Neither carries much traffic. Neither marvel of engineering has transformed the local economy. Instead what one really sees arching above these two capitals of vanished empires, over these two waterways where no armada has ever arrived with a historical solution, are two symbols. No less than the illiterates lining up to mark ballots, the Tagus and Bosporus bridges show how powerful even in these two least American of NATO allies— the one fundamentally Asian, the other essentially Latin-American—is the dream of modernity, progress, and freedom.

Americans of course intended no lesson for the Turks and Portuguese when they built the Golden Gate Bridge, no more than we set out to teach the world a course in constitutionalism with the Watergate crisis. But they, and all the rest we presume to tutor, will not fail to be instructed by what Jimmy Carter says when the sermon stops, by what he does when he is not in his pulpit. □

★★★

51

America's Foreign Policy: A Rake's Progress   Lewis H. Lapham

This essay uses the analogy of a "rich man" to explain the United States' involvement in foreign affairs. Lapham's argument is that we have been "squandering the national inheritance" in a number of ways, just as an unthinking rich man. In 1945, he contends, we were the dominant power in the world, and diplomacy was approached from the perspective of wealth. Have things changed since then? How so? Is wealth still an important variable affecting our foreign policy? He argues that we "see the world as a theater" in looking at our country as a major actor on the diplomatic stage. How was this bias reflected in our attitudes toward the Shah of Iran?

Another difficulty Lapham sees is that we are uninformed and inattentive to events around the world, and we very often are "wasteful" in making agreements with other nations. How is this reflected in our treatment of our allies? As a rich man, moreover, we feel "immune" from the full effects of our misdeeds. Since we have never fought any of the major world wars on American soil, has this "immunity" from the ravages of war bred in Americans a feeling of moral superiority and arrogance?

Another aspect of our attitude toward the world, says Lapham, is that even though we have suffered relatively little historically, we have a constant fear of losing everything, a "hypochondria" if you will. Has this perception encouraged us to overemphasize national security issues? Has it affected our foreign policy toward the Soviet Union? Lapham also asserts that the United States is "impatient," looking for simple solutions to complex problems. When we need advice about foreign affairs, we simply hire experts, or so-called "family retainers." Does this encourage administrations to select a group of "foreign policy establishment" regulars who conduct our diplomacy? Who are its members and what are its common bonds? A further comparison is drawn between the rich man and his "sentimental dreams." Our foreign policy, the author feels, is affected by images, visions, and values which eventually clash with harsh political realities. What evidence does Lapham give to support this view? Finally, he calls our attention to the fact that whenever the United States is rebuffed by small, less wealthy nations, we become "spiteful," as a rich man would upon being rebuffed by an unknown. Do we look for scapegoats, rather than seek to understand our own errors? Overall, do you think Lapham's parody based on the "rich man" is meaningful? In particular, do you think our foreign policy toward the poorer, underdeveloped nations of the world reflects these perceptions of a very wealthy superpower?

★ ★ ★

AMERICA'S FOREIGN POLICY: A RAKE'S PROGRESS

Squandering the national inheritance

by Lewis H. Lapham

Preamble

THE INCREASINGLY DISSOLUTE course of American foreign policy makes it difficult to characterize the spectacle of the United States in the world as anything other than a rake's progress. The country exhibits itself in the persona of a profligate heir, squandering his fortune in gambling hells and on speculations in organic farming and utopian politics. Bearing this portrait in mind, I can make sense of the accounts in the newspapers. Otherwise I'm at a loss to know what people mean when they talk about mutual-defense treaties, hegemonies, the China card, and arcs of crisis in Asia Minor and the Persian Gulf. On reading the communiqués from Washington, Peking, and Teheran (together with the supporting sophistry on the editorial pages of the *New York Times*), I see a soft-faced man in a nightclub at three A.M., earnestly seeking to persuade a bored demimondaine that he still worries about the higher things in life and that his inheritance has failed to bring him true peace and happiness. Through the dance music I can hear him saying, in a blurred but concerned voice, that he means to do what's right, but that this is a much harder thing to do than perhaps the young lady knows. He would have preferred to become a poet or a Protestant minister, or

possibly a guitar player hitchhiking across Arkansas with a girl who sings country songs. But his lawyers keep talking to him about the Russians (the boring, tedious Russians, who never laugh at his jokes), and his trust officers keep talking to him about money—about the goddam price of oil and the second-rate Shah who let him down in Iran, about the Chinese and the Japanese and the Taiwanese and the Vietnamese (all of whom look so much alike that it's hard to remember which ones are floating around in boats), and about the miserable Jews who failed him in the Middle East.

The persona of the spendthrift heir seems to be fitting because in 1945 the United States inherited the earth. During the first half of the twentieth century, the European powers twice attempted suicide, and at the end of World War II what was left of Western civilization passed into the American account.* The war also had prompted the country to invent a miraculous economic machine that seemed

---

* The United States came so suddenly into its inheritance that the fortune bears more of a resemblance to a family estate than to the wealth of a nation accumulated over centuries. It is no more than eighty-nine years from the closing of the frontier to the walk on the moon; the same span of time measures the building of Chartres Cathedral and the period between John D. Rockefeller's entry into business and his death amid incalculable riches. The alarms and excursions of the 1960s can best be understood as a family quarrel about the distribution of the estate.

Lewis H. Lapham is the editor of Harper's.

to grant as many wishes as were asked of it. The continental United States had escaped the plague of war, and so it was easy enough for the heirs to believe that they had been anointed by God. In their eager innocence, they made of foreign policy a game of transcendental poker, in which the ruthless self-interest of a commercial democracy (cf., the American policy toward the Plains Indians and the Mexicans) got mixed up with dreams, sermons, and the transmigration of souls. In Europe people may not know very much about foreign policy; as often as not they have no idea what to do about any particular crisis, but at least they can recognize the subjects under discussion. They know enough to know that the dealing between nations is a dull and sluggish business, unyielding in the financial details and encumbered with the usual displays of pride, greed, nastiness, and spite. The

Drawings by Paul Degen

Americans, who have little interest in tiresome details, prefer to imagine themselves playing cards with the Devil.

THE WEALTH of the United States in comparison to other nations of the world makes the figure of the rich man representative of the country's gargantuan extravagance. As the inheritors became increasingly profligate (cf., the rising levels of consumption, inflation, and debt through the 1960s), so also the assumptions of pecuniary privilege became habitual among larger segments of the population. I first encountered the prevailing attitude of mind in the fall of 1957, when, having studied history for a year in England, I returned to the United States with the notion of working for either the *Washington Post* or the CIA. My interest in foreign affairs had been awakened by the Suez and Hungarian incidents of 1956 and by my inability to understand, much less explain to a crowd of indignant Englishmen, the policy of John Foster Dulles. In 1957 the *Washington Post* and the CIA could be mistaken for different departments of the same corporation. Newspapermen traded rumors with intelligence agents, and although the gilding on the Pax Americana was beginning to wear a little thin, anybody who had been to Yale in the early 1950s couldn't help thinking the totalitarian hordes had to be prevented from sacking the holy cities of Christendom. Failing to find a job with the *Post*, I took the examinations for the CIA. These lasted a week, and afterward I was summoned to a preliminary interview with four or five young men introduced to me as "some of the junior guys." The interview took place in one of the temporary buildings put up during World War II in the vicinity of the Lincoln Memorial. The feeling of understated grandeur, of a building hastily assembled for an urgent, imperial purpose, was further exaggerated by the studied carelessness of the young men who asked the questions. All of them seemed to have graduated from Yale, and so they questioned me about whom I had known at New Haven and where I went in the summer. I had expected to discuss military history and the risings of the Danube; instead I found myself trying to remember the names of the girls who sailed boats off Fishers Island, or who had won the summer tennis tournaments in Southampton and Bedford Hills. As the conversation drifted through the ritual of polite inanity (about "personal goals" and "one's sense of achievement in life"), the young men every now and then exchanged an enigmatic reference to "that damn thing in Laos." Trying very hard not to be too obvious about it, they gave me **to** understand that they were playing the big varsity game of the Cold War. Before I got up to leave, apologizing for having applied to the wrong office, I understood that I had been invited to drop around to the common room of the best fraternity in the world so that the admissions committee could find out if I was "the right sort."

From that day forward I have never been surprised by the news of the CIA's vindictiveness and inattention. Good, clean-cut American boys, with all the best intentions in the world and convinced of their moral and social primogeniture, must be expected to make a few good-natured mistakes. If their innocent enthusiasm sometimes degenerates into sadism, well, that also must be expected. Nobody becomes more spiteful than the boy next door jilted by the beautiful Asian girl, especially after he has given her the beach house at Camranh Bay, $100 million in helicopters, and God knows how much in ideological support. It is a bitter thing to lose to Princeton and to find out that not even Dink Stover can make the world safe from Communism.

This same undergraduate insouciance has remained characteristic of American foreign policy for the past thirty years. Administrations have come and gone, and so have enemies and allies, but the attitude of mind remains constant, and so does the tone of voice. It is the voice of Henry Kissinger explaining to a lady at a dinner that a nation, like an ambitious Georgetown hostess, cannot afford to invite unsuccessful people to its parties. It is the voice of McGeorge Bundy, who told an audience of scholars in the early 1960s that he was getting out of Latin American studies because Latin America was such a second-rate place. It is the voice of James Reston finding something pleasant to say about this year's congenial dictator, or the State Department announcing its solidarity with Cambodia and expressing only mild regret about the regime's program of genocide.

After 1968 the inflection of the voice became slightly more irritable and petulant. During the early years of the decade the heir to the estate flattered himself with the gestures and exuberant rhetoric appropriate to an opulent idealism. He had access to unlimited resources (of moral authority as well as cash), and he stood willing to invest in anybody's scheme of political liberty. Nothing was too difficult or too expensive; no war or rural electrification was too small or inconsequential. The young heir undertook to invade Asia and to provide guns and wheat and computer tech-

nology to any beggar who stopped him in the street and asked him for a coin. After 1968, when the bills came due and things turned a little sour, the heir began muttering about scarcity and debts, about the damage done to the environment and the lack of first-class accommodation on spaceship earth. Nobody becomes more obsessive on the subject of money than the rich man who has suffered a financial loss. The fellow feels himself impoverished because he has to sell the yacht. President Nixon closed the gold window, and associate professors of social criticism dutifully taught their students that sometimes money weighs more heavily in the balance of human affairs than the romance of the zeitgeist.

Even so, the assumptions of entitlement remain intact. Although feeling himself somewhat diminished (as witness the success of the philosopher-merchants on the neoconservative Right) and somewhat older (as witness the dependence on sexual and spiritual rubber goods), the still-prodigal son continues to believe himself possessed of unlimited credit. He is still the heir to the fortune, no matter what anybody says about his horses and dogs, and he can damn well play his game of policy in any way that he damn well chooses. This assumption of grace begets a number of corollary attitudes, all of them as characteristic of a rich man going about his toys and pleasures as of the manner in which the United States conducts its foreign affairs. As follows:

I. The world as theater

CHILDREN ENCOURAGED to imagine themselves either rich or beautiful assume that nothing else will be required of them. What is important is the appearance of things, and if these can be properly maintained, then the heirs can look forward to a sequence of pleasant invitations. They will be entitled to a view from the box seats, and from the box seats, as every fortunate child knows, the world arranges itself into a decorous panorama. The point of view assumes that Australians will play tennis, that Italians will sing or kill one another, that Negroes will dance or riot (always at a safe distance), and that the holders of the season tickets will live happily ever after, or, if they are very, very rich, maybe forever. The complacence of this view implies a refusal to see anything that doesn't appear on the program. Nobody imagines that he can be dislodged by a social upheaval of no matter what force or velocity, and it is taken for granted that the embarrassments of death or failure will be vis-

"It is a bitter thing . . . to find out that not even Dink Stover can make the world safe from Communism."

ited upon people to whom one has never been properly introduced.

Since the end of World War II the people who make American foreign policy have assumed that the world is so much painted scenery. The impresarios in Washington assign all the parts and write all the last acts. Other people make exits and entrances. Thus President Carter, on the last night of 1977, offered a toast to the Shah of Iran in which he described the Shah as his "great friend" and Iran as an "island of stability" in the Middle East.* A year later Iran was in the midst of revolt and Washington was advising the Shah to abdicate in favor of any government, civil or military, that could restore production in the southern oil fields. In 1941 the Soviet Union appeared on the stage in the role of brave friend and courageous ally; six years later, the script was rewritten and the Soviet Union appeared as the villainous *éminence grise*, subverting the free world with the drug of Communism. China remained an implacable enemy of human freedom for the better part of thirty years, but in 1972 President Nixon announced the advent of democracy, and in 1978 President Carter proclaimed the miracle of redemption. Following the example set by the wall posters in Peking, the American press blossomed with praise for a regime previously celebrated for its brutality. The stagehands of the media took down the sets left over from the production of *Darkness at Noon* and replaced them with tableaux of happy Chinese workers eager to buy farm implements, military aircraft, and Coca-Cola.

In war, Napoleon once said, the greatest sin is to make pictures. But the man who has inherited a great fortune does nothing else except make pictures. Unlike the poor man, who must study other people's motives and

desires if he hopes to gain something from them, the rich man can afford to look only at what amuses or comforts him. He believes what he is told because he has no reason not to do so. What difference does it make? If everything is make-believe, then everything is as plausible as everything else. Asian dictators can promise to go among their peasants and instruct them in the mechanics of constitutional self-government; the Shah of Iran can say he means to make a democratic state among people who believe that they have won the blessing of Allah by burning to death 400 schoolchildren in a movie theater. The rich man applauds, admires the native costumes, and sends a gift of weapons. He believes that, once inspired by the American example, the repentant Asian despot will feel himself inwardly changed and seek to imitate the model of behavior established by Henry Cabot Lodge. Dictators don't really want to be dictators; they were raised in an unhealthy social environment, and if given enough tractors and a little moral encouragement, they will renounce the pleasures of sodomy and murder. The absurd political presentations that have found favor in Washington over the past thirty years resemble the farfetched rationalizations with which New York art dealers sell the latest school of modern painting to the nouveau riche. Like the visitors from abroad, the dealers retain a serene and justified confidence in the customer's willingness to be deceived.

II. The habit of inattention

THE PRESS and the politicians sometimes blame the CIA for being so poorly informed, not only about the events in Iran but also about events in China, Russia, Africa, and Vietnam. The recriminations seem to me unfair. The inattention of the CIA reflects and embodies the carelessness of the society for which it acts as agent. On leaving his club the rich man never looks behind him to see if the waiter is holding his coat; in much the same way the United States doesn't take the trouble to notice much of what goes on in the world's servants' quarters. The American press reports news from Africa that deals with disputes between whites and blacks; only large-scale civil wars between armies of blacks deserve mention in the dispatches, and then only if the Russians agree to sponsor one of the contenders. The rich man never knows why other people do what they do because it never occurs to him that they have obligations to anybody other than himself. Few among the

---

* It is instructive to quote Mr. Carter's toast at some length because it so nicely illustrates the somnambulism of American statesmen content to see whatever they wish to see. Mr. Carter explained that he decided to celebrate New Year's Eve with the Shah because he had asked his wife, Rosalynn, whom she wanted to be with on that occasion, and Rosalynn had said, "Above all others, I think, with the Shah and the empress Farah." The President then went on to say: "Iran, because of the great leadership of the Shah, is an island of stability in one of the more troubled areas of the world. This is a great tribute to you, Your Majesty, and to your leadership, and to the respect and the admiration and love which your people give to you. . . . We have no other nation on earth who is closer to us in planning for our mutual military security. We have no other with whom we have closer consultations on regional problems that concern us both. And there is no leader with whom I have a deeper sense of personal gratitude and personal friendship."

nation's more prominent journalists speak or read French. It would exceed the bounds of all decent patriotism to expect more than two or three of them to read or speak Russian, Chinese, or Arabic. The same thing can be said for members of Congress, for Presidents, Secretaries of State, ministers of defense, and almost the entire cadre of people who give shape and form to the discussion of foreign policy. Whenever I remark too loudly on the magnificent displays of American ignorance, somebody who has published an article in *Foreign Affairs* reminds me that the United States is the last, best hope of earth. This is undoubtedly true, but it has nothing to do with the subjects under discussion.

III. Wastefulness

WHEN PRESIDENT CARTER announced the Christmas demarche to Communist China, various mean-spirited critics observed that the United States had failed to gain any specific advantage from the deal. The United States ceased to recognize Taiwan as a sovereign state, abrogated the defense treaty, and agreed to withdraw its troops from the island. In return for these concessions, the Communist Chinese promised to be as friendly as possible and to do what they thought best for the Taiwanese.

The people who object to the slackness of this bargain overlook the rich man's unwillingness to set a vulgar price on metaphysics. The United States habitually makes poor bargains because it feels that it already owns everything worth owning, and so why haggle with the poor little fellows in Asia and the Middle East? Why make unreasonable demands on the Soviets in the SALT negotiations? It is the proof of a rich man's freedom that he can afford to pay an excessive price. It never occurs to him that political economy might be a form of destruction as ruthless although not quite so obvious as war, or that the world is full of hungry people still scrabbling around for anything they can get. The rich man considers it the height of fashion and good breeding to affect an aristocratic disdain for commerce.

Thus a rich nation's portfolio of treaties resembles a rich man's stock portfolio. It is full of issues that he inherited from his grandfather or his mother's uncles, and he has trouble remembering the assets and liabilities represented by NATO, SEATO, CENTO, and God knows how many other shares and securities for which he can't even recall the names. This explains his careless disregard for those coun-

tries denominated as allies. To the extent that none of them take precedence over any of the others, they can be bought and sold as the heir feels himself pressed by the need for cash or funds with which to stage an extravagant fireworks display.*

The habit of mind remains firmly ingrained despite the depleted value of the heir's investments. At the end of 1972 foreign banking interests controlled American assets of $26.8 billion; in 1978 the same interests controlled American assets worth $98 billion. During the first five months of 1978 the United States imported machinery and manufactured goods in the amount of $37 billion, as opposed to only $16 billion for foreign oil. The dollar continues to depreciate in the world markets, and American multinational corporations have begun to find themselves surpassed by their competitors in France, Germany, and Japan.

But the rich man intent upon his game of policy impatiently dismisses the accountants niggling at his sleeve. He feels compelled to place another bet in Indochina, this time backing the Cambodians (i.e., the friends of his new partners, the Communist Chinese) against the malevolent croupiers in Vietnam. He wants to make a grand and humanistic gesture in southern Africa, to do something visible and significant in Turkey, to effect a rapprochement in Central America. As recently as last summer, while listening to people with impeccable credentials discuss the prospects of American diplomacy, I heard a man say that nothing could happen in the world that could affect, in any serious way, the United States. Excepting only a nuclear miscalculation, he was happy to report that the country could consider itself invulnerable.

IV. Immunity

IN AMERICAN military circles, I'm told, it is considered poor form to discuss fortification and the strategies of attrition and civil defense. The whole notion of fortification is seen as stodgy, corrupting, somehow un-American. It brings to mind the depressing memory of stuffy French generals on the Maginot Line in the early weeks of World War II. The United States owes it to itself to cut a more dashing figure in the world. Where is the fun in fighting dreary rearguard actions? The young men in the Pen-

> **"If everything is make-believe, then everything is as plausible as everything else."**

---

* Thus, the Carter Administration didn't take the trouble to consult the NATO allies about its decision to postpone the deployment of the neutron bomb. In much the same spirit, the Nixon Administration didn't bother to consult with the Japanese in 1971 about the overtures to China, the shift in the monetary system, or the imposition of tariffs.

tagon and the military academies speak of forward thrusts, of broad-gauged advances, of assaults and landings and insertions.

All the fine talk conceals an ironic paradox. When it comes down to a question of how to go about these romantic maneuvers, the United States relies less on the daring and intelligence of its commanders than on the superiority of its expensive equipment. It is assumed that the wars will be won by the avalanche of American resources, matériel, production, logistics, and assembly lines—i.e., by the bureaucrats who need be neither impetuous nor brave. The faith in gadgetry and the "tech fix" accounts for the incalculable investment in missiles, bombs, airplanes, and anything else that can be bought in the finest sporting-goods stores. Nobody has the bad manners to insist that strategic bombing has yet to be proved a decisive factor in any of the century's wars. The rich man depends on his technology in the same way that he depends on his trust fund. Even if he makes no effort to think about the great bulk of his capital, it goes about the business of gathering its daily ransom of interest and dividends. The miraculous nature of this contrivance persuades the heir to believe in the divinity of machines.

His lack of acquaintance with the domesticity of war gives him further reason to think that he may have been granted an exemption from the scourges by which less fortunate men sometimes find themselves humiliated. The world is object, and the United States is subject, the fighting always takes place on somebody else's field. The politicians who currently hold office in England suffered the terror of the German bombing; in Moscow the present members of the Politburo watched German tank commanders sight their guns on the spires of the Kremlin. Their peers in Germany, China, Japan, and Italy all carry with them the memory of wives, fathers, brothers, and children killed by the armies of liberation. But in the United States these are tales that are told. Perhaps this is why the Americans were obliged to push the Vietnamese off the helicopters rising from the roof of the American embassy in Saigon. They hadn't been taught that defeats were as plausible as victories, and so they didn't know how to manage a courageous retreat.

V. Hypochondria

THE DISEASE IS popular with the rich because only the rich can afford it and because, being incurable, it gives them a constant occasion to talk about themselves. Never before in its history has the United States been so heavily armed a nation, and yet the newspapers and the literary gazettes ceaselessly bring reports of helplessness and alienation, of malignancies in the body politic and the encroaching shadow of Soviet hegemony. The fear of death provides a further excuse for the feverish rates of spending and the extravagant consumption of the estate's assets. Eat, drink, and be merry, for tomorrow we may have to pay one dollar for a gallon of gasoline and give up our chalets in Aspen. Like the society physicians who prey upon the anxieties of dowager heiresses, the learned doctors of foreign policy subtly remind the trembling patient of the illnesses that can befall the unwary traveler in the Third World who strays too far from supplies of safe drinking water.

The symptoms of hypochondria have been chronic since the early 1950s. The moods of euphoria and exultation ("How dare they defy us, those scrawny little peasants in Vietnam?") periodically give way to seizures of doubt and self-reproach. For no apparent reason, the stewards of the American empire suddenly become preoccupied with the phantoms of the missile gap or the energy crisis. Every now and then the consensus of alarmed opinion declares a "year of maximum danger." I have heard this moment in time variously given as 1954, 1962, 1968, 1974, and now—with President Carter's casting around for a credible portrait of himself as statesman and world leader—1979.

The obsession with security corresponds to the desire of the American rich to live in protected enclaves and to escape the filth and nuisance of the world. Howard Hughes ascends to the roof of a Las Vegas hotel, there to keep himself safe from bacteria; Hugh Hefner revolves on a round bed in a darkened room, arranging and rearranging pictures of paradise; David Rockefeller sits drinking milk among reports of poverty and overpopulation; Richard Nixon composes his memoirs in the brooding silence of San Clemente; and President Carter retires to the little study next to the Oval Office, listening to Wagnerian opera, checking off his list of things to say and do, communing with his God.

This inward gaze, and the delight in the chimpanzee's examination of the American self, contributes to the poor quality of the reporting from abroad. The diplomats and newspaper correspondents compose pictures that accord with their presuppositions when they signed up for the package tour. They see what they have been told to see (otherwise they wouldn't have been sent), and for the most part they notice that the world is a very poor and undeveloped place, not at all like Greenwich, Connecticut, or Far Hills, New Jersey. They assume that happiness cannot be separated from its natural setting amidst suburban lawns, and this leads them to suspect that the natives are dissatisfied and therefore angry. What man in his right mind would not want to drive a station wagon and ride in triumph through Grosse Pointe? The abyss looms on all sides, at all points of latitude and longitude. By confusing his money with his life, the rich heir imagines himself threatened by enemies of infinite number and variety— by thieves, dictators, IRS agents, hijackers, unscrupulous women, kings, radicals, kidnappers, and nationalist sentiment in South Yemen.

VI. Impatience

FORTUNE'S CHILD doesn't like to be bothered with details. He never has time to listen to the whole story or to read through the statistical memoranda and the volumes of supporting analysis. He has planes to catch and meetings to attend, and so he expects his advisers to provide him with summaries and conclusions. Unfortunately, this is a habit of mind that obliges him to conceive of foreign policy in extremely simple categories. A nation is slave or free, North or South, in the First World or the Third.

A man who must earn his own fortune learns to make subtle distinctions, and he knows that in all human undertakings, in diplomacy as well as in art or commerce, it is in the details that the issue is decided. So also the man who depends for his livelihood on the animals that he hunts and kills. He studies them with the fondness of a lover, watching them in all weathers, guessing their moods, admiring their grace, following their tracks.

The heir to the fortune doesn't have the patience for this sort of thing. He hires gunbearers and assumes that all wars will be short. Because he wants to do everything in a hurry and with the minimum loss to his own troops, he relies on the most brutal and undiscriminating means of warfare. In Vietnam the United States couldn't distinguish very clearly between friends and enemies, and so it had no choice but to send the bombers. The soldiers followed the rich man's simple rule of "shooting everything that moves," and the Eighty-second Airborne Division resolved the political difficulties by defining a Vietcong as any dead Vietnamese.

VII. Family retainers

IT IS BOTH customary and correct to say that when President Carter arrived in office he knew very little about diplomatic history, political economy, or geography. Had he been asked, prior to his election and without benefit of public-relations counsel, to give the approximate location of Namibia or Romania, I doubt whether he could have come within several hundred miles of a convincing answer. But among American Presidents, at least during their first years in office, the lack of sophistication in these matters is the rule rather than the exception. Who can expect a red-blooded American boy to bother himself with a lot of foreign names? After two years in office, President Ford still had trouble remembering the whereabouts of the Red Army in relation to Poland. Even President Kennedy, who had traveled in Europe and the South Pacific, remained charmingly vague about Asia and Latin America.

Although some schools take more trouble with geography than others, the heirs of the American fortune ordinarily have no occasion to learn much more than the broad outlines of the civilization in which they happen to be spending the money. The better schools also insist that the young men have the good manners to know the difference between a sonata and a logarithm table, but for the most part an American education (at Harvard as well as at the universities of Michigan or California) constitutes a social rather than an intellectual enterprise. It is also a means of acquiring a cash value, comparable to buying a seat on the stock exchange, and it qualifies the recipient for a place in the corporations and the bureaucracies. If the need arises for more refined intellectual goods and services, the heirs to the estate can always hire a Wall Street law firm or a Jew.

Thus do the tribunes of the people fall like sparrows into the nets of the foreign-policy establishment. For the past thirty years, the trustees of this establishment have been recruited from the banking and legal hierarchies in New York and Washington as well as from the prestigious universities deemed to be sufficiently sound in their distrust of the artistic or political imagination. Although innumerable critics and newspaper columnists have remarked on the primacy of this establishment (cf., President Carter's weaning at the dugs of the Trilateral Commission), the term itself causes confusion. The establishment does not define itself in terms of specific institutions, publications, or club memberships.

"Nobody has the bad manners to insist that strategic bombing has yet to be proved a decisive factor in any of the century's wars."

Rather it can be understood as organizational support, of both a financial and an intellectual nature, for the belief in the redeeming and transfiguring power of money. Sums in excess of $100 million have the properties of fairy gold: they can transform apes into men and frogs into princes. It is this doctrine, enforced with the rigor of an ecclesiastical court, that binds together counselors of such otherwise disparate views as Dean Rusk, John J. Mc-Cloy, Cyrus Vance, William Rogers, Henry Kissinger, Clark Clifford, Arthur Schlesinger, Jr., McGeorge Bundy, and Zbigniew Brzezinski. These men do not constitute a cabal; it is even probable that they have no wish to form or join an establishment, but because most of the people in the country prefer to avoid the company of foreigners they achieve their eminence by default. Perhaps this explains the shoddiness and the timidity of their policies. It is their submission to the rule of money that gives their advice, no matter what the partisan politics of the moment, its consistency of tone and emphasis.*

In periods of relative optimism and extravagance, when the world is young and all things seem possible, the family retainers permit the heir an occasional indulgence or youthful folly. President Kennedy's advisers made no objection to the assassination of Diem, and allowed him to toy with the hope of assassinating Fidel Castro. But the heir always likes to think well of himself, and so when going about these Machiavellian adventures of state, the family retainers perform the service of doing things in the heir's name but not in his sight. In this respect they resemble New York divorce lawyers, who for the sake of the children, find it prudent to blackmail the showgirl wife with photographs of her debut in a New Orleans brothel. During periods of reaction and constraint the family retainers warn the heir against doing anything that might injure the integrity of the trust fund. Thus Mr. Carter's advisers recommend that the United States curry favor with any nation, slave or free, that can guarantee commodities, raw materials, and markets.

The more desperate the circumstances of the heir, the more likely that he will be attended by retainers who are themselves consumed with avarice and ambition. It is the habit of the rich to have enemies for friends, and so they surround themselves with gossips and hairdressers whose sexual sterility presents no obvious claim against the fortune and who take pleasure in contributing to the dissolution of the estate. Similarly, President Nixon employed Henry Kissinger, who seldom bothered to disguise his contempt not only for the Western democracies but also for Mr. Nixon. He told people whatever secret and fantastic truths they most urgently wanted to hear, tapped his associates' telephones with the discrimination of a man making a guest list, and betrayed his nominal friends as blithely as he brought ruin to his enemies. He entered the Nixon Administration in the persona of the faithful squire and left it in the persona of the resourceful manservant, condescending to sell his court memoirs for $2 million. During the televised proceedings of the Republican National Convention in Kansas City in 1976 the camera paused briefly on Mr. Kissinger sitting in the balcony, listening to the speeches with an expression of unconcealed disgust. It was the expression of a fashion designer who has just been told that somebody else will receive the commission to make the dress for the Inaugural Ball.

* Mrs. Cornelius Vanderbilt in 1906 expressed this principle of American foreign policy when instructing her niece in the fine points of social politics. "One never meets Jews," Mrs. Vanderbilt said. The niece reminded Mrs. Vanderbilt that she took tea on Friday afternoons with Mrs. August Belmont. "Of course," Mrs. Vanderbilt said, "one chooses who a Jew is." Thus the Carter Administration can decide that the Nigerian generals have enough oil to exempt them from the status of dictators and that Mr. Marcos in the Philippines deserves to be paid $1 billion for the use of his facilities at Subic Bay.

VIII. Jeu d'esprit

FROM TIME TO TIME the rich man dreams sentimental dreams. He wonders what it would have been like to have wandered as a pilgrim in India or to have composed verses worthy of Lord Byron. Under the influence of this soft and elegiac humor he sometimes builds on his property the equivalent of what the eighteenth-century English nobility described as a folly. Traditionally this was a little gazebo or pavilion with a view of a river or meadow. The heir to the fortune could lean against a marble column, staring into the blue distance and thinking thoughts of the ineffable.

In much the same spirit the United States erected its policy toward Israel. The Middle East wasn't a particularly important place in 1948, and the Jews had been through some pretty rough times at Buchenwald and Auschwitz. Why not, as Nelson Rockefeller might say, do something nice for the fellas? What did it cost anybody? The United States could admire the pleasing prospect of its conscience stretching into the ennobling spaces of the Palestinian desert.

Besides, Zionist sentiment in the United States was both affluent and politically well-connected. The supporters of Israel could be counted upon for generous campaign contributions and vigorous arguments in the intellectual debates. Everything went well enough for many years, until, in cir-

cumstances much reduced, the geologists found oil in a neighboring pasture. Unhappily, the heir needed the money, and his advisers informed him that he would have to tear down his folly and shift the mise-en-scène of his musings to some other pavilion. The heir objected to this, protesting that he had become fond of looking at the little river. But the lawyers were firm and unrelenting. The Arab money from the desert weighed more heavily in the balance than the Jewish money from the sown. Or, as it was explained to me about a year ago by a director of one of the American oil corporations, "Over here at Z——, we get down every morning and pray to Mecca; if necessary we would kiss the ass of every Arab in Riyadh."

IX. Spitefulness and rage

NOTHING SO ANGERS the rich man as the discovery that his money cannot buy him the world's love and admiration. Being impatient of ambiguity and doubt, he wonders why his fortune

doesn't emancipate him from the slings and arrows of outrageous suffering or why, like Shakespeare's Richard II, he must "live with bread like you, feel want, taste grief, need friends." If he gives even $10,000 to a philanthropic charity, he counts upon receiving at least $1 million in services and flattery. President Carter anticipated sustained applause upon the announcement of his opening to China, and when this was not forthcoming he became petulant and sullen. Mr. Warren Christopher, the Deputy Secretary of State, traveled to Taipei only a few days after the United States had declared inoperative its treaty with Taiwan. He proceeded from the airport in a cavalcade of limousines, never for a moment thinking that his progress could be anything out of the ordinary. An angry crowd stopped Mr. Christopher's car and smeared it with insults. Mr. Christopher was lucky to escape with his life. The bad manners exhibited by the Taiwanese surprised and offended Mr. Christopher, and the State Department sent a note of reproval.

When things go wrong in the world (i.e., when the painted scenery shifts and moves and comes to life) the rich

man casts around for somebody to blame. Characteristically he blames his lawyers and investment managers. Why else does he employ Dean Rusk and Cyrus Vance if they can't straighten out his affairs? How is it possible that all the king's horses and all the king's men cannot put the Shah of Iran back together again? The lawyers and managers in their turn blame one another, as well as inflation, unemployment, and the rising cost of labor. Throughout Washington the bureaucracies ooze whispered recriminations. The White House blames the CIA for the poor quality of the intelligence from Teheran, and the CIA blames the White House for not listening to the early reports of discontent, possibly because Mr. Brzezinski couldn't hear anyone speak ill of his strategic hopes for the Persian Gulf or because he didn't want to think Iran couldn't accept delivery on $18 billion in arms shipments.

The rich man becomes particularly annoyed when he is forced to perceive that he is not behaving decently in the world, that he has associated himself with tyrants and criminals. More than anything else he expects his money to buy him the illusion of innocence. He resents being told that he might be soliciting the odd $1 billion here and there from people who stand willing to burn and mutilate Jews, or that weapons sold in the world markets fall into the hands of thugs who use them to commit murder. Reports or rumors of these unhappy accidents wound the rich man's self-esteem and cloud the flattering image that he expects to see in the mirrors held up to him by his retainers, his servants, and the press. In the paroxysm of his rage he comes upon the great truth that only the rich and the powerful have rights.*

---

* Justice Felix Frankfurter admirably stated the principle in question when in 1914, as a young lawyer in the War Department, he was asked to research the question as to whether the American occupation of Vera Cruz constituted an act of war. He explained that he didn't need to look up the relevant law. "It's an act of war against a great power," he said; "it's not an act of war against a small power."

He concludes that other people have failed him, that he has been betrayed by people in whom he placed so much of his trust, and it occurs to him that perhaps other people deserve whatever fate befalls them. The family retainers assemble in comfortably furnished conference rooms to prepare exquisite phrases of regret. They can't quite say that the Jews deserve what they get because Jews are pushy, or that the English lost the empire because they are selfish, or that the French are corrupt and the Latin Americans shiftless and greedy. This is what they mean, but the words don't make a good impression in the newspapers. The lawyers talk instead about treaties, trade balances, and the Arabian oil fields as the wellsprings of the democratic alliance. If there isn't time for the polite hypocrisies, or if the nations in question haven't shown a decent respect for the opinions of mankind, then the rich man simply sends the bombers over Hanoi on Christmas Eve.

Envoi

IN THE GREAT GAME of diplomacy, I don't count myself a professional, or even a particularly well-informed amateur. No doubt I do injustice to some of the American statesmen of the 1950s, and I'm sure that in various aspects of the preceding argument I have oversimplified the matter to the point of parody. Those apologies and qualifications having been duly made, I think it fair to say that the people who formulate the present American policies in the world misunderstand the strength of the American idea. The United States remains the most powerful country in the world not because of its wealth or its arsenal but because the Constitution and the Bill of Rights give practical meaning to the possibilities of human aspiration. The society raised up on those foundations allowed men to free themselves from the tyranny of kings and priests. Joined with a democratic form of government, this freedom of initiative gave rise to the enormous expansions, in all spheres of human thought and endeavor, that have

both created and defined the United States.

The present generation of would-be statesmen apparently labors under the delusion that the price of liberty, once paid (preferably by a man's ancestors), can be written off as a nonrecurring debt. Unfortunately the price of liberty must be paid every day. It requires people to renounce the pleasures of sadistic exploitation and self-aggrandizement and to work instead for the gradual process of evolutionary change. This is never easy, but it becomes all but impossible if people confuse the power of money with the power of the mind and the imagination.

The interests of the United States as a nation do not always correspond to its virtues as a democratic republic; in an increasingly dangerous world, the country sometimes has no choice but to deal with people who couldn't qualify for membership in the Century Club. Dealing with such people is a different thing from enthusing about them with the adulation of gossip columnists. No matter how expensive the barbarian gifts and tributes, and no matter how magnificent the silks and furs, the worship of money binds the worshiper to the past as surely as if he had been buried with the gold in Tutankhamen's tomb. Whenever possible, the United States should ally itself with the evolving future of man's mind, with those forces in the world (ideas, nations, movements, political parties, institutions) that encourage human beings to walk on two feet. Conversely, the country would stand against the forces in the world that require human beings to crawl on the ground like so many humiliated apes. The simplicity of this distinction would oblige the makers of American policy to ask of their allies a different set of questions. The health of a nation's people and the stability of its institutions might come to weigh more heavily in the balance than a Shah's capacity to give emeralds to the wives of magazine publishers and oil-company presidents. The more people who become fully human in the world, the more they can do for themselves; the fewer the number of apes, the less seductive the voices prophesying war.   □

★★★

52

Cyrus Vance Plays It Cool   Bernard Gwertzman

The secretary of state is responsible to the president for the conduct of foreign policy and is our primary spokesman for foreign policy. Some who have served in this office have been extraordinary, including such men as John Foster Dulles, who served under Eisenhower, and Henry Kissinger, who served under Presidents Nixon and Ford. This article by Bernard Gwertzman details the background, style, and goals of President Carter's secretary of state, Cyrus Vance. Gwertzman indicates that Vance was "born to a tradition of privilege, hard work and noblesse oblige." How important are these background characteristics in explaining a person's behavior? Do you see any evidence of these characteristics influencing foreign policy? As a lawyer, Vance brings a certain style and understanding to his work. Does his training as a lawyer help explain the difference in approaches and style of operations between Henry Kissinger, an academic, and Vance? Of course, any public office requires some adjustment on the part of the incumbent, and Gwertzman notes that Vance, upon taking office, had to abandon two reservations of personal conduct. What were they? Can the force of personality affect the temper of diplomacy? In the Carter administration, Gwertzman indicates that Vance and National Security Adviser Brzezinski do not perceive the Soviet Union in the same way. How do their views differ? Which man does Carter listen to, his secretary of state or his national security adviser? Can such a conflict of viewpoints act as a positive influence in policy-making? Can it act to frustrate policy-making?

Diplomacy is a complex activity and may involve the consideration of historical trends, international relations, and the balance of power, as well as a multiple number of actors among nations. To what extent do you think that single decision-makers, such as our secretary of state, can affect the course of foreign policy? Given what Cyrus Vance's accomplishments as secretary of state have been, has he been as important to foreign policy as most other secretaries of state have been?

★ ★ ★

CYRUS VANCE PLAYS IT COOL

With his old-fashioned ways and distrust of force, the Secretary of State is having more of an impact on foreign policy than his gray image might suggest.

By Bernard Gwertzman

It is a time to be stoic. Don't overreact. No Marines in Iran. There are limits to what the United States can do. Be calm. The storm will pass. The goals of our foreign policy are sound. They can be realized with patience. Patience. Patience.

As they walk along the woody paths of Camp David, this is the advice that the President has been getting of late from the tall, quiet Wall Street lawyer who is his Secretary of State. To Cyrus Roberts Vance, the words are only a restatement, in private counsel, of principles he has often enunciated in public. But to Jimmy Carter, they have apparently been a timely source of reassurance, a stiffening of his resolve.

The President's foreign policy has run into heavy weather. He has come under increasing attack on issues ranging from the "betrayal" of Taiwan to the "loss" of Iran, from "yielding" to the Russians on strategic arms to "rushing" into normalization of relations with China. On the right, he is charged with weakness; on the left, with being inept; in both camps, the critics accuse him of presiding over a retreat of American influence around the world.

The effect has been to draw Carter closer to the man who, perhaps more

Bernard Gwertzman, of The Times's Washington bureau, has been covering the State Department under four Secretaries of State.

than anyone else among his top advisers, shares his belief that the United States only stores up trouble for itself when it oversteps the limits of its ability to control events. That does not necessarily put distance between the President and Vance's friend, and occasional adversary, Zbigniew Brzezinski. The National Security Council director shares with Carter a fervent faith in America's dynamism and moral example, and he is able to frame their common purpose in geopolitical concepts for which Vance has little taste or talent. But what the President shares with his Secretary of State is a profound sense of caution, an almost religious view of the ambiguity of human events, a refusal to see every change as a gain or a loss for us or for the Russians.

When the President's standing in the polls fell last December because of seeming reverses abroad, it was Vance he turned to for consolation and counsel. At Camp David, where they and their wives spent a few days in a relaxed social atmosphere, the Secretary had with him, in his battered attaché case, a secret priority agenda for the next two years. The underlying imperatives: Work constructively with the Russians; be evenhanded between them and the Chinese; wrap up the Egyptian-Israeli peace treaty; press on with trade liberalization so as to help the underdeveloped countries; don't get caught up in useless rhetoric about regions of the world where we cannot shape developments to our liking. And,

first and last, be patient. Many problems that seem intractable today will yield to solutions tomorrow.

It was not the only time recently the two men met in the solitude of Catoctin Mountain for long discussions about the vicissitudes of foreign affairs. The lines of fatigue on the 62-year-old Secretary's face may owe something to the knowledge that some of these problems may get worse. Yet even if they do, the President seems to have emerged from these discourses with renewed determination to persevere with his policies — on the Persian Gulf, on the Middle East, on China, on SALT — whatever the attacks against them.

If this resolution holds up — as indicated by the President's risky peace mission to Cairo and Jerusalem — it will be a factor of some political importance. It will suggest that we may be witnessing the coming of age of a Secretary of State whose imprint on foreign policy during the past two years has been underrated because of his passion for self-effacement. The "dull" Vance image — so characterized by many in contrast to the Brzezinski flair — may be in line for some overhauling. The change, in that case, will be in the public perception of the man. The man himself is not likely to do more than go on doing his job the only way he knows how.

☐

Washington observers accustomed to sizing up people in terms of jockeying for position and the bureaucratic ploy have found Cyrus Vance difficult to fathom. He has never been known to sanction a leak for political gain. He passes up opportunities to plug the Administration's policies. When public television geared up for live coverage of Senate hearings on the new China policy — a splendid chance to court wider public understanding of the controversial decision to recognize Peking and sever official ties with Taiwan — he let the Deputy Secretary of State, Warren M. Christopher, do the talking.

Vance is publicity-shy, and has failed in his modest aim of holding at least one press conference a month. He is malice-proof, and no one has yet documented an instance of his ridiculing anyone. Milder forms of criticism, a staple of Washington conversation, seldom pass his lips. It is generally understood around his office that he finds corridor gossip distasteful. "He is," an aide says, "an old-fashioned gentleman."

This moralistic streak sets him apart as a negotiator from his predecessor, Henry Kissinger, who would use any device, however questionable, to save the world from itself. Simcha Dinitz, the former Israeli Ambassador to the United States, gives an example.

When Vance took a swing through the Middle East in the summer of 1977 to encourage movement toward a peace settlement, he went first to the Arab countries, to put some basic questions to their leaders. When he got to Israel and sat down with Prime Minister Menachem Begin and his aides, he pulled out his notes and read aloud the answers he had received from the Arabs. Almost in passing, he noted that Egypt, Syria and Jordan had told him they were ready to sign formal peace treaties with Israel as part of an overall accord.

"This," Dinitz says, "was a historic development. It was the first time the Arabs had said they would agree to a peace treaty. But Vance was so matter-of-fact that unless you were listening closely you wouldn't have heard him.

"If Kissinger had the same achievement, he would have told us: 'Look, I've got to go back to the Arab countries after leaving here. I *think* on the basis of my talks so far with the Arab leaders that I can get for you their agreement to sign peace treaties. But you'll have to give me something for them in return.'"

Negotiating with the Russians on strategic arms, Kissinger would try to involve his protagonists in the grand sweep of history, while dealing out American proposals like a magician flipping the cards. To Vance, each negotiation is just another lawyer's case. He has the latest American position typed out, double-spaced, and he goes over it many times before he presents it orally to Foreign Minister Andrei Gromyko, the Russian he most often faces across the table.

The atmosphere at these SALT talks is that of a litigation between opposing legal teams, each side respecting the other's abilities. In Moscow last April, Vance went out of his way to pay tribute to Gromyko, declaring to reporters that as a "thoroughly professional practitioner of the diplomatic trade," the Soviet negotiator — by now the dean of the world's foreign ministers — had "few peers." The two sides even have their jokes. During these same sessions in the Kremlin, one of Vance's aides saw a strange-looking bell, with a button on top. He examined it, and inadvertently pressed the button. A Soviet Deputy Foreign Minister, Georgi Korniyenko, said to the Americans, "Well, there goes Washington."

Beyond questions of negotiating style, what differentiates Vance from Kissinger is Vance's refusal to think of the Russians in terms of a grand design to encircle and undo the West, and his skeptical view of the more bellicose alternatives Kissinger has been offering lately for the Administration's policies in Africa and the Persian Gulf. In one respect, Vance may be closer to public opinion on these matters than the former Secretary: The latest New York Times / CBS News Poll this month, while showing only 30 percent support for Carter's overall foreign policy, found overwhelming approval of his decisions not to intervene in specific crises. But in official Washington, Vance's view of the Russians sets him apart from many opinion makers — and notoriously so from Brzezinski, whose evocation of the Soviet threat to Europe, Africa, the Far East, and now the "arc of crisis" in the Persian Gulf, often seems to be at odds with the soothing noises coming from the State Department. Vance appears to see the Russians as rivals for influence around the world who nevertheless have their own interest in the maintenance of peace, and who will respond to reason and enter into mutually advantageous agreements if the United States remains strong.

That is enough to tag him in some circles as Pollyanaish, and he himself confesses to a certain naïveté in one particular meeting with the Kremlin team. That was in March 1977, when he arrived in Moscow with a new set of proposals on SALT — and, to demonstrate the new Administration's openness, held a press conference on the progress of the negotiations every day. Alarmed by this mystifying candor, and not liking the proposals in the first place, Leonid Brezhnev rejected the whole American approach. The Vance mission collapsed. Looking back on it, the Secretary admits that discussing the negotiations so openly in Moscow had been a mistake.

All of which leads to an interesting question: Perhaps, in diplomacy, it takes a little less matter-of-factness and a little more guile and histrionics à la Kissinger to get results? A prevalent criticism of Vance has been that he is an admirable, plodding, rather humorless man — he never cracks a joke, although he laughs politely at others' quips — who flew more than 300,000 miles in quest of agreements during the first two years of the Carter Administration without scoring a single diplomatic triumph. "No-win Cy," some reporters dubbed him — words they were prepared to take back when the latest venture in Middle East jet diplomacy got under way this month.

Vance, during those two toilsome years, remained philosophic about the difficulty of reaching final agreements between nations. "Most of these problems are very complex," he says, and the only thing to do is to "slog it out." Even on the eve of his departure for Cairo with the President March 7, he was prosaic in discussing the efforts that led to the peace mission, and cautious about the prospects. "Quite frankly," he said in an interview, "we've just slogged away at it for two-plus years. And step by step we have put the various pieces together with the parties, and we're down close to what I hope will be the end of it." From his past observations, it would seem that he is equally prepared for huzzahs at times of success and knocks at times of failure. "Public opinion," he once said, "is very fickle. What people want to see is coonskins on the wall. They don't see enough coonskins on the wall at this point."

The reference to President Johnson's often-quoted exhortation during the Vietnam buildup of 1966 reflects his distrust of seemingly simple solutions. He was No. 2 to Robert McNamara at the Pentagon in those days, watching the optimism drain out of the Secretary of Defense in inverse proportion to the growing belligerence of the White House, and he was in a better position than most to assay the cost to the country of the coonskin L.B.J. thought he had nailed to the wall. But the experience that bred in him an intolerance for all thematic visions of reality — all "doctrines," to be implemented by military force or strong-arm diplomacy — goes farther back than his Washington years, to his training as corporate lawyer and his upbringing and education and family.

□

Cy Vance was born to a tradition of privilege, hard work and noblesse oblige. His mother belonged to the Philadelphia Main Line. His father, John Vance, was an insurance executive and landowner in Clarksburg, W. Va., where Cyrus was born in 1917. The father died when the boy was 5, and Cyrus came under the virtual guardianship of his father's first cousin and best friend, John W. Davis, the corporate lawyer, United States Congressman, Ambassador to Britain and Democratic candidate against Calvin Coolidge in 1924. "I used to browse in Mr. Davis's law library," Vance recalls. "I remember the smell of bound leather and those wonderfully big shelves of law books."

After prep school in Connecticut, he went to Yale, where he majored in economics and was remembered by classmates as giving 100 percent in everything he did. This included ice hockey, in which he earned the nickname Spider, for his gangly look on the ice. Socially he was very "white shoe" — the Fence Club fraternity, then Scroll and Key (not as prestigious as Skull and Bones but, to some Yalies, more upper crust). After college, he entered Yale Law School, graduating with honors in 1942. The next four years he spent in the Navy, seeing action aboard destroyers at Bougainville, Tarawa, the Philippines, Saipan and Guam and being discharged after the war with the rank of lieutenant.

His life fell into as sensible a pattern as that of any well-bred Episcopalian of his generation. He married Grace (Gay) Sloane, a Bryn Mawr graduate of the Sloane family of furniture and art dealers, and he went to work for the New York firm of Simpson Thacher & Bartlett, the traditional nesting place for bright Yale lawyers. For the next 10 years, he cultivated his career. Then, in 1957, when he was 40, he was persuaded to go to Washington as special counsel for a Senate subcommittee, thinking it would be only a short stint.

The stint grew longer than he had counted on, and in 1960, after John F. Kennedy's election, Robert McNamara tapped Cyrus Vance for his team for the Defense Department. Vance felt he could not refuse. He rose rapidly to the post of Secretary of the Army without attracting undue national attention or (a rare accomplishment) making any enemies. He got along equally well with liberals in Congress and right-wingers in the Pentagon, and McNamara, whose relations in both quarters were sometimes difficult, made him Deputy Secretary of Defense. He neither advocated the Vietnam War nor opposed it when it came. But he did, after resigning in 1967 because of severe back trouble, join with others in urging President Johnson to stop the bombing. That led to his appointment as W. Averell Harriman's No. 2 at the Paris peace talks of 1968. Other times he went troubleshooting for Johnson were during the Panama Canal rioting of 1964, the Cyprus dispute and the Detroit riots of 1967, and the seizure of the U.S.S. Pueblo by the North Koreans in 1968.

The next eight Republican years saw Cyrus Vance back at Simpson Thacher & Bartlett, raising his income from the partnership to as much as $260,000 a year and dabbling in the nomination campaigns of Edmund Muskie in 1972 and Sargent Shriver in 1976. Later that year, he joined up with Jimmy Carter. The President-elect asked him to be Secretary of State. Once again, Vance felt he could not refuse.

□

Among the resolutions he made upon becoming Secretary, two went by the board not long after he settled into the job. The first was to break with the airborne diplomacy of "Henry's Flying Circus." Vance found that the theoretical advantages of keeping the Secretary at home and negotiating through ambassadors abroad could not be reasserted in a world sold on high-level meetings and the precedents set by Kissinger and secretaries before him. At least, the Foreign Service veterans console themselves, Vance does not take the State Department with him in his briefcase, the way Kissinger did, but leaves it in the hands of his deputy, Warren Christopher, retaining control only of the object of his trip.

The second resolution was to take every Sunday off. Now, like Dean Rusk and Henry Kissinger before him, he works seven days a week, though he does try to keep his Saturday 4 o'clock indoor-tennis date with his wife.

Monday, Feb. 12, 1979, was a routine day. Up at 5 A.M., the Secretary was driven to work in his black Chrysler New Yorker limousine by his State Department security officer. On the way, he read a four-page overnight summary of important developments, and a four-page "think piece" by the department's intelligence division on some possible troubles ahead. Waiting for him in his office when he arrived at 6:52 were a dozen of the most urgent cables from overseas missions, and a set of briefing and "action" memos covering his appointments that day. At 7:50, a C.I.A. officer brought him the agency's special morning report, meant to be seen only by Carter, Vance, Brzezinski, Vice President Walter F. Mondale and Defense Secretary Harold Brown.

At 7:40, Christopher and three other close aides came into his office for a meeting. For the remainder of the day, the official record has 40 entries, items like "8:25 — Brzezinski called," "8:48 — [White House press spokesman] Jody Powell called,"

"12:55 — the President called," and "2:27 — [White House political adviser] Hamilton Jordan called." The other morning and afternoon entries include a meeting with the Ambassador to the United Nations, Andrew Young; a call to the Soviet Ambassador, Anatoly Dobrynin; two more calls from Brzezinski; meetings and phone conversations with State Department specialists on the Soviet Union, China, the Middle East, South Asia, policy planning, intelligence and research, politico-military problems, fisheries problems, legal problems and (one of the biggest problems of all) Congressional relations; a two-hour visit to the White House for a meeting on "Mexican problems" and a National Security Council session on SALT; more business in his office, including conversations with Christopher and department press spokesman Hodding Carter 3d and a call from Senator Jacob K. Javits of New York. He also found time to answer a call from Harry Mitchell, a friend from law school. Finally, the entry: "7:16 — departed for home."

On Fridays, the routine is adjusted for an 8 o'clock breakfast meeting at the White House with Carter, Brzezinski, Jordan and Mondale, at which many of the Administration's major foreign-policy decisions are made. (Another decision-making fixture is the weekly lunch for Vance, Brzezinski and Brown.) Some days, routine is a casualty to sudden crisis. Wednesday, Feb. 14, was such a day.

Shortly after midnight, Vance's "secure" phone rang at his home in the fashionable Spring Valley area of Washington. The American Ambassador to Afghanistan, Adolph (Spike) Dubs, had been kidnapped by a group of extremists. The Secretary was driven to work in his limousine by the State Department security agent on duty. No sooner was he in the department's Operations Center than the emergency in Afghanistan was overshadowed by the storming of the American Embassy in Iran. Ambassador William H. Sullivan and his staff were being held hostage.

One immediate decision for Vance and for Carter (who had been awakened shortly after the Secretary) was whether to proceed with the President's long-planned trip to Mexico that morning. The Secretary's recommendation came at about 6 A.M. — the Americans in Teheran had been freed; the Ambassador in Kabul was dead; the President should go ahead with his state visit.

In Mexico City, while Carter and President José López Portillo engaged in their now-famous public colloquy — the Mexican leader lecturing the *Yanquis* for their sinful ways and Carter trying to lighten the atmosphere with a tasteless joke — Vance, who was along for the ride, slipped away to the American Embassy to deal with the aftereffects of the misfortunes in Teheran and Kabul. At the Embassy, a new flash reached him: The Americans in the former French African colony of Chad were endangered by an outbreak of civil war. The State Department contacted the Quai d'Orsay; the French agreed to put the Americans under the protection of their paratroopers on the scene.

Two days later, things seemed to have simmered down. The Americans in Chad had been evacuated; the Embassy in Teheran was back in business; even the embarrassment in Mexico City was seen by some as having done more good than harm by clearing the air in United States-Mexican relations. But as Carter and Vance returned to Washington on the night of Friday, Feb. 16, top-secret intelligence from the Far East indicated that the Chinese were about to invade Vietnam. Before dawn the next day, the American C.I.A. station in Tokyo flashed the first word: The Chinese had struck across the border.

With Carter at Camp David for a badly needed rest, the Administration's crisis managers met in the Situation Room of the White House. The danger of spreading conflict was obvious; what was particularly unfortunate was that Deputy Prime Minister Deng Xiaoping had just completed a good-will tour of the United States, and it would be difficult to erase the impression that Carter had given him tacit approval for the attack. Here was an occasion for that Washington institution, the background briefing to present the Administration's case to the public. A few hours after the White House meeting broke up, the Secretary invited a reporter to his "back room," a small study behind his office.

That the Administration was unhappy about this Chinese adventure, and yet not surprised by it, did not have

★

to be explained to anyone who had followed the news during Deng's visit. The Chinese leader had made no secret of Peking's intention to "punish" the Vietnamese for their invasion of China's protégé, Cambodia. The Americans, who knew of the Chinese buildup on the Vietnamese border, had gone as far as they felt they could to dissuade him from that course. Now that the Chinese had gone ahead anyway, the United States had to make its attitude plain, and Vance read out loud, from a typed sheet, the principles agreed upon at the White House conference. The Chinese and the Russians were to be treated evenhandedly. Just as the United States had condemned the Soviet-approved Vietnamese invasion of Cambodia, so it would condemn the Chinese attack. And the Russians would be cautioned not to intervene.

He might have been reading from a legal brief on a corporate merger. No, he said, as unruffled as ever, he would not care to speculate on the consequences. Yes, that had been a "pretty tiring night" — the night before the morning of the Mexican trip.

An hour later, he kept his 4 o'clock tennis date with his wife. He did, however, return to the State Department after the game instead of proceeding with his wife to do the weekend shopping at their local Safeway.

□

To see Cyrus Vance off the job these days is to see a man well satisfied with the personal rewards of a virtuous life. He and his wife (who accompanies him on most of his diplomatic trips) have every right to be pleased with their five grown children. One daughter is a staff aide to Senator Gary Hart of Colorado; another is a New York lawyer; their son, Cyrus Jr., is working for a shipping firm in Greenwich, Conn. The Vances attend St. John's Episcopal Church in Georgetown. They wish they had more time for their weekend house in the horsy-set countryside of Far Hills, N.J., a house that used to be the barn of a working farm belonging to Mrs. Vance's father. Yet, on the job, a change of sorts seems to have come over Cyrus Vance.

At interagency conferences, Vance was long known for his distinctive style. As one of his aides once put it: "When Vance goes in to argue the case, he is very precise and very careful. He usually is not the first to speak. He listens to others. Then he starts asking questions that get beneath the rhetoric. After he puts others on the defensive, he comes in with his arguments, and I'd say that 90 percent of the time the President decides in his favor."

Lately, however, his patience has at times been wearing thin. At the committee meetings of the National Security Council that deal with current issues — and are always chaired by Brzezinski — Vance has been departing from his practice of waiting for others' opinions. Now he usually states his own position first — and often, according to one aide, "with considerable vehemence. He will say, 'I believe we must do this — this is the only way to handle it,' and thump the table with his hand."

At his meetings with his own people, he has never had Kissinger's relish for the lively bull session; he has always preferred to get specific recommendations from his aides and to decide among them on the spot (a procedure that leaves many of his senior officials without a real feel for his own views). Lately, his tolerance for inconclusive meetings and for "talking a subject to death" has become even lower.

Between meetings he has seemed more subdued than usual — even, at times, depressed. The ability to suffer critics gladly has come under a strain. At a Senate hearing Feb. 8, his reputation for never losing his temper in public came close to being impaired when the conservative Senator Jake Garn of Utah charged him with "negotiating from weakness" on SALT, accused him of seeking a treaty that would go against this country's interests, and impugned his integrity. Vance bristled and his face turned red. Staring at Garn, he said sharply: "We're bargaining long and tough. We could have had an agreement if we did what you suggested. When a SALT agreement comes, it will be a good treaty, and I look forward to debating you publicly."

His aides and admirers probably wouldn't mind at all if Vance occasionally gave vent to his feelings and let fly, but there has been evidence of another change in him that has disturbed some. Lately, it is said, he has been dealing with some issues within a deliberately narrowed circle of advisers, so as to prevent leaks to the press. This, however, has had the additional effect of restricting the flow of information around the department. The fear among some middle-level officials is of a return to the Kissinger days, when all major decisions were handled by a select few. This concern has been heightened by a recent episode, when Carter summoned the department's senior officials to the White House for a dressing-down, warning them that they would be fired if they could not prevent their subordinates from leaking unauthorized information.

What it is that has produced this heightened impression of impatience and reticence on the Secretary's part is anybody's guess. Perhaps it's a reaction to the bureaucratic infighting in which information is often used for partisan rather than national ends. Perhaps the two-year grind of Middle East and SALT diplomacy, with its wearying journeys, stubborn bargaining and grating arguments within the Administration, has been getting him down. Time has been running out for him to rack up the achievements he needs to validate his policy principles. The knowledge that the President's political fortunes are affected can only have deepened the frustrations he must have felt when historic agreements repeatedly eluded his grasp.

Some people even suggest that the Secretary may not be entirely content with all of the President's recent decisions. For it must be borne in mind that Vance is only the senior foreign-policy adviser, and that the decisions are made by Carter himself. On China, for instance, there is legitimate speculation as to whether the timing of the normalization move was cleared with Vance. He was in the Middle East when the President telephoned him to say that he intended to announce normalization on Dec. 15 and that he wanted Vance back in Washington by then. The immediate results were to fluster the Russians, who delayed completing a SALT agreement that seemed to be in hand, and to give the Chinese the security blanket they probably needed for their invasion of Vietnam. Both consequences would have been predictable for a diplomatist of Vance's experience, and the question is whether he would have joined in the decision had he been in Washington at the time. (Vance pooh-poohs this line of speculation, but a man of his code could no more dissociate himself from a Presidential decision, once made, than he could use a four-letter word in mixed company.)

Whatever the reasons for the Secretary's new mood, a lifting of spirits may be in store. Apart from the opportunities opened up by the new Middle East initiative, there are indications that a SALT agreement is finally on the point of being reached. Either accord would be as big a breakthrough as Vance could hope for. Prevailing upon the Egyptians and the Israelis to cut through the latest impediments to a treaty would surpass by far anything that any postwar Administration has been able to achieve in the Middle East conflict. And placing effective controls on the Soviet-American arms race, Vance has often said, would not only ease the burden of fear and economic cost for the United States and the Soviet Union but would have a marked effect upon the whole world, easing many of the strains that have characterized the past two decades. Either agreement would be a coonskin to do any President proud.

Whatever the triumph or renewed disappointment immediately ahead, one thing can be safely said. After the cheers or the groans die away, Cy Vance will be back on the job, resuming his tedious quest for still other agreements (and for these, too, if they have once again eluded him) — the workhorse of the Administration, unfazed, optimistic, unsurprised. The precepts that have guided him so far will govern him still: Force is not always helpful. Diplomacy is not a spectator sport. A good agreement is a win for both sides. These agreements can be achieved. Reason can prevail. The only thing to do is to slog it out. ∎

Constitution of the United States of America

★ ★ ★

PREAMBLE

We the people of the United States, in order to form a more perfect union, establish justice, insure domestic tranquillity, provide for the common defense, promote the general welfare, and secure the blessings of liberty to ourselves and our posterity, do ordain and establish this CONSTITUTION for the United States of America.

ARTICLE I

Section I

All legislative powers herein granted shall be vested in a Congress of the United States, which shall consist of a Senate and a House of Representatives.

Section II

The House of Representatives shall be composed of members chosen every second year by the people of the several States, and the electors in each State shall have the qualifications requisite for electors of the most numerous branch of the State Legislature.

No person shall be a Representative who shall not have attained to the age of twenty-five years, and been seven years a citizen of the United States, and who shall not, when elected, be an inhabitant of that State in which he shall be chosen.

Representatives and direct taxes shall be apportioned among the several States which may be included within this Union, according to their respective numbers, *which shall be determined by adding to the whole number of free persons, including those bound to service for a term of years and excluding Indians not taxed, three-fifths of all other persons.* The actual enumeration shall be made within three years after the first meeting of the Congress of the United States, and within every subsequent term of ten years, in such manner as they shall by law direct. The number of Representatives shall not exceed one for every thirty thousand, but each State shall have at least one Representative; *and until such enumeration shall be made, the State of New Hampshire shall be entitled to choose three, Massachusetts eight, Rhode Island and Providence Plantations one, Connecticut five, New York six, New Jersey four, Pennsylvania eight, Delaware one, Maryland six, Virginia ten, North Carolina five, South Carolina five, and Georgia three.*

NOTE: Passages that are no longer in effect are printed in italic type.

When vacancies happen in the representation from any State, the Executive authority thereof shall issue writs of election to fill such vacancies.

The house of Representatives shall choose their Speaker and other officers; and shall have the sole power of impeachment.

Section III

The Senate of the United States shall be composed of two Senators from each State, *chosen by the legislature thereof,* for six years; and each Senator shall have one vote.

Immediately after they shall be assembled in consequence of the first election, they shall be divided as equally as may be into three classes. The seats of the Senators of the first class shall be vacated at the expiration of the second year, of the second class at the expiration of the fourth year, and of the third class at the expiration of the sixth year, so that one-third may be chosen every second year; *and if vacancies happen by resignation or otherwise, during the recess of the legislature of any State, the Executive thereof may make temporary appointments until the next meeting of the legislature, which shall then fill such vacancies.*

No person shall be a Senator who shall not have attained to the age of thirty years, and been nine years a citizen of the United States, and who shall not, when elected, be an inhabitant of that State for which he shall be chosen.

The Vice-President of the United States shall be President of the Senate, but shall have no vote, unless they be equally divided.

The Senate shall choose their other officers, and also a President *pro tempore*, in the absence of the Vice-President, or when he shall exercise the office of President of the United States.

The Senate shall have the sole power to try all impeachments. When sitting for that purpose, they shall be on oath or affirmation. When the President of the United States is tried, the Chief Justice shall preside: and no person shall be convicted without the concurrence of two-thirds of the members present.

Judgment in cases of impeachment shall not extend further than to removal from office, and disqualification to hold and enjoy any office of honor, trust or profit under the United States: but the party convicted shall nevertheless be liable and subject to indictment, trial, judgment and punishment, according to law.

Section IV

The times, places and manner of holding elections for Senators and Representatives shall be prescribed in each State by the legislature thereof; but the Congress may at any time by law make or alter such regulations, except as to the places of choosing Senators.

The Congress shall assemble at least once in every year, and such meeting *shall be on the first Monday in December, unless they shall by law appoint a different day.*

Section V

Each house shall be the judge of the elections, returns and qualifications of its own members, and a majority of each shall constitute a quorum to do business; but a smaller number may adjourn from day to day, and may be authorized to compel the attendance of absent members, in such manner, and under such penalties, as each house may provide.

Each house may determine the rules of its proceedings, punish its members for disorderly behavior, and with the concurrence of two-thirds, expel a member.

Each house shall keep a journal of its proceedings, and from time to time publish the same, excepting such parts as may in their judgment require secrecy; and the yeas and nays of the members of either house on any question shall, at the desire of one-fifth of those present, be entered on the journal.

Neither house, during the session of Congress, shall, without the consent of the other, adjourn for more than three days, nor to any other place than that in which the two houses shall be sitting.

Section VI

The Senators and Representatives shall receive a compensation for their services, to be ascertained by law and paid out of the treasury of the United States. They shall in all cases except treason, felony and breach of the peace, be privileged from arrest during their attendance at the session of their respective houses, and in going to and returning from the same; and for any speech or debate in either house, they shall not be questioned in any other place.

No Senator or Representative shall, during the time for which he was elected, be appointed to any civil office under the authority of the United States, which shall have been created, or the emoluments whereof shall have been increased, during such time; and no person holding any office under the United States shall be a member of either house during his continuance in office.

Section VII

All bills for raising revenue shall originate in the House of Representatives; but the Senate may propose or concur with amendments as on other bills.

Every bill which shall have passed the House of Representatives and the Senate, shall, before it become a law, be presented to the President of the United States; if he approve he shall sign it, but if not he shall return it with objections to that house in which it originated, who shall enter the objections at large on their journal, and proceed to reconsider it. If after such reconsideration two-thirds of that house shall agree to pass the bill, it shall be sent, together with the objections, to the other house, by which it shall likewise be reconsidered, and, if approved by two-thirds of that house, it shall become a law. But in all such cases the votes of both houses shall be determined by yeas and nays, and the names of the persons voting for and against the bill shall be entered on the journal of each house respectively. If any bill shall not be returned by the President within ten days (Sundays excepted) after it shall have been presented to him, the same shall be a law, in like manner as if he had signed it, unless the Congress by their adjournment prevent its return, in which case it shall not be a law.

Every order, resolution, or vote to which the concurrence of the Senate and House of Representatives may be necessary (except on a question of adjournment) shall be presented to the President of the United States; and before the same shall take effect, shall be approved by him, or being disapproved by him, shall be repassed by two-thirds of the Senate and House of Representatives, according to the rules and limitations prescribed in the case of a bill.

Section VIII

The Congress shall have power

To lay and collect taxes, duties, imposts, and excises, to pay the debts and provide for the common defense and general welfare of the United States; but all duties, imposts and excises shall be uniform throughout the United States;

To borrow money on the credit of the United States;

To regulate commerce with foreign nations, and among the several States, and with the Indian tribes;

To establish an uniform rule of naturalization, and uniform laws on the subject of bankruptcies throughout the United States;

To coin money, regulate the value thereof, and of foreign coin, and fix the standard of weights and measures;

To provide for the punishment of counterfeiting the securities and current coin of the United States;

To establish post offices and post roads;

To promote the progress of science and useful arts by securing for limited times to authors and inventors the exclusive right to their respective writings and discoveries;

To constitute tribunals inferior to the Supreme Court;

To define and punish piracies and felonies committed on the high seas and offenses against the law of nations;

To declare war, grant letters of marque and reprisal, and make rules concerning captures on land and water;

To raise and support armies, but no appropriation of money to that use shall be for a longer term than two years;

To provide and maintain a navy;

To make rules for the government and regulation of the land and naval forces;

To provide for calling forth the militia to execute the laws of the Union, suppress insurrections, and repel invasions;

To provide for organizing, arming, and disciplining the militia, and for governing such part of them as may be employed in the service of the United States, reserving to the States respectively the appointment of the officers, and the authority of training the militia according to the discipline prescribed by Congress;

To exercise exclusive legislation in all cases whatsoever, over such district (not exceeding ten miles square) as may, by cession of particular States, and the acceptance of Congress, become the seat of government of the United States, and to exercise like authority over all places purchased by the consent of the legislature of the State, in which the same shall be, for the erection of forts, magazines, arsenals, dock-yards, and other needful buildings; — and

To make all laws which shall be necessary and proper for carrying into execution the foregoing powers, and all other powers vested by this Constitution in the government of the United States, or in any department or officer thereof.

Section IX

The migration or importation of such persons as any of the States now existing shall think proper to admit shall not be prohibited by the Congress prior to the year 1808; but a tax or duty may be imposed on such importation, not exceeding $10 for each person.

The privilege of the writ of habeas corpus shall not be suspended, unless when in cases of rebellion or invasion the public safety may require it.

No bill of attainder or ex post facto law shall be passed.

No capitation, or other direct, tax shall be laid, unless in proportion to the census or enumeration herein before directed to be taken.

No tax or duty shall be laid on articles exported from any State.

No preference shall be given by any regulation of commerce or revenue to the ports of one State over those of another; nor shall vessels bound to, or from, one State, be obliged to enter, clear, or pay duties in another.

No money shall be drawn from the treasury, but in consequence of appropriations made by law; and a regular statement and account of the receipts and expenditures of all public money shall be published from time to time.

No title of nobility shall be granted by the United States: and no person holding any office of profit or trust under them, shall, without the consent of the Congress, accept of any present, emolument, office, or title, of any kind whatever, from any king, prince, or foreign state.

Section X

No State shall enter into any treaty, alliance, or confederation; grant letters of marque and reprisal; coin money; emit bills of credit; make anything but gold and silver coin a tender in payment of debts; pass any bill of attainder, ex post facto law, or law impairing the obligation of contracts, or grant any title of nobility.

No State shall, without the consent of Congress, lay any imposts or duties on imports or exports, except what may be absolutely necessary for executing its inspection laws: and the net produce of all duties and imposts, laid by any State on imports or exports, shall be for the use of the treasury of the United States; and all such laws shall be subject to the revision and control of the Congress.

No State shall, without the consent of Congress, lay any duty of tonnage, keep troops or ships of war in time of peace, enter into any agreement or compact with another State, or with a foreign power, or engage in war, unless actually invaded, or in such imminent danger as will not admit of delay.

ARTICLE II

Section I

The executive power shall be vested in a President of the United States of America. He shall hold his office during the term of four years, and, together with the Vice-President, chosen for the same term, be elected as follows:

Each State shall appoint, in such manner as the legislature thereof may direct, a number of electors, equal to the whole number of Senators and Representatives to which the State may be entitled in the Congress; but no Senator or Representative, or person holding an office of trust or profit under the United States, shall be appointed an elector.

The electors shall meet in their respective States, and vote by ballot for two persons, of whom one at least shall not be an inhabitant of the same State with themselves. And they shall make a list of all the persons voted for, and of the number of votes for each; which list they shall sign and certify, and transmit sealed to the seat of government of the United States, directed to the President of the Senate. The President of the Senate shall, in the presence of the Senate and House of Representatives, open all the certificates, and the votes shall then be counted. The person having the greatest number of votes shall be the President, if such number be a majority of the whole number of electors appointed; and if there be more than one who have such majority, and have an equal number of votes, then the House of Representatives shall immediately choose by ballot one of them for President; and if no person have a majority, then from the five highest on the list said house shall in like manner choose the President. But in choosing the President the votes shall be taken by States, the representation from each State having one vote; a quorum for this purpose shall consist of a member or members from two-thirds of the States, and a majority of all the States shall be necessary to a choice. In every case, after the choice of the President, the person having the greatest number of votes of the electors shall be the Vice-President. But if there should remain two or more who have equal votes, the Senate shall choose from them by ballot the Vice-President.

The Congress may determine the time of choosing the electors and the day on which they shall give their votes; which day shall be the same throughout the United States.

No person except a natural-born citizen, *or a citizen of the United States at the time of the adoption of this Constitution,* shall be eligible to the office of President; neither shall any person be eligible to that office who shall not have attained to the age of thirty-five years, and been fourteen years a resident within the United States.

In case of the removal of the President from office or of his death, resignation, or inability to discharge the powers and duties of the said office, the same shall devolve on the Vice-President, and the Congress may by law provide for the case of removal, death, resignation, or inability, both of the President and Vice-President, declaring what officer shall then act as President, and such officer shall act accordingly, until the disability be removed, or a President shall be elected.

The President shall, at stated times, receive for his services a compensation, which shall neither be increased nor diminished during the period for which he shall have been elected, and he shall not receive within that period any other emolument from the United States, or any of them.

Before he enter on the execution of his office, he shall take the following oath or affirmation:—"I do solemnly swear (or affirm) that I will faithfully execute the office of the President of the United States, and will to the best of my ability preserve, protect and defend the Constitution of the United States."

Section II

The President shall be commander in chief of the army and navy of the United States, and of the militia of the several States, when called into the actual service of the United States; he may require the opinion, in writing, of the principal officer in each of the executive departments, upon any subject relating to the duties of their respective offices, and he shall have power to grant reprieves and pardons for offenses against the United States, except in cases of impeachment.

He shall have power, by and with the advice and consent of the Senate, to make treaties, provided two-thirds of the Senators present concur; and he shall nominate, and by and with the advice and consent of the Senate, shall appoint ambassadors, other public ministers and consuls, judges of the Supreme Court, and all other officers of the United States, whose appointments are not herein otherwise provided for, and which shall be established by law: but Congress may by law vest the appointment of such inferior officers, as they think proper, in the President alone, in the courts of law, or in the heads of departments.

The President shall have power to fill up all vacancies that may happen during the recess of the Senate, by granting commissions which shall expire at the end of their next session.

Section III

He shall from time to time give to the Congress information of the state of the Union, and recommend to their consideration such measures as he shall judge necessary and expedient; he may, on extraordinary occasions, convene both houses, or either of them, and in case of disagreement between them, with respect to the time of adjournment, he may adjourn them to such time as he shall think proper; he shall receive ambassadors and other public ministers; he shall take care that the laws be faithfully executed, and shall commission all the officers of the United States.

Section IV

The President, Vice-President and all civil officers of the United States shall be removed from office on impeachment for, and on conviction of, treason, bribery, or other high crimes and misdemeanors.

ARTICLE III

Section I

The judicial power of the United States shall be vested in one Supreme Court, and in such inferior courts as the Congress may from time to time ordain and establish. The judges, both of the Supreme and inferior courts, shall hold their offices during good behavior, and shall, at stated times, receive for their services a compensation which shall not be diminished during their continuance in office.

Section II

The judicial power shall extend to all cases, in law and equity, arising under this Constitution, the laws of the United States, and treaties made, or which shall be made, under their authority; — to all cases affecting ambassadors, other public ministers and consuls; — to all cases of admiralty and maritime jurisdiction; — to controversies to which the United States shall be a party; — to controversies between two or more States; — *between a State and citizens of another State;* — between citizens of different States; — between citizens of the same State claiming lands under grants of different States, and between a State, or the citizens thereof, and foreign states, citizens or subjects.

In all cases affecting ambassadors, other public ministers and consuls, and those in which a State shall be party, the Supreme Court shall have original jurisdiction. In all the other cases before mentioned, the Supreme Court shall have appellate jurisdiction, both as to law and fact, with such exceptions, and under such regulations, as the Congress shall make.

The trial of all crimes, except in cases of impeachment, shall be by jury; and such trial shall be held in the State where the said crimes shall have been committed; but when not committed within any State, the trial shall be at such place or places as the Congress may by law have directed.

Section III

Treason against the United States shall consist only in levying war against them, or in adhering to their enemies, giving them aid and comfort. No person shall be convicted of treason unless on the testimony of two witnesses to the same overt act, or on confession in open court.

The Congress shall have power to declare the punishment of treason, but no attainder of treason shall work corruption of blood, or forfeiture except during the life of the person attainted.

ARTICLE IV

Section I

Full faith and credit shall be given in each State to the public acts, records, and judicial proceedings of every other State. And the Congress may by general laws prescribe the manner in which such acts, records, and proceedings shall be proved, and the effect thereof.

Section II

The citizens of each State shall be entitled to all privileges and immunities of citizens in the several States.

A person charged in any State with treason, felony, or other crime, who shall flee from justice, and be found in another State, shall on demand of the executive authority of the State from which he fled, be delivered up, to be removed to the State having jurisdiction of the crime.

No person held to service or labor in one State, under the laws thereof, escaping into another, shall, in consequence of any law or regulation therein, be discharged from such service or labor, but shall be delivered up on claim of the party to whom such service or labor may be due.

Section III

New States may be admitted by the Congress into this Union; but no new State shall be formed or erected within the jurisdiction of any other State; nor any State be formed by the junction of two or more States, or parts of States, without the consent of the legislatures of the States concerned as well as of the Congress.

The Congress shall have power to dispose of and make all needful rules and regulations respecting the territory or other property belonging to the United States; and nothing in this Constitution shall be so construed as to prejudice any claims of the United States, or .of any particular State.

Section IV

The United States shall guarantee to every State in this Union a republican form of government, and shall protect each of them against invasion; and on application of the legislature, or of the executive (when the legislature cannot be convened), against domestic violence.

ARTICLE V

The Congress, whenever two-thirds of both houses shall deem it necessary, shall propose amendments to this Constitution, or, on the application of the legislatures of two-thirds of the several States, shall call a convention for proposing amendments, which, in either case, shall be valid to all intents and purposes, as part of this Constitution, when ratified by the legislatures of three-fourths of the several States, or by conventions in three-fourths thereof, as the one or the other mode of ratification may be proposed by the Congress; provided *that no amendments which may be made prior to the year one thousand eight hundred and eight shall in any manner affect the first and fourth clauses in the ninth section of the first article;* and that no State, without its consent, shall be deprived of its equal suffrage in the Senate.

ARTICLE VI

All debts contracted and engagements entered into, before the adoption of this Constitution, shall be as valid against the United States under this Constitution, as under the Confederation.

This Constitution, and the laws of the United States which shall be made in pursuance thereof; and all treaties made, or which shall be made, under the authority of the United States, shall be the supreme law of the land; and the judges in every State shall be bound thereby, anything in the Constitution or laws of any State to the contrary notwithstanding.

The Senators and Representatives before mentioned, and the members of the several State legislatures, and all executive and judicial officers, both of the United States and of the several States, shall be bound by oath or affirmation to support this Constitution; but no religious test shall ever be required as a qualification to any office or public trust under the United States.

ARTICLE VII

The ratification of the conventions of nine States shall be sufficient for the establishment of this Constitution between the States so ratifying the same.

Done in Convention by the unanimous consent of the States present, the seventeenth day of September in the year of our Lord one thousand seven hundred and eighty-seven and of the Independence of the United States of America the twelfth. In witness whereof we have hereunto subscribed our names.

[Signed by]
G⁰ WASHINGTON
Presidt and Deputy from Virginia
[and thirty-eight others]

AMENDMENTS TO THE CONSTITUTION

ARTICLE I*

Congress shall make no law respecting an establishment of religion, or prohibiting the free exercise thereof; or abridging the freedom of speech, or of the press; or the right of the people peaceably to assemble, and to petition the government for a redress of grievances.

ARTICLE II

A well-regulated militia being necessary to the security of a free State, the right of the people to keep and bear arms shall not be infringed.

ARTICLE III

No soldier shall, in time of peace, be quartered in any house without the consent of the owner, nor in time of war, but in a manner to be prescribed by law.

ARTICLE IV

The right of the people to be secure in their persons, houses, papers, and effects, against unreasonable searches and seizures, shall not be violated, and no warrants shall issue but upon probable cause, supported by oath or affirmation, and particularly describing the place to be searched, and the persons or things to be seized.

*The first ten Amendments (Bill of Rights) were adopted in 1791.

ARTICLE V

No person shall be held to answer for a capital, or otherwise infamous crime, unless on a presentment or indictment of a grand jury, except in cases arising in the land or naval forces, or in the militia, when in actual service in time of war or public danger; nor shall any person be subject for the same offense to be twice put in jeopardy of life or limb; nor shall be compelled in any criminal case to be a witness against himself, nor be deprived of life, liberty, or property, without due process of law; nor shall private property be taken for public use without just compensation.

ARTICLE VI

In all criminal prosecutions, the accused shall enjoy the right to a speedy and public trial, by an impartial jury of the State and district wherein the crime shall have been committed, which district shall have been previously ascertained by law, and to be informed of the nature and cause of the accusation; to be confronted with the witnesses against him; to have compulsory process for obtaining witnesses in his favor, and to have the assistance of counsel for his defense.

ARTICLE VII

In suits at common law, where the value in controversy shall exceed twenty dollars, the right of trial by jury shall be preserved, and no fact tried by a jury shall be otherwise reexamined in any court of the United States, than according to the rules of the common law.

ARTICLE VIII

Excessive bail shall not be required, nor excessive fines imposed, nor cruel and unusual punishments inflicted.

ARTICLE IX

The enumeration in the Constitution, of certain rights, shall not be construed to deny or disparage others retained by the people.

ARTICLE X

The powers not delegated to the United States by the Constitution, nor prohibited by it to the States, are reserved to the States respectively, or to the people.

ARTICLE XI [Adopted 1798]

The judicial power of the United States shall not be construed to extend to any suit in law or equity, commenced or prosecuted against one of the United States by citizens of another State, or by citizens or subjects of any foreign state.

ARTICLE XII [Adopted 1804]

The electors shall meet in their respective States, and vote by ballot for President and Vice-President, one of whom, at least, shall not be an inhabitant of the same State with themselves; they shall name in their ballots the person voted for as President, and in distinct ballots the person voted for as Vice-President, and they shall make distinct lists of all persons voted for as President, and of all persons voted for as Vice-President, and of the number of votes for each, which lists they shall sign and certify, and transmit sealed to the seat of government of the United States, directed to the President of the Senate;—the President of the Senate shall, in the presence of the Senate and House of Representatives, open all the certificates and the votes shall then be counted;—the person having the greatest number of votes for President shall be the President, if such number be a majority of the whole number of electors appointed; and if no person have such majority, then from the persons having the highest numbers not exceeding three on the list of those voted for as President, the House of Representatives shall choose immediately, by ballot, the President. But in choosing the President, the votes shall be taken by States, the representation from each State having one vote; a quorum for this purpose shall consist of a member or member from two-thirds of the States, and a majority of all the States shall be necessary to a choice. And if the House of Representatives shall not choose a President whenever the right of choice shall devolve upon them, before *the fourth day of March* next following, then the Vice-President shall act as President, as in the case of the death or other constitutional disability of the President.

The person having the greatest number of votes as Vice-President shall be the Vice-President, if such number be a majority of the whole number of electors appointed; and if no person have a majority, then from the two highest numbers on the list the Senate shall choose the Vice-President; a quorum for the purpose shall consist of two-thirds of the whole number of Senators, and a majority of the whole number shall be necessary to a choice. But no person constitutionally ineligible to the office of President shall be eligible to that of Vice-President of the United States.

ARTICLE XIII [Adopted 1865]

1. Neither slavery nor involuntary servitude, except as a punishment for crime whereof the party shall have been duly convicted, shall exist within the United States, or any place subject to their jurisdiction.

2. Congress shall have power to enforce this article by appropriate legislation.

ARTICLE XIV [Adopted 1868]

1. All persons born or naturalized in the United States, and subject to the jurisdiction thereof, are citizens of the United States and of the State wherein they reside. No State shall make or enforce any law which shall abridge the privileges or immunities of citizens of the United States; nor shall any State deprive any person of life, liberty, or property, without due process of law; nor deny to any person within its jurisdiction the equal protection of the laws.

2. Representatives shall be apportioned among the several States according to their respective numbers, counting the whole number of persons in each State, excluding Indians not taxed. But when the right to vote at any election for the choice of Electors for President and Vice-President of the United States, Representatives in Congress, the executive and judicial officers of a State, or the members of the legislature thereof, is denied to any of the male inhabitants of such State, being twenty-one years of age and citizens of the United States, or in any way abridged, except for participation in rebellion, or other crime, the basis of representation therein shall be reduced in the proportion which the number of such male citizens shall bear to the whole number of male citizens twenty-one years of age in such State.

3. No person shall be a Senator or Representative in Congress, or Elector of President and Vice-President, or hold any office, civil or military, under the United States, or under any State, who, having previously taken an oath, as a member of Congress, or as an officer of the United States, or as a member of any State legislature, or as an executive or judicial officer of any State, to support the Constitution of the United States, shall have engaged in insurrection or rebellion against the same, or given aid or comfort to the enemies thereof. But Congress may, by a vote of two-thirds of each house, remove such disability.

4. The validity of the public debt of the United States, authorized by law, including debts incurred for payment of pensions and bounties for services in suppressing insurrection or rebellion, shall not be questioned. But neither the United States nor any State shall assume or pay any debt or obligation incurred in aid of insurrection or rebellion against the United States, or any claim for the loss or emancipation of any slave; but all such debts, obligations, and claims shall be held illegal and void.

5. The Congress shall have power to enforce, by appropriate legislation, the provisions of this article.

ARTICLE XV [Adopted 1870]

1. The right of citizens of the United States to vote shall not be denied or abridged by the United States or by any State on account of race, color, or previous condition of servitude.

2. The Congress shall have power to enforce this article by appropriate legislation.

ARTICLE XVI [Adopted 1913]

The Congress shall have power to lay and collect taxes on incomes, from whatever source derived, without apportionment among the several States, and without regard to any census or enumeration.

ARTICLE · XVII [Adopted 1913]

1. The Senate of the United States shall be composed of two Senators from each State, elected by the people thereof, for six years; and each Senator shall have one vote. The electors in each State shall have the qualifications requisite for electors of [voters for] the most numerous branch of the State legislatures.

2. When vacancies happen in the representation of any State in the Senate, the executive authority of such State shall issue writs of election to fill such vacancies: Provided, that the Legislature of any State may empower the executive thereof to make temporary appointments until the people fill the vacancies by election as the Legislature may direct.

3. This amendment shall not be so construed as to affect the election or term of any Senator chosen before it becomes valid as part of the Constitution.

ARTICLE XVIII [Adopted 1919; Repealed 1933]

1. *After one year from the ratification of this article the manufacture, sale, or transportation of intoxicating liquors within, the importation thereof into, or the exportation thereof from the United States and all territory subject to the jurisdiction thereof, for beverage purposes, is hereby prohibited.*

2. *The Congress and the several States shall have concurrent power to enforce this article by appropriate legislation.*

3. *This article shall be inoperative unless it shall have been ratified as an amendment to the Constitution by the legislatures of the several States, as provided by the Constitution, within seven years from the date of the submission thereof to the States by the Congress.*

ARTICLE XIX [Adopted 1920]

1. The right of citizens of the United States to vote shall not be denied or abridged by the United States or by any State on account of sex.

2. The Congress shall have power to enforce this article by appropriate legislation.

ARTICLE XX [Adopted 1933]

1. The terms of the President and Vice-President shall end at noon on the 20th day of January, and the terms of Senators and Representatives at noon on the 3d day of January, of the years in which such terms would have ended if this article had not been ratified; and the terms of their successors shall then begin.

2. The Congress shall assemble at least once in every year, and such meeting shall begin at noon on the 3d day of January, unless they shall by law appoint a different day.

3. If, at the time fixed for the beginning of the term of the President, the President-elect shall have died, the Vice-President-elect shall become President. If a President shall not have been chosen before the time fixed for the beginning of his term, or if the President-

elect shall have failed to qualify, then the Vice-President-elect shall act as President until a President shall have qualified; and the Congress may by law provide for the case wherein neither a President-elect nor a Vice-President-elect shall have qualified, declaring who shall then act as President, or the manner in which one who is to act shall be selected, and such persons shall act accordingly until a President or Vice-President shall have qualified.

4. The Congress may by law provide for the case of the death of any of the persons from whom the House of Representatives may choose a President whenever the right of choice shall have devolved upon them, and for the case of the death of any of the persons from whom the Senate may choose a Vice-President whenever the right of choice shall have devolved upon them.

5. Sections 1 and 2 shall take effect on the 15th day of October following the ratification of this article.

6. This article shall be inoperative unless it shall have been ratified as an amendment to the Constitution by the Legislatures of three-fourths of the several States within seven years from the date of its submission.

ARTICLE XXI [Adopted 1933]

1. The eighteenth article of amendment to the Constitution of the United States is hereby repealed.

2. The transportation or importation into any State, Territory, or Possession of the United States for delivery or use therein of intoxicating liquors, in violation of the laws thereof, is hereby prohibited.

3. This article shall be inoperative unless it shall have been ratified as an amendment to the Constitution by conventions in the several States, as provided in the Constitution, within seven years from the date of submission thereof to the States by the Congress.

ARTICLE XXII [Adopted 1951]

1. No person shall be elected to the office of President more than twice, and no person who has held the office of President, or acted as President, for more than two years of a term to which some other person was elected President shall be elected to the office of President more than once. But this article shall not apply to any person holding the office of President when this article was proposed by the Congress, and shall not prevent any person who may be holding the office of President, or acting as President, during the term within which this article becomes operative from holding the office of President or acting as President during the remainder of such term.

2. This article shall be inoperative unless it shall have been ratified as an amendment to the Constitution by the legislatures of three-fourths of the several States within seven years from the date of its submission to the States by the Congress.

ARTICLE XXIII [Adopted 1961]

1. The District constituting the seat of Government of the United States shall appoint in such manner as the Congress may direct:
    A number of electors of President and Vice-President equal to the whole number of Senators and Representatives in Congress to which the District would be entitled if it were a State, but in no event more than the least populous State; they shall be in addition to those appointed by the States, but they shall be considered for the purposes of the election of President and Vice-President, to be electors appointed by a State; and they shall meet in the District and perform such duties as provided by the twelfth article of amendment.

2. The Congress shall have the power to enforce this article by appropriate legislation.

ARTICLE XXIV [Adopted 1964]

1. The right of citizens of the United States to vote in any primary or other election for President or Vice-President, for electors for President or Vice-President, or for Senator or

Representative in Congress, shall not be denied or abridged by the United States or any State by reason of failure to pay any poll tax or other tax.

2. The Congress shall have the power to enforce this article by appropriate legislation.

ARTICLE XXV [Adopted 1967]

1. In case of the removal of the President from office or of his death or resignation, the Vice President shall become President.

2. Whenever there is a vacancy in the office of the Vice President, the President shall nominate a Vice President who shall take office upon confirmation by a majority vote of both Houses of Congress.

3. Whenever the President transmits to the President pro tempore of the Senate and the Speaker of the House of Representatives his written declaration that he is unable to discharge the powers and duties of his office, and until he transmits to them a written declaration to the contrary, such powers and duties shall be discharged by the Vice President as Acting President.

4. Whenever the Vice President and a majority of either the principal officers of the executive departments or of such other body as Congress may by law provide, transmit to the President pro tempore of the Senate and the Speaker of the House of Representatives their written declaration that the President is unable to discharge the powers and duties of his office, the Vice President shall immediately assume the powers and duties of the office as Acting President.

Thereafter, when the President transmits to the President pro tempore of the Senate and the Speaker of the House of Representatives his written declaration that no inability exists, he shall resume the powers and duties of his office unless the Vice President and a majority of either the principal officers of the executive department[s] or of such other body as Congress may by law provide, transmit within four days to the President pro tempore of the Senate and the Speaker of the House of Representatives their written declaration that the President is unable to discharge the powers and duties of his office. Thereupon Congress shall decide the issue, assembling within forty-eight hours for that purpose if not in session. If the Congress, within twenty-one days after receipt of the latter written declaration, or, if Congress is not in session, within twenty-one days after Congress is required to assemble, determines by two-thirds vote of both Houses that the President is unable to discharge the powers and duties of his office, the Vice President shall continue to discharge the same as Acting President; otherwise, the President shall resume the powers and duties of his office.

ARTICLE XXVI [Adopted 1971]

1. The right of citizens of the United States, who are eighteen years of age or older, to vote shall not be denied or abridged by the United States or by any State on account of age.

2. The Congress shall have power to enforce this article by appropriate legislation.

ARTICLE XXVII [Sent to States, 1972]

1. Equality of rights under the law shall not be denied or abridged by the United States or by any State on account of sex.

2. The Congress shall have the power to enforce, by appropriate legislation, the provisions of this article.

3. This amendment shall take effect two years after the date of ratification.

1 2 3 4 5 6 7 8 9 0